MrExcel
LIBRARY

VBA and Macros: Microsoft® Excel® 2010

Bill Jelen

Tracy Syrstad

800 E. 96th Street
Indianapolis, Indiana   46240

Contents at a Glance

Introduction

1   Unleash the Power of Excel with VBA

2   This Sounds Like BASIC, So Why Doesn't It Look Familiar?

3   Referring to Ranges

4   User-Defined Functions

5   Looping and Flow Control

6   R1C1-Style Formulas

7   What Is New in Excel 2010 and What Has Changed

8   Create and Manipulate Names in VBA

9   Event Programming

10   Userforms—An Introduction

11   Creating Charts

12   Data Mining with Advanced Filter

13   Using VBA to Create Pivot Tables

14   Excel Power

15   Data Visualizations and Conditional Formatting

16   Reading from and Writing to the Web

17   Dashboarding with Sparklines in Excel 2010

18   Automating Word

19   Arrays

20   Text File Processing

21   Using Access as a Back End to Enhance Multiuser Access to Data

22   Creating Classes, Records, and Collections

23   Advanced Userform Techniques

24   Windows API

25   Handling Errors

26   Customizing the Ribbon to Run Macros

27   Creating Add-Ins

Index

VBA and Macros: Microsoft® Excel® 2010

Copyright © 2010 by Que Publishing

ISBN-13: 978-0-7897-4314-5
ISBN-10: 0-7897-4314-0

Library of Congress Cataloging-in-Publication Data:
Jelen, Bill.
  VBA and macros : Microsoft Excel 2010 / Bill Jelen, Tracy Syrstad.
    p. cm.
  Includes index.
  ISBN-13: 978-0-7897-4314-5
  ISBN-10: 0-7897-4314-0
  1. Microsoft Excel (Computer file) 2. Microsoft Visual Basic for applications. 3. Business—Computer programs. 4. Electronic spreadsheets. I. Syrstad, Tracy. II. Title.

  HF5548.4.M523J46 2010
  005.54—dc22
                                    2010018831
Printed in the United States of America

First Printing: June 2010

Trademarks

All terms mentioned in this book that are known to be trademarks or service marks have been appropriately capitalized. Que Publishing cannot attest to the accuracy of this information. Use of a term in this book should not be regarded as affecting the validity of any trademark or service mark.

Microsoft and Excel are a registered trademarks of Microsoft Corporation.

Warning and Disclaimer

Bulk Sales

Que Publishing offers excellent discounts on this book when ordered in quantity for bulk purchases or special sales. For more information, please contact

U.S. Corporate and Government Sales
1-800-382-3419
corpsales@pearsontechgroup.com

For sales outside the United States, please contact

International Sales
international@pearson.com

Associate Publisher
Greg Wiegand

Acquisitions Editor
Loretta Yates

Development Editor
Sondra Scott

Managing Editor
Sandra Schroeder

Senior Project Editor
Tonya Simpson

Copy Editor
Keith Kline

Indexer
Erika Millen

Proofreader
Language Logistics

Technical Editor
Bob Umlas

Publishing Coordinator
Cindy Teeters

Book Designer
Anne Jones

Compositor
Bronkella Publishing

Contents

Introduction 1
  Getting Results with VBA 1
  What Is in This Book? 1
    Reduce the Learning Curve 1
    Excel VBA Power 2
    Techie Stuff Needed to Produce Applications 2
    Does This Book Teach Excel? 2
  The Future of VBA and Windows Versions of Excel 4
    Versions of Excel 4
  Special Elements and Typographical Conventions 5
  Code Files 6
  Next Steps 6

1 Unleash the Power of Excel with VBA 7
  The Power of Excel 7
  Barriers to Entry 7
    The Macro Recorder Doesn't Work! 7
    Visual Basic Is Not Like BASIC 8
    Good News: Climbing the Learning Curve Is Easy 8
    Great News: Excel with VBA Is Worth the Effort 8
  Knowing Your Tools: The Developer Tab 9
  Macro Security 10
    Adding a Trusted Location 10
    Using Macro Settings to Enable Macros in Workbooks Outside of Trusted Locations 11
    Using Disable All Macros with Notification 12
  Overview of Recording, Storing, and Running a Macro 12
    Filling Out the Record Macro Dialog 13
  Running a Macro 14
    Creating a Macro Button on the Ribbon 14
    Creating a Macro Button on the Quick Access Toolbar 15
    Assigning a Macro to a Form Control, Text Box, or Shape 16
  Using New File Types in Excel 2010 18
  Understanding the VB Editor 19
    VB Editor Settings 19
    The Project Explorer 20
    The Properties Window 21
  Understanding Shortcomings of the Macro Recorder 21
    Examining Code in the Programming Window 23
    Running the Macro on Another Day Produces Undesired Results 25

Possible Solution: Use Relative References When Recording..26

Never Use the AutoSum Button While Recording a Macro 30

Three Tips When Using the Macro Recorder 31

Next Steps..32

2   This Sounds Like BASIC, So Why Doesn't It Look Familiar? 33

I Can't Understand This Code 33

Understanding the Parts of VBA "Speech"...34

VBA Is Not Really Hard 37

VBA Help Files: Using F1 to Find Anything..37

Using Help Topics 39

Examining Recorded Macro Code: Using the VB Editor and Help 39

Optional Parameters...41

Defined Constants 41

Properties Can Return Objects 46

Using Debugging Tools to Figure Out Recorded Code 46

Stepping Through Code...46

More Debugging Options: Breakpoints..49

Backing Up or Moving Forward in Code...49

Not Stepping Through Each Line of Code...50

Querying Anything While Stepping Through Code 50

Using a Watch to Set a Breakpoint 55

Using a Watch on an Object...55

Object Browser: The Ultimate Reference 56

Seven Tips for Cleaning Up Recorded Code 58

Tip 1: Don't Select Anything 58

Tip 2: Cells(2,5) Is More Convenient Than Range("E2") 59

Tip 3: Ride the Range from the Bottom to Find Last Row 59

Tip 4: Use Variables to Avoid Hard-Coding Rows and Formulas....................................60

Tip 5: R1C1 Formulas That Make Your Life Easier 61

Tip 6: Learn to Copy and Paste in a Single Statement..61

Tip 7: Use With...End With to Perform Multiple Actions 61

Next Steps..64

3   Referring to Ranges 65

The Range Object 65

Syntax to Specify a Range...66

Named Ranges...66

Shortcut for Referencing Ranges 66

Referencing Ranges in Other Sheets 67

Referencing a Range Relative to Another Range 68

Use the `Cells` Property to Select a Range...68

    Using the `Cells` Property in the `Range` Property 69

Use the `Offset` Property to Refer to a Range 69

Use the `Resize` Property to Change the Size of a Range 71

Using the Columns and Rows Properties to Specify a Range 72

Use the `Union` Method to Join Multiple Ranges..72

Use the `Intersect` Method to Create a New Range from Overlapping Ranges..............73

Use the `ISEMPTY` Function to Check Whether a Cell Is Empty....................................73

Use the `CurrentRegion` Property to Select a Data Range 74

Use the `Areas` Collection to Return a Noncontiguous Range 77

Referencing Tables 77

Next Steps..78

4   User-Defined Functions

4   **User-Defined Functions** **79**

Creating User-Defined Functions 79

Sharing UDFs 81

Useful Custom Excel Functions..82

    Set the Current Workbook's Name in a Cell 82

    Set the Current Workbook's Name and File Path in a Cell..................................82

    Check Whether a Workbook Is Open..83

    Check Whether a Sheet in an Open Workbook Exists...83

    Count the Number of Workbooks in a Directory 84

    Retrieve USERID..85

    Retrieve Date and Time of Last Save..86

    Retrieve Permanent Date and Time...87

    Validate an E-mail Address..88

    Sum Cells Based on Interior Color 89

    Count Unique Values 90

    Remove Duplicates from a Range..91

    Find the First Nonzero-Length Cell in a Range...93

    Substitute Multiple Characters 94

    Retrieve Numbers from Mixed Text 95

    Convert Week Number into Date...96

    Separate Delimited String 96

    Sort and Concatenate 97

    Sort Numeric and Alpha Characters 99

    Search for a String Within Text...100

    Reverse the Contents of a Cell 101

    Multiple Max 101

    Return Hyperlink Address...102

    Return the Column Letter of a Cell Address 103

Static Random 103

Using `Select Case` on a Worksheet 104

Next Steps..105

5 Looping and Flow Control 107

For...Next Loops 107

Using Variables in the `For` Statement..110

Variations on the `For...Next` Loop...110

Exiting a Loop Early After a Condition Is Met..111

Nesting One Loop Inside Another Loop 112

Do Loops 113

Using the `While` or `Until` Clause in Do Loops 115

`While...Wend` Loops 117

VBA Loop: `For Each` 117

Object Variables..117

Flow Control: Using `If...Then...Else` and `Select Case`...................................120

Basic Flow Control: `If...Then...Else`...121

Conditions 121

`If...Then...End If` 121

Either/Or Decisions: `If...Then...Else...End If` 122

Using `If...Else If...End If` for Multiple Conditions..122

Using `Select Case...End Select` for Multiple Conditions 123

Complex Expressions in `Case` Statements 124

Nesting `If` Statements 124

Next Steps..126

6 R1C1-Style Formulas 127

Referring to Cells: A1 Versus R1C1 References 127

Switching Excel to Display R1C1-Style References 128

The Miracle of Excel Formulas..129

Enter a Formula Once and Copy 1,000 Times..129

The Secret: It's Not That Amazing...130

Explanation of R1C1 Reference Style 132

Using R1C1 with Relative References...132

Using R1C1 with Absolute References 133

Using R1C1 with Mixed References..133

Referring to Entire Columns or Rows with R1C1 Style 134

Replacing Many A1 Formulas with a Single R1C1 Formula 134

Remembering Column Numbers Associated with Column Letters....................................136

Array Formulas Require R1C1 Formulas 137

Next Steps..138

7 What Is New in Excel 2010 and What Has Changed **139**

   If It Has Changed in the Front End, It Has Changed in VBA 139

      The Ribbon 139

      Charts 139

      Pivot Tables 140

      Slicers 140

      Conditional Formatting 140

      Tables 141

      Sorting...141

      SmartArt..142

   Learning the New Objects and Methods 143

   Compatibility Mode 144

      `Version`..144

      `Excel8CompatibilityMode`...145

   Next Steps...146

8 Create and Manipulate Names in VBA **147**

   Excel Names..147

   Global Versus Local Names 147

   Adding Names 148

   Deleting Names 149

   Adding Comments 150

   Types of Names...150

      Formulas..151

      Strings 151

      Numbers..152

      Tables 153

      Using Arrays in Names...153

      Reserved Names 154

   Hiding Names 155

   Checking for the Existence of a Name...155

   Next Steps...158

9 Event Programming **159**

   Levels of Events 159

   Using Events 160

      Event Parameters 160

      Enabling Events 161

   Workbook Events...161

      `Workbook_Activate()`...161

      `Workbook_Deactivate()`...161

Workbook_Open() 161
Workbook_BeforeSave(ByVal SaveAsUI As Boolean, Cancel As Boolean) 162
Workbook_BeforePrint(Cancel As Boolean) 163
Workbook_BeforeClose(Cancel As Boolean) 163
Workbook_NewSheet(ByVal Sh As Object) 164
Workbook_WindowResize(ByVal Wn As Window) 164
Workbook_WindowActivate(ByVal Wn As Window) 165
Workbook_WindowDeactivate(ByVal Wn As Window) 165
Workbook_AddInInstall() 165
Workbook_AddInUninstall 165
Workbook_Sync(ByVal SyncEventType As Office.MsoSyncEventType) 165
Workbook_PivotTableCloseConnection(ByVal Target As PivotTable) 165
Workbook_PivotTableOpenConnection(ByVal Target As PivotTable) 165
Workbook_RowsetComplete(ByVal Description As String, ByVal Sheet As
   String, ByVal Success As Boolean) 165
Workbook_BeforeXmlExport(ByVal Map As XmlMap, ByVal Url As String,
   Cancel As Boolean) 166
Workbook_AfterXmlExport(ByVal Map As XmlMap, ByVal Url As String, ByVal
   Result As XlXmlExportResult) 166
Workbook_BeforeXmlImport(ByVal Map As XmlMap, ByVal Url As String, ByVal
   IsRefresh As Boolean, Cancel As Boolean) 166
Workbook_AfterXmlImport(ByVal Map As XmlMap, ByVal IsRefresh As Boolean,
   ByVal Result As XlXmlImportResult) 166
Workbook Level Sheet and Chart Events 166
Worksheet Events 168
Worksheet_Activate() 168
Worksheet_Deactivate() 168
Worksheet_BeforeDoubleClick(ByVal Target As Range, Cancel As Boolean) 168
Worksheet_BeforeRightClick(ByVal Target As Range, Cancel As Boolean) 169
Worksheet_Calculate() 169
Worksheet_Change(ByVal Target As Range) 170
Worksheet_SelectionChange(ByVal Target As Range) 170
Worksheet_FollowHyperlink(ByVal Target As Hyperlink) 171
Worksheet_PivotTableUpdate(ByVal Target As PivotTable) 172
Chart Sheet Events 172
Embedded Charts 172
Chart_Activate() 173
Chart_BeforeDoubleClick(ByVal ElementID As Long, ByVal Arg1 As Long,
   ByVal Arg2 As Long, Cancel As Boolean) 173
Chart_BeforeRightClick(Cancel As Boolean) 173
Chart_Calculate() 173
Chart_Deactivate() 173
Chart_MouseDown(ByVal Button As Long, ByVal Shift As Long, ByVal x As
   Long, ByVal y As Long) 174
Chart_MouseMove(ByVal Button As Long, ByVal Shift As Long, ByVal x As
   Long, ByVal y As Long) 174

Chart_MouseUp(ByVal Button As Long, ByVal Shift As Long, ByVal x As Long, ByVal y As Long) 174
Chart_Resize() 174
Chart_Select(ByVal ElementID As Long, ByVal Arg1 As Long, ByVal Arg2 As Long) 174
Chart_SeriesChange(ByVal SeriesIndex As Long, ByVal PointIndex As Long) 175
Chart_DragOver() 175
Chart_DragPlot() 175
Application-Level Events 176
AppEvent_AfterCalculate() 176
AppEvent_NewWorkbook(ByVal Wb As Workbook) 177
AppEvent_ProtectedViewWindowActivate(ByVal Pvw As ProtectedViewWindow) 177
AppEvent_ProtectedViewWindowBeforeClose(ByVal Pvw As ProtectedViewWindow, ByVal Reason As XlProtectedViewCloseReason, Cancel As Boolean) 177
AppEvent_ProtectedViewWindowDeactivate(ByVal Pvw As ProtectedViewWindow) 177
AppEvent_ProtectedViewWindowOpen(ByVal Pvw As ProtectedViewWindow) 177
AppEvent_ProtectedViewWindowResize(ByVal Pvw As ProtectedViewWindow) 177
AppEvent_SheetActivate (ByVal Sh As Object) 177
AppEvent_SheetBeforeDoubleClick(ByVal Sh As Object, ByVal Target As Range, Cancel As Boolean) 178
AppEvent_SheetBeforeRightClick(ByVal Sh As Object, ByVal Target As Range, Cancel As Boolean) 178
AppEvent_SheetCalculate(ByVal Sh As Object) 178
AppEvent_SheetChange(ByVal Sh As Object, ByVal Target As Range) 178
AppEvent_SheetDeactivate(ByVal Sh As Object) 178
AppEvent_SheetFollowHyperlink(ByVal Sh As Object, ByVal Target As Hyperlink) 178
AppEvent_SheetSelectionChange(ByVal Sh As Object, ByVal Target As Range) 178
AppEvent_SheetPivotTableUpdate(ByVal Sh As Object, ByVal Target As PivotTable) 178
AppEvent_WindowActivate(ByVal Wb As Workbook, ByVal Wn As Window) 179
AppEvent_WindowDeactivate(ByVal Wb As Workbook, ByVal Wn As Window) 179
AppEvent_WindowResize(ByVal Wb As Workbook, ByVal Wn As Window) 179
AppEvent_WorkbookActivate(ByVal Wb As Workbook) 179
AppEvent_WorkbookAddinInstall(ByVal Wb As Workbook) 179
AppEvent_WorkbookAddinUninstall(ByVal Wb As Workbook) 179
AppEvent_WorkbookBeforeClose(ByVal Wb As Workbook, Cancel As Boolean) 179
AppEvent_WorkbookBeforePrint(ByVal Wb As Workbook, Cancel As Boolean) 180
AppEvent_WorkbookBeforeSave(ByVal Wb As Workbook, ByVal SaveAsUI As Boolean, Cancel As Boolean) 180
AppEvent_WorkbookNewSheet(ByVal Wb As Workbook, ByVal Sh As Object) 180
AppEvent_WorkbookOpen(ByVal Wb As Workbook) 180
AppEvent_WorkbookPivotTableCloseConnection(ByVal Wb As Workbook, ByVal Target As PivotTable) 180
AppEvent_WorkbookPivotTableOpenConnection(ByVal Wb As Workbook, ByVal Target As PivotTable) 180
AppEvent_WorkbookRowsetComplete(ByVal Wb As Workbook, ByVal Description As String, ByVal Sheet As String, ByVal Success As Boolean) 181

AppEvent_WorkbookSync(ByVal Wb As Workbook, ByVal SyncEventType As
  Office.MsoSyncEventType)..181
AppEvent_WorkbookBeforeXmlExport(ByVal Wb As Workbook, ByVal Map As
  XmlMap, ByVal Url As String, Cancel As Boolean)...181
AppEvent_WorkbookAfterXmlExport(ByVal Wb As Workbook, ByVal Map As
  XmlMap, ByVal Url As String, ByVal Result As XlXmlExportResult)..................181
AppEvent_WorkbookBeforeXmlImport(ByVal Wb As Workbook, ByVal Map As
  XmlMap, ByVal Url As String, ByVal IsRefresh As Boolean, Cancel As
  Boolean) 181
AppEvent_WorkbookAfterXmlImport(ByVal Wb As Workbook, ByVal Map As
  XmlMap, ByVal IsRefresh As Boolean, ByVal Result As XlXmlImportResult) 181

    Next Steps...182

10 Userforms: An Introduction **183**

    User Interaction Methods..183
        Input Boxes...183
        Message Boxes 184

    Creating a Userform...184

    Calling and Hiding a Userform 186

    Programming the Userform...186
        Userform Events 186

    Programming Controls 188

    Using Basic Form Controls..189
        Using Labels, Text Boxes, and Command Buttons 189
        Deciding Whether to Use List Boxes or Combo Boxes in Forms 191
        Adding Option Buttons to a Userform 194
        Adding Graphics to a Userform..195
        Using a Spin Button on a Userform...196
        Using the MultiPage Control to Combine Forms..198

    Verifying Field Entry 200

    Illegal Window Closing 200

    Getting a Filename 201

    Next Steps...202

11 Creating Charts **203**

    Charting in Excel 2010 203

    Referencing Charts and Chart Objects in VBA Code...203

    Creating a Chart..204
        Specifying the Size and Location of a Chart..204
        Later Referring to a Specific Chart 206

    Recording Commands from the Layout or Design Tabs 208
        Specifying a Built-in Chart Type 208
        Specifying a Template Chart Type 210
        Changing a Chart's Layout or Style 211

Using SetElement to Emulate Changes on the Layout Tab..213
Changing a Chart Title Using VBA...218
Emulating Changes on the Format Tab...218
  Using the Format Method to Access Formatting Options...218
Creating Advanced Charts..234
  Creating True Open-High-Low-Close Stock Charts..235
  Creating Bins for a Frequency Chart..236
  Creating a Stacked Area Chart..239
Exporting a Chart as a Graphic..244
  Creating a Dynamic Chart in a Userform..244
Creating Pivot Charts..246
Next Steps...248

12 Data Mining with Advanced Filter 249
Replacing a Loop with AutoFilter..249
  Using New AutoFilter Techniques...251
  Selecting Visible Cells Only..255
Advanced Filter Is Easier in VBA Than in Excel...257
  Using the Excel Interface to Build an Advanced Filter..258
Using Advanced Filter to Extract a Unique List of Values...258
  Extracting a Unique List of Values with the User Interface...259
  Extracting a Unique List of Values with VBA Code...260
  Getting Unique Combinations of Two or More Fields..263
Using Advanced Filter with Criteria Ranges..265
  Joining Multiple Criteria with a Logical OR...267
  Joining Two Criteria with a Logical AND...267
  Other Slightly Complex Criteria Ranges..267
  The Most Complex Criteria: Replacing the List of Values with a Condition Created as the Result of a Formula 268
Using Filter in Place in Advanced Filter..275
  Catching No Records When Using Filter in Place..276
  Showing All Records After Filter in Place..276
The Real Workhorse: xlFilterCopy with All Records Rather Than Unique Records Only...............276
  Copying All Columns...277
  Copying a Subset of Columns and Reordering...278
Using Filter in Place with Unique Records Only...283
  Excel in Practice: Turning Off a Few Drop-Downs in the AutoFilter..285
Next Steps...285

13 Using VBA to Create Pivot Tables...287
Introducing Pivot Tables...287
Understanding Versions...287
  New in Excel 2010..288
  New Beginning with Excel 2007...288

Creating a Vanilla Pivot Table in the Excel Interface 290
    Understanding Compact Layout 293
Building a Pivot Table in Excel VBA..294
    Defining the Pivot Cache 295
    Creating and Configuring the Pivot Table...295
    Adding Fields to the Data Area 296
    Learning Why You Cannot Move or Change Part of a Pivot Report...299
    Determining Size of a Finished Pivot Table to Convert the Pivot Table to Values 299
Using Advanced Pivot Table Features 302
    Using Multiple Value Fields 302
    Counting the Number of Records...303
    Grouping Daily Dates to Months, Quarters, or Years...303
    Changing the Calculation to Show Percentages 305
    Eliminating Blank Cells in the Values Area..308
    Controlling the Sort Order with AutoSort 308
    Replicating the Report for Every Product...309
Filtering a Data Set 312
    Manually Filtering Two or More Items in a Pivot Field...312
    Using the Conceptual Filters 313
    Using the Search Filter...316
    Setting Up Slicers to Filter a Pivot Table 319
    Filtering an OLAP Pivot Table Using Named Sets...321
Using Other Pivot Table Features...324
    Calculated Data Fields...324
    Calculated Items 325
    Using ShowDetail to Filter a Recordset 325
    Changing the Layout from the Design Tab 325
    Suppressing Subtotals for Multiple Row Fields...326
Next Steps..327

14 Excel Power **329**
File Operations...329
    List Files in a Directory...329
    Import CSV 331
    Read Entire TXT to Memory and Parse..332
Combining and Separating Workbooks 333
    Separate Worksheets into Workbooks...333
    Combine Workbooks 334
    Filter and Copy Data to Separate Worksheets...335
    Export Data to Word..336
Working with Cell Comments 337
    List Comments...337
    Resize Comments 339
    Resize Comments with Centering..340
    Place a Chart in a Comment..341

Utilities to Wow Your Clients 342
    Using Conditional Formatting to Highlight Selected Cell...342
    Highlight Selected Cell Without Using Conditional Formatting.................................344
    Custom Transpose Data 345
    Select/Deselect Noncontiguous Cells 347
Techniques for VBA Pros 349
    Pivot Table Drill-Down..349
    Speedy Page Setup 350
    Calculating Time to Execute Code 353
    Custom Sort Order 354
    Cell Progress Indicator 355
    Protected Password Box 356
    Change Case 359
    Selecting with SpecialCells 360
    ActiveX Right-Click Menu 360
Cool Applications 362
    Historical Stock/Fund Quotes 362
    Using VBA Extensibility to Add Code to New Workbooks...363
Next Steps..365

15 Data Visualizations and Conditional Formatting 367
Introduction to Data Visualizations...367
VBA Methods and Properties for Data Visualizations 368
Adding Data Bars to a Range 369
Adding Color Scales to a Range...374
Adding Icon Sets to a Range 375
    Specifying an Icon Set...376
    Specifying Ranges for Each Icon 377
Using Visualization Tricks 378
    Creating an Icon Set for a Subset of a Range 378
    Using Two Colors of Data Bars in a Range...380
Using Other Conditional Formatting Methods 382
    Formatting Cells That Are Above or Below Average 383
    Formatting Cells in the Top 10 or Bottom 5..383
    Formatting Unique or Duplicate Cells 384
    Formatting Cells Based on Their Value 385
    Formatting Cells That Contain Text..386
    Formatting Cells That Contain Dates 386
    Formatting Cells That Contain Blanks or Errors...387
    Using a Formula to Determine Which Cells to Format 387
    Using the New NumberFormat Property...388
Next Steps..389

16 Reading from and Writing to the Web **391**

    Getting Data from the Web 391

        Manually Creating a Web Query and Refreshing with VBA.......................................392

        Using VBA to Update an Existing Web Query...395

        Building Many Web Queries with VBA...396

    Using `Application.OnTime` to Periodically Analyze Data 399

        Scheduled Procedures Require Ready Mode 400

        Specifying a Window of Time for an Update 400

        Canceling a Previously Scheduled Macro 400

        Closing Excel Cancels All Pending Scheduled Macros...401

        Scheduling a Macro to Run x Minutes in the Future 401

        Scheduling a Verbal Reminder 402

        Scheduling a Macro to Run Every 2 Minutes...403

    Publishing Data to a Web Page 404

        Using VBA to Create Custom Web Pages 406

        Using Excel as a Content Management System 407

        Bonus: FTP from Excel..409

    Next Steps..410

17 Dashboarding with Sparklines in Excel 2010 ....**411**

    Creating Sparklines...412

    Scaling the Sparklines...414

    Formatting Sparklines 418

        Using Theme Colors 418

        Using RGB Colors 421

        Formatting Sparkline Elements 423

        Formatting Win/Loss Charts 426

    Creating a Dashboard 427

        Observations About Sparklines...428

        Creating 100's of Individual Sparklines in a Dashboard 428

    Next Steps..432

18 Automating Word **433**

    Early Binding 433

        Compile Error: Can't Find Object or Library 435

    Late Binding 436

    Creating and Referencing Objects..437

        The `New` Keyword 437

        `CreateObject` Function..438

        `GetObject` Function 438

    Using Constant Values 439

        Using the Watch Window to Retrieve the Real Value of a Constant 440

        Using the Object Browser to Retrieve the Real Value of a Constant.............................440

Understanding Word's Objects 441
 Document Object 442
 Selection Object 443
 Range Object...444
 Bookmarks...448
Controlling Form Fields in Word 450
Next Steps...452

19 Arrays **453**
Declare an Array 453
 Multidimensional Arrays..454
Fill an Array...455
Empty an Array 456
Arrays Make It Easier to Manipulate Data, but Is That All?.....................................457
Dynamic Arrays...459
Passing an Array 460
Next Steps...461

20 Text File Processing...**463**
Importing from Text Files 463
 Importing Text Files with Fewer Than 1,048,576 Rows.....................................463
 Reading Text Files with More Than 1,048,576 Rows 470
Writing Text Files..473
Next Steps...474

21 Using Access as a Back End to Enhance Multiuser Access to Data.....................**475**
ADO Versus DAO...476
The Tools of ADO 478
Adding a Record to the Database..480
Retrieving Records from the Database...481
Updating an Existing Record...483
Deleting Records via ADO 485
Summarizing Records via ADO..485
Other Utilities via ADO 487
 Checking for the Existence of Tables..487
 Checking for the Existence of a Field 488
 Adding a Table On the Fly...489
 Adding a Field On the Fly..489
SQL Server Examples...490
Next Steps...491

22 Creating Classes, Records, and Collections **493**

Inserting a Class Module 493

Trapping Application and Embedded Chart Events 494

   Application Events 494

   Embedded Chart Events 495

Creating a Custom Object 497

Using a Custom Object 498

Using `Property Let` and `Property Get` to Control How Users Utilize Custom Objects 499

Collections 501

   Creating a Collection in a Standard Module 501

   Creating a Collection in a Class Module 502

User-Defined Types 506

Next Steps 509

23 Advanced Userform Techniques **511**

Using the UserForm Toolbar in the Design of Controls on Userforms 511

More Userform Controls 511

   Check Boxes 512

   Tab Strips 513

   RefEdit 515

   Toggle Buttons 517

   Using a Scrollbar As a Slider to Select Values 517

Controls and Collections 519

Modeless Userforms 521

Using Hyperlinks in Userforms 522

Adding Controls at Runtime 523

   Resizing the Userform On-the-fly 524

   Adding a Control On-the-fly 525

   Sizing On-the-fly 525

   Adding Other Controls 525

   Adding an Image On-the-fly 526

   Putting It All Together 527

Adding Help to the Userform 529

   Showing Accelerator Keys 529

   Adding Control Tip Text 530

   Creating the Tab Order 530

   Coloring the Active Control 530

Transparent Forms 533

Next Steps 534

24 Windows API **535**

What Is the Windows API? 535

Understanding an API Declaration 536

Using an API Declaration 537

API Examples 537

    Retrieve the Computer Name 538

    Check Whether an Excel File Is Open on a Network 539

    Retrieve Display-Resolution Information 540

    Custom About Dialog 541

    Disable the X for Closing a Userform 541

    Running Timer 542

    Playing Sounds 543

    Retrieving a File Path 543

Finding More API Declarations 547

Next Steps 547

25 Handling Errors **549**

What Happens When an Error Occurs? 549

    Debug Error Inside Userform Code Is Misleading 551

Basic Error Handling with the On Error GoTo Syntax 552

Generic Error Handlers 554

    Handling Errors by Choosing to Ignore Them 554

    Suppressing Excel Warnings 556

    Encountering Errors on Purpose 556

Train Your Clients 557

Errors While Developing Versus Errors Months Later 557

    Runtime Error 9: Subscript Out of Range 557

    RunTime Error 1004: Method Range of Object Global Failed 558

The Ills of Protecting Code 559

More Problems with Passwords 560

Errors Caused by Different Versions 561

Next Steps 562

26 Customizing the Ribbon to Run Macros **563**

Out with the Old, In with the New 563

    Where to Add Your Code: customui Folder and File 564

Creating the Tab and Group 565

Adding a Control to Your Ribbon 566

Accessing the File Structure 571

Understanding the RELS File 571

Renaming the Excel File and Opening the Workbook 572

    Custom UI Editor Tool 572

Using Images on Buttons...572

    Microsoft Office Icons 573

    Custom Icon Images 574

Troubleshooting Error Messages...577

    The Attribute "Attribute Name" on the Element "customui Ribbon" Is Not Defined in the DTD/Schema 577

    Illegal Qualified Name Character 578

    Element "customui Tag Name" Is Unexpected According to Content Model of Parent Element "customui

      Tag Name"..578

    Excel Found Unreadable Content...579

    Wrong Number of Arguments or Invalid Property Assignment 580

    Nothing Happens..580

Other Ways to Run a Macro 580

    Keyboard Shortcut..580

    Attach a Macro to a Command Button 581

    Attach a Macro to a Shape...582

    Attach a Macro to an ActiveX Control 583

    Running a Macro from a Hyperlink 584

Next Steps..585

27 Creating Add-Ins 587

Characteristics of Standard Add-Ins...587

Converting an Excel Workbook to an Add-In 588

    Using Save As to Convert a File to an Add-In...589

    Using the VB Editor to Convert a File to an Add-In..590

Having Your Client Install the Add-In 591

    Standard Add-Ins Are Not Secure 592

    Closing Add-Ins 593

    Removing Add-Ins..593

Using a Hidden Workbook as an Alternative to an Add-In...593

Next Steps..595

Index 597

About the Authors

Bill Jelen, Excel MVP and the host of MrExcel.com, has been using spreadsheets since 1985, and he launched the MrExcel.com website in 1998. Bill was a regular guest on Call for Help with Leo Laporte and has produced more than 1,200 episodes of his daily video podcast, Learn Excel from MrExcel. He is the author of 30 books about Microsoft Excel and writes the monthly Excel column for *Strategic Finance* magazine. You will most frequently find Bill taking his show on the road, doing half-day Power Excel seminars wherever he can find a room full of accountants or Excellers. Before founding MrExcel.com, Jelen spent 12 years in the trenches—working as a financial analyst for finance, marketing, accounting, and operations departments of a $500 million public company. He lives near Akron, Ohio, with his wife, Mary Ellen, and his sons, Josh and Zeke.

Tracy Syrstad is the project manager for the MrExcel consulting team. She was introduced to Excel VBA by a co-worker who encouraged her to learn VBA by recording steps and then modifying the code as needed. Her first macro was a simple lookup and highlight for a parts index, although it hardly seemed simple then. But she was encouraged by this success and others to follow. She'll never forget the day when it all clicked. She hopes this book will bring that click to its readers sooner and with less frustration. She lives near Sioux Falls, South Dakota, with her husband, John.

Dedication

To everyone in the MrExcel.com message board community.
—*Bill Jelen*

To John, who would only accept perfection, even if it took four coats of paint.
—*Tracy Syrstad*

Acknowledgments

Thanks to Tracy Syrstad for being a great co-author and for doing a great job of managing all the consulting projects at MrExcel.com.

Bob Umlas is the smartest Excel guy I know and is an awesome technical editor. At Pearson, Loretta Yates is an excellent acquisitions editor.

Along the way, I've learned a lot about VBA programming from the awesome community at the MrExcel.com message board. VoG and Richard Schollar and Jon von der Heyden all stand out as having contributed posts that lead to ideas in this book. Thanks to Pam Gensel for Excel macro lesson #1. Mala Singh taught me about creating charts in VBA, and Oliver Holloway brought me up to speed with accessing SQL Server.

At MrExcel.com, thanks to Barb Jelen, Wei Jiang, Tracy Syrstad, Schar Oswald, and Scott Pierson. Thanks also to Josh and Zeke Jelen, who have been picking up hours after school learning how to edit and produce the MrExcel podcast.

Finishing five Excel books for Excel 2010 simultaneously has been a monumental task. My family was incredibly supportive during this time. Thanks for Josh, Zeke, and Mary Ellen Jelen.

—Bill

Thanks to Bill Jelen, whose trust in me to run the consulting side of his business has done so much in building my self-confidence. And to LKH, whose blog I've learned so much from about writing and balancing working in the home and still having a personal life.

Richard Schollar and Joe Miskey: You've both been invaluable managing member issues at the forum and I feel I don't say thank you often enough. Thank you! And thanks to all the moderators who keep the board organized, despite the best efforts of the spammers.

There have been so many MrExcel.com clients whose projects have shown myriad ways that Excel can be used. Your excitement and appreciation over the solution we provide you has brightened my day as often as your unique projects have kept this job interesting.

—Tracy

We Want to Hear from You!

As the reader of this book, *you* are our most important critic and commentator. We value your opinion and want to know what we're doing right, what we could do better, what areas you'd like to see us publish in, and any other words of wisdom you're willing to pass our way.

As an associate publisher for Que Publishing, I welcome your comments. You can email or write me directly to let me know what you did or didn't like about this book—as well as what we can do to make our books better.

Please note that I cannot help you with technical problems related to the topic of this book. We do have a User Services group, however, where I will forward specific technical questions related to the book.

When you write, please be sure to include this book's title and author as well as your name, email address, and phone number. I will carefully review your comments and share them with the author and editors who worked on the book.

Email: feedback@quepublishing.com

Mail: Greg Wiegand
        Associate Publisher
        Que Publishing
        800 East 96th Street
        Indianapolis, IN 46240 USA

Reader Services

Visit our website and register this book at quepublishing.com/register for convenient access to any updates, downloads, or errata that might be available for this book.

Getting Results with VBA

As corporate IT departments have found themselves with long backlogs of requests, Excel users have discovered they can produce the reports needed to run their business themselves using the macro language *Visual Basic for Applications* (VBA). VBA enables you to achieve tremendous efficiencies in your day-to-day use of Excel. This is both a good and bad thing. On the good side, without waiting for resources from IT, VBA helps you figure out how to import data and produce reports in Excel. On the bad side, you are now stuck importing data and producing reports in Excel.

What Is in This Book?

You have taken the right step by purchasing this book. I can help you reduce the learning curve so that you can write your own VBA macros and put an end to the burden of generating reports manually.

Reduce the Learning Curve

This Introduction provides a brief history of spreadsheets. Chapter 1 introduces the tools and confirms what you probably already know: The macro recorder does not work. Chapter 2 helps you understand the crazy syntax of VBA. Chapter 3 breaks the code on how to work efficiently with ranges and cells. By the time you get to Chapter 4, you will know enough to begin using the 25 sample user-defined functions in that chapter.

Chapter 5 covers the power of looping using VBA. The case study in this chapter creates a program to produce a department report, and then wraps that report routine in a loop to produce 46 reports.

IN THIS INTRODUCTION

Getting Results with VBA...............................1

What Is in This Book? 1

The Future of VBA and Windows Versions of Excel 4

Special Elements and Typographical Conventions..5

Code Files...6

Chapter 6 covers R1C1-style formulas. Chapter 7 looks at what changed in Excel VBA from Excel 2003 to Excel 2010. In the past, it was fairly straightforward to create VBA code that would run on any of the recent versions of Excel. Unfortunately, with the sweeping changes in Excel 2007 and Excel 2010, it became significantly more difficult to create this VBA code. Chapter 8 covers names. Chapter 9 includes some great tricks that use event programming. Chapter 10 introduces custom dialog boxes that you can use to collect information from the human using Excel.

Excel VBA Power

Chapters 11 through 13 provide an in-depth look at charting, Advanced Filter, and pivot tables. Any report automation tool will rely heavily on these concepts. Chapter 14 includes 25 code samples designed to exhibit the power of Excel VBA.

Chapters 15 through 18 handle data visualizations, web queries, sparklines, and automating another Office program such as Word.

Techie Stuff Needed to Produce Applications

Chapter 19 shows how to use arrays to build fast applications. Chapters 20 and 21 handle reading and writing to text files and Access databases. The techniques for using Access databases enable you to build an application with the multi-user features of Access while keeping the friendly front end of Excel.

Chapter 22, as it examines classes and collections, covers VBA from a Visual Basic programmer's point of view. Chapter 23 discusses advanced userform topics. Chapter 24 teaches some tricky ways to achieve tasks using the Windows application programming interface. Chapters 25 through 27 deal with error handling, custom menus, and add-ins.

Does This Book Teach Excel?

Microsoft believes the average Office user touches only 10 percent of the features in Office. I realize everyone reading this book is above average, and I have a pretty smart audience at MrExcel.com. Even so, a poll of 8,000 MrExcel.com readers shows that only 42 percent of smarter-than-average users are using any one of the top 10 power features in Excel.

I regularly present a Power Excel seminar for accountants. These are hard-core Excelers who use Excel 30 to 40 hours every week. Even so, two things come out in every seminar. First, half the audience gasps when they see how quickly you can do tasks with a particular feature such as automatic subtotals or pivot tables. Second, someone in the audience routinely trumps me. For example, someone asks a question, I answer, and someone in the second row raises a hand to give a better answer.

The point? You and I both know a lot about Excel. However, I will assume that in any given chapter, maybe 58 percent of the people have not used pivot tables before and maybe even fewer have used the "Top 10 Filter" feature of pivot tables. With this in mind, before I show how to automate something in VBA, I briefly cover how to do the same task in the

Excel interface. This book does not teach you how to do pivot tables, but it does alert you when you might need to explore a topic and learn more about it elsewhere.

CASE STUDY: MONTHLY ACCOUNTING REPORTS

This is a true story. Valerie is a business analyst in the accounting department of a medium-size corporation. Her company recently installed an overbudget $16 million ERP system. As the project ground to a close, there were no resources left in the IT budget to produce the monthly report that this corporation used to summarize each department.

However, Valerie had been close enough to the implementation process to think of a way to produce the report herself. She understood that she could export General Ledger data from the ERP system to a text file with comma-separated values. Using Excel, Valerie was able to import the G/L data from the ERP system into Excel.

Creating the report was not easy. Like many companies, there were exceptions in the data. Valerie knew that certain accounts in one particular cost center needed to be reclassed as an expense. She knew that other accounts needed to be excluded from the report entirely. Working carefully in Excel, Valerie made these adjustments. She created one pivot table to produce the first summary section of the report. She cut the pivot table results and pasted them into a blank worksheet. Then she created a new pivot table report for the second section of the summary. After about 3 hours, she had imported the data, produced five pivot tables, arranged them in a summary, and neatly formatted the report in color.

Becoming the Hero

Valerie handed the report to her manager. The manager had just heard from the IT department that it would be months before they could get around to producing "that convoluted report." When Valerie created the Excel report, she became the instant hero of the day. In 3 hours, Valerie had managed to do the impossible. Valerie was on cloud nine after a well-deserved "atta-girl."

More Cheers

The next day, Valerie's manager attended the monthly department meeting. When the department managers started complaining that they could not get the report from the ERP system, this manager pulled out his department report and placed it on the table. The other managers were amazed. How was he able to produce this report? Everyone was relieved to hear that someone had cracked the code. The company president asked Valerie's manager if he could have the report produced for each department.

Cheers Turn to Dread

You can probably see this coming. This particular company had 46 departments. That means 46 one-page summaries had to be produced once a month. Each report required importing data from the ERP system, backing out certain accounts, producing five pivot tables, and then formatting the reports in color. Even though it had taken Valerie 3 hours to produce the first report, after she got into the swing of things, she could produce the 46 reports in 40 hours. This is horrible. Valerie had a job to do before she became responsible of spending 40 hours a month producing these reports in Excel.

VBA to the Rescue

Valerie found my company, MrExcel Consulting, and explained her situation. In the course of about a week, I was able to produce a series of macros in Visual Basic that did all the mundane tasks. For example, it imported the data, backed out certain accounts, did five pivot tables, and applied the color formatting. From start to finish, the entire 40-hour manual process was reduced to two button clicks and about 4 minutes.

Right now, either you or someone in your company is probably stuck doing manual tasks in Excel that can be automated with VBA. I am confident that I can walk into any company with 20 or more Excel users and find a case equally amazing as Valerie's.

The Future of VBA and Windows Versions of Excel

Seven years ago, there were many rumblings that Microsoft might stop supporting VBA. There is now plenty of evidence to indicate that VBA will be around in Windows versions of Excel through 2025. When VBA was removed from the Mac version of Excel 2008, a huge outcry from customers led to it being included in the next Mac version of Excel.

Microsoft has stated that in Excel 15, which is the next version of Excel, it will stop providing support for XLM macros. These macros were replaced by VBA in 1993, and 17 years later, they are still supported. There is a chance that Microsoft will introduce a new programming language for the macro recorder in Excel 15. Assuming Microsoft continues to support VBA for 17 years after Excel 2012, you should be good through the mid-to-late 2020s.

However, you can see Microsoft's lack of commitment to VBA. Office 2003 offered a few features, such as the Research Pane and SmartTags, which could only be automated with Visual Basic.Net. The charting macro recorder, which was not finished in time to ship with Excel 2007, is included in Excel 2010.

The tools that you learn today will be good for the next 15 years. Even if Microsoft decides to scrap VBA in favor of another language, your coding skills will most likely transfer to the new platform.

Versions of Excel

This Third Edition of *VBA and Macros* is designed to work with Excel 2010. The previous editions of this book covered code for Excel 97 through Excel 2007. In 80 percent of the chapters, the code for Excel 2010 will be identical to code in previous versions. However, there are exceptions. For example, Microsoft offers new sorting logic, and charts have changed completely. In addition, the conditional formatting and data visualization tools in Chapter 15 are brand new. With Excel 2010, pivot tables offer new calculation options and slicers. The XML examples in Chapter 17 will work only with Excel 2003 or newer.

Differences for Mac Users

Although Excel for Windows and Excel for the Mac are similar in their user interface, there are a number of differences when you compare the VBA environment. Certainly, nothing in Chapter 24 that uses the Windows API will work on the Mac. The overall concepts discussed in the book apply to the Mac, but differences will exist. You can find a general list of differences as they apply to the Mac at http://www.mrexcel.com/macvba.html.

Special Elements and Typographical Conventions

The following typographical conventions are used in this book:

- *Italic*—Indicates new terms when they are defined, special emphasis, non-English words or phrases, and letters or words used as words
- Monospace—Indicates parts of VBA code such as object or method names, and filenames
- *Italic monospace*—Indicates placeholder text in code syntax
- **Bold monospace**—Indicates user input

In addition to these typographical conventions, there are several special elements. Each chapter has at least one case study that presents a real-world solution to common problems. The case study also demonstrates practical applications of topics discussed in the chapter.

In addition to the case studies, you will see New icons, Notes, Tips, and Cautions.

> **NOTE**
> Notes provide additional information outside the main thread of the chapter discussion that might be useful for you to know.

> **TIP**
> Tips provide quick workarounds and time-saving techniques to help you work more efficiently.

> **CAUTION**
> Cautions warn about potential pitfalls you might encounter. Pay attention to the Cautions; they alert you to problems that may otherwise cause you hours of frustration.

Code Files

As a thank you for buying this book, the authors have put together a set of 50 Excel workbooks that demonstrate the concepts included in this book. This set of files includes all the code from the book, sample data, additional notes from the authors, and 25 additional bonus macros. To download the code files, visit this book's web page at http://www.quepublishing.com or http://www.mrexcel.com/getcode2010.html.

Next Steps

Chapter 1 introduces the editing tools of the Visual Basic environment and shows why using the macro recorder is not an effective way to write VBA macro code.

Unleash the Power of Excel with VBA

The Power of Excel

Visual Basic for Applications (VBA) combined with Microsoft Excel is probably the most powerful tool available to you. VBA is sitting on the desktops of 500 million users of Microsoft Office, and most have never figured out how to harness the power of VBA in Excel. Using VBA, you can speed the production of any task in Excel. If you regularly use Excel to produce a series of monthly charts, you can have VBA do the same task for you in a matter of seconds.

IN THIS CHAPTER

The Power of Excel 7

Barriers to Entry 7

Knowing Your Tools: The Developer Tab 9

Macro Security 10

Overview of Recording, Storing, and Running a Macro 12

Running a Macro 14

Using New File Types in Excel 2010 18

Understanding the VB Editor 19

Understanding Shortcomings of the Macro Recorder 21

Barriers to Entry

There are two barriers to learning successful VBA programming. First, Excel's macro recorder is flawed and does not produce workable code for you to use as a model. Second, for many who learned a programming language such as BASIC, the syntax of VBA is horribly frustrating.

The Macro Recorder Doesn't Work!

Microsoft began to dominate the spreadsheet market in the mid-1990s. Although it was wildly successful in building a powerful spreadsheet program to which any Lotus 1-2-3 user could easily transition, the macro language was just too different. Anyone proficient in recording Lotus 1-2-3 macros who tried recording a few macros in Excel most likely failed. Although the Microsoft VBA programming language is much more powerful than the Lotus 1-2-3 macro language, the fundamental flaw is that the macro recorder does not work.

With Lotus 1-2-3, you could record a macro today, play it back tomorrow, and it would faithfully work.

When you attempt the same feat in Microsoft Excel, the macro might work today but not tomorrow. In 1995, when I tried to record my first Excel macro, I was horribly frustrated by this.

Visual Basic Is Not Like BASIC

The code generated by the macro recorder was unlike anything I had ever seen. It said this was "Visual Basic" (VB). I had the pleasure of learning half a dozen programming languages at various times; this bizarre-looking language was horribly unintuitive and did not resemble the BASIC language I had learned in high school.

To make matters worse, even in 1995 I was the spreadsheet wizard in my office. My company had forced everyone to convert from Lotus 1-2-3 to Excel, which meant I was faced with a macro recorder that didn't work and a language that I couldn't understand. This was not a good combination of events.

My assumption in writing this book is that you are pretty talented with a spreadsheet. You probably know more than 90 percent of the people in your office. I also assume that even though you are not a programmer, you might have taken a class in BASIC at some point. However, knowing BASIC is not a requirement—it actually is a barrier to entry into the ranks of being a successful VBA programmer. There is a good chance that you have recorded a macro in Excel and a similar chance that you were not happy with the results.

Good News: Climbing the Learning Curve Is Easy

Even if you've been frustrated with the macro recorder, it is really just a small speed bump on your road to writing powerful programs in Excel. This book will not only teach you why the macro recorder fails, but also how to change the recorded code into something useful. For all the former BASIC programmers in the audience, I will decode VBA so that you can easily pick through recorded macro code and understand what is happening.

Great News: Excel with VBA Is Worth the Effort

Although you probably have been frustrated with Microsoft over the inability to record macros in Excel, the great news is that Excel VBA is powerful. Absolutely anything you can do in the Excel interface can be duplicated with stunning speed in Excel VBA. If you find yourself routinely creating the same reports manually day after day or week after week, Excel VBA will greatly streamline those tasks.

The authors of this book work for MrExcel Consulting. In this role, we have automated reports for hundreds of clients. The stories are often similar: The MIS department has a several-month backlog of requests. Someone in accounting or engineering discovers that he or she can import some data into Excel and get the reports necessary to run the business. This is a liberating event—you no longer need to wait months for the IT department to write a program. However, the problem is that after you import the data into Excel and win accolades from your manager for producing the report, you will likely be asked to produce the same report every month or every week. This becomes very tedious.

Again, the great news is that with a few hours of VBA programming, you can automate the reporting process and turn it into a few button clicks. The reward is great. So, hang with me as we cover a few of the basics.

This chapter exposes why the macro recorder does not work. It also walks through an example of recorded code and demonstrates why it will work today but fail tomorrow. I realize that the code you see in this chapter might not be familiar to you, but that's okay. The point of this chapter is to demonstrate the fundamental problem with the macro recorder. You also learn the fundamentals of the Visual Basic environment.

Knowing Your Tools: The Developer Tab

Let's start with a basic overview of the tools needed to use VBA. By default, Microsoft hides the VBA tools. You need to complete the following steps to change a setting in Excel options to access the Developer tab.

1. Open the File menu to get to the new Backstage view.
2. Along the left navigation bar, select Options under Excel.
3. In the Excel Options dialog, select Customize Ribbon from the left navigation.
4. In the Right list box, the Developer tab is third from the bottom. Select the check box next to this item.
5. Click OK to return to Excel.

Excel displays the Developer tab shown in Figure 1.1.

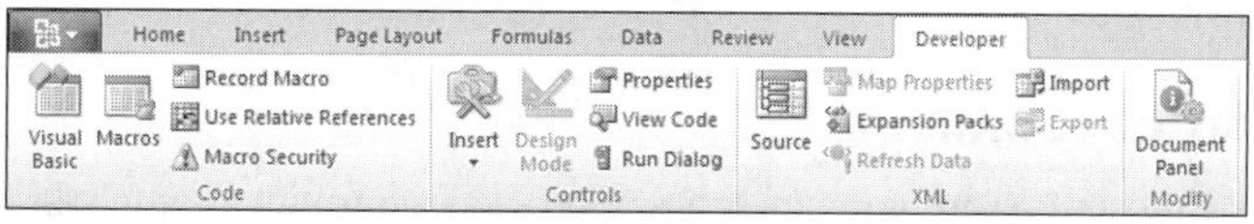

Figure 1.1
The Developer tab provides an interface for running and recording macros.

The Code group on the Developer tab contains the icons used for recording and playing back VBA macros, as listed here:

- **Visual Basic icon**—Opens the Visual Basic Editor.
- **Macros icon**—Displays the Macro dialog, where you can choose to run or edit a macro from the list of macros.
- **Record Macro icon**—Begins the process of recording a macro.
- **Use Relative Reference icon**—Toggles between using relative or absolute recording. With relative recording, Excel will record that you move down three cells. With absolute recording, Excel will record that you selected cell A4.
- **Macro Security icon**—Accesses the Trust Center, where you can choose to allow or disallow macros to run on this computer.

The Controls group of the Developer tab contains an Insert menu where you can access a variety of programming controls that can be placed on the worksheet. See "Assigning a Macro to a Form Control, Text Box, or Shape," later in this chapter. Other icons in this group enable you to work with the on-sheet controls. The Run Dialog button enables you to display a custom dialog box or userform that you designed in VBA. For more on user-forms, see Chapter 10, "Userforms: An Introduction."

> **NOTE**   The XML group of the Developer ribbon contains tools for importing and exporting XML documents.

Macro Security

After VBA macros were used as the delivery method for some high-profile viruses, Microsoft changed the default security settings to prevent macros from running. Therefore, before we can begin discussing the recording of a macro, we need to show you how to adjust the default settings.

In Excel 2010, you can either globally adjust the security settings or control macro settings for certain workbooks by saving the workbooks in a trusted location. Any workbooks stored in a folder that is marked as a trusted location will automatically have its macros enabled.

You can find the macro security settings under the Macro Security icon on the Developer tab. When you click this icon, the Macro Settings category of the Trust Center is displayed. You can use the left navigation bar in the dialog to access the Trusted Locations list.

Adding a Trusted Location

You can choose to store your macro workbooks in a folder that is marked as a trusted location. Any workbook stored in a trusted folder will have its macros enabled. Microsoft suggests that a trusted location should be on your hard drive. The default setting is that you cannot trust a location on a network drive.

To specify a trusted location, follow these steps:

1. Click Macro Security in the Developer tab.
2. Click Trusted Locations in the left navigation pane of the Trust Center.
3. If you want to trust a location on a network drive, select Allow Trusted Locations on My Network.
4. Click the Add New Location button. Excel displays the Microsoft Office Trusted Locations dialog (see Figure 1.2).
5. Click the Browse button. Excel displays the Browse dialog.
6. Browse to the parent folder of the folder you want to be a trusted location. Click the trusted folder. Although the folder name does not appear in the Folder Name box, click OK. The correct folder name will appear in the Browse dialog.

7. If you want to trust subfolders of the selected folder, select Subfolders of This Location Will Be Trusted.

8. Click OK to add the folder to the Trusted Locations list.

> **CAUTION**
>
> Use care when selecting a trusted location. When you double-click an Excel attachment in an e-mail, Outlook stores the file in a temporary folder on your C: drive. You will not want to globally add C:\ and all subfolders to the Trusted Locations list.

Figure 1.2
Manage trusted folders on the Trusted Locations category of the Trust Center.

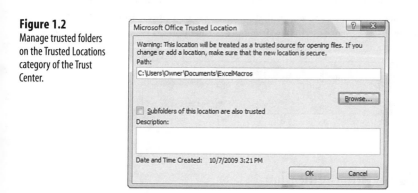

Although trusted locations are not new in Excel 2010, Microsoft has made the process of adding trusted locations more discoverable in Excel 2010.

Using Macro Settings to Enable Macros in Workbooks Outside of Trusted Locations

For all macros not stored in a trusted location, Excel relies on the macro settings. The Low, Medium, High, and Very High settings that were familiar in Excel 2003 have been renamed.

To access the macro settings, click Macro Security in the Developer tab. Excel displays the Macro Settings category of the Trust Center dialog. Select the second option, Disable All Macros with Notification. A description of each option follows:

- **Disable All Macros Without Notification**—This setting prevents all macros from running. This setting is for people who never intend to run macros. Because you are currently holding a book that teaches you how to use macros, it is assumed that this setting is not you. This setting is roughly equivalent to the old Very High Security setting in Excel 2003. With this setting, only macros in the Trusted Locations folders can run.

- **Disable All Macros with Notification**—This setting is similar to Medium security in Excel 2003 and is the recommended setting. In Excel 2003, a Medium setting caused a box to be displayed when you opened a file containing macros. This box forced the person to choose either Enable or Disable. Many novice Excel users randomly choose from this box. In Excel 2010, the message is displayed in the Message Area that macros have been disabled. You can choose to enable the content by clicking that option, as shown in Figure 1.3.

■ **Disable All Macros Except Digitally Signed Macros**—This setting requires you to obtain a digital signing tool from VeriSign or another provider. This might be appropriate if you are going to be selling add-ins to others, but a bit of a hassle if you just want to write macros for your own use.

■ **Enable All Macros (Not Recommended: Potentially Dangerous Code Can Run)**—This setting is similar to Low macro security in Excel 2003. Although it requires the least amount of hassle, it also opens your computer up to attacks from malicious Melissa-like viruses. Microsoft suggests that you do not use this setting.

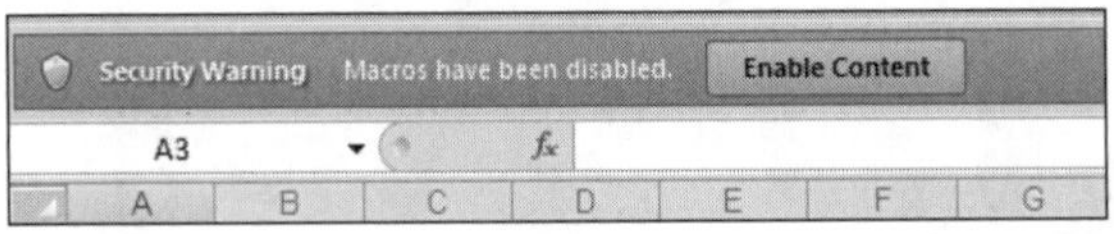

Figure 1.3
Open a macro workbook using the Disable All Macros with Notification setting to enable the macros.

Using Disable All Macros with Notification

It is recommended that you set your macro settings to Disable All Content with Notification. If you use this setting and open a workbook that contains macros, you will see a Security Warning in the area just above the formula bar. Assuming you were expecting macros in this workbook, click Enable Content.

If you do not want to enable macros for the current workbook, dismiss the Security Warning by clicking the *X* at the far right of the message bar.

If you forget to enable the macros and attempt to run a macro, Excel indicates that you cannot run the macro because all macros have been disabled. If this occurs, close the workbook and reopen it to access the message bar again.

> ┌ C A U T I O N ─────────────────────
> After you enable macros in a workbook stored on a local hard drive and then save the workbook, Excel will remember that you previously enabled macros in this workbook. The next time you open this workbook, macros will be automatically enabled.

Overview of Recording, Storing, and Running a Macro

Recording a macro is useful when you do not have experience in writing lines of code in a macro. As you gain more knowledge and experience, you will begin to record lines of code less frequently.

To begin recording a macro, select Record Macro from the Developer tab. Before recording begins, Excel displays the Record Macro dialog box, as shown in Figure 1.4.

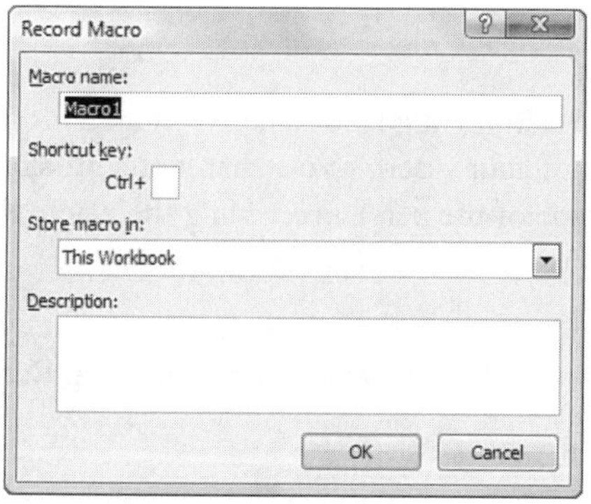

Figure 1.4
Use the Record Macro dialog box to assign a name and a shortcut key to the macro being recorded.

Filling Out the Record Macro Dialog

In the Macro Name field, type a name for the macro. Be sure to type continuous characters. For example, type Macro1 without a space, not Macro 1 with a space. Assuming you will soon be creating many macros, use a meaningful name for the macro. A name such as FormatReport is more useful than Macro1.

The second field in the Record Macro dialog box is a shortcut key. If you type J in this field, and then press Ctrl+J, this macro runs. Note that most of the lowercase shortcuts from Ctrl+a through Ctrl+z already have a use in Excel. Rather than being limited to the unassigned Ctrl+j, you can hold down the Shift key and type Shift+A through Shift+Z in the shortcut box. This will assign the macro to Ctrl+Shift+A.

> **CAUTION**
> You can reuse a shortcut key for a macro. If you assign a macro to Ctrl+c, Excel will run your macro instead of doing the normal action of copy.

In the Record Macro dialog box, choose where you want to save a macro when it is recorded: Personal Macro Workbook, New Workbook, This Workbook. It is recommended that you store macros related to a particular workbook in This Workbook.

The Personal Macro Workbook (Personal.xlsm) is not a visible workbook; it is created if you choose to save the recording in the Personal Macro Workbook. This workbook is used to save a macro in a workbook that will open automatically when you start Excel, thereby enabling you to use the macro. After Excel is started, the workbook is hidden. If you want to display it, select Unhide from the View tab.

> **TIP** It is not recommended you use the personal workbook for every macro you save. Save only those macros that assist you in general tasks—not in tasks that are performed in a specific sheet or workbook.

The fourth box in the Record Macro dialog is for a description. This description is added as a comment to the beginning of your macro. Note that legacy versions of Excel automatically noted the date and username of the person recording the macro. Excel 2010 no longer automatically inserts this information in the Description field.

After you select the location where you want to store the macro, click OK. Record your macro. When you are finished recording the macro, click the Stop Recording icon in the Developer tab.

> **TIP** You can also access a Stop Recording icon in the lower-left corner of the Excel window. Look for a small blue square to the right of the word *Ready* in the status bar. Using this Stop button might be more convenient than returning to the Developer tab. After you record your first macro, this area will usually have a Record Macro icon, which is a small red dot on an Excel worksheet.

Running a Macro

If you assigned a shortcut key to your macro, you can play it by pressing the key combination. Macros can also be assigned to toolbar buttons, forms controls, drawing objects, or you can run them from the Visual Basic toolbar.

Creating a Macro Button on the Ribbon

You can add an icon to a new group on the Ribbon to run your macro. This is appropriate for macros stored in the Personal Macro Workbook. Follow these steps to add a macro button to the Ribbon:

1. Click the File menu and select Excel Options to open the Excel Options dialog.
2. In the Excel Options dialog, select the Customize Ribbon category from the left-side navigation.

> **TIP** Note that a shortcut to replace steps 1 and 2 is to right-click the Ribbon and select Customize Ribbon.

3. In the list box on the right, choose the tab name where you want to add an icon.
4. Click the New Group button below the right list box. Excel adds a new entry called New Group (Custom) to the end of the groups in that ribbon tab.

5. To move the group to the left in the ribbon tab, click the up-arrow icon on the right side of the dialog several times.

6. To rename the group, click the Rename button. Type a new name, such as Report Macros. Click OK. Excel will show the group in the list box as Report Macros (Custom). Note that the word *Custom* will not appear in the Ribbon.

7. Open the upper-left drop-down and choose Macros from the list. The Macros category is fourth in the list. Excel displays a list of available macros in the left list box.

8. Choose a macro from the left list box. Click the Add button in the center of the dialog. Excel moves the macro to the right list box in the selected group. Excel uses a generic VBA icon for all macros. You can change the icon by following steps 9 and 10.

9. Click the macro in the right list box. Click the Rename button at the bottom of the right list box. Excel displays a list of 180 possible icons. Choose an icon. Alternatively, type a friendly label for the icon, such as Format Report.

10. Click OK to close Excel options. The new button appears on the selected Ribbon tab.

Creating a Macro Button on the Quick Access Toolbar

You can add an icon to the Quick Access toolbar to run your macro. If your macro is stored in the Personal Macro Workbook, you can have the button permanently displayed in the Quick Access toolbar. If the macro is stored in the current workbook, you can specify that the icon should appear only when the workbook is open. Follow these steps to add a macro button to the Quick Access toolbar:

1. Click the File menu and select Excel Options to open the Excel Options dialog.

2. In the Excel Options dialog select the Customize category from the left-side navigation.

> **TIP**
>
> Note that a shortcut to replace steps 1 and 2 is to right-click the Quick Access toolbar and select Customize Quick Access Toolbar.

3. If your macro should be available only when the current workbook is open, open the upper-right drop-down and change For All Documents (Default) to For <FileName. xlsm>. Any icons associated with the current workbook are displayed at the end of the Quick Access toolbar.

4. Open the upper-left drop-down and select Macros from the list. The Macros category is fourth in the list. Excel displays a list of available macros in the left list box.

5. Choose a macro from the left list box. Click the Add button in the center of the dialog. Excel moves the macro to the right list box. Excel uses a generic VBA icon for all macros. You can change the icon by following steps 6 through 8.

6. Click the macro in the right list box. Click the Modify button at the bottom of the right list box. Excel displays a list of 180 possible icons (see Figure 1.5).

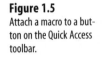

NOTE

Considering Excel 2003 offered 4,096 possible icons and an icon editor, the list of 180 is a major disappointment.

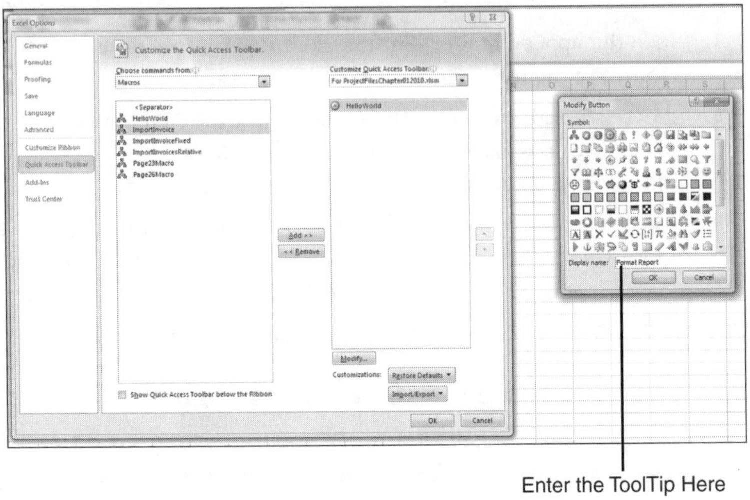

Figure 1.5
Attach a macro to a button on the Quick Access toolbar.

Enter the ToolTip Here

7. Choose an icon from the list. In the Display Name box, replace the macro name with a short name that will appear in the ToolTip for the icon.

8. Click OK to close the Modify Button dialog.

9. Click OK to close Excel options. The new button appears on the Quick Access toolbar.

Assigning a Macro to a Form Control, Text Box, or Shape

If you want to create a macro specific to a workbook, store the macro in the workbook and attach it to a form control or any object on the sheet.

Follow these steps to attach a macro to a form control on the sheet:

1. On the Developer tab, click the Insert button to open its drop-down list. Excel offers 12 form controls and 12 ActiveX controls. Many icons look similar in this drop-down. Click the Button Form Control icon at the upper-left icon in the drop-down.

2. Move your cursor over the worksheet; the cursor changes to a plus sign.

3. Draw a button on the sheet by clicking and holding the left mouse button while drawing a box shape. Release the button when you have finished.

4. Choose a macro from the Assign Macro dialog box and click OK. The button is created with generic text such as Button 1. To customize the text or the button appearance, follow steps 5 through 7.

5. Type a new label for the button. Note that while you are typing, the selection border around the button changes from dots to diagonal lines to indicate that you are in Text Edit mode. You cannot change the button color while in Text Edit mode. To exit Text Edit mode, either click the diagonal lines to change them to dots or Ctrl-click the button again. Note that if you accidentally click away from the button, you should Ctrl+click the button to select it. Then drag the cursor over the text on the button to select the text.

6. Right-click the dots surrounding the button and select Format Control. Excel displays the Format Control dialog with seven tabs across the top. If your Format Control dialog has only a Font tab, you failed to exit Text Edit mode. If this occurred, close the dialog, Ctrl-click the button, and repeat this step.

7. Use the settings in the Format Control dialog to change the font size, font color, margins, and similar settings for the control. Click OK to close the Format Control dialog when you have finished. Click on a cell to unselect the button.

8. Click the button to run the macro.

Macros can be assigned to any worksheet object such as clip art, a shape, SmartArt graphics, or text box. In Figure 1.6, the top button is a traditional button form control. The other images are clip art, a shape with WordArt, and a SmartArt graphic. To assign a macro to any object, right-click the object, and select Assign Macro.

Figure 1.6

Assigning a macro to a form control or an object appropriate for macros stored in the same workbook as the control. You can assign a macro to any of these objects.

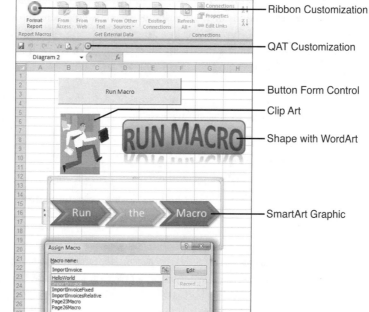

Using New File Types in Excel 2010

Excel 2010 offers support for four file types. Macros are not allowed to be stored in the default file type. You have to use the Save As setting for all of your macro workbooks, or you can change the default file type used by Excel 2010.

The available files types are as follows:

- **Excel Workbook (.xlsx)**—Files are stored as a series of XML objects and then zipped into a single file. This new file-saving paradigm in Excel 2010 allows for significantly smaller file sizes. It also allows other applications (even Notepad!) to edit or create Excel workbooks. Unfortunately, macros cannot be stored in files with an .xlsx extension.

- **Excel Macro-Enabled Workbook (.xlsm)**—This is similar to the default .xlsx format, except macros are allowed. The basic concept is that if someone has an .xlsx file, he or she will not need to worry about malicious macros. However, if they see an .xlsm file, they should be concerned that there might be macros attached.

- **Excel Binary Workbook (.xlsb)**—This is a binary format designed to handle the larger 1.1-million-row grid size in Excel 2010. Legacy versions of Excel stored their files in a proprietary binary format. Although binary formats might load quicker, they are more prone to corruption, and a few lost bits can destroy the whole file. Macros are allowed in this format.

- **Excel 97-2003 Workbook (.xls)**—This format produces files that can be read by anyone using legacy versions of Excel. Macros are allowed in this binary format; however, when you save in this format, you lose access to any cells outside of A1:IV65536. In addition, if someone opens the file in Excel 2003, he or she will lose access to anything that used features introduced in Excel 2007 or later.

To avoid having to choose a macro-enabled workbook in the Save As dialog, you can customize your copy of Excel to always save new files in the .xlsm format by following these steps:

1. Click the File menu and select Excel Options.
2. In the Excel Options dialog, select the Save category from the left navigation pane.
3. The first drop-down is Save Files in This Format. Open the drop-down and select Excel Macro-Enabled Workbook (*.xlsm). Click OK.

> **NOTE**
> Although you and I are not afraid to use macros, I have encountered some people who seem to freak out when they see the .xlsm file type. They actually seem angry that I sent them an .xlsm file that did not have any macros. Their reaction seemed reminiscent of King Arthur's "You got me all worked up!" line in *Monty Python and the Holy Grail*.

If you encounter someone who seems to have a fear of the .xlsm file type, remind them of these points:

- Every workbook created in the past 20 years could have had macros, but in fact, most did not.

- If someone is trying to avoid macros, they should use the security settings to prevent macros from running anyway (refer to Figure 1.3). They can still open the .xlsm file to get the data in the spreadsheet.

With these arguments, I hope you can overcome any fears of the .xlsm file type so that it can be your default file type.

Understanding the VB Editor

Figure 1.7 shows an example of the typical VB Editor screen. You can see three windows: Project Explorer, the Properties window, and the Programming window. Don't worry if your window doesn't look exactly like this because you will see how to display the windows you need in this review of the editor.

Figure 1.7
The VB Editor window.

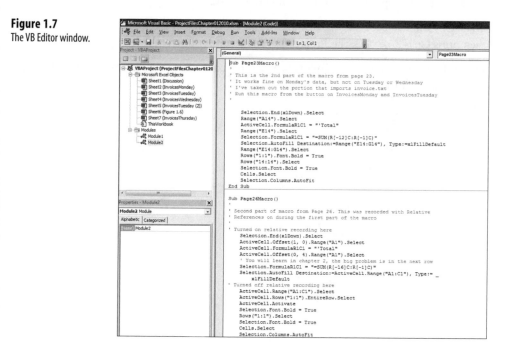

VB Editor Settings

Several settings in the VB Editor enable you to customize this editor. The following sub-section covers the setting that will help with your programming.

Customizing VB Editor Options Settings

Under Tools, Options, Editor, you will find several useful settings. All settings except for one are set correctly by default. The remaining setting requires some consideration on your part. This setting is Require Variable Declaration. By default, Excel does not require you to declare variables. I prefer this setting because it can save time when you create a program. My coauthor prefers to change this setting to require variable declaration. This change forces the compiler to stop if it finds a variable that it does not recognize, which reduces misspelled variable names. It is a matter of your personal preference if you turn this setting on or keep it off.

The Project Explorer

The Project Explorer lists any open workbooks and add-ins that are loaded. If you click the + icon next to the VBA Project, you will see that there is a folder with Microsoft Excel objects. There can also be folders for forms, class modules, and standard modules. Each folder includes one or more individual components.

Right-clicking a component and selecting View Code or just double-clicking the components brings up any code in the Programming window. The exception is userforms, where double-clicking displays the userform in Design view.

To display the Project Explorer window, select View, Project Explorer from the menu, and then press Ctrl+R or click the Project Explorer icon on the toolbar.

Figure 1.8 shows the Project Explorer pane. This pane can show Microsoft Excel objects, userforms, modules, and class modules.

Figure 1.8
The Project Explorer window displays different types of modules.

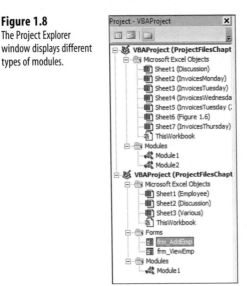

To insert a module, right-click your project, select Insert, and then choose the type of module you want. The available modules are as follows:

- **Microsoft Excel objects**—By default, a project consists of sheet modules for each sheet in the workbook and a single ThisWorkbook module. Code specific to a sheet such as controls or sheet events is placed on the corresponding sheet. Workbook events are placed in the ThisWorkbook module. You learn more about events in Chapter 9, "Event Programming."

- **Forms**—Excel allows you to design your own forms to interact with the user. You learn more about these forms in Chapter 10.

- **Modules**—When you record a macro, Excel automatically creates a module in which to place the code. Most of your code will reside in these types of modules.

- **Class modules**—Class modules are Excel's way of letting you create your own objects. They also allow pieces of code to be shared among programmers without the programmer needing to understand how it works. You will learn more about class modules in Chapter 22, "Creating Classes, Records, and Collections."

The Properties Window

The Properties window enables you to edit the properties of various components such as sheets, workbooks, modules, and form controls. The Property list varies according to what component is selected. To display this window, select View, Properties Window from the menu, press F4, or click the Project Properties icon on the toolbar.

Understanding Shortcomings of the Macro Recorder

Suppose you work in an accounting department. Each day you receive a text file from the company system showing all the invoices produced the prior day. This text file has commas separating each field. The columns in the file are InvoiceDate, InvoiceNumber, SalesRepNumber, CustomerNumber, ProductRevenue, ServiceRevenue, and ProductCost (see Figure 1.9).

Figure 1.9
Invoice.txt file.

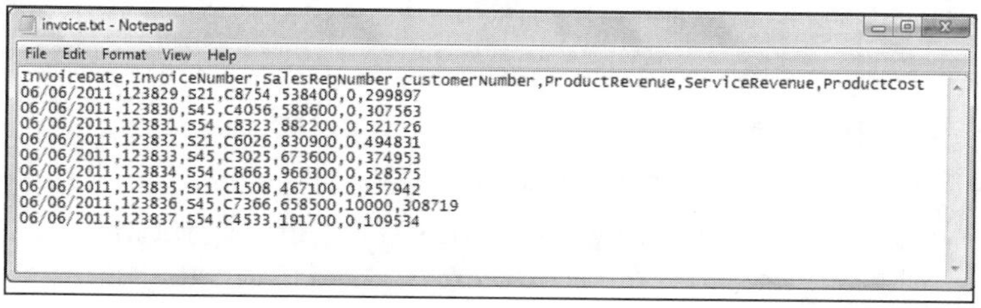

Each morning, you manually import this file into Excel. You add a total row to the data, bold the headings, and then print the report for distribution to a few managers.

This seems like a simple process that would be ideally suited to using the macro recorder. However, due to some problems with the macro recorder, your first few attempts might not be successful. The following case study explains how to overcome these problems.

CASE STUDY: PREPARING TO RECORD THE MACRO

The task mentioned in the previous section is perfect for a macro. However, before you record a macro, think about the steps you will use. In this case, the steps you will use are as follows:

1. Click the File menu and select Open.
2. Navigate to the folder where `Invoice.txt` is stored.
3. Select All Files(*.*) from the Files of Type drop-down list.
4. Select Invoice.txt.
5. Click Open.
6. In the Text Import Wizard—Step 1 of 3, select Delimited from the Original Data Type section.
7. Click Next.
8. In the Text Import Wizard—Step 2 of 3, clear the Tab key and select Comma in the Delimiters section.
9. Click Next.
10. In the Text Import Wizard—Step 3 of 3, select General in the Column Data Format section and change it to `Date: MDY`.
11. Click Finish to import the file.
12. Press the End key followed by the down arrow to move to the last row of data.
13. Press the down arrow one more time to move to the total row.
14. Type the word `Total`.
15. Press the right-arrow key four times to move to Column E of the total row.
16. Click the Autosum button and press Ctrl+Enter to add a total to the Product Revenue column while remaining in that cell.
17. Click the AutoFill handle and drag it from Column E to Column G to copy the total formula to Columns F and G.
18. Highlight Row 1 and click the Bold icon on the Home tab to set the headings in bold.
19. Highlight the Total row and click the Bold icon on the Home tab to set the totals in bold.
20. Press Ctrl+A to select all cells.
21. From the Home tab, select Format, AutoFit Column Width.

After you have rehearsed these steps in your head, you are ready to record your first macro. Open a blank workbook and save it with a name such as `MacroToImportInvoices.xlsm`. Click the Record Macro button on the Developer tab.

In the Record Macro dialog, the default macro name is Macro1. Change this to something descriptive like `ImportInvoice`. Make sure that the macros will be stored in This Workbook. You might want an easy way to run this macro later, so enter the letter `i` in the Shortcut Key field. In the Description field, add a little descriptive text to tell what the macro is doing (see Figure 1.10). Click OK when you are ready.

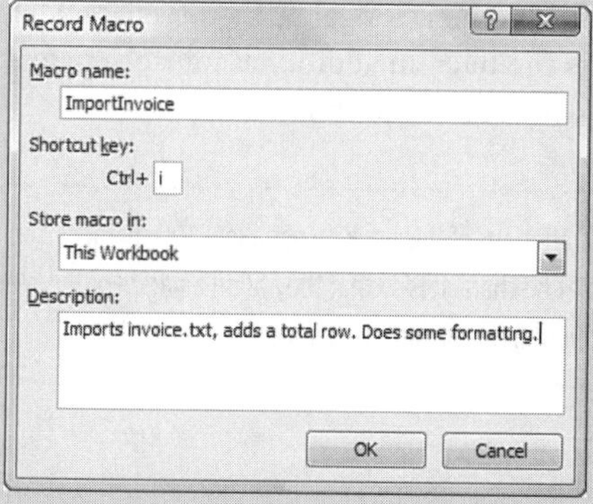

Figure 1.10
Before recording your
macro, complete the
Record Macro dialog box.

Recording the Macro

The macro recorder is now recording your every move, but don't be nervous. For this reason, perform your steps in exact order without extraneous actions. If you accidentally move to Column F, type a value, clear the value, and then move back to E to enter the first total, the recorded macro blindly makes that same mistake day after day after day. Recorded macros move fast, but there is nothing like watching the macro recorder play out your mistakes repeatedly.

Carefully, execute all the actions necessary to produce the report. After you have performed the final step, click the Stop button in the lower-left corner of the Excel window or click Stop Recording in the Developer tab.

Now it is time to look at your code. Switch to the VB Editor by selecting Visual Basic from the Developer tab or pressing Alt+F11.

Examining Code in the Programming Window

Let's look at the code you just recorded from the case study. Don't worry if it doesn't make sense yet.

To open the VB Editor, press Alt+F11. In your VBA Project (MacroToImportInvoices.xls), find the component Module1, right-click the module, and select View Code. Notice that some lines start with an apostrophe—these are comments and are ignored by the program. The macro recorder starts your macros with a few comments, using the description you entered in the Record Macro dialog. The comment for the Keyboard Shortcut is there to remind you of the shortcut.

> **NOTE**
> The comment does *not* assign the shortcut. If you change the comment to be Ctrl+J, it does not change the shortcut. You must change the setting in the Macro dialog box in Excel or run this line of code:
>
> ```
> Application.MacroOptions Macro:="ImportInvoice", _
>         Description:="", ShortcutKey:="j"
> ```

Recorded macro code is usually pretty neat (see Figure 1.11). Each noncomment line of code is indented four characters. If a line is longer than 100 characters, the recorder breaks it into multiple lines and indents the lines an additional four characters. To continue a line of code, type a space and an underscore at the end of the line.

> **NOTE**
>
> Note that the physical limitations of this book do not allow 100 characters on a single line. Therefore, the lines will be broken at 80 characters so that they fit on a page. For this reason, your recorded macro might look slightly different from the ones that appear in this book.

Figure 1.11

The recorded macro is neat looking and nicely indented.

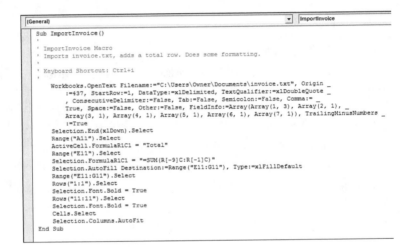

```
(General)                                                                    ▼  ImportInvoice

  Sub ImportInvoice()
  '
  '  ImportInvoice Macro
  '  Imports invoice.txt, adds a total row. Does some formatting.
  '
  '  Keyboard Shortcut: Ctrl+i
  '
      Workbooks.OpenText Filename:="C:\Users\Owner\Documents\invoice.txt", Origin _
          :=437, StartRow:=1, DataType:=xlDelimited, TextQualifier:=xlDoubleQuote _
          , ConsecutiveDelimiter:=False, Tab:=False, Semicolon:=False, Comma:= _
          True, Space:=False, Other:=False, FieldInfo:=Array(Array(1, 3), Array(2, 1), _
          Array(3, 1), Array(4, 1), Array(5, 1), Array(6, 1), Array(7, 1)), TrailingMinusNumbers _
          :=True
      Selection.End(xlDown).Select
      Range("A11").Select
      ActiveCell.FormulaR1C1 = "Total"
      Range("E11").Select
      Selection.FormulaR1C1 = "=SUM(R[-9]C:R[-1]C)"
      Selection.AutoFill Destination:=Range("E11:G11"), Type:=xlFillDefault
      Range("E11:G11").Select
      Rows("1:1").Select
      Selection.Font.Bold = True
      Rows("11:11").Select
      Selection.Font.Bold = True
      Cells.Select
      Selection.Columns.AutoFit
  End Sub
```

Consider that the following seven lines of recorded code is actually only one line of code that has been broken into seven lines for readability:

```
Workbooks.OpenText Filename:= _
    "C:\invoice.txt", Origin:=437, StartRow:=1, DataType:=xlDelimited, _
    TextQualifier:=xlDoubleQuote, ConsecutiveDelimiter:=False,  _
    Tab:=True, Semicolon:=False, Comma:=True, Space:=False,  _
    Other:=False, FieldInfo:=Array(Array(1, 3), Array(2, 1), Array(3, 1), _
    Array(4, 1), Array(5, 1), Array(6, 1), Array(7, 1)),  _
    TrailingMinusNumbers:=True
```

Counting this as one line, the macro recorder was able to record our 21-step process in 14 lines of code, which is pretty impressive.

> **NOTE**
>
> Each action you perform in the Excel user interface might equate to one or more lines of recorded code. Some actions might generate a dozen lines of code.

Test Each Macro

It is always a good idea to test macros. To test your new macro, return to the regular Excel interface by pressing Alt+F11. Close `Invoice.txt` without saving any changes. `MacroToImportInvoices.xls` is still open.

Press Ctrl+I to run the recorded macro. It should work beautifully if you completed the steps correctly. The data is imported, totals are added, bold formatting is applied, and the columns are made wider. This seems like a perfect solution (see Figure 1.12).

Figure 1.12
The macro formats the data in the sheet.

	A	B	C	D	E	F	G
1	InvoiceDate	InvoiceNumber	SalesRepNumber	CustomerNumber	ProductRevenue	ServiceRevenue	ProductCost
2	6/6/2011	123829 S21		C8754	538400	0	299897
3	6/6/2011	123830 S45		C4056	588600	0	307563
4	6/6/2011	123831 S54		C8323	882200	0	521726
5	6/6/2011	123832 S21		C6026	830900	0	494831
6	6/6/2011	123833 S45		C3025	673600	0	374953
7	6/6/2011	123834 S54		C8663	966300	0	528575
8	6/6/2011	123835 S21		C1508	467100	0	257942
9	6/6/2011	123836 S45		C7366	658500	10000	308719
10	6/6/2011	123837 S54		C4533	191700	0	109534
11	Total				5797300	10000	3203740
12							

Running the Macro on Another Day Produces Undesired Results

After testing the macro, be sure to save your macro file to use on another day. The next day, after receiving a new `Invoice.txt` file from the system, you open the macro, press Ctrl+I to run it, and disaster strikes. The data for June 6 happened to have 9 invoices, while the data for the June 7 has 17 invoices. However, the recorded macro blindly added the totals in Row 12 because this was where you put the totals when the macro was recorded (see Figure 1.13).

Figure 1.13
The intent of the recorded macro was to add a total at the end of the data, but the recorder made a macro that always adds totals at Row 11.

	A	B	C	D	E	F	G
1	InvoiceDate	InvoiceNumber	SalesRepNumber	CustomerNumber	ProductRevenue	ServiceRevenue	ProductCost
2	6/7/2011	123813 S82		C8754	716100	12000	423986
3	6/7/2011	123814		C4894	224200	0	131243
4	6/7/2011	123815 S43		C7278	277000	0	139208
5	6/7/2011	123816 S54		C6425	746100	15000	350683
6	6/7/2011	123817 S43		C6291	928300	0	488988
7	6/7/2011	123818 S43		C1000	723200	0	383069
8	6/7/2011	123819 S82		C6025	982600	0	544025
9	6/7/2011	123820 S17		C8026	490100	45000	243808
10	6/7/2011	123821 S43		C4244	615800	0	300579
11	Total	123822 S45		C1007	5703400	72000	3005589
12	6/7/2011	123823 S87		C1878	338100	0	165666
13	6/7/2011	123824 S43		C3068	567900	0	265775
14	6/7/2011	123825 S43		C7571	123456	0	55555
15	6/7/2011	123826 S55		C7181	37900	0	19811
16	6/7/2011	123827 S43		C7570	582700	0	292000
17	6/7/2011	123828 S87		C5302	495000	0	241504
18	6/7/2011	123828 S87		C5302	495000	0	241504
19							

This problem arises because the macro recorder is recording all your actions in absolute mode by default. Instead of using the default state of the macro recorder, the next section discusses relative recording and how this might get you closer to a final solution.

Possible Solution: Use Relative References When Recording

By default, the macro recorder records all actions as *absolute* actions. If you navigate to Row 11 when you record the macro on Monday, the macro will always go to Row 11 when the macro is run. This is rarely appropriate when dealing with variable numbers of rows of data. The better option is to use relative references when recording.

Macros recorded with absolute references note the actual address of the cell pointer, such as A11. Macros recorded with relative references note that the cell pointer should move a certain number of rows and columns from its current position. For example, if the cell pointer starts in cell A1, the code `ActiveCell.Offset(16, 1).Select` would move the cell pointer to B17, which is the cell 16 rows down and 1 column to the right.

Let's try the same case study again, this time using relative references. The solution will be much closer to working correctly.

CASE STUDY: RECORDING THE MACRO WITH RELATIVE REFERENCES

Let's try to record the macro again, but this time you will use relative references. Close `Invoice.txt` without saving changes. In the workbook `MacroToImportInvoices.xls`, record a new macro by selecting Record Macro from the Developer tab. Give the new macro a name of `ImportInvoicesRelative` and assign a different shortcut key such as Ctrl+Shift+J (see Figure 1.14).

Figure 1.14
Getting ready to record a second try.

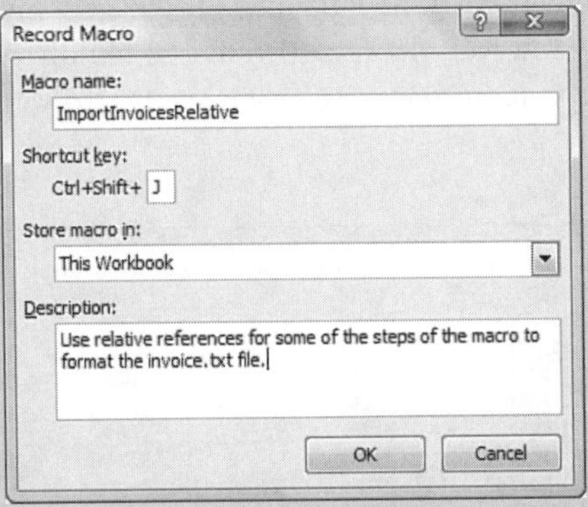

As you start to record the macro, go through the process of opening the `Invoice.txt` file. Before navigating to the last row of data by pressing the End key + then the down-arrow key, click the Use Relative Reference button on the Developer tab (refer to Figure 1.1).

Continue through the actions in the script from the case study:

1. Press the End key followed by the down-arrow key to move to the last row of data.

2. Press the down arrow one more time to move to the total row.

3. Type the word `Total`.

4. Press the right-arrow key four times to move to Column E of the Total row.

5. Click the Autosum button, and then press Ctrl+Enter to add a total to the Product Revenue column while remaining in that cell.

6. Click the AutoFill handle and drag from Column E to Column G to copy the total formula to Columns F and G.

7. Press Shift+spacebar to select the entire row. Type Ctrl+b to apply bold formatting to it. At this point, you need to move to Cell A1 to apply bold to the headings. You do not want the macro recorder to record the movement from Row 11 to Row 1 because it would record this as moving 10 rows up, which might not be correct tomorrow. Before moving to A1, toggle the Use Relative Recording button off, and then continue recording the rest of the macro.

8. Highlight Row 1 and click the Bold icon to set the headings in bold.

9. Press Ctrl+A to select all cells.

10. From the Home tab, select Format, AutoFit Column Width.

11. Select cell A1.

12. Stop recording.

Press Alt+F11 to go to the VB Editor to review your code. The new macro appears in Module1 below the previous macro.

If you close Excel between recording the first and second macro, Excel inserts a new module called Module2 for the newly recorded macro.

The following code has been edited with two comments that will help you remember where you turned the relative recording on and then off:

```
Sub ImportInvoicesRelative()
'
' ImportInvoicesRelative Macro
' Use relative references for some of the steps of the macro
' to format the invoice.txt file
'

    Workbooks.OpenText Filename:= _
        "C:\invoice.txt", Origin:=437, StartRow:=1, DataType:=xlDelimited, _
        TextQualifier:=xlDoubleQuote, ConsecutiveDelimiter:=False, _
        Tab:=True, Semicolon:=False, Comma:=True, Space:=False, _
        Other:=False, FieldInfo:=Array(Array(1, 3), Array(2, 1), Array(3, 1), _
        Array(4, 1), Array(5, 1), Array(6, 1), Array(7, 1)), _
        TrailingMinusNumbers:=True

' Turned on relative recording here
    Selection.End(xlDown).Select
    ActiveCell.Offset(1, 0).Range("A1").Select
    ActiveCell.FormulaR1C1 = "'Total"
    ActiveCell.Offset(0, 4).Range("A1").Select
    Selection.FormulaR1C1 = "=SUM(R[-16]C:R[-1]C)"
    Selection.AutoFill Destination:=ActiveCell.Range("A1:C1"), Type:= _
        xlFillDefault
```

```
' Turned off relative recording here
    ActiveCell.Range("A1:C1").Select
    ActiveCell.Rows("1:1").EntireRow.Select
    ActiveCell.Activate
    Selection.Font.Bold = True
    Rows("1:1").Select
    Selection.Font.Bold = True
    Cells.Select
    Selection.Columns.AutoFit
    Range("A1").Select
End Sub
```

To test the macro, close Invoice.txt without saving, and then run the macro with Ctrl+J. Everything should look good, and you should get the same results.

The next test is to see whether the program works on the next day when you might have more rows. Figure 1.15 shows the data for June 7.

Figure 1.15
Will the macro with relative references work with this data?

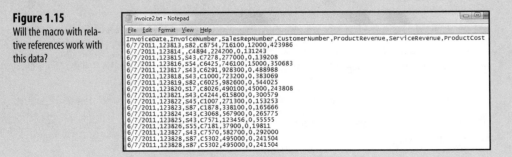

Open MacroToImportInvoices.xls and run the new macro with Ctrl+J. This time, everything should look good with the totals in the correct places. Look at Figure 1.16—see anything out of the ordinary?

Figure 1.16
The result of running the Relative macro.

	A	B	C	D	E	F	G
1	InvoiceDate	InvoiceNumber	SalesRepNumber	CustomerNumber	ProductRevenue	ServiceRevenue	ProductCost
2	6/7/2011	123813	S82	C8754	716100	12000	423986
3	6/7/2011	123814		C4894	224200	0	131243
4	6/7/2011	123815	S43	C7278	277000	0	139208
5	6/7/2011	123816	S54	C6425	746100	15000	350683
6	6/7/2011	123817	S43	C6291	928300	0	488988
7	6/7/2011	123818	S43	C1000	723200	0	383069
8	6/7/2011	123819	S82	C6025	982600	0	544025
9	6/7/2011	123820	S17	C8026	490100	45000	243808
10	6/7/2011	123821	S43	C4244	615800	0	300579
11	6/7/2011	123822	S45	C1007	271300	0	153253
12	6/7/2011	123823	S87	C1878	338100	0	165666
13	6/7/2011	123824	S43	C3068	567900	0	265775
14	6/7/2011	123825	S43	C7571	123456	0	55555
15	6/7/2011	123826	S55	C7181	37900	0	19811
16	6/7/2011	123827	S43	C7570	582700	0	292000
17	6/7/2011	123828	S87	C5302	495000	0	241504
18	6/7/2011	123828	S87	C5302	495000	0	241504
19	Total				3527156	0	1735647

If you aren't careful, you might print these reports for your manager. If you did, you would be in trouble. When you look in cell E19, Excel has inserted a green triangle to tell you to look at the cell. If you happened to try this back in Excel 95 or Excel 97 before SmartTags, there would not have been an indicator that anything was wrong.

When you move the cell pointer to E19, an alert indicator pops up near the cell. This indicator tells you the formula fails to include adjacent cells. If you look in the formula bar, you will see that the macro totaled only from Row 10 to Row 18. Neither the relative recording nor the nonrelative recording is smart enough to replicate the logic of the AutoSum button.

At this point, some people would give up. However, imagine that you might have had fewer invoice records on this particular day. Excel would have rewarded you with the illogical formula of =SUM(E6:E1048574) and a circular reference, as shown in Figure 1.17.

Figure 1.17
The result of running the Relative macro with fewer invoice records.

	A	B	C	D	E	F	G
1	InvoiceDate	InvoiceNumber	SalesRepNumber	CustomerNumber	ProductRevenue	ServiceRevenue	ProductCost
2	6/9/2011	123850		C1654	161000	0	90761
3	6/9/2011	123851		C6460	275500	10000	146341
4	6/9/2011	123852		C5143	925400	0	473515
5	6/9/2011	123853		C7868	148200	0	75700
6	6/9/2011	123854		C3310	890200	0	468333
7	Total				0	0	0

E7 — f_x =SUM(E6:E1048574)

If you have tried using the macro recorder, most likely you would run into similar problems as the ones produced in the last two case studies. Although this is frustrating, you should be happy to know that the macro recorder actually gets you 95 percent of the way to a useful macro.

Your job is to recognize where the macro recorder is likely to fail and then to be able to dive into the VBA code to fix the one or two lines that require adjusting to have a perfect macro. With some added human intelligence, you can produce awesome macros to speed up your daily work.

If you are like me, you are cursing Microsoft about now. We have wasted a good deal of time over a couple of days, and neither macro works. What makes it worse is that this sort of procedure would have been handled perfectly by the old Lotus 1-2-3 macro recorder introduced in 1983. Mitch Kapor solved this problem 24 years ago, and Microsoft still can't get it right.

Did you know that up through Excel 97, Microsoft Excel secretly ran Lotus command-line macros? I found this out right after Microsoft quit supporting Excel 97. At that time, a number of companies upgraded to Excel XP, which no longer supported the Lotus 1-2-3 macros. Many of these companies hired us to convert the old Lotus 1-2-3 macros to Excel VBA. It is interesting that from Excel 5, Excel 95, and Excel 97, Microsoft offered an interpreter that could handle the Lotus macros that solved this problem correctly, yet their own macro recorder couldn't (and still can't!) solve the problem.

Never Use the AutoSum Button While Recording a Macro

There actually is a macro-recorder solution to the current problem. It is important to recognize that the macro recorder will never correctly record the intent of the AutoSum button.

If you are in cell E99 and click the AutoSum button, Excel starts scanning from cell E98 upward until it locates a text cell, a blank cell, or a formula. It then proposes a formula that sums everything between the current cell and the found cell.

However, the macro recorder records the particular result of that search on the day that the macro was recorded. Rather than record something along the lines of "do the normal AutoSum logic," the macro recorder inserts a single line of code to add up the previous 98 cells.

The somewhat bizarre workaround is to type a SUM function that uses a mix of relative and absolute row references. If you type =SUM(E$2:E10) while the macro recorder is running, Excel correctly adds code that will always sum from a fixed row two down to the relative reference that is just above the current cell.

Here is the resulting code with a few comments:

```
Sub FormatInvoice3()
'
' FormatInvoice2 Macro
' Third try. Use relative. Don't touch AutoSum
'
' Keyboard Shortcut: Ctrl+Shift+K
'
    Workbooks.OpenText Filename:="C:\Users\Owner\Documents\invoice.txt", Ori-
gin _
        :=437, StartRow:=1, DataType:=xlDelimited,
TextQualifier:=xlDoubleQuote _
        , ConsecutiveDelimiter:=False, Tab:=False, Semicolon:=False, Comma:= _
        True, Space:=False, Other:=False, FieldInfo:=Array(Array(1, 3), Ar-
ray(2, 1), _
        Array(3, 1), Array(4, 1), Array(5, 1), Array(6, 1), Array(7, 1)),
TrailingMinusNumbers _
        :=True
    ' Relative turned on here
    Selection.End(xlDown).Select
    ActiveCell.Offset(1, 0).Range("A1").Select
    ActiveCell.FormulaR1C1 = "Total"
    ActiveCell.Offset(0, 4).Range("A1").Select
    ' Don't use AutoSum. Type this formula:
    Selection.FormulaR1C1 = "=SUM(R2C:R[-1]C)"
    Selection.AutoFill Destination:=ActiveCell.Range("A1:C1"), Type:= _
        xlFillDefault
    ActiveCell.Range("A1:C1").Select
    ' Relative turned off here
    ActiveCell.Rows("1:1").EntireRow.Select
    ActiveCell.Activate
```

```
        Selection.Font.Bold = True
        Cells.Select
        Selection.Columns.AutoFit
        Range("A1").Select
    End Sub
```

This third macro will consistently work with any size dataset.

To see a demo of recording this macro, search for Excel VBA 1 at YouTube.

Three Tips When Using the Macro Recorder

You will rarely be able to record 100 percent of your macros and have them work. However, you will get much closer by using these three tips demonstrated in the following subsections.

Tip 1: Use Relative References Setting Usually Needs to Be On

Microsoft should have made this setting be the default. Unless you specifically need to move to Row 1 from the bottom of a dataset, you should usually leave the Use Relative References button in the Developer tab turned on.

Tip 2: Use Special Navigation Keys to Move to Bottom of a Dataset

If you are at the top of a dataset and need to move to the last cell with data, you can press Ctrl+down arrow or press the End key and then the down-arrow key.

Similarly, to move to the last column in the current row of the dataset, press Ctrl+right arrow or press End and then press the right-arrow key.

By using these navigation keys, you can jump to the end of the dataset, no matter how many rows or columns you have today.

Tip 3: Never Touch the AutoSum Icon While Recording a Macro

The macro recorder will not record the "essence" of the AutoSum button. Instead, it will hard-code the formula that resulted from pressing the AutoSum button. This formula does not work any time you have more or fewer records in the dataset.

Instead, type a formula with a single dollar sign, such as =SUM(E$2:E10). When this is done, the macro recorder records the first E$2 as a fixed reference and starts the SUM range directly below the Row 1 headings. Provided the active cell is E11, the macro recorder recognizes E10 as a relative reference pointing directly above the current cell.

Next Steps

Chapter 2, "This Sounds Like BASIC, So Why Doesn't It Look Familiar?" examines the three macros you recorded in this chapter to make more sense out of them. After you know how to decode the VBA code, it will feel natural to either correct the recorded code or simply write code from scratch. Hang on through one more chapter. You'll soon learn that VBA is the solution, and you'll be writing useful code that works consistently.

This Sounds Like BASIC, So Why Doesn't It Look Familiar?

I Can't Understand This Code

As mentioned previously, if you have taken a class in a procedural language such as BASIC or COBOL, you might be confused when you look at VBA code. Even though VBA stands for *Visual Basic for Applications*, it is an *object-oriented* version of BASIC. Here is a bit of VBA code:

```
Selection.End(xlDown).Select
Range("A11").Select
ActiveCell.FormulaR1C1 = "Total"
Range("E11").Select
Selection.FormulaR1C1 = "=SUM(R[-9]C:R[-1] _
C)"
Selection.AutoFill
Destination:=Range("E11:G11"),
Type:=xlFillDefault
```

This code likely makes no sense to anyone who knows only procedural languages. Unfortunately, your first introduction to programming in school (assuming you are over 30 years old) would have been a procedural language.

Here is a section of code written in the BASIC language:

```
For x = 1 to 10
    Print Rpt$(" ",x);
    Print "*"
Next x
```

If you run this code, you get a pyramid of asterisks on your screen:

```
 *
  *
   *
    *
     *
      *
       *
        *
         *
          *
```

IN THIS CHAPTER

I Can't Understand This Code 33

Understanding the Parts of VBA "Speech" 34

VBA Is Not Really Hard 37

Examining Recorded Macro Code: Using the VB Editor and Help 39

Using Debugging Tools to Figure Out Recorded Code 46

Object Browser: The Ultimate Reference 46

Seven Tips for Cleaning Up Recorded Code 48

If you have ever been in a procedural programming class, you can probably look at the code and figure out what is going on because procedural languages are more English-like than object-oriented languages. The statement `Print "Hello World"` follows the verb-object format, which is how you would generally talk. Let's step away from programming for a second and think about a concrete example.

Understanding the Parts of VBA "Speech"

If you were going to write code for instructions to play soccer using BASIC, the instruction to kick a ball would look something like this:

"Kick the Ball"

Hey—this is how you talk! It makes sense. You have a verb (kick) and then a noun (ball). The BASIC code in the preceding section has a verb (print) and a noun (asterisk). Life is good.

Here is the problem. VBA doesn't work like this. In fact, no object-oriented language works like this. In an object-oriented language, the objects (nouns) are most important, hence the name: object-oriented. If you were going to write code for instructions to play soccer with VBA, the basic structure would be as follows:

```
Ball.Kick
```

You have a noun (ball), which comes first. In VBA, this is an *object*. Then you have the verb (kick), which comes next. In VBA, this is a *method*.

The basic structure of VBA is a bunch of lines of code where you have

```
Object.Method
```

Needless to say, this is not English. If you took a romance language in high school, you will remember that those languages use a "noun adjective" construct. However, no one uses "noun verb" to tell someone to do something:

```
Water.Drink
Food.Eat
Girl.Kiss
```

That is why VBA is confusing to someone who previously took a procedural programming class.

Let's carry the analogy a bit further. Imagine you walk onto a grassy field and there are five balls in front of you. There is a soccer ball, basketball, baseball, bowling ball, and tennis ball. You want to instruct the kid on your soccer team to "Kick the soccer ball."

If you tell him to kick the ball (or `ball.kick`), you really aren't sure which one of the five balls he will kick. Maybe he will kick the one closest to him, which could be a problem if he is standing in front of the bowling ball.

For almost any noun, or object in VBA, there is a collection of that object. Think about Excel. If you can have one row, you can have a bunch of rows. If you can have one cell, you can have a bunch of cells. If you can have one worksheet, you can have a bunch of worksheets. The only difference between an object and a collection is that you will add an *s* to the name of the object:

Row becomes Rows.

Cell becomes Cells.

Ball becomes Balls.

When you refer to something that is a collection, you have to tell the programming language to which item you are referring. There are a couple of ways to do this. You can refer to an item by using a number. For example, if the soccer ball is the second ball, you might say this:

```
Balls(2).Kick
```

This works fine, but it could be a dangerous way to program. For example, it might work on Tuesday. However, if you get to the field on Wednesday and someone has rearranged the balls, `Balls(2).Kick` might be a painful exercise.

A much safer way to go is to use a name for the object in a collection. You can say the following:

```
Balls("Soccer").Kick
```

With this method, you always know that it will be the soccer ball that is being kicked.

So far, so good. You know a ball will be kicked, and you know it will be the soccer ball. For most of the verbs, or methods in Excel VBA, there are *parameters* that tell *how* to do the action. These parameters act as adverbs. You might want the soccer ball to be kicked to the left and with a hard force. In this case, the method would have a number of parameters that tell how the program should perform the method:

```
Balls("Soccer").Kick Direction:=Left, Force:=Hard
```

When looking at VBA code, the colon-equals combination indicates that you are looking at parameters of how the verb should be performed.

Sometimes, a method will have a list of 10 parameters, some of which are optional. For example, if the `Kick` method has an `Elevation` parameter, you would have this line of code:

```
Balls("Soccer").Kick Direction:=Left, Force:=Hard, Elevation:=High
```

Here is the confusing part. Every method has a default order for its parameters. If you are not a conscientious programmer and you happen to know the order of the parameters, you can leave off the parameter names. The following code is equivalent to the previous line of code:

```
Balls("Soccer").Kick Left, Hard, High
```

This throws a monkey wrench into our understanding. Without the colon-equals, it is not obvious that you have parameters. Unless you know the parameter order, you might not understand what is being said. It is pretty easy with `Left`, `Hard`, and `High`, but when you have parameters like the following:

```
Shapes.AddShape type:=1, Left:=10, Top:=20, Width:=100, Height:=200
```

it gets confusing to see

```
Shapes.AddShape 1, 10, 20, 100, 200
```

The preceding is valid code. However, unless you know that the default order of the parameters for this `Add` method is `Type`, `Left`, `Top`, `Width`, `Height`, this code will not make sense. The default order for any particular method is the order of the parameters as shown in the help topic for that method.

To make life more confusing, you are allowed to start specifying parameters in their default order without naming them, and then switch to naming parameters when you hit one that does not match the default order. If you want to kick the ball to the left and high, but do not care about the force (you are willing to accept the default force), the following two statements are equivalent:

```
Balls("Soccer").Kick Direction:=Left, Elevation:=High
Balls("Soccer").Kick Left, Elevation:=High
```

However, keep in mind that as soon as you start naming parameters, they have to be named for the remainder of that line of code.

Some methods simply act on their own. To simulate pressing the F9 key, you use this code:

```
Application.Calculate
```

Other methods perform an action and create something. For example, you can add a worksheet using the following:

```
Worksheets.Add Before:=Worksheets(1)
```

However, because `Worksheets.Add` creates a new object, you can assign the results of this method to a variable. In this case, you must surround the parameters with parentheses:

```
Set MyWorksheet = Worksheets.Add(Before:=Worksheets(1))
```

One final bit of grammar is necessary: adjectives. Just as adjectives describe a noun, *properties* describe an object. Because you are Excel fans, let's switch from the soccer analogy to an Excel analogy midstream. There is an object to describe the active cell. Fortunately, it has a very intuitive name:

```
ActiveCell
```

Suppose you want to change the color of the active cell to yellow. There is a property called `InteriorColor` for a cell that uses a complex series of codes. However, you can turn a cell to yellow by using this code:

```
ActiveCell.Interior.ColorIndex = 6
```

You can see how this can be confusing. Again, there is the Noun-dot-Something construct, but this time it is `Object.Property` rather than `Object.Method`. Telling them apart is quite subtle—there is no colon before the equal sign. A property is almost always being set equal to something, or perhaps the value of a property is being assigned to something else.

To make this cell color the same as cell A1, you might say this:

```
ActiveCell.Interior.ColorIndex = Range("A1").Interior.ColorIndex
```

`Interior.ColorIndex` is a property. By changing the value of a property, you can make things look different. It is kind of bizarre—change an adjective, and you are actually doing something to the cell. Humans would say, "Color the cell yellow," whereas VBA says this:

```
ActiveCell.Interior.ColorIndex = 6
```

Table 2.1 summarizes the VBA "parts of speech."

Table 2.1 Parts of the VBA Programming Language

VBA Component	Analogous To	Notes
Object	Noun	
Collection	Plural noun	Usually specifies which object: `Worksheets(1)`.
Method	Verb	`Object.Method.`
Parameter	Adverb	Lists parameters after the method. Separate the parameter name from its value with `:=`.
Property	Adjective	You can set a property `activecell.height 10` or query the value of a property `x = activecell.height`.

VBA Is Not Really Hard

Knowing whether you are dealing with properties or methods will help you set up the correct syntax for your code. Don't worry if it all seems confusing right now. When you are writing VBA code from scratch, it is tough to know whether the process of changing a cell to yellow requires a verb or an adjective. Is it a method or a property?

This is where the beauty of the macro recorder comes in. When you don't know how to code something, you record a short little macro, look at the recorded code, and figure out what is going on.

VBA Help Files: Using F1 to Find Anything

This is a radically cool feature, but you need to jump through a few hoops first. If you are going to write VBA macros, you absolutely *must* have the VBA help topics installed. The problem: The VBA help topics are not installed in the default Office install. Follow these steps to see whether you have VBA help installed:

1. Open Excel and switch to the VB Editor by pressing Alt+F11. From the Insert menu, select Module (see Figure 2.1).

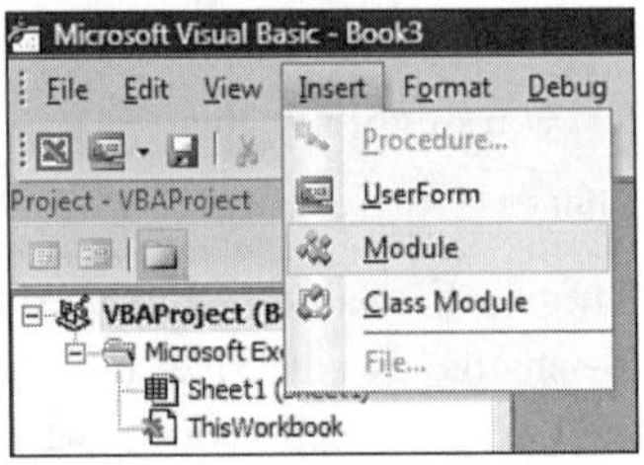
Microsoft Visual Basic - Book3
File Edit View Insert Format Debug
Procedure...
UserForm
Module
Class Module
File...
Project - VBAProject
VBAProject (B
Microsoft Ex
Sheet1
ThisWorkbook

Figure 2.1
Insert a new module in the blank workbook.

2

2. Type the three lines of code shown in Figure 2.2. Click inside the word *MsgBox*.

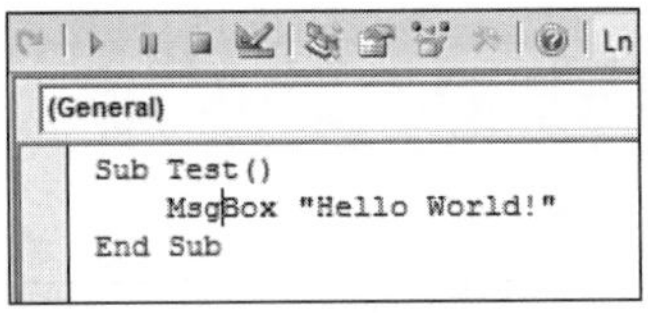
(General)
Sub Test()
MsgBox "Hello World!"
End Sub

Figure 2.2
Click inside the word *MsgBox* and press F1.

3. With the cursor in the word *MsgBox*, press F1. If the VBA help topics are installed, you will see the help topic shown in Figure 2.3.

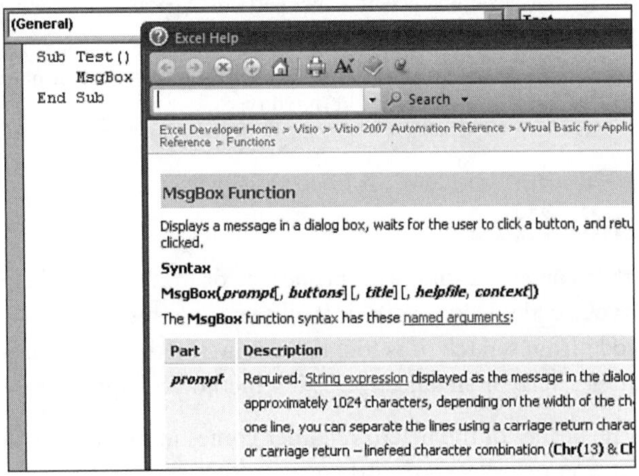
(General)
Sub Test()
MsgBox
End Sub
Excel Help
Search
Excel Developer Home > Visio > Visio 2007 Automation Reference > Visual Basic for Applic
Reference > Functions
MsgBox Function
Displays a message in a dialog box, waits for the user to click a button, and retu
clicked.
Syntax
MsgBox(prompt[, buttons] [, title] [, helpfile, context])
The MsgBox function syntax has these named arguments:
Part
Description
prompt
Required. String expression displayed as the message in the dialo
approximately 1024 characters, depending on the width of the ch
one line, you can separate the lines using a carriage return chara
or carriage return – linefeed character combination (Chr(13) & Ch

Figure 2.3
If the VBA help topics have been installed, you will get this screen.

However, if you get a message saying that help is not available on this topic, find the original CDs (or get your network administrator to grant rights to the installation folder) so that you can install the VBA help topics. Go through the process of doing a reinstall. During reinstall, select the custom install and be sure to select the VBA help files.

Using Help Topics

If you request help on a function or method, the help topic walks you through the various available arguments. If you browse to the bottom of the help topics, code samples are provided under the Example heading, which is a great resource (see Figure 2.4).

Figure 2.4
Most help topics include code samples.

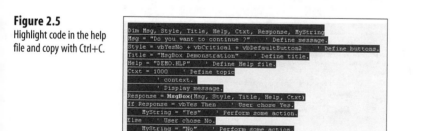

It is possible to select the code, copy it to the Clipboard by pressing Ctrl+C (see Figure 2.5), and then paste it into your module by pressing Ctrl+V.

After you record a macro, if there are objects or methods about which you are unsure, you can get help by inserting the cursor in any keyword and pressing F1.

Figure 2.5
Highlight code in the help file and copy with Ctrl+C.

Examining Recorded Macro Code: Using the VB Editor and Help

Let's take a look at the code that you recorded in Chapter 1, "Unleash the Power of Excel with VBA," to see whether it makes more sense now in the context of objects, properties, and methods. You can also see whether it's possible to correct the errors brought about by the macro recorder.

Figure 2.6 shows the first code that Excel recorded in the example from Chapter 1.

Figure 2.6
Recorded code from the example in Chapter 1.

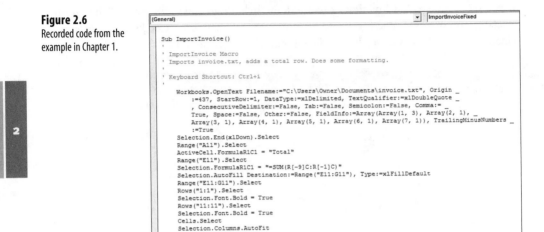

```
(General)                                                          ▼  ImportInvoiceFixed

    Sub ImportInvoice()
    '
    ' ImportInvoice Macro
    ' Imports invoice.txt, adds a total row. Does some formatting.
    '
    ' Keyboard Shortcut: Ctrl+i
    '
        Workbooks.OpenText Filename:="C:\Users\Owner\Documents\invoice.txt", Origin _
            :=437, StartRow:=1, DataType:=xlDelimited, TextQualifier:=xlDoubleQuote _
            , ConsecutiveDelimiter:=False, Tab:=False, Semicolon:=False, Comma:= _
            True, Space:=False, Other:=False, FieldInfo:=Array(Array(1, 3), Array(2, 1), _
            Array(3, 1), Array(4, 1), Array(5, 1), Array(6, 1), Array(7, 1)), TrailingMinusNumbers _
            :=True
        Selection.End(xlDown).Select
        Range("A11").Select
        ActiveCell.FormulaR1C1 = "Total"
        Range("E11").Select
        Selection.FormulaR1C1 = "=SUM(R[-9]C:R[-1]C)"
        Selection.AutoFill Destination:=Range("E11:G11"), Type:=xlFillDefault
        Range("E11:G11").Select
        Rows("1:1").Select
        Selection.Font.Bold = True
        Rows("11:11").Select
        Selection.Font.Bold = True
        Cells.Select
        Selection.Columns.AutoFit
    End Sub
```

Now that you understand the concept of Noun.Verb or Object.Method, consider the first line of code that says Workbooks.OpenText. In this case, Workbooks is an object, while OpenText is a method. Click your cursor inside the word OpenText and press F1 for an explanation of the OpenText method (see Figure 2.7).

The help file confirms that OpenText is a method or an action word. The default order for all the arguments that can be used with OpenText appears in the gray box. Notice that only one argument is required: FileName. All the other arguments are listed as optional.

Figure 2.7
Help topic for the OpenText method.

Excel Help

Search ▼

Excel Developer Home > Excel Object Model Reference > Workbooks Object > Methods

Excel Developer Reference

Workbooks.OpenText Method

Loads and parses a text file as a new workbook with a single sheet that contains the parsed text-file data.

expression.OpenText(*Filename, Origin, StartRow, DataType, TextQualifier, ConsecutiveDelimiter, Tab, Semicolon, Comma, Space, Other, OtherChar, FieldInfo, TextVisualLayout, DecimalSeparator, ThousandsSeparator, TrailingMinusNumbers, Local*)

expression A variable that represents a **Workbooks** object.

Parameters

Name	Required/Optional	Data Type	Description
Filename	Required	**String**	Specifies the file name of the text file to be opened and parsed.
Origin	Optional	**Variant**	Specifies the origin of the text file. Can be one of the following **XlPlatform** constants: **xlMacintosh**, **xlWindows**, or **xlMSDOS**. Additionally, this could be an integer representing the code page number of the desired code page. For example, "1256" would specify that the encoding of the source text file is Arabic (Windows). If this argument is omitted, the method uses the current setting of the **File Origin** option in the **Text Import Wizard**.
StartRow	Optional	**Variant**	The row number at which to start parsing text. The default value is 1.
DataType	Optional	**Variant**	Specifies the column format of the data in the file. Can be one of the following **XlTextParsingType** constants: **xlDelimited** or **xlFixedWidth**. If this argument is not specified, Microsoft Excel attempts to determine the

Developer Reference   Connected to Office Online

Optional Parameters

The help file can tell you if you happen to skip an optional parameter. For StartRow, the help file indicates that the default value is 1. If you leave out the StartRow parameter, Excel starts importing at Row 1. This is fairly safe.

Now look at the help file note about Origin. If this argument is omitted, you inherit whatever value was used for Origin the last time someone used this feature in Excel on this computer. That is a recipe for disaster. For example, your code may work 98 percent of the time. However, immediately after someone imports an Arabic file, Excel will remember the setting for Arabic and assume this is what your macro wants if you don't explicitly code this parameter.

Defined Constants

Look at the help file entry for DataType in Figure 2.7, which says it can be one of these constants: xlDelimited or xlFixedWidth. The help file says these are the valid xlTextParsingType constants that are predefined in Excel VBA. In the VB Editor, press Ctrl+G to bring up the Immediate window. In the Immediate window, type this line and press Enter:

```
Print xlFixedWidth
```

The answer appears in the Immediate window. xlFixedWidth is the equivalent of saying "2" (see Figure 2.8). Ask the Immediate window to Print xlDelimited, which is really the same as typing 1. Microsoft correctly assumes that it is easier for someone to read code that uses the somewhat English-like term xlDelimited rather than 1.

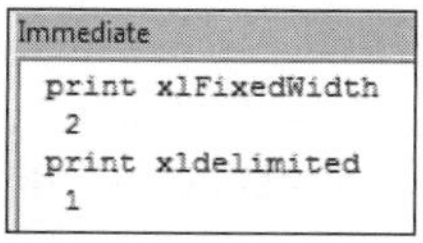

Figure 2.8
In the Immediate window of the VB Editor, query to see the true value of constants such as xlFixedWidth.

```
Immediate
  print xlFixedWidth
   2
  print xldelimited
   1
```

If you were an evil programmer, you could certainly memorize all these constants and write code using the numeric equivalents of the constants. However, the programming gods (and the next person who has to look at your code) will curse you for this.

In most cases, the help file either specifically calls out the valid values of the constants or offers a blue hyperlink that causes the help file to expand and show you the valid values for the constants (see Figure 2.9).

To see a demo of defined constants, search for Excel VBA 2 at YouTube.

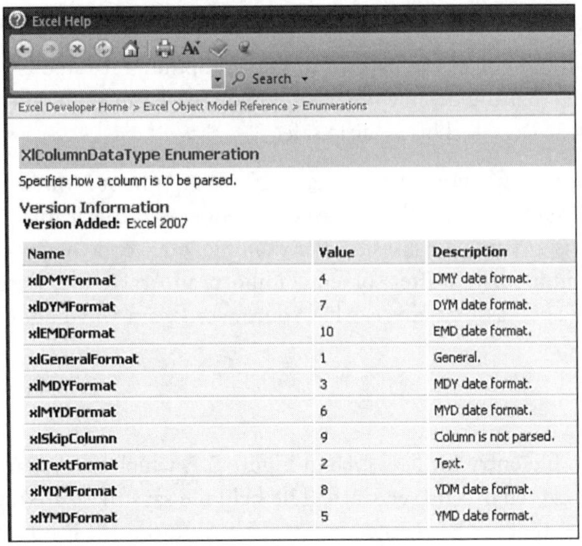
Excel Help

Excel Developer Home > Excel Object Model Reference > Enumerations

XlColumnDataType Enumeration

Specifies how a column is to be parsed.

Version Information

Version Added: Excel 2007

Name	Value	Description
xlDMYFormat	4	DMY date format.
xlDYMFormat	7	DYM date format.
xlEMDFormat	10	EMD date format.
xlGeneralFormat	1	General.
xlMDYFormat	3	MDY date format.
xlMYDFormat	6	MYD date format.
xlSkipColumn	9	Column is not parsed.
xlTextFormat	2	Text.
xlYDMFormat	8	YDM date format.
xlYMDFormat	5	YMD date format.

Figure 2.9
Click the blue hyperlink to see all the possible constant values. Here, the 10 possible `xlColumnDataType` constants are revealed in a new help topic.

One complaint with this excellent help system is that it does not identify which parameters may be new to a given version. In this particular case, `TrailingMinusNumbers` was introduced in Excel 2002. If you attempt to give this program to someone who is still using Excel 2000, the code will not run because it does not understand the `TrailingMinusNumbers` parameter. Sadly, the only way to learn to handle this frustrating problem is through trial and error.

If you read the help topic on `OpenText`, you can surmise that it is basically the equivalent of opening a file using the Text Import Wizard. In the first step of the wizard, you normally choose either Delimited or Fixed Width. You also specify the File Origin and at which row to start (see Figure 2.10). This first step of the wizard is handled by these parameters of the `OpenText` method:

```
Origin:=437
StartRow:=1
DataType:=xlDelimited
```

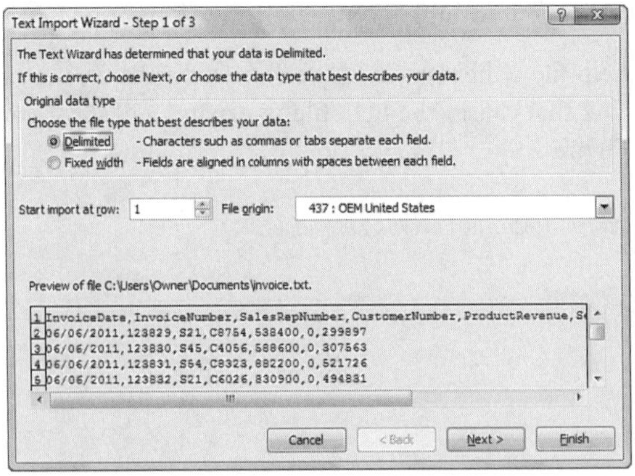

Figure 2.10
The first step of the Text Import Wizard in Excel is covered by three parameters of the `OpenText` method.

Step 2 of the Text to Columns Wizard enables you to specify that your fields be delimited by a comma. Because we do not want to treat two commas as a single comma, the Treat Consecutive Delimiters as One check box is not selected. Sometimes, a field may contain a comma, such as "XYZ, Inc." In this case, the field should have quotes around the value, as specified in the Text Qualifier box (see Figure 2.11). This second step of the wizard is handled by the following parameters of the OpenText method:

```
TextQualifier:=xlDoubleQuote
ConsecutiveDelimiter:=False
Tab:=False
Semicolon:=False
Comma:=True
Space:=False
Other:=False
```

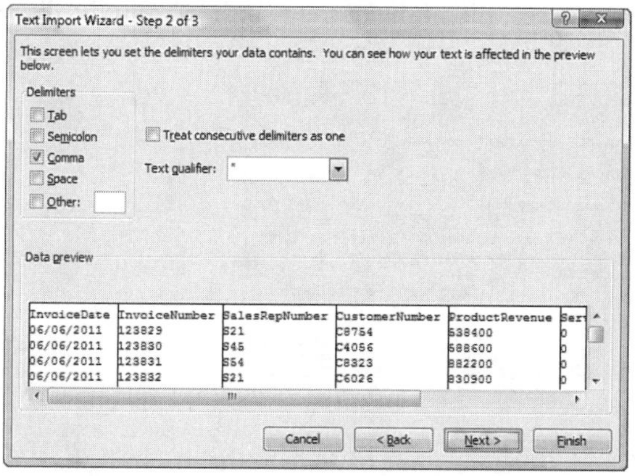

Figure 2.11
The second step Text Import Wizard is handled by the seven parameters of the OpenText method.

Step 3 of the wizard is where you actually identify the field types. In this case, you left all fields as General except for the first field, which was marked as a date in MDY (Month, Day, Year) format (see Figure 2.12). This is represented in code by the FieldInfo parameter.

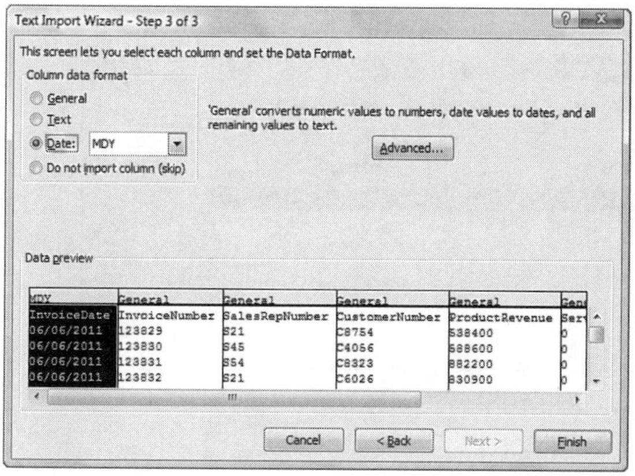

Figure 2.12
The third step of the Text Import Wizard is fairly complex. The entire FieldInfo parameter of the OpenText method duplicates the choices made on this step of the wizard.

If you happen to click the Advanced button on the third step of the wizard, you have an opportunity to specify something other than the default Decimal and Thousands separator, as well as the setting for Trailing Minus for negative numbers (see Figure 2.13).

> **TIP**
>
> Note that the macro recorder does not write code for DecimalSeparator or ThousandsSeparator unless you change these from the defaults. The macro recorder does always record the TrailingMinusNumbers parameter.

Every action that you perform in Excel while recording a macro gets translated to VBA code. In the case of many dialog boxes, the settings that you do not change will often get recorded along with the items that you do change. When you click OK to close the dialog, the macro recorder often records all the current settings from the dialog in the macro.

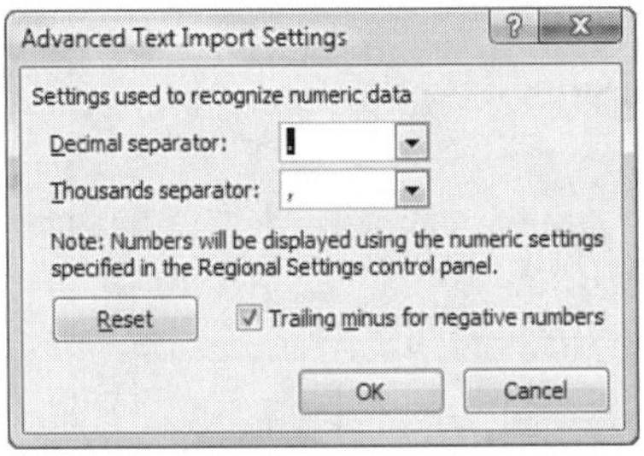

Figure 2.13
The TrailingMinus Numbers parameter comes from the Advanced Text Import Settings. If you change either of the separator fields, new parameters are recorded by the macro recorder.

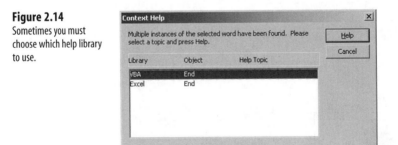

Here is another example. The next line of code in the macro is this:

```
Selection.End(xlDown).Select
```

You can click to get help for three topics in this line of code: Selection, End, and Select. Assuming that Selection and Select are somewhat self-explanatory, click in the word End and press F1 for help. A Context Help dialog box appears, saying that there are two possible help topics for End—one in the Excel library and one in the VBA library (see Figure 2.14).

Figure 2.14
Sometimes you must choose which help library to use.

If you are new to VBA, you might not know which help library to select. Select one and then click Help. In this case, the End help topic in the VBA library is talking about the End statement (see Figure 2.15), which is not what you need.

Close Help, press F1 again, and select the End object in the Excel library. This help topic says that End is a property. It returns a Range object that is equivalent to pressing End+Up or End+Down in the Excel interface (see Figure 2.16). If you click the blue hyperlink for xlDirection, you will see the valid parameters that can be passed to the End function.

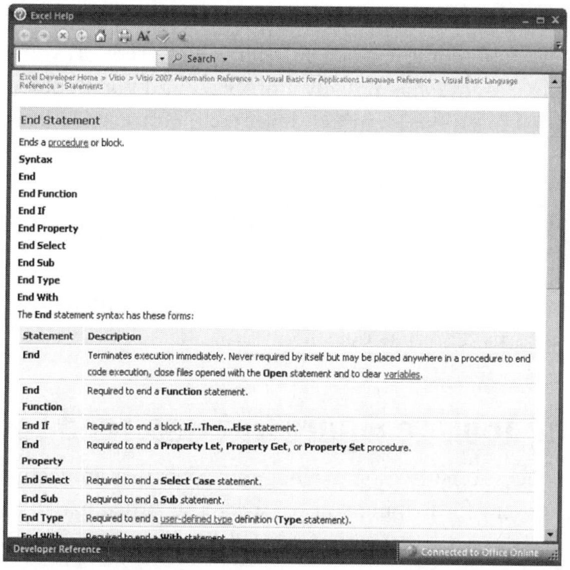

Figure 2.15
If the help topic is not the topic you need, it is easy enough to try again.

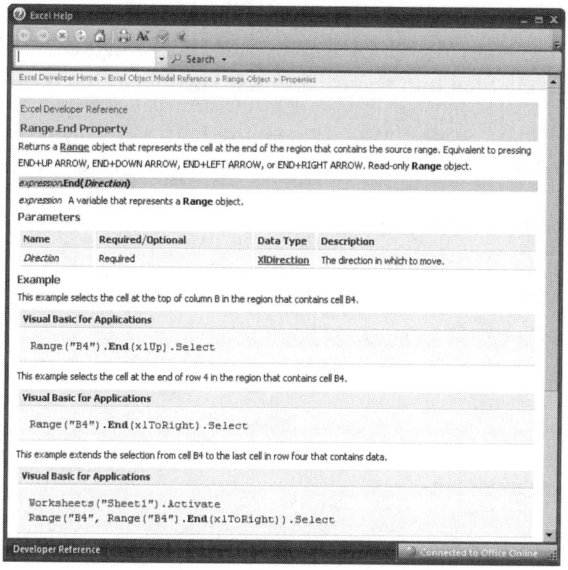

Figure 2.16
The correct help topic for the End property.

Properties Can Return Objects

Recall that the discussion at the start of this chapter said the basic syntax of VBA is Object. Method. Consider the line of code currently under examination:

```
Selection.End(xlDown).Select
```

In this particular line of code, the method is Select. The End keyword is a property, but from the help file, you see that it returns a Range object. Because the Select method can apply to a Range object, the method is actually appended to a property.

Based on this information, you might assume that Selection is the object in this line of code. If you click the mouse in the word Selection and press F1, you will see that according to the help topic, Selection is actually a property and not an object. In reality, the proper code would be to say Application.Selection. However, when you are running within Excel, VBA assumes you are referring to the Excel object model, so you can leave off the Application object. If you were to write a program in Word VBA to automate Excel, you would be required to include an object variable before the Selection property to qualify to which application you are referring.

In this case, the Application.Selection can return several different types of objects. If a cell is selected, it returns the Range object.

Using Debugging Tools to Figure Out Recorded Code

This section introduces some awesome debugging tools that are featured in VB Editor. These tools are excellent for helping you see what a recorded macro code is doing.

Stepping Through Code

Generally, a macro runs quickly—you start it, and less than a second later, it is done. If something goes wrong, you do not have an opportunity to figure out what it is doing. However, using Excel's Step Into feature makes it possible to run one line of code at a time.

To use this feature, make sure your cursor is in the ImportInvoice procedure, and then from the menu select Debug, Step Into, as shown in Figure 2.17. Alternatively, you can press F8.

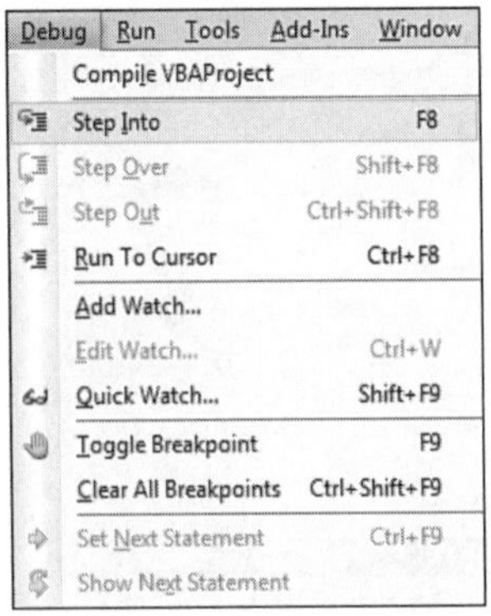

Figure 2.17
Using the Step Into feature allows you to run a single line of code at a time.

Debug	Run	Tools	Add-Ins	Window
Compile VBAProject				
Step Into				F8
Step Over				Shift+F8
Step Out				Ctrl+Shift+F8
Run To Cursor				Ctrl+F8
Add Watch...				
Edit Watch...				Ctrl+W
Quick Watch...				Shift+F9
Toggle Breakpoint				F9
Clear All Breakpoints				Ctrl+Shift+F9
Set Next Statement				Ctrl+F9
Show Next Statement				

The VB Editor is now in Break mode. The line about to be executed is highlighted in yellow with a yellow arrow in the margin before the code (see Figure 2.18).

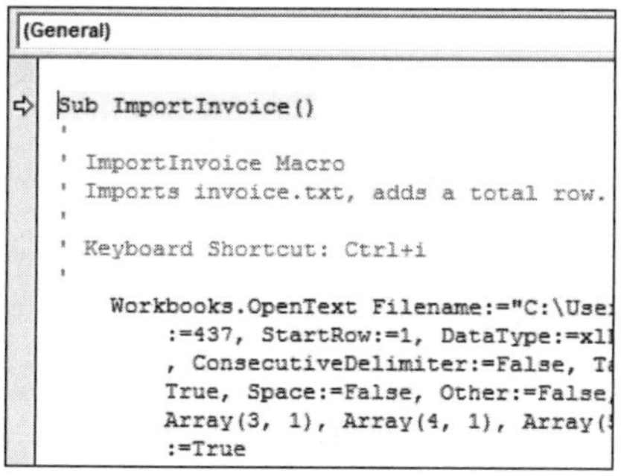

Figure 2.18
The first line of the macro is about to run.

In this case, the next line to be executed is the `Sub ImportInvoice()` line. This basically says, "You are about to start running this procedure." Press the F8 key to execute the line in yellow and move to the next line of code. The long code for `OpenText` is then highlighted. Press F8 to run this line of code. When you see that `Selection.End(xlDown).Select` is highlighted, you know that Visual Basic has finished running the `OpenText` command. At this point, you can press Alt+Tab to switch to Excel and see that the `Invoice.txt` file has been parsed into Excel. Note that A1 is selected (see Figure 2.19).

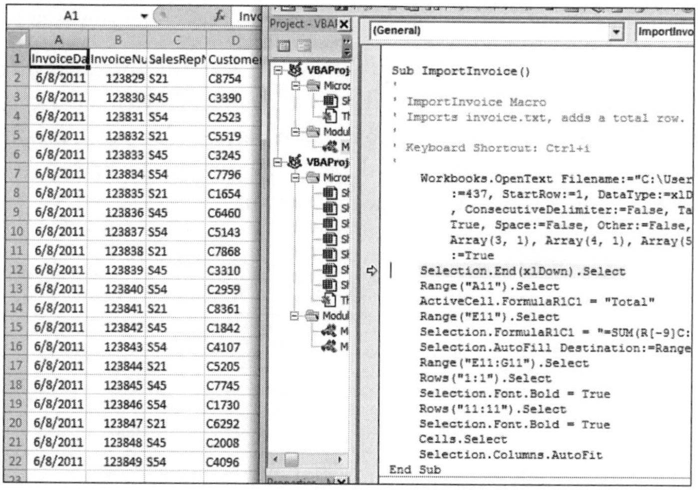

Figure 2.19
The Excel window behind the VBA Editor shows that the `Invoice.txt` file has been imported.

TIP   If you have a wide monitor, you can use the Restore Down icon at the top right of the VBA window to arrange the window so that you can see both the VBA window and the Excel window.

This is also a great trick while recording new code. You can actually watch the code appear as you do things in Excel.

Switch back to the VB Editor by pressing Alt+Tab. The next line about to be executed is `Selection.End(xlDown).Select`. Press F8 to run this code. Switch to Excel to see the results. Now A10 is selected (see Figure 2.20).

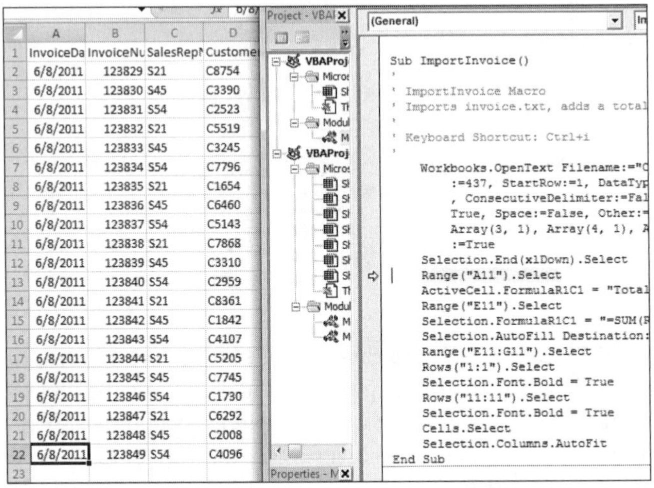

Figure 2.20

Verify that the `End(xlDown).Select` command worked as expected. This is equivalent to pressing the End key and then the down arrow.

Press F8 again to run the `Range("A11").Select` line. If you switch to Excel by pressing Alt+Tab, you will see that this is where the macro starts to have problems. Instead of moving to the first blank row, the program moved to the wrong row (see Figure 2.21).

Now that you have identified the problem area, you can stop the code execution by using the Reset command. You can start the Reset command by either selecting Run, Reset or by clicking the Reset button on the toolbar (see Figure 2.22). After clicking Reset, you should return to Excel and undo anything done by the partially completed macro. In this case, you need to close the `Invoice.txt` file without saving.

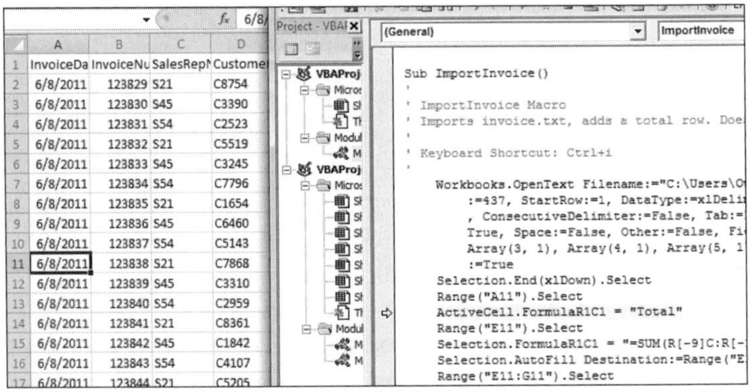

Figure 2.21

The recorded macro code blindly moves to Row 11 for the Total row.

Figure 2.22
The Reset button in the toolbar stops a macro that is in Break mode.

More Debugging Options: Breakpoints

If you have hundreds of lines of code, you might not want to step through each line one at a time. If you have a general idea that the problem is happening in one particular section of the program, you can set a breakpoint. You can then have the code start to run, but the macro breaks just before it executes the breakpoint line of code.

To set a breakpoint, click in the gray margin area to the left of the line of code on which you want to break. A large brown dot appears next to this code, and the line of code is highlighted in brown (see Figure 2.23). (If you don't see the margin area, go to Tools, Options, Editor Format and choose Margin Indicator Bar).

Figure 2.23
The large brown dot signifies a breakpoint.

```
Selection.End(xlDown).Select
Range("A11").Select
ActiveCell.FormulaR1C1 = "Total"
Range("E11").Select
Selection.FormulaR1C1 = "=SUM(R[-9]C:R[-1]C)"
Selection.AutoFill Destination:=Range("E11:G11"),
Range("E11:G11").Select
Rows("1:1").Select
Selection.Font.Bold = True
Rows("11:11").Select
```

Next, from the Start menu select Run, Run Sub or press F5. The program executes but stops just before the breakpoint. The VB Editor shows the breakpoint line highlighted in yellow. You can now press F8 to begin stepping through the code (see Figure 2.24).

After you have finished debugging your code, remove the breakpoints by clicking the dark brown dot in the margin to toggle off the breakpoint. Alternatively, you can select Debug, Clear All Breakpoints or press Ctrl+Shift+F9 to clear all breakpoints that you set in the project.

Figure 2.24
The yellow line signifies that the breakpoint line is about to be run.

```
ActiveCell.FormulaR1C1 = "Total"
Range("E11").Select
Selection.FormulaR1C1 = "=SUM(R[-9]C:R[-1]C)"
Selection.AutoFill Destination:=Range("E11:G11"),
Range("E11:G11").Select
```

Backing Up or Moving Forward in Code

When you are stepping through code, you might want to jump over some lines of code, or you might have corrected some lines of code that you want to run again. This is easy to do when you are working in Break mode. One favorite method is to use the mouse to grab the yellow arrow. The cursor changes to an icon, which means you can move the next line up or down. Drag the yellow line to whichever line you want to execute next (see Figure 2.25). The other option is to right-click the line to which you want to jump, and then select Set Next Statement.

Figure 2.25
The cursor as it appears when dragging the yellow line to a different line of code to be executed next.

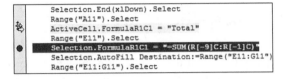

```
Selection.End(xlDown).Select
Range("A11").Select
ActiveCell.FormulaR1C1 = "Total"
Range("E11").Select
Selection.FormulaR1C1 = "=SUM(R[-9]C:R[-1]C)"
Selection.AutoFill Destination:=Range("E11:G11")
Range("E11:G11").Select
```

Not Stepping Through Each Line of Code

When you are stepping through code, you might want to run a section of code without stepping through each line, such as when you get to a loop. You might want VBA to run through the loop 100 times, so you can step through the lines after the loop. It is particularly monotonous to press the F8 key hundreds of times to step through a loop. Instead, click the cursor on the line you want to step to and press Ctrl+F8 or select Debug, Run to Cursor.

Querying Anything While Stepping Through Code

Even though variables have not yet been discussed, you can query the value of anything while in Break mode. However, keep in mind that the macro recorder never records a variable.

Using the Immediate Window

Press Ctrl+G to display the Immediate window in the VB Editor. While the macro is in Break mode, ask the VB Editor to tell you the currently selected cell, the name of the active sheet, or the value of any variable. Figure 2.26 shows several examples of queries typed into the Immediate window.

Figure 2.26
Queries and their answers that can be typed into the Immediate window while a macro is in Break mode.

```
Selection.End(xlDown).
Range("A11").Select
ActiveCell.FormulaR1C1
Range("E11").Select
Selection.FormulaR1C1
```

```
Immediate
Print Selection.Address
$E$11
print selection.value
 148200
print activesheet.name
invoice3
```

Instead of typing Print, you can type a question mark: ?Selection.Address. Read the question mark as "What is."

When invoked with Ctrl+G, the Immediate window usually appears at the bottom of the Code window. You can use the resize handle, which is located above the blue Immediate title bar, to make the Immediate window larger or smaller (see Figure 2.27).

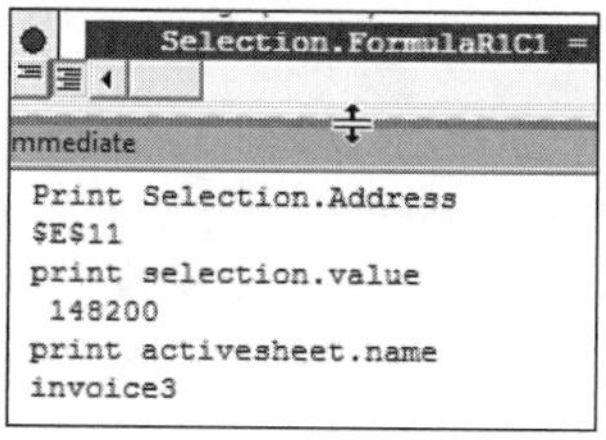

Figure 2.27
Resizing the Immediate window.

```
Selection.FormulaR1C1 =

mmediate
    Print Selection.Address
    $E$11
    print selection.value
     148200
    print activesheet.name
    invoice3
```

There is a scrollbar on the side of the Immediate window that can be used to scroll backward or forward through past entries in the Immediate window.

It is not necessary to run queries only at the bottom of the Immediate window. For example, if you have just run one line of code, in the Immediate window you can ask for the Selection.Address to ensure that this line of code worked (see Figure 2.28).

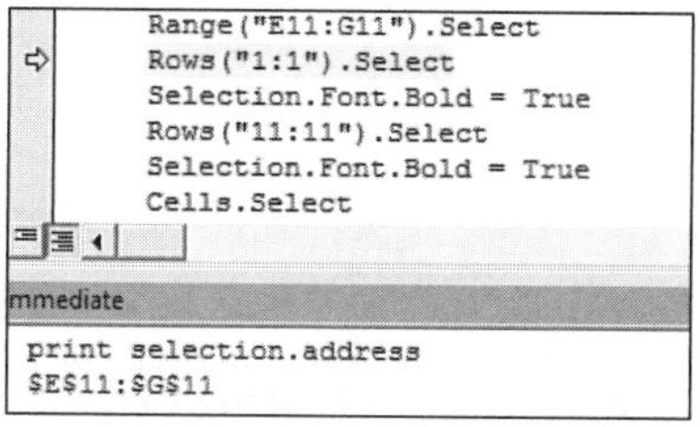

Figure 2.28
The Immediate window shows the results before the current line is executed.

```
        Range ("E11:G11").Select
 ⇨      Rows ("1:1").Select
        Selection.Font.Bold = True
        Rows ("11:11").Select
        Selection.Font.Bold = True
        Cells.Select

mmediate
    print selection.address
    $E$11:$G$11
```

Press the F8 key to run the next line of code. Instead of retyping the same query, click in the Immediate window at the end of the line containing the last query (see Figure 2.29).

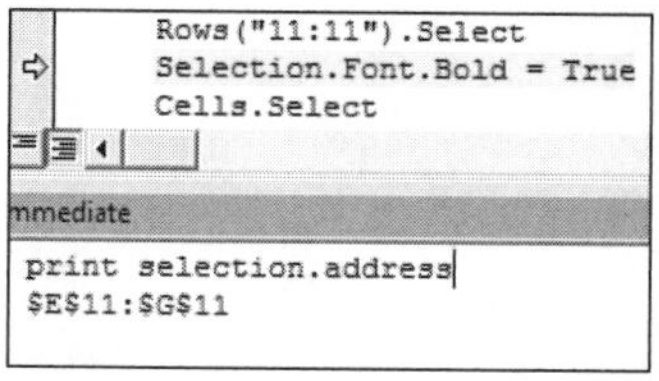

Figure 2.29
Place the cursor at the end of the previous command and press Enter to avoid typing the same commands over in the Immediate window.

```
        Rows ("11:11").Select
 ⇨      Selection.Font.Bold = True
        Cells.Select

mmediate
    print selection.address
    $E$11:$G$11
```

Press Enter, and the Immediate window runs this query again, displaying the results on the next line and pushing the old results farther down the window. In this case, the selected address is $11:$11. The previous answer, $E$11:$G$11, is pushed down the window (see Figure 2.30).

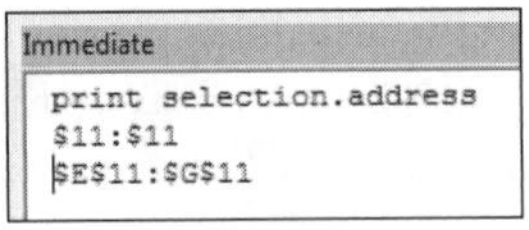

Figure 2.30

The prior answer ($E$11:$G$11) is shifted down, and the current answer ($11:$11) appears below the query.

```
Immediate
    print selection.address
    $11:$11
    $E$11:$G$11
```

Press F8 four more times to run through the line of code with `Cells.Select`. Again, position the cursor in the Immediate window just after `Print Selection.Address` and press Enter. The query is run again, and the most recent address is shown with the prior answers moved down in the Immediate window (see Figure 2.31).

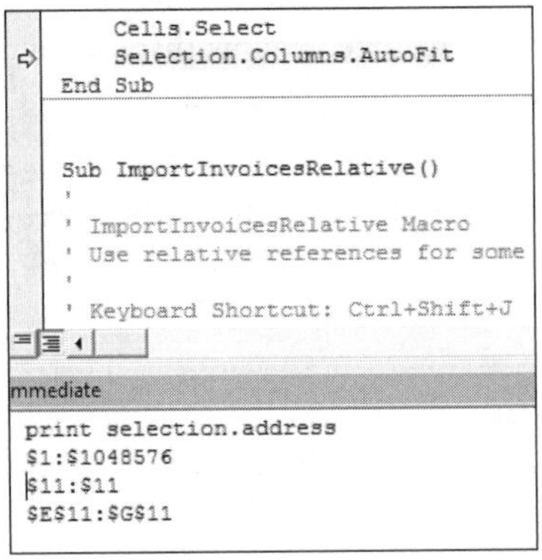

Figure 2.31

After selecting all cells with `Cells.Select`, place the cursor after the query in the Immediate window and press Enter. The new answer is that the selected range is all rows from 1 to 1,084,576.

```
        Cells.Select
        Selection.Columns.AutoFit
    End Sub


    Sub ImportInvoicesRelative()
    '
    ' ImportInvoicesRelative Macro
    ' Use relative references for some
    '
    ' Keyboard Shortcut: Ctrl+Shift+J
```
```
Immediate
    print selection.address
    $1:$1048576
    $11:$11
    $E$11:$G$11
```

You can also use this method to change the query by clicking to the right of the word `Address` in the Immediate window. Press the Backspace key to erase the word `Address` and instead type `Rows.Count`. Press Enter, and the Immediate window shows the number of rows in the selection (see Figure 2.32).

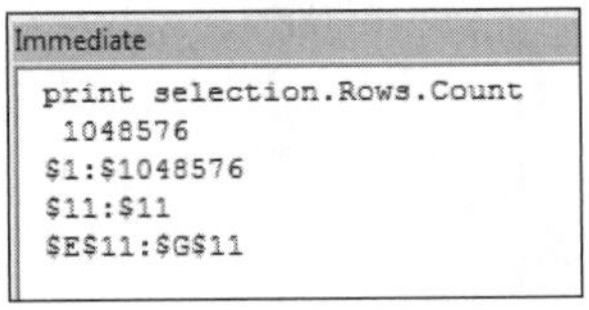

Figure 2.32

Delete part of a query, type something new, and press Enter. The previous answers are pushed down, and the current answer is displayed.

```
Immediate
    print selection.Rows.Count
     1048576
    $1:$1048576
    $11:$11
    $E$11:$G$11
```

This is an excellent technique to use when you are trying to figure out a sticky bit of code. For example, you can query the name of the active sheet (`Print Activesheet.Name`), the selection (`Print Selection.Address`), the active cell (`Print ActiveCell.Address`), the formula (`Print ActiveCell.Formula`) in the active cell, the value of the active cell (`Print ActiveCell.Value`, or `Print ActiveCell` because `Value` is the default property of a cell), and so on.

To dismiss the Immediate window, click the *X* in the upper-right corner of the Immediate window.

2

Querying by Hovering

In many instances, you can hover the cursor over an expression in the code, and then wait a second for a ToolTip to be displayed that shows the current value of the expression. This is an invaluable tool when you get to looping in Chapter 5, "Looping and Flow Control." It will also come in handy with recorded code. Note that the expression that you hover over does not have to be in the line of code just executed. In Figure 2.33, Visual Basic just selected Row 1, making A1 the `ActiveCell`. If you hover the cursor over `ActiveCell.` `Formula`, you will get a ToolTip showing that the formula in the `ActiveCell` is the word `InvoiceDate`.

Figure 2.33
Hover the mouse cursor over any expression for a few seconds, and a ToolTip shows the current value of the expression.

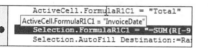

Sometimes the VBA window seems to not respond to hovering. Because some expressions are not supposed to show a value, it is difficult to tell whether VBA is not displaying the value on purpose or whether you are in the buggy "not responding" mode. Try hovering over something that you know should respond, such as a variable. If you get no response, hover, click into the variable, and continue to hover. This tends to wake Excel up from the stupor, and hovering will work again.

Are you impressed yet? This chapter started by complaining that this didn't seem much like BASIC. However, by now you have to admit that the Visual Basic environment is great to work in and that the debugging tools are excellent.

Querying by Using a Watch Window

In Visual Basic, a watch is not something you wear on your wrist; instead, it allows you to watch the value of any expression while you step through code. Let's say that in the current example, you want to watch to see what is selected as the code runs. You can do this by setting up a watch for `Selection.Address`.

From the VB Editor Debug menu, select Add Watch. In the Add Watch dialog, enter `Selection.Address` in the Expression text box and click OK (see Figure 2.34).

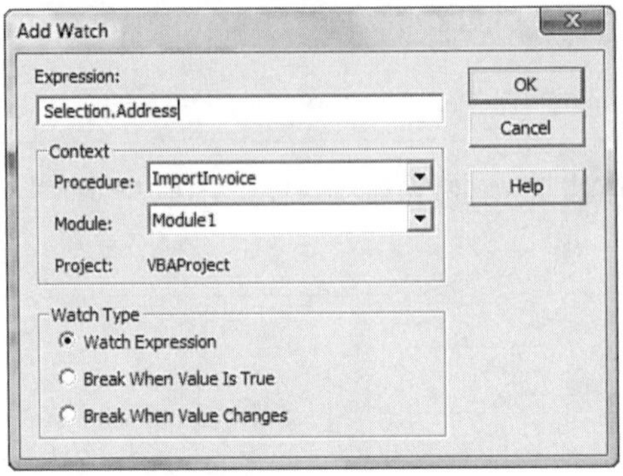

Figure 2.34
Setting up a watch to see the address of the current selection.

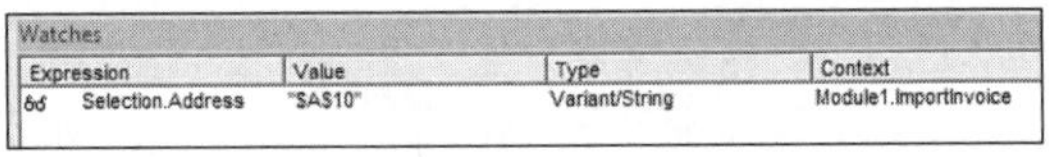

Figure 2.35
Without having to hover or type in the Immediate window, you can always see the value of watched expressions.

A Watches window is added to the busy Visual Basic window, usually at the bottom of the code window. When you start running the macro, import the file and press End+Down to move to the last row with data. Right after the End(xlDown) code is executed, the Watches window shows that Selection.Address is $A$10 (see Figure 2.35).

Press the F8 key to run the code Range("A11").Select. The Watches window is updated to show the current address of the Selection is now $A$11 (see Figure 2.36).

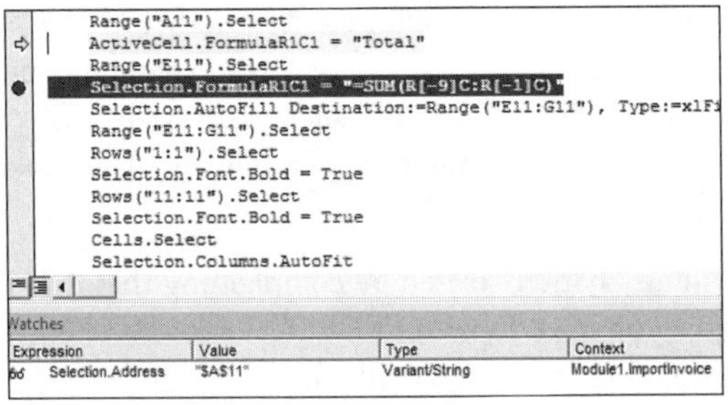

Figure 2.36
After running another line of code, the value in the Watches window updates to indicate the address of the new selection.

```
        Range("A11").Select
        ActiveCell.FormulaR1C1 = "Total"
        Range("E11").Select
        Selection.FormulaR1C1 = "=SUM(R[-9]C:R[-1]C)"
        Selection.AutoFill Destination:=Range("E11:G11"), Type:=xlFi
        Range("E11:G11").Select
        Rows("1:1").Select
        Selection.Font.Bold = True
        Rows("11:11").Select
        Selection.Font.Bold = True
        Cells.Select
        Selection.Columns.AutoFit
```

NOTE

In the Watch window, the value column is read/write (where possible)! You can type a new value here and see it change on the worksheet.

Using a Watch to Set a Breakpoint

Right-click any line in the Watches window and select Edit Watch. In the Watch Type section of the Edit Watch dialog, select Break When Value Changes (see Figure 2.37). Click OK.

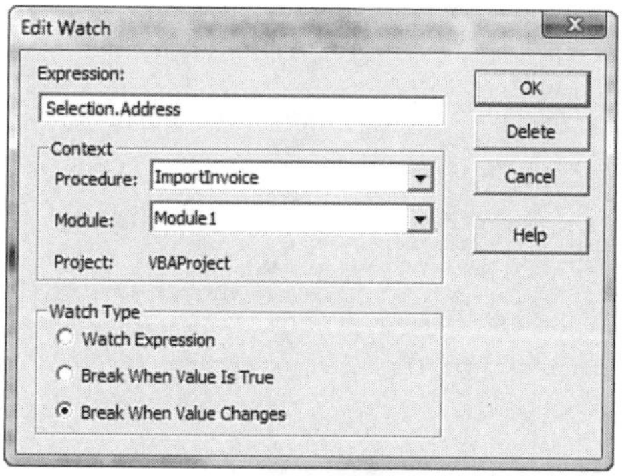

Figure 2.37
Select Break When Value Changes in the bottom of the Edit Watch dialog.

The glasses icon has changed to a hand with triangle icon. You can now press F5 to run the code. The macro starts running lines of code until something new is selected. This is very powerful. Instead of having to step through each line of code, you can now conveniently have the macro stop only when something important has happened. A watch can also be set up to stop when the value of a particular variable changes.

Using a Watch on an Object

In the preceding example, you watched a specific property: Selection.Address. It is also possible to watch an object such as Selection. In Figure 2.38, when a watch has been set up on Selection, you get the glasses icon and a + icon.

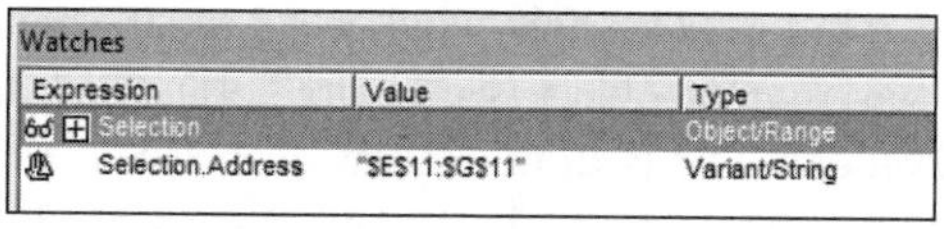

Figure 2.38
Setting a watch on an object gives you a + icon next to the glasses.

By clicking the + icon, you can see all the properties associated with Selection. When you look at Figure 2.39, you can see more than you ever wanted to know about Selection! There are properties that you probably never realized were available. You can also see that the AddIndent property is set to False and the AllowEdit property is set to True. There are useful properties in the list—you can see the Formula of the selection.

In this Watches window, some entries can be expanded. For example, the Borders collection has a plus next to it, which means that you can click any + icon to see more details.

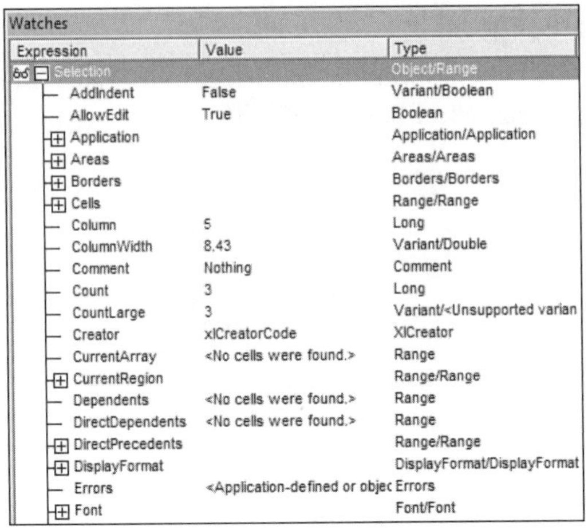

Figure 2.39
Clicking the + icon shows a plethora of properties and their current values.

Object Browser: The Ultimate Reference

In the VB Editor, press F2 to open the Object Browser, which lets you browse and search the entire Excel object library (see Figure 2.40). A 409-page book is available that is a reprint of this entire object model from the Object Browser. However, you do not need this book because the built-in Object Browser is much more powerful and always available at the touch of F2. The next few pages will teach you how to use the Object Browser.

Press F2 and the Object Browser appears where the code window normally appears. The topmost drop-down currently shows <All Libraries>. There is an entry in this drop-down for Excel, Office, VBA, each workbook that you have open, plus additional entries for anything that you check in Tools, References. For now, go to the drop-down and select only Excel.

In the left window of the Object Browser is a list of all classes available for Excel. Click the Application class in the left window. The right window adjusts to show all properties and methods that apply to the Application object (see Figure 2.41). Click something in the right window, such as ActiveCell. The bottom window of the Object Browser tells you that ActiveCell is a property that returns a range. It also tells you that ActiveCell is read-only (an alert that you cannot assign an address to ActiveCell to move the cell pointer).

You have learned from the Object Browser that ActiveCell returns a range. When you click the green hyperlink for Range in the bottom window, you will see all the properties and methods that apply to Range objects and, hence, to the ActiveCell property. Click any property or method, and then click the yellow question mark near the top of the Object Browser to go to the help topic for that property or method.

Type any term in the text box next to the binoculars, and click the binoculars to find all matching members of the Excel library.

Figure 2.40
Press F2 to display the
Object Browser.

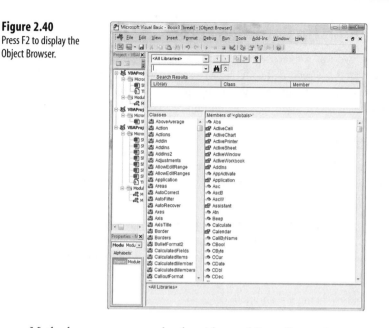

Methods appear as green books with speed lines. Properties appear as index cards with a
hand pointing to them.

The search capabilities and hyperlinks available in the Object Browser make it much more
valuable than an alphabetic printed listing of all of the information. Learn to make use of
the Object Browser in the VBA window by pressing F2. To close the Object Browser and
return to your code window, click the lower X in the upper-right corner (see Figure 2.41).

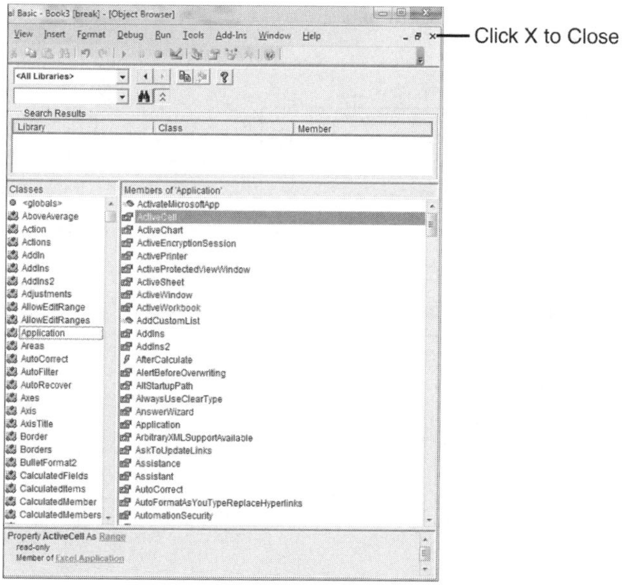

Figure 2.41
Select a class, and then a
member. The bottom win-
dow tells you the basics
about the particular
member.

————— Click X to Close

Seven Tips for Cleaning Up Recorded Code

At this point, you have two tips for recording code from Chapter 1. So far, this chapter has covered how to understand the recorded code, how to access VBA help for any word, and how to use the excellent VBA debugging tools to step through your code. The remainder of this chapter presents seven tips to use when cleaning up recorded code.

Tip 1: Don't Select Anything

Nothing screams "recorded code" more than having code that selects things before acting upon them. This makes sense—in the Excel interface, you have to select Row 1 before you can make it bold.

However, this is done rarely in VBA. There are a couple exceptions to this rule. For example, you need to select a cell when setting up a formula for conditional formatting. It is possible to directly turn on bold font to Row 1 without selecting it. The following two lines of code turn into one line.

Macro recorder code before being streamlined:

```
Cells.Select
Selection.Columns.AutoFit
```

After streamlining the recorded code

```
Cells.Columns.AutoFit
```

There are a couple of advantages to this method. First, there will be half as many lines of code in your program. Second, the program will run faster.

After recording code, highlight literally from before the word Select at the end of one line all the way to the dot after the word Selection on the next line and press Delete (see Figures 2.42 and 2.43).

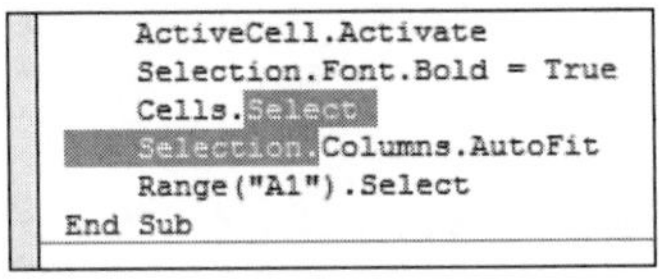

Figure 2.42
Select from here to here...

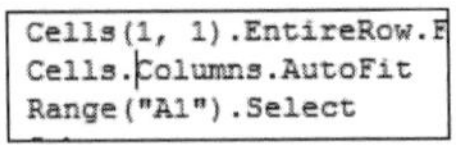

```
ActiveCell.Activate
Selection.Font.Bold = True
Cells.Select
Selection.Columns.AutoFit
Range("A1").Select
End Sub
```

Figure 2.43
...and press the Delete key. This is basic "101" of cleaning up recorded macros.

```
Cells(1, 1).EntireRow.F
Cells.Columns.AutoFit
Range("A1").Select
```

Tip 2: Cells(2,5) Is More Convenient Than Range("E2")

The macro recorder uses the `Range()` property frequently. If you follow the macro recorder's example, you will find yourself building a lot of complicated code. For example, if you have the row number for the total row stored in a variable, you might try to build this code:

```
Range("E" & TotalRow).Formula = "=SUM(E2:E" & TotalRow-1 & ")"
```

In this code, you are using concatenation to join the letter *E* with the current value of the `TotalRow` variable. This works, but eventually you will have to refer to a range where the column is stored in a variable. Say that `FinalCol` is `10`, which indicates Column J. To refer to this column in a `Range` command, you need to do something like this:

```
FinalColLetter = MID("ABCDEFGHIJKLMNOPQRSTUVWXYZ",FinalCol,1)
Range(FinalColLetter & "2").Select
```

Alternatively, perhaps you could do something like this:

```
FinalColLetter = CHR(64 + FinalCol)
Range(FinalColLetter & "2").Select
```

These approaches work for the first 26 columns but fail for the remaining 99.85 percent of the columns.

You could start to write 10-line functions to calculate that the column letter for column 15896 is WMJ, but it is not necessary. Instead of using `Range("WMJ17")`, you can use the `Cells(Row,Column)` syntax.

Chapter 3, "Referring to Ranges," covers this in complete detail. However, for now you need to understand that `Range("E10")` and `Cells(10, 5)` both point to the cell at the intersection of the fifth column and tenth row. Chapter 3 also shows you how to use `.Resize` to point to a rectangular range. `Cells(11, 5).Resize(1, 3)` is `E11:G11`.

Tip 3: Ride the Range from the Bottom to Find Last Row

It is difficult to trust data from just anywhere. If you are analyzing data in Excel, remember that the data can come from "who knows what" system written "who knows how long ago." The universal truth is that eventually some clerk will find a way to break the source system and enter a record without an invoice number. Maybe it will take a power failure to do it, but invariably, you cannot count on having every cell filled in.

This is a problem when using the End+Down shortcut. This key combination does not take you to the last row with data in the worksheet. It takes you to the last row with data in the current range. In Figure 2.44, pressing End+Down would move the cursor to cell A5 rather than cell A10.

Figure 2.44
End+Down fails in the user interface if a record is missing a value. Similarly, End(xlDown) fails in Excel VBA.

	A	B	C	D	E	F	G
1	InvoiceDa	InvoiceNu	SalesRepN	Customer	ProductRe	ServiceRe	ProductCost
2	6/8/2011	123829	S21	C8754	21000	0	9875
3	6/8/2011	123830	S45	C3390	188100	0	85083
4	6/8/2011	123831	S54	C2523	510600	0	281158
5	6/8/2011	123832	S21	C5519	86200	0	49967
6		123833	S45	C3245	800100	0	388277
7	6/8/2011	123834	S54	C7796	339000	0	195298
8	6/8/2011	123835	S21	C1654	161000	0	90761
9	6/8/2011	123836	S45	C6460	275500	10000	146341
10	6/8/2011	123837	S54	C5143	925400	0	473515
11							

The better solution is to start at the bottom of the Excel worksheet and press End+Up. This may seem silly in the Excel interface because it is easy to see whether you are at the end of the data. However, because it is easy in Excel VBA to start at the last row, get in the habit of using this code to find the true last row:

```
Cells(Rows.Count, 1).End(xlUp)
```

> **NOTE**
>
> From 1995 through 2006, Excel worksheets featured 65,536 rows. In the prior edition of this book, the coding style was to use Range("A65536").End(xlUp) to find the last row. With the expansion to 1,048,576 rows, you might be tempted to use Range("A1048576").End(xlUp) in Excel 2010.
>
> However, you cannot assume that your worksheet will have 1,048,576 rows. Someone might open an .xls file in Compatibility mode, and there will be only 65,536 rows. If someone else runs your macro in Excel 2003, there will be only 65,536 rows.
>
> The solution is to use Rows.Count to return the number of rows in the active workbook. This covers the possibility that the workbook is in Compatibility mode or that someone is running the code in Excel 2003.

Tip 4: Use Variables to Avoid Hard-Coding Rows and Formulas

The macro recorder never records a variable. Variables are easy to use, but just as in BASIC, a variable can remember a value. Variables are discussed in more detail in Chapter 5.

It is recommended that you set the last row with data to a variable. Be sure to use meaningful variable names such as FinalRow:

```
FinalRow = Cells(Rows.Count, 1).End(xlUp).Row
```

Now that you know the row number of the last record, put the word *Total* in Column A of the next row:

```
Cells(FinalRow + 1, 1).Value = "Total"
```

You can even use the variable when building the formula. This formula totals everything from E2 to the `FinalRow` of E:

```
Cells(FinalRow + 1, 5).Formula = "=SUM(E2:E" & FinalRow & ")"
```

Tip 5: R1C1 Formulas That Make Your Life Easier

The macro recorder often writes formulas in an arcane R1C1 style. However, most people change the code back to use a regular A1-style formula. After reading Chapter 6, "R1C1-Style Formulas," you will understand there are times when you can build an R1C1 formula that is much simpler than the corresponding A1-style formula. By using an R1C1 formula, you can add totals to all three cells in the Total row with the following:

```
Cells(FinalRow+1, 5).Resize(1, 3).FormulaR1C1 = "=SUM(R2C:R[-1]C)"
```

Tip 6: Learn to Copy and Paste in a Single Statement

Recorded code is notorious for copying a range, selecting another range, and then doing an `ActiveSheet.Paste`. The `Copy` method as it applies to a range is actually much more powerful. You can specify what to copy and specify the destination in one statement.

Recorded code:

```
Range("E14").Select
Selection.Copy
Range("F14:G14").Select
ActiveSheet.Paste
```

Better code:

```
Range("E14").Copy Destination:=Range("F14:G14")
```

Tip 7: Use With...End With to Perform Multiple Actions

If you were going to make the total row bold, double underline, with a larger font and a special color, you might get recorded code like this:

```
Range("A14:G14").Select
Selection.Font.Bold = True
Selection.Font.Size = 12
Selection.Font.ColorIndex = 5
Selection.Font.Underline = xlUnderlineStyleDoubleAccounting
```

For four of those lines of code, VBA must resolve the expression `Selection.Font`. Because you have four lines that all refer to the same object, you can name the object once at the top of a `With` block. Inside the `With...End With` block, everything that starts with a period is assumed to refer to the `With` object:

```
With Range("A14:G14").Font
    .Bold = True
    .Size = 12
    .ColorIndex = 5
    .Underline = xlUnderlineStyleDoubleAccounting
End With
```

CASE STUDY: PUTTING IT ALL TOGETHER: FIXING THE RECORDED CODE

Changing the Recorded Code

Using the seven tips discussed in the previous section, you can convert the recorded code into efficient, professional-looking code. Here is the code as recorded by the macro recorder at the end of Chapter 1:

```
Sub FormatInvoice3()
'
' FormatInvoice3 Macro
' Third try. Use relative. Don't touch AutoSum
'
' Keyboard Shortcut: Ctrl+Shift+K
'
    Workbooks.OpenText Filename:="C:\Users\Owner\Documents\invoice.txt", Origin _
        :=437, StartRow:=1, DataType:=xlDelimited, TextQualifier:=xlDoubleQuote _
        , ConsecutiveDelimiter:=False, Tab:=False, Semicolon:=False, Comma:= _
        True, Space:=False, Other:=False, FieldInfo:=Array(Array(1, 3), _
        Array(2, 1), _
        Array(3, 1), Array(4, 1), Array(5, 1), Array(6, 1), Array(7, 1)), _
        TrailingMinusNumbers _
        :=True
    ' Relative turned on here
    Selection.End(xlDown).Select
    ActiveCell.Offset(1, 0).Range("A1").Select
    ActiveCell.FormulaR1C1 = "Total"
    ActiveCell.Offset(0, 4).Range("A1").Select
    ' Don't use AutoSum. Type this formula:
    Selection.FormulaR1C1 = "=SUM(R2C:R[-1]C)"
    Selection.AutoFill Destination:=ActiveCell.Range("A1:C1"), Type:= _
        xlFillDefault
    ActiveCell.Range("A1:C1").Select
    ' Relative turned off here
    ActiveCell.Rows("1:1").EntireRow.Select
    ActiveCell.Activate
    Selection.Font.Bold = True
    Cells.Select
    Selection.Columns.AutoFit
    Range("A1").Select
End Sub
```

Follow these steps to clean up the macro:

1. The `Workbook.OpenText` lines are fine as recorded.

2. The following lines of code attempt to locate the final row of data so the program knows where to enter the total row:

    ```
    Selection.End(xlDown).Select
    ```

    You do not need to select anything to find the last row. It also helps to assign the row number of the final row and the total row to a variable so they can be used later. To handle the unexpected case where a single cell in Column A is blank, start at the bottom of the worksheet and go up to find the last used row:

    ```
    ' Find the last row with data. This might change every day
    FinalRow = Cells(Rows.Count, 1).End(xlUp).Row
    TotalRow = FinalRow + 1
    ```

3. These lines of code enter the word *Total* in Column A of the Total row:

```
Range("A14").Select
ActiveCell.FormulaR1C1 ="'Total"
```

The better code will use the `TotalRow` variable to locate where to enter the word *Total*. Again, there is no need to select the cell before entering the label:

```
' Build a Total row below this
Range("A" & TotalRow).Value = "Total"
```

4. These lines of code enter the `Total` formula in Column E and copy it to the next two columns:

```
Range("E14").Select
Selection.FormulaR1C1 = "=SUM(R[-12]C:R[-1]C)"
Selection.AutoFill Destination:=Range("E14:G14"), Type:=xlFillDefault
Range("E14:G14").Select
```

There is no reason to do all this selecting. The following line enters the formula in three cells. The R1C1 style of formulas is discussed in Chapter 6:

```
Range("E" & TotalRow).Resize(1, 3).FormulaR1C1 = "=SUM(R2C:R[-1]C)"
```

5. The macro recorder selects a range and then applies formatting:

```
Rows("1:1").Select
Selection.Font.Bold = True
Rows("14:14").Select
Selection.Font.Bold = True
```

There is no reason to select before applying the formatting. These two lines perform the same action and do it much quicker:

```
Rows("1:1").Font.Bold = True
Rows(TotalRow & ":" & TotalRow).Font.Bold = True
```

6. The macro recorder selects all cells before doing the `AutoFit` command:

```
Cells.Select
Selection.Columns.AutoFit
```

There is no need to select the cells before doing the

```
AutoFit:Cells.Columns.AutoFit
```

7. The macro recorder adds a short description to the top of each macro:

```
' ImportInvoice Macro
```

Now that you have changed the recorded macro code into something that will actually work, feel free to add your name as author to the description and mention what the macro will do:

```
' ImportInvoice Macro
' Written by Bill Jelen This macro will import invoice.txt and add totals.
```

Here is the final macro with the changes:

```
Sub ImportInvoiceFixed()
'
' ImportInvoice Macro
' Written by Bill Jelen This macro will import invoice.txt and add totals.
'
' Keyboard Shortcut: Ctrl+i
'
```

```
    Workbooks.OpenText Filename:= _
        "C:\invoice.txt", Origin _
        :=437, StartRow:=1, DataType:=xlDelimited, _
        TextQualifier:=xlDoubleQuote _
        , ConsecutiveDelimiter:=False, Tab:=True, Semicolon:=False, _
        Comma:=True _
        , Space:=False, Other:=False, FieldInfo:=Array(Array(1, 3), _
        Array(2, 1), _
        Array(3, 1), Array(4, 1), Array(5, 1), Array(6, 1), Array(7, 1)), _
        TrailingMinusNumbers:=True
    ' Find the last row with data. This might change every day
    FinalRow = Cells(Rows.Count, 1).End(xlUp).Row
    TotalRow = FinalRow + 1
    ' Build a Total row below this
    Range("A" & TotalRow).Value = "Total"
    Range("E" & TotalRow).Resize(1, 3).FormulaR1C1 = "=SUM(R2C:R[-1]C)"
    Rows("1:1").Font.Bold = True
    Rows(TotalRow & ":" & TotalRow).Font.Bold = True
    Cells.Columns.AutoFit
End Sub
```

Next Steps

By now, you should know how to record a macro. You should also be able to use help and debugging to figure out how the code works. This chapter provided seven tools for making the recorded code look like professional code.

The next chapters go into more detail about referring to ranges, looping, and the crazy, but useful R1C1 style of formulas that the macro recorder loves to use. In addition, you are introduced to 30 useful code samples.

Referring to Ranges

A *range* can be a cell, row, column, or a grouping of any of these. The RANGE object is probably the most frequently used object in Excel VBA—after all, you are manipulating data on a sheet. Although a range can refer to any grouping of cells on a sheet, it can refer to only one sheet at a time. If you want to refer to ranges on multiple sheets, you must refer to each sheet separately.

This chapter shows you different ways of referring to ranges such as specifying a row or column. You also will learn how to manipulate cells based on the active cell and how to create a new range from overlapping ranges.

The Range **Object**

The following is the Excel object hierarchy:

> Application > Workbook > Worksheet > Range

The Range object is a property of the Worksheet object. This means it requires that a sheet be active or it must reference a worksheet. Both of the following lines mean the same thing if Worksheets(1) is the active sheet:

```
Range("A1")
Worksheets(1).Range("A1")
```

There are several ways to refer to a Range object. Range("A1") is the most identifiable because that is how the macro recorder refers to it. However, each of the following is equivalent when referring to a range:

```
Range("D5")
[D5]
Range("B3").Range("C3")
Cells(5,4)
Range("A1").Offset(4,3)
Range("MyRange") 'assuming that D5 has a
Name 'of MyRange
```

3

IN THIS CHAPTER

The Range Object 65

Syntax to Specify a Range 66

Named Ranges... 66

Shortcut for Referencing Ranges 66

Referencing Ranges in Other Sheets 67

Referencing a Range Relative to Another Range 68

Use the Cells Property to Select a Range ... 68

Use the Offset Property to Refer to a Range 69

Use the Resize Property to Change the Size of a Range 71

Use the Columns and Rows Properties to Specify a Range... 72

Use the Union Method to Join Multiple Ranges 72

Use the Intersect Method to Create a New Range from Overlapping Ranges 73

Use the ISEMPTY Function to Check Whether the Cell Is Empty 73

Use the CurrentRegion Property to Select a Data Range 74

Use the Areas Collection to Return a Noncontiguous Range 77

Referencing Tables 77

Which format you use depends on your needs. Keep reading—it will all make sense soon!

Syntax to Specify a Range

The `Range` property has two acceptable syntaxes. To specify a rectangular range in the first syntax, specify the complete range reference just as you would in a formula in Excel:

```
Range("A1:B5").Select
```

In the alternative syntax, specify the upper-left corner and lower-right corner of the desired rectangular range. In this syntax, the equivalent statement might be this:

```
Range("A1", "B5").Select
```

For either corner, you can substitute a named range, the `Cells` property, or the `ActiveCell` property. The following line of code selects the rectangular range from A1 to the active cell:

```
Range("A1", ActiveCell).Select
```

The following statement selects from the active cell to five rows below the active cell and two columns to the right:

```
Range(ActiveCell, ActiveCell.Offset(5, 2)).Select
```

Named Ranges

You probably have already used named ranges on your worksheets and in formulas. You can also use them in VBA.

Use the following code to refer to the range `"MyRange"` in Sheet1:

```
Worksheets("Sheet1").Range("MyRange")
```

Notice that the name of the range is in quotes—unlike the use of named ranges in formulas on the sheet itself. If you forget to put the name in quotes, Excel thinks you are referring to a variable in the program. One exception is if you use the shortcut syntax discussed in the next section. In this case, quotes are not used.

Shortcut for Referencing Ranges

A shortcut is available when referencing ranges. The shortcut uses square brackets, as shown in Table 3.1.

Table 3.1   Shortcuts for Referencing Ranges

Standard Method	Shortcut
`Range("D5")`	`[D5]`
`Range("A1:D5")`	`[A1:D5]`

Standard Method	Shortcut
`Range ("A1:D5," "G6:I17")`	`[A1:D5, G6:I17]`
`Range("MyRange")`	`[MyRange]`

Referencing Ranges in Other Sheets

Switching between sheets by activating the needed sheet can dramatically slow down your code. To avoid this slowdown, you can refer to a sheet that is not active by first referencing the `Worksheet` object:

```
Worksheets("Sheet1").Range("A1")
```

This line of code references Sheet1 of the active workbook even if Sheet2 is the active sheet.

If you need to reference a range in another workbook, include the `Workbook` object, the `Worksheet` object, and then the `Range` object:

```
Workbooks("InvoiceData.xlsx").Worksheets("Sheet1").Range("A1")
```

Be careful if you use the `Range` property as an argument within another `Range` property. You must identify the range fully each time. For example, suppose that Sheet1 is your active sheet and you need to total data from Sheet2:

```
WorksheetFunction.Sum(Worksheets("Sheet2").Range(Range("A1"), Range("A7")))
```

This line does not work. Why not? Because `Range(Range("A1"), Range("A7"))` refers to an extra range at the beginning of the code line. Excel does not assume that you want to carry the `Worksheet` object reference over to the other `Range` objects. So what do you do? Well, you could write this:

```
WorksheetFunction.Sum(Worksheets("Sheet2").Range(Worksheets("Sheet2"). _
    Range("A1"), Worksheets("Sheet2").Range("A7")))
```

But this is not only a long line of code, it is difficult to read! Thankfully, there is a simpler way, using `With...End With`:

```
With Worksheets("Sheet2")
    WorksheetFunction.Sum(.Range(.Range("A1"), .Range("A7")))
End With
```

Notice now that there is a `.Range` in your code, but without the preceding object reference. That's because `With Worksheets("Sheet2")` implies that the object of the range is the worksheet.

3

Referencing a Range Relative to Another Range

Typically, the RANGE object is a property of a worksheet. It is also possible to have RANGE be the property of another range. In this case, the Range property is relative to the original range, which makes for unintuitive code. Consider this example:

```
Range("B5").Range("C3").Select
```

This code actually selects cell D7. Think about cell C3, which is located two rows below and two columns to the right of cell A1. The preceding line of code starts at cell B5. If we assume that B5 is in the A1 position, VBA finds the cell that would be in the C3 position relative to B5. In other words, VBA finds the cell that is two rows below and two columns to the right of B5, which is D7.

Again, I consider this coding style to be very unintuitive. This line of code mentions two addresses, and the actual cell selected is neither of these addresses! It seems misleading when you are trying to read this code.

You might consider using this syntax to refer to a cell relative to the active cell. For example, the following line of code activates the cell three rows down and four columns to the right of the currently active cell:

```
Selection.Range("E4").Select
```

This syntax is mentioned only because the macro recorder uses it. Recall that when you recorded a macro in Chapter 1, "Unleash the Power of Excel with VBA," with Relative References on, the following line was recorded:

```
ActiveCell.Offset(0, 4).Range("A2").Select
```

This line found the cell four columns to the right of the active cell, and from there it selected the cell that would correspond to A2. This is not the easiest way to write code, but that is the way the macro recorder does it.

Although a worksheet is usually the object of the Range property, occasionally, such as during recording, a range may be the property of a range.

Use the `Cells` Property to Select a Range

The Cells property refers to all the cells of the specified range object, which can be a worksheet or a range of cells. For example, this line selects all the cells of the active sheet:

```
Cells.Select
```

Using the Cells property with the Range object might seem redundant:

```
Range("A1:D5").Cells
```

This line refers to the original Range object. However, the Cells property has an Item property that makes the Cells property very useful. The Item property enables you to refer to a specific cell relative to the Range object.

The syntax for using the `Item` property with the `Cells` property is as follows:

```
Cells.Item(Row,Column)
```

You must use a numeric value for `Row`, but you may use the numeric value or string value for `Column`. Both of the following lines refer to cell C5:

```
Cells.Item(5,"C")
Cells.Item(5,3)
```

Because the `Item` property is the default property of the RANGE object, you can shorten these lines as follows:

```
Cells(5,"C")
Cells(5,3)
```

The ability to use numeric values for parameters is particularly useful if you need to loop through rows or columns. The macro recorder usually uses something like `Range("A1")`. `Select` for a single cell and `Range("A1:C5").Select` for a range of cells. If you are learning to code only from the recorder, you might be tempted to write code like this:

```
FinalRow = Cells(Rows.Count, 1).End(xlUp).Row
For i = 1 to FinalRow
    Range("A" & i & ":E" & i).Font.Bold = True
Next i
```

This little piece of code, which loops through rows and bolds the cells in Columns A through E, is awkward to read and write. But, how else can you do it?

```
FinalRow = Cells(Rows.Count, 1).End(xlUp).Row
For i = 1 to FinalRow
    Cells(i,"A").Resize(,5).Font.Bold = True
Next i
```

Instead of trying to type the range address, the new code uses the `Cells` and `Resize` properties to find the required cell, based on the active cell.

Using the `Cells` Property in the `Range` Property

`Cells` properties can be used as parameters in the `Range` property. The following refers to the range A1:E5:

```
Range(Cells(1,1),Cells(5,5))
```

This is particularly useful when you need to specify your variables with a parameter, as in the previous looping example.

Use the `Offset` Property to Refer to a Range

You have already seen a reference to `Offset` when the macro recorder used it when you recorded a relative reference. `Offset` enables you to manipulate a cell based off the location of the active cell. In this way, you do not need to know the address of a cell.

The syntax for the `Offset` property is as follows:

```
Range.Offset(RowOffset, ColumnOffset)
```

The syntax to affect cell F5 from cell A1 is

```
Range("A1").Offset(RowOffset:=4, ColumnOffset:=5)
```

Or, shorter yet, write this:

```
Range("A1").Offset(4,5)
```

The count of the rows and columns starts at A1 but does not include A1.

But what if you need to go over only a row or a column, but not both? You don't have to enter both the row and column parameter. If you need to refer to a cell one column over, use one of these lines:

```
Range("A1").Offset(ColumnOffset:=1)
Range("A1").Offset(,1)
```

Both lines mean the same, so the choice is yours. Referring to a cell one row up is similar:

```
Range("B2").Offset(RowOffset:=-1)
Range("B2").Offset(-1)
```

Once again, you can choose which one to use. It is a matter of readability of the code.

Suppose you have a list of produce with totals next to them. If you want to find any total equal to zero and place LOW in the cell next to it, do this:

```
Set Rng = Range("B1:B16").Find(What:="0", LookAt:=xlWhole, LookIn:=xlValues)
Rng.Offset(, 1).Value = "LOW"
Sub MyOffset()
With Range("B1:B16")
    Set Rng = .Find(What:="0", LookAt:=xlWhole, LookIn:=xlValues)
    If Not Rng Is Nothing Then
        firstAddress = Rng.Address
        Do
            Rng.Offset(, 1).Value = "LOW"
            Set Rng = .FindNext(Rng)
        Loop While Not Rng Is Nothing And Rng.Address <> firstAddress
    End If
End With
End Sub
```

The LOW totals are noted by the program, as shown in Figure 3.1.

> **NOTE**   Refer to the section "Object Variables" in Chapter 5 for more information on the Set statement.

Offsetting isn't only for single cells—it can be used with ranges. You can shift the focus of a range over in the same way you can shift the active cell. The following line refers to B2:D4 (see Figure 3.2):

```
Range("A1:C3").Offset(1,1)
```

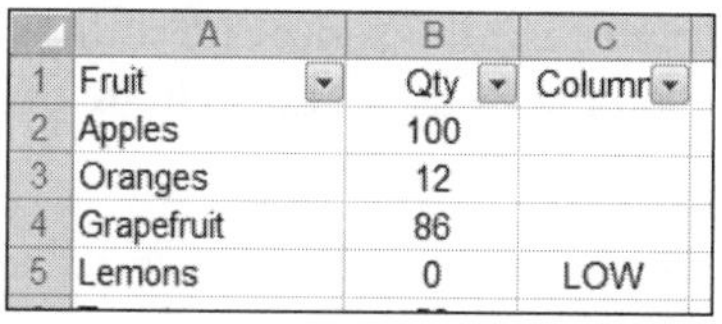

Figure 3.1
Find the produce with
zero totals.

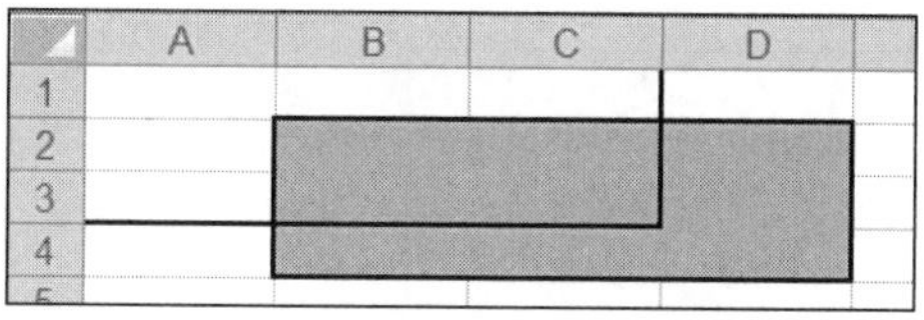

⬿	A		B		C	
1	Fruit	▾	Qty	▾	Columr	▾
2	Apples		100			
3	Oranges		12			
4	Grapefruit		86			
5	Lemons		0		LOW	

Figure 3.2
Offsetting a range:
Range("A1:C3").
Offset(1,1).
Select.

Use the `Resize` Property to Change the Size of a Range

The `Resize` property enables you to change the size of a range based on the location of the active cell. You can create a new range as needed. The syntax for the `Resize` property is

```
Range.Resize(RowSize, ColumnSize)
```

To create a range B3:D13, use the following:

```
Range("B3").Resize(RowSize:=11, ColumnSize:=3)
```

Or a simpler way to create this range:

```
Range("B3").Resize(11, 3)
```

But what if you need to resize by only a row or a column, not both? You do not have to enter both the row and column parameters.

If you need to expand by two columns, use one of the following:

```
Range("B3").Resize(ColumnSize:=2)
```

or

```
Range("B3").Resize(,2)
```

Both lines mean the same. The choice is yours. Resizing just the rows is similar. You can use either of the following:

```
Range("B3").Resize(RowSize:=2)
```

or

```
Range("B3").Resize(2)
```

Once again, the choice is yours. It is a matter of readability of the code.

From the list of produce, find the zero totals and color the cells of the total and corresponding produce (see Figure 3.3):

```
Set Rng = Range("B1:B16").Find(What:="0", LookAt:=xlWhole, LookIn:=xlValues)
Rng.Offset(, -1).Resize(, 2).Interior.ColorIndex = 15
```

Notice that the `Offset` property was used first to move the active cell over. When you are resizing, the upper-left corner cell must remain the same.

Resizing isn't only for single cells—it can be used to resize an existing range. For example, if you have a named range but need it and the column next to it, use this:

```
Range("Produce").Resize(,2)
```

Remember, the number you resize by is the total number of rows/columns you want to include.

Figure 3.3
Resizing a range to extend the selection.

◢	A	B	C
1	Apples	45	
2	Oranges	12	
3	Grapefruit	86	
4	Lemons	0	
5	Tomatos	58	

Use the Columns and Rows Properties to Specify a Range

Columns and Rows refer to the columns and rows of a specified Range object, which can be a worksheet or a range of cells. They return a Range object referencing the rows or columns of the specified object.

You have seen the following line used, but what is it doing?

```
FinalRow = Cells(Rows.Count, 1).End(xlUp).Row
```

This line of code finds the last row in a sheet in which Column A has a value and places the row number of that Range object into FinalRow. This can be useful when you need to loop through a sheet row by row—you will know exactly how many rows you need to go through.

> **CAUTION**
>
> Some properties of columns and rows require contiguous rows and columns to work properly. For example, if you were to use the following line of code, 9 would be the answer because only the first range would be evaluated:
>
> ```
> Range("A1:B9, C10:D19").Rows.Count
> ```
>
> However, if the ranges are grouped separately the answer would be 19.
>
> ```
> Range("A1:B9", "C10:D19").Rows.Count
> ```

Use the Union Method to Join Multiple Ranges

The Union method enables you to join two or more noncontiguous ranges. It creates a temporary object of the multiple ranges, which allows you to affect them together:

```
Application.Union(argument1, argument2, etc.)
```

The following code joins two named ranges on the sheet, inserts the =RAND() formula, and bolds them:

```
Set UnionRange = Union(Range("Range1"), Range("Range2"))
```

```
With UnionRange
    .Formula = "=RAND()"
    .Font.Bold = True
End With
```

Use the `Intersect` Method to Create a New Range from Overlapping Ranges

The `Intersect` method returns the cells that overlap between two or more ranges:

```
Application.Intersect(argument1, argument2, etc.)
```

The following code colors the overlapping cells of the two ranges.

```
Set IntersectRange = Intersect(Range("Range1"), Range("Range2"))
IntersectRange.Interior.ColorIndex = 6
```

Use the `ISEMPTY` Function to Check Whether a Cell Is Empty

The ISEMPTY function returns a Boolean value of whether a single cell is empty; True if empty, False if not. The cell must truly be empty. Even if it has a space that you cannot see, Excel does not consider the cell to be empty:

```
IsEmpty(Cell)
```

Figure 3.4 has several groups of data separated by a blank row. You want to make the separations a little more obvious.

Figure 3.4

Blank empty rows separating data.

	A	B	C	D
1	**Apples**	**Oranges**	**Grapefruit**	**Lemons**
2	45	12	86	15
3	51%	66%	57%	87%
4				
5	**Tomatos**	**Cabbage**	**Lettuce**	**Green Peppers**
6	58	24	31	0
7	63%	32%	97%	82%
8				
9	**Potatos**	**Yams**	**Onions**	**Garlic**
10	10	61	26	29
11	94%	19%	17%	79%
12				
13	**Green Beans**	**Brocolli**	**Peas**	**Carrots**
14	46	64	79	95
15	52%	7%	51%	85%

The following code goes down the data in Column A. When it finds an empty cell, it colors in the first four cells for that row (see Figure 3.5):

```
LastRow = Cells(Rows.Count, 1).End(xlUp).Row
For i = 1 To LastRow
    If IsEmpty(Cells(i, 1)) Then
        Cells(i, 1).Resize(1, 4).Interior.ColorIndex = 1
    End If
Next i
```

Figure 3.5
Colored rows separating data.

	A	B	C	D
1	Apples	Oranges	Grapefruit	Lemons
2	45	12	86	15
3	66%	88%	38%	26%
4				
5	Tomatoes	Cabbage	Lettuce	Green Peppers
6	58	24	31	0
7	70%	86%	79%	6%
8				
9	Potatoes	Yams	Onions	Garlic
10	10	61	26	29
11	43%	29%	43%	48%
12				
13	Green Beans	Broccoli	Peas	Carrots
14	46	64	79	95
15	33%	16%	2%	26%
16				

Use the `CurrentRegion` Property to Select a Data Range

`CurrentRegion` returns a `Range` object representing a set of contiguous data. As long as the data is surrounded by one empty row and one empty column, you can select the table with `CurrentRegion`:

```
RangeObject.CurrentRegion
```

The following line selects A1:D3 because this is the contiguous range of cells around cell A1 (see Figure 3.6):

```
Range("A1").CurrentRegion.Select
```

This is useful if you have a table whose size is in constant flux.

Figure 3.6
Use `CurrentRegion` to select a range of contiguous data around the active cell.

	A	B	C	D
1	Apples	Oranges	Grapefruit	Lemons
2	91	4	60	66
3	39%	41%	95%	49%
4				

CASE STUDY: USING THE SpecialCells METHOD TO SELECT SPECIFIC CELLS

Even Excel power users may not have encountered the Go To Special dialog box. If you press the F5 key in an Excel worksheet, you get the normal Go To dialog box (see Figure 3.7). In the lower-left corner of this dialog is a button labeled Special. Click that button to get to the super-powerful Go To Special dialog (see Figure 3.8).

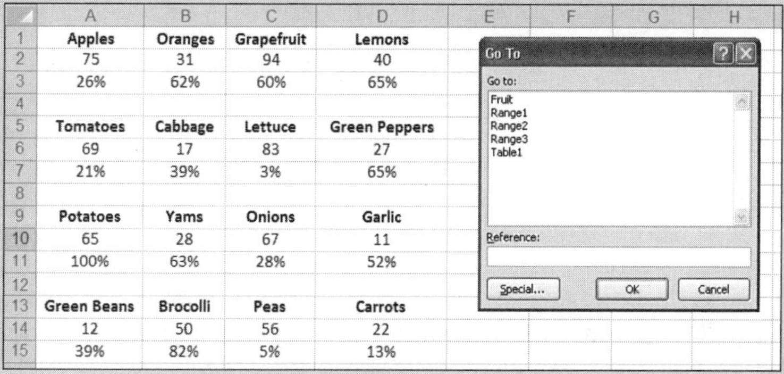

Figure 3.7
Although the Go To dialog doesn't seem useful, click the Special button in the lower-left corner.

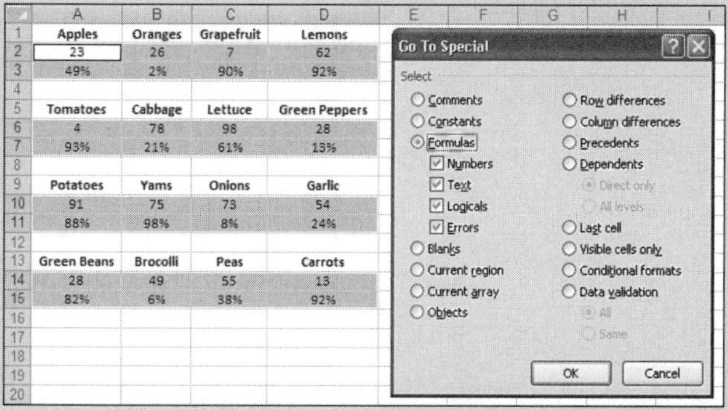

Figure 3.8
The Go To Special dialog has many incredibly useful selection tools.

In the Excel interface, the Go To Special dialog enables you to select only cells with formulas, only blank cells, or only the visible cells. Selecting only visible cells is excellent for grabbing the visible results of AutoFiltered data.

To simulate the Go To Special dialog in VBA, use the SpecialCells method. This enables you to act on cells that meet a certain criteria:

```
RangeObject.SpecialCells(Type, Value)
```

This method has two parameters: Type and Value. Type is one of the xlCellType constants:

```
xlCellTypeAllFormatConditions
xlCellTypeAllValidation
xlCellTypeBlanks
xlCellTypeComments
xlCellTypeConstants
xlCellTypeFormulas
xlCellTypeLastCell
```

```
xlCellTypeSameFormatConditions
xlCellTypeSameValidation
xlCellTypeVisible
```

`Value` is optional and can be one of the following:

```
xlErrors
xlLogical
xlNumbers
xlTextValues
```

The following code returns all the ranges that have conditional formatting set up. It produces an error if there are no conditional formats and adds a border around each contiguous section it finds:

```
Set rngCond = ActiveSheet.Cells.SpecialCells(xlCellTypeAllFormatConditions)
If Not rngCond Is Nothing Then
    rngCond.BorderAround xlContinuous
End If
```

Have you ever had someone send you a worksheet without all the labels filled in? Some people consider that the data shown in Figure 3.9 looks neat. They enter the Region field only once for each region. This might look aesthetically pleasing, but it is impossible to sort. Even Excel's pivot table routinely returns data in this annoying format.

Figure 3.9
The blank cells in the region column make it difficult to sort data tables such as this.

▲	A	B	C
1	Region	Product	Sales
2	North	ABC	766,469
3		DEF	776,996
4		XYZ	832,414
5	East	ABC	703,255
6		DEF	891,799
7		XYZ	897,949
8	West	ABC	631,646
9		DEF	494,919
10		XYZ	712,365
11			

Using the `SpecialCells` method to select all the blanks in this range is one way to fill in all the blank region cells quickly with the region found above them:

```
Sub FillIn()
    On Error Resume Next 'Need this because if there aren't any blank cells,
    'the code will error
    Range("A1").CurrentRegion.SpecialCells(xlCellTypeBlanks).FormulaR1C1 _
    = "=R[-1]C"
    Range("A1").CurrentRegion.Value = Range("A1").CurrentRegion.Value
End Sub
```

In this code, `Range("A1").CurrentRegion` refers to the contiguous range of data in the report. The `SpecialCells` method returns just the blank cells in that range. Although you can read more about R1C1 style formulas in Chapter 6, "R1C1-Style Formulas," this particular formula fills in all the blank cells with a formula that points to the cell above the blank cell. The second line of code is a fast way to simulate doing a Copy and then Paste Special Values. Figure 3.10 shows the results.

Figure 3.10
After the macro runs, the blank cells in the Region column have been filled in with data.

	A	B	C
1	Region	Product	Sales
2	North	ABC	766,469
3	North	DEF	776,996
4	North	XYZ	832,414
5	East	ABC	703,255
6	East	DEF	891,799
7	East	XYZ	897,949
8	West	ABC	631,646
9	West	DEF	494,919
10	West	XYZ	712,365
11			

Use the `Areas` Collection to Return a Noncontiguous Range

The Areas collection is a collection of noncontiguous ranges within a selection. It consists of individual `Range` objects representing contiguous ranges of cells within the selection. If the selection contains only one area, the `Areas` collection contains a single `Range` object corresponding to that selection.

You might be tempted to loop through the sheet, copy a row, and paste it to another section. However, there is an easier way (see Figure 3.11):

```
Range("A:D").SpecialCells(xlCellTypeConstants, 1).Copy Range("I1")
```

Figure 3.11
The `Areas` collection makes it easier to manipulate noncontiguous ranges.

	A	B	C	D	E	F	G	H	I	J	K	L
1	Apples	Oranges	Grapefruit	Lemons					45	12	86	15
2	45	12	86	15					58	24	31	0
3	31%	97%	71%	18%					10	61	26	29
4									46	64	79	95
5	Tomatoes	Cabbage	Lettuce	Green Peppers								
6	58	24	31	0								
7	45%	55%	26%	54%								
8												
9	Potatoes	Yams	Onions	Garlic								
10	10	61	26	29								
11	90%	21%	65%	73%								
12												
13	Green Beans	Broccoli	Peas	Carrots								
14	46	64	79	95								
15	73%	24%	13%	31%								
16												

Referencing Tables

With Excel 2007, you were introduced to a new way of interacting with ranges of data: tables. These special ranges offer the convenience of referencing named ranges, but they are not created in the same manner. For more information on how to create a named table, see Chapter 8, "Create and Manipulate Names in VBA."

The table itself is referenced using the standard method of referring to a ranged name. To refer to the data in Table1 in Sheet1, do this:

```
Worksheets(1).Range("Table1")
```

This references the data part of the table but does not include the header or total row. To include the header and total row, do this:

```
Worksheets(1).Range("Table1[#All]")
```

What I really like about this feature is the ease of referencing specific columns of a table. You don't have to know how many columns in from a starting position or the letter/number of the column, and you don't have to use a FIND function. Instead, you can use the header name of the column. For example, do this to reference the Qty column of the table:

```
Worksheets(1).Range("Table1[Qty]")
```

Next Steps

Now that you have an idea of how Excel works, it's time to apply it to useful situations. Chapter 4, "User-Defined Functions," uses the skills you have learned so far and introduces other programming methods that you will learn more about throughout this book.

3

User-Defined Functions

Creating User-Defined Functions

Excel provides many built-in formulas. However, sometimes you need a complex custom formula not offered, such as a formula that sums a range of cells based on their interior color.

So, what do you do? You could go down your list and copy the colored cells to another section. Or perhaps you have a calculator next to you as you work your way down your list—beware you don't enter the same number twice! Both methods are time-consuming and prone to accidents. What to do?

You could write a procedure to solve this problem—after all, that's what this book is about. However, you have another option: *user-defined functions* (UDFs).

Functions can be created in VBA that can be used just like Excel's built-in functions, such as SUM. After the custom function is created, a user needs to know only the function name and its arguments.

IN THIS CHAPTER

Creating User-Defined Functions 79

Sharing UDFs 81

Useful Custom Excel Functions 82

> **NOTE** UDFs can be entered only into standard modules. Sheet and ThisWorkbook modules are a special type of module. If you enter the function there, Excel will not recognize that you are creating a UDF.

CASE STUDY: CUSTOM FUNCTIONS: EXAMPLE AND EXPLANATION

Let's build a custom function used to add two values. After you have created it, you will use it on a worksheet.

Insert a new module in the VB Editor. Type the following function into the module. It is a function called ADD that will total two numbers in different cells. The function has two arguments:

```
Add(Number1,Number2)
```

Number1 is the first number to add; Number2 is the second number to add:

```
Function Add(Number1 As Integer, Number2 As Integer) As Integer
Add = Number1 + Number2
End Function
```

Let's break this down:

- Function name: ADD.
- Arguments are placed in parentheses after the name of the function. This example has two arguments: Number1 and Number2.
- As Integer defines the variable type of the result as a whole number.
- ADD =Number1 + Number2: The result of the function is returned.

Here is how to use the function on a worksheet:

1. Type numbers into cells A1 and A2.
2. Select cell A3.
3. Press Shift+F3 to open the Insert Function dialog box, or from the Formulas tab, choose Insert Function.
4. Select the User Defined category (see Figure 4.1).
5. Select the Add function.
6. In the first argument box, select cell A1 (see Figure 4.2).
7. In the second argument box, select cell A2.
8. Click OK.

Congratulations! You have created your first custom function.

> **NOTE** You can easily share custom functions because the users are not required to know how the function works. See the section "Sharing UDFs" in this chapter for more information.

Figure 4.1
You can find the UDFs under the User Defined category of the Insert Function dialog box.

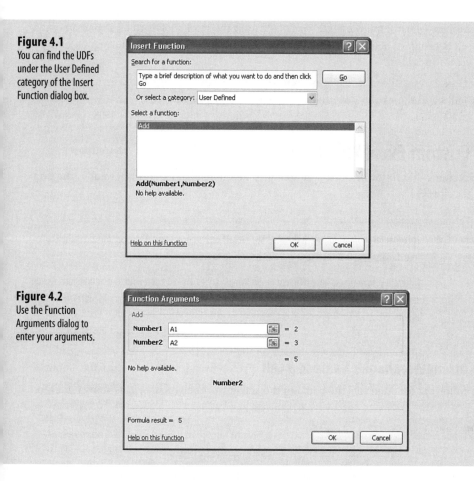

Figure 4.2
Use the Function Arguments dialog to enter your arguments.

4

Most of the functions used on sheets can also be used in VBA and vice versa. However, in VBA you call the UDF (ADD) from a procedure (Addition):

```
Sub Addition ()
Dim Total as Integer
Total = Add (1,10) 'we use a user-defined function Add
MsgBox "The answer is: " & Total
End Sub
```

Sharing UDFs

Where you store a UDF affects how you can share it:

- Personal.xlsb—Store the UDF in Personal.xlsb if it is just for your use and won't be used in a workbook opened on another computer.
- **Workbook**—Store the UDF in the workbook in which it is being used if it needs to be distributed to many people.

■ **Add-in**—Distribute the UDF via an add-in if the workbook is to be shared among a select group of people. See Chapter 27, "Creating Add-Ins," for information on how to create an add-in.

■ **Template**—Store the UDF in a template if it needs to be used to create several workbooks and the workbooks are distributed to many people.

Useful Custom Excel Functions

The sections that follow include a sampling of functions that can prove useful in the everyday Excel world.

> **NOTE**
>
> This chapter contains functions donated by several Excel programmers. These are functions they have found useful and that they hope will also be of help to you.
>
> Different programmers have different programming styles. We did not rewrite the submissions. As you review the lines of code, you might notice different ways of doing the same task such as referring to ranges.

Set the Current Workbook's Name in a Cell

The following function sets the name of the active workbook in a cell, as shown in Figure 4.3:

```
MyName()
```

Figure 4.3
Use a UDF to show the filename or the filename with directory path.

⊿	A	B
1	ProjectFilesChapter04.xlsm	=MyName()
2	\\Dzgnw41\e\Book 3\Chapter 4 - UDFs\ProjectFilesChapter04.xlsm	=MyFullname()
3		

No arguments are used with this function:

```
Function MyName() As String
    MyName = ThisWorkbook.Name
End Function
```

Set the Current Workbook's Name and File Path in a Cell

A variation of the previous function, the following function sets the file path and name of the active workbook in a cell, as shown previously in Figure 4.3:

```
MyFullName()
```

No arguments are used with this function:

```
Function MyFullName() As String
    MyFullName = ThisWorkbook.FullName
End Function
```

Check Whether a Workbook Is Open

There might be times when you need to check whether a workbook is open. The following function returns True if the workbook is open and False if it is not:

```
BookOpen(Bk)
```

The argument is Bk, which is the name of the workbook being checked:

```
Function BookOpen(Bk As String) As Boolean
Dim T As Excel.Workbook
Err.Clear 'clears any errors
On Error Resume Next 'if the code runs into an error, it skips it and
'continues
Set T = Application.Workbooks(Bk)
BookOpen = Not T Is Nothing
'If the workbook is open, then T will hold the workbook object and therefore
'will NOT be Nothing
Err.Clear
On Error GoTo 0
End Function
```

Here is an example of using the function:

```
Sub OpenAWorkbook()
Dim IsOpen As Boolean
Dim BookName As String
BookName = "ProjectFilesChapter04.xlsm"
IsOpen = BookOpen(BookName) 'calling our function - don't forget the parameter
If IsOpen Then
    MsgBox BookName & " is already open!"
Else
    Workbooks.Open (BookName)
End If
End Sub
```

Check Whether a Sheet in an Open Workbook Exists

This function requires that the workbook(s) it checks be open. It returns True if the sheet is found and False if it is not:

```
SheetExists(SName, WBName)
```

The arguments are as follows:

- SName—The name of the sheet being searched

- WBName—(Optional) The name of the workbook containing the sheet

```
Function SheetExists(SName As String, Optional WB As Workbook) As Boolean
    Dim WS As Worksheet
    ' Use active workbook by default
    If WB Is Nothing Then
```

4

```
        Set WB = ActiveWorkbook
    End If

    On Error Resume Next
        SheetExists = CBool(Not WB.Sheets(SName) Is Nothing)
    On Error GoTo 0

End Function
```

> **NOTE**
> Cbool is a function that converts the expression between the parentheses to a boolean value.

Here is an example of using this function:

```
Sub CheckForSheet()
Dim ShtExists As Boolean
ShtExists = SheetExists("Sheet9")
'notice that only one parameter was passed; the workbook name is optional
If ShtExists Then
    MsgBox "The worksheet exists!"
Else
    MsgBox "The worksheet does NOT exist!"
End If
End Sub
```

Count the Number of Workbooks in a Directory

This function searches the current directory, and its subfolders if you want, counting all Excel macro workbook files (XLSM) or just the ones starting with a string of letters:

```
NumFilesInCurDir (LikeText, Subfolders)
```

The arguments are as follows:

- `LikeText`—(Optional) A string value to search for must include an asterisk (*) such as `Mr*`
- `Subfolders`—(Optional) `True` to search subfolders, `False` (default) not to

> **NOTE**
> `FileSystemObject` requires the Microsoft Scripting Runtime reference library. To enable this setting, go to Tools, References and check Microsoft Scripting Runtime.

This function is a recursive function—it calls itself until a specific condition is met; in this case until all subfolders are processed.

```
Function NumFilesInCurDir(Optional strInclude As String = "", _
Optional blnSubDirs As Boolean = False)
Dim fso As FileSystemObject
Dim fld As Folder
Dim fil As File
Dim subfld As Folder
Dim intFileCount As Integer
Dim strExtension As String
  strExtension = "XLSM"
  Set fso = New FileSystemObject
  Set fld = fso.GetFolder(ThisWorkbook.Path)
  For Each fil In fld.Files
    If UCase(fil.Name) Like "*" & UCase(strInclude) & "*." & _
        UCase(strExtension) Then
      intFileCount = intFileCount + 1
    End If
  Next fil
  If blnSubDirs Then
    For Each subfld In fld.Subfolders
      intFileCount = intFileCount + NumFilesInCurDir(strInclude, True)
    Next subfld
  End If
  NumFilesInCurDir = intFileCount
  Set fso = Nothing
End Function
```

Here is an example of using this function:

```
Sub CountMyWkbks()
Dim MyFiles As Integer
MyFiles = NumFilesInCurDir("MrE*", True)
MsgBox MyFiles & " file(s) found"
End Sub
```

Retrieve USERID

Ever need to keep a record of who saves changes to a workbook? With the USERID function, you can retrieve the name of the user logged in to a computer. Combine it with the function discussed in the "Retrieve Permanent Date and Time" section and you have a nice log file. You can also use the USERID function to set up user rights to a workbook:

```
WinUserName ()
```

No arguments are used with this function.

> **NOTE** The USERID function is an advanced function that uses the *application programming interface* (API), which is reviewed in Chapter 24, "Windows Application Programming Interface."

This first section (`Private` declarations) must be at the top of the module:

```
Private Declare Function WNetGetUser Lib "mpr.dll" Alias "WNetGetUserA" _
    (ByVal lpName As String, ByVal lpUserName As String, _
lpnLength As Long) As Long
Private Const NO_ERROR = 0
Private Const ERROR_NOT_CONNECTED = 2250&
Private Const ERROR_MORE_DATA = 234
Private Const ERROR_NO_NETWORK = 1222&
Private Const ERROR_EXTENDED_ERROR = 1208&
Private Const ERROR_NO_NET_OR_BAD_PATH = 1203&
```

You can place the following section of code anywhere in the module as long as it is below the previous section:

```
Function WinUsername() As String
    'variables
    Dim strBuf As String, lngUser As Long, strUn As String
    'clear buffer for user name from api func
    strBuf = Space$(255)
    'use api func WNetGetUser to assign user value to lngUser
    'will have lots of blank space
    lngUser = WNetGetUser("", strBuf, 255)
    'if no error from function call
    If lngUser = NO_ERROR Then
        'clear out blank space in strBuf and assign val to function
        strUn = Left(strBuf, InStr(strBuf, vbNullChar) - 1)
        WinUsername = strUn
    Else
    'error, give up
        WinUsername = "Error :" & lngUser
    End If
End Function
```

Function example:

```
Sub CheckUserRights()
Dim UserName As String
UserName = WinUsername
Select Case UserName
    Case "Administrator"
        MsgBox "Full Rights"
    Case "Guest"
        MsgBox "You cannot make changes"
    Case Else
        MsgBox "Limited Rights"
End Select
End Sub
```

Retrieve Date and Time of Last Save

This function retrieves the saved date and time of any workbook, including the current one (see Figure 4.4).

```
LastSaved(FullPath)
```

Figure 4.4
Retrieve date and time of
last save.

	A	B
1	10/1/09 11:36 AM	=LastSaved("\\Dzgnw41\e\Book 3\Chapter 4 - UDFs\ProjectFilesChapter04.xlsm")

> **NOTE** The cell must be formatted properly to display the date/time.

The argument is `FullPath`, a string showing the full path and filename of the file in question:

```
Function LastSaved(FullPath As String) As Date
LastSaved = FileDateTime(FullPath)
End Function
```

Retrieve Permanent Date and Time

Because of the volatility of the NOW function, it isn't very useful for stamping a worksheet with the creation or editing date. Every time the workbook is opened or recalculated, the result of the NOW function is updated. The following function uses the NOW function. However, because you need to reenter the cell to update the function, it is much less volatile (see Figure 4.5):

```
DateTime()
```

Figure 4.5
Retrieve permanent date
and time.

	A	B
1	10/3/09 2:51 PM	=DateTime()

No arguments are used with this function:

```
DateTime()
```

> **NOTE** The cell must be formatted properly to display the date/time.

Function example:

```
Function DateTime()
    DateTime = Now
End Function
```

Validate an E-mail Address

If you manage an e-mail subscription list, you might receive invalid e-mail addresses, such as addresses with a space before the "at" symbol (@). The ISEMAILVALID function can check addresses and confirm that they are proper e-mail addresses (see Figure 4.6).

Figure 4.6
Validating e-mail addresses.

	A	B	C
1	Tracy@ MrExcel.com	FALSE	<-a space after the @
2	Bill@MrExcel.com	TRUE	
3	consult?@MrExcel/com	FALSE	<-invalid characters
4			

> **CAUTION**
>
> This function cannot verify that an e-mail address is an existing one. It only checks the syntax to verify that the address may be legitimate.
>
>   IsEmailValid (StrEmail)

The argument is strEmail, an e-mail address:

```
Function IsEmailValid(strEmail As String) As Boolean
Dim strArray As Variant
Dim strItem As Variant
Dim i As Long
Dim c As String
Dim blnIsItValid As Boolean
blnIsItValid = True
'count the @ in the string
i = Len(strEmail) - Len(Application.Substitute(strEmail, "@", ""))
'if there is more than one @, invalid email
If i <> 1 Then IsEmailValid = False: Exit Function
ReDim strArray(1 To 2)
'the following two lines place the text to the left and right
'of the @ in their own variables
strArray(1) = Left(strEmail, InStr(1, strEmail, "@", 1) - 1)
strArray(2) = Application.Substitute(Right(strEmail, Len(strEmail) - _
    Len(strArray(1))), "@", "")

For Each strItem In strArray
    'verify there is something in the variable.
'If there isn't, then part of the email is missing
    If Len(strItem) <= 0 Then
        blnIsItValid = False
        IsEmailValid = blnIsItValid
        Exit Function
    End If
    'verify only valid characters in the email
    For i = 1 To Len(strItem)
'lowercases all letters for easier checking
        c = LCase(Mid(strItem, i, 1))
        If InStr("abcdefghijklmnopqrstuvwxyz_-.", c) <= 0 _
        And Not IsNumeric Then
```

```
                blnIsItValid = False
                IsEmailValid = blnIsItValid
                Exit Function
            End If
        Next i
    'verify that the first character of the left and right aren't periods
        If Left(strItem, 1) = "." Or Right(strItem, 1) = "." Then
            blnIsItValid = False
            IsEmailValid = blnIsItValid
            Exit Function
        End If
    Next strItem
    'verify there is a period in the right half of the address
    If InStr(strArray(2), ".") <= 0 Then
        blnIsItValid = False
        IsEmailValid = blnIsItValid
        Exit Function
    End If
    i = Len(strArray(2)) - InStrRev(strArray(2), ".") 'locate the period
    'verify that the number of letters corresponds to a valid domain extension
    If i <> 2 And i <> 3 And i <> 4 Then
        blnIsItValid = False
        IsEmailValid = blnIsItValid
        Exit Function
    End If
    'verify that there aren't two periods together in the email
    If InStr(strEmail, "..") > 0 Then
        blnIsItValid = False
        IsEmailValid = blnIsItValid
        Exit Function
    End If
    IsEmailValid = blnIsItValid
End Function
```

Sum Cells Based on Interior Color

Let's say you have created a list of how much each of your clients owes. From this list, you want to sum just those cells you have colored to indicate clients who are 30 days past due.

> **NOTE**
> Cells colored by conditional formatting will not work; the cells must have an interior color.
>
> ```
> SumColor(CellColor, SumRange)
> ```

The arguments are as follows:

- CellColor—The address of a cell with the target color
- SumRange—The range of cells to be searched

```
Function SumByColor(CellColor As Range, SumRange As Range)
Dim myCell As Range
Dim iCol As Integer
```

```
Dim myTotal
iCol = CellColor.Interior.ColorIndex 'get the target color
For Each myCell In SumRange 'look at each cell in the designated range
'if the cell color matches the target color
If myCell.Interior.ColorIndex = iCol Then
'add the value in the cell to the total
myTotal = WorksheetFunction.Sum(myCell) + myTotal
    End If
Next myCell
SumByColor = myTotal
End Function
```

Figure 4.7 shows a sample worksheet using this function.

Figure 4.7
Sum cells based on interior color.

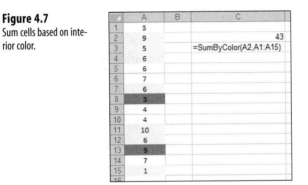

Count Unique Values

How many times have you had a long list of values and needed to know how many were unique values? This function goes through a range and provides that information, as shown in Figure 4.8:

```
NumUniqueValues(Rng)
```

Figure 4.8
Count the number of unique values in a range.

	A	B	C
1	A	11	=NumUniqueValues(A1:A16)
2	R		
3	T		
4	A		
5	V		
6	F		
7	EE		
8	1		
9	19		
10	V		
11	Q		
12	V		
13	GE		
14	V		
15	123		
16	1		

The argument is Rng, the range to search unique values.

Function example:

```
Function NumUniqueValues(Rng As Range) As Long
Dim myCell As Range
Dim UniqueVals As New Collection
Application.Volatile 'forces the function to recalculate when the range
changes
On Error Resume Next
'the following places each value from the range into a collection
'because a collection, with a key parameter, can contain only unique values,
'there will be no duplicates the error statements force the program to
'continue when the error messages appear for duplicate items in the collection
For Each myCell In Rng
    UniqueVals.Add myCell.Value, CStr(myCell.Value)
Next myCell
On Error GoTo 0
'returns the number of items in the collection
NumUniqueValues = UniqueVals.Count
End Function
```

Remove Duplicates from a Range

No doubt, you have also had a list of items and needed to list only the unique values. The following function goes through a range and stores only the unique values:

```
UniqueValues (OrigArray)
```

The argument is OrigArray, an array from which the duplicates will be removed.

This first section (Const declarations) must be at the top of the module:

```
Const ERR_BAD_PARAMETER = "Array parameter required"
Const ERR_BAD_TYPE = "Invalid Type"
Const ERR_BP_NUMBER = 20000
Const ERR_BT_NUMBER = 20001
```

You can place the following section of code anywhere in the module as long as it is below the previous section:

```
Public Function UniqueValues(ByVal OrigArray As Variant) As Variant
    Dim vAns() As Variant
    Dim lStartPoint As Long
    Dim lEndPoint As Long
    Dim lCtr As Long, lCount As Long
    Dim iCtr As Integer
    Dim col As New Collection
    Dim sIndex As String
    Dim vTest As Variant, vItem As Variant
    Dim iBadVarTypes(4) As Integer
    'Function does not work if array element is one of the
    'following types
    iBadVarTypes(0) = vbObject
    iBadVarTypes(1) = vbError
    iBadVarTypes(2) = vbDataObject
    iBadVarTypes(3) = vbUserDefinedType
    iBadVarTypes(4) = vbArray
```

4

```
'Check to see whether the parameter is an array
If Not IsArray(OrigArray) Then
    Err.Raise ERR_BP_NUMBER, , ERR_BAD_PARAMETER
    Exit Function
End If
lStartPoint = LBound(OrigArray)
lEndPoint = UBound(OrigArray)
For lCtr = lStartPoint To lEndPoint
    vItem = OrigArray(lCtr)
    'First check to see whether variable type is acceptable
    For iCtr = 0 To UBound(iBadVarTypes)
        If VarType(vItem) = iBadVarTypes(iCtr) Or _
          VarType(vItem) = iBadVarTypes(iCtr) + vbVariant Then
            Err.Raise ERR_BT_NUMBER, , ERR_BAD_TYPE
            Exit Function
        End If
    Next iCtr
    'Add element to a collection, using it as the index
    'if an error occurs, the element already exists
    sIndex = CStr(vItem)
    'first element, add automatically
    If lCtr = lStartPoint Then
        col.Add vItem, sIndex
        ReDim vAns(lStartPoint To lStartPoint) As Variant
        vAns(lStartPoint) = vItem
    Else
        On Error Resume Next
        col.Add vItem, sIndex
        If Err.Number = 0 Then
            lCount = UBound(vAns) + 1
            ReDim Preserve vAns(lStartPoint To lCount)
            vAns(lCount) = vItem
        End If
    End If
    Err.Clear
Next lCtr
UniqueValues = vAns
End Function
```

Here is an example of using this function. See Figure 4.9 for the result on a worksheet:

```
Function nodupsArray(rng As Range) As Variant
    Dim arr1() As Variant
    If rng.Columns.Count > 1 Then Exit Function
    arr1 = Application.Transpose(rng)
    arr1 = UniqueValues(arr1)
    nodupsArray = Application.Transpose(arr1)
End Function
```

Figure 4.9
List unique values from a range.

	A	B	C	D
1	Original Range		Array Function	
2	A		A	
3	R		R	
4	T		T	
5	A		V	
6	V		F	
7	F		EE	
8	EE		1	
9	1		19	
10	19		Q	
11	V		GE	
12	Q		123	
13	V			
14	GE			
15	V			
16	123			
17	1			

Find the First Nonzero-Length Cell in a Range

Suppose you imported a large list of data with many empty cells. Here is a function that evaluates a range of cells and returns the value of the first nonzero-length cell:

```
FirstNonZeroLength(Rng)
```

The argument is Rng, the range to search.

Function example:

```
Function FirstNonZeroLength(Rng As Range)
Dim myCell As Range
FirstNonZeroLength = 0#
For Each myCell In Rng
    If Not IsNull(myCell) And myCell <> "" Then
        FirstNonZeroLength = myCell.Value
        Exit Function
    End If
Next myCell
FirstNonZeroLength = myCell.Value
End Function
```

Figure 4.10 shows the function on a sample worksheet.

Figure 4.10
Find the value of the first nonzero-length cell in a range.

	A	B	C	D
1		2		
2		=FirstNonZeroLength(A1:A17)		
3	2			
4				
5	7			
6	8			
7	9			
8				

4

Substitute Multiple Characters

Excel has a substitute function, but it is a value-for-value substitution. What if you have several characters you need to substitute? Figure 4.11 shows several examples of how this function works:

```
MSubstitute(trStr, frStr, toStr)
```

Figure 4.11
Substitute multiple characters in a cell.

	A	B	C
1	1 Introduction	Introduction	=msubstitute(B1,"1","")
2	This wam a test	This was a test	=msubstitute(B2,"wam", "was")
3	123abc456	abc	=msubstitute(B3,"1234567890","")
4	Adnothyer Tuiest	Another Test	=msubstitute(B4,"dyui","")

The arguments are as follows:

- trStr—The string to be searched
- frStr—The text being searched for
- toStr—The replacement text

> **CAUTION**
>
> The toStr argument is assumed to be the same length as frStr. If not, the remaining characters are considered null (" "). The function is case sensitive. To replace all instances of a, use a and A. You cannot replace one character with two characters.
>
> ```
> =MSUBSTITUTE("This is a test","i","$@")
> ```
>
> This results in this:
>
> ```
> "Th$s $s a test"
> ```

Function example:

```
Function MSUBSTITUTE(ByVal trStr As Variant, frStr As String, _
        toStr As String) As Variant
Dim iCol As Integer
Dim j As Integer
Dim Ar As Variant
Dim vfr() As String
Dim vto() As String
ReDim vfr(1 To Len(frStr))
ReDim vto(1 To Len(frStr))
'place the strings into an array
For j = 1 To Len(frStr)
    vfr(j) = Mid(frStr, j, 1)
    If Mid(toStr, j, 1) <> "" Then
        vto(j) = Mid(toStr, j, 1)
    Else
        vto(j) = ""
    End If
Next j
'compare each character and substitute if needed
```

```
If IsArray(trStr) Then
    Ar = trStr
    For iRow = LBound(Ar, 1) To UBound(Ar, 1)
        For iCol = LBound(Ar, 2) To UBound(Ar, 2)
            For j = 1 To Len(frStr)
                Ar(iRow, iCol) = Application.Substitute(Ar(iRow, iCol), _
            vfr(j), vto(j))
            Next j
        Next iCol
    Next iRow
Else
    Ar = trStr
    For j = 1 To Len(frStr)
        Ar = Application.Substitute(Ar, vfr(j), vto(j))
    Next j
End If
MSUBSTITUTE = Ar
End Function
```

Retrieve Numbers from Mixed Text

This function extracts and returns numbers from text that is a mix of numbers and letters, as shown in Figure 4.12:

```
RetrieveNumbers (myString)
```

Figure 4.12
Extract numbers from mixed text.

▲	A	B	C	D	E
1	123abc456	123456			
2	1b2k3j34ioj	12334			
3	123 abc	123			

The argument is myString, the text containing the numbers to be extracted.

Function example:

```
Function RetrieveNumbers(myString As String)
Dim i As Integer, j As Integer
Dim OnlyNums As String
'starting at the END of the string and moving backwards (Step -1)
For i = Len(myString) To 1 Step -1
'IsNumeric is a VBA function that returns True if a variable is a number
'When a number is found, it is added to the OnlyNums string
    If IsNumeric(Mid(myString, i, 1)) Then
        j = j + 1
        OnlyNums = Mid(myString, i, 1) & OnlyNums
    End If
    If j = 1 Then OnlyNums = CInt(Mid(OnlyNums, 1, 1))
Next i
RetrieveNumbers = CLng(OnlyNums)
End Function
```

Convert Week Number into Date

Have you ever received a spreadsheet report in which all the headers showed the week number? This can be confusing because you probably don't know what Week 15 actually is. You would have to get out your calendar and count the weeks. This problem is exacerbated if you need to count weeks in a previous year. What you need is a nice little function that converts `Week ## Year` into the date of a particular day in a given week, as shown in Figure 4.13:

```
Weekday(Str)
```

Figure 4.13

Convert a week number into a date more easily referenced.

	A	B
1	Week 15 2010	April 5, 2010
2		=convertWEEKDAY(A1)
3		

The argument is `Str`, the week to be converted in `"Week ##, YYYY"` format.

> **NOTE**
> The result must be formatted as a date.

Function example:

```
Function ConvertWeekDay(Str As String) As Date
Dim Week As Long
Dim FirstMon As Date
Dim TStr As String
FirstMon = DateSerial(Right(Str, 4), 1, 1)
FirstMon = FirstMon - FirstMon Mod 7 + 2
TStr = Right(Str, Len(Str) - 5)
Week = Left(TStr, InStr(1, TStr, " ", 1)) + 0
ConvertWeekDay = FirstMon + (Week - 1) * 7
End Function
```

Separate Delimited String

In this example, you need to paste a column of delimited data. You could use Excel's Text to Columns, but you need only an element or two from each cell. Text to Columns parses the entire thing. What you need is a function that lets you specify the number of the element in a string that you need, as shown in Figure 4.14:

```
StringElement(str,chr,ind)
```

Figure 4.14
Extracting a single element from delimited text.

	A	B	C	D	E	F	G	H
1					ind			
2	str	chr	1	2	3	4	5	6
3	A|B|C|D|E|F	|	A	B	C	D	E	F
4			=StringElement($A$3,$B$3,C2)					
5								

The arguments are as follows:

- str—The string to be parsed
- chr—The delimiter
- ind—The position of the element to be returned

Function example:

```
Function StringElement(str As String, chr As String, ind As Integer)
Dim arr_str As Variant
arr_str = Split(str, chr) 'Not compatible with XL97
StringElement = arr_str(ind - 1)
End Function
```

Sort and Concatenate

The following function enables you to take a column of data, sort it, and concatenate it using a comma (,) as the delimiter (see Figure 4.15):

```
SortConcat(Rng)
```

Figure 4.15
Sort and concatenate a range of variables.

	A	B
1	Unsorted List	Sorted String
2	q	1,14,50,9,a,f,gg,q,r,rrrr
3	r	=sortConcat(A2:A11)
4	f	
5	a	
6	gg	
7	1	
8	9	
9	50	
10	14	
11	rrrrr	

The argument is Rng, the range of data to be sorted and concatenated. SortConcat calls another procedure, BubbleSort, that must be included.

Function example:

```
Function SortConcat(Rng As Range) As Variant
Dim MySum As String, arr1() As String
Dim j As Integer, i As Integer
Dim cl As Range
Dim concat As Variant
```

4

```
On Error GoTo FuncFail:
'initialize output
SortConcat = 0#
'avoid user issues
If Rng.Count = 0 Then Exit Function
'get range into variant variable holding array
ReDim arr1(1 To Rng.Count)
'fill array
i = 1
For Each cl In Rng
    arr1(i) = cl.Value
    i = i + 1
Next
'sort array elements
Call BubbleSort(arr1)
'create string from array elements
For j = UBound(arr1) To 1 Step -1
    If Not IsEmpty(arr1(j)) Then
        MySum = arr1(j) & ", " & MySum
    End If
Next j
'assign value to function
SortConcat = Left(MySum, Len(MySum) - 2)
'exit point
concat_exit:
Exit Function
'display error in cell
FuncFail:
SortConcat = Err.Number & " - " & Err.Description
Resume concat_exit
End Function
```

The following function is the ever-popular `BubbleSort`. Many developers use this program to do a simple sort of data:

```
Sub BubbleSort(List() As String)
'   Sorts the List array in ascending order
Dim First As Integer, Last As Integer
Dim i As Integer, j As Integer
Dim Temp
First = LBound(List)
Last = UBound(List)
For i = First To Last - 1
    For j = i + 1 To Last
        If UCase(List(i)) > UCase(List(j)) Then
            Temp = List(j)
            List(j) = List(i)
            List(i) = Temp
        End If
    Next j
Next i
End Sub
```

Sort Numeric and Alpha Characters

This function takes a mixed range of numeric and alpha characters and sorts them—first numerically and then alphabetically. The result is placed in an array that can be displayed on a worksheet by using an array formula, as shown in Figure 4.16:

```
sorter(Rng)
```

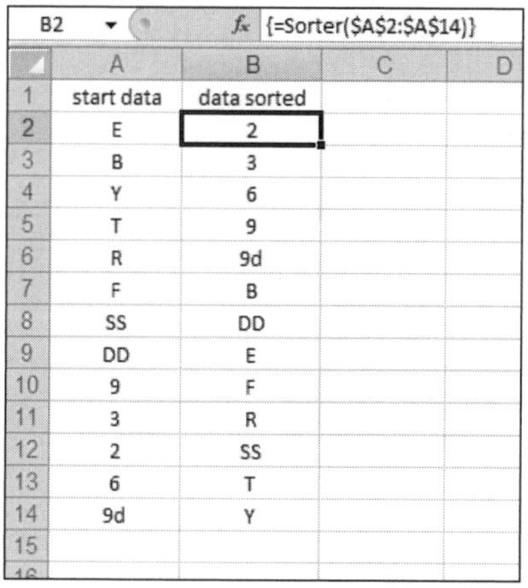

Figure 4.16

Sort a mixed alphanumeric list.

	A	B	C	D
B2	▼	f_x {=Sorter($A$2:$A$14)}		
1	start data	data sorted		
2	E	2		
3	B	3		
4	Y	6		
5	T	9		
6	R	9d		
7	F	B		
8	SS	DD		
9	DD	E		
10	9	F		
11	3	R		
12	2	SS		
13	6	T		
14	9d	Y		
15				

The argument is Rng, the range to be sorted.

Function example:

```
Function sorter(Rng As Range) As Variant
'returns an array
Dim arr1() As Variant
If Rng.Columns.Count > 1 Then Exit Function
arr1 = Application.Transpose(Rng)
QuickSort arr1
sorter = Application.Transpose(arr1)
End Function
```

The function uses the following two procedures to sort the data in the range:

```
Public Sub QuickSort(ByRef vntArr As Variant, _
    Optional ByVal lngLeft As Long = -2, _
    Optional ByVal lngRight As Long = -2)
Dim i, j, lngMid As Long
Dim vntTestVal As Variant
If lngLeft = -2 Then lngLeft = LBound(vntArr)
If lngRight = -2 Then lngRight = UBound(vntArr)
If lngLeft < lngRight Then
    lngMid = (lngLeft + lngRight) \ 2
    vntTestVal = vntArr(lngMid)
    i = lngLeft
    j = lngRight
    Do
        Do While vntArr(i) < vntTestVal
            i = i + 1
```

```
        Loop
        Do While vntArr(j) > vntTestVal
            j = j - 1
        Loop
        If i <= j Then
            Call SwapElements(vntArr, i, j)
            i = i + 1
            j = j - 1
        End If
    Loop Until i > j
    If j <= lngMid Then
        Call QuickSort(vntArr, lngLeft, j)
        Call QuickSort(vntArr, i, lngRight)
    Else
        Call QuickSort(vntArr, i, lngRight)
        Call QuickSort(vntArr, lngLeft, j)
    End If
End If
End Sub

Private Sub SwapElements(ByRef vntItems As Variant,
    ByVal lngItem1 As Long, _
    ByVal lngItem2 As Long)
Dim vntTemp As Variant
vntTemp = vntItems(lngItem2)
vntItems(lngItem2) = vntItems(lngItem1)
vntItems(lngItem1) = vntTemp
End Sub
```

Search for a String Within Text

Ever needed to find out which cells contain a specific string of text? This function can search strings in a range, looking for specified text. It returns a result identifying which cells contain the text, as shown in Figure 4.17:

```
ContainsText(Rng,Text)
```

Figure 4.17
Return a result identifying which cells contain a specified string.

	A	B	C
1	This is an apple	A3	=ContainsText(A1:A3,"banana")
2	This is an orange	A1,A2	=ContainsText(A1:A3,"This is")
3	Here is a banana		

The arguments are as follows:

- Rng—The range in which to search
- Text—The text for which to search

Function example:

```
Function ContainsText(Rng As Range, Text As String) As String
Dim T As String
Dim myCell As Range
```

```
    For Each myCell In Rng 'look in each cell
        If InStr(myCell.Text, Text) > 0 Then 'look in the string for the text
            If Len(T) = 0 Then 'if the text is found, add the address to my result
                T = myCell.Address(False, False)
            Else
                T = T & "," & myCell.Address(False, False)
            End If
        End If
    Next myCell
    ContainsText = T
    End Function
```

Reverse the Contents of a Cell

This function is mostly fun, but you might find it useful—it reverses the contents of a cell:

```
ReverseContents(myCell, IsText)
```

The arguments are as follows:

- myCell—The specified cell
- IsText—(Optional) If the cell value should be treated as text (default) or a number

Function example:

```
Function ReverseContents(myCell As Range, Optional IsText As Boolean = True)
Dim i As Integer
Dim OrigString As String, NewString As String
OrigString = Trim(myCell) 'remove leading and trailing spaces
For i = 1 To Len(OrigString)
'by adding the variable NewString to the character,
'instead of adding the character to NewStringthe string is reversed
    NewString = Mid(OrigString, i, 1) & NewString
Next i
If IsText = False Then
    ReverseContents = CLng(NewString)
Else
    ReverseContents = NewString
End If
End Function
```

Multiple Max

MAX finds and returns the maximum value in a range, but it doesn't tell you whether there is more than one maximum value. This function returns the addresses of the maximum values in a range, as shown in Figure 4.18:

```
ReturnMaxs(Rng)
```

The argument is Rng, the range to search for the maximum values.

Function example:

```
Function ReturnMaxs(Rng As Range) As String
Dim Mx As Double
Dim myCell As Range
'if there is only one cell in the range, then exit
```

```
    If Rng.Count = 1 Then ReturnMaxs = Rng.Address(False, False): Exit Function
    Mx = Application.Max(Rng) 'uses Excel's Max to find the max in the range
    'Because you now know what the max value is,
    'search the ranging finding matches and return the address
    For Each myCell In Rng
        If myCell = Mx Then
            If Len(ReturnMaxs) = 0 Then
                ReturnMaxs = myCell.Address(False, False)
            Else
                ReturnMaxs = ReturnMaxs & ", " & myCell.Address(False, False)
            End If
        End If
    Next myCell
End Function
```

Figure 4.18
Return the addresses of
all maximum values in
a range.

⊿	A	B
1	3	A9,A11
2	9	=ReturnMaxs(A1:A15)
3	5	
4	6	
5	6	
6	7	
7	6	
8	3	
9	10	
10	4	
11	10	
12	6	
13	9	
14	7	
15	1	
16		

Return Hyperlink Address

Let's say that you've received a spreadsheet with a list of hyperlinked information. You want
to see the actual links, not the descriptive text. You could just right-click the hyperlink and
select Edit Hyperlink, but you want something more permanent. This function extracts the
hyperlink address, as shown in Figure 4.19:

```
    GetAddress(Hyperlink)
```

Figure 4.19
Extract the hyperlink
address from behind a
hyperlink.

⊿	A	B	C
1	Tracy Syrstad	Tracy@MrExcel.com	=GetAddress(A1)
2	The Best Site for Excel Answers	http://www.mrexcel.com/	
3			

The argument is `HyperlinkCell`, the hyperlinked cell from which you want the address extracted.

Function example:

```
Function GetAddress(HyperlinkCell As Range)
    GetAddress = Replace(HyperlinkCell.Hyperlinks(1).Address, "mailto:", "")
End Function
```

Return the Column Letter of a Cell Address

You can use `CELL("Col")` to return a column number; but what if you need the column letter? This function extracts the column letter from a cell address, as shown in Figure 4.20:

```
ColName(Rng)
```

Figure 4.20
Return the column letter of a cell address.

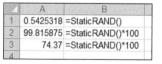

	A	B
1	A	=ColName(A1)
2	XFD	=ColName(XFD1048576)
3		

The argument is `Rng`, the cell for which you want the column letter.

Function example:

```
Function ColName(Rng As Range) As String
ColName = Left(Rng.Range("A1").Address(True, False), _
    InStr(1, Rng.Range("A1").Address(True, False), "$", 1) - 1)
End Function
```

Static Random

The function `=RAND()` can prove very useful for creating random numbers, but it constantly recalculates. What if you need random numbers but don't want them to change constantly? The following function places a random number, but the number changes only if you force the cell to recalculate, as shown in Figure 4.21:

```
StaticRAND()
```

Figure 4.21
Produce random numbers not quite so volatile.

	A	B
1	0.5425318	=StaticRAND()
2	99.815875	=StaticRAND()*100
3	74.37	=StaticRAND()*100
4		

There are no arguments for this function.

Function example:

```
Function StaticRAND() As Double
Randomize
STATICRAND = Rnd
End Function
```

Using Select Case on a Worksheet

At some point, you have probably nested an If...Then...Else on a worksheet to return a value. The Select...Case statement available in VBA makes this a lot easier, but you can't use Select...Case statements in a worksheet formula. Instead, you can create a UDF (see Figure 4.22).

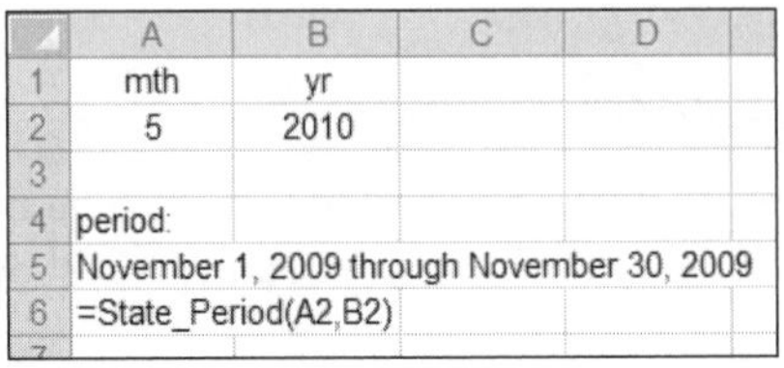

Figure 4.22

Example of using a Select...Case structure in a UDF rather than nested If...Then statements.

⊿	A	B	C	D
1	mth	yr		
2	5	2010		
3				
4	period:			
5	November 1, 2009 through November 30, 2009			
6	=State_Period(A2,B2)			
7				

The following function shows how you can use Select statements to produce the results of a nested If...Then statement:

```
Function state_period(mth As Integer, yr As Integer)
Select Case mth
  Case 1
     state_period = "July 1, " & yr - 1 & " through July 31, " & yr - 1
  Case 2
     state_period = "August 1, " & yr - 1 & " through August 31, " & yr - 1
  Case 3
     state_period = "September 1, " & yr - 1 & " through September 30, " & yr - 1
  Case 4
     state_period = "October 1, " & yr - 1 & " through October 31, " & yr - 1
  Case 5
     state_period = "November 1, " & yr - 1 & " through November 30, " & yr - 1
  Case 6
     state_period = "December 1, " & yr - 1 & " through December 31, " & yr - 1
  Case 7
     state_period = "January 1, " & yr & " through January 31, " & yr
  Case 8
     state_period = "February 1, " & yr & " through February 28, " & yr
  Case 9
     state_period = "March 1, " & yr & " through March 31, " & yr
  Case 10
     state_period = "April 1, " & yr & " through April 30, " & yr
  Case 11
     state_period = "May 1, " & yr & " through May 31, " & yr
  Case 12
     state_period = "June 1, " & yr & " through June 30, " & yr
  Case 13
     state_period = "Pre-Final"
  Case 14
     state_period = "Closeout"
End Select
End Function
```

Next Steps

Chapter 5, "Looping and Flow Control," describes a fundamental component of any programming language: loops. If you have taken a programming class, you will be familiar with basic loop structures. VBA supports all the usual loops. In the next chapter, you also learn about a special loop, For Each...Next, which is unique to object-oriented programming such as VBA.

4

Looping and Flow Control

Loops are a fundamental component of any programming language. If you've taken any programming classes, even BASIC, you've likely encountered a `For...Next` loop. Fortunately, VBA supports all the usual loops, plus a special loop that is excellent to use with VBA.

This chapter covers the basic loop constructs:

- `For...Next`
- `Do...While`
- `Do...Until`
- `While...Loop`
- `Until...Loop`

This chapter also discusses the useful loop construct that is unique to object-oriented languages:

- `For Each...Next`

5

For...Next **Loops**...................................107

Do **Loops** 113

The VBA Loop: For Each.......................117

Flow Control: Using If...Then...Else and Select Case...............................120

For...Next **Loops**

`For` and `Next` are common loop constructs. Everything between `For` and `Next` is run multiple times. Each time the code runs, a certain counter variable, specified in the `For` statement, has a different value.

Consider this code:

```
For I = 1 to 10
    Cells(I, I).Value = I
Next I
```

As this program starts to run, you need to give the counter variable a name of I. The first time through the code, the variable I is set to 1. The first time that the loop is executed, I is equal to 1, so the cell in Row 1, Column 1 will be set to 1 (see Figure 5.1).

Figure 5.1
After the first iteration through the loop, the cell in Row 1, Column 1 has the value of 1.

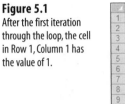

```
Microsoft Visual Basic - ProjectFilesChapter052010.xlsm [

File  Edit  View  Insert  Format  Debug  Run

(General)

Sub Chapter5a()
    ' Figure 5.1 through 5.7
    For i = 1 To 10
        Cells(i, i).Value = i
    Next i

End Sub
```

Let's take a close look at what happens as VBA gets to the line that says Next I. Before running this line, the variable I is equal to 1. During the execution of Next I, VBA must make a decision. VBA adds 1 to the variable I and compares it to the maximum value in the To clause of the For statement. If it is within the limits specified in the To clause, the loop is not finished. In this case, the value of I will be incremented to 2. Code execution then moves back to the first line of code after the For statement. Figure 5.2 shows the state of the program before running the Next line. Figure 5.3 shows what happens after executing the Next line.

Figure 5.2
Before running the Next I statement, I is equal to 1. VBA can safely add 1 to I, and it will be less than the 10 specified in the To clause of the For statement.

```
Sub Chapter5a()
    ' Figure 5.1 through 5.7
    For i = 1 To 10
        Cells(i, i).Value = i
    Next i                    i = 1

End Sub
```

Figure 5.3
After running the Next I statement, I is incremented to 2. Code execution continues with the line of code immediately following the For statement, which writes a 2 to cell B2.

```
Microsoft Visual Basic - ProjectFilesChapter052010.xlsm [bre

File  Edit  View  Insert  Format  Debug  Run

(General)

Sub Chapter5a()
    ' Figure 5.1 through 5.7
    For i = 1 To 10
        Cells(i, i).Value = i
    Next i                    i = 2

End Sub
```

The second time through the loop, the value of I is 2. The cell in Row 2, Column 2 (that is, cell B2) gets a value of 2.

As the process continues, the Next I statement advances I up to 3, 4, and so on. On the tenth pass through the loop, the cell in Row 10, Column 10 is assigned a value of 10.

It is interesting to watch what happens to the variable I on the last pass through Next I. In Figure 5.4, you can see that before executing Next I the tenth time, the variable I is equal to 10.

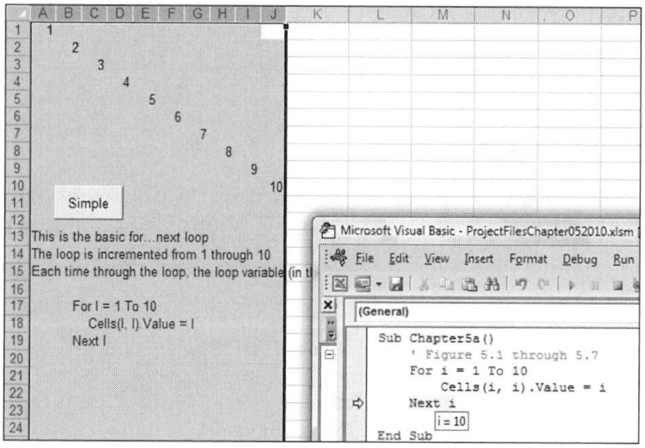

Figure 5.4
Before running Next I for the tenth time, the variable I is equal to 10.

VBA is now at a decision point. It adds 1 to the variable I. I is now equal to 11, which is greater than the limit in the For...Next loop. VBA then moves execution to the next line in the macro after the Next statement (see Figure 5.5). In case you are tempted to use the variable I later in the macro, it is important to realize that it might be incremented beyond the limit specified in the To clause of the For statement.

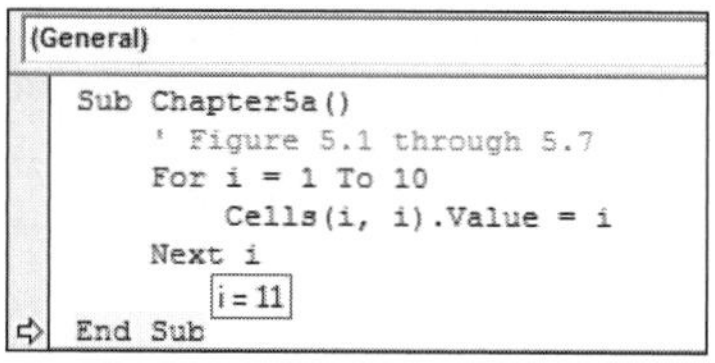

Figure 5.5
After incrementing I to 11, code execution moves to the line after the Next statement.

The common use for such a loop is to walk through all the rows in a dataset and decide to perform some action based on some criteria. For example, if you want to mark all the rows with positive service revenue in Column F, you could use this loop:

```
For I = 2 to 10
    If Cells(I, 6).Value > 0 Then
        Cells(I, 8).Value = "Service Revenue"
        Cells(I, 1).Resize(1, 8).Interior.ColorIndex = 4
    End If
Next i
```

This loop checks each item of data from Row 2 through Row 10. If there is a positive number in Column F, Column H of that row will have a new label, and the cells in Columns A:H of the row will be colored green. After running this macro, the results look like Figure 5.6.

Figure 5.6
After the loop completes all nine iterations, any rows with positive values in Column F are colored green and have the label "Service Revenue" added to Column H.

	A	B	C	D	E	F	G	H	I
1	InvoiceDate	InvoiceNumber	SalesRepNumber	CustomerNumber	ProductRevenue	ServiceRevenue	ProductCost		
2	6/7/2011	123829	S21	C8754	21000	0	9875		
3	6/7/2011	123834	S54	C7796	339000	0	195298		
4	6/7/2011	123835	S21	C1654	161000	0	90761		
5	6/7/2011	123836	S45	C6460	275500	10000	146341	Service Revenue	
6	6/7/2011	123837	S54	C5143	925400	0	473515		
7	6/7/2011	123841	S21	C8361	94400	0	53180		
8	6/7/2011	123842	S45	C1842	36500	55000	20696	Service Revenue	
9	6/7/2011	123843	S54	C4107	599700	0	276718		
10	6/7/2011	123844	S21	C5205	244900	0	143393		
11									

Using Variables in the For Statement

The previous example is not very useful in that it works only when there are exactly 10 rows of data. It is possible to use a variable to specify the upper/lower limit of the For statement. This code sample identifies FinalRow with data and then loops from Row 2 to that row:

```
FinalRow = Cells(Rows.Count, 1).End(xlUp).Row
For I = 2 to FinalRow
    If Cells(I, 6).Value > 0 Then
        Cells(I, 8).Value = "Service Revenue"
        Cells(I, 1).Resize(1, 8).Interior.ColorIndex = 4
    End If
Next I
```

> **CAUTION**
>
> Exercise caution when using variables. What if the imported file today is empty and has only a heading row? In this case, the FinalRow variable is equal to 1. This makes the first statement of the loop essentially say For I = 2 to 1. Because the start number is higher than the end number, the loop does not execute at all. The variable I is equal to 2, and code execution jumps to the line after Next.

Variations on the For...Next Loop

In a For...Next loop, it is possible to have the loop variable jump up by something other than 1. For example, you might use it to apply green-bar formatting to every other row in a dataset. In this case, you want to have the counter variable I examine every other row in the dataset. Indicate this by adding the Step clause to the end of the For statement:

```
FinalRow = Cells(Rows.Count, 1).End(xlUp).Row
For i = 2 to FinalRow Step 2
    Cells(i, 1).Resize(1, 8).Interior.ColorIndex = 35
Next i
```

While running this code, VBA adds a light green shading to Rows 2, 4, 6, and so on (see Figure 5.7).

To see a demo of this macro, search for Excel VBA 5 at YouTube.

The Step clause can be any number. You might want to check every tenth row of a dataset to extract a random sample. In this case, you would use Step 10:

```
FinalRow = Cells(Rows.Count, 1).End(xlUp).Row
NextRow = FinalRow + 5
Cells(NextRow-1, 1).Value = "Random Sample of Above Data"
For I = 2 to FinalRow Step 10
    Cells(I, 1).Resize(1, 8).Copy Destination:=Cells(NextRow, 1)
    NextRow = NextRow + 1
Next i
```

Figure 5.7
The Step clause in the For statement of the loop causes the action to occur on every other row.

	A	B	C	D	E	F	G
1	InvoiceDate	InvoiceNumber	SalesRepNumber	CustomerNumber	ProductRevenue	ServiceRevenue	ProductCost
2	6/7/2011	123829	S21	C8754	21000	0	9875
3	6/7/2011	123830	S45	C3390	188100	0	85083
4	6/7/2011	123831	S54	C2523	510600	0	281158
5	6/7/2011	123832	S21	C5519	86200	0	49967
6	6/7/2011	123833	S45	C3245	800100	0	388277
7	6/7/2011	123834	S54	C7796	339000	0	195298
8	6/7/2011	123835	S21	C1654	161000	0	90761
9	6/7/2011	123836	S45	C6460	275500	10000	146341
10	6/7/2011	123837	S54	C5143	925400	0	473515
11	6/7/2011	123838	S21	C7868	148200	0	75700
12	6/7/2011	123839	S45	C3310	890200	0	468333
13	6/7/2011	123840	S54	C2959	986000	0	528980
14	6/7/2011	123841	S21	C8361	94400	0	53180
15	6/7/2011	123842	S45	C1842	36500	55000	20696
16	6/7/2011	123843	S54	C4107	599700	0	276718
17	6/7/2011	123844	S21	C5205	244900	0	143393
18	6/7/2011	123845	S45	C7745	63000	0	35102
19	6/7/2011	123846	S54	C1730	212600	0	117787
20	6/7/2011	123847	S21	C6292	974700	0	478731
21	6/7/2011	123848	S45	C2008	327700	0	170968
22	6/7/2011	123849	S54	C4096	30700	0	18056

You can also have a For...Next loop run backward from high to low. This is particularly useful if you are selectively deleting rows. To do this, reverse the order of the For statement and have the Step clause specify a negative number:

```
' Delete all rows where column C is the Internal rep - S54
FinalRow = Cells(Rows.Count, 1).End(xlUp).Row
For I = FinalRow to 2 Step -1
    If Cells(I, 3).Value = "S54" Then
        Rows(I).Delete
    End If
Next i
```

5

> **NOTE**
> There is a faster way to delete the records, which is discussed in Chapter 12, "Deleting Records Using a Filter."

Exiting a Loop Early After a Condition Is Met

Sometimes you don't need to execute the whole loop. Perhaps you just need to read through the dataset until you find one record that meets a certain criteria. In this case, you want to find the first record and then stop the loop. A statement called Exit For does this.

The following sample macro looks for a row in the dataset where service revenue in Column F is positive and product revenue in Column E is 0. If such a row is found, you might indicate a message that the file needs manual processing today and move the cell pointer to that row:

```
' Are there any special processing situations in the data?
FinalRow = Cells(Rows.Count, 1).End(xlUp).Row
ProblemFound = False
For I = 2 to FinalRow
    If Cells(I, 6).Value > 0 Then
        If cells(I, 5).Value = 0 Then
            Cells(I, 6).Select
            ProblemFound = True
            Exit For
        End If
    End If
Next I
If ProblemFound Then
    MsgBox "There is a problem at row " & I
    Exit Sub
End If
```

Nesting One Loop Inside Another Loop

It is okay to run a loop inside another loop. The following code has the first loop run through all the rows in a recordset, while the second loop runs through all the columns:

```
' Loop through each row and column
' Add a checkerboard format
FinalRow = Cells(Rows.Count, 1).End(xlUp).Row
FinalCol = Cells(1, Columns.Count).End(xlToLeft).Column
For I = 2 to FinalRow
    ' For even numbered rows, start in column 1
    ' For odd numbered rows, start in column 2
    If I Mod 2 = 1 Then ' Divide I by 2 and keep remainder
        StartCol = 1
    Else
        StartCol = 2
    End If
    For J = StartCol to FinalCol Step 2
        Cells(I, J).Interior.ColorIndex = 35
    Next J
Next I
```

In this code, the outer loop is using the I counter variable to loop through all the rows in the dataset. The inner loop is using the J counter variable to loop through all the columns in that row. Because Figure 5.8 has seven data rows, the code runs through the I loop seven times. Each time through the I loop, the code runs through the J loop six or seven times. This means that the line of code that is inside the J loop ends up being executed several times for each pass through the I loop. Figure 5.8 shows the result.

Figure 5.8
The result of nesting one loop inside the other; VBA can loop through each row and then each column.

	A	B	C	D	E	F
1	Item	January	February	March	April	May
2	Hardware Revenue	1,972,637	1,655,321	1,755,234	1,531,060	1,345,699
3	Software Revenue	236,716	198,639	210,628	183,727	161,484
4	Service Revenue	473,433	397,277	421,256	367,454	322,968
5	Cost of Good Sold	1,084,951	910,427	965,379	842,083	740,135
6	Selling Expense	394,527	331,064	351,047	306,212	269,140
7	G&A Expense	150,000	150,000	150,000	150,000	150,000
8	R&D	125,000	125,000	125,000	125,000	125,000

Do **Loops**

There are several variations of the Do loop. The most basic Do loop is useful for doing a bunch of mundane tasks. For example, suppose someone sends you a list of addresses going down a column, as shown in Figure 5.9.

Figure 5.9
It would be more useful to have these addresses in a database format to use in a mail merge.

6	John Smith
7	123 Main Street
8	Akron OH 44308
9	
10	Jane Doe
11	245 State Street
12	Chicago IL 60011
13	
14	Ralph Emerson
15	345 2nd Ave
16	New York NY 10011
17	
18	George Washington
19	456 3rd St
20	Philadelphia PA 12345
21	

In this case, you might need to rearrange these addresses into a database with name in Column B, street in Column C, city and state in Column D. By setting Relative Recording (see Chapter 1, "Unleash the Power of Excel with VBA") and using a hot key of Ctrl+A, you can record this bit of useful code. The code is designed to copy one single address into database format. The code also navigates the cell pointer to the name of the next address in the list. Each time you press Ctrl+A, one address will be reformatted.

```
Sub Macro32010()
'
' Macro32010 Macro
'
' Keyboard Shortcut: Ctrl+Shift+A
'
    ActiveCell.Offset(1, 0).Range("A1").Select
    Selection.Cut
    ActiveCell.Offset(-1, 1).Range("A1").Select
    ActiveSheet.Paste
    ActiveCell.Offset(2, -1).Range("A1").Select
    Selection.Cut
    ActiveCell.Offset(-2, 2).Range("A1").Select
    ActiveSheet.Paste
    ActiveCell.Offset(1, -2).Range("A1:A3").Select
```

5

```
        Selection.EntireRow.Delete
        ActiveCell.Select
    End Sub
```

> **NOTE** Do not assume that the preceding code is suitable for a professional application. However, sometimes macros are written just to automate a one-time mundane task.

Without a macro, a lot of manual copying and pasting would be required. However, with the preceding recorded macro, you can simply place the cell pointer on a name in Column A and press Ctrl+Shift+A. That one address will be copied into three columns, and the cell pointer will move to the start of the next address (see Figure 5.10).

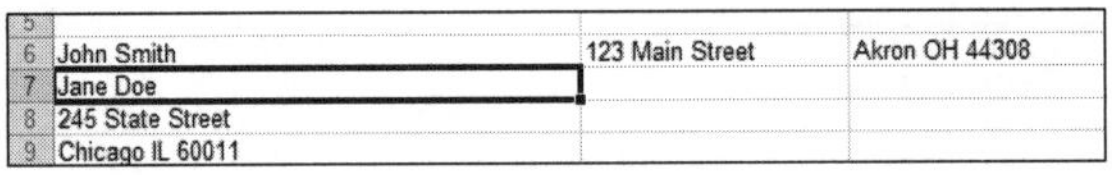

Figure 5.10

After running the macro once, one address is moved into the proper format, and the cell pointer is positioned to run the macro again.

5			
6	John Smith	123 Main Street	Akron OH 44308
7	Jane Doe		
8	245 State Street		
9	Chicago IL 60011		

When you use this macro, you will be able to process an address every second using the hot key. However, when you need to process 5,000 addresses, you will not want to keep running the same macro over and over.

In this case, a Do...Loop can be used to set up the macro to run continuously. You can have VBA run this code continuously by enclosing the recorded code with Do at the top and Loop at the end. Now you can sit back and watch the code perform this insanely boring task in minutes rather than hours.

Note that this particular Do...Loop will run forever because there is no mechanism to stop it. This will work for the task at hand because you can watch the progress on the screen and press Ctrl+Break to stop execution when the program advances past the end of this database.

This code uses a Do loop to fix the addresses.

```
    Sub Macro3()
    '
    ' Macro3 Macro
    ' Macro recorded 10/29/2003 by Bill Jelen
    ' Move one address into database format.
    ' Then move the cell pointer to the start of the next address.
    '
    ' Keyboard Shortcut: Ctrl+Shift+A
    '
    Do
        ActiveCell.Offset(1, 0).Range("A1").Select
        Selection.Cut
        ActiveCell.Offset(-1, 1).Range("A1").Select
```

```
        ActiveSheet.Paste
        ActiveCell.Offset(2, -1).Range("A1").Select
        Selection.Cut
        ActiveCell.Offset(-2, 2).Range("A1").Select
        ActiveSheet.Paste
        ActiveCell.Offset(1, -2).Range("A1:A3").Select
        Selection.EntireRow.Delete
        ActiveCell.Select
    Loop
    End Sub
```

These examples are "quick and dirty" loops that are great for when you need to accomplish a task quickly. The `Do...Loop` provides a number of options to allow you to have the program stop automatically when it accomplishes the end of the task.

The first option is to have a line in the `Do...Loop` that detects the end of the dataset and exits the loop. In the current example, this could be accomplished by using the `Exit Do` command in an `If` statement. If the current cell is on a cell that is empty, you can assume that you have reached the end of the data and stopped processing the loop:

```
    Do
        If Not Selection.Value > "" Then Exit Do
        ActiveCell.Offset(1, 0).Range("A1").Select
        Selection.Cut
        ActiveCell.Offset(-1, 1).Range("A1").Select
        ActiveSheet.Paste
        ActiveCell.Offset(2, -1).Range("A1").Select
        Selection.Cut
        ActiveCell.Offset(-2, 2).Range("A1").Select
        ActiveSheet.Paste
        ActiveCell.Offset(1, -2).Range("A1:A3").Select
        Selection.EntireRow.Delete
        ActiveCell.Select
    Loop
    End Sub
```

Using the `While` or `Until` Clause in Do Loops

There are four variations of using `While` or `Until`. These clauses can be added to either the `Do` statement or the `Loop` statement. In each case, the `While` or `Until` clause includes some test that evaluates to `True` or `False`.

With a `Do While <test expression>...Loop` construct, the loop is never executed if `<test expression>` is false. If you are reading records from a text file, you cannot assume that the file has one or more records. Instead, you need to test to see whether you are already at the end of file with the `EOF` function before you enter the loop:

```
    ' Read a text file, skipping the Total lines
        Open "C:\Invoice.txt" For Input As #1
        R = 1
        Do While Not EOF(1)
            Line Input #FileNumber, Data
            If Not Left (Data, 5) = "TOTAL" Then
                ' Import this row
                r = r + 1
```

5

```
            Cells(r, 1).Value = Data
        End If
    Loop
    Close #1
```

In this example, the `Not` keyword `EOF(1)` evaluates to `True` after there are no more records to be read from `Invoice.txt`. Some programmers believe it is hard to read a program that contains a lot of `Not`s. To avoid the use of `Not`, use the `Do Until <test expression>` ...`Loop` construct:

```
' Read a text file, skipping the Total lines
    Open "C:\Invoice.txt" For Input As #1
    R = 1
    Do Until EOF(1)
        Line Input #1, Data
        If Not (Data, 5) = "TOTAL" Then
            ' Import this row
            r = r + 1
            Cells(r, 1).Value = Data
        End If
    Loop
    Close #1
```

In other examples, you might always want the loop to be executed the first time. In these cases, move the `While` or `Until` instruction to the end of the loop. This code sample asks the user to enter sales amounts made that day. It continually asks them for sales amounts until they enter a zero:

```
TotalSales = 0
Do
    x = InputBox(Prompt:="Enter Amount of Next Invoice. Enter 0 when done." _
        Type:=1)
    TotalSales = TotalSales + x
Loop Until x = 0
MsgBox "The total for today is $" & TotalSales
```

In the following loop, a check amount is entered, and then it looks for open invoices to which the check can be applied. However, it is often the case that a single check is received that covers several invoices. The following program sequentially applies the check to the oldest invoices until 100 percent of the check has been applied:

```
' Ask for the amount of check received
AmtToApply = InputBox("Enter Amount of Check") + 0
' Loop through the list of open invoices.
' Apply the check to the oldest open invoices and Decrement AmtToApply
NextRow = 2
Do While AmtToApply > 0
    OpenAmt = Cells(NextRow, 3)
    If OpenAmt > AmtToApply Then
        ' Apply total check to this invoice
        Cells(NextRow, 4).Value = AmtToApply
        AmtToApply = 0
    Else
        Cells(NextRow, 4).Value = OpenAmt
        AmtToApply = AmtToApply - OpenAmt
    End If
```

```
        NextRow = NextRow + 1
    Loop
```

Because you can construct the `Do...Loop` with the `While` or `Until` qualifiers at the beginning or end, you have a great deal of subtle control over whether the loop is always executed once, even when the condition is true at the beginning.

While...Wend **Loops**

`While...Wend` loops are included in VBA for backward compatibility. In the VBA help file, Microsoft suggests that `Do...Loops` are more flexible. However, because you might encounter `While...Wend` loops in code written by others, a quick example is provided. In this loop, the first line is always `While <condition>`. The last line of the loop is always `Wend`. Note that there is no `Exit While` statement. In general, these loops are okay, but the `Do...Loop` construct is more robust and flexible. Because the `Do` loop offers either the `While` or `Until` qualifier, this qualifier can be used at the beginning or end of the loop, and there is the possibility to exit a `Do` loop early:

```
' Read a text file, adding the amounts
    Open "C:\Invoice.txt" For Input As #1
    TotalSales = 0
    While Not EOF(1)
        Line Input #1, Data
        TotalSales = TotalSales + Data
    Wend
    MsgBox "Total Sales=" & TotalSales
    Close #1
```

VBA Loop: `For Each`

Even though the VBA loop is an excellent loop, the macro recorder never records this type of loop. VBA is an object-oriented language. It is common to have a collection of objects in Excel such as a collection of worksheets in a workbook, cells in a range, pivot tables on a worksheet, or data series on a chart.

This special type of loop is great for looping through all the items in the collection. However, before discussing this loop in detail, you need to understand a special kind of variable called *object variables*.

Object Variables

At this point, you have seen a variable that contains a single value. When you have a variable such as `TotalSales = 0`, `TotalSales` is a normal variable and generally contains only a single value. It is also possible to have a more powerful variable called an *object variable* that holds many values. In other words, any property associated with the object is also associated with the object variable.

Generally, developers do not take the time to declare variables. Many books implore you to use the `DIM` statement to identify all your variables at the top of the procedure. This allows you to specify that a certain variable be of a certain type, such as Integer or Double. Although this saves a tiny bit of memory, it requires you to know up front which variables you plan on using. However, developers tend to whip up a new variable on-the-fly as the need arises. Even so, there are great benefits to declaring object variables. For example, the VBA AutoComplete feature turns on if you declare an object variable at the top of your procedure. The following lines of code declare three object variables: a worksheet, range, and a pivot table:

```
Sub Test()
    Dim WSD as Worksheet
    Dim MyCell as Range
    Dim PT as PivotTable
    Set WSD = ThisWorkbook.Worksheets("Data")
    Set MyCell = WSD.Cells(Rows.Count, 1).End(xlUp).Offset(1, 0)
    Set PT = WSD.PivotTables(1)
    ...
```

In this code, you can see that more than an equals statement is used to assign object variables. You also need to use the Set statement to assign a specific object to the object variable.

There are many good reasons to use object variables, not the least of which is the fact that it can be a great shorthand notation. It is easier to have a many lines of code refer to WSD rather than ThisWorkbook.Worksheets("Data"). In addition, as mentioned earlier, the object variable inherits all the properties of the object to which it refers.

The For Each...Loop employs an object variable rather than a Counter variable. The following code loops through all the cells in Column A. The code uses the .CurrentRegion property to define the current region and then uses the .Resize property to limit the selected range to a single column. The object variable is called Cell. Any name could be used for the object variable, but Cell seems more appropriate than does something arbitrary like Fred.

```
For Each cell in Range("A1").CurrentRegion.Resize(, 1)
    If cell.Value = "Total" Then
        cell.resize(1,8).Font.Bold = True
    End If
Next cell
```

This code sample searches all open workbooks, looking for a workbook where the first worksheet is called Menu:

```
For Each wb in Workbooks
    If wb.Worksheets(1).Name = "Menu" Then
    WBFound = True
    WBName = wb.Name
    Exit For
    End If
Next wb
```

In this code sample, all shapes on the current worksheet are deleted:

```
For Each Sh in ActiveSheet.Shapes
    Sh.Delete
Next Sh
```

This code sample deletes all pivot tables on the current sheet:

```
For Each pt in ActiveSheet.PivotTables
    pt.TableRange2.Clear
Next pt
```

CASE STUDY: LOOPING THROUGH ALL FILES IN A DIRECTORY

This case study includes some useful procedures that make extensive use of loops.

> **NOTE** Creating a list of all files in a directory used to be fairly simple using the `FileSearch` object. For inexplicable reasons, Microsoft stopped supporting `FileSearch` in Excel 2007.

The first procedure uses VBA's `Scripting.FileSystemObject` to find all JPG picture files in a certain directory. Each file is listed down a column in Excel.

```
Sub FindJPGFilesInAFolder()
    Dim fso As Object
    Dim strName As String
    Dim strArr(1 To 1048576, 1 To 1) As String, i As Long

    ' Enter the folder name here
    Const strDir As String = "C:\Artwork\"

    Let strName = Dir$(strDir & "*.jpg")
    Do While strName <> vbNullString
        Let i = i + 1
        Let strArr(i, 1) = strDir & strName
        Let strName = Dir$()
    Loop
    Set fso = CreateObject("Scripting.FileSystemObject")
    Call recurseSubFolders(fso.GetFolder(strDir), strArr(), i)
    Set fso = Nothing
    If i > 0 Then
        Range("A1").Resize(i).Value = strArr
    End If

    ' Next, loop through all found files
    ' and break into path and filename
    FinalRow = Cells(Rows.Count, 1).End(xlUp).Row
    For i = 1 To FinalRow
        ThisEntry = Cells(i, 1)
        For j = Len(ThisEntry) To 1 Step -1
            If Mid(ThisEntry, j, 1) = Application.PathSeparator Then
                Cells(i, 2) = Left(ThisEntry, j)
```

5

```
                    Cells(i, 3) = Mid(ThisEntry, j + 1)
                    Exit For
                End If
            Next j
        Next i

End Sub
Private Sub recurseSubFolders(ByRef Folder As Object, _
    ByRef strArr() As String, _
    ByRef i As Long)
Dim SubFolder As Object
Dim strName As String
For Each SubFolder In Folder.SubFolders
    Let strName = Dir$(SubFolder.Path & "*.jpg")
    Do While strName <> vbNullString
        Let i = i + 1
        Let strArr(i, 1) = SubFolder.Path & strName
        Let strName = Dir$()
    Loop
    Call recurseSubFolders(SubFolder, strArr(), i)
Next
End Sub
```

The idea in this situation is to organize the photos into new folders. In Column D, if you want to move a picture to a new folder, type the path of that folder. The following For…Each loop takes care of copying the pictures. Each time through the loop, the object variable named Cell will contain a reference to a cell in Column A. You can use Cell.Offset(0, 3) to return the value from the cell three columns to the right of the range represented by the variable Cell:

```
Sub CopyToNewFolder()
    FinalRow = Cells(Rows.Count, 1).End(xlUp).Row
    For Each Cell In Range("A2:A" & FinalRow)
        OrigFile = Cell.Value
        NewFile = Cell.Offset(0, 3) & Application.PathSeparator & _
            Cell.Offset(0, 2)
        FileCopy OrigFile, NewFile
    Next Cell
End Sub
```

Note that Application.PathSeparator is a backslash on Windows computers but might be different if the code is running on a Macintosh.

Flow Control: Using If...Then...Else and Select Case

Another aspect of programming that will never be recorded by the macro recorder is the concept of flow control. Sometimes you do not want every line of your program to be executed every time you run the macro. VBA offers two excellent choices for flow control: the If...Then...Else construct and the Select Case construct.

Basic Flow Control: If...Then...Else

The most common device for program flow control is the If statement. For example, suppose you have a list of products as shown in Figure 5.11. You want to loop through each product in the list and copy it to either a Fruits list or Vegetables list. Beginning programmers might be tempted to loop through the rows twice—once to look for fruit and a second time to look for vegetables. However, there is no need to loop through twice because you can use an If...Then...Else construct on a single loop to copy each row to the correct place.

Figure 5.11
A single loop can look for fruits or vegetables.

	A	B	C
1	Class	Product	Quantity
2	Fruit	Apples	1
3	Fruit	Apricots	3
4	Vegetable	Apsaragus	62
5	Fruit	Bananas	55
6	Fruit	Blueberry	17
7	Vegetable	Broccoli	56
8	Vegetable	Cabbage	35
9	Fruit	Cherries	59
10	Herbs	Dill	91
11	Vegetable	Eggplant	94
12	Fruit	Kiwi	86
13	Vegetable	Leeks	87
14	Vegetable	Lettuce	12
15	Vegetable	Onion	14
16	Fruit	Pears	21
17	Vegetable	Potatoes	94
18	Vegetable	Sprouts	79
19	Fruit	Starfruit	45
20	Fruit	Strawberry	20
21	Vegetable	Tomatoes	46
22	Fruit	Watermelon	25

Conditions

Any If statement needs a condition that is being tested. The condition should always evaluate to TRUE or FALSE. Here are some examples of simple and complex conditions:

- If Range("A1").Value = "Title" Then
- If Not Range("A1").Value = "Title" Then
- If Range("A1").Value = "Title" And Range("B1").Value = "Fruit" Then
- If Range("A1").Value = "Title" Or Range("B1").Value = "Fruit" Then

If...Then...End If

After the If statement, you may include one or more program lines that will be executed only if the condition is met. You should then close the If block with an End If line. Here is a simple example of an If statement:

```
Sub ColorFruitRedBold()
    FinalRow = Cells(Rows.Count, 1).End(xlUp).Row
```

```
        For i = 2 To FinalRow
            If Cells(i, 1).Value = "Fruit" Then
                Cells(i, 1).Resize(1, 3).Font.Bold = True
                Cells(i, 1).Resize(1, 3).Font.ColorIndex = 3
            End If
        Next i

        MsgBox "Fruit is now bold and red"
    End Sub
```

Either/Or Decisions: If...Then...Else...End If

Sometimes you will want to do one set of statements if the condition is true, and another set of statements if the condition is not true. To do this with VBA, the second set of conditions would be coded after the Else statement. There is still only one End If statement associated with this construct. For example, you could use the following code if you want to color the fruit red and the vegetables green:

```
    Sub FruitRedVegGreen()
        FinalRow = Cells(Rows.Count, 1).End(xlUp).Row

        For i = 2 To FinalRow
            If Cells(i, 1).Value = "Fruit" Then
                Cells(i, 1).Resize(1, 3).Font.ColorIndex = 3
            Else
                Cells(i, 1).Resize(1, 3).Font.ColorIndex = 50
            End If
        Next i

        MsgBox "Fruit is red / Veggies are green"
    End Sub
```

Using If...Else If...End If for Multiple Conditions

Notice that our product list includes one item that is classified as an herb. You have three conditions that can be used to test items on the list. It is possible to build an If...End If structure with multiple conditions. First, test to see whether the record is a fruit. Next, use an Else If to test whether the record is a vegetable. Then, test to see whether the record is an herb. Finally, if the record is none of those, highlight the record as an error.

```
    Sub MultipleIf()
        FinalRow = Cells(Rows.Count, 1).End(xlUp).Row

        For i = 2 To FinalRow
            If Cells(i, 1).Value = "Fruit" Then
                Cells(i, 1).Resize(1, 3).Font.ColorIndex = 3
            ElseIf Cells(i, 1).Value = "Vegetable" Then
                Cells(i, 1).Resize(1, 3).Font.ColorIndex = 50
            ElseIf Cells(i, 1).Value = "Herbs" Then
                Cells(i, 1).Resize(1, 3).Font.ColorIndex = 5
            Else
                ' This must be a record in error
                Cells(i, 1).Resize(1, 3).Interior.ColorIndex = 6
```

```
        End If
    Next i

    MsgBox "Fruit is red / Veggies are green / Herbs are blue"
End Sub
```

Using `Select Case...End Select` for Multiple Conditions

When you have many different conditions, it becomes unwieldy to use many `Else If` statements. For this reason, VBA offers another construct known as the `Select Case` construct. In your running example, always check the value of the Class in column A. This value is called the *test expression*. The basic syntax of this construct starts with the words `Select Case` followed by the test expression:

```
Select Case Cells(i, 1).Value
```

Thinking about this problem in English, you might say, "In cases where the record is fruit, color the record with red." VBA uses a shorthand version of this. You write the word `Case` followed by the literal `"Fruit"`. Any statements that follow `Case "Fruit"` will be executed whenever the test expression is a fruit. After these statements, you have the next `Case` statement: `Case "Vegetables"`. You continue in this fashion, writing a `Case` statement followed by the program lines that will be executed if that case is true.

After you have listed all the possible conditions you can think of, you may optionally include a `Case Else` section at the end. The `Case Else` section includes what the program should do if the test expression matches none of your cases. Finally, close the entire construct with the `End Select` statement.

The following program does the same operation as the previous macro but uses a `Select Case` statement:

```
Sub SelectCase()
    FinalRow = Cells(Rows.Count, 1).End(xlUp).Row

    For i = 2 To FinalRow
        Select Case Cells(i, 1).Value
            Case "Fruit"
                Cells(i, 1).Resize(1, 3).Font.ColorIndex = 3
            Case "Vegetable"
                Cells(i, 1).Resize(1, 3).Font.ColorIndex = 50
            Case "Herbs"
                Cells(i, 1).Resize(1, 3).Font.ColorIndex = 5
            Case Else
        End Select
    Next i

    MsgBox "Fruit is red / Veggies are green / Herbs are blue"
End Sub
```

5

Complex Expressions in Case Statements

It is possible to have fairly complex expressions in Case statements. You might want to perform the same actions for all berry records:

```
Case "Strawberry", "Blueberry", "Raspberry"
    AdCode = 1
```

If it makes sense, you might code a range of values in the Case statement:

```
Case 1 to 20
    Discount = 0.05
Case 21 to 100
    Discount = 0.1
```

You can include the keyword Is and a comparison operator, such as > or <:

```
Case Is < 10
    Discount = 0
Case Is > 100
    Discount = 0.2
Case Else
    Discount = 0.10
```

Nesting If Statements

It is not only possible, but also common to nest an If statement inside another If statement. In this situation, it is important to use proper indenting. You will often find that you have several End If lines at the end of the construct. By having proper indenting, it is easier to tell which End If is associated with a particular If.

The final macro has a lot of logic. Our discount rules are as follows:

- For Fruit, quantities under 5 cases get no discount.
- Quantities from 5 to 20 cases get a 10 percent discount.
- Quantities above 20 cases get a 15 percent discount.
- For Herbs, quantities under 10 cases get no discount.
- Quantities from 10 cases to 15 cases get a 3 percent discount.
- Quantities above 15 cases get a 6 percent discount.
- For Vegetables except Asparagus, 5 cases and above earn a 12 percent discount.
- Asparagus requires 20 cases for a discount of 12 percent.
- None of the discounts applies if the product is on sale this week. The sale price is 25 percent off the normal price. This week's sale items are Strawberry, Lettuce, and Tomatoes.

The code to execute this logic follows:

```
Sub ComplexIf()
    FinalRow = Cells(Rows.Count, 1).End(xlUp).Row

    For i = 2 To FinalRow
```

```
ThisClass = Cells(i, 1).Value
ThisProduct = Cells(i, 2).Value
ThisQty = Cells(i, 3).Value

' First, figure out if the item is on sale
Select Case ThisProduct
    Case "Strawberry", "Lettuce", "Tomatoes"
        Sale = True
    Case Else
        Sale = False
End Select

' Figure out the discount
If Sale Then
    Discount = 0.25
Else
    If ThisClass = "Fruit" Then
        Select Case ThisQty
            Case Is < 5
                Discount = 0
            Case 5 To 20
                Discount = 0.1
            Case Is > 20
                Discount = 0.15
        End Select
    ElseIf ThisClass = "Herbs" Then
        Select Case ThisQty
            Case Is < 10
                Discount = 0
            Case 10 To 15
                Discount = 0.03
            Case Is > 15
                Discount = 0.05
        End Select
    ElseIf ThisClass = "Vegetables" Then
        ' There is a special condition for asparagus
        If ThisProduct = "Asparagus" Then
            If ThisQty < 20 Then
                Discount = 0
            Else
                Discount = 0.12
            End If
        Else
            If ThisQty < 5 Then
                Discount = 0
            Else
                Discount = 0.12
            End If
        End If ' Is the product asparagus or not?
    End If ' Is the product a vegetable?
End If ' Is the product on sale?

Cells(i, 4).Value = Discount

If Sale Then
    Cells(i, 4).Font.Bold = True
End If
```

5

```
    Next i

    Range("D1").Value = "Discount"

    MsgBox "Discounts have been applied"

End Sub
```

Next Steps

Loops add a tremendous amount of power to your recorded macros. Any time you need to repeat a process over all worksheets or all rows in a worksheet, a loop is the way to go. Excel VBA supports the traditional programming loops of For...Next and Do...Loop and the object-oriented loop of For Each...Next. Next, Chapter 6, "R1C1-Style Formulas," discusses the seemingly arcane R1C1 style of formulas and shows why it is important in Excel VBA.

R1C1-Style Formulas

Referring to Cells: A1 Versus R1C1 References

We can trace the A1 style of referencing back to VisiCalc. Dan Bricklin and Bob Frankston used A1 to refer to the cell in the upper-left corner of the spreadsheet. Mitch Kapor used this same addressing scheme in Lotus 1-2-3. Upstart Multiplan from Microsoft attempted to buck the trend and used something called R1C1-style addressing. In R1C1 addressing, the cell known as A1 is referred to as R1C1 because it is in Row 1, Column 1.

With the dominance of Lotus 1-2-3 in the 1980s and early 1990s, the A1 style became the standard. Microsoft realized it was fighting a losing battle and eventually offered either R1C1-style addressing or A1-style addressing in Excel. When you open Excel today, the A1 style is used by default. Officially, however, Microsoft supports both styles of addressing.

You would think that this chapter would be a non-issue. Anyone who uses the Excel interface would agree that the R1C1 style is dead. However, we have what on the face of it seems to be an annoying problem: The macro recorder records formulas in the R1C1 style. So you might be thinking that you just need to learn R1C1 addressing so that you can read the recorded code and switch it back to the familiar A1 style.

I have to give Microsoft credit. After you understand R1C1-style formulas, they are actually more efficient, especially when you are dealing with writing formulas in VBA. Using R1C1-style addressing allows you to write more efficient code. Plus, there are some features such as setting up array formulas where you are required to enter the formula in R1C1 style.

6

IN THIS CHAPTER

Referring to Cells: A1 Versus R1C1
References.. 127

Switching Excel to Display R1C1-Style
References.. 128

The Miracle of Excel Formulas.................... 129

Explanation of R1C1 Reference Style........... 132

Array Formulas Require R1C1 Formulas....... 137

I can hear the collective groan from Excel users everywhere. You could skip these pages of this old-fashioned addressing style if it were only an annoyance or an efficiency issue. However, because it is necessary to understand R1C1 addressing to effectively use important features such as array formulas, you have to dive in and learn this style.

Switching Excel to Display R1C1-Style References

To switch to R1C1-style addressing, select Excel Options from the File menu. In the Formulas category, select the R1C1 reference style check box (see Figure 6.1).

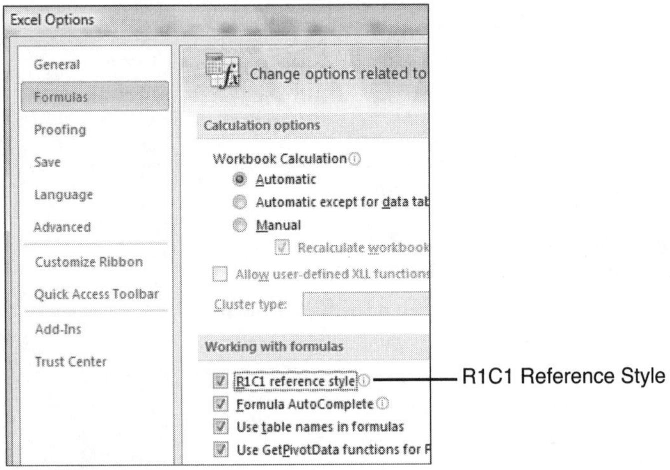

Figure 6.1
Selecting the R1C1 reference style on the Formulas category of the Excel Options dialog causes Excel to revert to R1C1 style in the Excel user interface.

After you switch to R1C1 style, the column letters A, B, C across the top of the worksheet are replaced by numbers 1, 2, 3 (see Figure 6.2).

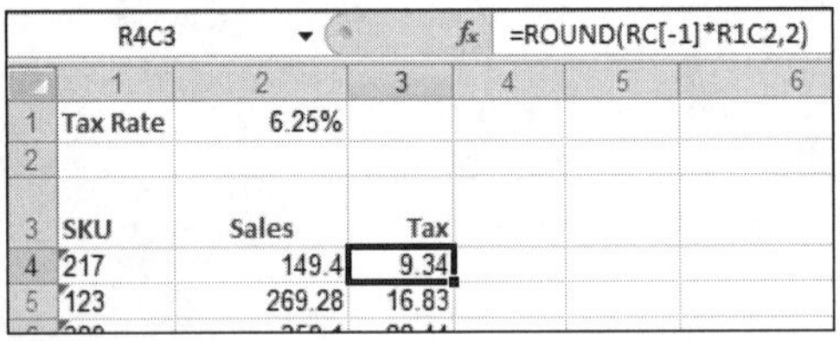

Figure 6.2
In R1C1 style, the column letters are replaced by numbers.

In this format, the cell that you know as B5 is called R5C2 because it is in Row 5, Column 2.

Every couple of weeks, someone manages to accidentally turn this option on, and we get an urgent support request at MrExcel. This style is foreign to 99 percent of spreadsheet users.

The Miracle of Excel Formulas

Automatically recalculating thousands of cells is the main benefit of electronic spreadsheets over the green ledger paper used up until 1979. However, a close second-prize award would be that you can enter one formula and copy that formula to thousands of cells.

Enter a Formula Once and Copy 1,000 Times

Consider this simple worksheet in Figure 6.3. Enter a simple formula such as =C4*B4 in cell D4, double-click the AutoFill handle, and the formula intelligently changes as at is copied down the range.

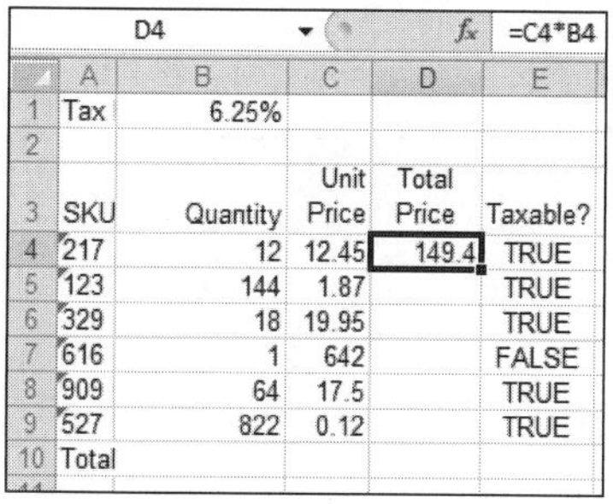

D4 =C4*B4

	A	B	C	D	E
1	Tax	6.25%			
2					
3	SKU	Quantity	Unit Price	Total Price	Taxable?
4	217	12	12.45	149.4	TRUE
5	123	144	1.87		TRUE
6	329	18	19.95		TRUE
7	616	1	642		FALSE
8	909	64	17.5		TRUE
9	527	822	0.12		TRUE
10	Total				

Figure 6.3
Double-click the AutoFill handle, and Excel intelligently copies this relative-reference formula down the column.

The formula in cell F4 includes both relative and absolute formulas: =IF(E4,ROUND(D4*$B$1,2),0). Thanks to the dollar signs inserted in cell B1, you can copy down this formula, and it always multiplies the Total Price in this row by the tax rate in cell B1.

The numeric results in Figure 6.4 are achieved by the formulas shown in Figure 6.5.

> **TIP** Ctrl+` in Excel switches between Normal view and Formula view.

Considering that you had to enter formulas only in Rows 4 and 10, it is amazing that Excel was able to intelligently copy the formulas down the column.

Excel users take this behavior for granted, but people in beginning Excel classes are amazed that the formula =F4+D4 in cell G4 automatically changed to =F5+D5 when it was copied to cell G5.

Figure 6.4

These results in Columns D, F, and G are achieved by the formulas shown in Figure 6.5.

▲	A	B	C	D	E	F	G
1	Tax	6.25%					
2							
3	SKU	Quantity	Unit Price	Total Price	Taxable?	Tax	Total
4	217	12	12.45	149.4	TRUE	9.34	158.74
5	123	144	1.87	269.28	TRUE	16.83	286.11
6	329	18	19.95	359.1	TRUE	22.44	381.54
7	616	1	642	642	FALSE	0	642.00
8	909	64	17.5	1120	TRUE	70	1190.00
9	527	822	0.12	98.64	TRUE	6.17	104.81
10	Total			2638.42		124.78	2763.2

Figure 6.5

Press Ctrl+` to switch to showing formulas rather than their results. It is amazing that Excel adjusts the cell references in each formula as you copy down the column.

f_x	=IF(E4,ROUND(D4*$B$1,2),0)		
D	**E**	**F**	**G**
Total Price	Taxable?	Tax	Total
=C4*B4	TRUE	=IF(E4,ROUND(D4*$B$1,2),0)	=F4+D4
=C5*B5	TRUE	=IF(E5,ROUND(D5*$B$1,2),0)	=F5+D5
=C6*B6	TRUE	=IF(E6,ROUND(D6*$B$1,2),0)	=F6+D6
=C7*B7	FALSE	=IF(E7,ROUND(D7*$B$1,2),0)	=F7+D7
=C8*B8	TRUE	=IF(E8,ROUND(D8*$B$1,2),0)	=F8+D8
=C9*B9	TRUE	=IF(E9,ROUND(D9*$B$1,2),0)	=F9+D9
=SUM(D4:D9)		=SUM(F4:F9)	=SUM(G4:G9)

The Secret: It's Not That Amazing

Remember that Excel does everything in R1C1-style formulas. Excel shows addresses and formulas in A1 style merely because it needs to adhere to the standard made popular by VisiCalc and Lotus.

If you switch the worksheet in Figure 6.5 to use R1C1 notation, you will notice that the "different" formulas in D4:D9 are all actually identical formulas in R1C1 notation. The same is true of F4:F9 and G4:G9.

Use the Options dialog to change the sample worksheet to R1C1-style addresses. If you examine the formulas in Figure 6.6, you will see that in R1C1 language, every formula in Column D is identical. Given that Excel is storing the formulas in R1C1 style, copying them, and then merely translating to A1 style for us to understand, it is no longer that amazing that Excel can easily manipulate A1-style formulas as it does.

This is one of the reasons why R1C1-style formulas are more efficient in VBA. You can enter the same formula in an entire range of data in a single statement.

Figure 6.6

The same formulas in R1C1 style. Note that every formula in Column 4 or Column 6 is the same as all other formulas in that column.

f_x	=IF(RC[-1],ROUND(RC[-2]*R1C2,2),0)		
4	**5**	**6**	**7**
Total Price	Taxable?	Tax	Total
=RC[-1]*RC[-2]	TRUE	=IF(RC[-1],ROUND(RC[-2]*R1C2,2),0)	=RC[-1]+RC[-3]
=RC[-1]*RC[-2]	TRUE	=IF(RC[-1],ROUND(RC[-2]*R1C2,2),0)	=RC[-1]+RC[-3]
=RC[-1]*RC[-2]	TRUE	=IF(RC[-1],ROUND(RC[-2]*R1C2,2),0)	=RC[-1]+RC[-3]
=RC[-1]*RC[-2]	FALSE	=IF(RC[-1],ROUND(RC[-2]*R1C2,2),0)	=RC[-1]+RC[-3]
=RC[-1]*RC[-2]	TRUE	=IF(RC[-1],ROUND(RC[-2]*R1C2,2),0)	=RC[-1]+RC[-3]
=RC[-1]*RC[-2]	TRUE	=IF(RC[-1],ROUND(RC[-2]*R1C2,2),0)	=RC[-1]+RC[-3]
=SUM(R[-6]C:R[-1])		=SUM(R[-6]C:R[-1]C)	=SUM(R[-6]C:R[-1]C)

CASE STUDY: ENTERING A1 VERSUS R1C1 IN VBA

Think about how you would set this spreadsheet up in the Excel interface. First, you enter a formula in cells D4, F4, G4. Next, you copy these cells, and paste them the rest of the way down the column. The code might look something like this:

```
Sub A1Style()
    ' Locate the FinalRow
    FinalRow = Cells(Rows.Count, 2).End(xlUp).Row
    ' Enter the first formula
    Range("D4").Formula = "=B4*C4"
    Range("F4").Formula = "=IF(E4,ROUND(D4*$B$1,2),0)"
    Range("G4").Formula = "=F4+D4"
    ' Copy the formulas from Row 4 down to the other cells
    Range("D4").Copy Destination:=Range("D5:D" & FinalRow)
    Range("F4:G4").Copy Destination:=Range("F5:G" & FinalRow)
    ' Enter the Total Row
    Cells(FinalRow + 1, 1).Value = "Total"
    Cells(FinalRow + 1, 6).Formula = "=SUM(G4:G" & FinalRow & ")"
End Sub
```

In this code, it takes three lines to enter the formulas at the top of the row and then another two lines to copy the formulas down the column.

The equivalent code in R1C1 style allows the formulas to be entered for the entire column in a single statement. Remember, the advantage of R1C1 style formulas is that all the formulas in Columns D, F, and most of G are identical:

```
Sub R1C1Style()
    ' Locate the FinalRow
    FinalRow = Cells(Rows.Count, 2).End(xlUp).Row
    ' Enter the first formula
    Range("D4:D" & FinalRow).FormulaR1C1 = "=RC[-1]*RC[-2]"
    Range("F4:F" & FinalRow).FormulaR1C1 = "=IF(RC[-1],ROUND(RC[-2]*R1C2,2),0)"
    Range("G4:G" & FinalRow).FormulaR1C1 = "=RC[-1]+RC[-3]"
    ' Enter the Total Row
    Cells(FinalRow + 1, 1).Value = "Total"
    Cells(FinalRow + 1, 6).FormulaR1C1 = "=SUM(R4C:R[-1]C)"
End Sub
```

In reality, you do not need to enter A1-style formulas in the top row and then copy them down. It seems counterintuitive, but when you specify an A1-style formula, Microsoft internally converts the formula to R1C1 and then enters that formula in the entire range. Thus, you can actually add the "same" A1-style formula to an entire range in a single line of code.

```
Sub A1StyleModified()
    ' Locate the FinalRow
    FinalRow = Cells(Rows.Count, 2).End(xlUp).Row
    ' Enter the first formula
    Range("D4:D" & FinalRow).Formula = "=B4*C4"
    Range("F4:F" & FinalRow).Formula = "=IF(E4,ROUND(D4*$B$1,2),0)"
    Range("G4:G" & FinalRow).Formula = "=F4+D4"
    ' Enter the Total Row
    Cells(FinalRow + 1, 1).Value = "Total"
    Cells(FinalRow + 1, 6).Formula = "=SUM(G4:G" & FinalRow & ")"
End Sub
```

6

Explanation of R1C1 Reference Style

An R1C1-style reference includes the letter R to refer to row and the letter C to refer to column. Because the most common reference in a formula is a relative reference, let's look at relative references in R1C1 style first.

Using R1C1 with Relative References

Imagine you are entering a formula in a cell. To point to a cell in a formula, you use the letters R and C. After each letter, enter the number of rows or columns in square brackets.

The following list explains the "rules" for using R1C1 relative references:

- For columns, a positive number means to move to the right a certain number of columns, and a negative number means to move to the left a certain number of columns. From cell E5, use RC[1] to refer to F5 and RC[-1] to refer to D5.

- For rows, a positive number means to move down the spreadsheet a certain number of rows. A negative number means to move toward the top of the spreadsheet a certain number of rows. From cell E5, use R[1]C to refer to E6 and use cell R[-1]C to refer to E4.

- If you leave off the square brackets for either the R or the C, it means that you are pointing to a cell in the same row or column as the cell with the formula

- If you enter =R[-1]C[-1] in cell E5, you are referring to a cell one row up and one column to the left. This would be cell D4.

- If you enter =RC[1] in cell E5, you are referring to a cell in the same row, but one column to the right. This would be cell F5.

- If you enter =RC in cell E5, you are referring to a cell in the same row and column, which is cell E5 itself. You would generally never do this because it would create a circular reference.

Figure 6.7 shows how you would enter a reference in cell E5 to point to various cells around E5.

One Row Above, Same Column

Figure 6.7
Here are various relative references. These would be entered in cell E5 to describe each cell around E5.

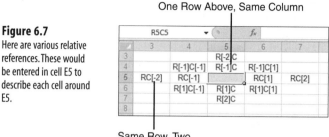

Same Row, Two
Columns to the Left

You can use R1C1 style to refer to a range of cells. If you want to add up the 12 cells to the left of the current cell, the formula is this:

```
=SUM(RC[-12]:RC[-1])
```

Using R1C1 with Absolute References

An absolute reference is one where the row and column remain fixed when the formula is copied to a new location. In A1-style notation, Excel uses a $ before the row number or column letter to keep that row or column absolute as the formula is copied.

To always refer to an absolute row or column number, just leave off the square brackets. This reference refers to cell $B$3 no matter where it is entered:

```
=R3C2
```

Using R1C1 with Mixed References

A mixed reference is one where the row is fixed and the column is allowed to be relative, or where the column is fixed and the row is allowed to be relative. This will be useful in many situations.

Imagine you have written a macro to import Invoice.txt into Excel. Using .End(xlUp), you find where the total row should go. As you are entering totals, you know that you want to sum from the row above the formula up to Row 2. The following code would handle that:

```
Sub MixedReference()
    TotalRow = Cells(Rows.Count, 1).End(xlUp).Row + 1
    Cells(TotalRow, 1).Value = "Total"
    Cells(TotalRow, 5).Resize(1, 3).FormulaR1C1 = "=SUM(R2C:R[-1]C)"
End Sub
```

In this code, the reference R2C:R[1]C indicates that the formula should add from Row 2 in the same column to the row just above the formula in the current column. Do you see the advantage to R1C1 formulas in this case? A single R1C1 formula with a mixed reference can be used to easily enter a formula to handle an indeterminate number of rows of data (see Figure 6.8).

6

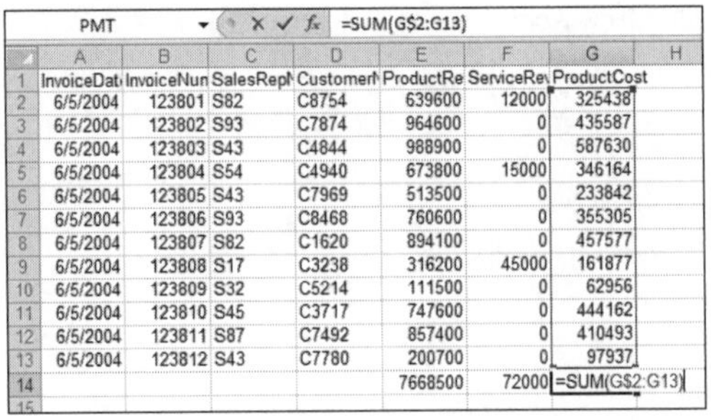

Figure 6.8

After running the macro, the formulas in Columns E:G of the total row will have a reference to a range that is locked to Row 2, but all other aspects are relative.

	A	B	C	D	E	F	G	H
							=SUM(G$2:G13)	
1	InvoiceDate	InvoiceNum	SalesRep	Customer	ProductRe	ServiceRe	ProductCost	
2	6/5/2004	123801	S82	C8754	639600	12000	325438	
3	6/5/2004	123802	S93	C7874	964600	0	435587	
4	6/5/2004	123803	S43	C4844	988900	0	587630	
5	6/5/2004	123804	S54	C4940	673800	15000	346164	
6	6/5/2004	123805	S43	C7969	513500	0	233842	
7	6/5/2004	123806	S93	C8468	760600	0	355305	
8	6/5/2004	123807	S82	C1620	894100	0	457577	
9	6/5/2004	123808	S17	C3238	316200	45000	161877	
10	6/5/2004	123809	S32	C5214	111500	0	62956	
11	6/5/2004	123810	S45	C3717	747600	0	444162	
12	6/5/2004	123811	S87	C7492	857400	0	410493	
13	6/5/2004	123812	S43	C7780	200700	0	97937	
14					7668500	72000	=SUM(G$2:G13)	
15								

Referring to Entire Columns or Rows with R1C1 Style

You will occasionally write a formula that refers to an entire column. For example, you might want to know the maximum value in Column G. If you don't know how many rows you will have in G, you can write =MAX($G:$G) in A1 style or =MAX(C7) in R1C1 style. To find the minimum value in Row 1, use =MIN($1:$1) in A1 style or =MIN(R1) in R1C1 style. You can use relative reference for either rows or columns. To find the average of the row above the current cell, use =AVERAGE(R[-1]).

Replacing Many A1 Formulas with a Single R1C1 Formula

After you get used to R1C1-style formulas, they actually seem a lot more intuitive to build. One classic example to illustrate R1C1-style formulas is building a multiplication table. It is easy to build a multiplication table in Excel using a single mixed-reference formula.

Building the Table

Enter the numbers 1 through 12 going across B1:M1. Copy and transpose these so the same numbers are going down A2:A13. Now the challenge is to build a single formula that works in all cells of B2:M13 and that shows the multiplication of the number in Row 1 times the number in Column 1. Using A1-style formulas, you must press the F4 key five times to get the dollar signs in the proper locations. The following is a far simpler formula in R1C1 style:

```
Sub MultiplicationTable()
    ' Build a multiplication table using a single formula
    Range("B1:M1").Value = Array(1, 2, 3, 4, 5, 6, 7, 8, 9, 10, 11, 12)
    Range("B1:M1").Font.Bold = True
    Range("B1:M1").Copy
    Range("A2:A13").PasteSpecial Transpose:=True
    Range("B2:M13").FormulaR1C1 = "=RC1*R1C"
    Cells.EntireColumn.AutoFit
End Sub
```

The R1C1-style reference =RC1*R1C could not be simpler. In English, it is saying, "Take this row's Column 1 and multiply it by Row 1 of this column." It works perfectly to build the multiplication table shown in Figure 6.9.

Figure 6.9

The macro creates a multiplication table. The formula in B2 uses two mixed references: =$A2*B$1.

CAUTION

After running the macro and producing the multiplication table in Figure 6.9, note that Excel still has the copied range from line 2 of the macro as the active clipboard item. If the user of this macro selects a cell and presses Enter, the contents of those cells will copy to the new location. However, this is generally not desirable. To get Excel out of Cut/Copy mode, add this line of code before your programs ends:

```
Application.CutCopyMode = False
```

An Interesting Twist

Try this experiment. Move the cell pointer to F6. Turn on macro recording using the Record Macro button on the Developer tab. Click the Use Relative Reference button on the Developer tab. Enter the formula =A1 and press Ctrl+Enter to stay in F6. Click the Stop Recording button on the floating toolbar.

You get this single-line macro, which enters a formula that points to a cell five rows up and five columns to the left:

```
Sub Macro1()
    ActiveCell.FormulaR1C1 = "=R[-5]C[-5]"
End Sub
```

Now, move the cell pointer to cell A1 and run the macro that you just recorded. You might think that pointing to a cell five rows above A1 would lead to the ubiquitous Run Time Error 1004. But it doesn't! When you run the macro, the formula in cell A1 is pointing to =XFA1048572, as shown in Figure 6.10, meaning that R1C1-style formulas actually wrap from the left side of the workbook to the right side. I cannot think of any instance where this would be actually useful, but for those of you who rely on Excel to error out when you ask for something that does not make sense, be aware that your macro will happily provide a result and probably not the one that you expected!

6

Figure 6.10
The formula to point to five rows above B1 wraps around to the bottom of the worksheet.

Remembering Column Numbers Associated with Column Letters

I like these formulas enough to use them regularly in VBA. I don't like them enough to change my Excel interface over to R1C1-style numbers. So, I routinely have to know that the cell known as U21 is really R21C21.

Knowing that *U* is the 21st letter of the alphabet is not something that comes naturally. We have 26 letters, so *A* is 1 and *Z* is 26. *M* is the halfway point of the alphabet and is Column 13. The rest of the letters are not particularly intuitive. If you play this little game for a few minutes each day, soon you will memorize the column numbers:

```
Sub QuizColumnNumbers()
    Do
        i = Int(Rnd() * 26) + 1
        Ans = InputBox("What column number is the letter " & _
        Chr(64 + i) & "?")
        If Ans = "" Then Exit Do
        If Not (Ans + 0) = i Then
            MsgBox "Letter " & Chr(64 + i) & " is column # " & i
        End If
    Loop
End Sub
```

If memorizing column numbers doesn't sound fun, or even if you have to figure out the column number of Column DGX someday, there is a straightforward way to do so using the Excel interface. Move the cell pointer to cell A1. Hold down the Shift key and start pressing the right-arrow key. For the first screen of columns, the column number appears in the name box to the left of the formula bar (see Figure 6.11).

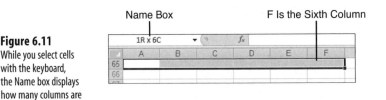

Figure 6.11
While you select cells with the keyboard, the Name box displays how many columns are selected for the first screen full of columns.

As you keep pressing the right-arrow key beyond the first screen, a ToolTip box to the right of the current cell tells you how many columns are selected. When you get to Column CS, it informs you that you are at Column 97 (see Figure 6.12).

You could also enter =COLUMN() in a cell to find the column number.

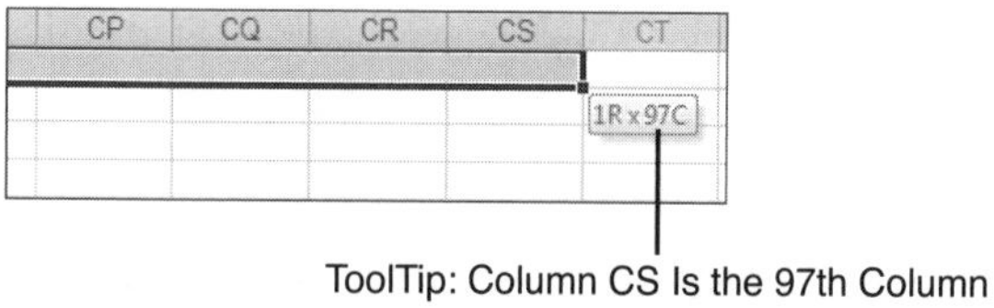

Figure 6.12
After the first screen of columns, a tool tip bar keeps track of the column number.

CP	CQ	CR	CS	CT
				1R x 97C

ToolTip: Column CS Is the 97th Column

Array Formulas Require R1C1 Formulas

Array formulas are powerful "super-formulas." At MrExcel.com, we call these CSE formulas because you have to use Ctrl+Shift+Enter to enter them. If you are not familiar with array formulas, they look like they should not work.

The array formula in E20, shown in Figure 6.13, is a formula that does 18 multiplications and then sums the result. It looks like this would be an illegal formula. In fact, if you happen to enter it without using Ctrl+Shift+Enter, you get the expected #VALUE! error. However, if you enter it with Ctrl+Shift+Enter, the formula miraculously multiplies row by row and then sums the result.

> **NOTE**
> You do not type the curly braces when entering the formula.

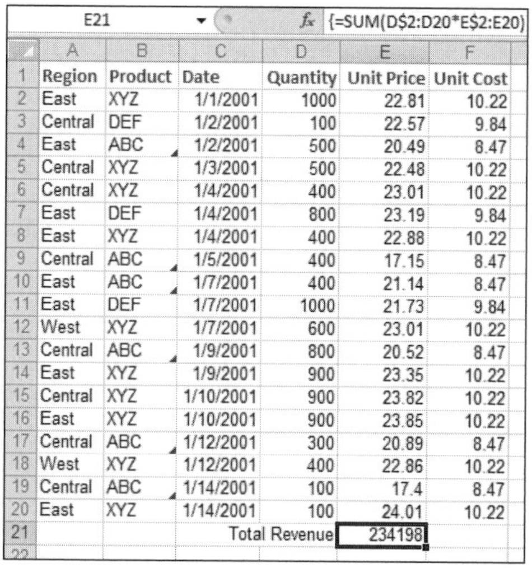

Figure 6.13
The array formula in E20 does 18 multiplications and then sums them. You must use Ctrl+Shift+Enter to enter this formula.

	E21	▼	f_x	{=SUM(D$2:D20*E$2:E20)	
	A	B	C	D	E	F
1	Region	Product	Date	Quantity	Unit Price	Unit Cost
2	East	XYZ	1/1/2001	1000	22.81	10.22
3	Central	DEF	1/2/2001	100	22.57	9.84
4	East	ABC	1/2/2001	500	20.49	8.47
5	Central	XYZ	1/3/2001	500	22.48	10.22
6	Central	XYZ	1/4/2001	400	23.01	10.22
7	East	DEF	1/4/2001	800	23.19	9.84
8	East	XYZ	1/4/2001	400	22.88	10.22
9	Central	ABC	1/5/2001	400	17.15	8.47
10	East	ABC	1/7/2001	400	21.14	8.47
11	East	DEF	1/7/2001	1000	21.73	9.84
12	West	XYZ	1/7/2001	600	23.01	10.22
13	Central	ABC	1/9/2001	800	20.52	8.47
14	East	XYZ	1/9/2001	900	23.35	10.22
15	Central	XYZ	1/10/2001	900	23.82	10.22
16	East	XYZ	1/10/2001	900	23.85	10.22
17	Central	ABC	1/12/2001	300	20.89	8.47
18	West	XYZ	1/12/2001	400	22.86	10.22
19	Central	ABC	1/14/2001	100	17.4	8.47
20	East	XYZ	1/14/2001	100	24.01	10.22
21			Total Revenue		234198	

The code to enter these formulas follows. Although the formulas appear in the user interface in A1-style notation, you must use R1C1-style notation for entering array formulas:

```
Sub EnterArrayFormulas()
    ' Add a formula to multiply unit price x quantity
    FinalRow = Cells(Rows.Count, 1).End(xlUp).Row
```

```
    Cells(FinalRow + 1, 5).FormulaArray = "=SUM(R2C[-1]:R[-1]C[-1]*R2C:R[-1] _
    C)"
End Sub
```

> **TIP**
> Use this trick to quickly find the R1C1 formula. Enter a regular A1-style formula or an array formula in any cell in Excel. Select that cell. Switch to the VBA editor. Press Ctrl+G to display the Immediate window. Type `Print ActiveCell.FormulaR1C1` and press Enter. Excel will convert the formula in the formula bar to an R1C1 style formula. You also can use a question mark instead of Print.

Next Steps

Read Chapter 7, "What's New in Excel 2010 and What's Changed," to learn about more features that have changed significantly in Excel 2010.

What Is New in Excel 2010 and What Has Changed

If It Has Changed in the Front End, It Has Changed in VBA

Thankfully, not too much of VBA doesn't work anymore, but a few things in the object model have changed. For most items, it's obvious that, because the Excel user interface changed, the VBA has changed.

→ See Chapter 8, "Create and Manipulate Names in VBA," for more information on working with names.

The Ribbon

If you have been working with a legacy version of Excel, the Ribbon is one of the first changes you'll notice when you open Excel 2010. Although the CommandBars object does still work to a point, if you want to flawlessly integrate your custom controls into the Ribbon, you need to make some major changes.

→ See Chapter 26, "Customizing the Ribbon to Run Macros," for more information.

Charts

Charts have many new features that are not backward-compatible with legacy versions of Excel. There's also a new type of mini-chart called Sparklines that are inserted within a cell.

IN THIS CHAPTER

If It Has Changed in the Front End, It Has Changed in VBA 139

Learning the New Objects and Methods 143

Compatibility Mode 144

Sparklines are not backward-compatible, not even to Excel 2007.

→ See Chapter 11, "Creating Charts," for more information.

Pivot Tables

Pivot tables have a few new features available that aren't backward-compatible, such as subtotals at the top and the report layout options.

→ Tables 13.1 and 13.2 in Chapter 13, "Using VBA to Create Pivot Tables," list the new methods and properties in Excel 2010 that you have to watch out for if you need to make a backward-compatible workbook.

Slicers

A slicer is a new feature in Excel 2010 that is not backward-compatible, not even to Excel 2007. It's useful in pivot tables, allowing for an easy to see and use filtering option. If you open a workbook with a slicer in an older version of Excel, the slicer is replaced with a shape, including text explaining what the shape is there for and that the feature is not available.

→ See Chapter 13, "Using VBA to Create Pivot Tables," for more information.

Conditional Formatting

Conditional formatting has been completely reinvented. Where we were once limited to three conditions and changing a few cell formatting options, it seems now the sky is the limit.

> **NOTE**
>
> To get an idea of how much the conditional formatting feature has changed, consider this: *Excel 2010 in Depth* (Sams, ISBN 0789743086) has a 30-page chapter just to review the options available. Compare that to almost any Excel 2003 or earlier book, in which conditional formatting coverage was just a footnote or two scattered throughout the book.

This feature has come a long way, which means so has the code. Compare the following two recorded macros. They both are relatively simple. A cell's fill is changed to red if the value in the cell is between 1 and 5. Notice, however, how much more code is involved with the new options that you now need to set in 2010.

Excel 2003 recorded macro:

```
Sub Macro2()
```

7

```
'
' Macro2 Macro
'


'
    Selection.FormatConditions.Delete
    Selection.FormatConditions.Add Type:=xlCellValue, Operator:=xlBetween, _
        Formula1:="1", Formula2:="5"
    Selection.FormatConditions(1).Interior.ColorIndex = 3
    ActiveCell.FormulaR1C1 = "2"
    Range("A2").Select
End Sub
```

Excel 2010 recorded macro:

```
Sub Macro2()
'
' Macro2 Macro
'


'
    Selection.FormatConditions.AddColorScale ColorScaleType:=2
    Selection.FormatConditions(Selection.FormatConditions.Count).SetFirstPri-
ority
    Selection.FormatConditions(1).ColorScaleCriteria(1).Type = _
        xlConditionValueNumber
    Selection.FormatConditions(1).ColorScaleCriteria(1).Value = 1
    With Selection.FormatConditions(1).ColorScaleCriteria(1).FormatColor
        .Color = 255
        .TintAndShade = 0
    End With
    Selection.FormatConditions(1).ColorScaleCriteria(2).Type = _
        xlConditionValueNumber
    Selection.FormatConditions(1).ColorScaleCriteria(2).Value = 5
    With Selection.FormatConditions(1).ColorScaleCriteria(2).FormatColor
        .Color = 255
        .TintAndShade = 0
    End With
    ActiveCell.FormulaR1C1 = "2"
    Range("A2").Select
End Sub
```

Tables

Tables are a convenient way to deal with data that is already set up as tables (multiple records set up beneath a row of column headers). For this new functionality, there are corresponding new objects, properties, and methods.

→ To learn more, **see** "Referencing Tables," **p. 77** and "Tables," **p. 153**.

Sorting

Because of the increased sorting options such as sorting by color, sort code has gone through a few changes. Instead of a single line of code with a few options to set, you need to configure the sort options and then do the sort, as shown here:

7

```
Sub Macro2()
'
' Macro2 Macro
'

'
    Range("A1:A4").Select
    'clear current sort options
    ActiveWorkbook.Worksheets("Sheet1").Sort.SortFields.Clear
    'set the new sort option - this is just a simple A-Z sort
    ActiveWorkbook.Worksheets("Sheet1").Sort.SortFields.Add Key:=Range("A1"), _
        SortOn:=xlSortOnValues, Order:=xlAscending, DataOption:=xlSortNormal
    'do the actual sort
    With ActiveWorkbook.Worksheets("Sheet1").Sort
        .SetRange Range("A1:A4")
        .Header = xlYes
        .MatchCase = False
        .Orientation = xlTopToBottom
        .SortMethod = xlPinYin
        .Apply
    End With
End Sub
```

SmartArt

SmartArt is the new function that has replaced the Diagram feature of legacy versions of Excel. Recording is very limited, but it will help you find the correct schema. After that, the recorder doesn't capture text entry or format changes.

The following example created the art in Figure 7.1. The name of the schema used is hChevron3. I changed the schemecolor for the middle chevron, leaving the other two with the default colors:

```
Sub AddDiagram()
With ActiveSheet
    Call .Shapes.AddSmartArt(Application.SmartArtLayouts( _
        "urn:microsoft.com/office/officeart/2005/8/layout/hChevron3")).Select
    .Shapes.Range(Array("Diagram 5")).GroupItems(1).TextEffect.Text = "Bill"
    .Shapes.Range(Array("Diagram 5")).GroupItems(3).TextEffect.Text = "Tracy"
    With .Shapes.Range(Array("Diagram 5")).GroupItems(2)
        .Fill.BackColor.SchemeColor = 7
        .TextEffect.Text = "Barb"
    End With
End With
End Sub
```

Figure 7.1
The macro recorder is limited when recording the creation of SmartArt. You'll need to trace through the object's properties to find what you need.

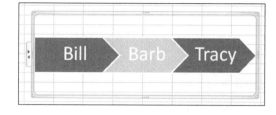

Learning the New Objects and Methods

Excel's VBA Help files have several tables of changes for objects and methods in Excel to which you can refer. They're even broken up by version number, as shown in Figure 7.2. To access these tables, click the Help icon in the VB Editor toolbar and select What's New from the dialog that appears.

Figure 7.2
Excel's VBA Help has several sections to help you find what will and won't work in the new Excel.

Excel Help

Excel 2010 Developer Reference

What's New

Topics
Object Model Changes Since Microsoft Office 97
Object Model Changes Since Microsoft Office 2000
Object Model Changes Since Microsoft Office XP (2002)
Object Model Changes Since Microsoft Office 2003

When you review the "Object Model Changes Since" sections, you may be wondering what Microsoft means when they say an item's status is Hidden (see Figure 7.3). If you use one of these items in your code, such as FileSearch, the program will compile just fine, but it won't run in Excel 2010.

> **CAUTION**
>
> Microsoft has allowed you to include a Hidden item in your code for legacy usage and will compile it, but when you try to run it, the program won't know what to do with it. Unless you have some kind of compatibility mode check in your code, your program will debug at runtime.

7

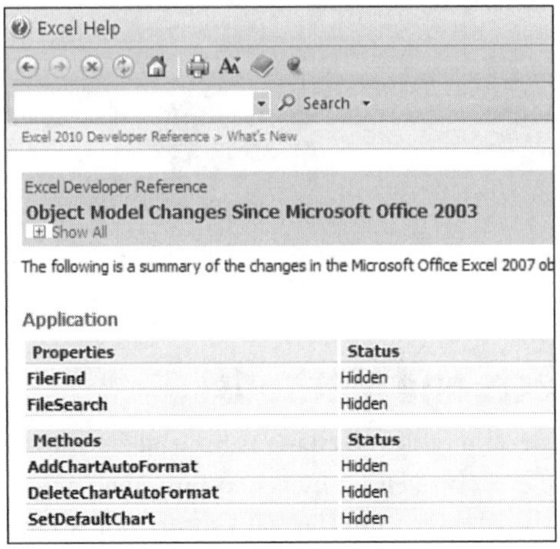

Figure 7.3
Some items appear as
Hidden in the Object
Model Changes reference
tables. This means Excel
will compile them for use
in legacy versions, but
they won't actually work
in Excel 2010.

Compatibility Mode

With all the changes in Excel 2010, now more than ever it's important to verify the application's version. Two ways you can do this are `Version` and `Excel8CompatibilityMode`.

Dealing with Compatibility Issues

Creating a compatibility mode workbook can be problematic. Most code will still run in legacy versions of Excel, as long as the program doesn't run into an item from the Excel 2010 object model. If you use any items from the Excel 2010 object model, however, the code will not compile in legacy versions. To work around this, comment out the 2010-specific lines of code, compile, and then comment the lines back in.

If your only Excel 2010 issue is the use of constant values, partially treat your code as if you were doing late binding to an external application. If you have only constant values that are incompatible, treat them like late binding arguments, assigning a variable the numeric value of the constant. The following section shows an example of this.

→   **See** "Using Constant Values" **p. 439**, for more information on using constant values.

Version

The `Version` property returns a string containing the active Excel application version. For 2010, this is 14. This can prove useful if you've developed an add-in to use across versions; but some parts of it, such as saving the active workbook, are version-specific:

```
Sub wkbkSave()
Dim xlVersion As String
Dim myxlOpenXMLWorkbook As String
```

```
myxlOpenXMLWorkbook = "51" 'non-macro enabled workbook

xlVersion = Application.Version

Select Case xlVersion
    Case Is = "9.0", "10.0", "11.0"
        ActiveWorkbook.SaveAs Filename:="LegacyVersionExcel.xls"
    Case Is = "12.0", "14.0" '12.0 is Excel 2007
        ActiveWorkbook.SaveAs Filename:="Excel2010Version", _
        FileFormat:=myxlOpenXMLWorkbook
End Select
End Sub
```

> **CAUTION**
>
> Note that for the FileFormat property of the Excel 2010 case, I had to create my own variable,
> myxlOpenXMLWorkbook, to hold the constant value of xlOpenXMLWorkbook. If I were to try to
> run this in a legacy version of Excel just using the Excel 2010 constant, xlOpenXMLWorkbook, the
> code would not even compile.

Excel8CompatibilityMode

This property returns a Boolean, to let you know whether a workbook is in Compatibility
mode—that is, saved as an Excel 97-2003 file. You use this, for example, if you have
an add-in using the new conditional formatting, but you wouldn't want the user to try
and use it on the workbook. The following function, CompatibilityCheck, returns True
if the active workbook is in Compatibility mode and False if it is not. The procedure,
CheckCompatibility, uses the result to inform the user of an incompatible feature, as shown
in Figure 7.4:

```
Function CompatibilityCheck() As Boolean
Dim blMode As Boolean

If Application.Version = "12.0" or Application.Version = "14.0" Then
    blMode = ActiveWorkbook.Excel8CompatibilityMode
    If blMode = True Then
        CompatibilityCheck = True
    ElseIf blMode = False Then
        CompatibilityCheck = False
    End If
End If
End Function

Sub CheckCompatibility()
Dim xlCompatible As Boolean

xlCompatible = CompatibilityCheck

If xlCompatible = True Then
    MsgBox "You are attempting to use an Excel 2010 function " & Chr(10) & _
    "in a 97-2003 Compatibility Mode workbook"
End If
End Sub
```

7

Figure 7.4
Use Excel8-
Compatibility-
Check to inform a user
that certain features in
your add-in won't work
in a 97–2003 Excel file
opened in Excel 20010.

Next Steps

Now that you have an idea about the differences you might run into in Excel 2010, you're ready to move on to the next chapter, which discusses using named ranges to simplify your coding including one of my favorite new methods—the Table method.

Create and Manipulate Names in VBA

8

Excel Names

You have probably named ranges in a worksheet by highlighting a range and typing a name in the Name box to the left of the formula field. You also might have created more complicated names containing formulas. For example, perhaps you created a name with a formula that finds the last row in a column. The ability to set a name to a range makes it much easier to write formulas and set tables.

The ability to create and manipulate names is also available in VBA and provides the same benefits as naming ranges in a worksheet. For example, you can store a new range in a name.

This chapter explains different types of names and the various ways you can use them.

Global Versus Local Names

Names can be *global*, which means they are available anywhere in the workbook. Names can also be *local*, which means they are available only on a specific worksheet. With local names, you can have multiple references in the workbook with the same name. Global names must be unique to the workbook.

In previous versions of Excel, it was difficult to tell whether you were looking at a global or local name. In fact, you had to be on the correct sheet and compare the list of names on different sheets. Beginning with Excel 2007, you have the Name Manager dialog box, which lists all the names in a workbook, even a name that has been assigned to both the global and local levels. The Scope column lists the scope of the name, whether it is the workbook or a specific sheet such as Sheet1.

IN THIS CHAPTER

Excel Names...147

Global Versus Local Names........................147

Adding Names 148

Deleting Names 149

Adding Comments.....................................150

Types of Names 150

Hiding Names 155

Checking for the Existence of a Name 155

8

For example, in Figure 8.1 the name Apples is assigned to Sheet1, but also to the workbook.

Figure 8.1
The Name Manager lists all local and global names.

Name	Value	Refers To	Scope	Comment
Apples	Apples	=Sheet1!$A$2	Sheet1	
Apples	Apples	=Sheet1!$A$2	Workbook	
Bananas	Bananas	=Sheet1!$A$6	Workbook	
Company	CompanyA	="CompanyA"	Workbook	
Criteria	Apples	=Sheet4!$A$1	Sheet4	
Current	111111111111111...	111111111111111...	Workbook	
Database	{"Column1","1/1/20...	=Sheet1!$A$1:$F$6	Workbook	
Extract	{"","","",""}	=Sheet4!$G$1:$K$1	Sheet4	
FirstArray	{...}	={#N/A,#N/A,#N/...	Workbook	
Fruits	{"Column1","1/1/20...	=Sheet1!$A$1:$F$6	Sheet1	
Fruits	{"","1/1/2003","1/2...	=Sheet2!$A$1:$F$6	Workbook	
Kiwis	Kiwis	=Sheet1!$A$5	Sheet1	
Kiwis	Kiwis	=Sheet1!$A$5	Workbook	
Lemons	Lemons	=Sheet1!$A$4	Workbook	

Refers to:
=Sheet1!$A$2

Adding Names

If you record the creation of a named range and then view the code, you see something like this:

```
ActiveWorkbook.Names.Add Name:="Fruits", RefersToR1C1:="=Sheet2!R1C1:R6C6"
```

This creates a global name `"Fruits"`, which includes the range A1:F6 (`R1C1:R6C6`). The formula is enclosed in quotes, and the equal sign in the formula must be included. In addition, the range reference must be absolute (include the $ sign) or in R1C1 notation. If the sheet on which the name is created is the active sheet, the sheet reference does not have to be included. However, it can make the code easier to understand.

> **NOTE**
> If the reference is not absolute, the name might be created, but it will not point to the correct range. For example, if you run this line of code the name is created in the workbook. However, as you can see in Figure 8.2, it hasn't actually been assigned to the range.
>
> ```
> ActiveWorkbook.Names.Add Name:="Citrus", _
>         RefersToR1C1:="=Sheet1!R1C1"
> ```

Figure 8.2
Cell A1 doesn't have the name Citrus assigned to it because the name formula lacks absolute referencing and is not properly recognized by Excel.

To create a local name, include the sheet name:

```
ActiveWorkbook.Names.Add Name:="Sheet2!Fruits", _
    RefersToR1C1:="=Sheet2!R1C1:R6C6"
```

Alternatively, specify that the Names collection belongs to a worksheet:

```
Worksheets("Sheet1").Names.Add Name:="Fruits", _
    RefersToR1C1:="=Sheet1!R1C1:R6C6"
```

The preceding example is what you would learn from the macro recorder. There is a simpler way:

```
Range("A1:F6").Name = "Fruits"
```

Alternatively, for a local variable only, you can use this:

```
Range("A1:F6").Name = "Sheet1!Fruits"
```

When creating names with this method, absolute referencing is not required.

> **NOTE** Table names were a new feature in Excel 2007. You can use them like defined names, but you don't create them the same way. See the "Tables" section, later in this chapter, for more information about creating table names.

Although this is much easier and quicker than what the macro recorder creates, it is limited in that it works only for ranges. Formulas, strings, numbers, and arrays require the use of the Add method.

The Name property of the name ObjectName is an object but still has a Name property. The following line renames an existing name:

```
Names("Fruits").Name = "Produce"
```

Fruits no longer exists; Produce is now the name of the range.

When you are renaming names in which a local and global reference both carry the same name, the previous line renames the local reference first.

Deleting Names

Use the Delete method to delete a name:

```
Names("ProduceNum").Delete
```

An error occurs if you attempt to delete a name that does not exist.

> **CAUTION**
>
> If both local and global references with the same name exist, be more specific as to which name is being deleted.

Adding Comments

Beginning with Excel 2007, you can add comments about names. You can add any additional information such as why the name was created or where it is used. To insert a comment for the local name LocalOffice, do this:

```
ActiveWorkbook.Worksheets("Sheet7").Names("LocalOffice").Comment = _
"Holds the name of the current office"
```

The comments will appear in a column in the Name Manager, as shown in Figure 8.3.

> **CAUTION**
>
> The name must exist before a comment can be added to it.

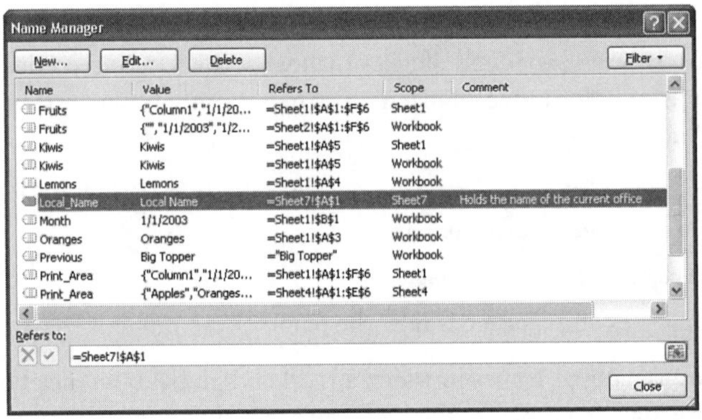

Figure 8.3
You can add comments
about names to help
remember their purpose.

Types of Names

The most common use of names is for storing ranges; however, names can store more than just ranges. After all, that's what they're for: Names store information. Names make it simple to remember and use potentially complex or large amounts of information. In addition, unlike variables, names remember what they store beyond the life of the program.

You have covered creating range names, but you can also assign names to name formulas, strings, numbers, and arrays.

Formulas

The syntax for storing a formula in a name is the same as for a range because the range is essentially a formula:

```
Names.Add Name:="ProductList", _
    RefersTo:="=OFFSET(Sheet2!$A$2,0,0,COUNTA(Sheet2!$A:$A))"
```

The preceding code allows for a dynamic named column, which is useful for creating dynamic tables or for referencing any dynamic listing on which calculations may be performed, as shown in Figure 8.4.

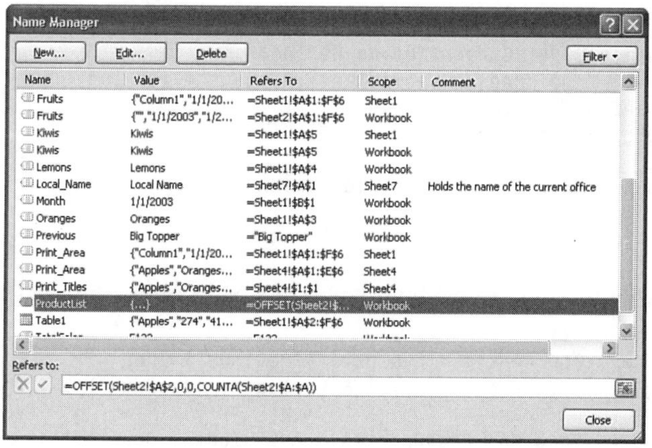

Figure 8.4
Dynamic formulas can be assigned to names.

Strings

When using names to hold strings such as the name of the current fruit producer, enclose the string value in quotes. Because there is no formula involved, an equal sign is not needed. If you were to include an equal sign, Excel would treat the value as a formula. Let Excel include the equal sign shown in the Name Manager.

```
Names.Add Name: = "Company", RefersTo:="CompanyA"
```

Figure 8.5 shows how the coded name will appear in the Name Manager window.

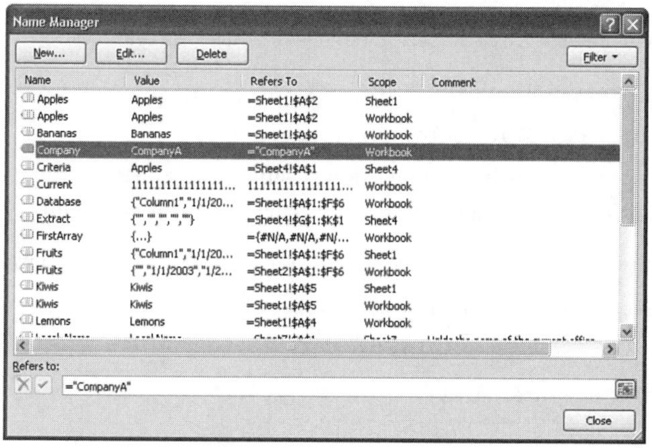

Figure 8.5
A string value can be assigned to a name.

Using Names to Store Values

Because names do not lose their references between sessions, this is a great way to store values as opposed to storing values in cells from which the information would have to be retrieved. For example, to track the leading producer between seasons, create a name Leader. If the new season's leading producer matches the name reference, a special report comparing the seasons could be created. The other option is to create a special sheet to track the values between sessions and then retrieve the values when needed. With names, the values are readily available.

The following procedure shows how cells in a variable sheet are used to retain information between sessions:

```
Sub NoNames(ByRef CurrentTop As String)
TopSeller = Worksheets("Variables").Range("A1").Value
If CurrentTop = TopSeller Then
    MsgBox ("Top Producer is " & TopSeller & " again.")
Else
    MsgBox ("New Top Producer is " & CurrentTop)
End If
End Sub
```

The following procedure shows how names are used to store information between sessions:

```
Sub WithNames()
If Evaluate("Current") = Evaluate("Previous") Then
    MsgBox ("Top Producer is " & Evaluate("Previous") & " again.")
Else
    MsgBox ("New Top Producer is " & Evaluate("Current"))
End If
End Sub
```

If Current and Previous are previously declared names, you access them directly rather than create variables in which to pass them. Note the use of the Evaluate method to extract the values in names. The string being stored cannot have more than 255 characters.

Numbers

You can also use names to store numbers between sessions. Use this:

```
NumofSales = 5123
Names.Add Name:="TotalSales", RefersTo:=NumofSales
```

Alternatively, you can use this:

```
Names.Add Name:="TotalSales", RefersTo:=5123
```

Notice the lack of quotes or an equal sign. Using quotes changes the number to a string. With the addition of an equal sign, the number changes to a formula.

To retrieve the value in the name, you have a longer and a shorter option:

```
NumofSales = Names("TotalSales").Value
```

or

```
NumofSales = [TotalSales]
```

Keep in mind that someone reading your code might not be familiar with the use of the `Evaluate` method (square brackets). If you know that someone else will be reading your code, avoid the use of the `Evaluate` method or add a comment explaining it.

Tables

Excel tables share some of the properties of defined names, but they also have their own unique methods. Unlike defined names, which are what you are used to dealing with, tables cannot be created manually. In other words, you cannot select a range on a sheet and type a name in the Name field. However, you can manually create them via VBA.

Tables are not created using the same method as the defined names. Instead of `Range(xx).Add` or `Names.Add`, use `ListObjects.Add`.

To create a table from cells A1:F6, and assuming the table has column headers, as shown in Figure 8.6, do this:

```
ActiveSheet.ListObjects.Add(xlSrcRange, Range("$A$1:$F$6"), , xlYes).Name = _
  "Table1"
```

Figure 8.6
You can assign a special name to a data table.

	A	B	C	D	E	F
1	Column1	1/1/2010	1/2/2010	1/3/2010	1/4/2010	1/5/2010
2	Apples	274	412	159	314	837
3	Oranges	228	776	344	245	487
4	Lemons	160	183	502	583	100
5	Kiwis	478	724	755	618	778
6	Bananas	513	438	600	456	51
7	Total					2253

`xlSrcRange` (the `SourceType`) tells Excel the source of the data is an Excel range. You then need to specify the range (the source) of the table. If you have headers in the table, include that row when indicating the range. The next argument, which is not used in the preceding example, is the `LinkSource`, a Boolean indicating whether there is an external data source and is not used if the `SourceType` is `xlSrcRange`. `xlYes` lets Excel know the data table has column headers; otherwise, Excel automatically generates them. The final argument, which is not shown in the preceding example, is the destination. This is used when the `SourceType` is `xlSrcExternal`, indicating the upper-left cell where the table will begin.

Using Arrays in Names

A name can also store the data stored in an array. The array size is limited by available memory. See Chapter 19, "Arrays," for more information about arrays.

An array reference is stored in a name the same way as a numeric reference:

```
Sub NamedArray()
Dim myArray(10, 5)
Dim i As Integer, j As Integer
'The following For loops fill the array myArray
```

```
    For i = 1 To 10
        For j = 1 To 5
            myArray(i, j) = i + j
        Next j
    Next i
    'The following line takes our array and gives it a name
    Names.Add Name:="FirstArray", RefersTo:=myArray
    End Sub
```

Because the name is referencing a variable, no quotes or equal signs are required.

Reserved Names

Excel uses local names of its own to keep track of information. These local names are considered reserved, and if you use them for your own references, they might cause problems.

Highlight an area on a sheet. Then from the Page Layout tab, select Print Area, Set Print Area.

As shown in Figure 8.7, a Print_Area listing is in the Range Name field. Deselect the area and look again in the Range Name field. The name is still there. Select it, and the print area previously set is now highlighted. If you save, close, and reopen the workbook, Print_Area is still set to the same range. Print_Area is a name reserved by Excel for its own use.

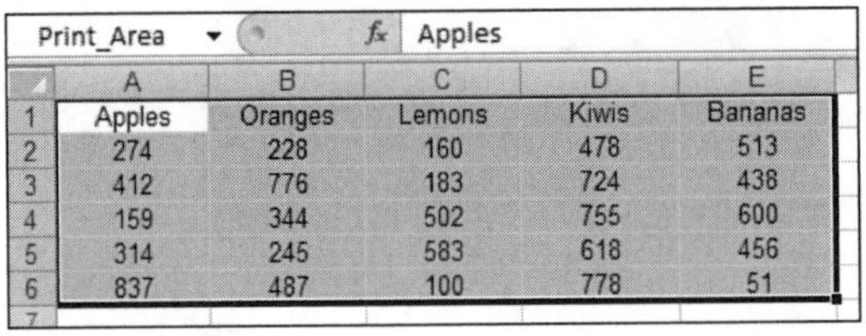

Figure 8.7
Excel creates its own names.

	A	B	C	D	E
1	Apples	Oranges	Lemons	Kiwis	Bananas
2	274	228	160	478	513
3	412	776	183	724	438
4	159	344	502	755	600
5	314	245	583	618	456
6	837	487	100	778	51
7					

Print_Area ▼   *fx*   Apples

> **CAUTION**
>
> Each sheet has its own print area. In addition, setting a new print area on a sheet with an existing print area overwrites the original print area name.

Fortunately, Excel does not have a large list of reserved names:

> Criteria
>
> Database
>
> Extract
>
> Print_Area
>
> Print_Titles

Criteria and Extract are used when the Advanced Filter (on the Data tab, select Advanced Filter) is configured to extract the results of the filter to a new location.

Database is no longer required in Excel. However, some features, such as Data Form, still recognize it. Legacy versions of Excel used it to identify the data you wanted to manipulate in certain functions.

Print_Area is used when a print area is set (from the Page Layout tab, select Print Area, Set Print Area) or when Page Setup options that designate the print area (from the Page Layout tab, Scale) are changed.

Print_Titles is used when print titles are set (Page Layout, Print Titles).

These names should be avoided and variations used with caution. For example, if you create a name PrintTitles, you might accidentally code this:

```
Worksheets("Sheet4").Names("Print_Titles").Delete
```

You have just deleted the Excel name rather than your custom name.

Hiding Names

Names are incredibly useful, but you don't necessarily want to see all the names you have created. Like many other objects, names have a `Visible` property. To hide a name, set the `Visible` property to `False`. To unhide a name, set the `Visible` property to `True`:

```
Names.Add Name:="ProduceNum", RefersTo:="=$A$1", Visible:=False
```

> **CAUTION**
>
> If a user creates a Name object with the same name as your hidden one, the hidden name is overwritten without any warning message. To prevent this, protect the worksheet.

Checking for the Existence of a Name

You can use the following function to check for the existence of a user-defined name, even a hidden one. Keep in mind that this function does not return the existence of Excel's reserved names. Even so, this is a handy addition to your arsenal of "programmer's useful code":

```
Function NameExists(FindName As String) As Boolean
Dim Rng As Range
Dim myName As String
On Error Resume Next
myName = ActiveWorkbook.Names(FindName).Name
If Err.Number = 0 Then
    NameExists = True
Else
    NameExists = False
End If
End Function
```

The preceding code is also an example of how to use errors to your advantage. If the name for which you are searching does not exist, an error message is generated. By adding the On Error Resume Next line at the beginning, you force the code to continue. Then you use Err.Number to tell you whether it ran into an error. If you didn't, Err.Number is zero, which means the name exists. Otherwise, you had an error and the name does not exist.

CASE STUDY: USING NAMED RANGES FOR VLOOKUP

Every day, you import a file of sales data from a chain of retail stores. The file includes the store number but not the store name. You obviously don't want to have to type store names every day, but you would like to have store names appear on all the reports that you run.

Normally, you would enter a table of store numbers and names in an out-of-the way spot on a back worksheet. You can use VBA to help maintain the list of stores each day and then use the VLOOKUP function to get store names from the list into your data set.

The basic steps are as follows:

1. Import the data file.
2. Find all the unique store numbers in today's file.
3. See whether any of these store numbers are not in your current table of store names.
4. For any stores that are new, add them to the table and ask the user for a store name.
5. The Store Names table is now larger, so reassign the named range used to describe the store table.
6. Use a VLOOKUP function in the original dataset to add a store name to all records. This VLOOKUP references the named range of the newly expanded Store Names table.

The following code handles these six steps:

```
Sub ImportData()
' This routine imports sales.csv to the data sheet
' Check to see whether any stores in column A are new
' If any are new, then add them to the StoreList table

Dim WSD As Worksheet
Dim WSM As Worksheet
Dim WB As Workbook

Set WB = ThisWorkbook
' Data is stored on the Data worksheet
Set WSD = WB.Worksheets("Data")
' StoreList is stored on a menu worksheet
Set WSM = WB.Worksheets("Menu")

' Open the file..This makes the csv file active
Workbooks.Open Filename:="C:\Sales.csv"
' Copy the data to WSD and close
ActiveWorkbook.Range("A1").CurrentRegion.Copy Destination:=WSD.Range("A1")
ActiveWorkbook.Close SaveChanges:=False
```

```vba
' Find a list of unique stores from column A
FinalRow = WSD.Cells(WSD.Rows.Count, 1).End(xlUp).Row
WSD.Range("A1").Resize(FinalRow, 1).AdvancedFilter Action:=xlFilterCopy, _
    CopyToRange:=WSD.Range("Z1"), Unique:=True

' For all the unique stores, see whether they are in the
' current store list.
FinalStore = WSD.Range("Z" & WSD.Rows.Count).End(xlUp).Row
WSD.Range("AA1").Value = "There?"
WSD.Range("AA2:AA" & FinalStore).FormulaR1C1 = _
    "=ISNA(VLOOKUP(RC[-1],StoreList,1,False))"

' Find the next row for a new store. Because StoreList starts in A1
' of the Menu sheet, find the next available row
NextRow = WSM.Range("A" & WSM.Rows.Count).End(xlUp).Row + 1

' Loop through the list of today 's stores.If they are shown
' as missing, then add them at the bottom of the StoreList
For i = 2 To FinalStore
    If WSD.Cells(i, 27).Value = True Then
        ThisStore = Cells(i, 26).Value
        WSM.Cells(NextRow, 1).Value = ThisStore
        WSM.Cells(NextRow, 2).Value = _
            InputBox(Prompt:="What is name of store " _
            & ThisStore, Title:="New Store Found")
        NextRow = NextRow + 1
    End If
Next i

' Delete the temporary list of stores in Z &AA
WSD.Range("Z1:AA" & FinalStore).Clear

' In case any stores were added, re-define StoreList name
FinalStore = WSM.Range("A" & WSM.Rows.Count).End(xlUp).Row
WSM.Range("A1:B" & FinalStore).Name = "StoreList"

' Use VLOOKUP to add StoreName to column B of the dataset
WSD.Range("B1").EntireColumn.Insert
WSD.Range("B1").Value = "StoreName"
WSD.Range("B2:B" & FinalRow).FormulaR1C1 = "=VLOOKUP(RC1,StoreList,2,False)"

' Change Formulas to Values
WSD.Range("B2:B" & FinalRow).Value = Range("B2:B" & FinalRow).Value

'Release our variables to free system memory
Set WB = Nothing
Set WSD = Nothing
Set WSM = Nothing
End Sub
```

Next Steps

In Chapter 9, "Event Programming," you will learn how code can be written to run automatically based on users' actions such as activating a sheet or selecting a cell. This is done with events, which are actions in Excel that can be captured and used to your advantage.

Event Programming

Levels of Events

Earlier in the book, you read about workbook events and you have seen examples of worksheet events. *Events* are Excel's way of letting you execute code based on certain actions that take place in a workbook.

These events can be found at the following levels:

- **Application level**—Control based on application actions such as `Application_NewWorkbook`
- **Workbook level**—Control based on workbook actions such as `Workbook_Open`
- **Worksheet level**—Control based on worksheet actions such as `Worksheet_SelectionChange`
- **Chart sheet level**—Control based on chart actions such as `Chart_Activate`

Listed here are where different types of events should be placed:

- Workbook events go into the ThisWorkbook module.
- Worksheet events go into the module of the sheet they affect such as Sheet1.
- Chart sheet events go into the module of the chart sheet they affect such as Chart1.
- Embedded charts and application events go into class modules.

The events can still make procedure or function calls outside their own modules. Therefore, if you want the same action to take place for two different sheets, you don't have to copy the code. Instead, place the code in a module and have each sheet event call the procedure.

IN THIS CHAPTER

Levels of Events	159
Using Events	160
Workbook Events	161
Worksheet Events	168
Chart Sheet Events	172
Application-Level Events	176

In this chapter, you learn about different levels of events, where to find them, and how to use the events.

NOTE   Userform and control events are discussed in Chapter 10, "Userforms: An Introduction," and Chapter 23, "Advanced Userform Techniques."

Using Events

Each level consists of several types of events, and memorizing the syntax of them all would be a feat. Excel makes it easy to view and insert the available events in their proper modules right from the VB Editor.

When a ThisWorkbook, Sheet, Chart Sheet, or Class module is active, the corresponding events are available through the Object and Procedure drop-downs, as shown in Figure 9.1.

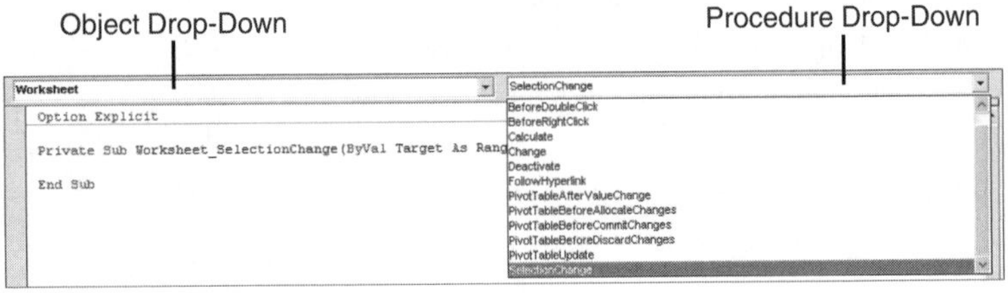

Object Drop-Down   Procedure Drop-Down

Figure 9.1
The different events are easy to access from the VB Editor Object and Procedure drop-downs.

After the object is selected, the Procedure drop-down updates to list the events available for that object. Selecting a procedure automatically places the procedure header (`Private Sub`) and footer (`End Sub`) in the editor, as shown in Figure 9.2.

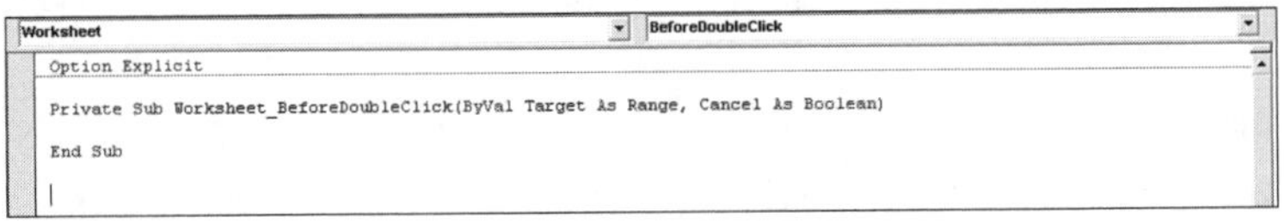

Figure 9.2
The procedure header and footer are automatically placed.

Event Parameters

Some events have parameters, such as `Target` or `Cancel`, that allow values to be passed into the procedure. For example, some procedures are triggered before the actual event, such as `BeforeRightClick`. Assigning `True` to the `Cancel` parameter prevents the default action from taking place. In this case, the shortcut menu is prevented from appearing:

```
Private Sub Worksheet_BeforeRightClick(ByVal Target As Range, Cancel As _
Boolean)
Cancel = True
End Sub
```

Enabling Events

Some events can trigger other events including themselves. For example, the `Worksheet_Change` event is triggered by a change in a cell. If the event is triggered and the procedure itself changes a cell, the event gets triggered again, which changes a cell, triggering another the event, and so on. The procedure gets stuck in an endless loop.

To prevent this, disable the events and then reenable them at the end of the procedure:

```
Private Sub Worksheet_Change(ByVal Target As Range)
Application.EnableEvents = False
Range("A1").Value = Target.Value
Application.EnableEvents = True
End Sub
```

9

> **TIP**
>
> To interrupt a macro, press Esc or Ctrl+Break. To restart it, use Run on the toolbar or press F5.

Workbook Events

The following event procedures are available at the workbook level. Some events, such as `Workbook_SheetActivate`, are sheet events available at the workbook level. This means you don't have to copy and paste the code in each sheet in which you want it to run.

Workbook_Activate()

`Workbook_Activate` occurs when the workbook containing this event becomes the active workbook.

Workbook_Deactivate()

`Workbook_Deactivate` occurs when the active workbook is switched from the workbook containing the event to another workbook.

Workbook_Open()

`Workbook_Open` is the default workbook event. This procedure is activated when a workbook is opened; no user interface is required. The procedure has a variety of uses, such as checking the username and then customizing the user's privileges in the workbook.

The following code checks the `UserName`. If it is not Admin, this code protects each sheet from user changes.

> **TIP**
>
> `UserInterfaceOnly` allows macros to make changes, but not the user.

```
Private Sub Workbook_Open()
Dim sht As Worksheet
If Application.UserName <> "Admin" Then
    For Each sht In Worksheets
        sht.Protect UserInterfaceOnly:=True
    Next sht
End If
End Sub
```

You can also use Workbook_Open to create custom menus or toolbars. The following code adds the menu MrExcel Programs to the Add-ins tab with two options underneath it (see Figure 9.3).

→ For more information about custom menus, **see** Chapter 26, "Customizing the Ribbon to Run Macros."

```
Sub Workbook_Open()
```

Figure 9.3
You can use the Open event to create custom menus under the Add-ins tab.

```
Dim cbWSMenuBar As CommandBar
Dim Ctrl As CommandBarControl, muCustom As CommandBarControl
Set cbWSMenuBar = Application.CommandBars("Worksheet menu bar")
Set muCustom = cbWSMenuBar.Controls.Add(Type:=msoControlPopup, _
    Temporary:=True)
For Each Ctrl In cbWSMenuBar.Controls
    If Ctrl.Caption = "&MrExcel Programs" Then
        cbWSMenuBar.Controls("MrExcel Programs").Delete
    End If
Next Ctrl
With muCustom
    .Caption = "&MrExcel Programs"
    With .Controls.Add(Type:=msoControlButton)
        .Caption = "&Import and Format"
        .OnAction = "ImportFormat"
    End With
    With .Controls.Add(Type:=msoControlButton)
        .Caption = "&Calculate Year End"
        .OnAction = "CalcYearEnd"
    End With
End With
End Sub
```

Workbook_BeforeSave(ByVal SaveAsUI As Boolean, Cancel As Boolean)

Workbook_BeforeSave occurs when the workbook is saved. SaveAsUI is set to True if the Save As dialog box is to be displayed. Cancel set to True prevents the workbook from being saved.

Workbook_BeforePrint(Cancel As Boolean)

Workbook_BeforePrint occurs when any print command is used, whether it is in the ribbon, keyboard, or macro. Cancel set to True prevents the workbook from being printed.

The following code tracks each time a sheet is printed. It logs the date, time, username, and the sheet printed in a hidden print log (see Figure 9.4):

```
Private Sub Workbook_BeforePrint(Cancel As Boolean)
Dim LastRow As Long
Dim PrintLog As Worksheet
Set PrintLog = Worksheets("PrintLog")
LastRow = PrintLog.Cells(PrintLog.Rows.Count, 1).End(xlUp).Row + 1
With PrintLog
    .Cells(LastRow, 1).Value = Now()
    .Cells(LastRow, 2).Value = Application.UserName
    .Cells(LastRow, 3).Value = ActiveSheet.Name
End With
End Sub
```

Figure 9.4
Use the BeforePrint event to keep a hidden print log in a workbook.

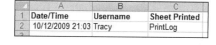

	A	B	C
1	Date/Time	Username	Sheet Printed
2	10/12/2009 21:03	Tracy	PrintLog

You also can use the BeforePrint event to add information to a header or footer before the sheet is printed. Although you can enter the file path into a header or footer through the Page Setup, before Office XP the only way to add the file path was with code. In legacy versions of Office, the following code was commonly used:

```
Private Sub Workbook_BeforePrint(Cancel As Boolean)
    ActiveSheet.PageSetup.RightFooter = ActiveWorkbook.FullName
End Sub
```

Workbook_BeforeClose(Cancel As Boolean)

Workbook_BeforeClose occurs when a workbook is closed. Cancel set to True prevents the workbook from closing.

If the Open event is used to create a custom menu, the BeforeClose event is used to delete it:

```
Private Sub Workbook_BeforeClose(Cancel As Boolean)
Dim cbWSMenuBar As CommandBar
On Error Resume Next
Set cbWSMenuBar = Application.CommandBars("Worksheet menu bar")
cbWSMenuBar.Controls("MrExcel Programs").Delete
End Sub
```

This is a nice little procedure, but there is one problem: If changes are made to the workbook and it isn't saved, Excel displays the Do You Want to Save? dialog box after the BeforeClose event has run. This means that if the user decides to cancel, the menu is now gone.

The solution is to create your own Save dialog in the event:

```
Private Sub Workbook_BeforeClose(Cancel As Boolean)
Dim Msg As String
Dim Response
Dim cbWSMenuBar As CommandBar
If Not ThisWorkbook.Saved Then
    Msg = "Do you want to save the changes you made to " & Me.Name & "?"
    Response = MsgBox(Msg, vbQuestion + vbYesNoCancel)
    Select Case Response
        Case vbYes
            ThisWorkbook.Save
        Case vbNo
            ThisWorkbook.Saved = True
        Case vbCancel
            Cancel = True
            Exit Sub
    End Select
End If
On Error Resume Next
Set cbWSMenuBar = Application.CommandBars("Worksheet menu bar")
cbWSMenuBar.Controls("MrExcel Programs").Delete
End Sub
```

Workbook_NewSheet(ByVal Sh As Object)

Workbook_NewSheet occurs when a new sheet is added to the active workbook. Sh is the new Worksheet or Chart Sheet object.

Workbook_WindowResize(ByVal Wn As Window)

Workbook_WindowResize occurs when the active workbook is resized. Wn is the window.

> **NOTE** Only resizing the active workbook window starts this event. Resizing the application window is an application-level event that is not affected by the workbook-level event.

This code disables the resizing of the active workbook:

```
Private Sub Workbook_WindowResize(ByVal Wn As Window)
Wn.EnableResize = False
End Sub
```

> **CAUTION** If you disable the capability to resize, the minimize and maximize buttons are removed, and the workbook cannot be resized. To undo this, type **ActiveWindow.EnableResize = True** in the Immediate window.

Workbook_WindowActivate(ByVal Wn As Window)

`Workbook_WindowActivate` occurs when any workbook window is activated. `Wn` is the window. Only activating the workbook window starts this event.

Workbook_WindowDeactivate(ByVal Wn As Window)

`Workbook_WindowDeactivate` occurs when any workbook window is deactivated. `Wn` is the window. Only deactivating the workbook window starts this event.

Workbook_AddInInstall()

`Workbook_AddInInstall` occurs when the workbook is installed as an add-in (by selecting the Microsoft Office button, Excel Options, Add-ins). Double-clicking an XLAM file (an add-in) to open it does not activate the event.

Workbook_AddInUninstall

`Workbook_AddInUninstall` occurs when the workbook (add-in) is uninstalled. The add-in is not automatically closed.

Workbook_Sync(ByVal SyncEventType As Office.MsoSyncEventType)

`Workbook_Sync` occurs when the local copy of a sheet in a workbook that is part of a Document Workspace is synchronized with the copy on the server. `SyncEventType` is the status of the synchronization.

Workbook_PivotTableCloseConnection(ByVal Target As PivotTable)

`Workbook_PivotTableCloseConnection` occurs when a pivot table report closes its connection to its data source. `Target` is the pivot table that has closed the connection.

Workbook_PivotTableOpenConnection(ByVal Target As PivotTable)

`Workbook_PivotTableOpenConnection` occurs when a pivot table report opens a connection to its data source. `Target` is pivot table that has opened the connection.

Workbook_RowsetComplete(ByVal Description As String, ByVal Sheet As String, ByVal Success As Boolean)

`Workbook_RowsetComplete` occurs when the user drills through a recordset or calls upon the rowset action on an OLAP PivotTable. `Description` is a description of the event; `Sheet` is the name of the sheet on which the recordset is created; `Success` indicates success or failure.

```
Workbook_BeforeXmlExport(ByVal Map As XmlMap, ByVal Url As
String, Cancel As Boolean)
```

Workbook_BeforeXmlExport occurs when XML data is exported or saved. Map is the map used to export or save the data; Url is the location of the XML file; Cancel set to True cancels the export operation.

```
Workbook_AfterXmlExport(ByVal Map As XmlMap, ByVal Url As String,
ByVal Result As XlXmlExportResult)
```

Workbook_AfterXmlExport occurs after XML data is exported or saved. Map is the map used to export or save the data; Url is the location of the XML file; Result indicates success or failure.

```
Workbook_BeforeXmlImport(ByVal Map As XmlMap, ByVal Url As
String, ByVal IsRefresh As Boolean, Cancel As Boolean)
```

Workbook_BeforeXmlImport occurs when XML data is imported or refreshed. Map is the map used to import the data; Url is the location of the XML file; IsRefresh returns True if the event was triggered by refreshing an existing connection and False if triggered by importing from a new data source; Cancel set to True cancels the import or refresh operation.

```
Workbook_AfterXmlImport(ByVal Map As XmlMap, ByVal IsRefresh As
Boolean, ByVal Result As XlXmlImportResult)
```

Workbook_AfterXmlImport occurs when XML data is exported or saved. Map is the map used to export or save the data; IsRefresh returns True if the event was triggered by refreshing an existing connection and False if triggered by importing from a new data source; Result indicates success or failure.

Workbook Level Sheet and Chart Events

The following are sheet and chart events available at the workbook level. These events affect all sheets in the workbook. Unless otherwise indicated, to affect a specific sheet, replace the text Workbook_Sheet with Worksheet_ or Chart_ to access the sheet or chart level event. For example, if the event is Workbook_SheetSelectionChange, the sheet level event is Worksheet_SelectChange. This does not apply to pivot table events.

Workbook_SheetActivate(ByVal Sh As Object)

Workbook_SheetActivate occurs when any chart sheet or worksheet in the workbook is activated. Sh is the active sheet.

Workbook_SheetBeforeDoubleClick (ByVal Sh As Object, ByVal Target As Range, Cancel As Boolean)

`Workbook_SheetBeforeDoubleClick` occurs when the user double-clicks any chart sheet or worksheet in the active workbook. `Sh` is the active sheet; `Target` is the object double-clicked; `Cancel` set to `True` prevents the default action from taking place.

Workbook_SheetBeforeRightClick(ByVal Sh As Object, ByVal Target As Range, Cancel As Boolean)

`Workbook_SheetBeforeRightClick` occurs when the user right-clicks any worksheet in the active workbook. `Sh` is the active worksheet; `Target` is the object right-clicked; `Cancel` set to `True` prevents the default action from taking place.

Workbook_SheetCalculate(ByVal Sh As Object)

`Workbook_SheetCalculate` occurs when any worksheet is recalculated or any updated data is plotted on a chart. `Sh` is the active sheet.

Workbook_SheetChange (ByVal Sh As Object, ByVal Target As Range)

`Workbook_SheetChange` occurs when any range in a worksheet is changed. `Sh` is the worksheet; `Target` is the changed range.

There is no Chart version of this event.

Workbook_SheetDeactivate (ByVal Sh As Object)

`Workbook_SheetDeactivate` occurs when any chart sheet or worksheet in the workbook is deactivated. `Sh` is the sheet being switched from.

Workbook_SheetFollowHyperlink (ByVal Sh As Object, ByVal Target As Hyperlink)

`Workbook_SheetFollowHyperlink` occurs when any hyperlink is clicked in Excel. `Sh` is the active worksheet; `Target` is the hyperlink.

There is no Chart version of this event.

Workbook_SheetSelectionChange(ByVal Sh As Object, ByVal Target As Range)

`Workbook_SheetSelectionChange` occurs when a new range is selected on any sheet. `Sh` is the active sheet; `Target` is the affected range.

There is no Chart version of this event.

Workbook_SheetPivotTableUpdate(ByVal Sh As Object, ByVal Target As PivotTable)

`Workbook_SheetPivotTableUpdate` occurs when a pivot table is updated. `Sh` is the active sheet; `Target` is the updated pivot table.

Worksheet Events

The following event procedures are available at the worksheet level.

Worksheet_Activate()

Worksheet_Activate occurs when the sheet on which the event is located becomes the active sheet.

Worksheet_Deactivate()

Worksheet_Deactivate occurs when another sheet becomes the active sheet.

> **NOTE**
> If a Deactivate event is on the active sheet and you switch to a sheet with an Activate event, the Deactivate event runs first, followed by the Activate event.

Worksheet_BeforeDoubleClick(ByVal Target As Range, Cancel As Boolean)

Worksheet_BeforeDoubleClick allows control over what happens when the user double-clicks the sheet. Target is the selected range on the sheet; Cancel is set to False by default, but if set to True, it prevents the default action, such as entering a cell, from happening.

The following code prevents the user from entering a cell with a double-click. In addition, if the formula field is hidden, this code does not allow the user to enter information in the traditional way:

```
Private Sub Worksheet_BeforeDoubleClick(ByVal Target As Range, _
    Cancel As Boolean)
Cancel = True
End Sub
```

> **NOTE**
> The preceding code does not prevent the user from double-clicking to size a row or column.

Preventing the double-click from entering a cell allows it to be used for something else such as highlighting a cell. The following code changes a cell's interior color to red when it is double-clicked:

```
Private Sub Worksheet_BeforeDoubleClick(ByVal Target As Range, _
    Cancel As Boolean)
Dim myColor As Integer
Target.Interior.ColorIndex = 3
End Sub
```

Worksheet_BeforeRightClick(ByVal Target As Range, Cancel As Boolean)

`Worksheet_BeforeRightClick` is triggered when the user right-clicks a range. `Target` is the object right-clicked; `Cancel` set to `True` prevents the default action from taking place.

Worksheet_Calculate()

`Worksheet_Calculate` occurs after a sheet is recalculated.

The following example compares a month's profits between the previous and current year. If profit has fallen, a red down arrow appears below the month; if profit has risen, a green up arrow appears (see Figure 9.5):

```
Private Sub Worksheet_Calculate()
Select Case Range("C3").Value
    Case Is < Range("C4").Value
        SetArrow 10, msoShapeDownArrow
    Case Is > Range("C4").Value
        SetArrow 3, msoShapeUpArrow
End Select
End Sub

Private Sub SetArrow(ByVal ArrowColor As Integer, ByVal ArrowDegree)
' The following code is added to remove the prior shapes
For Each sh In ActiveSheet.Shapes
    If sh.Name Like "*Arrow*" Then
        sh.Delete
    End If
Next sh
ActiveSheet.Shapes.AddShape(ArrowDegree, 22, 40, 5, 10).Select
With Selection.ShapeRange
    With .Fill
        .Visible = msoTrue
        .Solid
        .ForeColor.SchemeColor = ArrowColor
        .Transparency = 0#
    End With
    With .Line
        .Weight = 0.75
        .DashStyle = msoLineSolid
        .Style = msoLineSingle
        .Transparency = 0#
        .Visible = msoTrue
        .ForeColor.SchemeColor = 64
        .BackColor.RGB = RGB(255, 255, 255)
    End With
End With
Range("A3").Select 'Place the selection back on the dropdown
End Sub
```

9

Figure 9.5
Use the Calculate event to add graphics that emphasize the change in profits.

	A	B	C
1		2008 vs 2009 Profit	
2			
3	June	Current	3307
4	⇑	Previous	1383
5			
6			
7	Month	2008	2009
8	January	4000	7258
9	February	9704	3459
10	March	3950	3874
11	April	7518	3907
12	May	4542	9774
13	June	1383	3307
14	July	2888	4741
15	August	8493	8232
16	September	642	9775
17	October	5308	2090
18	November	6040	7490
19	December	6845	6845
20			

Worksheet_Change(ByVal Target As Range)

`Worksheet_Change` is triggered by a change to a cell's value such as when text is entered, edited, or deleted. `Target` is the cell that has been changed.

> **NOTE**
> The event can also be triggered by pasting values. Recalculation of a value does not trigger the event. Therefore, the `Calculation` event should be used instead.

Worksheet_SelectionChange(ByVal Target As Range)

`Worksheet_SelectionChange` occurs when a new range is selected. `Target` is the newly selected range.

The following example helps identify a single selected cell by highlighting the row and column:

> **CAUTION**
> This example makes use of conditional formatting and overwrites any existing conditional formatting on the sheet. The code may also clear the clipboard, which makes it difficult to copy and paste on the sheet.

```
Private Sub Worksheet_SelectionChange(ByVal Target As Range)
Dim iColor As Integer
On Error Resume Next
iColor = Target.Interior.ColorIndex
If iColor < 0 Then
    iColor = 36
Else
```

```
        iColor = iColor + 1
    End If
    If iColor = Target.Font.ColorIndex Then iColor = iColor + 1
    Cells.FormatConditions.Delete
    With Range("A" & Target.Row, Target.Address)
        .FormatConditions.Add Type:=2, Formula1:="TRUE"
        .FormatConditions(1).Interior.ColorIndex = iColor
    End With
    With Range(Target.Offset(1 - Target.Row, 0).Address & ":" & _
        Target.Offset(-1, 0).Address)
        .FormatConditions.Add Type:=2, Formula1:="TRUE"
        .FormatConditions(1).Interior.ColorIndex = iColor
    End With
    End Sub
```

Worksheet_FollowHyperlink(ByVal Target As Hyperlink)

Worksheet_FollowHyperlink occurs when a hyperlink is clicked. Target is the hyperlink.

CASE STUDY: QUICKLY ENTERING MILITARY TIME INTO A CELL

You're entering arrival and departure times and want the times to be formatted with a 24-hour clock, which is also known as *military time.* You have tried formatting the cell, but no matter how you enter the times, they are displayed in the 0:00 hours and minutes format.

The only way to get the time to appear as military time such as 23:45, is to have the time entered in the cell in this manner. Because typing the colon is time-consuming, it would be more efficient to enter the numbers and let Excel format it for you.

The solution is to use a Change event to take what is in the cell and insert the colon for you:

```
Private Sub Worksheet_Change(ByVal Target As Range)
Dim ThisColumn As Integer
Dim UserInput As String, NewInput As String
ThisColumn = Target.Column
If ThisColumn < 3 Then
    If Target.Count > 1 Then Exit Sub 'check that only 1 cell is selected
    UserInput = Target.Value
    If UserInput > 1 Then
        NewInput = Left(UserInput, Len(UserInput) - 2) & ":" & _
        Right(UserInput, 2)
        Application.EnableEvents = False
        Target = NewInput
        Application.EnableEvents = True
    End If
End If
End Sub
```

An entry of 2345 will display as 23:45. Note that the code limits this format change to Columns A and B (If ThisColumn < 3). Without this limitation, entering numbers anywhere on a sheet such as in a totals column would force it to be reformatted.

> TIP
>
> Use `Application.EnableEvents` = `False` to prevent the procedure from calling itself when the value in the target is updated.

Worksheet_PivotTableUpdate(ByVal Target As PivotTable)

`Worksheet_PivotTableUpdate` occurs when a pivot table is updated. `Target` is the updated pivot table.

Chart Sheet Events

Chart events occur when a chart is changed or activated. Embedded charts require the use of class modules to access the events. For more information about class modules, see Chapter 22, "Creating Classes, Records, and Collections."

Embedded Charts

Because embedded charts do not create chart sheets, the chart events are not as readily available. However, you can make them available by adding a class module, as follows:

1. Insert a class module.

2. Rename the module to `cl_ChartEvents`.

3. Enter the following line of code in the class module:

   ```
   Public WithEvents myChartClass As Chart
   ```
   The chart events are now available to the chart, as shown in Figure 9.6. They are accessed in the class module rather than on a chart sheet.

4. Insert a standard module.

5. Enter the following lines of code in a standard module:

   ```
   Dim myClassModule As New cl_ChartEvents
   Sub InitializeChart()
       Set myClassModule.myChartClass = _
           Worksheets(1).ChartObjects(1).Chart
   End Sub
   ```

These lines initialize the embedded chart to be recognized as a Chart object. The procedure must be run once per session.

> TIP
>
> `Workbook_Open` can be used to automate this procedure.

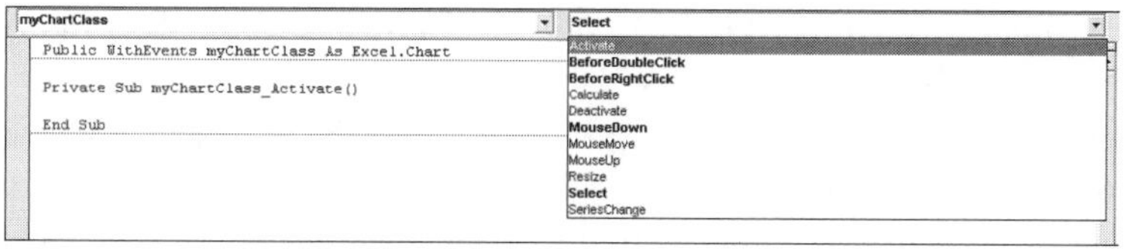

Figure 9.6
Embedded chart events are now available in the class module.

Chart_Activate()

Chart_Activate occurs when a chart sheet is activated or changed.

Chart_BeforeDoubleClick(ByVal ElementID As Long, ByVal Arg1 As Long, ByVal Arg2 As Long, Cancel As Boolean)

Chart_BeforeDoubleClick occurs when any part of a chart is double-clicked. ElementID is the part of the chart that is double-clicked, such as the legend. Arg1 and Arg2 are dependent upon the ElementID; Cancel set to True prevents the default double-click action from occurring.

The following sample hides the legend when it is double-clicked, while double-clicking either axis brings back the legend:

```
Private Sub MyChartClass_BeforeDoubleClick(ByVal ElementID As Long, _
    ByVal Arg1 As Long, ByVal Arg2 As Long, Cancel As Boolean)
Select Case ElementID
    Case xlLegend
        Me.HasLegend = False
        Cancel = True
    Case xlAxis
        Me.HasLegend = True
        Cancel = True
End Select
End Sub
```

Chart_BeforeRightClick(Cancel As Boolean)

Chart_BeforeRightClick occurs when a chart is right-clicked. Cancel set to True prevents the default right-click action from occurring.

Chart_Calculate()

Chart_Calculate occurs when a chart's data is changed.

Chart_Deactivate()

Chart_Deactivate occurs when another sheet becomes the active sheet.

Chart_MouseDown(ByVal Button As Long, ByVal Shift As Long, ByVal x As Long, ByVal y As Long)

Chart_MouseDown occurs when the cursor is over the chart and any mouse button is pressed. Button is the mouse button that was clicked; Shift is whether a Shift, Ctrl, or Alt key was pressed; X is the X coordinate of the cursor when the button is pressed; Y is the Y coordinate of the cursor when the button is pressed.

The following code zooms in on a left mouse click and zooms out on a right mouse click. Use the Cancel argument in the BeforeRightClick event to handle the menus that appear when you right-click a chart.

```
Private Sub MyChartClass_MouseDown(ByVal Button As Long, ByVal Shift _
    As Long, ByVal x As Long, ByVal y As Long)
If Button = 1 Then
    ActiveChart.Axes(xlValue).MaximumScale = _
    ActiveChart.Axes(xlValue).MaximumScale - 50
End If
If Button = 2 Then
    ActiveChart.Axes(xlValue).MaximumScale = _
    ActiveChart.Axes(xlValue).MaximumScale + 50
End If
End Sub
```

Chart_MouseMove(ByVal Button As Long, ByVal Shift As Long, ByVal x As Long, ByVal y As Long)

Chart_MouseMove occurs as the cursor is moved over a chart. Button is the mouse button being held down, if any; Shift is whether a Shift, Ctrl, or Alt key was pressed; X is the X coordinate of the cursor on the chart; Y is the Y coordinate of the cursor on the chart.

Chart_MouseUp(ByVal Button As Long, ByVal Shift As Long, ByVal x As Long, ByVal y As Long)

Chart_MouseUp occurs when any mouse button is released while the cursor is on the chart. Button is the mouse button that was clicked; Shift is whether a Shift, Ctrl, or Alt key was pressed; X is the X coordinate of the cursor when the button is released; Y is the Y coordinate of the cursor when the button is released.

Chart_Resize()

Chart_Resize occurs when a chart is resized using the sizing handles. However, this does not occur when the size is changed using the size control on the Format tab of the chart tools.

Chart_Select(ByVal ElementID As Long, ByVal Arg1 As Long, ByVal Arg2 As Long)

Chart_Select occurs when a chart element is selected. ElementID is the part of the chart selected such as the legend. Arg1 and Arg2 are dependent upon the ElementID.

The following code highlights the data set when a point on the chart is selected—assuming the series starts in A1 and each row is a point to plot—as shown in Figure 9.7:

```
Private Sub MyChartClass_Select(ByVal ElementID As Long, ByVal Arg1 _
        As Long, ByVal Arg2 As Long)
If Arg1 = 0 Then Exit Sub
Sheets("Sheet1").Cells.Interior.ColorIndex = xlNone
    If ElementID = 3 Then
        If Arg2 = -1 Then
            ' Selected the entire series in Arg1
            Sheets("Sheet1").Range("A2:A22").Offset(0, Arg1).Interior.ColorIndex _
            = 19
        Else
            ' Selected a single point in range Arg1, Point Arg2
            Sheets("Sheet1").Range("A1").Offset(Arg2, Arg1).Interior.ColorIndex _
            = 19
        End If
    End If
End Sub
```

Figure 9.7
Use the Chart_ Select event to highlight the data used to create a point on the chart.

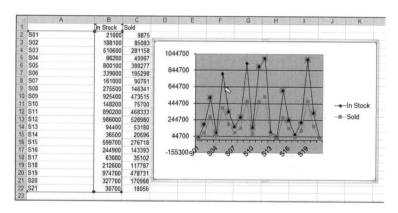

Chart_SeriesChange(ByVal SeriesIndex As Long, ByVal PointIndex As Long)

Chart_SeriesChange occurs when a chart data point is updated. SeriesIndex is the offset in the Series collection of updated series; PointIndex is the offset in the Point collection of updated point.

Chart_DragOver()

Chart_DragOver occurs when a range is dragged over to a chart. This event no longer works in Excel 2007 or Excel 2010. However, a program using it will compile for use in legacy versions of Excel.

Chart_DragPlot()

Chart_DragPlot occurs when a range is dragged and dropped on a chart. This event no longer works in Excel 2007 or Excel 2010. However, a program using it will compile for use in legacy versions of Excel.

Application-Level Events

Application-level events affect all open workbooks in an Excel session. They require a class module to access them. This is similar to the class module used to access events for embedded chart events. Follow these steps to create the class module:

1. Insert a class module.

2. Rename the module `cl_AppEvents`.

3. Enter the following line of code in the class module:

```
Public WithEvents AppEvent As Application
```

The application events are now available to the workbook as shown in Figure 9.8. They are accessed in the class module rather than in a standard module.

4. Insert a standard module.

5. Enter the following lines of code in the standard module:

```
Dim myAppEvent As New cl_AppEvents
Sub InitializeAppEvent()
    Set myAppEvent.AppEvent = Application
End Sub
```

These lines initialize the application to recognize application events. The procedure must be run once per session.

> **TIP**
>
> `Workbook_Open` can be used to automate the procedure to run the event once per session.

Figure 9.8
Application events are now available through the class module.

> **NOTE**
>
> The object in front of the event such as `AppEvent` is dependent on the name given in the class module.

AppEvent_AfterCalculate()

`AppEvent_AfterCalculate` occurs after all calculations are complete and there aren't any outstanding queries or incomplete calculations.

> **NOTE**
> This event occurs after all other `Calculation`, `AfterRefresh`, and `SheetChange` events and after `Application.CalculationState` is set to `xlDone`.

AppEvent_NewWorkbook(ByVal Wb As Workbook)

`AppEvent_NewWorkbook` occurs when a new workbook is created. `Wb` is the new workbook. The following code arranges the open workbooks in a tiled configuration:

```
Private Sub AppEvent_NewWorkbook(ByVal Wb As Workbook)
    Application.Windows.Arrange xlArrangeStyleTiled
End Sub
```

AppEvent_ProtectedViewWindowActivate(ByVal Pvw As ProtectedViewWindow)

`ProtectedViewWindowActivate` occurs when a workbook in Protected View mode is activated. `PVW` is the workbook being activated.

AppEvent_ProtectedViewWindowBeforeClose(ByVal Pvw As ProtectedViewWindow, ByVal Reason As XlProtectedViewCloseReason, Cancel As Boolean)

`ProtectedViewWindowBeforeClose` occurs when a workbook in Protected View mode is closed. `PVW` is the workbook being deactivated; `Reason` is why the workbook closed; `Cancel` set to `True` prevents the workbook from closing.

AppEvent_ProtectedViewWindowDeactivate(ByVal Pvw As ProtectedViewWindow)

`ProtectedViewWindowDeactivate` occurs when a workbook in Protected View mode is deactivated. `PVW` is the workbook being deactivated.

AppEvent_ProtectedViewWindowOpen(ByVal Pvw As ProtectedViewWindow)

`ProtectedViewWindowOpen` occurs when a workbook is open in Protected View mode. `PVW` is the workbook being opened.

AppEvent_ProtectedViewWindowResize(ByVal Pvw As ProtectedViewWindow)

`ProtectedViewWindowResize` occurs when the window of the protected workbook is resized. However, this does not occur in the application itself. `PVW` is the workbook being resized.

AppEvent_SheetActivate (ByVal Sh As Object)

`AppEvent_SheetActivate` occurs when a sheet is activated. `Sh` is the worksheet or chart sheet.

9

9

AppEvent_SheetBeforeDoubleClick(ByVal Sh As Object, ByVal Target As Range, Cancel As Boolean)

AppEvent_SheetBeforeDoubleClick occurs when the user double-clicks a worksheet. Target is the selected range on the sheet; Cancel is set to False by default. However, when set to True, it prevents the default action such as entering a cell from happening.

AppEvent_SheetBeforeRightClick(ByVal Sh As Object, ByVal Target As Range, Cancel As Boolean)

AppEvent_SheetBeforeRightClick occurs when the user right-clicks any worksheet. Sh is the active worksheet; Target is the object right-clicked; Cancel set to True prevents the default action from taking place.

AppEvent_SheetCalculate(ByVal Sh As Object)

AppEvent_SheetCalculate occurs when any worksheet is recalculated or any updated data is plotted on a chart. Sh is the active sheet.

AppEvent_SheetChange(ByVal Sh As Object, ByVal Target As Range)

AppEvent_SheetChange occurs when the value of any cell is changed. Sh is the worksheet; Target is the changed range.

AppEvent_SheetDeactivate(ByVal Sh As Object)

AppEvent_SheetDeactivate occurs when any chart sheet or worksheet in a workbook is deactivated. Sh is the sheet being deactivated.

AppEvent_SheetFollowHyperlink(ByVal Sh As Object, ByVal Target As Hyperlink)

AppEvent_SheetFollowHyperlink occurs when any hyperlink is clicked in Excel. Sh is the active worksheet; Target is the hyperlink.

AppEvent_SheetSelectionChange(ByVal Sh As Object, ByVal Target As Range)

AppEvent_SheetSelectionChange occurs when a new range is selected on any sheet. Sh is the active sheet; Target is the selected range.

AppEvent_SheetPivotTableUpdate(ByVal Sh As Object, ByVal Target As PivotTable)

AppEvent_SheetPivotTableUpdate occurs when a pivot table is updated. Sh is the active sheet; Target is the updated pivot table.

AppEvent_WindowActivate(ByVal Wb As Workbook, ByVal Wn As Window)

AppEvent_WindowActivate occurs when any workbook window is activated. Wb is the workbook being deactivated; Wn is the window. Works only if there are multiple windows.

AppEvent_WindowDeactivate(ByVal Wb As Workbook, ByVal Wn As Window)

AppEvent_WindowDeactivate occurs when any workbook window is deactivated. Wb is the active workbook; Wn is the window. Works only if there are multiple windows.

AppEvent_WindowResize(ByVal Wb As Workbook, ByVal Wn As Window)

AppEvent_WindowResize occurs when the active workbook is resized. Wb is the active workbook; Wn is the window. Works only if there are multiple windows.

> **CAUTION**
>
> If you disable the capability to resize (EnableResize = False), the minimize and maximize buttons are removed, and the workbook cannot be resized. To undo this, type ActiveWindow. EnableResize = True in the Immediate window.

AppEvent_WorkbookActivate(ByVal Wb As Workbook)

AppEvent_WorkbookActivate occurs when any workbook is activated. Wn is the window. The following sample maximizes any workbook when it is activated:

```
Private Sub AppEvent_WorkbookActivate(ByVal Wb as Workbook)
    Wb.WindowState = xlMaximized
End Sub
```

AppEvent_WorkbookAddinInstall(ByVal Wb As Workbook)

AppEvent_WorkbookAddinInstall occurs when a workbook is installed as an add-in (File, Options, Add-ins). Double-clicking an XLAM file to open it does not activate the event. Wb is the workbook being installed.

AppEvent_WorkbookAddinUninstall(ByVal Wb As Workbook)

AppEvent_WorkbookAddinUninstall occurs when a workbook (add-in) is uninstalled. The add-in is not automatically closed. Wb is the workbook being uninstalled.

AppEvent_WorkbookBeforeClose(ByVal Wb As Workbook, Cancel As Boolean)

AppEvent_WorkbookBeforeClose occurs when a workbook closes. Wb is the workbook; Cancel set to True prevents the workbook from closing.

AppEvent_WorkbookBeforePrint(ByVal Wb As Workbook, Cancel As Boolean)

AppEvent_WorkbookBeforePrint occurs when any print command is used (via the ribbon, keyboard, or a macro). Wb is the workbook; Cancel set to True prevents the workbook from being printed.

The following code places the username in the footer of the active sheet printed:

```
Private Sub AppEvent_WorkbookBeforePrint(ByVal Wb As Workbook, _
    Cancel As Boolean)
Wb.ActiveSheet.PageSetup.LeftFooter = Application.UserName
End Sub
```

AppEvent_WorkbookBeforeSave(ByVal Wb As Workbook, ByVal SaveAsUI As Boolean, Cancel As Boolean)

AppEvent_Workbook_BeforeSave occurs when the workbook is saved. Wb is the workbook; SaveAsUI is set to True if the Save As dialog box is to be displayed; Cancel set to True prevents the workbook from being saved.

AppEvent_WorkbookNewSheet(ByVal Wb As Workbook, ByVal Sh As Object)

AppEvent_WorkbookNewSheet occurs when a new sheet is added to the active workbook. Wb is the workbook; Sh is the new worksheet or chart sheet object.

AppEvent_WorkbookOpen(ByVal Wb As Workbook)

AppEvent_WorkbookOpen occurs when a workbook is opened. Wb is the workbook that was just opened.

AppEvent_WorkbookPivotTableCloseConnection(ByVal Wb As Workbook, ByVal Target As PivotTable)

AppEvent_PivotTableCloseConnection occurs when a pivot table report closes its connection to its data source. Wb is the workbook containing the pivot table that triggered the event; Target is pivot table that has closed the connection.

AppEvent_WorkbookPivotTableOpenConnection(ByVal Wb As Workbook, ByVal Target As PivotTable)

AppEvent_PivotTableOpenConnection occurs when a pivot table report opens a connection to its data source. Wb is the workbook containing the pivot table that triggered the event; Target is the pivot table that has opened the connection.

AppEvent_WorkbookRowsetComplete(ByVal Wb As Workbook, ByVal Description As String, ByVal Sheet As String, ByVal Success As Boolean)

AppEvent_RowsetComplete occurs when the user drills through a recordset or calls upon the rowset action on an OLAP pivot table. Wb is the workbook that triggered the event; Description is a description of the event; Sheet is the name of the sheet on which the recordset is created; Success indicates success or failure.

AppEvent_WorkbookSync(ByVal Wb As Workbook, ByVal SyncEventType As Office.MsoSyncEventType)

AppEvent_Workbook_Sync occurs when the local copy of a sheet in a workbook that is part of a Document Workspace is synchronized with the copy on the server. Wb is the workbook that triggered the event; SyncEventType is the status of the synchronization.

AppEvent_WorkbookBeforeXmlExport(ByVal Wb As Workbook, ByVal Map As XmlMap, ByVal Url As String, Cancel As Boolean)

AppEvent_WorkbookBeforeXmlExport occurs when XML data is exported or saved. Wb is the workbook that triggered the event; Map is the map used to export or save the data; Url is the location of the XML file; Cancel set to True cancels the export operation.

AppEvent_WorkbookAfterXmlExport(ByVal Wb As Workbook, ByVal Map As XmlMap, ByVal Url As String, ByVal Result As XlXmlExportResult)

AppEvent_WorkbookAfterXmlExport occurs after XML data is exported or saved. Wb is the workbook that triggered the event; Map is the map used to export or save the data; Url is the location of the XML file; Result indicates success or failure.

AppEvent_WorkbookBeforeXmlImport(ByVal Wb As Workbook, ByVal Map As XmlMap, ByVal Url As String, ByVal IsRefresh As Boolean, Cancel As Boolean)

AppEvent_WorkbookBeforeXmlImport occurs when XML data is imported or refreshed. Wb is the workbook that triggered the event; Map is the map used to import the data; Url is the location of the XML file; IsRefresh returns True if the event was triggered by refreshing an existing connection and False if triggered by importing from a new data source; Cancel set to True cancels the import or refresh operation.

AppEvent_WorkbookAfterXmlImport(ByVal Wb As Workbook, ByVal Map As XmlMap, ByVal IsRefresh As Boolean, ByVal Result As XlXmlImportResult)

AppEvent_WorkbookAfterXmlImport occurs when XML data is exported or saved. Wb is the workbook that triggered the event; Map is the map used to export or save the data; IsRefresh returns True if the event was triggered by refreshing an existing connection and False if triggered by importing from a new data source; Result indicates success or failure.

Next Steps

In this chapter, you learned more about interfacing with Excel. Chapter 10 introduces you to tools you can use to interact with users. You learn how to prompt users for information to use in your code, warn them of illegal actions, or provide them with an interface to work with other than the spreadsheet.

9

Userforms: An Introduction

User Interaction Methods

Userforms enable you to display information and allow the user to input information. `InputBox` and `MsgBox` controls are simple ways of doing this. You can use the userform controls in the VB Editor to create forms that are more complex.

This chapter covers simple user interfaces using input boxes and message boxes and the basics of creating userforms in the VB Editor.

→ To learn more about advanced userform programming, **see** Chapter 23, "Advanced Userform Techniques."

Input Boxes

The `InputBox` function is used to create a basic interface element that requests input from the user before the program can continue. You can configure the prompt, the title for the window, a default value, the window position, and user help files. The only two buttons provided are the OK and Cancel buttons. The returned value is a string.

10

IN THIS CHAPTER

User Interaction Methods 183

Creating a Userform 184

Calling and Hiding a Userform 186

Programming the Userform 186

Programming Controls 188

Using Basic Form Controls 189

Verifying Field Entry 200

Illegal Window Closing 200

Getting a Filename 201

The following code asks the user for the number of months to be averaged. Figure 10.1 shows the resulting InputBox.

```
AveMos = InputBox(Prompt:="Enter the number " & _
" of months to average", Title:="Enter Months", _
Default:="3")
```

Figure 10.1
A simple but effective input box.

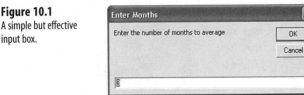

Message Boxes

The MsgBox function creates a message box that displays information and waits for the user to click a button before continuing. Whereas InputBox only has OK and Cancel buttons, the MsgBox function allows you to choose from several configurations of buttons, including Yes, No, OK, and Cancel. You can also configure the prompt, the window title, and help files. The following code produces a prompt to find out whether the user wants to continue. A Select Case statement is then used to continue the program with the appropriate action. Figure 10.2 shows the resulting customized message box.

```
myTitle = "Sample Message"
MyMsg = "Do you want to Continue?"
Response = MsgBox(myMsg, vbExclamation + vbYesNoCancel, myTitle)
Select Case Response
    Case Is = vbYes
        ActiveWorkbook.Close SaveChanges:=False
```

Figure 10.2
The MsgBox function is used to display information and obtain a basic response from the user.

```
    Case Is = vbNo
        ActiveWorkbook.Close SaveChanges:=True
    Case Is = vbCancel
        Exit Sub
End Select
```

Creating a Userform

Userforms combine the capabilities of InputBox and MsgBox to create a more efficient way of interacting with the user. For example, rather than have the user fill out personal information on a sheet, you can create a userform that prompts for the required data (see Figure 10.3).

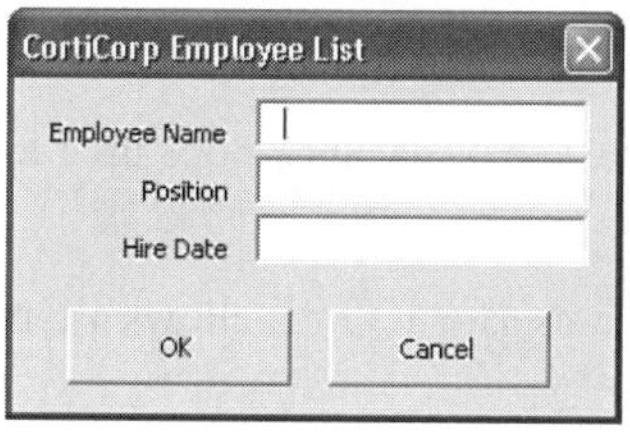

Figure 10.3
Create a custom userform to get more information from the user.

Insert a userform in the VB Editor by selecting Insert, UserForm from the main menu. When a UserForm module is added to the Project Explorer, a blank form appears in the window where your code usually is, and the Controls toolbox appears.

You can resize the form by grabbing and dragging the handles on the right side, bottom edge, or lower-right corner of the userform. To add controls to the form, click the desired control in the toolbox and draw it on the form. Controls can be moved and resized at any time.

> **NOTE**
> By default, the toolbox displays the most common controls. To access more controls, right-click the toolbox and select Additional Controls. However, be careful; other users may not have the same additional controls as you do. If you send these users a form with a control they do not have installed, the program will generate an error.

After a control is added to a form, its properties can be changed from the Properties window. These properties can be set manually now or set later programmatically. If the Properties window is not visible, you can bring it up by selecting View, Properties Window. Figure 10.4 shows the Properties window for a text box.

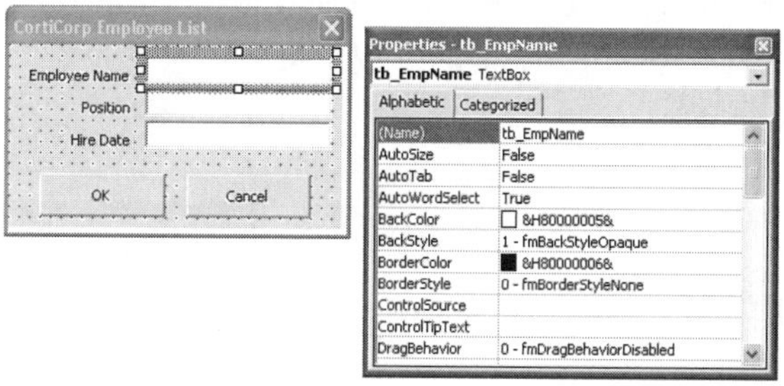

Figure 10.4
Use the Properties window to change the properties of a control.

Calling and Hiding a Userform

A userform can be called from any module. `FormName.Show` pops up a form for the user:

```
frm_AddEmp.Show
```

The `Load` method can also be used to call a userform. This allows a form to be loaded but remain hidden:

```
Load frm_AddEmp
```

To hide a userform, use the `Hide` method. The form is still active but hidden from the user. However, the controls on the form can still be accessed programmatically:

```
Frm_AddEmp.Hide
```

The `Unload` method unloads the form from memory and removes it from the user's view, which means the form cannot be accessed by the user or programmatically:

```
Unload Me
```

> **TIP**
>
> Me is a keyword that can be used to refer to the userform itself. It can be used in the code of any control to refer to itself.

Programming the Userform

The code for a control goes in the Forms module. Unlike the other modules, double-clicking the Forms module opens up the form in Design view. To view the code, you can right-click either the module or the userform in Design mode and select View Code.

Userform Events

Just like a worksheet, a userform has events triggered by actions. After the userform has been added to the project, the events are available in the Properties drop-down list at the top-right of the code window (see Figure 10.5) by selecting UserForm from the Objects drop-down on the left.

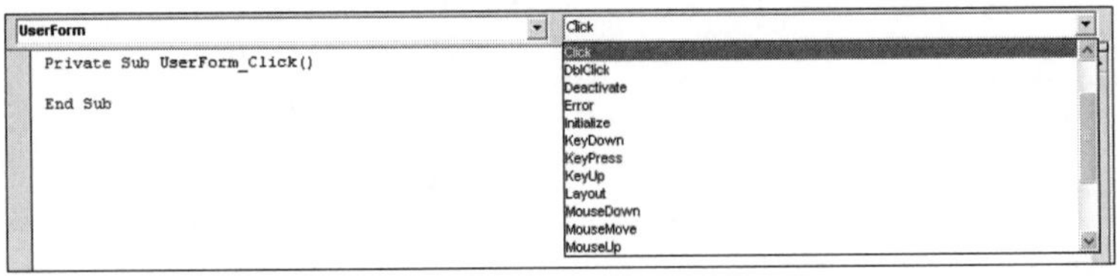

Figure 10.5
Various events for the userform can be selected from the drop-down list at the top of the code window.

The available events for userforms are described in Table 10.1.

Table 10.1   The Events for Userforms

Event	Description
Activate	Occurs when a userform is shown either from being loaded or unhidden. This event is triggered after the Initialize event.
AddControl	Occurs when a control is added to a userform at runtime. Does not run at design time or upon userform initialization.
BeforeDragOver	Occurs while the user does a drag and drop onto the userform.
BeforeDroporPaste	Occurs right before the user is about to drop or paste data into the userform.
Click	Occurs when the user clicks the userform with the mouse.
DblClick	Occurs when the user double-clicks the userform with the mouse. If a click event is also in use, the double-click event will not work.
Deactivate	Occurs when a userform is deactivated.
Error	Occurs when the userform runs into an error and cannot return the error information.
Initialize	Occurs when the userform is first loaded, before the Activate event. If you hide then show a form, Initialize will not trigger.
KeyDown	Occurs when the user presses a key on the keyboard.
KeyPress	Occurs when the user presses an ANSI key. An ANSI key is a typeable character such as the letter *A*. An example of a nontypeable character is the Tab key.
KeyUp	Occurs when the user releases a key on the keyboard.
Layout	Occurs when the control changes size.
MouseDown	Occurs when the user presses the mouse button within the borders of the userform.
MouseMove	Occurs when the user moves the mouse within the borders of the userform.
MouseUp	Occurs when the user releases the mouse button within the borders of the userform.
QueryClose	Occurs before a userform closes. It allows you to recognize the method used to close a form and have code respond accordingly.
RemoveControl	Occurs when a control is deleted from within the userform.
Resize	Occurs when the userform is resized.
Scroll	Occurs when a visible scrollbar box is repositioned.
Terminate	Occurs after the userform has been unloaded. This is triggered after QueryClose.
Zoom	Occurs when the zoom value is changed.

10

Programming Controls

To program a control, highlight the control and select View, Code. The footer, header, and default action for the control is entered in the programming field automatically. To see the other actions that are available for a control, select the control from the Object drop-down and view the actions in the Properties drop-down, as shown in Figure 10.6.

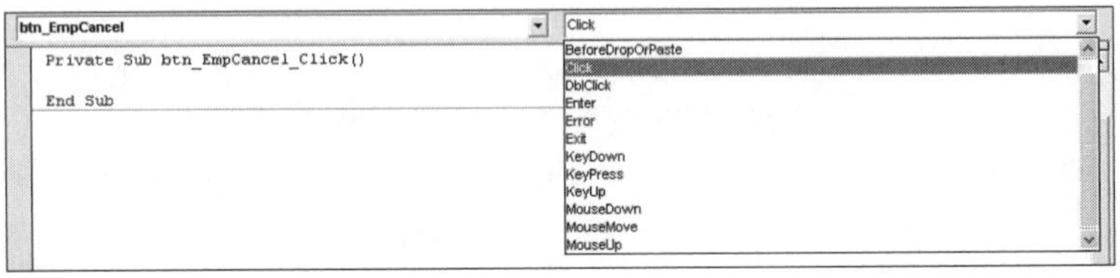

Figure 10.6

Various actions for a control can be selected from the VB Editor drop-downs.

The controls are objects, like `ActiveWorkbook`. They have properties and methods, dependent on the type of control. Most of the programming for the controls is done behind the form. However, if another module needs to refer to a control, the parent, which is the form, needs to be included with the object. Here's how this is done:

```
Private Sub btn_EmpCancel_Click()
Unload Me
End Sub
```

The preceding code can be broken down into three sections:

- `btn_EmpCancel`—Name given to the control
- `Click`—Action of the control
- `Unload Me`—The code behind the control, which, in this case, is unloading the form)

> **TIP**
>
> Change the (Name) property in the control's Properties window to rename a control from the default assigned by the editor.

CASE STUDY: BUG FIX WHEN ADDING CONTROLS TO AN EXISTING FORM

If you have been using a userform for some time and later try to add a new control, you might find that Excel seems to get confused about the control. You will see that the control is added to the form, but when you right-click the control and select View Code, the code module does not seem to acknowledge that the control exists. The control name will not be available in the left drop-down at the top of the code module.

To work around this situation, follow these steps:

1. Add all the controls you need to add to the existing userform.
2. In the Project Explorer, right-click the userform and select Export File. Select Save to save the file in the default location.
3. In the Project Explorer, right-click the userform and select Remove. Because you just exported the userform, click No to the question about exporting.
4. Right-click anywhere in the Project Explorer and select Import File. Select the filename that you saved in step 2.

The new controls will now be available in the code pane of the userform.

Using Basic Form Controls

Each control has different events associated with it, which allows you to code what happens based on the user's actions. A table reviewing the control events is available at the end of each of the sections that follow.

Using Labels, Text Boxes, and Command Buttons

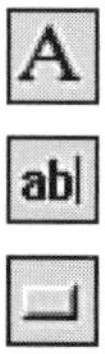

The basic form shown in Figure 10.7 consists of labels, text boxes, and command buttons. It is a simple yet effective method of requesting information from the user. After the text boxes have been filled in, the user clicks OK, and the information is added to a sheet (see Figure 10.8).

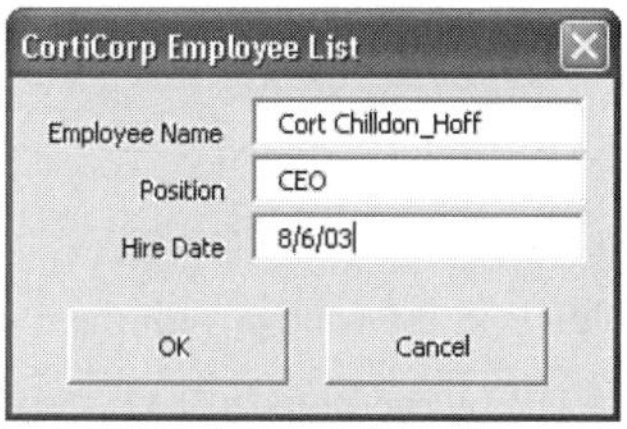

Figure 10.7
A simple form to collect information from the user.

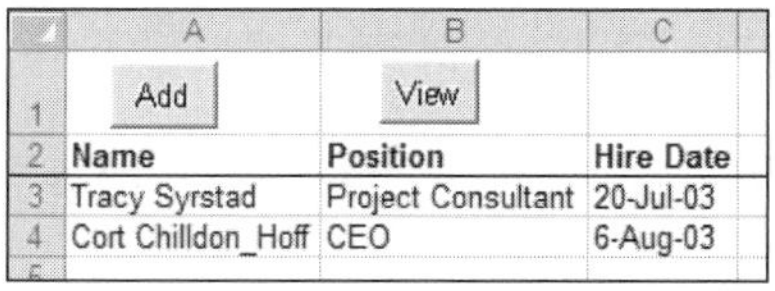

	A	B	C
1	Add	View	
2	Name	Position	Hire Date
3	Tracy Syrstad	Project Consultant	20-Jul-03
4	Cort Chilldon_Hoff	CEO	6-Aug-03

Figure 10.8
The information is added to the sheet.

```
Private Sub btn_EmpOK_Click()
Dim LastRow As Long
LastRow = Worksheets("Employee").Cells(Worksheets("Employee").Rows.Count, 1) _
.End(xlUp).Row + 1
Cells(LastRow, 1).Value = tb_EmpName.Value
Cells(LastRow, 2).Value = tb_EmpPosition.Value
Cells(LastRow, 3).Value = tb_EmpHireDate.Value
End Sub
```

With a change in the code shown in the following sample, the same form design can be used
to retrieve information. The following code retrieves the position and hire date after the
employee's name is entered:

```
Private Sub btn_EmpOK_Click()
Dim EmpFound As Range
With Range("EmpList") 'a named range on a sheet listing the employee names
    Set EmpFound = .Find(tb_EmpName.Value)
    If EmpFound Is Nothing Then
        MsgBox "Employee not found!"
        tb_EmpName.Value = ""

    Else
        With Range(EmpFound.Address)
            tb_EmpPosition = .Offset(0, 1)
            tb_HireDate = .Offset(0, 2)
        End With
    End If
End With
Set EmpFound = Nothing
End Sub
```

The available events for Label, TextBox, and CommandButton controls are described in Table 10.2.

Table 10.2   The Events for Label, TextBox, and CommandButton Controls

Event	Description
AfterUpdate[2]	Occurs after the control's data has been changed by the user.
BeforeDragOver	Occurs while the user drags and drops data onto the control.
BeforeDropOrPaste	Occurs right before the user is about to drop or paste data into the control.
BeforeUpdate[2]	Occurs before the data in the control is changed.
Change[2]	Occurs when the value of the control is changed.
Click[1,3]	Occurs when the user clicks the control with the mouse.
DblClick	Occurs when the user double-clicks the control with the mouse.
DropButtonClick[2]	Occurs when the user presses F4 on the keyboard. This is similar to the drop-down control on the combo box, but there is no drop-down on a text box.
Enter[2,3]	Occurs right before the control receives the focus from another control on the same userform.
Error	Occurs when the control runs into an error and cannot return the error information.

Exit[2,3]	Occurs right after the control loses focus to another control on the same userform.
KeyDown[2,3]	Occurs when the user presses a key on the keyboard.
KeyPress[2,3]	Occurs when the user presses an ANSI key. An ANSI key is a typeable character such as the letter *A*. An example of a nontypeable character is the Tab key.
KeyUp[2,3]	Occurs when the user releases a key on the keyboard.
MouseDown	Occurs when the user presses the mouse button within the borders of the control.
MouseMove	Occurs when the user moves the mouse within the borders of the control.
MouseUp	Occurs when the user releases the mouse button within the borders of the control.

[1]Label *control only*

[2]TextBox *control only*

[3]CommandButton *control only*

Deciding Whether to Use List Boxes or Combo Boxes in Forms

You can let users type in an employee name to search for, but what if they misspell the name? You need a way to make sure that the name is typed correctly. Which do you use: a list box or a combo box?

- A list box displays a list of values from which the user can choose.

- A combo box displays a list of values from which the user can choose and allows the user to enter a new value.

In this case, when you want to limit user options, you should use a list box to list the employee names, as shown in Figure 10.9.

Figure 10.9
Use a list box to control user input.

CortiCorp Employee List - Search	☒
Employee Name	Tracy Syrstad Cort Chilldon-Hoff John Doe
Position	
Hire Date	
OK	Cancel

In the RowSource property of the list box, enter the range from which the control should draw its data. Use a dynamic named range to keep the list updated if employees are added, as shown in the following code:

```
Private Sub btn_EmpOK_Click()
```

```
Dim EmpFound As Range
With Range("EmpList")
    Set EmpFound = .Find(lb_EmpName.Value)
    If EmpFound Is Nothing Then
        MsgBox ("Employee not found!")
        lb_EmpName.Value = ""
        Exit Sub
    Else
        With Range(EmpFound.Address)
            tb_EmpPosition = .Offset(0, 1)
            tb_HireDate = .Offset(0, 2)
        End With
    End If
End With
End Sub
```

Using the MultiSelect Property of a List Box

List boxes have a MultiSelect property, which allows the user to select multiple items from the choices in the list box, as shown in Figure 10.10:

- ■ fmMultiSelectSingle—The default setting allows only a single item selection at a time.

- ■ fmMultiSelectMulti—Allows an item to be deselected by clicking it again; multiple items can also be selected.

- ■ fmMultiSelectExtended—Allows the Ctrl and Shift keys to be used to select multiple items.

If multiple items are selected, the Value property cannot be used to retrieve the items. Instead, check to see whether the item is selected, and then manipulate it as needed using the following code:

```
Private Sub btn_EmpOK_Click()
Dim LastRow As Long, i As Integer
LastRow = Worksheets("Sheet2").Cells(Worksheets("Sheet2").Rows.Count, 1) _
.End(xlUp).Row + 1
Cells(LastRow, 1).Value = tb_EmpName.Value
'check the selection status of the items in the ListBox
For i = 0 To lb_EmpPosition.ListCount - 1
'if the item is selected, add it to the sheet
    If lb_EmpPosition.Selected(i) = True Then
        Cells(LastRow, 2).Value = Cells(LastRow, 2).Value & _
        lb_EmpPosition.List(i) & ","
    End If
Next i
Cells(LastRow, 2).Value = Left(Cells(LastRow, 2).Value, _
Len(Cells(LastRow, 2).Value) - 1)
Cells(LastRow, 3).Value = tb_HireDate.Value
End Sub
```

The items in a list box start counting at zero. For this reason, if you use the ListCount property, you must subtract one from the result:

```
For i = 0 To lb_EmpPosition.ListCount - 1
```

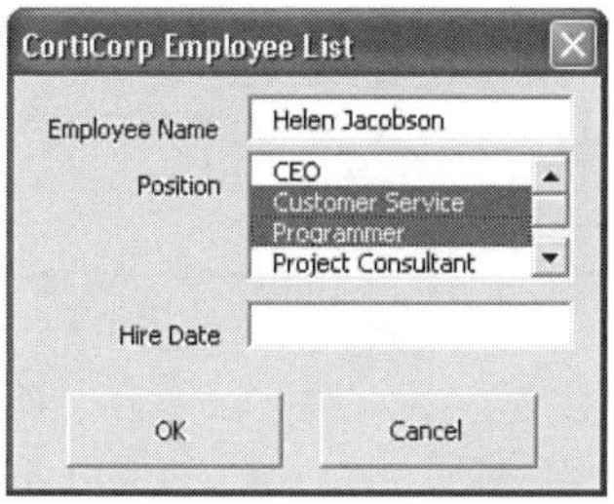

Figure 10.10
MultiSelect allows the user to select multiple items from a list box.

The available events for ListBox controls and ComboBox controls are described in Table 10.3.

Table 10.3   Events for ListBox **and** ComboBox **Controls**

Event	Description
AfterUpdate	Occurs after the control's data has been changed by the user.
BeforeDragOver	Occurs while the user drags and drops data onto the control.
BeforeDropOrPaste	Occurs right before the user is about to drop or paste data into the control.
BeforeUpdate	Occurs before the data in the control is changed.
Change	Occurs when the value of the control is changed.
Click	Occurs when the user selects a value from the list box or combo box.
DblClick	Occurs when the user double-clicks the control with the mouse.
DropButtonClick[1]	Occurs when the drop-down list appears after the user clicks the drop-down arrow of the combo box or presses F4 on the keyboard.
Enter	Occurs right before the control receives the focus from another control on the same userform.
Error	Occurs when the control runs into an error and can't return the error information.
Exit	Occurs right after the control loses focus to another control on the same userform.
KeyDown	Occurs when the user presses a key on the keyboard.
KeyPress	Occurs when the user presses an ANSI key. An ANSI key is a typeable character such as the letter *A*. An example of a nontypeable character is the Tab key.
KeyUp	Occurs when the user releases a key on the keyboard.
MouseDown	Occurs when the user presses the mouse button within the borders of the control.

10

`MouseMove`	Occurs when the user moves the mouse within the borders of the control.
`MouseUp`	Occurs when the user releases the mouse button within the borders of the control.

[1]`ComboBox` *control only*

Adding Option Buttons to a Userform

 Option buttons are similar to check boxes in that they can be used to make a selection. However, unlike check boxes, option buttons can be configured to allow only one selection out of a group.

 Using the Frame tool, draw a frame to separate the next set of controls from the other controls on the userform. The frame is used to group option buttons together, as shown in Figure 10.11.

Figure 10.11
Use a frame to group option buttons together.

Option buttons have a `GroupName` property. If you assign the same group name, Buildings, to a set of option buttons, you force them to act collectively as a toggle, so that only one button in the set can be selected. Selecting an option button automatically deselects the other buttons in the same group or frame. To prevent this behavior, either leave the `GroupName` property blank or enter another name.

> **TIP**
>
> For users who prefer to select the option button's label rather than the button itself, create a separate label and add code to the label to trigger the option button.
>
> ```
> Private Sub Lbl_Bldg1_Click()
>     Obtn_Bldg1.Value = True
> End Sub
> ```

The available events for `OptionButton` controls and `Frame` controls are described in Table 10.4.

Table 10.4   Events for `OptionButton` **and** `Frame` **Controls**

Event	Description
`AfterUpdate`[1]	Occurs after the control's data has been changed by the user.
`AddControl`[2]	Occurs when a control is added to a frame on a form at runtime. Does not run at design time or upon userform initialization.
`BeforeDragOver`	Occurs while the user does a drag and drop onto the control.
`BeforeDropOrPaste`	Occurs right before the user is about to drop or paste data into the control.
`BeforeUpdate`[1]	Occurs before the data in the control is changed.
`Change`[1]	Occurs when the value of the control is changed.
`Click`	Occurs when the user clicks the control with the mouse.
`DblClick`	Occurs when the user double-clicks the control with the mouse.
`Enter`	Occurs right before the control receives the focus from another control on the same userform.
`Error`	Occurs when the control runs into an error and cannot return the error information.
`Exit`	Occurs right after the control loses focus to another control on the same userform.
`KeyDown`	Occurs when the user presses a key on the keyboard.
`KeyPress`	Occurs when the user presses an ANSI key. An ANSI key is a typeable character such as the letter *A*. An example of a nontypeable character is the Tab key.
`KeyUp`	Occurs when the user releases a key on the keyboard.
`Layout`[2]	Occurs when the frame changes size.
`MouseDown`	Occurs when the user presses the mouse button within the borders of the control.
`MouseMove`	Occurs when the user moves the mouse within the borders of the control.
`MouseUp`	Occurs when the user releases the mouse button within the borders of the control.
`RemoveControl`[2]	Occurs when a control is deleted from within the frame control.
`Scroll`[2]	Occurs when the scrollbar box, if visible, is repositioned.
`Zoom`[2]	Occurs when the zoom value is changed.

[1]`OptionButton` *control only*

[2]`Frame` *control only*

Adding Graphics to a Userform

 A listing on a form can be even more helpful if a corresponding graphic is added to the form. The following code displays the photograph corresponding to the selected employee from the list box:

```
Private Sub lb_EmpName_Change()
Dim EmpFound As Range
With Range("EmpList")
    Set EmpFound = .Find(lb_EmpName.Value)
    If EmpFound Is Nothing Then
        MsgBox "Employee not found!"
        lb_EmpName.Value = ""
    Else
        With Range(EmpFound.Address)
            tb_EmpPosition = .Offset(0, 1)
            tb_HireDate = .Offset(0, 2)
            On Error Resume Next
            Img_Employee.Picture = LoadPicture _
        ("C:\Excel VBA 2007 by Jelen & Syrstad\" & EmpFound & ".bmp")
            On Error GoTo 0
        End With
    End If
End With
Set EmpFound = Nothing
Exit Sub
```

The available events for Graphic controls are described in Table 10.5.

Table 10.5   Events for Graphic Controls

Event	Description
BeforeDragOver	Occurs while the user drags and drops data onto the control.
BeforeDropOrPaste	Occurs right before the user is about to drop or paste data into the control.
Click	Occurs when the user clicks the image with the mouse.
DblClick	Occurs when the user double-clicks the image with the mouse.
Error	Occurs when the control runs into an error and can't return the error information.
MouseDown	Occurs when the user presses the mouse button within the borders of the image.
MouseMove	Occurs when the user moves the mouse within the borders of the image.
MouseUp	Occurs when the user releases the mouse button within the borders of the control.

Using a Spin Button on a Userform

As it is, the Hire Date field allows the user to enter the date in any format including 1/1/1 or January 1, 2001. This possible inconsistency can create problems later on if you need to use or search for dates. The solution? Force users to enter dates in a unified manner.

 Spin buttons allow the user to increment/decrement through a series of numbers. In this way, the user is forced to enter numbers rather than text.

Draw a spin button for a Month entry on the form. In the Properties, set the Min to 1 for January and the Max to 12 for December. In the Value property, enter 1, the first month. Next, draw a text box next to the spin button. This text box reflects the value of the spin button. In addition, labels can be used.

```
Private Sub SpBtn_Month_Change()
tb_Month.Value = SpBtn_Month.Value
End Sub
```

Finish building the form. Use a Min of 1 and Max of 31 for days or a Min of 1900 and a Max of 2100 for Year:

```
Private Sub btn_EmpOK_Click()
Dim LastRow As Long, i As Integer
LastRow = Worksheets("Sheet2").Cells(Worksheets("Sheet2").Rows.Count, 1) _
.End(xlUp).Row + 1
Cells(LastRow, 1).Value = tb_EmpName.Value
For i = 0 To lb_EmpPosition.ListCount - 1
    If lb_EmpPosition.Selected(i) = True Then
        Cells(LastRow, 2).Value = Cells(LastRow, 2).Value & _
        lb_EmpPosition.List(i) & ","
    End If
Next i
'Concatenate the values from the textboxes to create the date
Cells(LastRow, 3).Value = tb_Month.Value & "/" & tb_Day.Value & _
    "/" & tb_Year.Value
End Sub
```

The available events for `SpinButton` controls are described in Table 10.6.

Table 10.6   Events for `SpinButton` Controls

Event	Description
AfterUpdate	Occurs after the control's data has been changed by the user.
BeforeDragOver	Occurs while the user drags and drops data onto the control.
BeforeDropOrPaste	Occurs right before the user is about to drop or paste data into the control.
BeforeUpdate	Occurs before the data in the control is changed.
Change	Occurs when the value of the control is changed.
DblClick	Occurs when the user double-clicks the control.
Enter	Occurs right before the control receives the focus from another control on the same userform.
Error	Occurs when the control runs into an error and cannot return the error information.
Exit	Occurs right after the control loses focus to another control on the same userform.
KeyDown	Occurs when the user presses a key on the keyboard.
KeyPress	Occurs when the user presses an ANSI key. An ANSI key is a typeable character such as the letter *A*. An example of a nontypeable character is the Tab key.

10

KeyUp	Occurs when the user releases a key on the keyboard.
SpinDown	Occurs when the user clicks the lower or left spin button, decreasing the value.
SpinUp	Occurs when the user clicks the upper or right spin button, increasing the value.

Using the MultiPage Control to Combine Forms

The MultiPage control provides a neat way of organizing multiple forms. Instead of having a form for personal employee information and one for on-the-job information, combine the information into one multipage form, as shown in Figures 10.12 and 10.13.

Figure 10.12
Use the MultiPage control to combine multiple forms. This is the first page of the form.

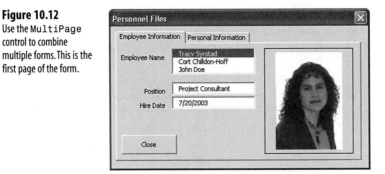

Figure 10.13
This is the second page of the form.

> **TIP**
> Adding multipage forms after the rest of the form is created is not an easy task. Therefore, plan multi-page forms the beginning. If you decide later that you need a multipage form, insert a new form, draw the multipage, and copy/paste the controls from the other forms to the new form.

> **NOTE** Do not right-click in the tab area to view the MultiPage code. Instead, right-click in the MultiPage's main area to get the View Code option.

You can modify a page by right-clicking the tab of the page, which displays the following menu of options: New Page, Delete Page, Rename, or Move.

Unlike many of the other controls where the Value property holds a user-entered or selected value, the Value property of the MultiPage control holds the number of the active page, starting at zero. For example, if you have a five-page form and want to activate the fourth page, do this:

```
MultiPage1.Value = 3
```

If you have a control you want all the pages to share, such as the Save or Cancel buttons, place the control on the main userform rather than on the individual pages, as shown in Figure 10.14.

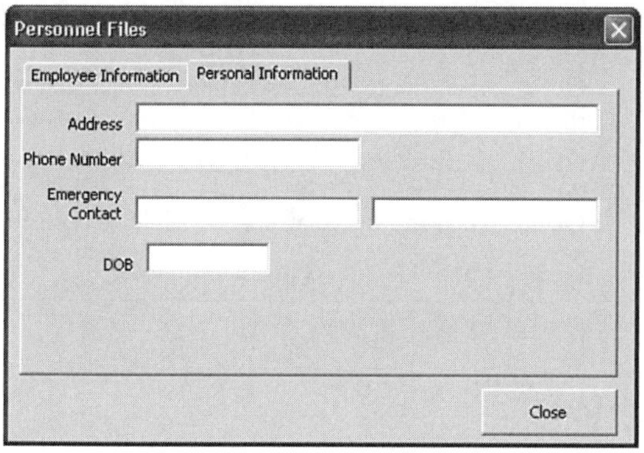

Figure 10.14
Place common controls like the Close button on the main userform.

The available events for MultiPage controls are described in Table 10.7.

Table 10.7   Events for the MultiPage **Control**

Event	Description
AddControl	Occurs when a control is added to a page of the MultiPage control. Does not run at design time or upon userform initialization.
BeforeDragOver	Occurs while the user drags and drops data onto a page of the MultiPage control.
BeforeDropOrPaste	Occurs right before the user is about to drop or paste data onto a page of the MultiPage control.
Change	Occurs when the user changes pages of a multipage.

`Click`	Occurs when the user clicks on a page of the `MultiPage` control.
`DblClick`	Occurs when the user double-clicks a page of the `MultiPage` control with the mouse.
`Enter`	Occurs right before the multipage receives the focus from another control on the same userform.
`Error`	Occurs when the `MultiPage` control runs into an error and cannot return the error information.
`Exit`	Occurs right after the multipage loses focus to another control on the same userform.
`KeyDown`	Occurs when the user presses a key on the keyboard.
`KeyPress`	Occurs when the user presses an ANSI key. An ANSI key is a typeable character, such as the letter *A*. An example of a nontypeable character is the Tab key.
`KeyUp`	Occurs when the user releases a key on the keyboard.
`MouseDown`	Occurs when the user presses the mouse button within the borders of the control.
`MouseMove`	Occurs when the user moves the mouse within the borders of the control.
`MouseUp`	Occurs when the user releases the mouse button within the borders of the control.
`RemoveControl`	Occurs when a control is removed from a page of the multipage.
`Scroll`	Occurs when the scrollbar box, if visible, is repositioned.
`Zoom`	Occurs when the zoom value is changed.

Verifying Field Entry

Even if users are told to fill in all the fields, there is no way to force them to do so—except with an electronic form. As a programmer, you can ensure that all required fields are filled in by not allowing the user to continue until all requirements are met. Here's how to do this:

```
If tb_EmpName.Value = "" Then
    frm_AddEmp.Hide
    MsgBox ("Please enter an Employee Name")
    frm_AddEmp.Show
    Exit Sub
End If
```

Illegal Window Closing

The userforms created in the VB Editor are not that different from normal windows: They also include the *X* close button in the upper-right corner. Although using the button is not wrong, it can cause problems, depending on the objective of the userform. In cases like this, you might want to control what happens if the user presses the button. Use the `QueryClose` event of the userform to find out what method is used to close the form and code an appropriate action:

```
Private Sub UserForm_QueryClose(Cancel As Integer, CloseMode As Integer)
If CloseMode = vbFormControlMenu Then
    MsgBox "Please use the OK or Cancel buttons to close the form", vbCritical
    Cancel = True
End If
End Sub
```

After you know the method the user used to try to close the form, you can create a message box similar to Figure 10.15 to warn the user that the method was illegal.

Figure 10.15
Control what happens when the user clicks the *X* button.

10

The `QueryClose` event can be triggered in four ways:

- `vbFormControlMenu`—The user right-clicks either on the form's title bar and selects the Close command or clicks the *X* in the upper-right corner of the form..
- `vbFormCode`—The `Unload` statement is used.
- `vbAppWindows`—Windows shuts down.
- `vbAppTaskManager`—The application is shut down by the Task Manager.

Getting a Filename

One of the most common client interactions is when you need the client to specify a path and filename. Excel VBA has a built-in function to display the File Open dialog box, as shown in Figure 10.16. The client browses to and selects a file. When the client selects the Open button, instead of opening the file, Excel VBA returns the full path and filename to the code.

```
Sub SelectFile()
' Ask which file to copy
x = Application.GetOpenFilename( _
    FileFilter:="Excel Files (*.xls*), *.xls*", _
    Title:="Choose File to Copy", MultiSelect:=False)
```

```
' check in case no files were selected
If x = "False" Then Exit Sub

MsgBox "You selected " & x
End Sub
```

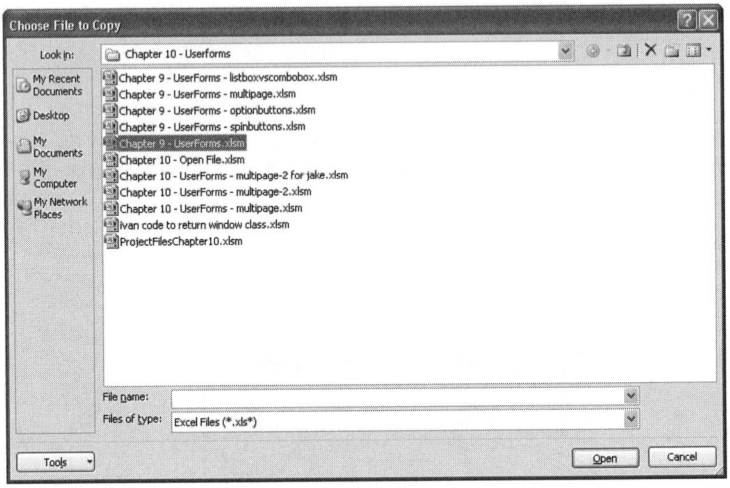

Figure 10.16
Use the File Open dialog box to allow the user to select a file.

The preceding code allows the client to select one file. If you want them to specify multiple files, use this code:

```
Sub ManyFiles()
Dim x As Variant

x = Application.GetOpenFilename( _
    FileFilter:="Excel Files (*.xls*), *.xls*", _
    Title:="Choose Files", MultiSelect:=True)

On Error Resume Next
If Ubound(x) > 0 Then
    For i = 1 To UBound(x)
        MsgBox "You selected " & x(i)
    Next i
ElseIf x = "False" Then Exit Sub
End If
On Error GoTo 0

End Sub
```

In a similar fashion, you can use `Application.GetSaveAsFileName` to find the path and file-name that should be used to save a file.

Next Steps

Now that you have seen how to work with userforms, the next chapter examines charts. In Chapter 11, you learn how spreadsheet charting has become a highly customizable resource capable of handling large amounts of data.

Creating Charts

Charting in Excel 2010

Microsoft rewrote the Excel charting engine for Excel 2007. Most code from Excel 2003 will continue to work in Excel 2010.

The following are some important methods and features available in Excel 2010:

- **ApplyLayout**—This method applies one of the chart layouts available on the Design tab.
- **SetElement**—This method chooses any of the built-in element choices from the Layout tab.
- **ChartFormat**—This object enables you to change the fill, glow, line, reflection, shadow, soft edge, or 3-D format of most individual chart elements. This is similar to settings on the Format tab.
- **AddChart**—This method enables you to add a chart to an existing worksheet.

Referencing Charts and Chart Objects in VBA Code

If you go back far enough in Excel history, you find that all charts used to be created as their own chart sheets. Then, in the mid-1990s, Excel added the amazing capability to embed a chart right onto an existing worksheet. This allowed a report to be created with tables of numbers and charts all on the same page, something we take for granted today.

These two different ways of dealing with charts make it necessary for you to deal with two separate object models for charts. When a chart is on its own standalone chart sheet, you are dealing with a Chart object. When a chart is embedded in a worksheet, you are dealing with a ChartObject object.

11

IN THIS CHAPTER

Charting in Excel 2010 203

Referencing Charts and Chart Objects in VBA Code 203

Creating a Chart 204

Recording Commands from the Layout or Design Tabs 208

Using SetElement to Emulate Changes on the Layout Tab 213

Changing a Chart Title Using VBA 218

Emulating Changes on the Format Tab 218

Creating Advanced Charts 234

Exporting a Chart as a Graphic 244

Creating Pivot Charts 246

Excel 2010 includes a third evolutionary branch because objects on a worksheet are also members of the Shapes collection.

In legacy versions of Excel, to reference the color of the chart area for an embedded chart, you must refer to the chart in this manner:

```
Worksheets("Jan").ChartObjects("Chart 1").Chart.ChartArea.Interior.ColorIndex _
    = 4
```

In Excel 2010, you can use the Shapes collection:

```
Worksheets("Jan").Shapes("Chart 1").Chart.ChartArea.Interior.ColorIndex = 4
```

In any version of Excel, if a chart is on its own chart sheet, you don't have to specify the container; you can simply refer to the Chart object:

```
Sheets("Chart1").ChartArea.Interior.ColorIndex = 4
```

Creating a Chart

In legacy versions of Excel, you used the Charts.Add command to add a new chart. Next, you specified the source data, type of chart, and whether the chart should be on a new sheet or embedded on an existing worksheet. The first three lines of the following code create a clustered column chart on a new chart sheet. The fourth line moves the chart back to be an embedded object in Sheet1:

```
Charts.Add
ActiveChart.SetSourceData Source:=Worksheets("Sheet1").Range("A1:E4")
ActiveChart.ChartType = xlColumnClustered
ActiveChart.Location Where:=xlLocationAsObject, Name:="Sheet1"
```

If you plan to share your macros with people who still use Excel 2003, you should use the Charts.Add method. However, if your application will be running only Excel 2007 or Excel 2010, you can use the new AddChart method. The code for the AddChart method can be as simple as the following:

```
' Create chart on the current sheet
ActiveSheet.Shapes.AddChart.Select
ActiveChart.SetSourceData Source:=Range("A1:E4")
ActiveChart.ChartType = xlColumnClustered
```

Alternatively, you can specify the chart type, size, and location as part of the AddChart method, as described in the next section.

Specifying the Size and Location of a Chart

The AddChart method has additional parameters you can use to specify the type of chart, the chart's location on the worksheet, and the size of the chart.

The location and size of a chart are specified in points (72 points = 1 inch). For example, the Top parameter requires the number of points from the top of Row 1 to the top edge of the worksheet.

The following code creates a chart that roughly covers the Range C11:J30:

```
Sub SpecifyLocation()
    Dim WS As Worksheet
    Set WS = Worksheets("Sheet1")
    WS.Shapes.AddChart(xlColumnClustered, _
        Left:=100, Top:=150, _
        Width:=400, Height:=300).Select
    ActiveChart.SetSourceData Source:=WS.Range("A1:E4")
End Sub
```

It requires a lot of trial and error to randomly figure out the exact distance in points to cause a chart to line up with a certain cell. Fortunately, you can ask VBA to tell you the distance in points to a certain cell. If you ask for the Left property of any cell, you find the distance to the top-left corner of that cell. You can also ask for the width of a range or the height of a range. For example, the following code creates a chart in exactly C11:J30:

```
Sub SpecifyExactLocation()
    Dim WS As Worksheet
    Set WS = Worksheets("Sheet1")
    WS.Shapes.AddChart(xlColumnClustered, _
        Left:=WS.Range("C11").Left, _
        Top:=WS.Range("C11").Top, _
        Width:=WS.Range("C11:J11").Width, _
        Height:=WS.Range("C11:C30").Height).Select
    ActiveChart.SetSourceData Source:=WS.Range("A1:E4")
End Sub
```

In this case, you are not moving the location of the Chart object. Instead, you are moving the location of the container that contains the chart. In Excel 2010, it is either the ChartObject or the Shape object. If you try to change the actual location of the chart, you move it within the container. Because you can actually move the chart area a few points in either direction inside the container, the code will run, but you will not get the desired results.

To see a demo of specifying chart location, search for Excel VBA 11 at YouTube.

To move a chart that has already been created, you can reference either the ChartObject or the Shape and change the Top, Left, Width, and Height properties, as shown in the following macro:

```
Sub MoveAfterTheFact()
    Dim WS As Worksheet
    Set WS = Worksheets("Sheet1")
    With WS.ChartObjects("Chart 9")
        .Left = WS.Range("C21").Left
        .Top = WS.Range("C21").Top
        .Width = WS.Range("C1:H1").Width
        .Height = WS.Range("C21:C25").Height
    End With
End Sub
```

11

Later Referring to a Specific Chart

When a new chart is created, it is given a sequential name, such as Chart 1. If you select a chart and then look in the name box, you see the name of the chart. In Figure 11.1, the name of the chart is Chart 14. This does not mean that there are 14 charts on the worksheet. In this particular case, many individual charts have been created and deleted.

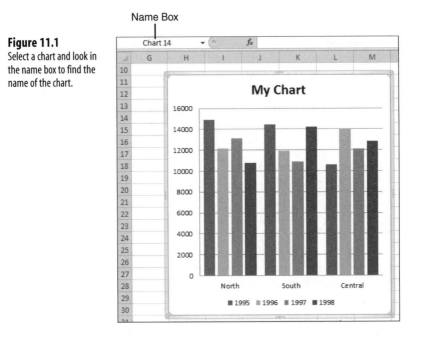

Figure 11.1
Select a chart and look in the name box to find the name of the chart.

This means that on any given day that your macro runs, the Chart object might have a different name. If you need to reference the chart later in the macro, perhaps after you have selected other cells and the chart is no longer active, you might ask VBA for the name of the chart and store it in a variable for later use, as shown here:

```
Sub RememberTheName()
    Dim WS As Worksheet
    Set WS = Worksheets("Sheet1")
    WS.Shapes.AddChart(xlColumnClustered, _
        Left:=WS.Range("C11").Left, _
        Top:=WS.Range("C11").Top, _
        Width:=WS.Range("C11:J11").Width, _
        Height:=WS.Range("C11:C30").Height _
        ).Select
    ActiveChart.SetSourceData Source:=WS.Range("A1:E4")
    ' Remember the name in a variable
    ThisChartObjectName = ActiveChart.Parent.Name
    ' more lines of code...
    ' then later in the macro, you need to re-assign the chart
    With WS.Shapes(ThisChartObjectName)
```

```
        .Chart.SetSourceData Source:=WS.Range("A20:E24"), PlotBy:=xlColumns
        .Top = WS.Range("C26").Top
    End With
End Sub
```

In the preceding macro, the variable `ThisChartObjectName` contains the name of the `Chart` object. This method works great if your changes will happen later in the same macro. However, after the macro finishes running, the variable will be out of scope, and you won't be able to access the name later.

If you want to be able to remember a chart name, you could store the name in an out-of-the-way cell on the worksheet. The first macro here stores the name in Cell Z1, and the second macro then later modifies the chart using the name stored in Cell Z1:

```
Sub StoreTheName()
    Dim WS As Worksheet
    Set WS = Worksheets("Sheet1")
    WS.Shapes.AddChart(xlColumnClustered, _
        Left:=WS.Range("C11").Left, _
        Top:=WS.Range("C11").Top, _
        Width:=WS.Range("C11:J11").Width, _
        Height:=WS.Range("C11:C30").Height _
        ).Select
    ActiveChart.SetSourceData Source:=WS.Range("A1:E4")
    Range("Z1").Value = ActiveChart.Parent.Name
End Sub
```

After the previous macro stored the name in Cell Z1, the following macro will use the value in Z1 to figure out which chart to change:

```
Sub ChangeTheChartLater()
    Dim WS As Worksheet
    Set WS = Worksheets("Sheet1")
    MyName = WS.Range("Z1").Value
    With WS.Shapes(MyName)
        .Chart.SetSourceData Source:=WS.Range("A20:E24"), PlotBy:=xlColumns
        .Top = WS.Range("C26").Top
    End With

End Sub
```

If you need to modify a preexisting chart—such as a chart that you did not create—and there is only one chart on the worksheet, you can use this line of code:

```
WS.ChartObjects(1).Chart.Interior.ColorIndex = 4
```

If there are many charts, and you need to find the one with the upper-left corner located in Cell A4, you can loop through all the `Chart` objects until you find one in the correct location, like this:

```
For each Cht in ActiveSheet.ChartObjects
    If Cht.TopLeftCell.Address = "$A$4" then
        Cht.Interior.ColorIndex = 4
    end if
Next Cht
```

11

Recording Commands from the Layout or Design Tabs

With charts in Excel 2010, there are three levels of chart changes. The global chart settings that indicate the chart type and style are on the Design tab. Selections from the built-in element settings appear on the Layout tab. You make microchanges by using the Format tab.

The macro recorder was not finished in Excel 2007, but it is working in Excel 2010. If you need to make certain changes, this enables you to quickly record a macro and then copy its code.

Specifying a Built-in Chart Type

Excel 2010 has 73 built-in chart types. To change a chart to one of the 73 types, you use the ChartType property. This property can be applied either to a chart or to a series within a chart. Here is an example that changes the type for the entire chart:

```
ActiveChart.ChartType = xlBubble
```

To change the second series on a chart to a line chart, you use this:

```
ActiveChart.Series(2).ChartType = xlLine
```

Table 11.1 lists the 73 chart type constants that you can use to create various charts. The sequence of Table 11.1 matches the sequence of the charts in the Chart Type dialog.

Table 11.1   Chart Types for Use in VBA

Chart Type	Constant
Clustered Column	xlColumnClustered
Stacked Column	xlColumnStacked
100% Stacked Column	xlColumnStacked100
3-D Clustered Column	xl3DColumnClustered
Stacked Column in 3-D	xl3DColumnStacked
100% Stacked Column in 3-D	xl3DColumnStacked100
3-D Column	xl3DColumn
Clustered Cylinder	xlCylinderColClustered
Stacked Cylinder	xlCylinderColStacked
100% Stacked Cylinder	xlCylinderColStacked100
3-D Cylinder	xlCylinderCol
Clustered Cone	xlConeColClustered
Stacked Cone	xlConeColStacked
100% Stacked Cone	xlConeColStacked100
3-D Cone	xlConeCol

Chart Type	Constant
Clustered Pyramid	`xlPyramidColClustered`
Stacked Pyramid	`xlPyramidColStacked`
100% Stacked Pyramid	`xlPyramidColStacked100`
3-D Pyramid	`xlPyramidCol`
Line	`xlLine`
Stacked Line	`xlLineStacked`
100% Stacked Line	`xlLineStacked100`
Line with Markers	`xlLineMarkers`
Stacked Line with Markers	`xlLineMarkersStacked`
100% Stacked Line with Markers	`xlLineMarkersStacked100`
3-D Line	`xl3DLine`
Pie	`xlPie`
Pie in 3-D	`xl3DPie`
Pie of Pie	`xlPieOfPie`
Exploded Pie	`xlPieExploded`
Exploded Pie in 3-D	`xl3DPieExploded`
Bar of Pie	`xlBarOfPie`
Clustered Bar	`xlBarClustered`
Stacked Bar	`xlBarStacked`
100% Stacked Bar	`xlBarStacked100`
Clustered Bar in 3-D	`xl3DBarClustered`
Stacked Bar in 3-D	`xl3DBarStacked`
100% Stacked Bar in 3-D	`xl3DBarStacked100`
Clustered Horizontal Cylinder	`xlCylinderBarClustered`
Stacked Horizontal Cylinder	`xlCylinderBarStacked`
100% Stacked Horizontal Cylinder	`xlCylinderBarStacked100`
Clustered Horizontal Cone	`xlConeBarClustered`
Stacked Horizontal Cone	`xlConeBarStacked`
100% Stacked Horizontal Cone	`xlConeBarStacked100`
Clustered Horizontal Pyramid	`xlPyramidBarClustered`
Stacked Horizontal Pyramid	`xlPyramidBarStacked`
100% Stacked Horizontal Pyramid	`xlPyramidBarStacked100`
Area	`xlArea`
Stacked Area	`xlAreaStacked`

11

11

Table 11.1 Continued

Chart Type	Constant
100% Stacked Area	xlAreaStacked100
3-D Area	xl3DArea
Stacked Area in 3-D	xl3DAreaStacked
100% Stacked Area in 3-D	xl3DAreaStacked100
Scatter with only Markers	xlXYScatter
Scatter with Smooth Lines and Markers	xlXYScatterSmooth
Scatter with Smooth Lines	xlXYScatterSmoothNoMarkers
Scatter with Straight Lines and Markers	xlXYScatterLines
Scatter with Straight Lines	xlXYScatterLinesNoMarkers
High-Low-Close	xlStockHLC
Open-High-Low-Close	xlStockOHLC
Volume-High-Low-Close	xlStockVHLC
Volume-Open-High-Low-Close	xlStockVOHLC
3-D Surface	xlSurface
Wireframe 3-D Surface	xlSurfaceWireframe
Contour	xlSurfaceTopView
Wireframe Contour	xlSurfaceTopViewWireframe
Doughnut	xlDoughnut
Exploded Doughnut	xlDoughnutExploded
Bubble	xlBubble
Bubble with a 3-D Effect	xlBubble3DEffect
Radar	xlRadar
Radar with Markers	xlRadarMarkers
Filled Radar	xlRadarFilled

Specifying a Template Chart Type

Excel 2010 allows you to create a custom chart template with all your preferred settings such as colors and fonts. This technique is a great way to save time when you are creating a chart with a lot of custom formatting.

A VBA macro can make use of a custom chart template, provided you plan to distribute the custom chart template to each person who will run your macro.

In Excel 2010, you save custom chart types as `.crtx` files and store them in the `%appdata%\Microsoft\Templates\Charts\` folder.

To apply a custom chart type, you use the following:

```
ActiveChart.ApplyChartTemplate "MyChart.crtx"
```

If the chart template does not exist, VBA returns an error. If you would like Excel to continue without displaying a debug error, you can instruct the error handler to resume with the next line. After applying the chart template, go back to the default state of the error handler so that you will see any errors. Here's how you do this:

```
On Error Resume Next
ActiveChart.ApplyChartTemplate ("MyChart.crtx")
On Error GoTo 0 ' that final character is a zero
```

Changing a Chart's Layout or Style

Two galleries—the Chart Layout gallery and the Styles gallery—make up the bulk of the Design tab.

The Chart Layout gallery offers from 4 to 12 combinations of chart elements. These combinations are different for various chart types. When you look at the gallery shown in Figure 11.2, the ToolTips for the layouts show that the layouts are named imaginatively as Layout 1 through Layout 11.

Layout 1   Layout 3

Figure 11.2
The built-in layouts are numbered 1 through 11. For other chart types, you might have from 4 to 12 layouts.

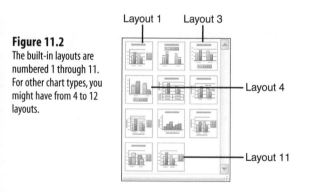

Layout 4

Layout 11

To apply one of the built-in layouts in a macro, you have to use the `ApplyLayout` method with a number from 1 through 12 to correspond to the built-in layouts. The following code applies Layout 1 to the active chart:

```
ActiveChart.ApplyLayout 1
```

11

11

> **CAUTION**
>
> Whereas line charts offer 12 built-in layouts, other types such as radar charts offer as few as four built-in layouts. If you attempt to specify a layout number that is larger than the layouts available for the current chart type, Excel returns a runtime error 5. Unless you just created the active chart in the same macro, there is always the possibility that the person running the macro changed your line charts to radar charts, so include some error handling before you use the `ApplyLayout` command.

Therefore, to use a built-in layout effectively, you must have actually built a chart by hand and found a layout that you like.

As shown in Figure 11.3, the Styles gallery contains 48 styles. These styles are also numbered sequentially, with Styles 1 through 8 in Row 1, Styles 9 through 16 in Row 2, and so on. These styles follow a bit of a pattern:

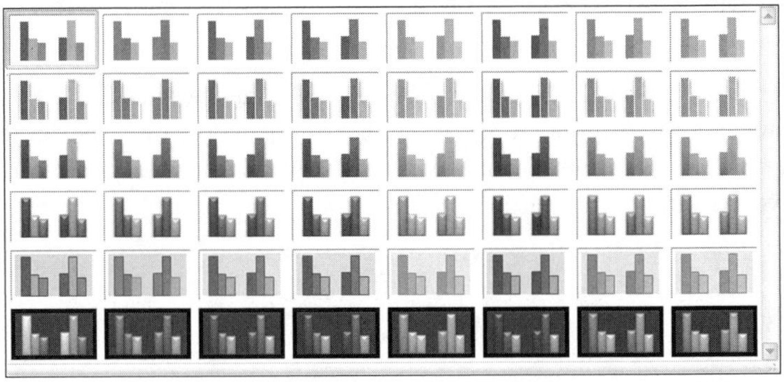

Figure 11.3
The built-in styles are numbered 1 through 48.

- Styles 1, 9, 17, 25, 33, and 41 (that is, the styles in Column 1) are monochrome.
- Styles 2, 10, 18, 26, 34, and 42 (that is, the styles in Column 2) use different colors for each point.
- All the other styles use hues of a particular theme color.
- Styles 1 through 8 are simple styles.
- Styles 17 through 24 use moderate effects.
- Styles 33 through 40 have intense effects.
- Styles 41 through 48 appear on a dark background.

> **TIP**
>
> If you are going to mix styles in a single workbook, consider staying within a single row or a single column of the gallery.

To apply a style to a chart, you use the `ChartStyle` property, assigning it a value from 1 to 48:

```
ActiveChart.ChartStyle = 1
```

The `ChartStyle` property changes the colors in the chart. However, a number of formatting changes from the Format tab are not overwritten when you change the `ChartStyle` property. For example, suppose that you had applied glow or a clear glass bezel to a chart. Running the preceding code will not clear that formatting.

To clear any previous formatting, you use the `ClearToMatchStyle` method:

```
ActiveChart.ChartStyle = 1
ActiveChart.ClearToMatchStyle
```

Using `SetElement` to Emulate Changes on the Layout Tab

The Layout tab contains a number of built-in settings. Figure 11.4 shows a few of the built-in menu items for the Legend tab. There are similar menus for each of the icons in the figure.

If you use a built-in menu item to change the titles, legend, labels, axes, gridlines, or background, it is probably handled in code that uses the `SetElement` method that is available in Excel 2010.

> **TIP**
> `SetElement` does not work with the More choices at the bottom of each menu. It also does not work with the 3-D Rotation button. Other than that, you can use `SetElement` to change everything in the Labels, Axes, Background, and Analysis groups.

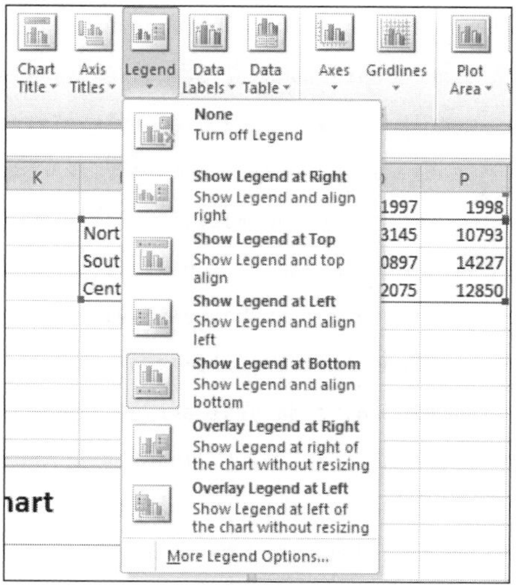

Figure 11.4
There are built-in menus similar to this one for each icon. If your choice is in the menu, the VBA code uses the SetElement method.

The macro recorder always works for the built-in settings on the Layout tab. If you do not feel like looking up the proper constant in this book, you can always quickly record a macro.

The SetElement method is followed by a constant that specifies which menu item to select. For example, if you want to choose Show Legend at Left, you can use this code:

```
ActiveChart.SetElement msoElementLegendLeft
```

Table 11.2 shows all the available constants that you can use with the SetElement method. These constants are in roughly the same order as they appear on the Layout tab.

Table 11.2   Constants Available with SetElement

Layout Tab	Chart Element Constant Icon
Chart Title	msoElementChartTitleNone
Chart Title	msoElementChartTitleCenteredOverlay
Chart Title	msoElementChartTitleAboveChart
Axis Titles	msoElementPrimaryCategoryAxisTitleNone
Axis Titles	msoElementPrimaryCategoryAxisTitleBelowAxis
Axis Titles	msoElementPrimaryCategoryAxisTitleAdjacentToAxis
Axis Titles	msoElementPrimaryCategoryAxisTitleHorizontal
Axis Titles	msoElementPrimaryCategoryAxisTitleVertical
Axis Titles	msoElementPrimaryCategoryAxisTitleRotated
Axis Titles	msoElementSecondaryCategoryAxisTitleAdjacentToAxis
Axis Titles	msoElementSecondaryCategoryAxisTitleBelowAxis
Axis Titles	msoElementSecondaryCategoryAxisTitleHorizontal
Axis Titles	msoElementSecondaryCategoryAxisTitleNone
Axis Titles	msoElementSecondaryCategoryAxisTitleRotated
Axis Titles	msoElementSecondaryCategoryAxisTitleVertical
Axis Titles	msoElementPrimaryValueAxisTitleAdjacentToAxis
Axis Titles	msoElementPrimaryValueAxisTitleBelowAxis
Axis Titles	msoElementPrimaryValueAxisTitleHorizontal
Axis Titles	msoElementPrimaryValueAxisTitleNone
Axis Titles	msoElementPrimaryValueAxisTitleRotated
Axis Titles	msoElementPrimaryValueAxisTitleVertical
Axis Titles	msoElementSecondaryValueAxisTitleBelowAxis
Axis Titles	msoElementSecondaryValueAxisTitleHorizontal
Axis Titles	msoElementSecondaryValueAxisTitleNone
Axis Titles	msoElementSecondaryValueAxisTitleRotated

Layout Tab	Chart Element Constant Icon
Axis Titles	`msoElementSecondaryValueAxisTitleVertical`
Axis Titles	`msoElementSeriesAxisTitleHorizontal`
Axis Titles	`msoElementSeriesAxisTitleNone`
Axis Titles	`msoElementSeriesAxisTitleRotated`
Axis Titles	`msoElementSeriesAxisTitleVertical`
Axis Titles	`msoElementSecondaryValueAxisTitleAdjacentToAxis`
Legend	`msoElementLegendNone`
Legend	`msoElementLegendRight`
Legend	`msoElementLegendTop`
Legend	`msoElementLegendLeft`
Legend	`msoElementLegendBottom`
Legend	`msoElementLegendRightOverlay`
Legend	`msoElementLegendLeftOverlay`
Data Labels	`msoElementDataLabelCenter`
Data Labels	`msoElementDataLabelInsideEnd`
Data Labels	`msoElementDataLabelNone`
Data Labels	`msoElementDataLabelInsideBase`
Data Labels	`msoElementDataLabelOutSideEnd`
Data Labels	`msoElementDataLabelTop`
Data Labels	`msoElementDataLabelBottom`
Data Labels	`msoElementDataLabelRight`
Data Labels	`msoElementDataLabelLeft`
Data Labels	`msoElementDataLabelShow`
Data Labels	`msoElementDataLabelBestFit`
Data Table	`msoElementDataTableNone`
Data Table	`msoElementDataTableShow`
Data Table	`msoElementDataTableWithLegendKeys`
Axis	`msoElementPrimaryCategoryAxisNone`
Axis	`msoElementPrimaryCategoryAxisShow`
Axis	`msoElementPrimaryCategoryAxisWithoutLabels`
Axis	`msoElementPrimaryCategoryAxisReverse`
Axis	`msoElementPrimaryCategoryAxisThousands`
Axis	`msoElementPrimaryCategoryAxisMillions`
Axis	`msoElementPrimaryCategoryAxisBillions`

11

Table 11.2 Continued

Layout Tab	Chart Element Constant Icon
Axis	msoElementPrimaryCategoryAxisLogScale
Axis	msoElementSecondaryCategoryAxisNone
Axis	msoElementSecondaryCategoryAxisShow
Axis	msoElementSecondaryCategoryAxisWithoutLabels
Axis	msoElementSecondaryCategoryAxisReverse
Axis	msoElementSecondaryCategoryAxisThousands
Axis	msoElementSecondaryCategoryAxisMillions
Axis	msoElementSecondaryCategoryAxisBillions
Axis	msoElementSecondaryCategoryAxisLogScaIe
Axis	msoElementPrimaryValueAxisNone
Axis	msoElementPrimaryValueAxisShow
Axis	msoElementPrimaryValueAxisThousands
Axis	msoElementPrimaryValueAxisMillions
Axis	msoElementPrimaryValueAxisBillions
Axis	msoElementPrimaryValueAxisLogScale
Axis	msoElementSecondaryValueAxisNone
Axis	msoElementSecondaryValueAxisShow
Axis	msoElementSecondarWalueAxisThousands
Axis	msoElementSecondaryValueAxisMillions
Axis	msoElementSecondaryValueAxisBillions
Axis	msoElementSecondaryValueAxisLogScale
Axis	msoElementSeriesAxisNone
Axis	msoElementSeriesAxisShow
Axis	msoElementSeriesAxisReverse
Axis	msoElementSeriesAxisWithoutLabeling
GridLines	msoElementPrimaryCategoryGridLinesNone
GridLines	msoElementPrimaryCategoryGridLinesMajor
GridLines	msoElementPrimaryCategoryGridLinesMinor
GridLines	msoElementPrimaryCategoryGridLinesMinorMajor
GridLines	msoElementSecondaryCategoryGridLinesNone
GridLines	msoElementSecondaryCategoryGridLinesMajor
GridLines	msoElementSecondaryCategoryGridLinesMinor
GridLines	msoElementSecondaryCategoryGridLinesMinorMajor

11

Layout Tab	Chart Element Constant Icon
GridLines	msoElementPrimaryValueGridLinesNone
GridLines	msoElementPrimaryValueGridLinesMajor
GridLines	msoElementPrimaryValueGridLinesMinor
GridLines	msoElementPrimaryValueGridLinesMinorMajor
GridLines	msoElementSecondaryValueGridLinesNone
GridLines	msoElementSecondaryValueGridLinesMajor
GridLines	msoElementSecondaryValueGridLinesMinor
GridLines	msoElementSecondaryValueGridLinesMinorMajor
GridLines	msoElementSeriesAxisGridLinesNone
GridLines	msoElementSeriesAxisGridLinesMajor
GridLines	msoElementSeriesAxisGridLinesMinor
GridLines	msoElementSeriesAxisGridLinesMinorMajor
Plot Area	msoElementPlotAreaNone
Plot Area	msoElementPlotAreaShow
Chart Wall	msoElementChartWallNone
Chart Wall	msoElementChartWallShow
Chart Floor	msoElementChartFloorNone
Chart Floor	msoElementChartFloorShow
Trendline	msoElementTrendlineNone
Trendline	msoElementTrendlineAddLinear
Trendline	msoElementTrendlineAddExponential
Trendline	msoElementTrendlineAddLinearForecast
Trendline	msoElementTrendlineAddTwoPeriodMovingAverage
Lines	msoElementLineNone
Lines	msoElementLineDropLine
Lines	msoElementLineHiLoLine
Lines	msoElementLineDropHiLoLine
Lines	msoElementLineSeriesLine
Up/Down Bars	msoElementUpDownBarsNone
Up/Down Bars	msoElementUpDownBarsShow
Error Bar	msoElementErrorBarNone
Error Bar	msoElementErrorBarStandardError
Error Bar	msoElementErrorBarPercentage
Error Bar	msoElementErrorBarStandardDeviation

11

> ┌─ CAUTION ───┐
> If you attempt to format an element that is not present, Excel will return a −2147467259 Method
> Failed error.

Changing a Chart Title Using VBA

The Layout tab's built-in menus enable you to add a title above a chart, but they do not
enable you to change the characters in a chart title or axis title.

In the Excel interface, you can double-click the chart title text and type a new title to
change the title.

To specify a chart title in VBA, use this code:

```
ActiveChart.ChartTitle.Caption = "My Chart"
```

Similarly, you can specify the axis titles by using the Caption property. The following code
changes the axis title along the category axis:

```
ActiveChart.Axes(xlCategory, xlPrimary).AxisTitle.Caption = "Months"
```

Emulating Changes on the Format Tab

The Format tab offers icons for changing colors and effects for individual chart elements.
While many people call the Shadow, Glow, Bevel, and Material settings "chart junk," there
are ways in VBA to apply these formats.

Using the Format Method to Access Formatting Options

Excel 2010 includes an object called the ChartFormat object that contains the settings for
Fill, Glow, Line, PictureFormat, Shadow, SoftEdge, TextFrame2, and ThreeD. You can access
the ChartFormat object by using the Format method on many chart elements. Table 11.3
lists a sampling of chart elements that can be formatted using the Format method.

Table 11.3   Chart Elements to Which Formatting Applies

Chart Element	VBA to Refer to This Chart
Chart Title	`ChartTitle`
Axis Title - Category	`Axes(xlCategory, xlPrimary).AxisTitle`
Axis Title - Value	`Axes(xlValue, xlPrimary).AxisTitle`
Legend	`Legend`
Data Labels for Series 1	`SeriesCollection(1).DataLabels`
Data Labels for Point 2	`SeriesCollection(1).DataLabels(2) or` `SeriesCollection(1).Points(2).DataLabel`

Chart Element	VBA to Refer to This Chart
Data Table	`DataTable`
Axes – Horizontal	`Axes(xlCategory, xlPrimary)`
Axes – Vertical	`Axes(xlValue, xlPrimary)`
Axis – Series (Surface Charts Only)	`Axes(xlSeries, xlPrimary)`
Major Gridlines	`Axes(xlValue, xlPrimary).MajorGridlines`
Minor Gridlines	`Axes(xlValue, xlPrimary).MinorGridlines`
Plot Area	`PlotArea`
Chart Area	`ChartArea`
Chart Wall	`Walls`
Chart Back Wall	`BackWall`
Chart Side Wall	`SideWall`
Chart Floor	`Floor`
Trendline for Series 1	`SeriesCollection(1).TrendLines(1)`
Droplines	`ChartGroups(1).DropLines`
Up/Down Bars	`ChartGroups(1).UpBars`
Error Bars	`SeriesCollection(1).ErrorBars`
Series(1)	`SeriesCollection(1)`
Series(1) DataPoint	`SeriesCollection(1).Points(3)`

The `Format` method is the gateway to settings for `Fill`, `Glow`, and so on. Each of those objects has different options. The following sections provide examples of how to set up each type of format.

Changing an Object's Fill

As shown in Figure 11.5, the Shape Fill drop-down on the Format tab enables you to choose a single color, a gradient, a picture, or a texture for the fill.

To apply a specific color, you can use the RGB (red, green, blue) setting. To create a color, you specify a value from 0 to 255 for levels of red, green, and blue. The following code applies a simple blue fill:

```
Dim cht As Chart
Dim upb As UpBars
Set cht = ActiveChart
Set upb = cht.ChartGroups(1).UpBars
upb.Format.Fill.ForeColor.RGB = RGB(0, 0, 255)
```

If you would like an object to pick up the color from a specific theme accent color, you use the `ObjectThemeColor` property. The following code changes the bar color of the first series to accent color 6, which is an orange color in the Office theme. However, this might be another color if the workbook is using a different theme.

```
Sub ApplyThemeColor()
    Dim cht As Chart
    Dim ser As Series
    Set cht = ActiveChart
    Set ser = cht.SeriesCollection(1)
    ser.Format.Fill.ForeColor.ObjectThemeColor = msoThemeColorAccent6
End Sub
```

To apply a built-in texture, you use the PresetTextured method. The following code applies a green marble texture to the second series. However, you can apply any of the 20 different textures:

```
Sub ApplyTexture()
    Dim cht As Chart
    Dim ser As Series
    Set cht = ActiveChart
    Set ser = cht.SeriesCollection(2)
    ser.Format.Fill.PresetTextured msoTextureGreenMarble
End Sub
```

Figure 11.5
Fill options include a solid color, a gradient, a texture, or a picture.

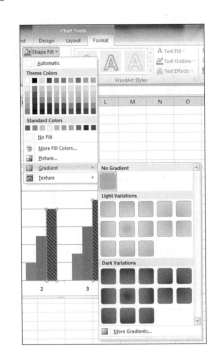

> **TIP**
> When you type PresetTextured followed by a space, the VB Editor offers a complete list of possible texture values.

To fill the bars of a data series with a picture, you use the `UserPicture` method and specify the path and filename of an image on the computer, as in the following example:

```
Sub FormatWithPicture()
    Dim cht As Chart
    Dim ser As Series
    Set cht = ActiveChart
    Set ser = cht.SeriesCollection(1)
    MyPic = "C:\PodCastTitle1.jpg"
    ser.Format.Fill.UserPicture MyPic
End Sub
```

Microsoft removed patterns as fills from Excel 2007. However, this method was restored in Excel 2010 because of the outcry from customers who used patterns to differentiate columns printed on monochrome printers.

In Excel 2010, you can apply a pattern using the `.Patterned` method. Patterns have a type such as `msoPatternPlain`, as well as a foreground and background color. The following code creates dark red vertical lines on a white background:

```
Sub FormatWithPicture()
    Dim cht As Chart
    Dim ser As Series
    Set cht = ActiveChart
    Set ser = cht.SeriesCollection(1)
    With ser.Format.Fill
        .Patterned msoPatternDarkVertical
        .BackColor.RGB = RGB(255,255,255)
        .ForeColor.RGB = RGB(255,0,0)
    End With
End Sub
```

> **CAUTION**
>
> Code that uses patterns will work in every version of Excel except Excel 2007. Therefore, do not use this code if you will be sharing the macro with coworkers who use Excel 2007.

Gradients are more difficult to specify than fills. Excel 2010 provides three methods that help you set up the common gradients. The `OneColorGradient` and `TwoColorGradient` methods require that you specify a gradient direction such as `msoGradientFromCorner`. You can then specify one of four styles, numbered 1 through 4, depending on whether you want the gradient to start at the top left, top right, bottom left, or bottom right. After using a gradient method, you need to specify the `ForeColor` and the `BackColor` settings for the object. The following macro sets up a two-color gradient using two theme colors:

```
Sub TwoColorGradient()
    Dim cht As Chart
    Dim ser As Series
    Set cht = ActiveChart
    Set ser = cht.SeriesCollection(1)
```

11

```
        ser.Format.Fill.TwoColorGradient msoGradientFromCorner, 3
        ser.Format.Fill.ForeColor.ObjectThemeColor = msoThemeColorAccent6
        ser.Format.Fill.BackColor.ObjectThemeColor = msoThemeColorAccent2
    End Sub
```

When using the OneColorGradient method, you specify a direction, a style (1 through 4), and a darkness value between 0 and 1 (0 for darker gradients or 1 for lighter gradients).

When using the PresetGradient method, you specify a direction, a style (1 through 4), and the type of gradient such as msoGradientBrass, msoGradientLateSunset, or msoGradientRainbow. Again, as you are typing this code in the VB Editor, the AutoComplete tool provides a complete list of the available preset gradient types.

Formatting Line Settings

The LineFormat object formats either a line or the border around an object. You can change numerous properties for a line, such as the color, arrows, dash style, and so on.

The following macro formats the trendline for the first series in a chart:

```
    Sub FormatLineOrBorders()
        Dim cht As Chart
        Set cht = ActiveChart
        With cht.SeriesCollection(1).Trendlines(1).Format.Line
            .DashStyle = msoLineLongDashDotDot
            .ForeColor.RGB = RGB(50, 0, 128)
            .BeginArrowheadLength = msoArrowheadShort
            .BeginArrowheadStyle = msoArrowheadOval
            .BeginArrowheadWidth = msoArrowheadNarrow
            .EndArrowheadLength = msoArrowheadLong
            .EndArrowheadStyle = msoArrowheadTriangle
            .EndArrowheadWidth = msoArrowheadWide
        End With
    End Sub
```

When you are formatting a border, the arrow settings are not relevant, so the code is shorter than the code for formatting a line. The following macro formats the border around a chart:

```
    Sub FormatBorder()
        Dim cht As Chart
        Set cht = ActiveChart
        With cht.ChartArea.Format.Line
            .DashStyle = msoLineLongDashDotDot
            .ForeColor.RGB = RGB(50, 0, 128)
        End With
    End Sub
```

Formatting Glow Settings

To create a glow, you have to specify a color and a radius. The radius value can be from 1 to 20. A radius of 1 is barely visible, whereas a radius of 20 is often too thick.

The following macro adds a line around the title and adds a glow around that line:

```
Sub AddGlowToTitle()
    Dim cht As Chart
    Set cht = ActiveChart
    cht.ChartTitle.Format.Line.ForeColor.RGB = RGB(255, 255, 255)
    cht.ChartTitle.Format.Line.DashStyle = msoLineSolid
    cht.ChartTitle.Format.Glow.Color.ObjectThemeColor = msoThemeColorAccent6
    cht.ChartTitle.Format.Glow.Radius = 8
End Sub
```

Formatting Shadow Settings

A shadow is composed of a color, a transparency, and the number of points by which the shadow should be offset from the object. If you increase the number of points, it appears that the object is farther from the surface of the chart. The horizontal offset is known as OffsetX, and the vertical offset is known as OffsetY.

The following macro adds a light blue shadow to the box surrounding a legend:

```
Sub FormatShadow()
    Dim cht As Chart
    Set cht = ActiveChart
    With cht.Legend.Format.Shadow
        .ForeColor.RGB = RGB(0, 0, 128)
        .OffsetX = 5
        .OffsetY = -3
        .Transparency = 0.5
        .Visible = True
    End With
End Sub
```

Formatting Reflection Settings

No chart elements can have reflections applied. The Reflection settings on the Format tab are grayed-out continuously when a chart is selected. Similarly, the ChartFormat object does not have a reflection object.

Formatting Soft Edges

There are six levels of soft edge settings. The settings feather the edges by 1, 2.5, 5, 10, 25, or 50 points. The first setting is barely visible. The biggest settings are usually larger than most of the chart elements you are likely to format.

Microsoft says that the following is the proper syntax for SoftEdge:

```
Chart.Seriess(1).Points(i).Format.SoftEdge.Type = msoSoftEdgeType1
```

11

However, `msoSoftEdgeType1` and words like it are really variables defined by Excel. To try a cool trick, go to the VB Editor and open the Immediate window by pressing Ctrl+G. In the Immediate window, type `Print msoSoftEdgeType2` and press Enter. The Immediate window tells you that using this word is equivalent to typing 2. Therefore, you can use either `mso-SoftEdgeType2` or the value 2.

If you use `msoSoftEdgeType2`, your code will be slightly easier to understand than if you use simply 2. However, if you hope to format each point of a data series with a different format, you might want to use a loop such as this one, in which case it is far easier to use just the numbers 1 through 6 than `msoSoftEdgeType1` through `msoSoftEdgeType6`, as shown in this macro:

```
Sub FormatSoftEdgesWithLoop()
    Dim cht As Chart
    Dim ser As Series
    Set cht = ActiveChart
    Set ser = cht.SeriesCollection(1)
    For i = 1 To 6
        ser.Points(i).Format.SoftEdge.Type = i
    Next i
End Sub
```

> **CAUTION**
>
> It is a bit strange that the soft edges are defined as a fixed number of points. In a chart that is sized to fit an entire sheet of paper, a 10-point soft edge might work fine. However, if you resize the chart so that you can fit six charts on a page, a 10-point soft edge applied to all sides of a column might make the column completely disappear.

Formatting 3-D Rotation Settings

The 3-D settings handle three different menus on the Format tab. In the Shape Effects drop-down, settings under Preset, Bevel, and 3-D are all actually handled by the `ThreeD` object in the `ChartFormat` object. This section discusses settings that affect the 3-D rotation. The next section discusses settings that affect the bevel and 3-D format.

The methods and properties that can be set for the `ThreeD` object are very broad. In fact, the 3-D settings in VBA include more preset options than do the menus on the Format tab.

Figure 11.6 shows the presets available in the 3-D Rotation fly-out menu.

To apply one of the 3-D rotation presets to a chart element, you use the `SetPresetCamera` method, as shown here:

```
Sub Assign3DPreset()
    Dim cht As Chart
    Dim shp As Shape
    Set cht = ActiveChart
    Set shp = cht.Shapes(1)
    shp.ThreeD.SetPresetCamera msoCameraIsometricLeftDown
End Sub
```

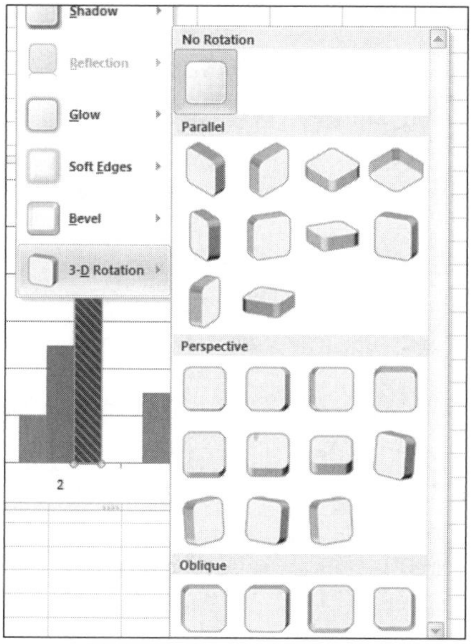

Figure 11.6
Whereas the 3-D Rotation menu offers 25 presets, VBA offers 62 presets.

Table 11.4 lists all the possible `SetPresetCamera` values.

> **T I P**
>
> If the first column indicates that it is a bonus or an Excel 2003 style, you know the value is a preset that is available in VBA. However, the value was not chosen by Microsoft to be included in the 3-D Rotation fly-out menu. You can make some charts in Excel 2010 that no one else will be able to replicate using the Excel interface.

Table 11.4   3-D Preset Formats and Their VBA Constant Values

Menu Location	Description	VBA Value
Parallel group, row 1, column 1	Isometric Left Down	msoCameraIsometricLeftDown
Parallel group, row 1, column 2	Isometric Right Up	msoCameraIsometricRightUp
Parallel group, row 1, column 3	Isometric Top Up	msoCameraIsometricTopUp
Parallel group, row 1, column 4	Isometric Bottom Down	msoCameraIsometricBottomDown
Parallel group, row 2, column 1	Isometric OffAxis1 Left	msoCameraIsometricOffAxis1Left
Parallel group, row 2, column 2	Isometric OffAxis1 Right	msoCameraIsometricOffAxis1Right

Table 11.4   Continued

Menu Location	Description	VBA Value
Parallel group, row 2, column 3	Isometric OffAxis1 Top	`msoCameraIsometricOffAxis1Top`
Parallel group, row 2, column 4	Isometric OffAxis2 Left	`msoCameraIsometricOffAxis2Left`
Parallel group, row 3, column 1	Isometric OffAxis2 Right	`msoCameraIsometricOffAxis2Right`
Parallel group, row 3, column 2	Isometric OffAxis2 Top	`msoCameraIsometricOffAxis2Top`
Parallel group, bonus selection	Isometric Bottom Up	`msoCameraIsometricBottomUp`
Parallel group, bonus selection	Isometric Left Up	`msoCameraIsometricLeftUp`
Parallel group, bonus selection	Isometric OffAxis3 Bottom	`msoCameraIsometricOffAxis3Bottom`
Parallel group, bonus selection	Isometric OffAxis3 Left	`msoCameraIsometricOffAxis3Left`
Parallel group, bonus selection	Isometric OffAxis3 Right	`msoCameraIsometricOffAxis3Right`
Parallel group, bonus selection	Isometric OffAxis4 Bottom	`msoCameraIsometricOffAxis4Bottom`
Parallel group, bonus selection	Isometric OffAxis4 Left	`msoCameraIsometricOffAxis4Left`
Parallel group, bonus selection	Isometric OffAxis4 Right	`msoCameraIsometricOffAxis4Right`
Parallel group, bonus selection	Isometric Right Down	`msoCameraIsometricRightDown`
Parallel group, bonus selection	Isometric Top Down	`msoCameraIsometricTopDown`
Perspective group, row 1, column 1	Perspective Front	`msoCameraPerspectiveFront`
Perspective group, row 1, column 2	Perspective Left	`msoCameraPerspectiveLeft`
Perspective group, row 1, column 3	Perspective Right	`msoCameraPerspectiveRight`
Perspective group, row 1, column 4	Perspective Below	`msoCameraPerspectiveBelow`
Perspective group, row 2, column 1	Perspective Above	`msoCameraPerspectiveAbove`
Perspective group, row 2, column 2	Perspective Relaxed Moderately	`msoCameraPerspectiveRelaxedModerately`

11

Menu Location	Description	VBA Value
Perspective group, row 2, column 3	Perspective Relaxed	`msoCameraPerspectiveRelaxed`
Perspective group, row 2, column 4	Perspective Contrasting Left Facing	`msoCameraPerspectiveContrastingLeft-Facing`
Perspective group, row 3, column 1	Perspective Contrasting Right Facing	`msoCameraPerspectiveContrastingRight-Facing`
Perspective group, row 3, column 2	Perspective Heroic Extreme Left Facing	`msoCameraPerspectiveHeroicEx-tremeLeftFacing`
Perspective group, row 3, column 3	Perspective Heroic Extreme Right Facing	`msoCameraPerspectiveHeroicExtremeR-ightFacing`
Perspective group, bonus selection	Perspective Above Left Facing	`msoCameraPerspectiveAboveLeftFacing`
Perspective group, bonus selection	Perspective Above Right Facing	`msoCameraPerspectiveAboveRightFacing`
Perspective group, bonus selection	Perspective Heroic Left Facing	`msoCameraPerspectiveHeroicLeftFacing`
Perspective group, bonus selection	Perspective Heroic Right Facing	`msoCameraPerspectiveHeroicRightFacing`
Perspective group, Excel 2003 styles	Legacy Perspective Bottom	`msoCameraLegacyPerspectiveBottom`
Perspective group, Excel 2003 styles	Legacy Perspective Lower Left	`msoCameraLegacyPerspectiveBottomLeft`
Perspective group, Excel 2003 styles	Legacy Perspective Lower Right	`msoCameraLegacyPerspectiveBottomRight`
Perspective group, Excel 2003 styles	Legacy Perspective Front	`msoCameraLegacyPerspectiveFront`
Perspective group, Excel 2003 styles	Legacy Perspective Left	`msoCameraLegacyPerspectiveLeft`
Perspective group, Excel 2003 styles	Legacy Perspective Right	`msoCameraLegacyPerspectiveRight`
Perspective group, Excel 2003 styles	Legacy Perspective Top	`msoCameraLegacyPerspectiveTop`
Perspective group, Excel 2003 styles	Legacy Perspective Upper Left	`msoCameraLegacyPerspectiveTopLeft`
Perspective group, Excel 2003 styles	Legacy Perspective Upper Right	`msoCameraLegacyPerspectiveTopRight`
Oblique group, row 1, column 1	Oblique Upper Left	`msoCameraObliqueTopLeft`
Oblique group, row 1, column 2	Oblique Upper Right	`msoCameraObliqueTopRight`

11

Table 11.4 Continued

Menu Location	Description	VBA Value
Oblique group, row 1, column 3	Oblique Lower Left	`msoCameraObliqueBottomLeft`
Oblique group, row 1, column 4	Oblique Lower Right	`msoCameraObliqueBottomRight`
Oblique group, bonus selection	Oblique Bottom	`msoCameraObliqueBottom`
Oblique group, bonus selection	Oblique Left	`msoCameraObliqueLeft`
Oblique group, bonus selection	Oblique Right	`msoCameraObliqueRight`
Oblique group, bonus selection	Oblique Top	`msoCameraObliqueTop`
Oblique group, bonus selection	Orthographic Front	`msoCameraOrthographicFront`
Oblique group, Excel 2003 styles	Legacy Oblique Bottom	`msoCameraLegacyObliqueBottom`
Oblique group, Excel 2003 styles	Legacy Oblique Lower Left	`msoCameraLegacyObliqueBottomLeft`
Oblique group, Excel 2003 styles	Legacy Oblique Lower Right	`msoCameraLegacyObliqueBottomRight`
Oblique group, Excel 2003 styles	Legacy Oblique Front	`msoCameraLegacyObliqueFront`
Oblique group, Excel 2003 styles	Legacy Oblique Left	`msoCameraLegacyObliqueLeft`
Oblique group, Excel 2003 styles	Legacy Oblique Right	`msoCameraLegacyObliqueRight`
Oblique group, Excel 2003 styles	Legacy Oblique Top	`msoCameraLegacyObliqueTop`
Oblique group, Excel 2003 styles	Legacy Oblique Upper Left	`msoCameraLegacyObliqueTopLeft`
Oblique group, Excel 2003 styles	Legacy Oblique Upper Right	`msoCameraLegacyObliqueTopRight`

If you prefer not to use the presets, you can explicitly control the rotation around the x-, y-, or z-axis. You can use the following properties and methods to change the rotation of an object:

- RotationX—Returns or sets the rotation of the extruded shape around the x-axis, in degrees. This can be a value from -90 through 90. A positive value indicates upward rotation; a negative value indicates downward rotation.

- RotationY—Returns or sets the rotation of the extruded shape around the y-axis, in degrees. This can be a value from -90 through 90. A positive value indicates rotation to the left; a negative value indicates rotation to the right.

- RotationZ—Returns or sets the rotation of the extruded shape around the z-axis, in degrees. This can be a value from -90 through 90. A positive value indicates upward rotation; a negative value indicates downward rotation.

- IncrementRotationX—Changes the rotation of the specified shape around the x-axis by the specified number of degrees. You specify an increment from -90 to 90. Negative degrees tip the object down, and positive degrees tip the object up.

> **TIP**
>
> You can use the RotationX property to set the absolute rotation of the shape around the x-axis.

- IncrementRotationY—Changes the rotation of the specified shape around the y-axis by the specified number of degrees. A positive value tilts the object left, and a negative value tips the object right.

> **TIP**
>
> You can use the RotationY property to set the absolute rotation of the shape around the y-axis.

- IncrementRotationZ—Changes the rotation of the specified shape around the z-axis by the specified number of degrees. A positive value tilts the object left, and a negative value tips the object right.

> **TIP**
>
> You can use the RotationZ property to set the absolute rotation of the shape around the z-axis.

- IncrementRotationHorizontal—Changes the rotation of the specified shape horizontally by the specified number of degrees. You specify an increment from -90 to 90 to specify how much (in degrees) the rotation of the shape is to be changed horizontally. A positive value moves the shape left; a negative value moves it right.

- IncrementRotationVertical—Changes the rotation of the specified shape vertically by the specified number of degrees. You specify an increment from -90 to 90 to specify how much (in degrees) the rotation of the shape is to be changed horizontally. A positive value moves the shape left; a negative value moves it right.

- ResetRotation—Resets the extrusion rotation around the x-axis and the y-axis to 0 so that the front of the extrusion faces forward. This method does not reset the rotation around the z-axis.

11

Changing the Bevel and 3-D Format

There are 12 presets in the Bevel fly-out menu. These presets affect the bevel on the top face of the object. In charts, you usually see the top face. However, there are some bizarre rotations of a 3-D chart where you see the bottom face of charting elements.

The Format Shape dialog contains the same 12 presets as the Bevel fly-out but allows you to apply the preset to the top or bottom face. You can also control the width and height of the bevel. The VBA properties and methods correspond to the settings on the 3-D Format category of the Format Shape dialog (see Figure 11.7).

You set the type of bevel by using the BevelTopType and BevelBottomType properties. You can further modify the bevel type by setting the BevelTopInset value to set the width and the BevelTopDepth value to set the height. The following macro adds a bevel to the columns of Series 1:

```
Sub AssignBevel()
    Dim cht As Chart
    Dim ser As Series
    Set cht = ActiveChart
    Set ser = cht.SeriesCollection(1)
    ser.Format.ThreeD.Visible = True
    ser.Format.ThreeD.BevelTopType = msoBevelCircle
    ser.Format.ThreeD.BevelTopInset = 16
    ser.Format.ThreeD.BevelTopDepth = 6
End Sub
```

11

Figure 11.7
You can control the 3-D Format settings such as bevel, surface, and lighting.

The 12 possible settings for the bevel type are shown in Table 11.5; these settings correspond to the thumbnails in the fly-out menu. To turn off the bevel, you use msoBevelNone.

Table 11.5 Bevel Types

Location in Figure 11.17	Constant	Value
Row 1, column 1	msoBevelCircle	3
Row 1, column 2	msoBevelRelaxedInset	2
Row 1, column 3	msoBevelCross	5
Row 1, column 4	msoBevelCoolSlant	9
Row 2, column 1	msoBevelAngle	6
Row 2, column 2	msoBevelSoftRound	7
Row 2, column 3	msoBevelConvex	8
Row 2, column 4	msoBevelSlope	4
Row 3, column 1	msoBevelDivot	10
Row 3, column 2	msoBevelRiblet	11
Row 3, column 3	msoBevelHardEdge	12
Row 3, column 4	msoBevelArtDeco	13

Usually, the accent color used in a bevel is based on the color used to fill the object. However, if you would like control over the extrusion color, you should first specify that the extrusion color type is custom and then specify either a theme accent color or an RGB color. Here's an example:

```
ser.Format.ThreeD.ExtrusionColorType = msoExtrusionColorCustom
' either use this:
ser.Format.ThreeD.ExtrusionColor.ObjectThemeColor = msoThemeColorAccent1
' or this:
ser.Format.ThreeD.ExtrusionColor.RGB = RGB(255, 0, 0)
```

You use the Depth property to control the amount of extrusion in the bevel, and you specify the depth in points. Here's an example:

```
ser.Format.ThreeD.Depth = 5
```

For the contour, you can specify either a color or a size of the contour or both. You can specify the color as an RGB value or a theme color. You specify the size in points, using the ContourWidth property. Here's an example:

```
ser.Format.ThreeD.ContourColor.RGB = RGB(0, 255, 0)
ser.Format.ThreeD.ContourWidth = 10
```

The Surface drop-downs are controlled by the following properties:

- PresetMaterial—Contains choices from the Material drop-down
- PresetLighting—Contains choices from the Lighting drop-down
- LightAngle—Controls the angle from which the light is shining on the object

The Material drop-down menu from the 3-D category of the Format dialog box offers 11 settings, although it appears that Microsoft designed a 12th setting in the object model. It is not clear why Microsoft does not offer the SoftMetal style in the dialog box, but you can use it in VBA.

In addition, there are three legacy styles in the object model, which are not available in the Format dialog box. In theory, the new Plastic2 material is better than the old Plastic material. Table 11.6 shows the settings for each thumbnail.

Table 11.6   VBA Constants for Material Types

Type	VBA Constant	Value
Matte	msoMaterialMatte2	5
Warm Matte	msoMaterialWarmMatte	8
Plastic	msoMaterialPlastic2	6
Metal	msoMaterialMetal2	7
Dark Edge	msoMaterialDarkEdge	11
Soft Edge	msoMaterialSoftEdge	12
Flat	msoMaterialFlat	14
Wire Frame	msoMaterialWireFrame	4
Powder	msoMaterialPowder	10
Translucent Powder	msoMaterialTranslucentPowder	9
Clear	msoMaterialClear	13
Bonus	msoMaterialMatte	1
Bonus	msoMaterialPlastic	2
Bonus	msoMaterialMetal	3
Bonus	msoMaterialSoftMetal	15

In legacy versions of Excel, the material property was limited to matte, metal, plastic, and wire frame. Microsoft apparently was not happy with the old matte, metal, and plastic settings. It left those values in place to support legacy charts but created the new Matte2, Plastic2, and Metal2 settings. These settings are actually available in the dialog box. In VBA, you are free to use either the old or the new settings.

The columns in Figure 11.8 compare the new and old settings. The final column is for the SoftMetal setting that Microsoft left out of the Format dialog box. This was probably an aesthetic decision instead of an "oh no; this setting crashes the computer" decision. You should feel free to use msoMaterialSoftMetal to create a look that has a subtle difference from charts others create using the settings in the Format dialog box.

The Lighting drop-down menu from the 3-D category of the Format dialog box offers 15 settings. The object model offers these 15 settings, plus 13 legacy settings from the Excel 2003 Lighting toolbar. Table 11.7 shows the settings for each of these thumbnails.

Figure 11.8
Comparison of some new and old material presets.

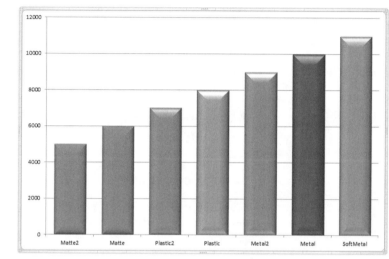

Table 11.7   VBA Constants for Lighting Types

Type	VBA Constant	Value
Neutral Category		
ThreePoint	msoLightRigThreePoint	13
Balanced	msoLightRigBalanced	14
Soft	msoLightRigSoft	15
Harsh	msoLightRigHarsh	16
Flood	msoLightRigFlood	17
Contrasting	msoLightRigContrasting	18
Warm Category		
Morning	msoLightRigMorning	19
Sunrise	msoLightRigSunrise	20
Sunset	msoLightRigSunset	21
Cool Category		
Chilly	msoLightRigChilly	22
Freezing	msoLightRigFreezing	23

11

Table 11.7   Continued

Type	VBA Constant	Value
Special Category		
Flat	msoLightRigFlat	24
TwoPoint	msoLightRigTwoPoint	25
Glow	msoLightRigGlow	26
BrightRoom	msoLightRigBrightRoom	27
Legacy Category		
Flat 1	msoLightRigLegacyFlat1	1
Flat 2	msoLightRigLegacyFlat2	2
Flat 3	msoLightRigLegacyFlat3	3
Flat 4	msoLightRigLegacyFlat4	4
Harsh 1	msoLightRigLegacyHarsh1	9
Harsh 2	msoLightRigLegacyHarsh2	10
Harsh 3	msoLightRigLegacyHarsh3	11
Harsh 4	msoLightRigLegacyHarsh4	12
Normal 1	msoLightRigLegacyNormal1	5
Normal 2	msoLightRigLegacyNormal2	6
Normal 3	msoLightRigLegacyNormal3	7
Normal 4	msoLightRigLegacyNormal4	8
Mixed	msoLightRigMixed	–2

Creating Advanced Charts

In *Charts & Graphs for Microsoft Excel 2010* (Que, ISBN 0789743124), I included some amazing charts that do not look like they can possibly be created using Excel. Building these charts usually involves adding a rogue data series that appears in the chart as an XY series to complete some effect.

The process of creating these charts manually is very tedious, which ensures that most people will never resort to creating such charts. However, if the process could be automated, the creation of the charts starts to become feasible.

The next sections explain how to use VBA to automate the process of creating these rather complex charts.

Creating True Open-High-Low-Close Stock Charts

If you are a fan of stock charts in the *Wall Street Journal* or finance.yahoo.com, you will recognize the chart type known as Open-High-Low-Close (OHLC) chart. Excel does not offer such a chart. Its High-Low-Close (HLC) chart is missing the left-facing dash that represents the opening for each period. You might think that HLC charts are close enough to OHLC charts. However, one of my personal pet peeves is that the WSJ can create better-looking charts than Excel can.

In Figure 11.9, you can see a true OHLC chart.

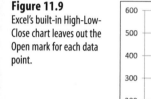

Figure 11.9
Excel's built-in High-Low-Close chart leaves out the Open mark for each data point.

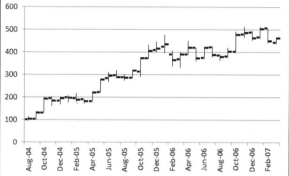

> **NOTE**
> In Excel 2010, you can specify a custom picture that you can use as the marker in a chart. Given that Excel has a right-facing dash but not a left-facing dash, you need to use Photoshop to create a left-facing dash as a GIF file. This tiny graphic makes up for the fundamental flaw in Excel's chart marker selection.

> **TIP**
> You can also download a LeftDash.gif file from http://www.mrexcel.com/getcode2010.html.

In the Excel user interface, you will indicate that the Open series should have a custom picture and then specify LeftDash.gif as the picture. In VBA code, you use the UserPicture method, as shown here:

```
ActiveChart Cht.SeriesCollection(1).Fill.UserPicture "C:\leftdash.gif"
```

To create a true OHLC chart, follow these steps:

1. Create a line chart from four series; Open, High, Low, Close.
2. Change the line style to none for all four series.
3. Eliminate the marker for the High and Low series.
4. Add a High-Low line to the chart.

5. Change the marker for Close to a right-facing dash, which is called a dot in VBA, with a size of 9.

6. Change the marker for Open to a custom picture and load `LeftDash.gif` as the fill for the series.

The following code creates the top chart in Figure 11.9:

```
Sub CreateOHCLChart()
    ' Download leftdash.gif from the sample files for this book
    ' and save it in the same folder as this workbook
    Dim Cht As Chart
    Dim Ser As Series

    ActiveSheet.Shapes.AddChart(xlLineMarkers).Select
    Set Cht = ActiveChart
    Cht.SetSourceData Source:=Range("Sheet1!$A$1:$E$33")
    ' Format the Open Series
    With Cht.SeriesCollection(1)
        .MarkerStyle = xlMarkerStylePicture
        .Fill.UserPicture ("C:\leftdash.gif")
        .Border.LineStyle = xlNone
        .MarkerForegroundColorIndex = xlColorIndexNone
    End With
    ' Format High & Low Series
    With Cht.SeriesCollection(2)
        .MarkerStyle = xlMarkerStyleNone
        .Border.LineStyle = xlNone
    End With
    With Cht.SeriesCollection(3)
        .MarkerStyle = xlMarkerStyleNone
        .Border.LineStyle = xlNone
    End With
    ' Format the Close series
    Set Ser = Cht.SeriesCollection(4)
    With Ser
        .MarkerBackgroundColorIndex = 1
        .MarkerForegroundColorIndex = 1
        .MarkerStyle = xlDot
        .MarkerSize = 9
        .Border.LineStyle = xlNone
    End With
    ' Add High-Low Lines
    Cht.SetElement (msoElementLineHiLoLine)
    Cht.SetElement (msoElementLegendNone)

End Sub
```

Creating Bins for a Frequency Chart

Suppose that you have results from 3,000 scientific trials. There must be a good way to produce a chart of those results. However, if you just select the results and create a chart, you will end up with chaos (see Figure 11.10).

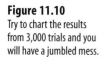

Figure 11.10
Try to chart the results
from 3,000 trials and you
will have a jumbled mess.

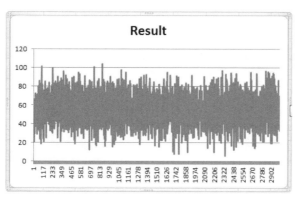

The trick to creating an effective frequency distribution is to define a series of categories, or *bins*. A FREQUENCY array function counts the number of items from the 3,000 results that fall within each bin.

The process of creating bins manually is rather tedious and requires knowledge of array formulas. It is better to use a macro to perform all of the tedious calculations.

The macro in this section requires you to specify a bin size and a starting bin. If you expect results in the 0 to 100 range, you might specify bins of 10 each, starting at 0. This would create bins of 0–10, 11–20, 21–30, and so on. If you specify bin sizes of 15 with a starting bin of 5, the macro will create bins of 5–20, 21–35, 36–50, and so on.

To use the following macro, your trial results should start in Row 2 and should be in the rightmost column of a dataset. Three variables near the top of the macro define the starting bin, the ending bin, and the bin size:

```
' Define Bins
BinSize = 10
FirstBin = 0
LastBin = 100
```

After that, the macro skips a column and then builds a range of starting bins. In Cell D4 in Figure 11.11, the 10 is used to tell Excel that you are looking for the number of values larger than the 0 in D3, but equal to or less than the 10 in D4.

Although the bins extend from D3:D13, the FREQUENCY function entered in Column E needs to include one extra cell, in case any results are larger than the last bin. This single formula returns many results. Formulas that return more than one answer are called *array formulas*. In the Excel user interface, you specify an array formula by holding down Ctrl+Shift while pressing Enter to finish the formula. In Excel VBA, you need to use the FormulaArray property. The following lines of the macro set up the array formula in Column E:

```
' Enter the Frequency Formula
Form = "=FREQUENCY(R2C" & FinalCol & ":R" & FinalRow & "C" & FinalCol & _
    ",R3C" & NextCol & ":R" & _
    LastRow & "C" & NextCol & ")"
Range(Cells(FirstRow, NextCol + 1), Cells(LastRow, NextCol + 1)). _
    FormulaArray = Form
```

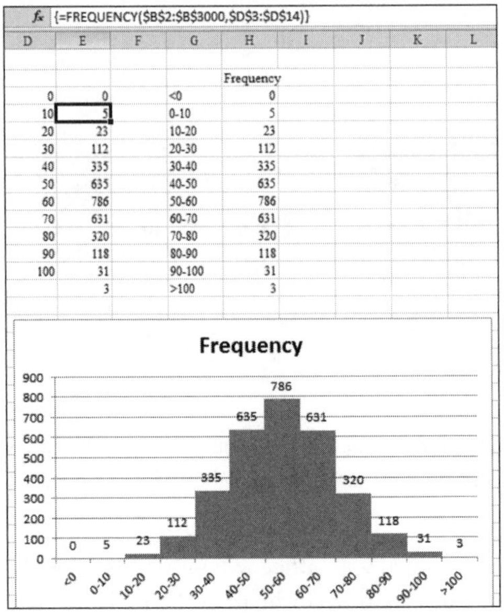

Figure 11.11

The macro summarizes the results into bins and provides a meaningful chart of the data.

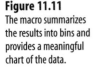

It is not evident to the reader if the bin indicated in Column D is the upper or lower limit. The macro builds readable labels in Column G and then copies the frequency results over to Column H.

After the macro builds a simple column chart, the following line eliminates the gap between columns, creating the traditional histogram view of the data:

```
Cht.ChartGroups(1).GapWidth = 0
```

The macro to create the chart in Figure 11.11 follows:

```
Sub CreateFrequencyChart()
    ' Find the last column
    FinalCol = Cells(1, Columns.Count).End(xlToLeft).Column
    ' Find the FinalRow
    FinalRow = Cells(Rows.Count, FinalCol).End(xlUp).Row

    ' Define Bins
    BinSize = 10
    FirstBin = 0
    LastBin = 100

    'The bins will go in row 3, two columns after FinalCol
    NextCol = FinalCol + 2
    FirstRow = 3
    NextRow = FirstRow - 1

    ' Set up the bins for the Frequency function
    For i = FirstBin To LastBin Step BinSize
        NextRow = NextRow + 1
        Cells(NextRow, NextCol).Value = i
```

```
Next i

' The Frequency function has to be one row larger than the bins
LastRow = NextRow + 1

' Enter the Frequency Formula
Form = "=FREQUENCY(R2C" & FinalCol & ":R" & FinalRow & "C" & FinalCol & _
    ",R3C" & NextCol & ":R" & _
    LastRow & "C" & NextCol & ")"
Range(Cells(FirstRow, NextCol + 1), Cells(LastRow, NextCol + 1)). _
    FormulaArray = Form

' Build a range suitable a chart source data
LabelCol = NextCol + 3
Form = "=R[-1]C[-3]&""-""&RC[-3]"
Range(Cells(4, LabelCol), Cells(LastRow - 1, LabelCol)).FormulaR1C1 = _
    Form
' Enter the > Last formula
Cells(LastRow, LabelCol).FormulaR1C1 = "="">""&R[-1]C[-3]"
' Enter the < first formula
Cells(3, LabelCol).FormulaR1C1 = "=""<""&RC[-3]"

' Enter the formula to copy the frequency results
Range(Cells(3, LabelCol + 1), Cells(LastRow, LabelCol + 1)).FormulaR1C1 = _
    "=RC[-3]"
' Add a heading
Cells(2, LabelCol + 1).Value = "Frequency"

' Create a column chart
Dim Cht As Chart
ActiveSheet.Shapes.AddChart(xlColumnClustered).Select
Set Cht = ActiveChart
Cht.SetSourceData Source:=Range(Cells(2, LabelCol), _
    Cells(LastRow, LabelCol + 1))
Cht.SetElement (msoElementLegendNone)
Cht.ChartGroups(1).GapWidth = 0
Cht.SetElement (msoElementDataLabelOutSideEnd)

End Sub
```

Creating a Stacked Area Chart

The stacked area chart shown in Figure 11.12 is incredibly difficult to create in the Excel user interface. Although the chart appears to contain four independent charts, this chart actually contains nine series:

- The first series contains the values for the East region.
- The second series contains 1,000 minus the East values. This series is formatted with a transparent fill.
- Series 3, 5, and 7 contain values for Central, Northwest, and Southwest.
- Series 4, 6, and 8 contain 1,000 minus the preceding series.

■ The final series is a XY series used to add labels for the left axis. There is one point for each gridline. The markers are positioned at an X position of 0. Custom data labels are added next to invisible markers to force the labels along the axis to start again at 0 for each region.

Figure 11.12
A single chart appears to hold four different charts.

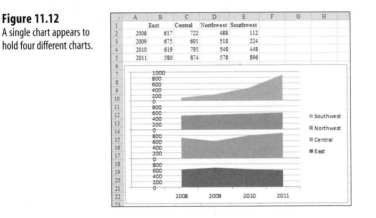

To use the macro provided here, your data should begin in Column A and Row 1. The macro adds new columns to the right of the data and new rows below the data, so the rest of the worksheet should be blank.

Two variables at the top of the macro define the height of each chart. In the current example, leaving a height of 1000 allows the sales for each region to fit comfortably. The LabSize value should indicate how frequently labels should appear along the left axis. This number must be evenly divisible into the chart height. In this example, values of 500, 250, 200, 125, or 100 would work:

```
' Define the height of each area chart
ChtHeight = 1000
' Define Tick Mark Size
' ChtHeight should be an even multiple of LabSize
LabSize = 200
```

The macro builds a copy of the data to the right of the original data. New "dummy" series are added to the right of each region to calculate 1,000 minus the data point. In Figure 11.13, this series is shown in G1:O5.

The macro then creates a stacked area chart for the first eight series. The legend for this chart indicates values of East, dummy, Central, dummy, and so on. To delete every other legend entry, use this code:

```
' Fill the dummy series with no fill
For i = FinalSeriesCount To 2 Step -2
    Cht.SeriesCollection(i).Interior.ColorIndex = xlNone
Next i
```

Figure 11.13

Extra data to the right and below the original data are created by the macro to create the chart.

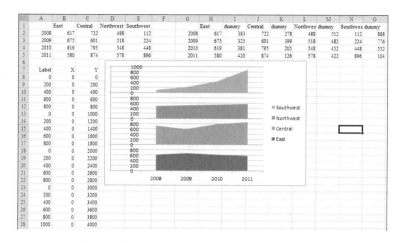

Similarly, the fill for each even numbered series in the chart needs to be set to transparent:

```
' Fill the dummy series with no fill
For i = FinalSeriesCount To 2 Step -2
    Cht.SeriesCollection(i).Interior.ColorIndex = xlNone
Next i
```

The trickiest part of the process is adding a new final series to the chart. This series will have far more data points than the other series. Range B8:C28 contains the X and Y values for the new series. You will see that each point has an X value of 0 to ensure that it appears along the left side of the plot area. The Y values increase steadily by the value indicated in the LabSize variable. In Column A next to the X and Y points are the actual labels that will be plotted next to each marker. These labels give the illusion that the chart starts over with a value of 0 for each region.

The process of adding the new series is actually much easier in VBA than in the Excel user interface. The following code identifies each component of the series and specifies that it should be plotted as an XY chart:

```
' Add the new series to the chart
Set Ser = Cht.SeriesCollection.NewSeries
With Ser
    .Name = "Y"
    .Values = Range(Cells(AxisRow + 1, 3), Cells(NewFinal, 3))
    .XValues = Range(Cells(AxisRow + 1, 2), Cells(NewFinal, 2))
    .ChartType = xlXYScatter
    .MarkerStyle = xlMarkerStyleNone
End With
```

Finally, code applies a data label from Column A to each point in the final series:

```
' Label each point in the series
' This code actually adds fake labels along left axis
For i = 1 To TickMarkCount
    Ser.Points(i).HasDataLabel = True
    Ser.Points(i).DataLabel.Text = Cells(AxisRow + i, 1).Value
Next i
```

The complete code to create the stacked chart in Figure 11.13 is shown here:

```
Sub CreatedStackedChart()
    Dim Cht As Chart
    Dim Ser As Series
    FinalRow = Cells(Rows.Count, 1).End(xlUp).Row
    FinalCol = Cells(1, Columns.Count).End(xlToLeft).Column
    OrigSeriesCount = FinalCol - 1
    FinalSeriesCount = OrigSeriesCount * 2

    ' Define the height of each area chart
    ChtHeight = 1000
    ' Define Tick Mark Size
    ' ChtHeight should be an even multiple of LabSize
    LabSize = 200

    ' Make a copy of the data
    NextCol = FinalCol + 2
    Cells(1, 1).Resize(FinalRow, FinalCol).Copy _
        Destination:=Cells(1, NextCol)
    FinalCol = Cells(1, Columns.Count).End(xlToLeft).Column

    ' Add in new columns to serve as dummy series
    MyFormula = "=" & ChtHeight & "-RC[-1]"
    For i = FinalCol + 1 To NextCol + 2 Step -1
        Cells(1, i).EntireColumn.Insert
        Cells(1, i).Value = "dummy"
        Cells(2, i).Resize(FinalRow - 1, 1).FormulaR1C1 = MyFormula
    Next i

    ' Figure out the new Final Column
    FinalCol = Cells(1, Columns.Count).End(xlToLeft).Column

    ' Build the Chart
    ActiveSheet.Shapes.AddChart(xlAreaStacked).Select
    Set Cht = ActiveChart
    Cht.SetSourceData Source:=Range(Cells(1, NextCol), Cells(FinalRow, _
        FinalCol))
    Cht.PlotBy = xlColumns

    ' Clear out the even number series from the Legend
    For i = FinalSeriesCount - 1 To 1 Step -2
        Cht.Legend.LegendEntries(i).Delete
    Next i

    ' Set the axis Maximum Scale & Gridlines
    TopScale = OrigSeriesCount * ChtHeight
    With Cht.Axes(xlValue)
        .MaximumScale = TopScale
        .MinorUnit = LabSize
        .MajorUnit = ChtHeight
    End With
    Cht.SetElement (msoElementPrimaryValueGridLinesMinorMajor)

    ' Fill the dummy series with no fill
    For i = FinalSeriesCount To 2 Step -2
```

```
            Cht.SeriesCollection(i).Interior.ColorIndex = xlNone
    Next i

    ' Hide the original axis labels
    Cht.Axes(xlValue).TickLabelPosition = xlNone

    ' Build a new range to hold a rogue XY series that will
    ' be used to create left axis labels
    AxisRow = FinalRow + 2
    Cells(AxisRow, 1).Resize(1, 3).Value = Array("Label", "X", "Y")
    TickMarkCount = OrigSeriesCount * (ChtHeight / LabSize) + 1
    ' Column B contains the X values. These are all zero
    Cells(AxisRow + 1, 2).Resize(TickMarkCount, 1).Value = 0
    ' Column C contains the Y values.
    Cells(AxisRow + 1, 3).Resize(TickMarkCount, 1).FormulaR1C1 = _
        "=R[-1]C+" & LabSize
    Cells(AxisRow + 1, 3).Value = 0
    ' Column A contains the labels to be used for each point
    Cells(AxisRow + 1, 1).Value = 0
    Cells(AxisRow + 2, 1).Resize(TickMarkCount - 1, 1).FormulaR1C1 = _
        "=IF(R[-1]C+" & LabSize & ">=" & ChtHeight & ",0,R[-1]C+" & LabSize _
        & ")"
    NewFinal = Cells(Rows.Count, 1).End(xlUp).Row
    Cells(NewFinal, 1).Value = ChtHeight

    ' Add the new series to the chart
    Set Ser = Cht.SeriesCollection.NewSeries
    With Ser
        .Name = "Y"
        .Values = Range(Cells(AxisRow + 1, 3), Cells(NewFinal, 3))
        .XValues = Range(Cells(AxisRow + 1, 2), Cells(NewFinal, 2))
        .ChartType = xlXYScatter
        .MarkerStyle = xlMarkerStyleNone
    End With

    ' Label each point in the series
    ' This code actually adds fake labels along left axis
    For i = 1 To TickMarkCount
        Ser.Points(i).HasDataLabel = True
        Ser.Points(i).DataLabel.Text = Cells(AxisRow + i, 1).Value
    Next i

    ' Hide the Y label in the legend
    Cht.Legend.LegendEntries(Cht.Legend.LegendEntries.Count).Delete
End Sub
```

NOTE The websites of Andy Pope (http://www.andypope.info) and Jon Peltier (http://peltiertech.com) are filled with examples of unusual charts that require extraordinary effort. If you find that you will regularly be creating stacked charts or any other chart like those on their websites, taking the time to write the VBA will ease the pain of creating the charts in the Excel user interface.

Exporting a Chart as a Graphic

You can export any chart to an image file on your hard drive. The `ExportChart` method requires you to specify a filename and a graphic type. The available graphic types depend on graphic file filters installed in your Registry. It is a safe bet that JPG, BMP, PNG, and GIF will work on most computers.

For example, the following code exports the active chart as a GIF file:

```
Sub ExportChart()
    Dim cht As Chart
    Set cht = ActiveChart
    cht.Export Filename:="C:\Chart.gif", Filtername:="GIF"
End Sub
```

> **CAUTION**
>
> Since Excel 2003, Microsoft has supported an Interactive argument in the Export method. Excel Help indicates that if you set Interactive to TRUE, Excel asks for additional settings depending on the file type. However, the dialog that asks for additional settings never appears—at least not for the four standard types of JPG, GIF, BMP, or PNG. To prevent any questions from popping up in the middle of your macro, set Interactive:=False.

Creating a Dynamic Chart in a Userform

With the ability to export a chart to a graphic file, you can also load a graphic file into an `Image` control in a userform. This means you can create a dialog box in which someone can dynamically control values used to plot a chart.

To create the dialog shown in Figure 11.14, follow these steps:

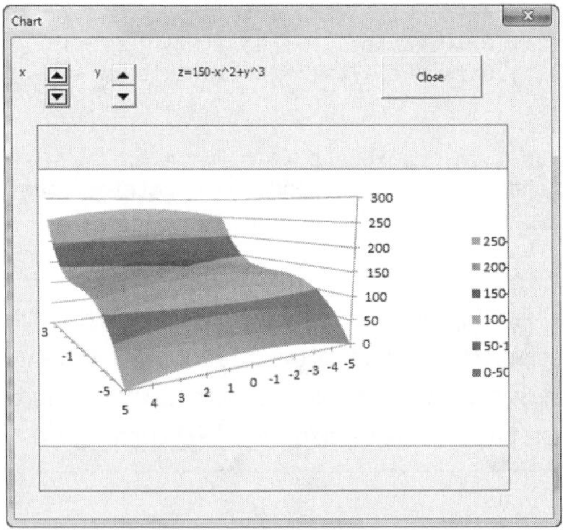

Figure 11.14
This dialog box is a VBA userform displaying a chart. The chart redraws based on changes to the dialog controls.

1. In the VBA window, select Insert, UserForm. In the Properties window, rename the form frmChart.

2. Resize the userform.

3. Add a large Image control to the userform.

4. Add two spin buttons named sbX and sbY. Set them to have a minimum of 1 and a maximum of 5.

5. Add a Label3 control to display the formula.

6. Add a command button labeled Close.

7. Enter this code in the code window behind the form:

```
Private Sub CommandButton1_Click()
    Unload Me
End Sub

Private Sub sbX_Change()
    MyPath = ThisWorkbook.Path & Application.PathSeparator & "Chart.gif"
    Worksheets("Surface").Range("O2").Value = Me.sbX.Value
    Worksheets("Surface").Shapes("Chart 1").Chart.Export MyPath
    Me.Label3.Caption = Worksheets("Surface").Range("O4").Value
    Me.Image1.Picture = LoadPicture(MyPath)
End Sub

Private Sub sbY_Change()
    MyPath = ThisWorkbook.Path & Application.PathSeparator & "Chart.gif"
    Worksheets("Surface").Range("O3").Value = Me.sbY.Value
    Worksheets("Surface").Shapes("Chart 1").Chart.Export MyPath
    Me.Label3.Caption = Worksheets("Surface").Range("O4").Value
    Me.Image1.Picture = LoadPicture(MyPath)
End Sub

Private Sub UserForm_Initialize()
    MyPath = ThisWorkbook.Path & Application.PathSeparator & "Chart.gif"
    Me.sbX = Worksheets("Surface").Range("O2").Value
    Me.sbY = Worksheets("Surface").Range("O3").Value
    Me.Label3.Caption = Worksheets("Surface").Range("O4").Value
    Worksheets("Surface").Shapes("Chart 1").Chart.Export MyPath
    Me.Image1.Picture = LoadPicture(MyPath)
End Sub
```

8. Use Insert, Module to add a Module1 component with this code:

```
Sub ShowForm()
    frmChart.Show
End Sub
```

As someone changes the spin buttons in the userform, Excel writes new values to the worksheet. This causes the chart to update. The userform code then exports the chart and displays it in the userform, as shown in Figure 11.14.

Creating Pivot Charts

A *pivot chart* is a chart that uses a pivot table as the underlying data source. Unfortunately, pivot charts do not have the cool "show pages" functionality that regular pivot tables have. You can overcome this problem with a quick VBA macro that creates a pivot table and then a pivot chart based on the pivot table. The macro then adds the customer field to the report filter area of the pivot table. It then loops through each customer and exports the chart for each customer.

In Excel 2010, you first create a pivot cache by using the `PivotCache.Create` method. You can then define a pivot table based on the pivot cache. The usual procedure is to turn off pivot table updating while you add fields to the pivot table. Then you update the pivot table to have Excel perform the calculations.

It takes a bit of finesse to figure out the final range of the pivot table. If you have turned off the column and row totals, the chartable area of the pivot table starts one row below the `PivotTableRange1` area. You have to resize the area to include one fewer row to make your chart appear correctly.

After the pivot table is created, you can switch back to the `Charts.Add` code discussed earlier in this chapter. You can use any formatting code to get the chart formatted as you desire.

The following code creates a pivot table and a single pivot chart that summarize revenue by region and product:

```
Sub CreateSummaryReportUsingPivot()
    Dim WSD As Worksheet
    Dim PTCache As PivotCache
    Dim PT As PivotTable
    Dim PRange As Range
    Dim FinalRow As Long
    Dim ChartDataRange As Range
    Dim Cht As Chart
    Set WSD = Worksheets("Data")

    ' Delete any prior pivot tables
    For Each PT In WSD.PivotTables
        PT.TableRange2.Clear
    Next PT
    WSD.Range("I1:Z1").EntireColumn.Clear

    ' Define input area and set up a Pivot Cache
    FinalRow = WSD.Cells(Application.Rows.Count, 1).End(xlUp).Row
    FinalCol = WSD.Cells(1, Application.Columns.Count). _
        End(xlToLeft).Column
    Set PRange = WSD.Cells(1, 1).Resize(FinalRow, FinalCol)
```

```
        Set PTCache = ActiveWorkbook.PivotCaches.Create(SourceType:= _
            xlDatabase, SourceData:=PRange.Address)

        ' Create the Pivot Table from the Pivot Cache
        Set PT = PTCache.CreatePivotTable(TableDestination:=WSD. _
            Cells(2, FinalCol + 2), TableName:="PivotTable1")

        ' Turn off updating while building the table
        PT.ManualUpdate = True

        ' Set up the row fields
        PT.AddFields RowFields:="Region", ColumnFields:="Product", _
            PageFields:="Customer"

        ' Set up the data fields
        With PT.PivotFields("Revenue")
            .Orientation = xlDataField
            .Function = xlSum
            .Position = 1
        End With

        With PT
            .ColumnGrand = False
            .RowGrand = False
            .NullString = "0"
        End With

        ' Calc the pivot table
        PT.ManualUpdate = False
        PT.ManualUpdate = True

        ' Define the Chart Data Range
        Set ChartDataRange = _
            PT.TableRange1.Offset(1, 0).Resize(PT.TableRange1.Rows.Count - 1)

        ' Add the Chart
        WSD.Shapes.AddChart.Select
        Set Cht = ActiveChart
        Cht.SetSourceData Source:=ChartDataRange
        ' Format the Chart
        Cht.ChartType = xlColumnClustered
        Cht.SetElement (msoElementChartTitleAboveChart)
        Cht.ChartTitle.Caption = "All Customers"
        Cht.SetElement msoElementPrimaryValueAxisThousands
        ' Excel 2010 only. Next line will not work in 2007
        Cht.ShowAllFieldButtons = False
    End Sub
```

Figure 11.15 shows the resulting chart and pivot table.

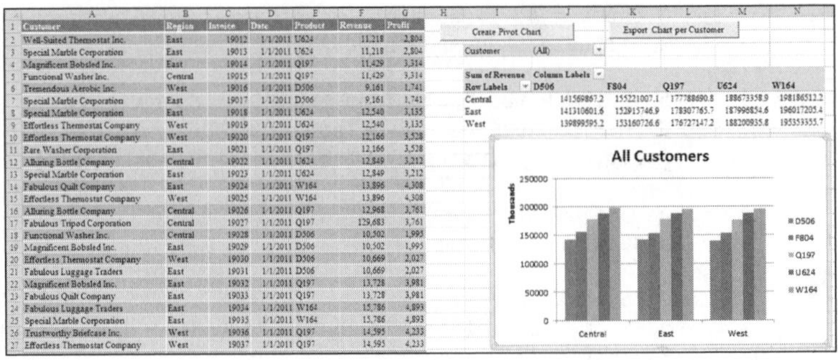

Figure 11.15
VBA creates a pivot table and then a chart from the pivot table. Excel automatically displays the PivotChart Filter window in response.

Next Steps

Charts provide a visual picture that can help to summarize data for a manager. In Chapter 12, "Data Mining with Advanced Filter," you learn about using the Advanced Filter tools to produce reports quickly.

Data Mining with Advanced Filter

12

Read this chapter.

This chapter was among the best chapters in the previous edition of this book. In the three years since that edition was released, I have discovered even more uses for Advanced Filter, AutoFilter, and even GoTo Special. In "Replacing a Loop With AutoFilter," you will see a topic that I first discovered while researching the book, *Excel Gurus Gone Wild*. This technique is dramatically faster than looking through records.

I am writing this on a Continental flight from Cleveland to Dallas after co-presenting at the Power Analyst Boot Camp. Several attendees had specific problems that needed to be solved with VBA. New filtering methods solved all of those problems. You will see those problems as case studies in this chapter.

I will estimate that I end up using one of these filtering techniques as the core of a macro in 80 percent of the macros that I develop for clients. Given that Advanced Filter is used in less than 1 percent of Excel sessions, this is a dramatic statistic.

So even if you hardly ever use Advanced Filter in regular Excel, you should study this chapter for powerful VBA techniques.

IN THIS CHAPTER

Replacing a Loop With AutoFilter................250

Advanced Filter Is Easier in VBA Than in Excel 257

Using Advanced Filter to Extract a Unique List of Values......................................258

Using Advanced Filter with Criteria Ranges. 265

Using Filter in Place in Advanced Filter........275

The Real Workhorse: xlFilterCopy with All Records Rather than Unique Records Only... 276

Using Filter in Place with Unique Records Only..283

Replacing a Loop with AutoFilter

In Chapter 6, "R1C1-Style Formulas," you read about several ways to loop through a dataset to format records that match certain criteria. By using the AutoFilter, you can achieve the same result much faster.

Let's say that you have a dataset as shown in Figure 12.1, and you want to perform some action on all the records that match a certain criteria.

Figure 12.1
Find all Ford records and mark them.

	A	B	C	D	E	F	G	H
1	Region	Product	Date	Customer	Quantity	Revenue	COGS	Profit
504	Central	ABC	10/16/2009	Phillip Morris	800	15312	6776	8536
505	East	XYZ	10/17/2009	Verizon	900	19161	9198	9963
506	East	XYZ	10/18/2009	CitiGroup	500	10940	5110	5830
507	**Central**	**ABC**	**10/19/2009**	**Ford**	**1000**	**21010**	**8470**	**12540**
508	East	ABC	10/21/2009	Bank of Americ:	900	18576	7623	10953
509	East	DEF	10/21/2009	General Electric	700	13797	6888	6909
510	Central	DEF	10/21/2009	CitiGroup	200	4484	1968	2516

In Chapter 6, you learned to write code like this to color all the Ford records green:

```
Sub OldLoop()
    FinalRow = Cells(Rows.Count, 1).End(xlUp).Row
    For i = 2 To FinalRow
        If Cells(i, 4) = "Ford" Then
            Cells(i, 1).Resize(1, 8).Interior.ColorIndex = 4
        End If
    Next i
End Sub
```

If you needed to delete records, you had to be careful to run the loop from the bottom of the dataset to the top using code like this:

```
Sub OldLoopToDelete()
    FinalRow = Cells(Rows.Count, 1).End(xlUp).Row
    For i = FinalRow To 2 Step -1
        If Cells(i, 4) = "Ford" Then
            Rows(i).Delete
        End If
    Next i
End Sub
```


The `AutoFilter` method enables you to isolate all the Ford records in a single line of code:

```
Range("A1").AutoFilter Field:=4, Criteria1:="Ford"
```

After isolating the matching records, you do not need to use the VisibleCellsOnly setting to format the matching records. Instead, the following line of code will format all the matching records to be green:

```
Range("A1").CurrentRegion.Interior.ColorIndex = 4
```

> **NOTE** Note that the `.CurrentRegion` property extends the A1 reference to include the entire dataset.

There are two problems with the current two-line macro. First, the program leaves the AutoFilter drop-downs in the dataset. Second, the heading row is also formatted in green.

If you want to turn off the AutoFilter drop-downs and clear the filter, this single line of code will work:

```
Range("A1").AutoFilter
```

If you want to leave the AutoFilter drop-downs on but clear the Column D drop-down from showing Ford, you can use this line of code:

```
ActiveSheet.ShowAllData
```

The second problem is a bit more difficult. After you apply the filter, select `Range("A1")`. `CurrentRegion` includes the headers automatically in the selection. Any formatting is also applied to the header row.

If you did not care about the first blank row below the data, you could simply add an `OFFSET(1)` to move the current region down to start in A2. This would be fine if your goal were to delete all the Ford records:

```
Sub DeleteFord()
    ' skips header, but also deletes blank row below
    Range("A1:A1").AutoFilter Field:=4, Criteria1:="Ford"
    Range("A1").CurrentRegion.Offset(1).EntireRow.Delete
    Range("A1").AutoFilter

End Sub
```

> **NOTE** The OFFSET property usually requires the number of rows and the number of columns. Using `.OFFSET(-2, 5)` moves two rows up and five columns right. If you do not want to adjust by any columns, you can leave off the column parameter. `.OFFSET(1)` means one row down and zero columns over.

The preceding code works because you do not mind if the first blank row below the data is deleted. However, if you are applying a green format to those rows, the code will apply the green format to the blank row below the dataset, which would not look right.

If you will be doing some formatting, you can determine the height of the dataset and use `.Resize` to reduce the height of the current region while you use `OFFSET`:

```
Sub ColorFord()
    DataHt = Range("A1").CurrentRegion.Rows.Count
    Range("A1").AutoFilter Field:=4, Criteria1:="Ford"

    With Range("A1").CurrentRegion.Offset(1).Resize(DataHt - 1)
    ' No need to use VisibleCellsOnly for formatting
        .Interior.ColorIndex = 4
        .Font.Bold = True
    End With
    ' Clear the AutoFilter & remove drop-downs
    Range("A1").AutoFilter

End Sub
```

Using New AutoFilter Techniques

Excel 2007 introduced the possibility of selecting multiple items from a filter, filtering by color, filtering by icon, filtering by top 10, and filtering to virtual date filters. Excel 2010

12

introduces the new search box in the filter drop-down. All these new filters have VBA equivalents, although some of them are implemented in VBA using legacy filtering methods.

Selecting Multiple Items

Legacy versions of Excel allowed you to select two values, joined by AND or OR. In this case, you would specify xlAND or xlOR as the operator:

```
Range("A1").AutoFilter Field:=4, _
    Criteria1:="Ford", _
    Operator:=xlOr, _
    Criteria2:="General Motors"
```

As the AutoFilter command became more flexible, Microsoft continued to use the same three parameters, even if they didn't quite make sense. For example, Excel lets you filter a field by asking for the top five items or the bottom 8 percent of records. To use this type of filter, specify either "5" or "8" as the Criteria1 argument, and then specify xlTop10Items, xlTop10Percent, xlBottom10Items, xlBottom10Percent as the operator. The following code produces the top 12 revenue records:

```
Sub Top10Filter()
    ' Top 12 Revenue Records
    Range("A1").AutoFilter Field:=6, _
        Criteria1:="12", _
        Operator:=xlTop10Items
End Sub
```

There are a lot of numbers (5, 12, 10) in the code for this AutoFilter. Field 5 indicates that you are looking at the fifth column. xlTop10Items is the name of the filter, but the filter is not limited to 10 items. The criteria of 12 indicates the number of items that you want the filter to return.

Excel 2010 offers several new filter options. Excel continues to force these filter options to fit in the old object model where the filter command must fit in an operator and up to two criteria fields.

If you want to choose three or more items, change the operator to the newly introduced Operator:=xlFilterValues and specify the list of items as an array in the Criteria1 argument:

```
Range("A1").AutoFilter Field:=4, _
    Criteria1:=Array("General Motors", "Ford", "Fiat"), _
    Operator:=xlFilterValues
```

Selecting Using the Search Box

Excel 2010 introduces the new Search box in the AutoFilter drop-down. After typing something in the Search box, you can use the Select All Search Results item in the Filter drop-down, as shown in Figure 12.2.

Figure 12.2
Find all records containing "AT."

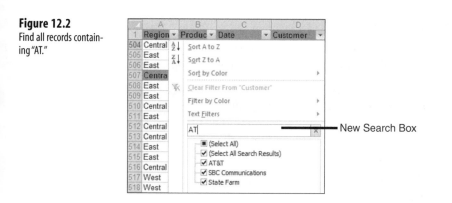

The macro recorder does a poor job of recording the Search box. The macro recorder hard-codes a list of customers who matched the search at the time you ran the macro.

Think about the Search box. It is really a shortcut way of selecting Text Filters, Contains. In addition, the Contains filter is actually a shortcut way of specifying the search string surrounded by asterisks. Therefore, to filter to all the records that contain "AT," use this:

```
Range("A1").AutoFilter, Field:=4, Criteria1:="*at*"
```

Filtering by Color

To find records that have a particular font color, use an operator of xlFilterFontColor and specify a particular RGB value as the criteria. This code finds all cells with a red font in Column F:

```
Sub FilterByFontColor()
    Range("A1").AutoFilter Field:=6, _
        Criteria1:=RGB(255, 0, 0), Operator:=xlFilterFontColor
End Sub
```

To find records that have no particular font color, use an operator of xlFilterAutomatic-FillColor and do not specify any criteria.

```
Sub FilterNoFontColor()
    Range("A1").AutoFilter Field:=6, _
        Operator:=xlFilterAutomaticFontColor
End Sub
```

To find records that have a particular fill color, use an operator of xlFilterCellColor and specify a particular RGB value as the criteria. This code finds all red cells in Column F:

```
Sub FilterByFillColor()
    Range("A1").AutoFilter Field:=6, _
        Criteria1:=RGB(255, 0, 0), Operator:=xlFilterCellColor
End Sub
```

To find records that have no fill color, use an operator of xlFilterNoFill and do not specify any criteria.

12

Filtering by Icon

If you are expecting the dataset to have an icon set applied, you can filter to show only records with one particular icon by using the xlFilterIcon operator.

For the criteria, you have to know which icon set has been applied and which icon within the set. The icon sets are identified using the names shown in Column A of Figure 12.3. The items range from 1 through 5. The following code filters the Revenue column to show the rows containing an upward-pointing arrow in the 5 Arrows Gray icon set:

```
Sub FilterByIcon()
    Range("A1").AutoFilter Field:=6, _
        Criteria1:=ActiveWorkbook.IconSets(xl5ArrowsGray).Item(5), _
        Operator:=xlFilterIcon
End Sub
```

Figure 12.3
To search for a particular icon, you need to know the icon set from Column A and the item number from Row 1.

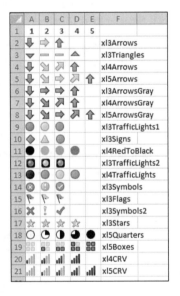

To find records that have no conditional formatting icon, use an operator of xlFilterNoIcon and do not specify any criteria.

Selecting a Dynamic Date Range Using AutoFilters

Perhaps the most powerful feature in Excel 2010 filters are the dynamic filters. These filters enable you to choose records that are above average or with a date field to select virtual periods, such as Next Week or Last Year.

To use a dynamic filter, specify xlFilterDynamic as the operator and then use one of 34 values as Criteria1. The following code finds all dates that are in next year:

```
Sub DynamicAutoFilter()
    Range("A1").AutoFilter Field:=3, _
        Criteria1:=xlFilterNextYear, _
        Operator:=xlFilterDynamic
End Sub
```

The following lists all the dynamic filter criteria options. Specify these values as `Criteria1` in the `AutoFilter` method:

- **Criteria for values**—Use `xlFilterAboveAverage` or `xlFilterBelowAverage` to find all the rows that are above or below average. Note that in Lake Wobegon, using `xlFilterBelowAverage` will likely return no records.

- **Criteria for future periods**—Use `xlFilterTomorrow`, `xlFilterNextWeek`, `xlFilterNextMonth`, `xlFilterNextQuarter`, or `xlFilterNextYear` to find rows that fall in a certain future period. Note that next week starts on Sunday and ends on Saturday.

- **Criteria for current periods**—Use `xlFilterToday`, `xlFilterThisWeek`, `xlFilterThisMonth`, `xlFilterThisQuarter`, or `xlFilterThisYear` to find rows that fall within the current period. Excel will use the system clock to find the current day.

- **Criteria for past periods**—Use `xlFilterYesterday`, `xlFilterLastWeek`, `xlFilterLastMonth`, `xlFilterLastQuarter`, `xlFilterLastYear`, or `xlFilterYearToDate` to find rows that fell within a previous period.

- **Criteria for specific quarters**—Use `xlFilterDatesInPeriodQuarter1`, `xlFilterDatesInPeriodQuarter2`, `xlFilterDatesInPeriodQuarter3`, or `xlFilterDatesInPeriodQuarter4` to filter to rows that fall within a specific quarter. Note that these filters do not differentiate based on a year. If you ask for quarter 1, you might get records from this January, last February, and next March.

- **Criteria for specific months**—Use `xlFilterDatesInPeriodJanuary` through `xlFilterDatesInPeriodDecember` to filter to records that fall during a certain month. Like the quarters, the filter does not filter to any particular year.

Unfortunately, you cannot combine criteria. You might think that you can specify `xlFilterDatesInPeriodJanuary` as `Criteria1` and `xlFilterDatesNextYear` as `Criteria2`. Even though this is a brilliant thought, Microsoft does not support this syntax (yet).

Selecting Visible Cells Only

Once you apply a filter, most commands only operate on the visible rows in the selection. If you need to delete the records, format the records, apply a conditional format to the records, you can simply refer to the `.CurrentRegion` of the first heading cell and perform the command.

However, if you have a dataset where the rows have been hidden using the Hide Rows command, any formatting applied to the `.CurrentRegion` will apply to the hidden rows, too. In these cases, you should use the Visible Cells Only option of the Go To Special dialog, as shown in Figure 12.4.

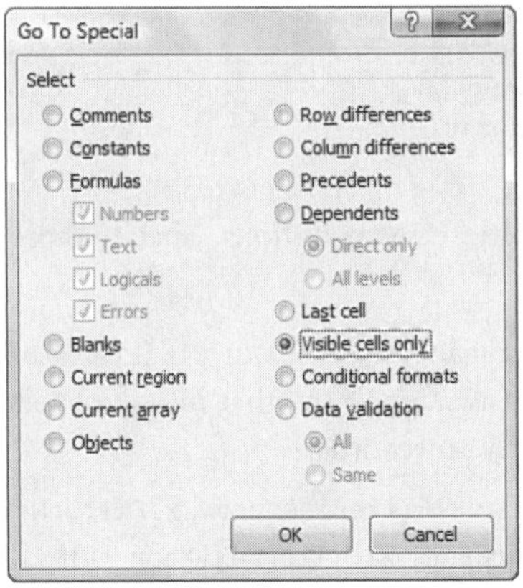

Figure 12.4
If rows have been manually hidden, use Visible Cells Only of the Go To Special dialog.

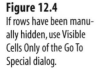

To use Visible Cells Only in code, use the `SpecialCells` property:

```
Range("A1").CurrentRegion.SpecialCells(xlCellTypeVisible)
```

CASE STUDY: GO TO SPECIAL INSTEAD OF LOOPING

The Go To Special dialog also plays a role in the following case study:

At the 2009 Data Analyst Boot Camp, one of the attendees had a macro that was taking a long time to run. The workbook had a number of selection controls. A complex `IF` function in cells H10:H750 was choosing which records should be included in a report. While that `IF` statement had many nested conditions, the formula was inserting either `KEEP` or `HIDE` in each cell:

```
=IF(True,"KEEP","HIDE")
```

The following section of code was hiding individual rows:

```
For Each cell In Range("H10:H750")
    If cell.Value = "HIDE" Then
        cell.EntireRow.Hidden = True
    End If
Next cell
```

The macro was taking several minutes to run. `SUBTOTAL` formulas that excluded hidden rows were recalculating after each pass through the loop. The first attempts to speed up the macro involved turning off screen updating and calculation:

```
Application.ScreenUpdating = False
Application.Calculation = xlCalculationManual
For Each cell In Range("H10:H750")
    If cell.Value = "HIDE" Then
        cell.EntireRow.Hidden = True
    End If
Next cell
Application.Calculation = xlCalculationAutomatic
Application.ScreenUpdating = True
```

12

For some reason, it was still taking too long to loop through all the records. We tried using AutoFilter to isolate the HIDE records, then hiding those rows, but you lose the manual row hiding after turning off the AutoFilter.

The solution was to make use of the Special Cells dialog's ability to limit the selection to text results of formulas. First, the formula in Column H was changed to return either HIDE or a number:

```
=IF(True,"KEEP",1)
```

Then, the following single line of code was able to hide the rows that evaluated to a text value in Column H:

```
Range("H10:H750") _
    .SpecialCells(xlCellTypeFormulas, xlTextValues) _
    .EntireRow.Hidden = True
```

Because all the rows were hidden in a single command, that section of the macro ran in seconds rather than minutes.

📹 *To see a demo of this case study, search for Excel VBA 12 at YouTube.*

Advanced Filter Is Easier in VBA Than in Excel

Using the arcane Advanced Filter command is so difficult in the Excel user interface that it is pretty rare to find someone who enjoys using it regularly.

However, in VBA, advanced filters are a joy to use. With a single line of code, you can rapidly extract a subset of records from a database or quickly get a unique list of values in any column. This is critical when you want to run reports for a specific region or customer. Two advanced filters are used most often in the same procedure—one to get a unique list of customers and a second to filter to each individual customer, as shown in Figure 12.5. The rest of this chapter builds toward such a routine.

Figure 12.5
A typical macro uses two advanced filters.

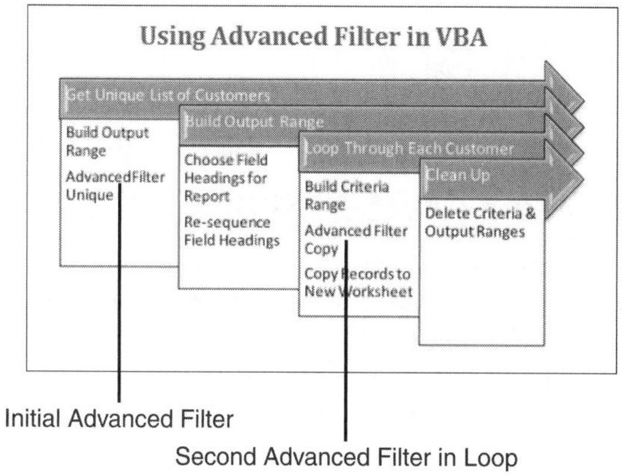

Using Advanced Filter in VBA

Get Unique List of Customers
Build Output Range
Loop Through Each Customer
Clean Up

Build Output Range
AdvancedFilter Unique

Choose Field Headings for Report
Re-sequence Field Headings

Build Criteria Range
Advanced Filter Copy
Copy Records to New Worksheet

Delete Criteria & Output Ranges

Initial Advanced Filter

Second Advanced Filter in Loop

12

Using the Excel Interface to Build an Advanced Filter

Because not many people use the Advanced Filter feature, this section walks you through examples using the user interface to build an advanced filter and then shows you the analogous code. You will be amazed at how complex the user interface seems and yet how easy it is to program a powerful advanced filter to extract records.

One reason why Advanced Filter is hard to use is that you can use the filter in several different ways. You must make three basic choices in the Advanced Filter dialog box. Because each choice has two options, there are eight (2 x 2 x 2) possible combinations of these choices. The three choices are shown in Figure 12.6 and described here:

- **Action**—You can select Filter the List, In-Place, or Copy to Another Location. If you choose to filter the records in place, the nonmatching rows are hidden. Choosing to copy to a new location copies the records that match the filter to a new range.

- **Criteria**—You can filter with or without criteria. Filtering with criteria is appropriate for getting a subset of rows. Filtering without criteria is still useful when you want a subset of columns or when you are using the Unique Records Only option.

- **Unique**—You can choose to request Unique Records Only or all matching records. The Unique option makes the Advanced Filter command one of the fastest ways to find a unique list of values in one field. By placing the "Customer" heading in the output range, you will get a unique list of values for that one column.

Figure 12.6
The Advanced Filter dialog is complicated to use in the Excel user interface. Luckily, it is much easier in VBA.

Using Advanced Filter to Extract a Unique List of Values

One of the simplest uses of Advanced Filter is to extract a unique list of a single field from a dataset. In this example, you want to get a unique list of customers from a sales report. You know that customer is in Column D of the dataset. You have an unknown number of records starting in cell A2, and Row 1 is the header row. There is nothing located to the right of the dataset.

Extracting a Unique List of Values with the User Interface

To extract a unique list of values, follow these steps:

1. With the cursor anywhere in the data range, select Advanced from the Sort & Filter group on the Data tab. The first time that you use the Advanced Filter command on a worksheet, Excel automatically populates the List Range text box with the entire range of your dataset. On subsequent uses of the Advanced Filter command, this dialog box remembers the settings from the prior advanced filter.

2. Select the Unique Records Only check box at the bottom of the dialog.

3. In the Action section, select Copy to Another Location.

4. Type J1 in the Copy To text box.

By default, Excel copies all the columns in the dataset. You can filter just the Customer column by either limiting the List Range to include only Column D or by specifying one or more headings in the Copy To range. Either method has its own drawbacks.

Change the List Range to a Single Column

Edit the List Range to point to the Customer column. In this case, it means changing the default $A$1:$H$1127 to $D$1:$D$1127. The Advanced Filter dialog should appear.

> **TIP**
> When you initially edit any range in the dialog box, Excel might be in Point mode. In this mode, pressing a left- or right-arrow key will insert a cell reference in the text box. If you see the word *Point* in the lower-left corner of your Excel window, press the F2 key to change from Point mode to Edit mode.

The drawback of this method is that Excel remembers the list range on subsequent uses of the Advanced Filter command. If you later want to get a unique list of regions, you will be constantly specifying the list range.

Copy the Customer Heading Before Filtering

With a little forethought before invoking the Advanced Filter command, you can allow Excel to keep the default list range of $A$1:$H$1127. In cell J1, type the Customer heading. In Figure 12.6, you leave the List Range field pointing to Columns A through H. Because the Copy To range of J1 already contains a valid heading from the list range, Excel copies data only from the Customer column. This is the preferred method, particularly if you will be doing multiple advanced filters. Because Excel remembers the prior settings from the last advanced filter, it is more convenient to always filter the entire columns of the list range and limit the columns by setting up headings in the Copy To range.

After you use either of these methods to perform the advanced filter, a concise list of the unique customers appears in Column J (see Figure 12.7).

12

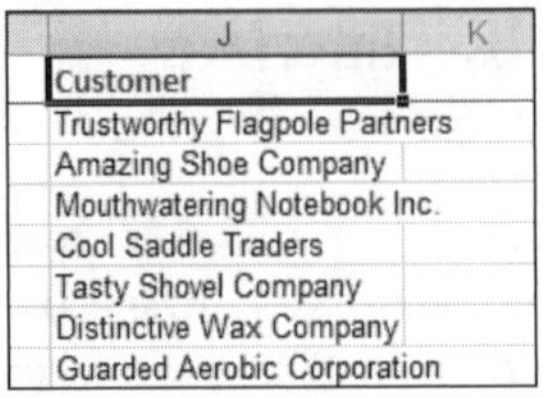

Figure 12.7
The advanced filter extracted a unique list of customers from the dataset and copied it to Column J.

J	K
Customer	
Trustworthy Flagpole Partners	
Amazing Shoe Company	
Mouthwatering Notebook Inc.	
Cool Saddle Traders	
Tasty Shovel Company	
Distinctive Wax Company	
Guarded Aerobic Corporation	

Extracting a Unique List of Values with VBA Code

In VBA, you use the `AdvancedFilter` method to carry out the Advanced Filter command. Again, you have three choices to make:

■ **Action**—Choose to either filter in place with the parameter `Action:=xlFilterInPlace` or to copy with `Action:=xlFilterCopy`. If you want to copy, you also have to specify the parameter `CopyToRange:=Range("J1")`.

■ **Criteria**—To filter with criteria, include the parameter `CriteriaRange:=Range("L 1:L2")`. To filter without criteria, omit this optional parameter.

■ **Unique**—To return only unique records, specify the parameter `Unique:=True`.

The following code sets up a single column output range two columns to the right of the last-used column in the data range:

```
Sub GetUniqueCustomers()
    Dim IRange As Range
    Dim ORange As Range

    ' Find the size of today's dataset
    FinalRow = Cells(Rows.Count, 1).End(xlUp).Row
    NextCol = Cells(1, Columns.Count).End(xlToLeft).Column + 2

    ' Set up output range. Copy heading from D1 there
    Range("D1").Copy Destination:=Cells(1, NextCol)
    Set ORange = Cells(1, NextCol)

    ' Define the Input Range
    Set IRange = Range("A1").Resize(FinalRow, NextCol - 2)

    ' Do the Advanced Filter to get unique list of customers
    IRange.AdvancedFilter Action:=xlFilterCopy, CopyToRange:=ORange, _
        Unique:=True

End Sub
```

By default, an advanced filter copies all columns. If you just want one particular column, use that column heading as the heading in the output range.

The first bit of code finds the final row and column in the dataset. Although it is not necessary to do so, you can define an object variable for the output range (`ORange`) and for the input range (`IRange`).

This code is generic enough that it will not have to be rewritten if new columns are added to the dataset at a later time. Setting up the object variables for the input and output range is done for readability rather than out of necessity. The previous code could be written just as easily like this shortened version:

```
Sub UniqueCustomerRedux()
    ' Copy a heading to create an output range
    Range("J1").Value = Range("D1").Value
    ' Do the Advanced Filter
    Range("A1").CurrentRegion.AdvancedFilter xlFilterCopy, _
        CopyToRange:=Range("J1"), Unique:=True
End Sub
```

When you run either of the previous blocks of code on the sample dataset, you get a unique list of customers off to the right of the data. In Figure 12.7, you saw the original dataset in Columns A:H and the unique customers in Column J. The key to getting a unique list of customers is copying the header from the Customer field to a blank cell and specifying this cell as the output range.

After you have the unique list of customers, you can sort the list and add a SUMIF formula to get total revenue by customer. The following code gets the unique list of customers, sorts it, and then builds a formula to total revenue by customer. Figure 12.8 shows the results:

```
Sub RevenueByCustomers()
    Dim IRange As Range
    Dim ORange As Range

    ' Find the size of today's data set
    FinalRow = Cells(Rows.Count, 1).End(xlUp).Row
    NextCol = Cells(1, Columns.Count).End(xlToLeft).Column + 2

    ' Set up output range. Copy heading from D1 there
    Range("D1").Copy Destination:=Cells(1, NextCol)
    Set ORange = Cells(1, NextCol)

    ' Define the Input Range
    Set IRange = Range("A1").Resize(FinalRow, NextCol - 2)

    ' Do the Advanced Filter to get unique list of customers
    IRange.AdvancedFilter Action:=xlFilterCopy, _
        CopyToRange:=ORange, Unique:=True

    ' Determine how many unique customers we have
    LastRow = Cells(Rows.Count, NextCol).End(xlUp).Row

    ' Sort the data
    Cells(1, NextCol).Resize(LastRow, 1).Sort Key1:=Cells(1, NextCol), _
        Order1:=xlAscending, Header:=xlYes

    ' Add a SUMIF formula to get totals
    Cells(1, NextCol + 1).Value = "Revenue"
    Cells(2, NextCol + 1).Resize(LastRow - 1).FormulaR1C1 = _
        "=SUMIF(R2C4:R" & FinalRow & _
        "C4,RC[-1],R2C6:R" & FinalRow & "C6)")

End Sub
```

12

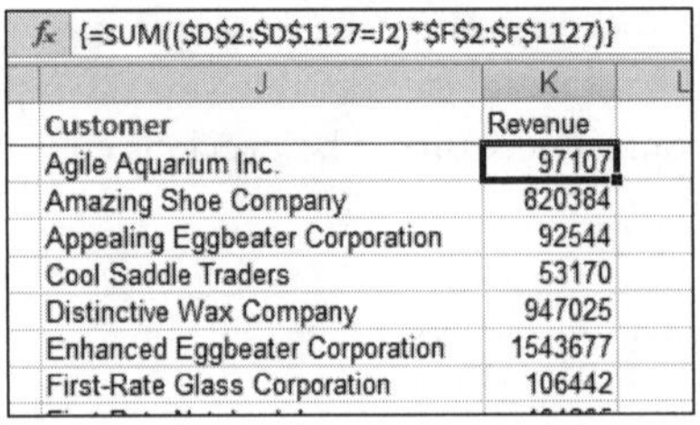

Figure 12.8
This macro produced a summary report by customer from a lengthy dataset. Using `AdvancedFilter` is the key to powerful macros such as these.

	J	K	L
	Customer	Revenue	
	Agile Aquarium Inc.	97107	
	Amazing Shoe Company	820384	
	Appealing Eggbeater Corporation	92544	
	Cool Saddle Traders	53170	
	Distinctive Wax Company	947025	
	Enhanced Eggbeater Corporation	1543677	
	First-Rate Glass Corporation	106442	

Formula bar: `{=SUM(($D$2:$D$1127=J2)*$F$2:$F$1127)}`

Another use of a unique list of values is to quickly populate a list box or a combo box on a userform. For example, suppose that you have a macro that can run a report for any one specific customer. To allow your clients to choose which customers to report, create a simple userform. Add a list box to the userform and set the list box's `MultiSelect` property to `1-fmMultiSelectMulti`. In this case, the form is named frmReport. In addition to the list box, there are four command buttons: OK, Cancel, Mark All, Clear All. The code to run the form follows. Note the `Userform_Initialize` procedure includes an advanced filter to get the unique list of customers from the dataset:

```
Private Sub CancelButton_Click()
    Unload Me
End Sub

Private Sub cbSubAll_Click()
    For i = 0 To lbCust.ListCount - 1
        Me.lbCust.Selected(i) = True
    Next i
End Sub

Private Sub cbSubClear_Click()
    For i = 0 To lbCust.ListCount - 1
        Me.lbCust.Selected(i) = False
    Next i
End Sub

Private Sub OKButton_Click()
    For i = 0 To lbCust.ListCount - 1
        If Me.lbCust.Selected(i) = True Then
            ' Call a routine to produce this report
            RunCustReport WhichCust:=Me.lbCust.List(i)
        End If
    Next i
    Unload Me
End Sub

Private Sub UserForm_Initialize()
    Dim IRange As Range
    Dim ORange As Range

    ' Find the size of today's data set
```

12

```
        FinalRow = Cells(Rows.Count, 1).End(xlUp).Row
        NextCol = Cells(1, Columns.Count).End(xlToLeft).Column + 2

        ' Set up output range. Copy heading from D1 there
        Range("D1").Copy Destination:=Cells(1, NextCol)
        Set ORange = Cells(1, NextCol)

        ' Define the Input Range
        Set IRange = Range("A1").Resize(FinalRow, NextCol - 2)

        ' Do the Advanced Filter to get unique list of customers
        IRange.AdvancedFilter Action:=xlFilterCopy, _
            CopyToRange:=ORange, Unique:=True

        ' Determine how many unique customers we have
        LastRow = Cells(Rows.Count, NextCol).End(xlUp).Row

        ' Sort the data
        Cells(1, NextCol).Resize(LastRow, 1).Sort Key1:=Cells(1, NextCol), _
            Order1:=xlAscending, Header:=xlYes

With Me.lbCust
    .RowSource = ""
    .List = Cells(2, NextCol).Resize(LastRow - 1, 1).Value
End With

        ' Erase the temporary list of customers
        Cells(1, NextCol).Resize(LastRow, 1).Clear
End Sub
```

Launch this form with a simple module such as this:

```
Sub ShowCustForm()
    frmReport.Show
End Sub
```

Your clients are presented with a list of all valid customers from the dataset. Because the list box's `MultiSelect` property is set to allow it, they can select any number of customers, as shown in Figure 12.9.

Getting Unique Combinations of Two or More Fields

To get all unique combinations of two or more fields, build the output range to include the additional fields. This code sample builds a list of unique combinations of two fields, Customer and Product:

```
Sub UniqueCustomerProduct()
    Dim IRange As Range
    Dim ORange As Range

    ' Find the size of today's data set
    FinalRow = Cells(Rows.Count, 1).End(xlUp).Row
    NextCol = Cells(1, Columns.Count).End(xlToLeft).Column + 2
```

12

```
' Set up output range. Copy headings from D1 & B1
Range("D1").Copy Destination:=Cells(1, NextCol)
Range("B1").Copy Destination:=Cells(1, NextCol + 1)
Set ORange = Cells(1, NextCol).Resize(1, 2)

' Define the Input Range
Set IRange = Range("A1").Resize(FinalRow, NextCol - 2)

' Do the Advanced Filter to get unique list of customers & product
IRange.AdvancedFilter Action:=xlFilterCopy, _
    CopyToRange:=ORange, Unique:=True

' Determine how many unique rows we have
LastRow = Cells(Rows.Count, NextCol).End(xlUp).Row

' Sort the data
Cells(1, NextCol).Resize(LastRow, 2).Sort Key1:=Cells(1, NextCol), _
    Order1:=xlAscending, Key2:=Cells(1, NextCol + 1), _
    Order2:=xlAscending, Header:=xlYes

End Sub
```

In the result shown in Figure 12.10, you can see that Enhanced Eggbeater buys only one product, and Agile Aquarium buys three products. This might be useful to use as a guide in running reports on either customer by product or product by customer.

Figure 12.9
Your clients will have a list of customers from which to select. Using an advanced filter on even a 1,000,000-row dataset is much faster than setting up a class to populate the list box.

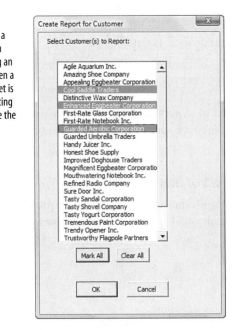

Figure 12.10
By including two columns in the output range on a Unique Values query, we get every combination of Customer and Product.

J	K
Customer	Product
Agile Aquarium Inc.	M556
Agile Aquarium Inc.	R537
Agile Aquarium Inc.	W435
Amazing Shoe Company	M556
Amazing Shoe Company	R537
Amazing Shoe Company	W435
Appealing Eggbeater Corporation	M556
Appealing Eggbeater Corporation	R537
Appealing Eggbeater Corporation	W435
Cool Saddle Traders	M556
Cool Saddle Traders	R537
Cool Saddle Traders	W435
Distinctive Wax Company	M556
Distinctive Wax Company	R537
Distinctive Wax Company	W435
Enhanced Eggbeater Corporation	R537
First-Rate Glass Corporation	M556

Using Advanced Filter with Criteria Ranges

As the name implies, Advanced Filter is usually used to filter records—in other words, to get a subset of data. You specify the subset by setting up a criteria range. Even if you are familiar with criteria, be sure to check out using the powerful Boolean formula in criteria ranges later in this chapter, in the section "The Most Complex Criteria: Replacing the List of Values with a Condition Created as the Result of a Formula."

Set up a criteria range in a blank area of the worksheet. A criteria range always includes two or more rows. The first row of the criteria range contains one or more field header values to match the one(s) in the data range you want to filter. The second row contains a value showing what records to extract. In Figure 12.11, Range J1:J2 is the criteria range, and Range L1 is the output range.

In the Excel user interface, to extract a unique list of products that were purchased by a particular customer, select Advanced Filter and set up the Advanced Filter dialog, as shown in Figure 12.11. Figure 12.12 shows the results.

Figure 12.11
To learn a unique list of products purchased by Cool Saddle Traders, set up the criteria range shown in J1:J2.

J	K	L
Customer		Product
Cool Saddle Traders		

Advanced Filter

Action
○ Filter the list, in-place
● Copy to another location

List range: $A$1:$H$1127
Criteria range: port!$J$1:$J$2
Copy to: SalesReport!$L$1

☑ Unique records only

OK   Cancel

Figure 12.12
The results of the advanced filter that uses a criteria range and asks for a unique list of products. Of course, more complex and interesting criteria can be built.

J	K	L	M
Customer		Product	
Cool Saddle Traders		R537	
		M556	
		W435	

In VBA, you use the following code to perform an equivalent advanced filter:

```
Sub UniqueProductsOneCustomer()
    Dim IRange As Range
    Dim ORange As Range
    Dim CRange As Range

    ' Find the size of today's dataset
    FinalRow = Cells(Rows.Count, 1).End(xlUp).Row
    NextCol = Cells(1, Columns.Count).End(xlToLeft).Column + 2

    ' Set up the Output Range with one customer
    Cells(1, NextCol).Value = Range("D1").Value
    ' In reality, this value should be passed from the userform
    Cells(2, NextCol).Value = Range("D2").Value
    Set CRange = Cells(1, NextCol).Resize(2, 1)

    ' Set up output range. Copy heading from B1 there
    Range("B1").Copy Destination:=Cells(1, NextCol + 2)
    Set ORange = Cells(1, NextCol + 2)

    ' Define the Input Range
    Set IRange = Range("A1").Resize(FinalRow, NextCol - 2)

    ' Do the Advanced Filter to get unique list of customers & product
    IRange.AdvancedFilter Action:=xlFilterCopy, _
        CriteriaRange:=CRange, CopyToRange:=ORange, Unique:=True
    ' The above could also be written as:
    'IRange.AdvancedFilter xlFilterCopy, CRange, ORange, True

    ' Determine how many unique rows we have
    LastRow = Cells(Rows.Count, NextCol + 2).End(xlUp).Row

    ' Sort the data
    Cells(1, NextCol + 2).Resize(LastRow, 1).Sort Key1:=Cells(1, NextCol + 2), _
        Order1:=xlAscending, Header:=xlYes

End Sub
```

Joining Multiple Criteria with a Logical OR

You might want to filter records that match one criteria or another. For example, you can extract customers who purchased either product M556 or product R537. This is called a *logical OR* criteria.

When your criteria should be joined by a logical OR, place the criteria on subsequent rows of the criteria range. For example, the criteria range shown in J1:J3 of Figure 12.13 tells you which customers order product M556 or product R357.

Figure 12.13
Place criteria on succes-sive rows to join them with an OR. This criteria range gets customers who ordered either prod-uct M556 or R537.

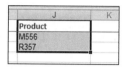

Joining Two Criteria with a Logical AND

Other times, you will want to filter records that match one criteria and another criteria. For example, you might want to extract records where the product sold was W435 and the region was the West region. This is called a *logical AND*.

To join two criteria by AND, put both criteria on the same row of the criteria range. For example, the criteria range shown in J1:K2 of Figure 12.14 gets the customers who ordered product W435 in the West region.

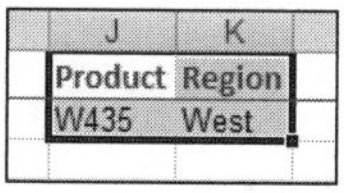

Figure 12.14
Place criteria on the same row to join them with an AND. The criteria range in J1:K2 gets customers from the West region who ordered product W435.

Other Slightly Complex Criteria Ranges

The criteria range shown in Figure 12.15 is based on two different fields that are joined with an OR. The query finds all records from either the West region or records where the product is W435.

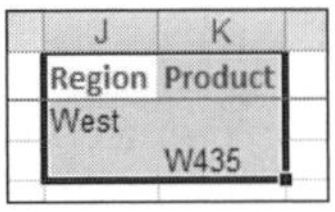

Figure 12.15
The criteria range in J1:K3 returns records where either the Region is West or the Product is W435.

> **TIP**
> Joining two criteria with OR might be useful where new California legislation will impact shipments made to California or products sourced at the California plant.

The Most Complex Criteria: Replacing the List of Values with a Condition Created as the Result of a Formula

It is possible to have a criteria range with multiple logical AND and logical OR criteria joined together. Although this might work in some situations, in other scenarios it quickly gets out of hand. Fortunately, Excel allows for criteria where the records are selected as the result of a formula to handle this situation.

CASE STUDY: WORKING WITH VERY COMPLEX CRITERIA

Your clients so loved the "Create a Customer" report, they hired you to write a new report. In this case, they could select any customer, any product, any region, or any combination of them. You can quickly adapt the frmReport userform to show three list boxes, as shown in Figure 12.16.

In your first test, imagine that you select two customers and two products. In this case, your program has to build a five-row criteria range, as shown in Figure 12.17. This isn't too bad.

This gets crazy if someone selects 10 products, all regions but the house region, and all customers except the internal customer. Your criteria range would need unique combinations of the selected fields. This could easily be 10 products times 9 regions times 499 customers, or more than 44,000 rows of criteria range. You can quickly end up with a criteria range that spans thousands of rows and three columns. I was once foolish enough to actually try running an advanced filter with such a criteria range. It would still be trying to compute if I hadn't rebooted the computer.

The solution for this report is to replace the lists of values with a formula-based condition.

Figure 12.16
This super-flexible form lets clients run any types of reports that they can imagine. It creates some nightmarish criteria ranges, unless you know the way out.

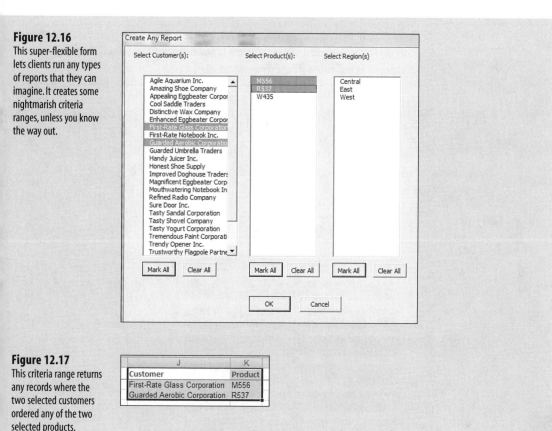

Figure 12.17
This criteria range returns any records where the two selected customers ordered any of the two selected products.

Setting Up a Condition as the Result of a Formula

Amazingly, there is an incredibly obscure version of Advanced Filter criteria that can replace the 44,000-row criteria range in the previous case study. In the alternative form of criteria range, the top row is left blank. There is no heading above the criteria. The criteria set up in Row 2 are a formula that results in True or False. If the formula contains any relative references to Row 2 of the data range, Excel compares that formula to every row of the data range, one by one.

For example, if you want all records where the Gross Profit Percentage is below 53 percent, the formula built in J2 will reference the Profit in H2 and the Revenue in F2. To do this, leave J1 blank to tell Excel that you are using a computed criterion. Cell J2 contains the formula =(H2/F2)<0.53. The criteria range for the advanced filter would be specified as J1:J2.

As Excel performs the advanced filter, it logically copies the formula and applies it to all rows in the database. Anywhere that the formula evaluates to True, the record is included in the output range.

This is incredibly powerful and runs remarkably fast. You can combine multiple formulas in adjacent columns or rows to join the formula criteria with AND or OR, just as you do with regular criteria.

N O T E Row 1 of the criteria range doesn't have to be blank, but it cannot contain any words that are headings in the data range. You could perhaps use that row to explain that someone should look to this page in this book for an explanation of these computed criteria.

CASE STUDY: USING FORMULA-BASED CONDITIONS IN THE EXCEL USER INTERFACE

You can use formula-based conditions to solve the report introduced in the previous case study. Figure 12.18 shows the flow of setting up a formula-based criteria.

Figure 12.18
Data in O:Q is used in formulas in J2:L2.

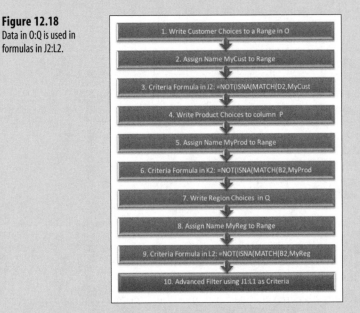

1. Write Customer Choices to a Range in O

2. Assign Name MyCust to Range

3. Criteria Formula in J2: =NOT(ISNA(MATCH(D2,MyCust

4. Write Product Choices to column P

5. Assign Name MyProd to Range

6. Criteria Formula in K2: =NOT(ISNA(MATCH(B2,MyProd

7. Write Region Choices in Q

8. Assign Name MyReg to Range

9. Criteria Formula in L2: =NOT(ISNA(MATCH(B2,MyReg

10. Advanced Filter using J1:L1 as Criteria

To illustrate, off to the right of the criteria range set up a column of cells with the list of selected customers. Assign a name to the range, such as MyCust. In cell J2 of the criteria range, enter a formula such as =Not(ISNA(Match(D2,MyCust,0))).

To the right of the MyCust range, set up a range with a list of selected products. Assign this range the name of MyProd. In the K2 of the criteria range, add a formula to check products, =NOT(ISNA(Match(B2,MyProd,0))).

To the right of the MyProd range, set up a range with a list of selected regions. Assign this range the name of MyRegion. In L2 of the criteria range, add a formula to check for selected regions, =NOT(ISNA(Match(A2,MyRegion,0))).

Now, with a criteria range of J1:L2, you can effectively retrieve the records matching any combination of selections from the userform.

Using Formula-Based Conditions with VBA

The following is the code for this userform. Note the logic in `OKButton_Click` that builds the formula. Figure 12.19 shows the Excel sheet just before the advanced filter is run.

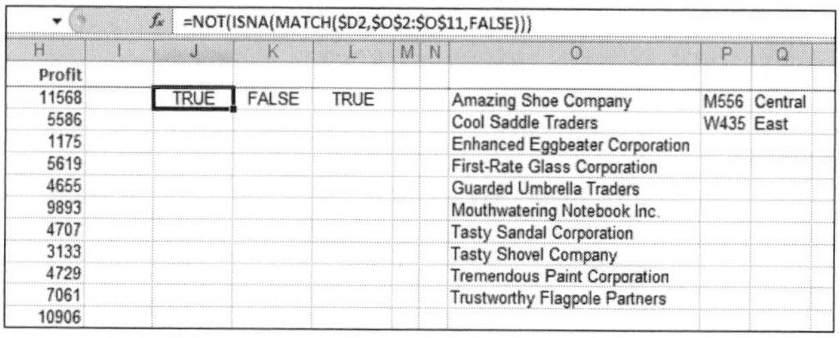
=NOT(ISNA(MATCH($D2,$O$2:$O$11,FALSE)))

H	I	J	K	L	M	N	O	P	Q
Profit									
11568		TRUE	FALSE	TRUE			Amazing Shoe Company	M556	Central
5586							Cool Saddle Traders	W435	East
1175							Enhanced Eggbeater Corporation		
5619							First-Rate Glass Corporation		
4655							Guarded Umbrella Traders		
9893							Mouthwatering Notebook Inc.		
4707							Tasty Sandal Corporation		
3133							Tasty Shovel Company		
4729							Tremendous Paint Corporation		
7061							Trustworthy Flagpole Partners		
10906									

Figure 12.19
The worksheet just before the macro runs the advanced filter.

The following code initializes the user form. Three advanced filters find the unique list of customers, products, and regions:

```
Private Sub UserForm_Initialize()
    Dim IRange As Range
    Dim ORange As Range

    ' Find the size of today's data set
    FinalRow = Cells(Rows.Count, 1).End(xlUp).Row
    NextCol = Cells(1, Columns.Count).End(xlToLeft).Column + 2

    ' Define the input range
    Set IRange = Range("A1").Resize(FinalRow, NextCol - 2)

    ' Set up output range for Customer. Copy heading from D1 there
    Range("D1").Copy Destination:=Cells(1, NextCol)
    Set ORange = Cells(1, NextCol)

    ' Do the Advanced Filter to get unique list of customers
    IRange.AdvancedFilter Action:=xlFilterCopy, CriteriaRange:="", _
        CopyToRange:=ORange, Unique:=True

    ' Determine how many unique customers we have
    LastRow = Cells(Rows.Count, NextCol).End(xlUp).Row

    ' Sort the data
    Cells(1, NextCol).Resize(LastRow, 1).Sort Key1:=Cells(1, NextCol), _
        Order1:=xlAscending, Header:=xlYes

    With Me.lbCust
        .RowSource = ""
        .List = Application.Transpose(Cells(2,NextCol).Resize(LastRow-1,1))
    End With

    ' Erase the temporary list of customers
    Cells(1, NextCol).Resize(LastRow, 1).Clear

    ' Set up output range for product. Copy heading from D1 there
```

```
Range("B1").Copy Destination:=Cells(1, NextCol)
Set ORange = Cells(1, NextCol)

' Do the Advanced Filter to get unique list of customers
IRange.AdvancedFilter Action:=xlFilterCopy, _
    CopyToRange:=ORange, Unique:=True

' Determine how many unique customers we have
LastRow = Cells(Rows.Count, NextCol).End(xlUp).Row

' Sort the data
Cells(1, NextCol).Resize(LastRow, 1).Sort Key1:=Cells(1, NextCol), _
    Order1:=xlAscending, Header:=xlYes

With Me.lbProduct
    .RowSource = ""
    .List = Application.Transpose(Cells(2,NextCol).Resize(LastRow-1,1))
End With

' Erase the temporary list of customers
Cells(1, NextCol).Resize(LastRow, 1).Clear

' Set up output range for Region. Copy heading from A1 there
Range("A1").Copy Destination:=Cells(1, NextCol)
Set ORange = Cells(1, NextCol)

' Do the Advanced Filter to get unique list of customers
IRange.AdvancedFilter Action:=xlFilterCopy, CopyToRange:=ORange, _
    Unique:=True

' Determine how many unique customers we have
LastRow = Cells(Rows.Count, NextCol).End(xlUp).Row

' Sort the data
Cells(1, NextCol).Resize(LastRow, 1).Sort Key1:=Cells(1, NextCol), _
    Order1:=xlAscending, Header:=xlYes

With Me.lbRegion
    .RowSource = ""
    .List = Application.Transpose(Cells(2,NextCol).Resize(LastRow-1,1))
End With

' Erase the temporary list of customers
Cells(1, NextCol).Resize(LastRow, 1).Clear

End Sub
```

These tiny procedures run when someone clicks Mark All or Clear All:

```
Private Sub CancelButton_Click()
    Unload Me
End Sub

Private Sub cbSubAll_Click()
    For i = 0 To lbCust.ListCount - 1
        Me.lbCust.Selected(i) = True
```

```
        Next i
    End Sub

    Private Sub cbSubClear_Click()
        For i = 0 To lbCust.ListCount - 1
            Me.lbCust.Selected(i) = False
        Next i
    End Sub

    Private Sub CommandButton1_Click()
        ' Clear all products
        For i = 0 To lbProduct.ListCount - 1
            Me.lbProduct.Selected(i) = False
        Next i
    End Sub

    Private Sub CommandButton2_Click()
        ' Mark all products
        For i = 0 To lbProduct.ListCount - 1
            Me.lbProduct.Selected(i) = True
        Next i
    End Sub

    Private Sub CommandButton3_Click()
        ' Clear all regions
        For i = 0 To lbRegion.ListCount - 1
            Me.lbRegion.Selected(i) = False
        Next i
    End Sub

    Private Sub CommandButton4_Click()
        ' Mark all regions
        For i = 0 To lbRegion.ListCount - 1
            Me.lbRegion.Selected(i) = True
        Next i
    End Sub
```

The following code is attached to the OK button. This code builds three ranges in O, P, and Q that list the selected customers, products, and regions. The actual criteria range is comprised of three blank cells in J1:L1 and then three formulas in J2:L2.

```
    Private Sub OKButton_Click()
        Dim CRange As Range, IRange As Range, ORange As Range
        ' Build a complex criteria that ANDS all choices together
        NextCCol = 10
        NextTCol = 15

        For j = 1 To 3
            Select Case j
                Case 1
                    MyControl = "lbCust"
                    MyColumn = 4
                Case 2
                    MyControl = "lbProduct"
                    MyColumn = 2
                Case 3
                    MyControl = "lbRegion"
```

12

```
                    MyColumn = 1
        End Select
        NextRow = 2
        ' Check to see what was selected.
        For i = 0 To Me.Controls(MyControl).ListCount - 1
            If Me.Controls(MyControl).Selected(i) = True Then
                Cells(NextRow, NextTCol).Value = _
                    Me.Controls(MyControl).List(i)
                NextRow = NextRow + 1
            End If
        Next i
        ' If anything was selected, build a new criteria formula
        If NextRow > 2 Then
            ' the reference to Row 2 must be relative in order to work
            MyFormula = "=NOT(ISNA(MATCH(RC" & MyColumn & ",R2C" & NextTCol & _
                ":R" & NextRow - 1 & "C" & NextTCol & ",0)))"
            Cells(2, NextCCol).FormulaR1C1 = MyFormula
            NextTCol = NextTCol + 1
            NextCCol = NextCCol + 1
        End If
    Next j
    Unload Me

    ' Figure 12.19 shows the worksheet at this point
    ' if we built any criteria, define the criteria range
    If NextCCol > 10 Then
        Set CRange = Range(Cells(1, 10), Cells(2, NextCCol - 1))
        Set IRange = Range("A1").CurrentRegion
        Set ORange = Cells(1, 20)
        IRange.AdvancedFilter xlFilterCopy, CRange, ORange

        ' Clear out the criteria
        Cells(1, 10).Resize(1, 10).EntireColumn.Clear
    End If

    ' At this point, the matching records are in T1

End Sub
```

Figure 12.19 shows the worksheet just before the AdvancedFilter method is called. The user has selected customers, products, and regions. The macro has built temporary tables in Columns O, P, Q to show which values the user selected. The criteria range is J1:L2. That criteria formula in J2 looks to see whether the value in $D2 is in the list of selected customers in O. The formulas in K2 and L2 compare $B2 to Column P and $A2 to Column Q.

> **CAUTION**
>
> Excel VBA Help says that if you do not specify a criteria range, no criteria is used. This is not true in Excel 2010. When working with Excel 2010, if no criteria range is specified, the advanced filter inherits the criteria range from the prior advanced filter. You should include CriteriaRange:="" to clear the prior value.

Using Formula-Based Conditions to Return Above-Average Records

The formula-based conditions formula criteria are cool but are a rarely used feature in a rarely used function. Some interesting business applications use this technique. For example, this criteria formula would find all the above-average rows in the dataset:

```
=$A2>Average($A$2:$A$60000)
```

Using Filter in Place in Advanced Filter

It is possible to filter a large dataset in place. In this case, you do not need an output range. You would normally specify criteria range—otherwise you return 100 percent of the records and there is no need to do the advanced filter!

In the user interface of Excel, running a Filter in Place makes sense: You can easily peruse the filtered list looking for something in particular.

Running a Filter in Place in VBA is a little less convenient. The only good way to programmatically peruse through the filtered records is to use the `xlCellTypeVisible` option of the `SpecialCells` method. In the Excel user interface, the equivalent action is to select Find & Select, Go to Special from the Home tab. In the Go to Special dialog, select Visible Cells Only, as shown in Figure 12.20.

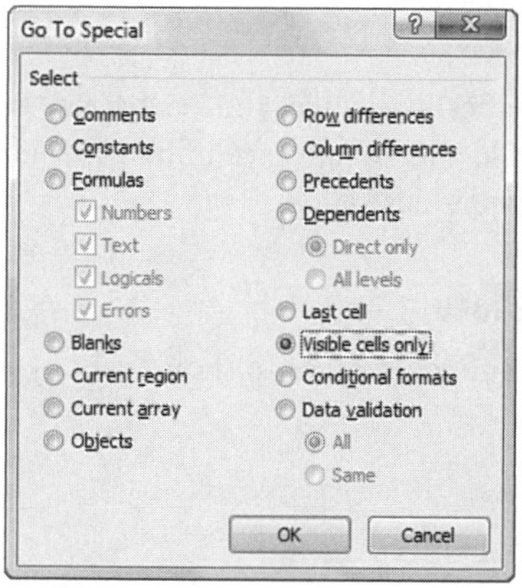

Figure 12.20
The Filter in Place option hides rows that do not match the selected criteria. However, the only way to programmatically see the matching records is to do the equivalent of selecting Visible Cells Only from the Go To Special dialog box.

To run a Filter in Place, use the constant `XLFilterInPlace` as the Action parameter in the `AdvancedFilter` command and remove the `CopyToRange` from the command:

```
IRange.AdvancedFilter Action:=xlFilterInPlace, CriteriaRange:=CRange, _
    Unique:=False
```

Then, the programmatic equivalent to loop through Visible Cells Only is this code:

```
For Each cell In Range("A2:A" & FinalRow).SpecialCells(xlCellTypeVisible)
    Ctr = Ctr + 1
Next cell
MsgBox Ctr & " cells match the criteria"
```

If you know that there would be no blanks in the visible cells, you could eliminate the loop with

```
Ctr = Application.Counta(Range("A2:A" & FinalRow).SpecialCells(xlCellTypeVisi
ble))
```

Catching No Records When Using Filter in Place

Just as when using `Copy`, you have to watch out for the possibility of having no records match the criteria. However, in this case it is more difficult to realize that nothing is returned. You generally find out when the `.SpecialCells` method returns a Runtime Error 1004—no cells were found.

To catch this condition, you have to set up an error trap to anticipate the 1004 error with the `SpecialCells` method.

→ **See** Chapter 25, "Handling Errors," for more information on catching errors.

```
On Error GoTo NoRecs
    For Each cell In Range("A2:A" & FinalRow).SpecialCells(xlCellTypeVisible)
        Ctr = Ctr + 1
    Next cell
    On Error GoTo 0
    MsgBox Ctr & " cells match the criteria"
    Exit Sub
NoRecs:
    MsgBox "No records match the criteria"
End Sub
```

This error trap works because it specifically excludes the header row from the `SpecialCells` range. The header row is always visible after an advanced filter. Including it in the range would prevent the 1004 error from being raised.

Showing All Records After Filter in Place

After doing a Filter in Place, you can get all records to show again by using the `ShowAllData` method:

```
ActiveSheet.ShowAllData
```

The Real Workhorse: `xlFilterCopy` with All Records Rather Than Unique Records Only

The examples at the beginning of this chapter talked about using `xlFilterCopy` to get a unique list of values in a field. You used unique lists of customer, region, and product to populate the list boxes in your report-specific userforms.

However, a more common scenario is to use an advanced filter to return all records that match the criteria. After the client selects which customer to report, an advanced filter can extract all records for that customer.

In all the examples in the following sections, you want to keep the Unique Records Only check box cleared. You do this in VBA by specifying `Unique:=False` as a parameter to the `AdvancedFilter` method.

This is not difficult to do, and you have some powerful options. If you need only a subset of fields for a report, copy only those field headings to the output range. If you want to resequence the fields to appear exactly as you need them in the report, you can do this by changing the sequence of the headings in the output range.

The next sections walk you through three quick examples to show the options available.

Copying All Columns

To copy all columns, specify a single blank cell as the output range. You will get all columns for those records that match the criteria, as shown in Figure 12.21:

```
Sub AllColumnsOneCustomer()
    Dim IRange As Range
    Dim ORange As Range
    Dim CRange As Range

    ' Find the size of today's dataset
    FinalRow = Cells(Rows.Count, 1).End(xlUp).Row
    NextCol = Cells(1, Columns.Count).End(xlToLeft).Column + 2

    ' Set up the criteria range with one customer
    Cells(1, NextCol).Value = Range("D1").Value
    ' In reality, this value should be passed from the userform
    Cells(2, NextCol).Value = Range("D2").Value
    Set CRange = Cells(1, NextCol).Resize(2, 1)

    ' Set up output range. It is a single blank cell
    Set ORange = Cells(1, NextCol + 2)

    ' Define the Input Range
    Set IRange = Range("A1").Resize(FinalRow, NextCol - 2)

    ' Do the Advanced Filter to get unique list of customers & product
    IRange.AdvancedFilter Action:=xlFilterCopy, _
        CriteriaRange:=CRange, CopyToRange:=ORange

End Sub
```

Figure 12.21
When using xlFil-terCopy with a blank output range, you get all columns in the same order as they appear in the original list range.

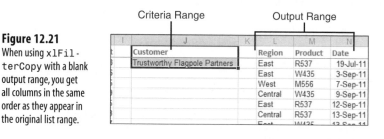

Criteria Range		Output Range		
I	J	K	L	M	N
Customer			Region	Product	Date
Trustworthy Flagpole Partners			East	R537	19-Jul-11
			East	W435	3-Sep-11
			West	M556	7-Sep-11
			Central	W435	9-Sep-11
			East	R537	12-Sep-11
			Central	R537	13-Sep-11
			East	W435	13-Sep-11

12

Copying a Subset of Columns and Reordering

If you are doing the advanced filter to send records to a report, it is likely that you might only need a subset of columns and you might need them in a different sequence.

This example finishes the frmReport example that was presented earlier in this chapter. As you recall, frmReport allows the client to select a customer. The OK button then calls the RunCustReport routine, passing a parameter to identify for which customer to prepare a report.

Imagine this is a report being sent to the customer. The customer really does not care about the surrounding region, and you do not want to reveal your cost of goods sold or profit. Assuming that you will put the customer's name in the title of the report, the fields that you need to produce the report are Date, Quantity, Product, Revenue.

The following code copies those headings to the output range. The advanced filter produces data, as shown in Figure 12.22. The program then goes on to copy the matching records to a new workbook. A title and total row is added, and the report is saved with the customer's name. Figure 12.23 shows the final report.

```
Sub RunCustReport(WhichCust As Variant)
    Dim IRange As Range
    Dim ORange As Range
    Dim CRange As Range
    Dim WBN As Workbook
    Dim WSN As Worksheet
    Dim WSO As Worksheet

    Set WSO = ActiveSheet
    ' Find the size of today's dataset
    FinalRow = Cells(Rows.Count, 1).End(xlUp).Row
    NextCol = Cells(1, Columns.Count).End(xlToLeft).Column + 2

    ' Set up the criteria range with one customer
    Cells(1, NextCol).Value = Range("D1").Value
    Cells(2, NextCol).Value = WhichCust
    Set CRange = Cells(1, NextCol).Resize(2, 1)

    ' Set up output range. We want Date, Quantity, Product, Revenue
    ' These columns are in C, E, B, and F
    Cells(1, NextCol + 2).Resize(1, 4).Value = _
        Array(Cells(1, 3), Cells(1, 5), Cells(1, 2), Cells(1, 6))
    Set ORange = Cells(1, NextCol + 2).Resize(1, 4)

    ' Define the Input Range
    Set IRange = Range("A1").Resize(FinalRow, NextCol - 2)

    ' Do the Advanced Filter to get unique list of customers & products
    IRange.AdvancedFilter Action:=xlFilterCopy, _
        CriteriaRange:=CRange, CopyToRange:=ORange

    ' Create a new workbook with one blank sheet to hold the output
    ' xlWBATWorksheet is the template name for a single worksheet
    Set WBN = Workbooks.Add(xlWBATWorksheet)
```

```
    Set WSN = WBN.Worksheets(1)

    ' Set up a title on WSN
    WSN.Cells(1, 1).Value = "Report of Sales to " & WhichCust

    ' Copy data from WSO to WSN
    WSO.Cells(1, NextCol + 2).CurrentRegion.Copy Destination:=WSN.Cells(3, 1)
    TotalRow = WSN.Cells(Rows.Count, 1).End(xlUp).Row + 1
    WSN.Cells(TotalRow, 1).Value = "Total"
    WSN.Cells(TotalRow, 2).FormulaR1C1 = "=SUM(R2C:R[-1]C)"
    WSN.Cells(TotalRow, 4).FormulaR1C1 = "=SUM(R2C:R[-1]C)"

    ' Format the new report with bold
    WSN.Cells(3, 1).Resize(1, 4).Font.Bold = True
    WSN.Cells(TotalRow, 1).Resize(1, 4).Font.Bold = True
    WSN.Cells(1, 1).Font.Size = 18

    WBN.SaveAs "C:\" & WhichCust & ".xls"
    WBN.Close SaveChanges:=False

    WSO.Select

    ' clear the output range, etc.
    Range("J:Z").Clear

End Sub
```

Figure 12.22

Immediately after the advanced filter, you have just the columns and records needed for the report.

J	K	L	M	N	O
Customer		Date	Product	Quantity	Revenue
Trustworthy Flagpole Partners		19-Jul-11	R537	1000	22810
		3-Sep-11	W435	200	4742
		7-Sep-11	M556	300	5700
		9-Sep-11	W435	600	13282

Figure 12.23

After copying the filtered data to a new sheet and applying some formatting, you have a good-looking report to send to each customer.

	A	B	C	D	E	F
1	Report of Sales to Cool Saddle Traders					
2						
3	Date	Quantity	Product	Revenue		
4	22-Jul-11	400	R537	9152		
5	25-Jul-11	600	R537	13806		
6	16-Aug-11	400	M556	7136		
7	23-Sep-11	100	R537	2358		
8	29-Sep-11	100	R537	1819		
9	21-Oct-11	100	R537	2484		
10	2-Mar-12	200	W435	4270		
11	17-Aug-12	700	W435	12145		
12	Total	2600		53170		
13						

12

CASE STUDY: UTILIZING TWO KINDS OF ADVANCED FILTERS TO CREATE A REPORT FOR EACH CUSTOMER

The final advanced filter example for this chapter uses several advanced filter techniques. Let's say that after importing invoice records, you want to send a purchase summary to each customer. The process would be as follows:

1. Run an advanced filter requesting unique values to get a list of customers in J. This `AdvancedFilter` specifies the `Unique:=True` parameter and uses a `CopyToRange` that includes a single heading for Customer:

   ```
   ' Set up output range. Copy heading from D1 there
   Range("D1").Copy Destination:=Cells(1, NextCol)
   Set ORange = Cells(1, NextCol)

   ' Define the Input Range
   Set IRange = Range("A1").Resize(FinalRow, NextCol - 2)

   ' Do the Advanced Filter to get unique list of customers
   IRange.AdvancedFilter Action:=xlFilterCopy, CriteriaRange:="", _
       CopyToRange:=ORange, Unique:=True
   ```

2. For each customer in the list of unique customers in Column J, perform steps 3 through 7. Find the number of customers in the output range from step 1. Then, use a `For Each Cell` loop to loop through the customers:

   ```
   ' Loop through each customer
   FinalCust = Cells(Rows.Count, NextCol).End(xlUp).Row
   For Each cell In Cells(2, NextCol).Resize(FinalCust - 1, 1)
       ThisCust = cell.Value
       ' ... Steps 3 through 7 here
   Next Cell
   ```

3. Build a criteria range in L1:L2 to be used in a new advanced filter. The criteria range would include a heading of Customer in L1 and the customer name from this iteration of the loop in cell L2:

   ```
   ' Set up the Criteria Range with one customer
   Cells(1, NextCol + 2).Value = Range("D1").Value
   Cells(2, NextCol + 2).Value = ThisCust
   Set CRange = Cells(1, NextCol + 2).Resize(2, 1)
   ```

4. Do an advanced filter to copy matching records for this customer to Column N. This `Advanced Filter` statement specifies the `Unique:=False` parameter. Because you want only the columns for Date, Quantity, Product, and Revenue, the `CopyToRange` specifies a four-column range with those headings copied in the proper order:

   ```
   ' Set up output range. We want Date, Quantity, Product, Revenue
   ' These columns are in C, E, B, and F
   Cells(1, NextCol + 4).Resize(1, 4).Value = _
       Array(Cells(1, 3), Cells(1, 5), Cells(1, 2), Cells(1, 6))
   Set ORange = Cells(1, NextCol + 4).Resize(1, 4)

   ' Do the Advanced Filter to get unique list of customers & product
   IRange.AdvancedFilter Action:=xlFilterCopy, CriteriaRange:=CRange, _
       CopyToRange:=Orange
   ```

5. Copy the customer records to a report sheet in a new workbook. The VBA code uses the `Workbooks.Add` method to create a new blank workbook. The extracted records from step 4 are copied to Cell A3 of the new workbook:

```
' Create a new workbook with one blank sheet to hold the output
Set WBN = Workbooks.Add(xlWBATWorksheet)
Set WSN = WBN.Worksheets(1)

' Copy data from WSO to WSN
WSO.Cells(1, NextCol + 4).CurrentRegion.Copy _
    Destination:=WSN.Cells(3, 1)
```

6. Format the report with a title and totals. In VBA, add a title that reflects the customer's name in cell A1. Make the headings bold and add a total below the final row:

```
' Set up a title on WSN
WSN.Cells(1, 1).Value = "Report of Sales to " & ThisCust

TotalRow = WSN.Cells(Rows.Count, 1).End(xlUp).Row + 1
WSN.Cells(TotalRow, 1).Value = "Total"
WSN.Cells(TotalRow, 2).FormulaR1C1 = "=SUM(R2C:R[-1]C)"
WSN.Cells(TotalRow, 4).FormulaR1C1 = "=SUM(R2C:R[-1]C)"

' Format the new report with bold
WSN.Cells(3, 1).Resize(1, 4).Font.Bold = True
WSN.Cells(TotalRow, 1).Resize(1, 4).Font.Bold = True
WSN.Cells(1, 1).Font.Size = 18
```

7. Use `SaveAs` to save the workbook based on customer name. After the workbook is saved, close the new workbook. Return to the original workbook and clear the output range to prepare for the next pass through the loop:

```
WBN.SaveAs "C:\Reports\" & ThisCust & ".xls"
WBN.Close SaveChanges:=False

WSO.Select
' Free up memory by setting object variables to nothing
Set WSN = Nothing
Set WBN = Nothing
' clear the output range, etc.
Cells(1, NextCol + 2).Resize(1, 10).EntireColumn.Clear
```

The complete code is as follows:

```
Sub RunReportForEachCustomer()
    Dim IRange As Range
    Dim ORange As Range
    Dim CRange As Range
    Dim WBN As Workbook
    Dim WSN As Worksheet
    Dim WSO As Worksheet

    Set WSO = ActiveSheet
    ' Find the size of today's dataset
    FinalRow = Cells(Rows.Count, 1).End(xlUp).Row
    NextCol = Cells(1, Columns.Count).End(xlToLeft).Column + 2
    ' First - get a unique list of customers in J
    ' Set up output range. Copy heading from D1 there
```

12

```
Range("D1").Copy Destination:=Cells(1, NextCol)
Set ORange = Cells(1, NextCol)

' Define the Input Range
Set IRange = Range("A1").Resize(FinalRow, NextCol - 2)

' Do the Advanced Filter to get unique list of customers
 IRange.AdvancedFilter Action:=xlFilterCopy, CriteriaRange:="", _
    CopyToRange:=ORange, Unique:=True

' Loop through each customer
FinalCust = Cells(Rows.Count, NextCol).End(xlUp).Row
For Each cell In Cells(2, NextCol).Resize(FinalCust - 1, 1)
    ThisCust = cell.Value

    ' Set up the Criteria Range with one customer
    Cells(1, NextCol + 2).Value = Range("D1").Value
    Cells(2, NextCol + 2).Value = ThisCust
    Set CRange = Cells(1, NextCol + 2).Resize(2, 1)

    ' Set up output range. We want Date, Quantity, Product, Revenue
    ' These columns are in C, E, B, and F
    Cells(1, NextCol + 4).Resize(1, 4).Value = _
        Array(Cells(1, 3), Cells(1, 5), Cells(1, 2), Cells(1, 6))
    Set ORange = Cells(1, NextCol + 4).Resize(1, 4)

    ' Do the Advanced Filter to get unique list of customers & product
    IRange.AdvancedFilter Action:=xlFilterCopy, CriteriaRange:=CRange, _
        CopyToRange:=ORange

    ' Create a new workbook with one blank sheet to hold the output
    Set WBN = Workbooks.Add(xlWBATWorksheet)
    Set WSN = WBN.Worksheets(1)
    ' Copy data from WSO to WSN
    WSO.Cells(1, NextCol + 4).CurrentRegion.Copy _
        Destination:=WSN.Cells(3, 1)

    ' Set up a title on WSN
    WSN.Cells(1, 1).Value = "Report of Sales to " & ThisCust

    TotalRow = WSN.Cells(Rows.Count, 1).End(xlUp).Row + 1
    WSN.Cells(TotalRow, 1).Value = "Total"
    WSN.Cells(TotalRow, 2).FormulaR1C1 = "=SUM(R2C:R[-1]C)"
    WSN.Cells(TotalRow, 4).FormulaR1C1 = "=SUM(R2C:R[-1]C)"

    ' Format the new report with bold
    WSN.Cells(3, 1).Resize(1, 4).Font.Bold = True
    WSN.Cells(TotalRow, 1).Resize(1, 4).Font.Bold = True
    WSN.Cells(1, 1).Font.Size = 18

    WBN.SaveAs "C:\Reports\" & ThisCust & ".xlsx"
    WBN.Close SaveChanges:=False
    WSO.Select
    Set WSN = Nothing
```

```
            Set WBN = Nothing

            ' clear the output range, etc.
            Cells(1, NextCol + 2).Resize(1, 10).EntireColumn.Clear
        Next cell

        Cells(1, NextCol).EntireColumn.Clear
        MsgBox FinalCust - 1 & " Reports have been created!"
    End Sub
```

This is a remarkable 45 lines of code. Incorporating a couple of advanced filters and not much else, you have managed to produce a tool that created 27 reports in less than 1 minute. Even an Excel power user would normally take 2 to 3 minutes per report to create these manually. In less than 60 seconds, this code will save someone a few hours every time these reports need to be created. Imagine the real scenario where there are hundreds of customers. Undoubtedly, there are people in every city who are manually creating these reports in Excel because they simply don't realize the power of Excel VBA.

Using Filter in Place with Unique Records Only

It is possible to use Filter in Place and Unique Records Only. Only columns that should be evaluated for unique combinations of values should be specified as the input range.

In Figure 12.24, the dataset has a common problem: Each account number appears with many different spellings of the customer name. You would like a unique list of customer numbers. For each unique customer number, you would like to include any of the various spellings for that customer.

Figure 12.24

Each account number has various variations of customer name.

	C	D
	Cust #	Customer
08	C826	CitiGroup
08	C826	CitiGroup
08	C826	CitiGroup
08	C826	CitiGroup
09	C826	Citi Group
08	C826	CitiGroup
09	C826	Citi Group
09	D267	Duke Energy
08	D267	Duke
08	D267	Duke Energy
08	D267	Duke Energy
09	E847	Exxon

To solve this problem, you can specify Column C as the input range, filter in place, and ask for unique records using this code:

```
FinalRow = Cells(Rows.Count, 4).End(xlUp).Row
Range("C1").Resize(FinalRow, 1).AdvancedFilter _
    Action:=xlFilterInPlace, _
    Unique:=True
```

12

Figure 12.25 shows the result: Each account number appears just once.

Figure 12.25

Because Column C was the input range, you only see one line per customer number.

	A	B	C	D	E
1	Region	Date	Cust #	Customer	Revenue
2	Central	6/24/2009	A158	AIG	4060
6	Central	1/13/2009	A180	AT&T	1740
46	East	5/13/2008	B151	Boeing	9635
50	West	5/15/2008	B689	Bank of America	6156
78	East	8/6/2009	C586	Compaq	4380
82	West	10/12/2008	C725	Chevron	7032
86	Central	2/8/2008	C826	CitiGroup	1817
134	East	8/28/2009	D267	Duke Energy	5532
138	West	12/9/2008	E847	Exxon	1878
204	East	8/19/2008	F293	Ford Motor	1836
260	West	9/16/2009	G225	G.E.	1741
312	West	3/12/2009	G351	General Motors	1704

Column D contains the first instance of each customer name. To copy those results to another place, use this code.

```
Range("C1").Resize(FinalRow, 2).Copy _
    Destination:=Worksheets("Customers").Range("A1")
ActiveSheet.ShowAllData
```

Figure 12.26 shows a unique list of customer numbers with the first customer name found for each customer number. This is significantly different than using Remove Duplicates on Customer Number and Customer. That command would show each variant of spelling of the customer name as a new row.

Figure 12.26

A unique list of customer numbers, along with one of the spellings of the customer name.

	A	B
1	Cust #	Customer
2	A158	AIG
3	A180	AT&T
4	B151	Boeing
5	B689	Bank of America
6	C586	Compaq
7	C725	Chevron
8	C826	CitiGroup
9	D267	Duke Energy
10	E847	Exxon
11	F293	Ford Motor
12	G225	G.E.
13	G351	General Motors
14	H268	HP
15	H636	Home Depot
16	I714	IBM
17	K772	Kroger
18	L922	Lucent
19	M254	Motorola
20	M719	Merck
21	P618	Phillip Morris
22	P665	P&G
23	S160	SBC Communications
24	S497	State Farm
25	S842	Sears
26	T610	Texaco
27	V742	Verizon
28	W285	Wal-Mart

Excel in Practice: Turning Off a Few Drop-Downs in the AutoFilter

One cool feature is available only in Excel VBA. When you AutoFilter a list in the Excel user interface, every column in the dataset gets a field drop-down in the heading row. Sometimes you have a field that does not make a lot of sense to AutoFilter. For example, in your current dataset, you might want to provide AutoFilter drop-downs for Region, Product, Customer, but not the numeric or date fields. After setting up the AutoFilter, you need one line of code to turn off each drop-down that you do not want to appear. The following code turns off the drop-downs for Columns C, E, F, G, and H:

```
Sub AutoFilterCustom()
    Range("A1").AutoFilter Field:=3, VisibleDropDown:=False
    Range("A1").AutoFilter Field:=5, VisibleDropDown:=False
    Range("A1").AutoFilter Field:=6, VisibleDropDown:=False
    Range("A1").AutoFilter Field:=7, VisibleDropDown:=False
    Range("A1").AutoFilter Field:=8, VisibleDropDown:=False
End Sub
```

Using this tool is a fairly rare treat. Most of the time, Excel VBA lets you to do things that are possible in the user interface—although it lets us do them very rapidly. The VisibleDropDown parameter actually enables you to do something in VBA that is generally not available in the Excel user interface. Your knowledgeable clients will be scratching their heads trying to figure out how you set up the cool auto filter with only a few filterable columns (see Figure 12.27).

Figure 12.27
Using VBA, you can set up an auto filter where only certain columns have the AutoFilter drop-down.

To clear the filter from the customer column, you use this code:

```
Sub SimpleFilter()
    Worksheets("SalesReport").Select
    Range("A1").AutoFilter
    Range("A1").AutoFilter Field:=4
End Sub
```

Next Steps

Using techniques from this chapter, you have many reporting techniques available to you by using the arcane Advanced Filter tool. Chapter 13, "Using VBA to Create Pivot Tables," introduces the most powerful feature in Excel: the pivot table. The combination of advanced filters and pivot tables creates reporting tools that enable amazing applications.

Using VBA to Create Pivot Tables

13

Introducing Pivot Tables

Pivot tables are the most powerful tools that Excel has to offer. The concept was first put into practice by Lotus with its Improv product.

I love pivot tables because they are a fast way to summarize massive amounts of data. The name *pivot table* comes from the ability you have to drag fields in the drop zones and have them recalculate. You can use the basic vanilla pivot table to produce a concise summary in seconds. However, pivot tables come in so many flavors that they can be the tools of choice for many different uses. You can build pivot tables to act as the calculation engine to produce reports by store, by style, or to quickly find the top 5 or bottom 10 of anything.

I am not suggesting you use VBA to build pivot tables to give to your user. I am suggesting you use pivot tables as a means to an end—use a pivot table to extract a summary of data and then take this summary on to better uses.

Understanding Versions

As Microsoft invests in making Excel the premier choice in business intelligence, pivot tables continue to evolve. They were introduced in Excel 5 and perfected in Excel 97. In Excel 2000, pivot table creation in VBA was dramatically altered. Some new parameters were added in Excel 2002. A few new properties such as `PivotFilters` and `TableStyle2` were added in Excel 2007. Slicers and new choices for Show Values As were added in Excel 2010. Therefore, you need to be extremely careful when writing code in Excel 2010 that might be run in legacy versions.

IN THIS CHAPTER

Introducing Pivot Tables.............................287

Understanding Versions 287

Creating a Vanilla Pivot Table in the Excel Interface..290

Building a Pivot Table in Excel VBA.............294

Using Advanced Pivot Table Features 302

Filtering a Data Set 312

Using Other Pivot Table Features 324

Much of the code in this chapter is backward-compatible all the way to Excel 2000. Pivot table creation in Excel 97 required using the `PivotTableWizard` method. Although this book will not include code for Excel 97, one example has been included in the sample file for this chapter.

New in Excel 2010

Excel 2010 offers many new features in pivot tables. If you use any of these features in VBA, the code will work in Excel 2010 but crash in any legacy versions of Excel.

Table 13.1 shows items that are available in Excel 2010 VBA for pivot tables.

> **NOTE** The items included in Table 13.1 will cause incompatibilities when run in Excel 2007.

Table 13.1   Properties and Methods New in Excel 2010

Feature	Properties and Methods
Slicers	Anything with the word Slicer will not work in Excel 2007, including `SlicerCaches`, `Slicers`, and `SlicerItems`.
Write-Back	You can write-back to OLAP datasets. Properties include `AllocateChanges`, `Allocation`, `AllocationMethod`, `AllocationValue`, `AllocationWeightExpression`, `ChangeList`, and `EnableWriteback`. Methods include `AllocateChanges`, `CommitChanges`, `DiscardChanges`, `RefreshDataSourceValues`. Objects include `PivotTableChangeList`. Also, `PivotCell.AllocateChange`, `PivotCell.CellChanged`, `PivotCell.DataSourceValue`, `PivotCell.DiscardChange`, `PivotCell.MDX`.
Repeat Labels	`RepeatAllLabels` method, `RepeatLabels` property.
Sets	`AlternativeText`, `CalculatedMembersInFilters`, `DisplayContextTooltips`, `ShowValuesRow`, `Summary`, `VisualTotalsForSets`.
Show Values As	These values from `xlPivotFieldCalculation` are new in Excel 2010: `xlPercentOfParentColumn`, `xlPercentOfParentRow`, `xlPercentRunningTotal`, `xlRankAscending`, `xlRankDescending`.

New Beginning with Excel 2007

If there is some chance that your code will run in Excel 2003, there are even more possible incompatibilities. Many concepts on the Design tab, such as subtotals at the top, the report layout options, blank rows, and the new pivot table styles, were introduced in Excel 2007. Excel 2007 offered better filters than legacy versions of Excel. Every new feature adds one or more methods or properties to VBA.

Table 13.2 shows the methods that were added in Excel 2007. If you record a macro that uses these methods, you cannot share the macro with someone using a legacy version of Excel.

Table 13.2   Methods That Were New in Excel 2007

Method	Description
`ClearAllFilters`	Clears all filters in the pivot table.
`ClearTable`	Removes all fields from the pivot table but keeps the pivot table intact.
`ConvertToFormulas`	Converts a pivot table to cube formulas. This method is valid only for pivot tables based on OLAP data sources.
`DisplayAllMember`	Equivalent to Options, Display, Show Properties `PropertiesInTooltip` in ToolTips.
`RowAxisLayout`	Changes the layout for all fields in the row area. Valid values are `xlCompactRow`, `xlTabularRow`, or `xlOutlineRow`.
`SubtotalLocation`	Controls whether subtotals appear at the top or bottom of each group. Valid arguments are `xlAtTop` or `xlAtBottom`.

Table 13.3 lists the properties that were new in Excel 2007. If you record a macro that refers to these properties, you cannot share the macro with someone using a legacy version of Excel.

Table 13.3   Properties That Were New in Excel 2007

Property	Description
`ActiveFilters`	Indicates the active filters in the pivot table; this is a read-only property.
`AllowMultipleFilters`	Indicates whether a pivot field can have multiple filters applied to it at the same time.
`CompactLayoutColumnHeader`	Specifies the caption that is displayed in the column header of a pivot table when in compact row layout form.
`CompactLayoutRowHeader`	Specifies the caption that displays in the row header of a pivot table when in compact row layout form.

13

Table 13.3   Continued

Property	Description
CompactRowIndent	Indicates the indent increment for pivot items when compact row layout form is turned on.
DisplayContextTooltips	Controls whether ToolTips display for pivot table cells.
DisplayFieldCaptions	Controls whether filter buttons and pivot field captions for rows and columns display in the grid.
DisplayMemberPropertyTooltips	Controls whether to display member properties in ToolTips.
FieldListSortAscending	Controls the sort order of fields in the PivotTable Field List. When this property is True, the fields are sorted in alphabetic order. When it is set to False, the fields are presented in the same sequence as the data source columns.
InGridDropZones	Controls whether you can drag and drop fields onto the grid. Changing the pivot table layout also changes this property. Changing this property forces the layout back to a table layout.
LayoutRowDefault	Specifies the layout settings for pivot fields when they are added to the pivot table for the first time. Valid values are xlCompactRow, xlTabularRow, or xlOutlineRow.
PivotColumnAxis	Returns a PivotAxis object representing the entire column axis.
PivotRowAxis	Returns a PivotAxis object representing the entire row axis.
PrintDrillIndicators	Specifies whether drill indicators are printed with the pivot table.
ShowDrillIndicators	Specifies whether drill indicators are shown in the pivot table.
ShowTableStyleColumnHeaders	Controls whether table style 2 should affect the column headers.
ShowTableStyleColumnStripes	Controls whether table style 2 should show banded columns.
ShowTableStyleLastColumn	Controls whether table style 2 should format the final column.
ShowTableStyleRowHeaders	Controls whether table style 2 should affect the row headers.
ShowTableStyleRowStripes	Controls whether table style 2 should show banded columns.
SortUsingCustomLists	Controls whether custom lists are used for sorting items of fields, both initially and later when applying a sort. Setting this property to False can optimize performance for fields with many items and allows you to avoid using custom-list-based sorting.
TableStyle2	Specifies the pivot table style currently applied to the pivot table. Note that previous versions of Excel offered a weak AutoFormat option. That feature's settings were held in the TableStyle property, so Microsoft had to use TableStyle2 as the property name for the new pivot table styles. The property might have a value such as PivotStyleLight17.

Creating a Vanilla Pivot Table in the Excel Interface

Even though pivot tables are the most powerful feature in Excel, Microsoft estimates they are used by only 7 percent of Excel users overall. Based on surveys at MrExcel.com, about

42 percent of advanced Excel users have used pivot tables. Because a significant portion of Excel users has not used pivot tables, this section walks through the steps of building a pivot table in the user interface.

NOTE If you are already a pivot table pro, jump ahead to the next section.

Let's say you have 5,000 or 500,000 rows of data, as shown in Figure 13.1. You want a summary of revenue by region and product. Regions should go down the side, products across the top.

Figure 13.1
If you need to summarize 500,000 rows of transactional data quickly, a pivot table can do so in seconds. Your goal is to produce a summary of revenue by region and product.

	A	B	C	D	E	F	G	H
1	Region	Product	Date	Customer	Quantity	Revenue	COGS	Profit
2	West	D625	1/4/2011	Guarded Kettle Corporation	430	10937	6248	4689
3	Central	A292	1/4/2011	Mouthwatering Jewelry Company	400	8517	4564	3953
4	West	B722	1/4/2011	Agile Glass Supply	940	23188	11703	11485
5	Central	E438	1/4/2011	Persuasive Kettle Inc.	190	5520	2958	2562
6	East	E438	1/4/2011	Safe Saddle Corporation	130	3933	2024	1909
7	West	C409	1/4/2011	Agile Glass Supply	440	11304	5936	5368
8	West	C409	1/4/2011	Guarded Kettle Corporation	770	20382	10387	9995
9	Central	E438	1/4/2011	Matchless Yardstick Inc.	570	17584	8875	8709
10	East	D625	1/4/2011	Unique Marble Company	380	10196	5521	4675

To build the pivot table to the right of the data, follow these steps:

1. Select a single cell in the transaction data. Select the PivotTable icon from the Insert tab. Excel displays the Create PivotTable dialog.

2. Verify that Excel filled in the proper address for the table range. Provided your data has no completely blank rows or blank columns, this address is usually correct.

3. Select to create the pivot table on an existing worksheet. Click the Location reference box and select Cell J1, as shown in Figure 13.2.

Figure 13.2
Verify that Excel selected the correct data and specify a location for the pivot table.

> **Create PivotTable**
>
> Choose the data that you want to analyze
> - ◉ Select a table or range
>   - Table/Range: `PivotTable!$A$1:$H$4989`
> - ○ Use an external data source
>   - Choose Connection...
>   - Connection name:
>
> Choose where you want the PivotTable report to be placed
> - ○ New Worksheet
> - ◉ Existing Worksheet
>   - Location: `PivotTable!$J$1`
>
> OK   Cancel

13

4. Click OK to create a blank pivot table. Instructions in the blank pivot table tell you to choose fields from the PivotTable Field List. The PivotTable Field List appears at the right side of your screen. A list of available fields is in the top of the task pane. The following four drop zones appear at the bottom of the task pane: Report Filter, Column Labels, Row Labels, and Values (see Figure 13.3).

Figure 13.3
Excel presents you with a list of available fields and four drop zones in the PivotTable Field List.

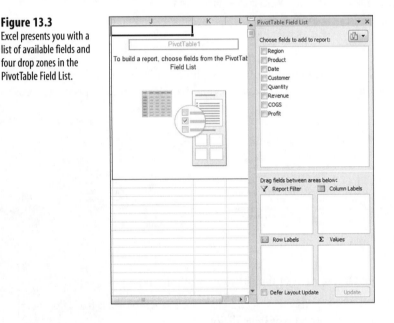

5. Click the Region and Revenue fields in the top section of the PivotTable Field List. Because the region field contains text data, it is automatically moved to the Row Labels drop zone. Because Revenue contains numeric data, it is automatically moved to the Values drop zone.

6. Click the Product field in the top section of the PivotTable Field List and drag to the Column Labels drop zone in the bottom half of the PivotTable Field List. This adds a list of products stretching across the top row of your pivot table.

Excel has built a concise summary of your data in the pivot table, as shown in Figure 13.4.

After a pivot table has been created on your worksheet, you can easily change the data summarized in the report by dragging fields within the drop zones of the PivotTable Field List. In Figure 13.5, Customer was added to the Row Labels section of the existing pivot table.

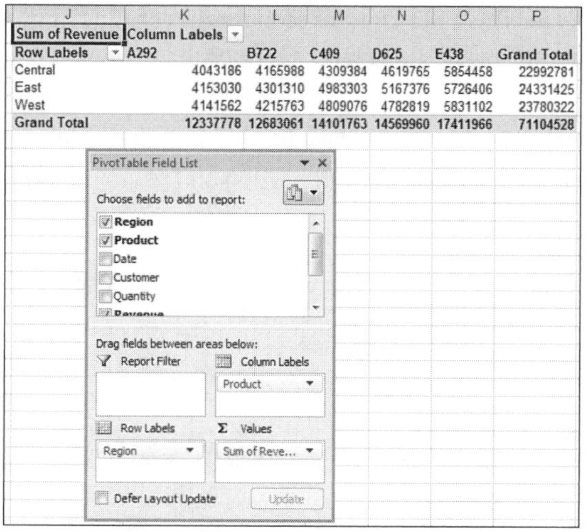

Figure 13.4
Only six clicks were required to create this summary.

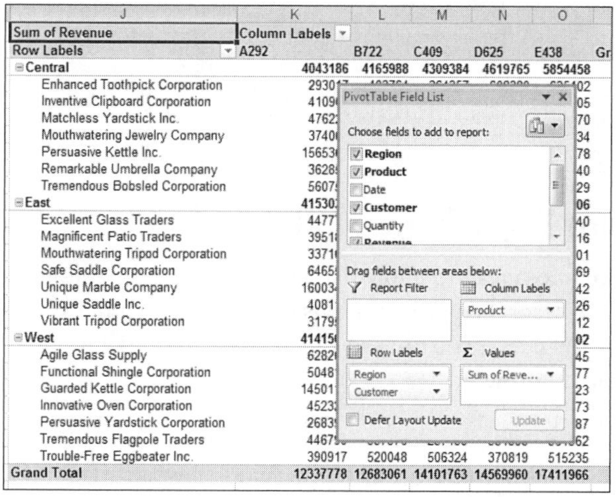

Figure 13.5
In a couple of clicks, you can move Region across the top, move Product down the side, and add a summary by Customer.

Understanding Compact Layout

Beginning with Excel 2007, all pivot tables created in the Excel interface are created in a new layout called Compact Form. In this layout, multiple Row fields appear in a single column at the left of the pivot table. Excel also puts the subtotals above the detail rows.

Although these changes might make for a better live pivot table, most of the pivot tables in this chapter will be converted to values to produce a static summary of the data. In these cases, you want to perform the following steps in the user interface:

1. On the Design tab, select Report Layout, Show in Tabular Form, and then select Repeat All Item Labels.

2. On the Design tab, select Subtotals, Do Not Show Subtotals.

13

3. On the Options tab, select the Options icon on the left side of the ribbon. In the Layout & Format tab of the PivotTable Options dialog, type a 0 next to For Empty Cells Show.

4. On the Design tab, select Grand Totals, Off for Rows and Columns.

After implementing these changes, you will have a solid, contiguous block of data, as shown in Figure 13.6.

Figure 13.6

If you plan to reuse the output of the pivot table for further analysis, a few changes to the default settings are required.

Sum of Reven		Product				
Region	Customer	A292	B722	C409	D625	E438
⊟ Central	Enhanced Toothpick Corporati	293017	403764	364357	602380	635402
Central	Inventive Clipboard Corporation	410968	440937	422647	292109	346605
Central	Matchless Yardstick Inc.	476223	352550	260833	392890	578970
Central	Mouthwatering Jewelry Compa	374000	446290	471812	291793	522434
Central	Persuasive Kettle Inc.	1565368	1385296	1443434	1584759	2030578
Central	Remarkable Umbrella Compar	362851	425325	469054	653531	645140
Central	Tremendous Bobsled Corporat	560759	711826	877247	802303	1095329
⊟ East	Excellent Glass Traders	447771	386804	723888	522227	454540
East	Magnificent Patio Traders	395186	483856	484067	430971	539616
East	Mouthwatering Tripod Corpora	337100	310841	422036	511184	519701
East	Safe Saddle Corporation	646559	857573	730463	1038371	1053369
East	Unique Marble Company	1600347	1581665	1765305	1707140	2179242
East	Unique Saddle Inc.	408114	311970	543737	458428	460826
East	Vibrant Tripod Corporation	317953	368601	313807	499055	519112
⊟ West	Agile Glass Supply	628204	652845	905059	712285	978745
West	Functional Shingle Corporation	504818	289670	408567	505071	484777
West	Guarded Kettle Corporation	1450110	1404742	1889149	1842751	2302023
West	Innovative Oven Corporation	452320	364200	420624	539300	582773
West	Persuasive Yardstick Corporat	268394	426882	441914	257998	402987
West	Tremendous Flagpole Traders	446799	557376	237439	554595	564562
West	Trouble-Free Eggbeater Inc.	390917	520048	506324	370819	515235

Building a Pivot Table in Excel VBA

This chapter does not mean to imply that you should use VBA to build pivot tables to give to your clients. Instead, the purpose of this chapter is to remind you that pivot tables can be used as a means to an end; you can use a pivot table to extract a summary of data and then use that summary elsewhere.

> **NOTE**
>
> The code listings from this chapter are available for download at http://www.MrExcel.com/getcode2010.html.

CAUTION

Although the Excel user interface has new names for the various sections of a pivot table, VBA code continues to refer to the old names. Microsoft had to use this choice; otherwise, millions of lines of code would stop working in Excel 2007 when they referred to a page field rather than a filter field. Although the four sections of a pivot table in the Excel user interface are Report Filter, Column Labels, Row Labels, and Values, VBA continues to use the old terms of Page fields, Column fields, Row fields, and Data fields.

Defining the Pivot Cache

In Excel 2000 and later, you first build a pivot cache object to describe the input area of the data:

```
Dim WSD As Worksheet
Dim PTCache As PivotCache
Dim PT As PivotTable
Dim PRange As Range
Dim FinalRow As Long
Dim FinalCol As Long
Set WSD = Worksheets("PivotTable")

' Delete any prior pivot tables
For Each PT In WSD.PivotTables
    PT.TableRange2.Clear
Next PT

' Define input area and set up a Pivot Cache
FinalRow = WSD.Cells(Rows.Count, 1).End(xlUp).Row
FinalCol = WSD.Cells(1, Columns.Count).End(xlToLeft).Column
Set PRange = WSD.Cells(1, 1).Resize(FinalRow, FinalCol)
Set PTCache = ActiveWorkbook.PivotCaches.Add(SourceType:=xlDatabase, _
    SourceData:=PRange)
```

Creating and Configuring the Pivot Table

After defining the pivot cache, use the CreatePivotTable method to create a blank pivot table based on the defined pivot cache:

```
Set PT = PTCache.CreatePivotTable(TableDestination:=WSD.Cells(2, _
    FinalCol + 2), TableName:="PivotTable1")
```

In the CreatePivotTable method, you specify the output location and optionally give the table a name. After running this line of code, you have a strange-looking blank pivot table, like the one shown in Figure 13.7. You now have to use code to drop fields onto the table.

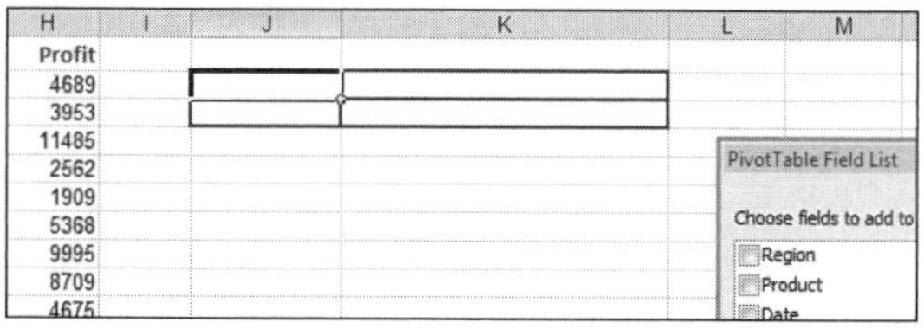

Figure 13.7
When you use the CreatePivotTable method, Excel gives you a four-cell blank pivot table that is not very useful.

If you choose the Defer Layout Update setting in the user interface to build the pivot table, Excel does not recalculate the pivot table after you drop each field onto the table. By default in VBA, Excel calculates the pivot table as you execute each step of building the table. This could require the pivot table to be executed a half-dozen times before you get the final result. To speed up your code execution, you can temporarily turn off calculation of the pivot table by using the ManualUpdate property:

```
PT.ManualUpdate = True
```

You can now run through the steps needed to lay out the pivot table. In the `.AddFields` method, you can specify one or more fields that should be in the row, column, or filter area of the pivot table.

The `RowFields` parameter enables you to define fields that appear in the Row Labels drop zone of the PivotTable Field List. The `ColumnFields` parameter corresponds to the Column Labels drop zone. The `PageFields` parameter corresponds to the Report Filter drop zone.

The following line of code populates a pivot table with two fields in the row area and one field in the column area:

```
' Set up the row & column fields
PT.AddFields RowFields:=Array("Region", "Customer"), _
    ColumnFields:="Product"
```

To add a field such as Revenue to the values area of the table, you change the `Orientation` property of the field to be `xlDataField`.

Adding Fields to the Data Area

When you are adding fields to the Data area of the pivot table, there are many settings you should control instead of letting Excel's intellisense decide.

For example, say you are building a report with revenue in which you will likely want to sum the revenue. If you don't explicitly specify the calculation, Excel scans through the data in the underlying data. If 100 percent of the revenue columns are numeric, Excel will sum those columns. If one cell is blank or contains text, Excel will decide on that day to count the revenue, which will produce confusing results.

Because of this possible variability, you should never use the `DataFields` argument in the `AddFields` method. Instead, change the property of the field to `xlDataField`. You can then specify the `Function` to be `xlSum`.

While you are setting up the data field, you can change several other properties within the same `With...End With` block.

The `Position` property is useful when adding multiple fields to the data area. Specify 1 for the first field, 2 for the second field, and so on.

By default, Excel will rename a Revenue field to have a strange name like Sum of Revenue. You can use the `.Name` property to change that heading back to something normal.

> **TIP**
> Note that you cannot reuse the word "Revenue" as a name. Instead, you should use "Revenue " (with a space).

You are not required to specify a number format, but it can make the resulting pivot table easier to understand, and only takes an extra line of code.

```
' Set up the data fields
With PT.PivotFields("Revenue")
    .Orientation = xlDataField
    .Function = xlSum
    .Position = 1
    .NumberFormat = "#,##0"
    .Name = "Revenue "
End With
```

At this point, you have given VBA all the settings required to generate the pivot table correctly. If you set `ManualUpdate` to `False`, Excel calculates and draws the pivot table. You can immediately thereafter set this back to `True`:

```
' Calc the pivot table
PT.ManualUpdate = False
PT.ManualUpdate = True
```

Your pivot table inherits the table style settings selected as the default on whatever computer happens to run the code. If you want control over the final format, you can explicitly choose a table style. The following code applies banded rows and a medium table style:

```
' Format the pivot table
PT.ShowTableStyleRowStripes = True
PT.TableStyle2 = "PivotStyleMedium10"
```

If you want to reuse the data from the pivot table, turn off the grand totals and subtotals and fill in the labels along the left column. For an explanation of why this code turns off the subtotals, see "Suppressing Subtotals for Multiple Row Fields" near the end of this chapter.

```
With PT
    .ColumnGrand = False
    .RowGrand = False
    .RepeatAllLabels xlRepeatLabels ' New in Excel 2010
End With
PT.PivotFields("Region").Subtotals(1) = True
PT.PivotFields("Region").Subtotals(1) = False
```

At this point, you have a complete pivot table like the one shown in Figure 13.8.

Figure 13.8
Fewer than 50 lines of code created this pivot table in less than a second.

Region	Customer	A292	B722	C409	D625	E438
Central	Enhanced Toothpick Corporation	293,017	403,764	364,357	602,380	635,402
Central	Inventive Clipboard Corporation	410,968	440,937	422,647	292,109	346,605
Central	Matchless Yardstick Inc.	476,223	352,550	260,833	392,890	578,970
Central	Mouthwatering Jewelry Company	374,000	446,290	471,812	291,793	522,434
Central	Persuasive Kettle Inc.	1,565,368	1,385,296	1,443,434	1,584,759	2,030,578
Central	Remarkable Umbrella Company	362,851	425,325	469,054	653,531	645,140
Central	Tremendous Bobsled Corporation	560,759	711,826	877,247	802,303	1,095,329
East	Excellent Glass Traders	447,771	386,804	723,888	522,227	454,540
East	Magnificent Patio Traders	395,186	483,856	484,067	430,971	539,616
East	Mouthwatering Tripod Corporation	337,100	310,841	422,036	511,184	519,701
East	Safe Saddle Corporation	646,559	857,573	730,463	1,038,371	1,053,369
East	Unique Marble Company	1,600,347	1,581,665	1,765,305	1,707,140	2,179,242
East	Unique Saddle Inc.	408,114	311,970	543,737	458,428	460,826
East	Vibrant Tripod Corporation	317,953	368,601	313,807	499,055	519,112
West	Agile Glass Supply	628,204	652,845	905,059	712,285	978,745
West	Functional Shingle Corporation	504,818	289,670	408,567	505,071	484,777
West	Guarded Kettle Corporation	1,450,110	1,404,742	1,889,149	1,842,751	2,302,023
West	Innovative Oven Corporation	452,320	364,200	420,624	539,300	582,773
West	Persuasive Yardstick Corporation	268,394	426,882	441,914	257,998	402,987
West	Tremendous Flagpole Traders	446,799	557,376	237,439	554,595	564,562
West	Trouble-Free Eggbeater Inc.	390,917	520,048	506,324	370,819	515,235

13

Listing 13.1 shows the complete code used to generate the pivot table.

Listing 13.1   Code to Generate a Pivot Table

```
Sub CreatePivot()
    Dim WSD As Worksheet
    Dim PåTCache As PivotCache
    Dim PT As PivotTable
    Dim PRange As Range
    Dim FinalRow As Long
    Set WSD = Worksheets("PivotTable")

    ' Delete any prior pivot tables
    For Each PT In WSD.PivotTables
        PT.TableRange2.Clear
    Next PT

    ' Define input area and set up a Pivot Cache
    FinalRow = WSD.Cells(Application.Rows.Count, 1).End(xlUp).Row
    FinalCol = WSD.Cells(1, Application.Columns.Count). _
        End(xlToLeft).Column
    Set PRange = WSD.Cells(1, 1).Resize(FinalRow, FinalCol)
    Set PTCache = ActiveWorkbook.PivotCaches.Add(SourceType:= _
        xlDatabase, SourceData:=PRange.Address)

    ' Create the Pivot Table from the Pivot Cache
    Set PT = PTCache.CreatePivotTable(TableDestination:=WSD. _
        Cells(2, FinalCol + 2), TableName:="PivotTable1")

    ' Turn off updating while building the table
    PT.ManualUpdate = True

    ' Set up the row & column fields
    PT.AddFields RowFields:=Array("Region", "Customer"), _
        ColumnFields:="Product"

    ' Set up the data fields
    With PT.PivotFields("Revenue")
        .Orientation = xlDataField
        .Function = xlSum
        .Position = 1
        .NumberFormat = "#,##0"
        .Name = "Revenue "
    End With

    ' Calc the pivot table
    PT.ManualUpdate = False
    PT.ManualUpdate = True

    'Format the pivot table
    PT.ShowTableStyleRowStripes = True
    PT.TableStyle2 = "PivotStyleMedium10"
    With PT
        .ColumnGrand = False
        .RowGrand = False
        .RepeatAllLabels xlRepeatLabels ' New in Excel 2010
    End With
```

```
PT.PivotFields("Region").Subtotals(1) = True
PT.PivotFields("Region").Subtotals(1) = False
WSD.Activate
Range("J2").Select

End Sub
```

Learning Why You Cannot Move or Change Part of a Pivot Report

Although pivot tables are incredible, they have annoying limitations; for example, you cannot move or change just part of a pivot table. Try to run a macro that clears Row 2. The macro comes to a screeching halt with an error 1004, as shown in Figure 13.9. To get around this limitation, you can copy the pivot table and paste as values.

Figure 13.9
You cannot delete just part of a pivot table.

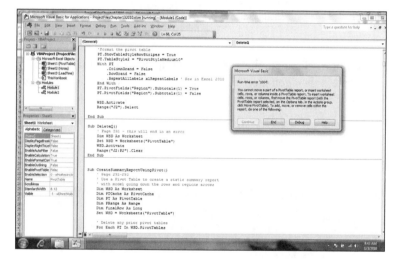

Determining Size of a Finished Pivot Table to Convert the Pivot Table to Values

Knowing the size of a pivot table in advance is difficult. If you run a report of transactional data on one day, you may or may not have sales from the West region, for example. This could cause your table to be either six or seven columns wide. Therefore, you should use the special property `TableRange2` to refer to the entire resultant pivot table.

`PT.TableRange2` includes the entire pivot table. In Figure 13.10, `TableRange2` includes the extra row at the top with the button Sum of Revenue. To eliminate that row, the code copies `PT.TableRange2` but offsets this selection by one row by using `.Offset(1, 0)`. Depending on the nature of your pivot table, you might need to use an offset of two or more rows to get rid of extraneous information at the top of the pivot table.

The code copies `PT.TableRange2` and uses `PasteSpecial` on a cell five rows below the current pivot table. At that point in the code, your worksheet appears as shown in Figure 13.10. The table in J2 is a live pivot table, and the table in J12 is just the copied results.

13

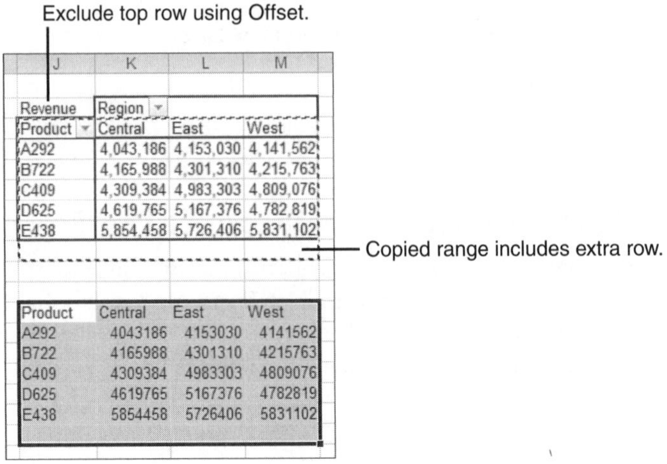

Exclude top row using Offset.

Figure 13.10
This figure shows an intermediate result of the macro. Only the summary in J12:M17 will remain after the macro finishes.

Copied range includes extra row.

You can then eliminate the pivot table by applying the Clear method to the entire table. If your code is then going on to do additional formatting, you should remove the pivot cache from memory by setting PTCache equal to Nothing.

The code in Listing 13.2 uses a pivot table to produce a summary from the underlying data. At the end of the code, the pivot table will be copied to static values and the pivot table will be cleared.

Listing 13.2   Code to Produce a Static Summary from a Pivot Table

```
Sub CreateSummaryReportUsingPivot()
    ' Use a Pivot Table to create a static summary report
    ' with product going down the rows and regions across
    Dim WSD As Worksheet
    Dim PTCache As PivotCache
    Dim PT As PivotTable
    Dim PRange As Range
    Dim FinalRow As Long
    Set WSD = Worksheets("PivotTable")

    ' Delete any prior pivot tables
    For Each PT In WSD.PivotTables
        PT.TableRange2.Clear
    Next PT
    WSD.Range("J1:Z1").EntireColumn.Clear

    ' Define input area and set up a Pivot Cache
    FinalRow = WSD.Cells(Application.Rows.Count, 1).End(xlUp).Row
    FinalCol = WSD.Cells(1, Application.Columns.Count). _
        End(xlToLeft).Column
    Set PRange = WSD.Cells(1, 1).Resize(FinalRow, FinalCol)
    Set PTCache = ActiveWorkbook.PivotCaches.Add(SourceType:= _
        xlDatabase, SourceData:=PRange.Address)

    ' Create the Pivot Table from the Pivot Cache
```

```
    Set PT = PTCache.CreatePivotTable(TableDestination:=WSD. _
        Cells(2, FinalCol + 2), TableName:="PivotTable1")

    ' Turn off updating while building the table
    PT.ManualUpdate = True

    ' Set up the row fields
    PT.AddFields RowFields:="Product", ColumnFields:="Region"

    ' Set up the data fields
    With PT.PivotFields("Revenue")
        .Orientation = xlDataField
        .Function = xlSum
        .Position = 1
        .NumberFormat = "#,##0"
        .Name = "Revenue "
    End With

    With PT
        .ColumnGrand = False
        .RowGrand = False
        .NullString = "0"
    End With

    ' Calc the pivot table
    PT.ManualUpdate = False
    PT.ManualUpdate = True

    ' PT.TableRange2 contains the results. Move these to J12
    ' as just values and not a real pivot table.
    PT.TableRange2.Offset(1, 0).Copy
    WSD.Cells(5 + PT.TableRange2.Rows.Count, FinalCol + 2). _
        PasteSpecial xlPasteValues

    ' At this point, the worksheet looks like Figure 13.10
    ' Stop

    ' Delete the original Pivot Table & the Pivot Cache
    PT.TableRange2.Clear
    Set PTCache = Nothing

    WSD.Activate
    Range("J12").Select
End Sub
```

The code in Listing 13.2 creates the pivot table. It then copies the results and pastes them as values in J12:M13. Figure 13.10, which was shown previously, includes an intermediate result just before the original pivot table is cleared.

So far, this chapter has walked you through building the simplest of pivot table reports. Pivot tables offer far more flexibility. The sections that follow present more complex reporting examples.

Using Advanced Pivot Table Features

In this section, you will take the detailed transactional data and produce a series of reports for each product line manager. This section covers the following advanced pivot table features that are required in these reports:

- Group the daily dates up to yearly dates
- Add multiple fields to the value area
- Control the sort order so the largest customers are listed first
- Use the ShowPages feature to replicate the report for each product line manager
- After producing the pivot tables, convert the pivot table to values and do some basic formatting

Figure 13.11 shows the report for one product line manager so that you can understand the final goal.

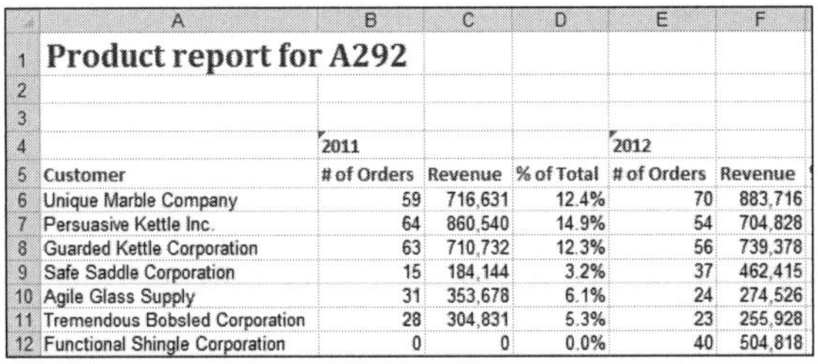

Figure 13.11
Using pivot tables simplifies the creation of the report.

	A	B	C	D	E	F
1	**Product report for A292**					
2						
3						
4		2011			2012	
5	Customer	# of Orders	Revenue	% of Total	# of Orders	Revenue
6	Unique Marble Company	59	716,631	12.4%	70	883,716
7	Persuasive Kettle Inc.	64	860,540	14.9%	54	704,828
8	Guarded Kettle Corporation	63	710,732	12.3%	56	739,378
9	Safe Saddle Corporation	15	184,144	3.2%	37	462,415
10	Agile Glass Supply	31	353,678	6.1%	24	274,526
11	Tremendous Bobsled Corporation	28	304,831	5.3%	23	255,928
12	Functional Shingle Corporation	0	0	0.0%	40	504,818

Using Multiple Value Fields

The report has three fields in the values area; Count of Orders, Revenue, and % of Total Revenue. Anytime you have two or more fields in the values area, a new virtual field named Data becomes available in your pivot table.

In Excel 2010, this field appears as sigma values in the drop zone of the Pivot Table Field List. When creating your pivot table, you can specify Data as one of the column fields or row fields.

The position of the Data field is important. It usually works best as the innermost column field.

When you define your pivot table in VBA, you will have two columns fields: the Date field and the Data field. To specify two or more fields in the AddFields method, you wrap those fields in an array function.

Use this code to define the pivot table:

```
' Set up the row fields
PT.AddFields RowFields:="Customer", _
    ColumnFields:=Array("Date", "Data"), _
    PageFields:="Product"
```

This is the first time you have seen the PageFields parameter in this chapter. If you were creating a pivot table for someone to use, the fields in the PageField allow for easy ad hoc analysis. In this case, the value in the PageField is going to make it easy to replicate the report for every product line manager.

Counting the Number of Records

So far, the .Function property of the data fields has always been .xlSum. There are a total of 11 functions available: xlSum, xlCount, xlAverage, xlStdDev, xlMin, xlMax, and so on.

Count is the only function that works for text fields. To count the number of records, and hence the number of orders, add a text field to the data area and choose .xlCount as the function.

```
With PT.PivotFields("Region")
    .Orientation = xlDataField
    .Function = xlCount
    .Position = 1
    .NumberFormat = "#,##0"
    .Name = "# of Orders "
End With
```

> **CAUTION**
>
> This is a count of the number of records. It is not a count of the distinct values in a field. This has always been difficult to do in a pivot table. It is now fairly easy to do with the PowerPivot add-in. Unfortunately, you cannot use VBA to build a PowerPivot pivot table.

Grouping Daily Dates to Months, Quarters, or Years

Pivot tables have the amazing ability to group daily dates up to months, quarters, and/or years. In VBA, this feature is a bit annoying because you must select a date cell before issuing the command. As you saw in Figure 13.10, your pivot table usually stays as four blank cells until the end of the macro, so there really is not a date field to select.

However, if you need to group a date field, you will have to let the pivot table redraw. To do this, use this code:

```
' Pause here to group daily dates up to years
' Need to draw the pivot table so you can select date heading
PT.ManualUpdate = False
PT.ManualUpdate = True
```

> **TIP**
>
> I used to go through all sorts of gyrations to figure out where the first date field was. In fact, you can simply refer to PT.PivotFields("Date").LabelRange to point to the date heading.

13

There are seven ways to group times or dates: Seconds, Minutes, Hours, Days, Months, Quarters, and Years. Note that you can group a field by multiple items. You specify a series of seven True/False values corresponding to Seconds, Minutes, and so on.

For example, to group by Months, Quarters, and Years, you would use the following:

```
PT.PivotFields("Date").LabelRange.Group , Periods:= _
    Array(False, False, False, False, True, True, True)
```

> **CAUTION**
>
> Never choose to group by only months without including years. If you do this, Excel combines January from this year and January from last year into a single item called January. Although this is great for seasonality analyses, it is rarely what you want in a summary. Always choose Years and Months in the Grouping dialog.

If you want to group by week, you group only by day and use 7 as the value for the By parameter:

```
PT.PivotFields("Date").LabelRange.Group _
    Start:=True, End:=True, By:=7, _
    Periods:=Array(False, False, False, True, False, False, False)
```

Specifying True for Start and End will start the first week at the earliest date in the data. If you only want to show weeks starting from Monday January 3, 2011 through Sunday January 1, 2012, use this code:

```
With PT.PivotFields("Date")
    .LabelRange.Group _
        Start:=DateSerial(2011, 1, 3), _
        End:=DateSerial(2012, 1, 1), _
        By:=7, _
        Periods:=Array(False, False, False, True, False, False, False)
    On Error Resume Next
    .PivotItems("<1/3/2011").Visible = False
    .PivotItems(">1/1/2012").Visible = False
    On Error Goto 0
End With
```

To see a demo of grouping by week, search for Excel VBA 13 at YouTube.

> **CAUTION**
>
> There is one limitation to grouping by week. When you group by week, you cannot also group by any other measure. For example, grouping by week and quarter is not valid.

For this report, you only need to group by year, so the code is as follows:

```
' Group daily dates up to years
PT.PivotFields("Date").LabelRange.Group , Periods:= _
    Array(False, False, False, False, False, False, True)
```

CAUTION

Before grouping the daily dates up to years, you had about 500 date columns across this report. After grouping, you have two date columns plus a total. I prefer to group the dates as soon as possible in the macro. If you added the other two data fields to the report before grouping, your report would be 1500 columns wide. While this is not a problem since Excel 2007 increased the column limit from 256 to 16,384, it still creates an unusually large report when you ultimately only need a few columns.

Figure 13.12 shows the report before grouping the dates up to years. Figure 13.13 shows the report after grouping to years.

Figure 13.12
Five hundred daily dates stretch across the report.

Product	(All)			
# of Orders	Date			
Customer	1/4/2011	1/5/2011	1/6/2011	1/7/2011
Agile Glass Supply	3	1		
Enhanced Toothpick Corporation	1			1
Excellent Glass Traders				
Functional Shingle Corporation				
Guarded Kettle Corporation	2	1		1
Innovative Oven Corporation				
Inventive Clipboard Corporation	1	1		

Figure 13.13
After one line of code, the dates are rolled up to years.

Product	(All)		
# of Orders	Date		
Customer	2011	2012	Grand Total
Agile Glass Supply	148	130	278
Enhanced Toothpick Corporation	85	71	156
Excellent Glass Traders	87	80	167
Functional Shingle Corporation		157	157
Guarded Kettle Corporation	316	290	606

NOTE

After you issue this command, the years field is still called Date. This may not always be true. If you roll daily dates up to months and to years, the Date field will contain months, and a new Year field will be added to the field list to hold years.

Changing the Calculation to Show Percentages

Excel 2010 offers a new Show Values As drop-down in the Options tab. Although some of the options in that drop-down are truly new to Excel 2010, most of the options have been hidden away on a back tab of the Field Settings dialog.

These calculations allow you to change how a field is displayed in the report. Instead of showing sales, you could show the sales as a percentage of the total sales. You could show a running total. You could show each day's sales as a percentage of the previous day's sales.

All these settings are controlled through the `.Calculation` property of the pivot field. Each calculation has its own unique set of rules. Some, such as % of column, work without any further settings. Others, such as Running Total In, require a base field. Others, such as running total, require a base field and a base item.

To get the percentage of the total, specify `xlPercentOfTotal` as the `.Calculation` property for the page field:

```
.Calculation = xlPercentOfTotal
```

To set up a running total, you have to specify a `BaseField`. Say that you need a running total along a date column:

```
' Set up Running Total
    .Calculation = xlRunningTotal
    .BaseField = "Date"
```

With ship months going down the columns, you might want to see the percentage of revenue growth from month to month. You can set up this arrangement with the `xlPercent-DifferenceFrom` setting. In this case, you must specify that the `BaseField` is `"Date"` and that the `BaseItem` is something called `(previous)`:

```
' Set up % change from prior month
With PT.PivotFields("Revenue")
    .Orientation = xlDataField
    .Function = xlSum
    .Caption = "%Change"
    .Calculation = xlPercentDifferenceFrom
    .BaseField = "Date"
    .BaseItem = "(previous)"
    .NumberFormat = "#0.0%"
End With
```

Note that with positional calculations, you cannot use the `AutoShow` or `AutoSort` method. This is too bad; it would be interesting to sort the customers high to low and to see their sizes in relation to each other.

You can use the `xlPercentDifferenceFrom` setting to express revenues as a percentage of the West region sales:

```
' Show revenue as a percentage of California
With PT.PivotFields("Revenue")
    .Orientation = xlDataField
    .Function = xlSum
    .Caption = "% of West"
    .Calculation = xlPercentDifferenceFrom
    .BaseField = "State"
    .BaseItem = "California"
    .Position = 3
    .NumberFormat = "#0.0%"
End With
```

Table 13.4 shows the complete list of `.Calculation` options. The second column indicates whether the calculation is compatible with earlier versions of Excel. The third column indicates if you need a base field and base item.

Table 13.4   Complete List of `.Calculation` **Options**

Calculation	Version	BaseField/BaseItem
`xlDifferenceFrom`	All	Both required
`xlIndex`	All	Neither
`xlNoAdditionalCalculation`	All	Neither
`xlPercentDifferenceFrom`	All	Both required
`xlPercentOf`	All	Both required
`xlPercentOfColumn`	All	Neither
`xlPercentOfParent`	2010 Only	BaseField only
`xlPercentOfParentColumn`	2010 Only	Both required
`xlPercentOfParentRow`	2010 Only	Both required
`xlPercentOfRow`	All	Neither
`xlPercentOfTotal`	All	Neither
`xlPercentRunningTotal`	2010 Only	BaseField only
`xlRankAscending`	2010 Only	BaseField only
`xlRankDescending`	2010 Only	BaseField only
`xlRunningTotal`	All	BaseField only

After that long explanation of the `.Calculation` property, you can build the other two pivot table fields for the product line report.

Add `Revenue` to the report twice. The first time, there is no calculation. The second time, calculate the percentage of total:

```
' Set up the data fields - Revenue
With PT.PivotFields("Revenue")
    .Orientation = xlDataField
    .Function = xlSum
    .Position = 2
    .NumberFormat = "#,##0"
    .Name = "Revenue "
End With

' Set up the data fields - % of total Revenue
With PT.PivotFields("Revenue")
    .Orientation = xlDataField
    .Function = xlSum
    .Position = 3
    .NumberFormat = "0.0%"
    .Name = "% of Total "
    .Calculation = xlPercentOfColumn
End With
```

13

> **TIP**
>
> Take careful note of the name of the first field above. By default, Excel would use Sum of Revenue. Like me, if you think this is a goofy title, you can change it. However, you cannot change it to Revenue because there is already a field in the pivot table field list with that name.
>
> In the preceding code, I used the name "Revenue " (with a trailing space). This works fine, and no one notices the extra space. However, in the rest of the macro, when you refer to this field, remember to refer to it as "Revenue " (with a trailing space).

Eliminating Blank Cells in the Values Area

If you have some customers who were new in year 2, their sales will appear blank in year 1. Anyone using Excel 97 or later can replace blank cells with zeros. In the Excel interface, you can find the setting on the Layout & Format tab of the PivotTable Options dialog box. Select the For Empty Cells, Show option and type 0 in the box.

The equivalent operation in VBA is to set the `NullString` property for the pivot table to "0":

```
PT.NullString = "0"
```

> **NOTE**
>
> Although the proper code is to set this value to a text zero, Excel actually puts a real zero in the empty cells.

Controlling the Sort Order with AutoSort

The Excel interface offers an AutoSort option that enables you to show customers in descending order based on revenue. The equivalent code in VBA to sort the product field by descending revenue uses the `AutoSort` method:

```
PT.PivotFields("Customer").AutoSort Order:=xlDescending, _
    Field:="Revenue "
```

After applying some formatting in the macro, you now have one report with totals for all products, as shown in Figure 13.14.

Figure 13.14
Replicate this report for each product.

Customer	2011 # of Orders	Revenue	% of Total	2012 # of Orders	Revenue	% of Total	Total # of Orders	Total Revenue	Total % of Total
Guarded Kettle Corporation	316	4,501,310	13.2%	290	4,387,465	11.9%	606	8,888,775	12.5%
Unique Marble Company	307	4,418,324	13.0%	316	4,415,375	11.9%	623	8,833,699	12.4%
Persuasive Kettle Inc.	268	3,870,414	11.4%	295	4,139,021	11.2%	563	8,009,435	11.3%
Safe Saddle Corporation	135	1,979,144	5.8%	160	2,347,191	6.3%	295	4,326,335	6.1%
Tremendous Bobsled Corporation	146	1,991,712	5.8%	148	2,055,752	5.6%	294	4,047,464	5.7%
Agile Glass Supply	148	2,128,660	6.2%	130	1,748,478	4.7%	278	3,877,138	5.5%
Remarkable Umbrella Company	98	1,445,685	4.2%	79	1,110,216	3.0%	177	2,555,901	3.6%
Excellent Glass Traders	87	1,304,899	3.8%	80	1,230,331	3.3%	167	2,535,230	3.6%
Tremendous Flagpole Traders	72	960,387	2.8%	95	1,400,384	3.8%	167	2,360,771	3.3%
Innovative Oven Corporation	84	1,106,089	3.2%	83	1,253,128	3.4%	167	2,359,217	3.3%
Magnificent Patio Traders	80	1,134,692	3.3%	84	1,199,004	3.2%	164	2,333,696	3.3%
Trouble-Free Eggbeater Inc.	84	1,173,096	3.4%	78	1,130,247	3.1%	162	2,303,343	3.2%
Enhanced Toothpick Corporation	85	1,210,506	3.6%	71	1,088,414	2.9%	156	2,298,920	3.2%
Functional Shingle Corporation	0	0	0.0%	157	2,192,903	5.9%	157	2,192,903	3.1%
Unique Saddle Inc.	76	1,093,908	3.2%	73	1,089,167	2.9%	149	2,183,075	3.1%
Mouthwatering Jewelry Company	79	1,104,468	3.2%	72	1,001,861	2.7%	151	2,106,329	3.0%
Mouthwatering Tripod Corporation	67	952,918	2.8%	85	1,147,944	3.1%	152	2,100,862	3.0%
Matchless Yardstick Inc.	71	944,109	2.8%	74	1,117,357	3.0%	145	2,061,466	2.9%
Vibrant Tripod Corporation	63	903,394	2.6%	83	1,115,134	3.0%	146	2,018,528	2.8%
Inventive Clipboard Corporation	72	1,005,355	2.9%	67	907,911	2.6%	139	1,913,266	2.7%
Persuasive Yardstick Corporation	68	862,022	2.5%	62	936,153	2.5%	130	1,798,175	2.5%
Grand Total	2,406	34,091,092	100.0%	2,582	37,013,436	100.0%	4,988	71,104,528	100.0%

Replicating the Report for Every Product

As long as your pivot table was not built on an OLAP data source, you now have access to one of the most powerful, but least-well-known features in pivot tables. The command is called Show Report Filter Pages, and it will take your pivot table and replicate it for every item in one of the fields in the Report Filter area.

Because you built the report with Product as a filter field, it takes only one line of code to replicate the pivot table for every product.

```
' Replicate the pivot table for each product
PT.ShowPages PageField:="Product"
```

After running this line of code, you will have a new worksheet for every product in the dataset.

From there, you have some simple formatting and calculations. Check the end of the macro for these techniques, which should be second nature by this point in the book.

Listing 13.3 shows the complete macro.

Listing 13.3 The Complete Macro

```
Sub CustomerByProductReport()
    ' Use a Pivot Table to create a report for each product
    ' with customers in rows and years in columns
    Dim WSD As Worksheet
    Dim PTCache As PivotCache
    Dim PT As PivotTable
    Dim PT2 As PivotTable
    Dim WS As Worksheet
    Dim WSF As Worksheet
    Dim PRange As Range
    Dim FinalRow As Long
    Set WSD = Worksheets("PivotTable")

    ' Delete any prior pivot tables
    For Each PT In WSD.PivotTables
        PT.TableRange2.Clear
    Next PT
```

13

```
WSD.Range("J1:Z1").EntireColumn.Clear

' Define input area and set up a Pivot Cache
FinalRow = WSD.Cells(Application.Rows.Count, 1).End(xlUp).Row
FinalCol = WSD.Cells(1, Application.Columns.Count). _
    End(xlToLeft).Column
Set PRange = WSD.Cells(1, 1).Resize(FinalRow, FinalCol)
Set PTCache = ActiveWorkbook.PivotCaches.Add(SourceType:= _
    xlDatabase, SourceData:=PRange.Address)

' Create the Pivot Table from the Pivot Cache
Set PT = PTCache.CreatePivotTable(TableDestination:=WSD. _
    Cells(2, FinalCol + 2), TableName:="PivotTable1")

' Turn off updating while building the table
PT.ManualUpdate = True

' Set up the row fields
PT.AddFields RowFields:="Customer", _
    ColumnFields:=Array("Date", "Data"), _
    PageFields:="Product"

' Set up the data fields - count of orders
With PT.PivotFields("Region")
    .Orientation = xlDataField
    .Function = xlCount
    .Position = 1
    .NumberFormat = "#,##0"
    .Name = "# of Orders "
End With

' Pause here to group daily dates up to years
' Need to draw the pivot table so you can select date heading
PT.ManualUpdate = False
PT.ManualUpdate = True

' Group daily dates up to years
PT.PivotFields("Date").LabelRange.Group , Periods:= _
    Array(False, False, False, False, False, False, True)

' Set up the data fields - Revenue
With PT.PivotFields("Revenue")
    .Orientation = xlDataField
    .Function = xlSum
    .Position = 2
    .NumberFormat = "#,##0"
    .Name = "Revenue "
End With

' Set up the data fields - % of total Revenue
With PT.PivotFields("Revenue")
    .Orientation = xlDataField
    .Function = xlSum
    .Position = 3
    .NumberFormat = "0.0%"
    .Name = "% of Total "
    .Calculation = xlPercentOfColumn
End With
```

```
' Sort the customers so the largest is at the top
PT.PivotFields("Customer").AutoSort Order:=xlDescending, _
    Field:="Revenue "


With PT
    .ShowTableStyleColumnStripes = True
    .ShowTableStyleRowStripes = True
    .TableStyle2 = "PivotStyleMedium10"
    .NullString = "0"
End With

' Calc the pivot table
PT.ManualUpdate = False
PT.ManualUpdate = True

' Replicate the pivot table for each product
PT.ShowPages PageField:="Product"

Ctr = 0
For Each WS In ActiveWorkbook.Worksheets
    If WS.PivotTables.Count > 0 Then
        If WS.Cells(1, 1).Value = "Product" Then
            ' Save some info
            WS.Select
            ThisProduct = Cells(1, 2).Value
            Ctr = Ctr + 1
            If Ctr = 1 Then
                Set WSF = ActiveSheet
            End If
            Set PT2 = WS.PivotTables(1)
            CalcRows = PT2.TableRange1.Rows.Count - 3

            PT2.TableRange2.Copy
            PT2.TableRange2.PasteSpecial xlPasteValues

            Range("A1:C3").ClearContents
            Range("A1:B2").Clear
            Range("A1").Value = "Product report for " & ThisProduct
            Range("A1").Style = "Title"

            ' Fix some headings
            Range("b5:d5").Copy Destination:=Range("H5:J5")
            Range("H4").Value = "Total"
            Range("I4:J4").Clear

            ' Copy the format
            Range("J1").Resize(CalcRows + 5, 1).Copy
            Range("K1").Resize(CalcRows + 5, 1).PasteSpecial xlPasteFormats
            Range("K5").Value = "% Rev Growth"
            Range("K6").Resize(CalcRows, 1).FormulaR1C1 = _
                "=IFERROR(RC6/RC3-1,1)"

            Range("A2:K5").Style = "Heading 4"
            Range("A1").Resize(CalcRows + 2, 11).Columns.AutoFit

        End If
    End If
```

```
Next WS

WSD.Select
PT.TableRange2.Clear
Set PTCache = Nothing

WSF.Select
MsgBox Ctr & " product reports created."

End Sub
```

Filtering a Data Set

There are many ways to filter a pivot table, from the new Excel 2010 slicers, to the Excel 2007 conceptual filters, to simply selecting and clearing items from one of the many field drop-downs.

Manually Filtering Two or More Items in a Pivot Field

When you open a field heading drop-down and select or clear items from the list, you are applying a manual filter.

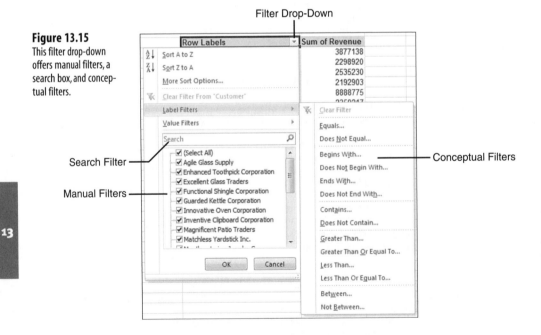

Figure 13.15
This filter drop-down offers manual filters, a search box, and conceptual filters.

For example, you have one client who sells shoes. In the report showing sales of sandals, he wants to see just the stores that are in warm-weather states. The code to hide a particular store is as follows:

```
PT.PivotFields("Store").PivotItems("Minneapolis").Visible = False
```

This process is easy in VBA. After building the table with Product in the page field, loop through to change the Visible property to show only the total of certain products:

```
' Make sure all PivotItems along line are visible
For Each PivItem In _
    PT.PivotFields("Product").PivotItems
    PivItem.Visible = True
Next PivItem

' Now - loop through and keep only certain items visible
For Each PivItem In _
    PT.PivotFields("Product").PivotItems
    Select Case PivItem.Name
        Case "Landscaping/Grounds Care", _
            "Green Plants and Foliage Care"
            PivItem.Visible = True
        Case Else
            PivItem.Visible = False
    End Select
Next PivItem
```

Using the Conceptual Filters

Excel 2007 introduced new conceptual filters for date fields, numeric fields, and text fields. Open the drop-down for any field label in the pivot table. In the drop-down that appears, you can choose Label Filters, Date Filters, or Value Filters. The Date filters offer the ability to filter to a conceptual period such as last month or next year (see Figure 13.16).

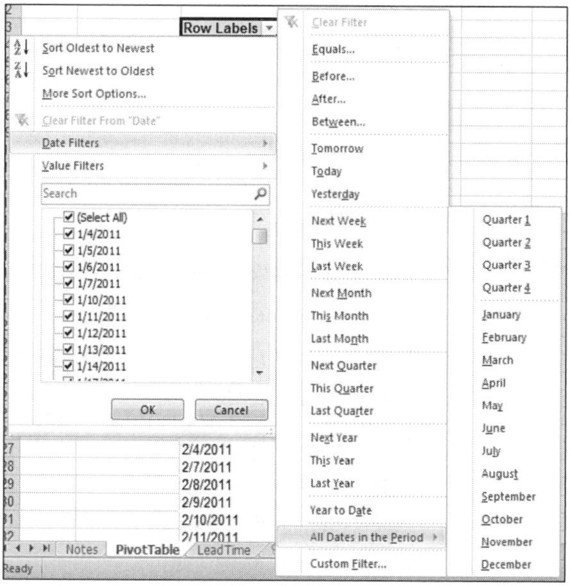

Figure 13.16
These date filters were introduced in Excel 2007.

To apply a label filter in VBA, use the `PivotFilters.Add` method. The following code filters to the customers that start with the letter *E*:

```
PT.PivotFields("Customer").PivotFilters.Add _
    Type:=xlCaptionBeginsWith, Value1:="E"
```

To clear the filter from the Customer field, use the `ClearAllFilters` method:

```
PT.PivotFields("Customer").ClearAllFilters
```

To apply a date filter to the date field to find records from this week, use this code:

```
PT.PivotFields("Date").PivotFilters.Add Type:=xlThisWeek
```

The value filters allow you to filter one field based on the value of another field. For example, to find all the markets where the total revenue is over $100,000, you would use this code:

```
PT.PivotFields("Market").PivotFilters.Add _
    Type:=xlValueIsGreaterThan, _
    DataField:=PT.PivotFields("Sum of Revenue"), _
    Value1:=100000
```

Other value filters might allow you to specify that you want branches where the revenue is between $50,000 and $100,000. In this case, you would specify one limit as `Value1` and the second limit as `Value2`:

```
PT.PivotFields("Market").PivotFilters.Add _
    Type:=xlValueIsBetween, _
    DataField:=PT.PivotFields("Sum of Revenue"), _
    Value1:=50000, Value2:=100000
```

Table 13.5 lists all the possible filter types.

Table 13.5   Filter Types

Filter Type	Description
xlBefore	Filters for all dates before a specified date
xlBeforeOrEqualTo	Filters for all dates on or before a specified date
xlAfter	Filters for all dates after a specified date
xlAfterOrEqualTo	Filters for all dates on or after a specified date
xlAllDatesInPeriodJanuary	Filters for all dates in January
xlAllDatesInPeriodFebruary	Filters for all dates in February
xlAllDatesInPeriodMarch	Filters for all dates in March
xlAllDatesInPeriodApril	Filters for all dates in April
xlAllDatesInPeriodMay	Filters for all dates in May
xlAllDatesInPeriodJune	Filters for all dates in June
xlAllDatesInPeriodJuly	Filters for all dates in July

13

Filter Type	Description
xlAllDatesInPeriodAugust	Filters for all dates in August
xlAllDatesInPeriodSeptember	Filters for all dates in September
xlAllDatesInPeriodOctober	Filters for all dates in October
xlAllDatesInPeriodNovember	Filters for all dates in November
xlAllDatesInPeriodDecember	Filters for all dates in December
xlAllDatesInPeriodQuarter1	Filters for all dates in Quarter 1
xlAllDatesInPeriodQuarter2	Filters for all dates in Quarter 2
xlAllDatesInPeriodQuarter3	Filters for all dates in Quarter 3
xlAllDatesInPeriodQuarter4	Filters for all dates in Quarter 4
xlBottomCount	Filters for the specified number of values from the bottom of a list
xlBottomPercent	Filters for the specified percentage of values from the bottom of a list
xlBottomSum	Sums the values from the bottom of the list
xlCaptionBeginsWith	Filters for all captions beginning with the specified string
xlCaptionContains	Filters for all captions that contain the specified string
xlCaptionDoesNotBeginWith	Filters for all captions that do not begin with the specified string
xlCaptionDoesNotContain	Filters for all captions that do not contain the specified string
xlCaptionDoesNotEndWith	Filters for all captions that do not end with the specified string
xlCaptionDoesNotEqual	Filters for all captions that do not match the specified string
xlCaptionEndsWith	Filters for all captions that end with the specified string
xlCaptionEquals	Filters for all captions that match the specified string
xlCaptionIsBetween	Filters for all captions that are between a specified range of values
xlCaptionIsGreaterThan	Filters for all captions that are greater than the specified value
xlCaptionIsGreaterThanOrEqualTo	Filters for all captions that are greater than or match the specified value
xlCaptionIsLessThan	Filters for all captions that are less than the specified value
xlCaptionIsLessThanOrEqualTo	Filters for all captions that are less than or match the specified value
xlCaptionIsNotBetween	Filters for all captions that are not between a specified range of values
xlDateBetween	Filters for all dates that are between a specified range of dates
xlDateLastMonth	Filters for all dates that apply to the previous month
xlDateLastQuarter	Filters for all dates that apply to the previous quarter
xlDateLastWeek	Filters for all dates that apply to the previous week
xlDateLastYear	Filters for all dates that apply to the previous year

13

Table 13.5 (continued)

Filter Type	Description
xlDateNextMonth	Filters for all dates that apply to the next month
xlDateNextQuarter	Filters for all dates that apply to the next quarter
xlDateNextWeek	Filters for all dates that apply to the next week
xlDateNextYear	Filters for all dates that apply to the next year
xlDateThisMonth	Filters for all dates that apply to the current month
xlDateThisQuarter	Filters for all dates that apply to the current quarter
xlDateThisWeek	Filters for all dates that apply to the current week
xlDateThisYear	Filters for all dates that apply to the current year
xlDateToday	Filters for all dates that apply to the current date
xlDateTomorrow	Filters for all dates that apply to the next day
xlDateYesterday	Filters for all dates that apply to the previous day
xlNotSpecificDate	Filters for all dates that do not match a specified date
xlSpecificDate	Filters for all dates that match a specified date
xlTopCount	Filters for the specified number of values from the top of a list
xlTopPercent	Filters for the specified percentage of values from a list
xlTopSum	Sums the values from the top of the list
xlValueDoesNotEqual	Filters for all values that do not match the specified value
xlValueEquals	Filters for all values that match the specified value
xlValueIsBetween	Filters for all values that are between a specified range of values
xlValueIsGreaterThan	Filters for all values that are greater than the specified value
xlValueIsGreaterThanOrEqualTo	Filters for all values that are greater than or match the specified value
xlValueIsLessThan	Filters for all values that are less than the specified value
xlValueIsLessThanOrEqualTo	Filters for all values that are less than or match the specified value
xlValueIsNotBetween	Filters for all values that are not between a specified range of values
xlYearToDate	Filters for all values that are within 1 year of a specified date

Using the Search Filter

Excel 2010 added a Search box to the filter drop-down. While this is a slick feature in the Excel interface, there is no equivalent magic in VBA. Whereas the drop-down offers the Select All Search Results check box, the equivalent VBA just lists all the items that match the selection.

There is nothing new in Excel 2010 VBA to emulate the search box. To achieve the same results in VBA, use the xlCaptionContains filter described in the previous style.

CASE STUDY: FILTERING TO TOP FIVE OR TOP 10 USING A FILTER

If you are designing an executive dashboard utility, you might want to spotlight the top five customers. As with the AutoSort option, you could be a pivot table pro and never have stumbled across the Top 10 AutoShow feature in Excel. This setting lets you select either the top or the bottom *n* records based on any Data field in the report.

The code to use AutoShow in VBA uses the .AutoShow method:

```
' Show only the top 5 Customers
PT.PivotFields("Customer").AutoShow Top:=xlAutomatic, Range:=xlTop, _
    Count:=5, Field:= "Sum of Revenue"
```

When you create a report using the .AutoShow method, it is often helpful to copy the data and then go back to the original pivot report to get the totals for all markets. In the code, this is achieved by removing the Customer field from the pivot table and copying the grand total to the report. The code produces the report shown in Figure 13.17.

Figure 13.17

The Top 5 Customers report contains two pivot tables.

	A	B	C	D	E	F	G
1	Top 5 Customers						
2							
3	Customer	A292	B722	C409	D625	E438	Grand Total
4	Guarded Kettle Corporation	1,450,110	1,404,742	1,889,149	1,842,751	2,302,023	8,888,775
5	Unique Marble Company	1,600,347	1,581,665	1,765,305	1,707,140	2,179,242	8,833,699
6	Persuasive Kettle Inc.	1,565,368	1,385,296	1,443,434	1,584,759	2,030,578	8,009,435
7	Safe Saddle Corporation	646,559	857,573	730,463	1,038,371	1,053,369	4,326,335
8	Tremendous Bobsled Corporation	560,759	711,826	877,247	802,303	1,095,329	4,047,464
9	Top 5 Total	5,823,143	5,941,102	6,705,598	6,975,324	8,660,541	34,105,708
10							
11	Total Company		12,337,778	12,683,061	14,101,763	14,569,960	17,411,966	71,104,528

```
Sub Top5Customers()
    ' Listing 13.4
    ' Produce a report of the top 5 customers
    Dim WSD As Worksheet
    Dim WSR As Worksheet
    Dim WBN As Workbook
    Dim PTCache As PivotCache
    Dim PT As PivotTable
    Dim PRange As Range
    Dim FinalRow As Long
    Set WSD = Worksheets("PivotTable")

    ' Delete any prior pivot tables
    For Each PT In WSD.PivotTables
        PT.TableRange2.Clear
    Next PT
    WSD.Range("J1:Z1").EntireColumn.Clear

    ' Define input area and set up a Pivot Cache
    FinalRow = WSD.Cells(Application.Rows.Count, 1).End(xlUp).Row
```

13

```
FinalCol = WSD.Cells(1, Application.Columns.Count). _
    End(xlToLeft).Column
Set PRange = WSD.Cells(1, 1).Resize(FinalRow, FinalCol)
Set PTCache = ActiveWorkbook.PivotCaches.Add(SourceType:= _
    xlDatabase, SourceData:=PRange.Address)

' Create the Pivot Table from the Pivot Cache
Set PT = PTCache.CreatePivotTable(TableDestination:=WSD. _
    Cells(2, FinalCol + 2), TableName:="PivotTable1")

' Turn off updating while building the table
PT.ManualUpdate = True

' Set up the row fields
PT.AddFields RowFields:="Customer", ColumnFields:="Product"

' Set up the data fields
With PT.PivotFields("Revenue")
    .Orientation = xlDataField
    .Function = xlSum
    .Position = 1
    .NumberFormat = "#,##0"
    .Name = "Total Revenue"
End With

' Ensure that we get zeros instead of blanks in the data area
PT.NullString = "0"

' Sort customers descending by sum of revenue
PT.PivotFields("Customer").AutoSort Order:=xlDescending, _
    Field:="Total Revenue"

' Show only the top 5 customers
PT.PivotFields("Customer").AutoShow Type:=xlAutomatic, Range:=xlTop, _
    Count:=5, Field:="Total Revenue"

' Calc the pivot table to allow the date label to be drawn
PT.ManualUpdate = False
PT.ManualUpdate = True

' Create a new blank workbook with one worksheet
Set WBN = Workbooks.Add(xlWBATWorksheet)
Set WSR = WBN.Worksheets(1)
WSR.Name = "Report"
' Set up ritle for report
With WSR.[A1]
    .Value = "Top 5 Customers"
    .Font.Size = 14
End With

' Copy the pivot table data to row 3 of the report sheet
' Use offset to eliminate the title row of the pivot table
```

```
PT.TableRange2.Offset(1, 0).Copy
WSR.[A3].PasteSpecial Paste:=xlPasteValuesAndNumberFormats
LastRow = WSR.Cells(Rows.Count, 1).End(xlUp).Row
WSR.Cells(LastRow, 1).Value = "Top 5 Total"

' Go back to the pivot table to get totals without the AutoShow
PT.PivotFields("Customer").Orientation = xlHidden
PT.ManualUpdate = False
PT.ManualUpdate = True
PT.TableRange2.Offset(2, 0).Copy
WSR.Cells(LastRow + 2, 1).PasteSpecial Paste:= _
    xlPasteValuesAndNumberFormats
WSR.Cells(LastRow + 2, 1).Value = "Total Company"

' Clear the pivot table
PT.TableRange2.Clear
Set PTCache = Nothing

' Do some basic formatting

' Autofit columns, bold the headings, right-align
WSR.Range(WSR.Range("A3"), WSR.Cells(LastRow + 2, 6)).Columns.AutoFit
Range("A3").EntireRow.Font.Bold = True
Range("A3").EntireRow.HorizontalAlignment = xlRight
Range("A3").HorizontalAlignment = xlLeft

Range("A2").Select
MsgBox "CEO Report has been Created"
End Sub
```

The Top 5 Customers report actually contains two snapshots of a pivot table. After using the AutoShow feature to grab the top five markets with their totals, the macro went back to the pivot table, removed the AutoShow option, and grabbed the total of all customers to produce the Total Company row.

Setting Up Slicers to Filter a Pivot Table

Excel 2010 introduced the concept of slicers to filter a pivot table. A *slicer* is a visual filter. Slicers can be resized and repositioned. You can control the color of the slicer and control the number of columns in a slicer. You can also select or unselect items from a slicer using VBA.

Figure 13.18 shows a pivot table with five slicers. The Date slicer has been modified to have three.

13

Figure 13.18
Slicers provide a visual filter of several fields.

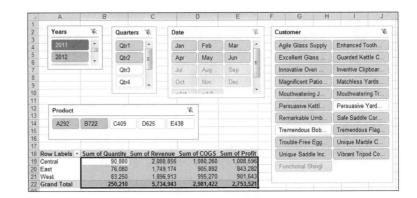

A slicer consists of a slicer cache and a slicer. To define a slicer cache, you need to specify a pivot table as the source and a field name as the SourceField. The slicer cache is defined at the workbook level. This would allow you to have the slicer on a different worksheet than the actual pivot table:

```
Dim SCP as SlicerCache
Dim SCR as SlicerCache
Set SCP = ActiveWorkbook.SlicerCaches.Add(Source:=PT, SourceField:="Product")
Set SCR = ActiveWorkbook.SlicerCaches.Add(Source:=PT, SourceField:="Region")
```

After you have defined the slicer cache, you can add the slicer. The slicer is defined as an object of the slicer cache. Specify a worksheet as the destination. The name argument controls the internal name for the slicer. The Caption argument is the heading that will be visible in the slicer. This might be useful if you would like to show the name Region, but the IT department defined the field as IDKRegn. Specify the size of the slicer using height and width in points. Specify the location using top and left in point.

In the followimg code, the values for top, left, height, and width are assigned to be equal to the location or size of certain cell ranges:

```
Dim SLP as Slicer
Set SLP = SCP.Slicers.Add(SlicerDestination:=WSD, Name:="Product", _
    Caption:="Product", _
    Top:=WSD.Range("A12").Top, _
    Left:=WSD.Range("A12").Left + 10, _
    Width:=WSR.Range("A12:C12").Width, _
    Height:=WSD.Range("A12:A16").Height)
```

All slicers start out as one column. You can change the style and number of columns with this code:

```
' Format the color and number of columns
With SLS
    .Style = "SlicerStyleLight6"
    .NumberOfColumns = 5
End With
```

13

I find that when I create slicers in the Excel interface, I spend many mouse clicks making adjustments to the slicers. After adding two or three slicers, they are arranged in an overlapping tile arrangement. I always tweak the location, size, number of columns, and so on. In my seminars, I always brag that I can create a complex pivot table in six mouse clicks. Slicers are admittedly powerful but seem to take 20 mouse clicks before they look right. Having a macro make all of these adjustments at once is a time-saver.

Once the slicer is defined, you can actually use VBA to choose which items are activated in the slicer. It seems counter-intuitive, but to choose items in the slicer, you have to change the `SlicerItem`, which is a member of the `SlicerCache`, not a member of the `Slicer`:

```
With SCP
     .SlicerItems("A292").Selected = True
     .SlicerItems("B722").Selected = True
     .SlicerItems("C409").Selected = False
     .SlicerItems("D625").Selected = False
     .SlicerItems("E438").Selected = False
End With
```

You might need to deal with slicers that already exist. If a slicer is created for the product field, the name of the `SlicerCache` will be `"Slicer_Product"`. The following code will format existing slicers:

```
Sub MoveAndFormatSlicer()
     Dim SCP As SlicerCache
     Dim SLP as Slicer
     Dim WSD As Worksheet
     Set WSD = ActiveSheet
     Set SCP = ActiveWorkbook.SlicerCaches("Slicer_Product")
     Set SLS = SCS.Slicers("Product")
     With SLS
          .Style = "SlicerStyleLight6"
          .NumberOfColumns = 5
          .Top = WSD.Range("A1").Top + 5
          .Left = WSD.Range("A1").Left + 5
          .Width = WSD.Range("A1:B14").Width - 60
          .Height = WSD.Range("A1:B14").Height
     End With
End Sub
```

Filtering an OLAP Pivot Table Using Named Sets

Ready for some good news, bad news, and sneaky news?

Good News: Named Sets

Microsoft added an amazing feature to Excel 2010 pivot tables called named sets. This feature allows you to create filters that were never possible before. For example, in Figure 13.19, the pivot table shows Actuals and Budget for FY2009 and FY2010. It would have been impossible to show an asymmetric report with only FY2009 Actuals and FY 2010 Budget: when you turned off Budget for 2009, it would have been turned off for all years. Named sets allow you to overcome this.

13

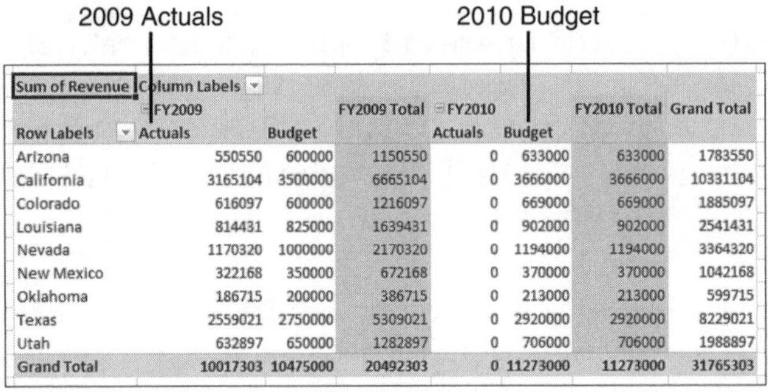

Sum of Revenue	Column Labels						
	FY2009		FY2009 Total	FY2010		FY2010 Total	Grand Total
Row Labels	Actuals	Budget		Actuals	Budget		
Arizona	550550	600000	1150550	0	633000	633000	1783550
California	3165104	3500000	6665104	0	3666000	3666000	10331104
Colorado	616097	600000	1216097	0	669000	669000	1885097
Louisiana	814431	825000	1639431	0	902000	902000	2541431
Nevada	1170320	1000000	2170320	0	1194000	1194000	3364320
New Mexico	322168	350000	672168	0	370000	370000	1042168
Oklahoma	186715	200000	386715	0	213000	213000	599715
Texas	2559021	2750000	5309021	0	2920000	2920000	8229021
Utah	632897	650000	1282897	0	706000	706000	1988897
Grand Total	10017303	10475000	20492303	0	11273000	11273000	31765303

Figure 13.19
You want to show 2009 Actuals and 2010 Budget.

Bad News Named Sets Limitations

Named sets only work for data coming from OLAP pivot tables. If you are dealing with pivot tables based on regular Excel data, you will have to wait until a future release of Excel to tap into the power of named sets.

Sneaky News: Workaround

A pivot table produced using the PowerPivot add-in is actually an OLAP pivot table. To create the pivot table shown in Figure 13.19, I copied the Excel data, pasted as a new table in the PowerPivot add-in, and then returned to Excel to create the pivot table.

> **NOTE**
> PowerPivot is a free add-in for Excel 2010 brought to you by the SQL Server Analysis Services team at Microsoft. Because you cannot control PowerPivot from VBA, it is not covered in this book. However, it is a great add-in. You can use PowerPivot to mash up datasets from multimillion row datasets. You can use PowerPivot to define calculations not possible in regular Excel pivot tables. I have written an entire book about PowerPivot: *PowerPivot for the Excel Data Analyst*.

13

This is a minor use for a powerful tool. The PowerPivot add-in is designed to mash-up multimillion row recordsets from various sources. To take a single flat table and paste it into the powerful tool is admittedly underutilizing the tool. However, it is one great way to get an unbalanced pivot table report.

Using a Named Set for Asymmetric Pivot Table

A common request is to show an asymmetric selection from two column fields. In Figure 13.19, you would like to show 2009 year's actual and 2010 budget.

To define a named set, you will have to build a formula that uses the MDX language. MDX stands for Multidimensional Expressions Language. There are many MDX tutorials on the Internet. Luckily, you can turn on the macro recorder while you define a named set using the Excel 2010 interface and have the macro recorder write the MDX formula for you.

When you are defining a named set, you will define both a `CalculatedMember` and then add a `CubeField` set. These declarations at the top of the macro will initialize two calculated members:

```
Dim CM1 As CalculatedMember
```

The MDX formula is the key to the named set. In this code, the formula contains 2009 Actuals and 2010 Budget. The formula starts and ends with curly braces indicating that the formula contains an array of values. Each line of code is adding another column to the array:

```
' Set up a formula to get FY2009 actuals and FY2010 Budget
FText = "{([Financials].[Year].&[FY2009],[Financials].[Measure].&[Actuals]),"
FText = FText & _
    "([Financials].[Year].&[FY2010],[Financials].[Measure].&[Budget])}"
```

After you have defined the formula, use the following code to add the calculated member to the dataset:

```
' Define a Calculated Member to replace Year & Measure
Set CM1 = ActiveWorkbook.Connections("PowerPivot Data"). _
    OLEDBConnection.CalculatedMembers.Add( _
    Name:="[ActVBud]", _
    Formula:=FText, _
    Type:=xlCalculatedSet, _
    Dynamic:=False, _
    HierarchizeDistinct:=False)
CM1.FlattenHierarchies = False
PT.CubeFields.AddSet Name:="[ActVBud]", Caption:="ActVBud"
```

This code will add a new folder to the pivot table field list called Sets. In that folder, an item called ActVBud will be available as field, just like the field called Year or Measure. In your code, you will want to replace the Year and Measure field in the pivot table with the ActVBud field:

```
' Remove the Measure and Year fields, replace it with the Set
PT.CubeFields("[Financials].[Measure]").Orientation = xlHidden
PT.CubeFields("[Financials].[Year]").Orientation = xlHidden
PT.CubeFields("[ActVBud]").Orientation = xlColumnField
```

Figure 13.20 shows the asymmetric report.

13

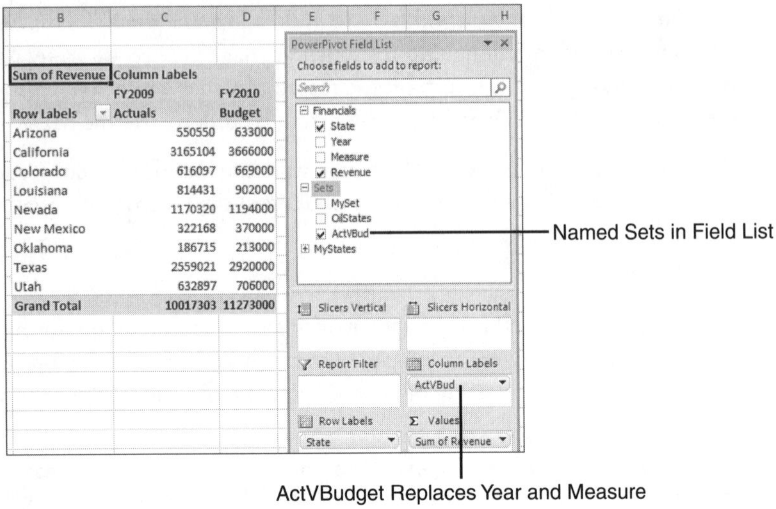

Figure 13.20
Named sets enable asym-
metric reporting.

Named Sets in Field List

ActVBudget Replaces Year and Measure

Using Other Pivot Table Features

This section covers a few additional features in pivot tables that you might need to code
with VBA.

Calculated Data Fields

Pivot tables offer two types of formulas. The most useful type defines a formula for a calculated field. This adds a new field to the pivot table. Calculations for calculated fields are
always done at the summary level. If you define a calculated field for average price as revenue divided by units sold, Excel first adds the total revenue and total quantity, and then
it does the division of these totals to get the result. In many cases, this is exactly what you
need. If your calculation does not follow the associative law of mathematics, it might not
work as you expect.

To set up a Calculated field, use the Add method with the CalculatedFields object. You
have to specify a field name and a formula.

> **NOTE**
> Note that if you create a field called Profit Percent, the default pivot table produces a field called Sum
> of Profit Percent. This title is misleading and downright silly. The solution is to use the Name property
> when defining the Data field to replace Sum of Profit Percent with something such as GP Pct. Keep in
> mind that this name must differ from the name for the Calculated field.

```
' Define Calculated Fields
    PT.CalculatedFields.Add Name:="ProfitPercent", Formula:="=Profit/Revenue"
    With PT.PivotFields("ProfitPercent")
        .Orientation = xlDataField
        .Function = xlSum
```

```
                .Position = 3
                .NumberFormat = "#0.0%"
                .Name = "GP Pct"
         End With
```

Calculated Items

Suppose you have a Measure field with two items, Budget and Actual. You would like to add a new position to calculate Variance as Actual-Budget. You can do this with a calculated item by using this code:

```
' Define calculated item along the product dimension
PT.PivotFields("Measure").CalculatedItems _
    .Add "Variance", "='Actual'-'Budget'"
```

Using `ShowDetail` to Filter a Recordset

When you take any pivot table in the Excel user interface and then double-click any number in the table, Excel will insert a new sheet in the workbook and copies all the source records that represent that number. In the Excel user interface, this is a great way to perform a drill-down query into a dataset.

The equivalent VBA property is `ShowDetail`. By setting this property to `True` for any cell in the pivot table, you generate a new worksheet with all the records that make up that cell:

```
PT.TableRange2.Offset(2, 1).Resize(1, 1).ShowDetail = True
```

Changing the Layout from the Design Tab

The Layout group of the Design tab contains four drop-downs that control the following:

- Location of subtotals (top or bottom)
- Presence of grand totals
- Report layout including if outer row labels are repeated
- Presence of blank rows

Subtotals can appear either at the top or at the bottom of a group of pivot items. The `SubtotalLocation` property applies to the entire pivot table; valid values are `xlAtBottom` or `xlAtTop`:

```
PT.SubtotalLocation:=xlAtTop
```

Grand totals can be turned on or off for rows or columns. Because these two settings can be confusing, remember that at the bottom of a report, there is a total line that most people would call the Grand Total Row. To turn off that row, you have to use the following:

```
PT.ColumnGrand = False
```

13

You need to turn off the `ColumnGrand` when you want to suppress the total row because Microsoft calls that row the "grand total for columns." Get it? In other words, they are saying that the row at the bottom contains the total of the columns above it. I finally started doing better when I would decide which one to turn off, and then turn off the opposite one.

To suppress what you would call the Grand Total Column along the right side of the report, you have to suppress what Microsoft calls the Total for Rows with the following code:

```
PT.RowGrand = False
```

Settings for the Report Layout

There are three settings for the report layout.

- **Tabular layout**—Similar to the default layout in Excel 2003
- **Outline layout**—Optionally available in Excel 2003
- **Compact layout**—Introduced in Excel 2007

When you create a pivot table in the Excel interface, you will get compact layout. When you build a pivot table in VBA, you will get the tabular layout. You can change to one of the other layouts with one of these lines:

```
PT.RowAxisLayout xlTabularRow
PT.RowAxisLayout xlOutlineRow
PT.RowAxisLayout = xlCompactRow
```

Starting in Excel 2007, you can add a blank line to the layout after each group of pivot items. Although the Design tab offers a single setting to affect the entire pivot table, the setting is actually applied to each individual pivot field individually. The macro recorder responds by recording a dozen lines of code for a pivot table with 12 fields. You can intelligently add a single line of code for the outer Row fields:

```
PT.PivotFields("Region").LayoutBlankLine = True
```

Suppressing Subtotals for Multiple Row Fields

As soon as you have more than one row field, Excel automatically adds subtotals for all but the innermost row field. That extra row field can get in the way if you plan on reusing the results of the pivot table as a new dataset for some other purpose. Although accomplishing this task manually can be relatively simple, the VBA code to suppress subtotals is surprisingly complex.

Most people do not realize that it is possible to show multiple types of subtotals. For example, you can choose to show Total, Average, Min, and Max in the same pivot table.

To suppress subtotals for a field, you must set the `Subtotals` property equal to an array of 12 `False` values. The first `False` turns off automatic subtotals, the second `False` turns off the `Sum` subtotal, the third `False` turns off the `Count` subtotal, and so on. This line of code suppresses the `Region` subtotal:

```
PT.PivotFields("Region").Subtotals = Array(False, False, False, False, _
    False, False, False, False, False, False, False, False)
```

A different technique is to turn on the first subtotal. This method automatically turns off the other 11 subtotals. You can then turn off the first subtotal to make sure that all subtotals are suppressed:

```
PT.PivotFields("Region").Subtotals(1) = True
PT.PivotFields("Region").Subtotals(1) = False
```

CASE STUDY: APPLYING A DATA VISUALIZATION

Beginning with Excel 2007, fantastic data visualizations such as icon sets, color gradients, and in-cell data bars are offered. When you apply visualization to a pivot table, you should exclude the total rows from the visualization.

If you have 20 customers that average $3,000,000 in revenue each, the total for the 20 customers is $60 million. If you include the total in the data visualization, the total gets the largest bar, and all the customer records have tiny bars.

In the Excel user interface, you always want to use the Add Rule or Edit Rule choice to select the option All Cells Showing "Sum of Revenue" for "Customer."

The code to add a data bar to the Revenue field is as follows:

```
' Apply a Databar
PT.TableRange2.Cells(3, 2).Select
Selection.FormatConditions.AddDatabar
Selection.FormatConditions(1).ShowValue = True
Selection.FormatConditions(1).SetFirstPriority
With Selection.FormatConditions(1)
    .MinPoint.Modify newtype:=xlConditionValueLowestValue
    .MaxPoint.Modify newtype:=xlConditionValueHighestValue
End With
With Selection.FormatConditions(1).BarColor
    .ThemeColor = xlThemeColorAccent3
    .TintAndShade = -0.5
End With
Selection.FormatConditions(1).ScopeType = xlFieldsScope
```

13

Next Steps

If you cannot already tell, pivot tables are my favorite feature in Excel. They are incredibly powerful and flexible. Combined with VBA, they provide an excellent calculation engine and power many of the reports I build for clients. In Chapter 14, "Excel Power," you learn multiple techniques for handling various tasks in VBA.

Excel Power

A major secret of successful programmers is to never waste time writing the same code twice. They all have little bits—or even big bits—of code that are used over and over again. Another big secret is to never take 8 hours doing something that can be done in 10 minutes—which is what this book is about!

This chapter contains programs donated by several Excel power programmers. These are programs they have found useful, and they hope these will help you too. Not only can they save you time, but they may also teach you new ways of solving common problems.

Different programmers have different programming styles, and we did not rewrite the submissions. As you review the lines of code, you will notice different ways of doing the same task such as referring to ranges.

14

IN THIS CHAPTER

File Operations..............................329

Combining and Separating Workbooks.......333

Working with Cell Comments....................337

Utilities to Wow Your Clients.....................342

Techniques for VBA Pros............................349

Cool Applications.....................................362

File Operations

The following utilities deal with handling files in folders. Being able to loop through a list of files in a folder is a useful task.

List Files in a Directory

Submitted by Nathan P. Oliver of Minneapolis, Minnesota. Nathan is a financial consultant and application developer.

This program returns the filename, size, and date modified of all specified file types in the selected directory and its subfolders.

```
Sub ExcelFileSearch()
Dim srchExt As Variant, srchDir As Vari-
ant, i As
Long, j As Long
Dim strName As String, varArr(1 To
1048576, 1 To
3) As Variant
```

```
Dim strFileFullName As String
Dim ws As Worksheet
Dim fso As Object

Let srchExt = Application.InputBox("Please Enter File Extension", "Info Re-
quest")
If srchExt = False And Not TypeName(srchExt) = "String" Then
    Exit Sub
End If

Let srchDir = BrowseForFolderShell
If srchDir = False And Not TypeName(srchDir) = "String" Then
    Exit Sub
End If

Application.ScreenUpdating = False

Set ws = ThisWorkbook.Worksheets.Add(Sheets(1))
On Error Resume Next
Application.DisplayAlerts = False
ThisWorkbook.Worksheets("FileSearch Results").Delete
Application.DisplayAlerts = True
On Error GoTo 0
ws.Name = "FileSearch Results"

Let strName = Dir$(srchDir & "\*" & srchExt)
Do While strName <> vbNullString
    Let i = i + 1
    Let strFileFullName = srchDir & strName
    Let varArr(i, 1) = strFileFullName
    Let varArr(i, 2) = FileLen(strFileFullName) \ 1024
    Let varArr(i, 3) = FileDateTime(strFileFullName)
    Let strName = Dir$()
Loop

Set fso = CreateObject("Scripting.FileSystemObject")
Call recurseSubFolders(fso.GetFolder(srchDir), varArr(), i, CStr(srchExt))
Set fso = Nothing

ThisWorkbook.Windows(1).DisplayHeadings = False
With ws
    If i > 0 Then
        .Range("A2").Resize(i, UBound(varArr, 2)).Value = varArr
        For j = 1 To i
            .Hyperlinks.Add anchor:=.Cells(j + 1, 1), Address:=varArr(j, 1)
        Next
    End If
    .Range(.Cells(1, 4), .Cells(1, .Columns.Count)).EntireColumn.Hidden = True
    .Range(.Cells(.Rows.Count, 1).End(xlUp)(2), _
        .Cells(.Rows.Count, 1)).EntireRow.Hidden = True
    With .Range("A1:C1")
        .Value = Array("Full Name", "Kilobytes", "Last Modified")
        .Font.Underline = xlUnderlineStyleSingle
        .EntireColumn.AutoFit
        .HorizontalAlignment = xlCenter
    End With
End With
Application.ScreenUpdating = True
```

```
End Sub

Private Sub recurseSubFolders(ByRef Folder As Object, _
    ByRef varArr() As Variant, _
    ByRef i As Long, _
    ByRef srchExt As String)
Dim SubFolder As Object
Dim strName As String, strFileFullName As String
For Each SubFolder In Folder.SubFolders
    Let strName = Dir$(SubFolder.Path & "\*" & srchExt)
    Do While strName <> vbNullString
        Let i = i + 1
        Let strFileFullName = SubFolder.Path & "\" & strName
        Let varArr(i, 1) = strFileFullName
        Let varArr(i, 2) = FileLen(strFileFullName) \ 1024
        Let varArr(i, 3) = FileDateTime(strFileFullName)
        Let strName = Dir$()
    Loop
    If i > 1048576 Then Exit Sub
    Call recurseSubFolders(SubFolder, varArr(), i, srchExt)
Next
End Sub

Private Function BrowseForFolderShell() As Variant
Dim objShell As Object, objFolder As Object
Set objShell = CreateObject("Shell.Application")
Set objFolder = objShell.BrowseForFolder(0, "Please select a folder", 0,
"C:\")
If Not objFolder Is Nothing Then
    On Error Resume Next
    If IsError(objFolder.Items.Item.Path) Then
        BrowseForFolderShell = CStr(objFolder)
    Else
        On Error GoTo 0
        If Len(objFolder.Items.Item.Path) > 3 Then
            BrowseForFolderShell = objFolder.Items.Item.Path & _
            Application.PathSeparator
        Else
            BrowseForFolderShell = objFolder.Items.Item.Path
        End If
    End If
Else
    BrowseForFolderShell = False
End If
Set objFolder = Nothing: Set objShell = Nothing
End Function
```

Import CSV

Submitted by Masaru Kaji of Kobe-City, Japan. Masaru provides Excel consultation through Colo's Excel Junk Room (www.puremis.net/excel).

If you find yourself importing a lot of comma-separated variable (CSV) files and then having to go back and delete them, this program is for you. It quickly opens a CSV in Excel and permanently deletes the original file:

```
Option Base 1
```

```
Sub OpenLargeCSVFast()
    Dim buf(1 To 16384) As Variant
    Dim i As Long
    'Change the file location and name here
    Const strFilePath As String = "C:\temp\Test.CSV"

    Dim strRenamedPath As String
    strRenamedPath = Split(strFilePath, ".")(0) & "txt"

    With Application
        .ScreenUpdating = False
        .DisplayAlerts = False
    End With
    'Setting an array for FieldInfo to open CSV
    For i = 1 To 16384
        buf(i) = Array(i, 2)
    Next
    Name strFilePath As strRenamedPath
    Workbooks.OpenText Filename:=strRenamedPath, DataType:=xlDelimited, _
                    Comma:=True, FieldInfo:=buf
    Erase buf
    ActiveSheet.UsedRange.Copy ThisWorkbook.Sheets(1).Range("A1")
    ActiveWorkbook.Close False
    Kill strRenamedPath
    With Application
        .ScreenUpdating = True
        .DisplayAlerts = True
    End With
End Sub
```

Read Entire TXT to Memory and Parse

Submitted by Suat Mehmet Ozgur of Istanbul, Turkey. Suat develops applications in Excel, Access, and Visual Basic.

This sample takes a different approach to reading a text file. Instead of reading one record at a time, the macro loads the entire text file into memory in a single string variable. The macro then parses the string into individual records. The advantage of this method is that you access the file on disk only one time. All subsequent processing occurs in memory and is very fast:

```
Sub ReadTxtLines()
'No need to install Scripting Runtime library since we used late binding
Dim sht As Worksheet
Dim fso As Object
Dim fil As Object
Dim txt As Object
Dim strtxt As String
Dim tmpLoc As Long

    'Working on active sheet
    Set sht = ActiveSheet
    'Clear data in the sheet
    sht.UsedRange.ClearContents
```

```
            'File system object that we need to manage files
            Set fso = CreateObject("Scripting.FileSystemObject")

            'File that we like to open and read
            Set fil = fso.GetFile("c:\test.txt")

            'Opening file as a TextStream
            Set txt = fil.OpenAsTextStream(1)

            'Reading file include into a string variable at once
            strtxt = txt.ReadAll

            'Close textstream and free the file. We don't need it anymore.
            txt.Close

            'Find the first placement of new line char
            tmpLoc = InStr(1, strtxt, vbCrLf)

            'Loop until no more new line
            Do Until tmpLoc = 0
                'Use A column and next empty cell to write the text file line
                sht.Cells(sht.Rows.Count, 1).End(xlUp).Offset(1).Value = _
                    Left(strtxt, tmpLoc - 1)

                'Remove the parsed line from the variable that we stored file include
                strtxt = Right(strtxt, Len(strtxt) - tmpLoc - 1)

                'Find the next placement of new line char
                tmpLoc = InStr(1, strtxt, vbCrLf)
            Loop

            'Last line that has data but no new line char
            sht.Cells(sht.Rows.Count, 1).End(xlUp).Offset(1).Value = strtxt

            'It will be already released by the ending of this procedure but
            ' as a good habit, set the object as nothing.
            Set fso = Nothing
        End Sub
```

Combining and Separating Workbooks

The next four utilities demonstrate how to combine worksheets into single workbooks or separate a single workbook into individual worksheets or Word documents.

Separate Worksheets into Workbooks

Submitted by Tommy Miles of Houston, Texas.

This sample goes through the active workbook and saves each sheet as its own workbook in the same path as the original workbook. It names the new workbooks based on the sheet name, and it will overwrite files without prompting. You will also notice that you need to choose whether you save the file as XLSM (macro-enabled) or XLSX (macros will be stripped). In the following code, both lines are included—xlsm and xlsx—but the xlsx lines are commented out, making them inactive:

14

```
Sub SplitWorkbook()

Dim ws As Worksheet
Dim DisplayStatusBar As Boolean

DisplayStatusBar = Application.DisplayStatusBar
Application.DisplayStatusBar = True
Application.ScreenUpdating = False
Application.DisplayAlerts = False

For Each ws In ThisWorkbook.Sheets
    Dim NewFileName As String
    Application.StatusBar = ThisWorkbook.Sheets.Count & " Remaining Sheets"
    If ThisWorkbook.Sheets.Count <> 1 Then
        NewFileName = ThisWorkbook.Path & "\" & ws.Name & ".xlsm" 'Macro _
            -Enabled
'        NewFileName = ThisWorkbook.Path & "\" & ws.Name & ".xlsx" _
            'Not Macro-Enabled
        ws.Copy
        ActiveWorkbook.Sheets(1).Name = "Sheet1"
        ActiveWorkbook.SaveAs Filename:=NewFileName, _
            FileFormat:=xlOpenXMLWorkbookMacroEnabled
'        ActiveWorkbook.SaveAs Filename:=NewFileName, _
            FileFormat:=xlOpenXMLWorkbook
        ActiveWorkbook.Close SaveChanges:=False
    Else
        NewFileName = ThisWorkbook.Path & "\" & ws.Name & ".xlsm"
'        NewFileName = ThisWorkbook.Path & "\" & ws.Name & ".xlsx"
        ws.Name = "Sheet1"
    End If
Next

Application.DisplayAlerts = True
Application.StatusBar = False
Application.DisplayStatusBar = DisplayStatusBar
Application.ScreenUpdating = True
End Sub
```

Combine Workbooks

Submitted by Tommy Miles.

This sample goes through all the Excel files in a specified directory and combines them into a single workbook. It renames the sheets based on the name of the original workbook:

```
Sub CombineWorkbooks()
    Dim CurFile As String, DirLoc As String
    Dim DestWB As Workbook
    Dim ws As Object 'allows for different sheet types

    DirLoc = ThisWorkbook.Path & "\tst\" 'location of files
    CurFile = Dir(DirLoc & "*.xls*")

    Application.ScreenUpdating = False
    Application.EnableEvents = False

    Set DestWB = Workbooks.Add(xlWorksheet)
```

```
        Do While CurFile <> vbNullString
            Dim OrigWB As Workbook
            Set OrigWB = Workbooks.Open(Filename:=DirLoc & CurFile,
    ReadOnly:=True)

            ' Limit to valid sheet names and removes .xls*
            CurFile = Left(Left(CurFile, Len(CurFile) - 5), 29)

            For Each ws In OrigWB.Sheets
                ws.Copy After:=DestWB.Sheets(DestWB.Sheets.Count)

                If OrigWB.Sheets.Count > 1 Then
                    DestWB.Sheets(DestWB.Sheets.Count).Name = CurFile & ws.Index
                Else
                    DestWB.Sheets(DestWB.Sheets.Count).Name = CurFile
                End If
            Next

            OrigWB.Close SaveChanges:=False
            CurFile = Dir
        Loop

        Application.DisplayAlerts = False
        DestWB.Sheets(1).Delete
        Application.DisplayAlerts = True

        Application.ScreenUpdating = True
        Application.EnableEvents = True

        Set DestWB = Nothing
    End Sub
```

Filter and Copy Data to Separate Worksheets

Submitted by Dennis Wallentin of Ostersund, Sweden. Dennis provides Excel tips and tricks at www.xldennis.com.

This sample uses a specified column to filter data and copies the results to new worksheets in the active workbook:

```
Sub Filter_NewSheet()
Dim wbBook As Workbook
Dim wsSheet As Worksheet
Dim rnStart As Range, rnData As Range
Dim i As Long

Set wbBook = ThisWorkbook
Set wsSheet = wbBook.Worksheets("Sheet1")

With wsSheet
    'Make sure that the first row contains headings.
    Set rnStart = .Range("A2")
    Set rnData = .Range(.Range("A2"), .Cells(.Rows.Count, 3).End(xlUp))
End With

Application.ScreenUpdating = True
```

14

```
For i = 1 To 5
    'Here we filter the data with the first criterion.
    rnStart.AutoFilter Field:=1, Criteria1:="AA" & i
    'Copy the filtered list
    rnData.SpecialCells(xlCellTypeVisible).Copy
    'Add a new worksheet to the active workbook.
    Worksheets.Add Before:=wsSheet
    'Name the added new worksheets.
    ActiveSheet.Name = "AA" & i
    'Paste the filtered list.
    Range("A2").PasteSpecial xlPasteValues
Next i

'Reset the list to its original status.
rnStart.AutoFilter Field:=1

With Application
    'Reset the clipboard.
    .CutCopyMode = False
    .ScreenUpdating = False
End With

End Sub
```

Export Data to Word

Submitted by Dennis Wallentin.

This program transfers data from Excel to the first table found in a Word document. It uses early binding, so a reference must be established in the VB Editor using Tools, References to the Microsoft Word object library:

```
Sub Export_Data_Word_Table()
Dim wdApp As Word.Application
Dim wdDoc As Word.Document
Dim wdCell As Word.Cell
Dim i As Long
Dim wbBook As Workbook
Dim wsSheet As Worksheet
Dim rnData As Range
Dim vaData As Variant

Set wbBook = ThisWorkbook
Set wsSheet = wbBook.Worksheets("Sheet1")

With wsSheet
    Set rnData = .Range("A1:A10")
End With

'Add the values in the range to a one-dimensional variant-array.
vaData = rnData.Value

'Here we instantiate the new object.
Set wdApp = New Word.Application
'Here the target document resides in the same folder as the workbook.
Set wdDoc = wdApp.Documents.Open(ThisWorkbook.Path & "\Test.docx")
```

14

```
'Import data to the first table and in the first column of a ten-row table.
For Each wdCell In wdDoc.Tables(1).Columns(1).Cells
    i = i + 1
    wdCell.Range.Text = vaData(i, 1)
Next wdCell

'Save and close the document.
With wdDoc
    .Save
    .Close
End With

'Close the hidden instance of Microsoft Word.
wdApp.Quit
'Release the external variables from the memory
Set wdDoc = Nothing
Set wdApp = Nothing

MsgBox "The data has been transfered to Test.docx.", vbInformation

End Sub
```

Working with Cell Comments

Cell comments are often underused features of Excel. The following four utilities help you to get the most out of cell comments.

List Comments

Submitted by Tommy Miles.

Excel allows the user to print the comments in a workbook, but it does not specify the workbook or worksheet on which the comments appear, only the cell, as shown in Figure 14.1.

The following sample places comments, author, and location of each comment on a new sheet for easy viewing, saving, or printing. Figure 14.2 shows a sample result.

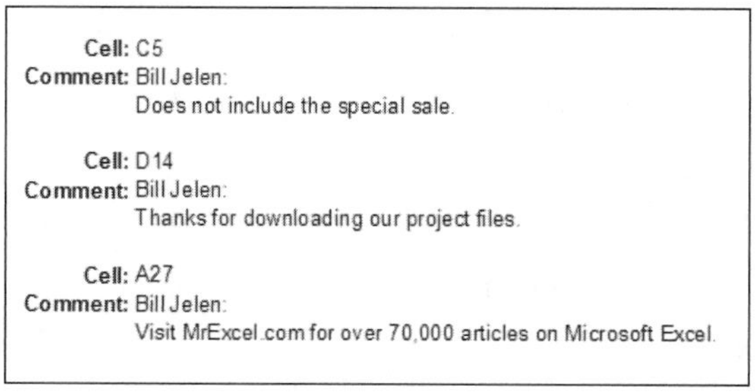

Figure 14.1

Excel prints only the origin cell address and its comment.

> Cell: C5
> Comment: Bill Jelen:
>   Does not include the special sale.
>
> Cell: D14
> Comment: Bill Jelen:
>   Thanks for downloading our project files.
>
> Cell: A27
> Comment: Bill Jelen:
>   Visit MrExcel.com for over 70,000 articles on Microsoft Excel.

14

Figure 14.2
Easily list all the information pertaining to comments.

	A	B	C	D	E	F	G	H	I	J
1	Author	Book	Sheet	Range	Comment					
2	Bill Jelen	ProjectFilesChapter14.xlsm	ListComments	$C$5	Does not include the special sale.					
3	Bill Jelen	ProjectFilesChapter14.xlsm	ListComments	$D$14	Thanks for downloading our project files.					
4	Bill Jelen	ProjectFilesChapter14.xlsm	ListComments	$A$27	Visit MrExcel.com for over 70,000 articles on Microsoft Excel.					

```vba
Sub ListComments()
    Dim wb As Workbook
    Dim ws As Worksheet

    Dim cmt As Comment

    Dim cmtCount As Long

    cmtCount = 2

    On Error Resume Next
        Set ws = ActiveSheet
            If ws Is Nothing Then Exit Sub
    On Error GoTo 0

    Application.ScreenUpdating = False

    Set wb = Workbooks.Add(xlWorksheet)

    With wb.Sheets(1)
        .Range("$A$1") = "Author"
        .Range("$B$1") = "Book"
        .Range("$C$1") = "Sheet"
        .Range("$D$1") = "Range"
        .Range("$E$1") = "Comment"
    End With

    For Each cmt In ws.Comments
        With wb.Sheets(1)
            .Cells(cmtCount, 1) = cmt.author
            .Cells(cmtCount, 2) = cmt.Parent.Parent.Parent.Name
            .Cells(cmtCount, 3) = cmt.Parent.Parent.Name
            .Cells(cmtCount, 4) = cmt.Parent.Address
            .Cells(cmtCount, 5) = CleanComment(cmt.author, cmt.Text)
        End With

        cmtCount = cmtCount + 1
    Next

    wb.Sheets(1).UsedRange.WrapText = False

    Application.ScreenUpdating = True

    Set ws = Nothing
    Set wb = Nothing
End Sub

Private Function CleanComment(author As String, cmt As String) As String
    Dim tmp As String
```

```
        tmp = Application.WorksheetFunction.Substitute(cmt, author & ":", "")
        tmp = Application.WorksheetFunction.Substitute(tmp, Chr(10), "")

        CleanComment = tmp
    End Function
```

Resize Comments

Submitted by Tom Urtis of San Francisco, California. Tom is the principal owner of Atlas Programming Management, an Excel consulting firm in the Bay Area.

Excel doesn't automatically resize cell comments. In addition, if you have several on a sheet, as shown in Figure 14.3, it can be a hassle to resize them one at a time. The following sample code resizes all the comment boxes on a sheet so that, when selected, the entire comment is easily viewable, as shown in Figure 14.4.

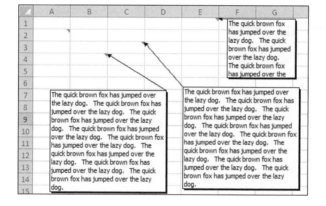

Figure 14.3
By default, Excel doesn't size the comment boxes to show all the entered text.

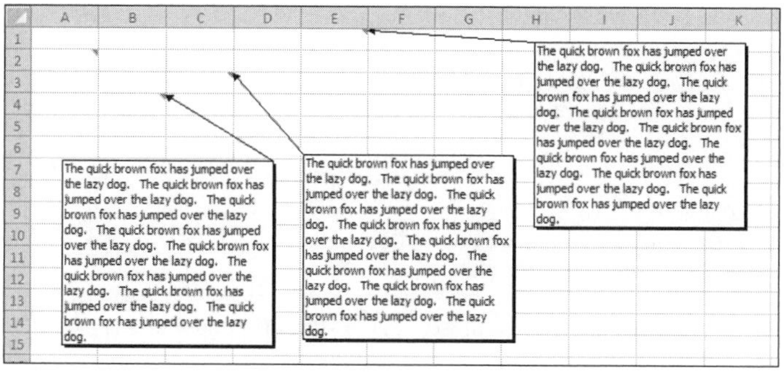

Figure 14.4
Resize the comment boxes to fit all the text.

14

```
Sub CommentFitter1()
Application.ScreenUpdating = False
Dim x As Range, y As Long

For Each x In Cells.SpecialCells(xlCellTypeComments)
    Select Case True
        Case Len(x.NoteText) <> 0
            With x.Comment
                .Shape.TextFrame.AutoSize = True
                If .Shape.Width > 250 Then
                    y = .Shape.Width * .Shape.Height
                    .Shape.Width = 150
                    .Shape.Height = (y / 200) * 1.3
                End If
            End With
    End Select
Next x
Application.ScreenUpdating = True
End Sub
```

Resize Comments with Centering

Submitted by Tom Urtis.

This sample resizes all the comment boxes on a sheet by centering the comments (see Figure 14.5).

Figure 14.5
Center all the comments on a sheet.

The Comment Box Resized and Centered

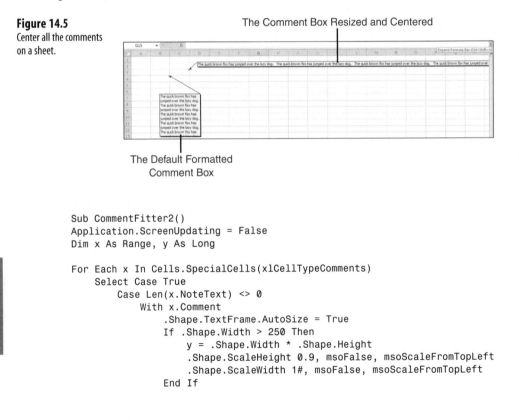

The Default Formatted
Comment Box

```
Sub CommentFitter2()
Application.ScreenUpdating = False
Dim x As Range, y As Long

For Each x In Cells.SpecialCells(xlCellTypeComments)
    Select Case True
        Case Len(x.NoteText) <> 0
            With x.Comment
                .Shape.TextFrame.AutoSize = True
                If .Shape.Width > 250 Then
                    y = .Shape.Width * .Shape.Height
                    .Shape.ScaleHeight 0.9, msoFalse, msoScaleFromTopLeft
                    .Shape.ScaleWidth 1#, msoFalse, msoScaleFromTopLeft
                End If
```

```
            End With
        End Select
    Next x
    Application.ScreenUpdating = True
    End Sub
```

Place a Chart in a Comment

Submitted by Tom Urtis.

A live chart cannot exist in a shape, but you can take a picture of the chart and load it into the comment shape, as shown in Figure 14.6.

Figure 14.6

Place a chart in a cell comment.

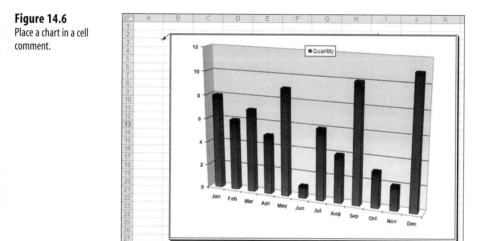

The steps to do this manually are as follows:

1. Create and save the picture image you want the comment to display.
2. If you have not already done so, create the comment and select the cell in which the comment is located.
3. From the Review tab, select Edit Comment, or right-click the cell and select Edit Comment.
4. Right-click the comment border and select Format Comment.
5. Select the Colors and Lines tab, and click the down arrow belonging to the Color field of the Fill section.
6. Select Fill Effects, select the Picture tab, and then click the Select Picture button.
7. Navigate to your desired image, select the image, and click OK twice.

The effect of having a "live chart" in a comment can be achieved if, for example, the code is part of a SheetChange event when the chart's source data is being changed. In addition, business charts are updated often, so you might want a macro to keep the comment updated and to avoid repeating the same steps.

14

The following macro does just that—it modifies the macro for file path name, chart name, destination sheet, cell, and size of comment shape, depending on the size of the chart:

```
Sub PlaceGraph()
Dim x As String, z As Range

Application.ScreenUpdating = False

'assign a temporary location to hold the image
x = "C:\XWMJGraph.gif"

'assign the cell to hold the comment
Set z = Worksheets("ChartInComment").Range("A3")

'delete any existing comment in the cell
On Error Resume Next
z.Comment.Delete
On Error GoTo 0

'select and export the chart
ActiveSheet.ChartObjects("Chart 1").Activate
ActiveChart.Export x

'add a new comment to the cell, set the size and insert the chart
With z.AddComment
    With .Shape
        .Height = 322
        .Width = 465
        .Fill.UserPicture x
    End With
End With

'delete the temporary image
Kill x

Range("A1").Activate
Application.ScreenUpdating = True

Set z = Nothing
End Sub
```

Utilities to Wow Your Clients

The next four utilities will amaze and impress your clients.

Using Conditional Formatting to Highlight Selected Cell

Submitted by Ivan F. Moala of Auckland, New Zealand. Ivan is the site author of The XcelFiles (www.xcelfiles.com), where you will find out how to do things you thought you could not do in Excel.

Conditional formatting is used to highlight the row and column of the active cell to help you visually locate it, as shown in Figure 14.7.

> **CAUTION**
>
> Do *not* use this method if you already have conditional formats on the worksheet. Any existing conditional formats will be overwritten. In addition, this program clears the Clipboard. Therefore, it is not possible to use this method while doing copy, cut, or paste.

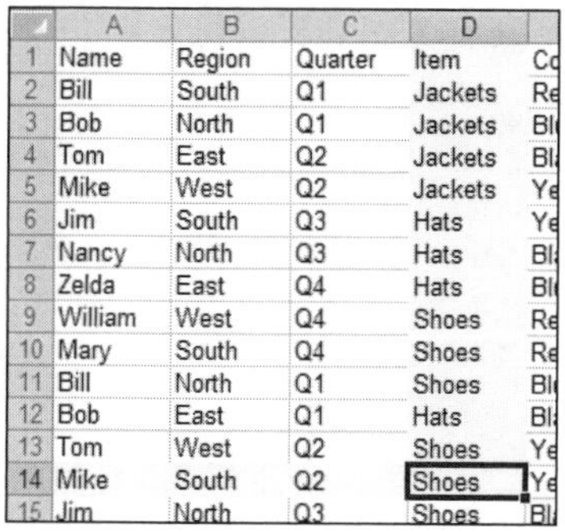

	A	B	C	D	
1	Name	Region	Quarter	Item	Co
2	Bill	South	Q1	Jackets	Re
3	Bob	North	Q1	Jackets	Bl
4	Tom	East	Q2	Jackets	Bl
5	Mike	West	Q2	Jackets	Ye
6	Jim	South	Q3	Hats	Ye
7	Nancy	North	Q3	Hats	Bl
8	Zelda	East	Q4	Hats	Bl
9	William	West	Q4	Shoes	Re
10	Mary	South	Q4	Shoes	Re
11	Bill	North	Q1	Shoes	Bl
12	Bob	East	Q1	Hats	Bl
13	Tom	West	Q2	Shoes	Ye
14	Mike	South	Q2	Shoes	Ye
15	Jim	North	Q3	Shoes	Bl

Figure 14.7
Use conditional formatting to highlight the selected cell in a table.

```
Const iInternational As Integer = Not (0)

Private Sub Worksheet_SelectionChange(ByVal Target As Range)
Dim iColor As Integer
'// On error resume in case
'// user selects a range of cells
On Error Resume Next
iColor = Target.Interior.ColorIndex
'// Leave On Error ON for Row offset errors

If iColor < 0 Then
    iColor = 36
Else
    iColor = iColor + 1
End If

'// Need this test in case font color is the same
If iColor = Target.Font.ColorIndex Then iColor = iColor + 1

Cells.FormatConditions.Delete

'// Horizontal color banding
With Range("A" & Target.Row, Target.Address) 'Rows(Target.Row)
    .FormatConditions.Add Type:=2, Formula1:=iInternational 'Or just 1 '"TRUE"
    .FormatConditions(1).Interior.ColorIndex = iColor
End With

'// Vertical color banding
With Range(Target.Offset(1 - Target.Row, 0).Address & ":" & _
    Target.Offset(-1, 0).Address)
    .FormatConditions.Add Type:=2, Formula1:=iInternational 'Or just 1 '"TRUE"
    .FormatConditions(1).Interior.ColorIndex = iColor
```

```
End With

End Sub
```

Highlight Selected Cell Without Using Conditional Formatting

Submitted by Ivan F. Moala.

This example visually highlights the active cell without using conditional formatting when the keyboard arrow keys are used to move around the sheet.

Place the following in a standard module:

```
Dim strCol As String
Dim iCol As Integer
Dim dblRow As Double

Sub HighlightRight()
    HighLight 0, 1
End Sub

Sub HighlightLeft()
    HighLight 0, -1
End Sub

Sub HighlightUp()
    HighLight -1, 0, -1
End Sub

Sub HighlightDown()
    HighLight 1, 0, 1
End Sub

Sub HighLight(dblxRow As Double, iyCol As Integer, Optional dblZ As _
Double = 0)

On Error GoTo NoGo
strCol = Mid(ActiveCell.Offset(dblxRow, iyCol).Address, _
        InStr(ActiveCell.Offset(dblxRow, iyCol).Address, "$") + 1, _
        InStr(2, ActiveCell.Offset(dblxRow, iyCol).Address, "$") - 2)
iCol = ActiveCell.Column
dblRow = ActiveCell.Row

Application.ScreenUpdating = False

With Range(strCol & ":" & strCol & "," & dblRow + dblZ & ":" & dblRow + dblZ)
    .Select
    Application.ScreenUpdating = True
    .Item(dblRow + dblxRow).Activate
End With

NoGo:
End Sub

Sub ReSet() 'manual reset
    Application.OnKey "{RIGHT}"
    Application.OnKey "{LEFT}"
```

```
        Application.OnKey "{UP}"
        Application.OnKey "{DOWN}"
    End Sub
```

Place the following in the ThisWorkbook module:

```
Private Sub Workbook_Open()
    Application.OnKey "{RIGHT}", "HighlightRight"
    Application.OnKey "{LEFT}", "HighlightLeft"
    Application.OnKey "{UP}", "HighlightUp"
    Application.OnKey "{DOWN}", "HighlightDown"
    Application.OnKey "{DEL}", "DisableDelete"
End Sub

Private Sub Workbook_BeforeClose(Cancel As Boolean)
    Application.OnKey "{RIGHT}"
    Application.OnKey "{LEFT}"
    Application.OnKey "{UP}"
    Application.OnKey "{DOWN}"
    Application.OnKey "{DEL}"
End Sub
```

Custom Transpose Data

Submitted by Masaru Kaji.

You have a report where the data is set up in rows (see Figure 14.8). However, you need the data formatted so each date and batch is in a single row, with the Value and Finish Position going across. Note that the Finish Position is not shown in Figure 14.9. The following program does a customized data transposition based on the specified column, as shown in Figure 14.9.

Figure 14.8
The original data has similar records in separate rows.

	A	B	C	D	E
1	ItemName	ItemDate	Batch#	FinishPosition	Value
2	Thermal	10/23/2002	1	8	2.15
3	Thermal	10/23/2002	1	3	3.2
4	Thermal	10/23/2002	1	2	4.9
5	Thermal	10/23/2002	1	1	6.1
6	Thermal	10/23/2002	1	7	6.2
7	Thermal	10/23/2002	1	4	12.9
8	Thermal	10/23/2002	1	9	23
9	Thermal	10/23/2002	1	5	36
10	Thermal	10/23/2002	1	6	36.25
11	Thermal	10/23/2002	2	2	1.05
12	Thermal	10/23/2002	2	1	2.5
13	Thermal	10/23/2002	2	8	7.3
14	Thermal	10/23/2002	2	3	10.9
15	Thermal	10/23/2002	2	4	12.1
16	Thermal	10/23/2002	2	9	21.7

14

Figure 14.9
The formatted data transposes the data so that identical dates and batches are merged into a single row.

	A	B	C	D	E	F	G	H	I	J	K	L	M	N	O	
1	ItemName	ItemDate	Batch#	V1	V2	V3	V4	V5	V6	V7	V8	V9	V10	V11	V12	V
2	Thermal	10/23/2009	1	2.15	3.2	4.9	6.1	6.2	12.9	23	36	36.25				
3	Thermal	10/23/2009	2	1.05	2.5	7.3	10.9	12.1	21.7	33.25	43	43.25				
4	Thermal	10/23/2009	3	1.65	3.1	3.1	3.75	7.1	7.1	7.7	18.7	34	55.5			
5	Thermal	10/23/2009	4	1.1	2.75	4	9.5	14.3	25	37.75						
6	Thermal	10/23/2009	5	0.9	3.75	7.1	9	16	18.1	19.5	22.5	74.75				
7	Thermal	10/23/2009	6	1.6	3.4	5.2	7.8	8.2	9.4	11.5						
8	Thermal	10/23/2009	7	0.8	4.2	4.9	9.6	15	21.2	24.75	63.25					
9	Thermal	10/23/2009	8	0.7	6.2	8.4	10.3	10.6	12.3	28.75	31.75	52	76.75			
10	Thermal	10/23/2009	9	2.9	3.9	4.4	5.9	7	11.4	13.5	18.4	26.25	66.25			
11	Thermal	10/24/2009	1	1.4	3.85	6.2	8.1	10	12.3	17.2	27.5	37.5	55.5			
12	Thermal	10/24/2009	2	1.75	2.95	6	6.5	7.8	8.3	16.8						
13	Thermal	10/24/2009	3	1.15	5.4	8.7	9.9	10.9	11.8	13.3	17.1	24	37			
14	Thermal	10/24/2009	4	1.05	1.9	5.2	6.8	19.9								
15	Thermal	10/24/2009	5	2.5	3.15	3.15	4.2	6	12.2	12.3	19.9	23.2	25.25	42.25	150	
16	Thermal	10/24/2009	6	2.4	2.95	4.4	6.5	8.7	14.2	22.9	22.9	25.75	51	58.25	59.5	
17	Thermal	10/24/2009	7	1.2	3.35	6.3	9.5	11.3	12	14.4	36.25					

```
Sub TransposeData()
Dim shOrg As Worksheet, shRes As Worksheet
Dim rngStart As Range, rngPaste As Range
Dim lngData As Long

Application.ScreenUpdating = False
On Error Resume Next
Application.DisplayAlerts = False
Sheets("TransposeResult").Delete
Application.DisplayAlerts = True
On Error GoTo 0

On Error GoTo terminate

Set shOrg = Sheets("TransposeData")
Set shRes = Sheets.Add(After:=shOrg)
shRes.Name = "TransposeResult"
With shOrg
    '--Sort
    .Cells.CurrentRegion.Sort Key1:=.[B2], Order1:=1, Key2:=.[C2], _
       Order2:=1, Key3:=.[E2], Order3:=1, Header:=xlYes
    '--Copy title
    .Rows(1).Copy shRes.Rows(1)
    '--Set start range
    Set rngStart = .[C2]
    Do Until IsEmpty(rngStart)
        Set rngPaste = shRes.Cells(shRes.Rows.Count, 1).End(xlUp).Offset(1)
        lngData = GetNextRange(rngStart)
        rngStart.Offset(, -2).Resize(, 5).Copy rngPaste

        'Copy to V1 toV14
        rngStart.Offset(, 2).Resize(lngData).Copy
        rngPaste.Offset(, 5).PasteSpecial Paste:=xlAll, Operation:=xlNone, _
         SkipBlanks:=False, Transpose:=True
        'Copy to V1FP to V14FP
        rngStart.Offset(, 1).Resize(lngData).Copy
        rngPaste.Offset(, 19).PasteSpecial Paste:=xlAll, Operation:=xlNone, _
         SkipBlanks:=False, Transpose:=True
        Set rngStart = rngStart.Offset(lngData)
    Loop
End With

Application.Goto shRes.[A1]
```

```
With shRes
    .Cells.Columns.AutoFit
    .Columns("D:E").Delete shift:=xlToLeft
End With

Application.ScreenUpdating = True
Application.CutCopyMode = False

If MsgBox("Do you want to delete the original worksheet?", 36) = 6 Then
    Application.DisplayAlerts = False
    Sheets("TransposeData").Delete
    Application.DisplayAlerts = True
End If

Set rngPaste = Nothing
Set rngStart = Nothing
Set shRes = Nothing

Exit Sub

terminate:
End Sub

Function GetNextRange(ByVal rngSt As Range) As Long
    Dim i As Long
    i = 0

    Do Until rngSt.Value <> rngSt.Offset(i).Value
        i = i + 1
    Loop

    GetNextRange = i
End Function
```

Select/Deselect Noncontiguous Cells

Submitted by Tom Urtis.

Ordinarily, to deselect a single cell or range on a sheet, you must click an unselected cell to deselect all cells and then start over by reselecting all the correct cells. This is inconvenient if you need to reselect a lot of noncontiguous cells.

This sample adds two new options to the contextual menu of a selection: Deselect ActiveCell and Deselect ActiveArea. With the noncontiguous cells selected, hold down the Ctrl key, click the cell you want to deselect to make it active, release the Ctrl key, and then right-click the cell you want to deselect. The contextual menu shown in Figure 14.10 appears. Click the menu item that deselects either that one active cell or the contiguously selected area of which it is a part.

14

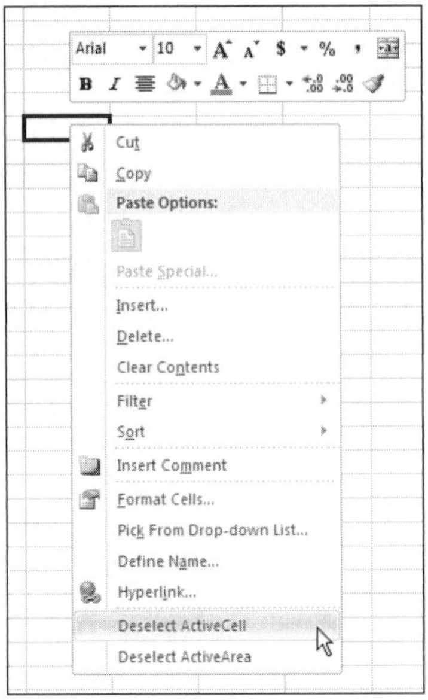

Figure 14.10
The `ModifyRight`
`Click` procedure pro-
vides a custom contextual
menu for deselecting
noncontiguous cells.

Enter the following procedures in a standard module:

```
Sub ModifyRightClick()
'add the new options to the right-click menu
Dim O1 As Object, O2 As Object

'delete the options if they exist already
On Error Resume Next
With CommandBars("Cell")
    .Controls("Deselect ActiveCell").Delete
    .Controls("Deselect ActiveArea").Delete
End With
On Error GoTo 0

'add the new options
Set O1 = CommandBars("Cell").Controls.Add

With O1
    .Caption = "Deselect ActiveCell"
    .OnAction = "DeselectActiveCell"
End With

Set O2 = CommandBars("Cell").Controls.Add

With O2
    .Caption = "Deselect ActiveArea"
    .OnAction = "DeselectActiveArea"
End With

End Sub

Sub DeselectActiveCell()
```

```
        Dim x As Range, y As Range

        If Selection.Cells.Count > 1 Then
            For Each y In Selection.Cells
                If y.Address <> ActiveCell.Address Then
                    If x Is Nothing Then
                        Set x = y
                    Else
                        Set x = Application.Union(x, y)
                    End If
                End If
            Next y
            If x.Cells.Count > 0 Then
                x.Select
            End If
        End If

        End Sub

        Sub DeselectActiveArea()
        Dim x As Range, y As Range

        If Selection.Areas.Count > 1 Then
            For Each y In Selection.Areas
                If Application.Intersect(ActiveCell, y) Is Nothing Then
                    If x Is Nothing Then
                        Set x = y
                    Else
                        Set x = Application.Union(x, y)
                    End If
                End If
            Next y
            x.Select
        End If
        End Sub
```

Add the following procedures to the ThisWorkbook module:

```
        Private Sub Workbook_Activate()
        ModifyRightClick
        End Sub

        Private Sub Workbook_Deactivate()
        Application.CommandBars("Cell").Reset
        End Sub
```

Techniques for VBA Pros

The next 10 utilities amaze me. In the various message board communities on the Internet, VBA programmers are constantly coming up with new ways to do something faster or better. When someone posts some new code that obviously runs circles around the prior generally accepted best code, everyone benefits.

Pivot Table Drill-Down

Submitted by Tom Urtis.

14

When you are double-clicking the data section, a pivot table's default behavior is to insert a new worksheet and display that drill-down information on the new sheet. The following example serves as an option for convenience, to keep the drilled-down recordsets on the same sheet as the pivot table (see Figure 14.11) and letting you delete them as you want.

To use this macro, double-click the data section or the Totals section to create stacked drill-down recordsets in the next available row of this sheet. To delete any drill-down recordsets you have created, double-click anywhere in their respective current region.

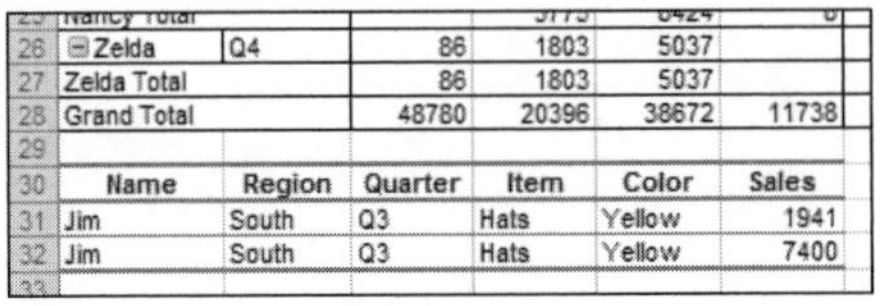

26	⊟Zelda	Q4	86	1803	5037	
27	Zelda Total		86	1803	5037	
28	Grand Total		48780	20396	38672	11738
29						
30	Name	Region	Quarter	Item	Color	Sales
31	Jim	South	Q3	Hats	Yellow	1941
32	Jim	South	Q3	Hats	Yellow	7400

Figure 14.11
Show the drill-down recordset on the same sheet as the pivot table.

```
Private Sub Worksheet_BeforeDoubleClick(ByVal Target As Range, Cancel As _
  Boolean)
Application.ScreenUpdating = False
Dim LPTR&

With ActiveSheet.PivotTables(1).DataBodyRange
    LPTR = .Rows.Count + .Row - 1
End With

Dim PTT As Integer
On Error Resume Next
PTT = Target.PivotCell.PivotCellType
If Err.Number = 1004 Then
    Err.Clear
    If Not IsEmpty(Target) Then
        If Target.Row > Range("A1").CurrentRegion.Rows.Count + 1 Then
            Cancel = True
            With Target.CurrentRegion
                .Resize(.Rows.Count + 1).EntireRow.Delete
            End With
        End If
    Else
        Cancel = True
    End If
Else
    CS = ActiveSheet.Name
End If
Application.ScreenUpdating = True
End Sub
```

Speedy Page Setup

Submitted by Juan Pablo Gonzàlez Ruiz of Bogotà, Colombia. Juan Pablo is an Excel consultant and runs his photography business at http://www.juanpg.com.

The following examples compare the runtimes of variations on changing the margins from the defaults to 1.5 inches and the footer/header to 1 inch in the Page Setup. The macro recorder was used to create Macro1. Macros 2, 3, and 4 show how the recorded code's runtime can be decreased. Figure 14.12 shows the results of the speed test running each variation.

Figure 14.12
Page setup speed tests.

	A	B	C	D
1	Macro1	Macro1_Version2	Macro1_Version3	Macro1_Version4
2	0.5663	0.1234	0.1161	0.0212
3	0.4886	0.1063	0.1373	0.0219
4	0.4943	0.1131	0.1277	0.0204
5	0.4624	0.1189	0.1057	0.0216
6	0.4837	0.1154	0.113	0.0203
7	0.5063	0.1408	0.1141	0.0203
8	0.4819	0.1093	0.1318	0.0215
9	0.469	0.1188	0.1311	0.0138
10	0.481	0.1176	0.1233	0.02
11	0.4833	0.119	0.1068	0.019
12	0.4835	0.1472	0.1162	0.0199
13	0.5423	0.1208	0.1369	0.0191
14	0.5502	0.1206	0.1255	0.0199
15	0.4623	0.1372	0.094	0.0197
16	0.4602	0.1112	0.131	0.0193
17	0.455	0.1172	0.1236	0.02
18	0.4569	0.1189	0.1299	0.0191
19	0.4805	0.1168	0.1248	0.0168
20	0.4706	0.1148	0.0996	0.0193
21	0.4516	0.1182	0.1391	0.0197
22	0.49	0.12	0.12	0.02
23	4	2	3	1
24	On my system, Version4 runs in 4% of the time of the recorded version.			

```
Sub Macro1()
'
' Macro1 Macro
' Macro recorded 11/3/2009
'
    With ActiveSheet.PageSetup
        .PrintTitleRows = ""
        .PrintTitleColumns = ""
    End With
    ActiveSheet.PageSetup.PrintArea = ""
    With ActiveSheet.PageSetup
        .LeftHeader = ""
        .CenterHeader = ""
        .RightHeader = ""
        .LeftFooter = ""
        .CenterFooter = ""
        .RightFooter = ""
        .LeftMargin = Application.InchesToPoints(1.5)
        .RightMargin = Application.InchesToPoints(1.5)
        .TopMargin = Application.InchesToPoints(1.5)
        .BottomMargin = Application.InchesToPoints(1.5)
        .HeaderMargin = Application.InchesToPoints(1)
        .FooterMargin = Application.InchesToPoints(1)
        .PrintHeadings = False
        .PrintGridlines = False
        .PrintComments = xlPrintNoComments
```

```
          .PrintQuality = -3
          .CenterHorizontally = False
          .CenterVertically = False
          .Orientation = xlPortrait
          .Draft = False
          .PaperSize = xlPaperLetter
          .FirstPageNumber = 1
          .Order = xlDownThenOver
          .BlackAndWhite = False
          .Zoom = False
          .FitToPagesWide = 1
          .FitToPagesTall = 1
          .PrintErrors = xlPrintErrorsDisplayed
          .OddAndEvenPagesHeaderFooter = False
          .DifferentFirstPageHeaderFooter = False
          .ScaleWithDocHeaderFooter = True
          .AlignMarginsHeaderFooter = False
          .EvenPage.LeftHeader.Text = ""
          .EvenPage.CenterHeader.Text = ""
          .EvenPage.RightHeader.Text = ""
          .EvenPage.LeftFooter.Text = ""
          .EvenPage.CenterFooter.Text = ""
          .EvenPage.RightFooter.Text = ""
          .FirstPage.LeftHeader.Text = ""
          .FirstPage.CenterHeader.Text = ""
          .FirstPage.RightHeader.Text = ""
          .FirstPage.LeftFooter.Text = ""
          .FirstPage.CenterFooter.Text = ""
          .FirstPage.RightFooter.Text = ""
     End With
     Application.PrintCommunication = True
End Sub
```

The macro recorder is doing a lot of extra work, which requires extra processing time. Considering this, along with the fact that the PageSetup object is one of the slowest objects to update, you can have quite a mess. So, a cleaner version that uses just the Delete key to clean out extraneous lines follows:

```
Sub Macro1_Version2()
    With ActiveSheet.PageSetup
        .LeftMargin = Application.InchesToPoints(1.5)
        .RightMargin = Application.InchesToPoints(1.5)
        .TopMargin = Application.InchesToPoints(1.5)
        .BottomMargin = Application.InchesToPoints(1.5)
        .HeaderMargin = Application.InchesToPoints(1)
        .FooterMargin = Application.InchesToPoints(1)
    End With
End Sub
```

Okay, this runs faster than Macro1. The average reduction is around 70 percent on some simple tests! However, it can be improved even further.

As noted earlier, the PageSetup object takes a long time to process. Therefore, if you reduce the number of operations that VBA has to make and include some IF functions to update only the properties that require changing, you can get better results.

14

In the following case, the `Application.InchesToPoints` function was hard-coded to the inches value. The third version of Macro1 looks like this:

```
Sub Macro1_Version3()
    With ActiveSheet.PageSetup
        If .LeftMargin <> 108 Then .LeftMargin = 108
        If .RightMargin <> 108 Then .RightMargin = 108
        If .TopMargin <> 108 Then .TopMargin = 108
        If .BottomMargin <> 108 Then .BottomMargin = 108
        If .HeaderMargin <> 72 Then .HeaderMargin = 72
        If .FooterMargin <> 72 Then .FooterMargin = 72
    End With
End Sub
```

You will see the difference on this third version when you are not changing all the default margins.

Another option can reduce the runtime by more than 95 percent. This option uses the `PAGE.SETUP` XLM method. The necessary parameters are `left`, `right`, `top`, `bot`, `head_margin`, and `foot_margin`. These parameters are measured in inches, not points. Therefore, using the same margins that we have been changing already, a fourth version of Macro1 looks like this:

```
Sub Macro1_Version4()
    Dim St As String
    St = "PAGE.SETUP(, , " & _
                    "1.5, 1.5, 1.5, 1.5" & _
                    ", 0, False, False, False, 1, 1, True, 1, 1,False, , _
                    " & "1, 1" & _
                    ", False)"
    Application.ExecuteExcel4Macro St
End Sub
```

> **CAUTION**
>
> The second and fourth lines of St correspond to these parameters. However, you need to follow some simple precautions. First, this macro relies on XLM language, which is still included in Excel for backward compatibility. However, we do not know when Microsoft will drop it. Second, be care-ful when setting the parameters of PAGE.SETUP because if one of them is wrong, the PAGE.SETUP is not executed and does not generate an error, which can possibly leave you with the wrong page setup.

Calculating Time to Execute Code

You might wonder how to calculate elapsed time down to the thousandth of a second, as shown earlier in Figure 14.12.

This is the code used to generate the time results for the macros in this section:

```
Public Declare Function QueryPerformanceFrequency _
    Lib "kernel32" (lpFrequency As Currency) As Long
```

14

```
Public Declare Function QueryPerformanceCounter _
    Lib "kernel32.dll" (lpPerformanceCount As Currency) As Long

Sub CalculateTime()
    Dim Ar(1 To 20, 1 To 4) As Currency, WS As Worksheet
    Dim n As Currency, str As Currency, fin As Currency
    Dim y As Currency

    Dim i As Long, j As Long

    Application.ScreenUpdating = False
    For i = 1 To 4
        For j = 1 To 20
            Set WS = ThisWorkbook.Sheets.Add
            WS.Range("A1").Value = 1
            QueryPerformanceFrequency y
            QueryPerformanceCounter str
            Select Case i
            Case 1: Macro1
            Case 2: Macro1_Version2
            Case 3: Macro1_Version3
            Case 4: Macro1_Version4
            End Select
            QueryPerformanceCounter fin
            Application.DisplayAlerts = False
            WS.Delete
            Application.DisplayAlerts = True
            n = (fin - str)
            Ar(j, i) = CCur(Format(n, "#########.###########") / y)
        Next j
    Next i
    With Range("A1").Resize(1, 4)
        .Value = Array("Macro1", "Macro2", "Macro3", " Macro4")
        .Font.Bold = True
    End With
    Range("A2").Resize(20, 4).Value = Ar

    With Range("A22").Resize(1, 4)
        .FormulaR1C1 = "=AVERAGE(R2C:R21C)"
        .Offset(1).FormulaR1C1 = "=RANK(R22C,R22C1:R22C4,1)"
        .Resize(2).Font.Bold = True
    End With
    Application.ScreenUpdating = True
End Sub
```

Custom Sort Order

Submitted by Wei Jiang of Wuhan City, China. Jiang is a consultant for MrExcel.com.

By default, Excel enables you to sort lists numerically or alphabetically, but sometimes that is not what is needed. For example, a client might need each day's sales data sorted by the default division order of belts, handbags, watches, wallets, and everything else. This sample uses a custom sort order list to sort a range of data into default division order and then deletes the custom sort order. Figure 14.13 shows the results.

Figure 14.13
When you use the macro, the list in A:C is sorted first by date, then by the custom sort list in Column I.

	A	B	C	D	E	F	G	H	I	J
1	Date	Category	# sold						Belts	
2	1/1/2009	Belts	15						Handbags	
3	1/1/2009	Handbags	23						Watches	
4	1/1/2009	Watches	42						Wallets	
5	1/1/2009	Wallets	17						Everything Else	
6	1/1/2009	Everything Else	36							
7	1/2/2009	Belts	17							
8	1/2/2009	Handbags	21							
9	1/2/2009	Watches	43							
10	1/2/2009	Wallets	18							
11	1/2/2009	Everything Else	42							
12	1/3/2009	Belts	21							
13	1/3/2009	Handbags	20							
14	1/3/2009	Watches	35							
15	1/3/2009	Wallets	19							
16	1/3/2009	Everything Else	45							

```
Sub CustomSort()

    ' add the custom list to Custom Lists
    Application.AddCustomList ListArray:=Range("I1:I5")

    ' get the list number
    nIndex = Application.GetCustomListNum(Range("I1:I5").Value)

    ' Now, we could sort a range with the custom list.
    ' Note, we should use nIndex + 1 as the custom list number here,
    ' for the first one is Normal order
    Range("A2:C16").Sort Key1:=Range("B2"), Order1:=xlAscending, _
                            Header:=xlNo, Orientation:=xlSortColumns, _
                            OrderCustom:=nIndex + 1
    Range("A2:C16").Sort Key1:=Range("A2"), Order1:=xlAscending, _
                            Header:=xlNo, Orientation:=xlSortColumns

    ' At the end, we should remove this custom list...
    Application.DeleteCustomList nIndex
End Sub
```

Cell Progress Indicator

Submitted by Tom Urtis.

I have to admit, the new conditional formatting options in Excel such as data bars are fantastic. However, there still isn't an option for a visual like that shown in Figure 14.14. The following example builds a progress indicator in Column C based on entries in Columns A and B.

Figure 14.14
Use indicators in cells to show progress.

C21 fx

	A	B	C
1	Progress made	Progress required	Visual representation of progress made vs progress completed
2	11	15	■■■■■■■■■■■□□□□
3	14	20	■■■■■■■■■■■■■■□□□□□□
4	1	5	■□□□□
5	4	10	■■■■□□□□□□
6	4	10	■■■■□□□□□□
7	10	10	■■■■■■■■■■
8	8	15	■■■■■■■■□□□□□□□
9		10	□□□□□□□□□□
10		10	□□□□□□□□□□
11		10	□□□□□□□□□□

```
Private Sub Worksheet_Change(ByVal Target As Range)
If Target.Column > 2 Or Target.Cells.Count > 1 Then Exit Sub
If Application.IsNumber(Target.Value) = False Then
    Application.EnableEvents = False
    Application.Undo
    Application.EnableEvents = True
    MsgBox "Numbers only please."
    Exit Sub
End If
Select Case Target.Column
    Case 1
        If Target.Value > Target.Offset(0, 1).Value Then
            Application.EnableEvents = False
            Application.Undo
            Application.EnableEvents = True
            MsgBox "Value in column A may not be larger than value in column _
                B."
            Exit Sub
        End If
    Case 2
        If Target.Value < Target.Offset(0, -1).Value Then
            Application.EnableEvents = False
            Application.Undo
            Application.EnableEvents = True
            MsgBox "Value in column B may not be smaller " & _
                "than value in column A."
            Exit Sub
        End If
End Select
Dim x As Long
x = Target.Row
Dim z As String
z = Range("B" & x).Value - Range("A" & x).Value
With Range("C" & x)
    .Formula = "=IF(RC[-1]<=RC[-2],REPT(""n"",RC[-1]) _
        &REPT(""n"",RC[-2]-RC[-1]),REPT(""n"",RC[-2]) _
        &REPT(""o"",RC[-1]-RC[-2]))"
    .Value = .Value
    .Font.Name = "Wingdings"
    .Font.ColorIndex = 1
    .Font.Size = 10
    If Len(Range("A" & x)) <> 0 Then
        .Characters(1, (.Characters.Count - z)).Font.ColorIndex = 3
        .Characters(1, (.Characters.Count - z)).Font.Size = 12
    End If
End With
End Sub
```

Protected Password Box

Submitted by Daniel Klann of Sydney, Australia. Daniel works mainly with VBA in Excel and Access, but dabbles in all sorts of languages.

Using an input box for password protection has a major security flaw: The characters being entered are easily viewable. This program changes the characters to asterisks as they are entered—just like a real password field (see Figure 14.15).

Figure 14.15
Use an input box as a
secure password field.

```
Private Declare Function CallNextHookEx Lib "user32" (ByVal hHook As Long, _
ByVal ncode As Long, ByVal wParam As Long, lParam As Any) As Long

Private Declare Function GetModuleHandle Lib "kernel32" _
    Alias "GetModuleHandleA" (ByVal lpModuleName As String) As Long

Private Declare Function SetWindowsHookEx Lib "user32" _
    Alias "SetWindowsHookExA" _
    (ByVal idHook As Long, ByVal lpfn As Long, _
    ByVal hmod As Long,ByVal dwThreadId As Long) As Long

Private Declare Function UnhookWindowsHookEx Lib "user32" _
    (ByVal hHook As Long) As Long

Private Declare Function SendDlgItemMessage Lib "user32" _
    Alias "SendDlgItemMessageA" _
    (ByVal hDlg As Long, _
    ByVal nIDDlgItem As Long, ByVal wMsg As Long, _
    ByVal wParam As Long, ByVal lParam As Long) As Long

Private Declare Function GetClassName Lib "user32" _
    Alias "GetClassNameA" (ByVal hwnd As Long, _
    ByVal lpClassName As String, _
    ByVal nMaxCount As Long) As Long

Private Declare Function GetCurrentThreadId _
    Lib "kernel32" () As Long

'Constants to be used in our API functions
Private Const EM_SETPASSWORDCHAR = &HCC
Private Const WH_CBT = 5
Private Const HCBT_ACTIVATE = 5
Private Const HC_ACTION = 0

Private hHook As Long

Public Function NewProc(ByVal lngCode As Long, _
    ByVal wParam As Long, ByVal lParam As Long) As Long
    Dim RetVal
```

14

```
        Dim strClassName As String, lngBuffer As Long

        If lngCode < HC_ACTION Then
            NewProc = CallNextHookEx(hHook, lngCode, wParam, lParam)
            Exit Function
        End If

        strClassName = String$(256, " ")
        lngBuffer = 255

        If lngCode = HCBT_ACTIVATE Then      'A window has been activated

            RetVal = GetClassName(wParam, strClassName, lngBuffer)

            'Check for class name of the Inputbox
            If Left$(strClassName, RetVal) = "#32770" Then
                'Change the edit control to display the password character *.
                'You can change the Asc("*") as you please.
                SendDlgItemMessage wParam, &H1324, EM_SETPASSWORDCHAR, _
                    Asc("*"), &H0
            End If

        End If

        'This line will ensure that any other hooks that may be in place are
        'called correctly.
        CallNextHookEx hHook, lngCode, wParam, lParam

End Function

Public Function InputBoxDK(Prompt, Optional Title, _
    Optional Default, Optional XPos, _
Optional YPos, Optional HelpFile, Optional Context) As String
    Dim lngModHwnd As Long, lngThreadID As Long

    lngThreadID = GetCurrentThreadId
    lngModHwnd = GetModuleHandle(vbNullString)

    hHook = SetWindowsHookEx(WH_CBT, AddressOf NewProc, lngModHwnd, _
        lngThreadID)
    On Error Resume Next
    InputBoxDK = InputBox(Prompt, Title, Default, XPos, YPos, HelpFile, _
        Context)
    UnhookWindowsHookEx hHook

End Function

Sub PasswordBox()
If InputBoxDK("Please enter password", "Password Required") <> "password" Then
        MsgBox "Sorry, that was not a correct password."
    Else
        MsgBox "Correct Password!  Come on in."
    End If
End Sub
```

14

Change Case

Submitted by Ivan F. Moala.

Word can change the case of selected text, but that capability is notably lacking in Excel. This program enables the Excel user to change the case of text in any selected range, as shown in Figure 14.16.

Figure 14.16
You can now change the case of words, just like in Word.

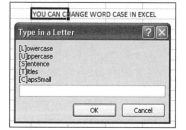

```
Sub TextCaseChange()
Dim RgText As Range
Dim oCell As Range
Dim Ans As String
Dim strTest As String
Dim sCap As Integer, _
    lCap As Integer, _
    i As Integer

'// You need to select a range to alter first!

Again:
Ans = Application.InputBox("[L]owercase" & vbCr & "[U]ppercase" & vbCr & _
        "[S]entence" & vbCr & "[T]itles" & vbCr & "[C]apsSmall", _
        "Type in a Letter", Type:=2)

If Ans = "False" Then Exit Sub
If InStr(1, "LUSTC", UCase(Ans), vbTextCompare) = 0 _
    Or Len(Ans) > 1 Then GoTo Again

On Error GoTo NoText
If Selection.Count = 1 Then
    Set RgText = Selection
Else
    Set RgText = Selection.SpecialCells(xlCellTypeConstants, 2)
End If
On Error GoTo 0

For Each oCell In RgText
    Select Case UCase(Ans)
        Case "L": oCell = LCase(oCell.Text)
        Case "U": oCell = UCase(oCell.Text)
        Case "S": oCell = UCase(Left(oCell.Text, 1)) & _
            LCase(Right(oCell.Text, Len(oCell.Text) - 1))
        Case "T": oCell = Application.WorksheetFunction.Proper(oCell.Text)
        Case "C"
```

```
                        lCap = oCell.Characters(1, 1).Font.Size
                        sCap = Int(lCap * 0.85)
                        'Small caps for everything.
                        oCell.Font.Size = sCap
                        oCell.Value = UCase(oCell.Text)
                        strTest = oCell.Value
                        'Large caps for 1st letter of words.
                        strTest = Application.Proper(strTest)
                        For i = 1 To Len(strTest)
                            If Mid(strTest, i, 1) = UCase(Mid(strTest, i, 1)) Then
                                oCell.Characters(i, 1).Font.Size = lCap
                            End If
                        Next i
            End Select
    Next

    Exit Sub
    NoText:
    MsgBox "No text in your selection @ " & Selection.Address

    End Sub
```

Selecting with SpecialCells

Submitted by Ivan F. Moala.

Typically, when you want to find certain values, text, or formulas in a range, the range is selected and each cell is tested. The following example shows how SpecialCells can be used to select only the desired cells. Having fewer cells to check will speed up your code.

The following code ran in the blink of an eye on my machine. However, the version that checked each cell in the range (A1:Z20000) took 14 seconds—an eternity in the automation world!

```
    Sub SpecialRange()
    Dim TheRange As Range
    Dim oCell As Range

        Set TheRange = Range("A1:Z20000").SpecialCells(__
        xlCellTypeConstants, xlTextValues)

        For Each oCell In TheRange
            If oCell.Text = "Your Text" Then
                MsgBox oCell.Address
                MsgBox TheRange.Cells.Count
            End If
        Next oCell

    End Sub
```

ActiveX Right-Click Menu

Submitted by Tom Urtis.

There is no built-in menu for the right-click event of ActiveX objects on a sheet. This is a utility for that, using a command button for the example in Figure 14.17. Set the Take Focus on Click property of the command button to False.

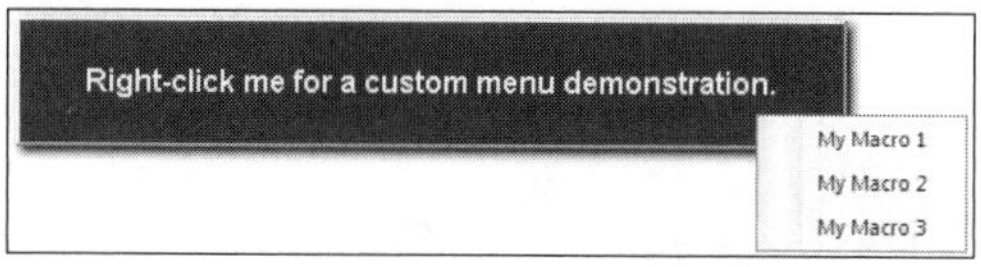

Figure 14.17
Customize the contextual (right-click) menu of an ActiveX control.

Place the following in the ThisWorkbook module:

```
Private Sub Workbook_Open()
With Application
    .CommandBars("Cell").Reset
    .WindowState = xlMaximized
    .Goto Sheet1.Range("A1"), True
End With
End Sub

Private Sub Workbook_Activate()
Application.CommandBars("Cell").Reset
End Sub

Private Sub Workbook_SheetBeforeRightClick(ByVal Sh As Object, _
    ByVal Target As Range, Cancel As Boolean)
Application.CommandBars("Cell").Reset
End Sub

Private Sub Workbook_Deactivate()
Application.CommandBars("Cell").Reset
End Sub

Private Sub Workbook_BeforeClose(Cancel As Boolean)
With Application
    .CommandBars("Cell").Reset
    .WindowState = xlMaximized
    .Goto Sheet1.Range("A1"), True
End With
ThisWorkbook.Save
End Sub
```

Place the following in a standard module:

```
Sub MyRightClickMenu()
Application.CommandBars("Cell").Reset
Dim cbc As CommandBarControl
  For Each cbc In Application.CommandBars("cell").Controls
      cbc.Visible = False
  Next cbc
With Application.CommandBars("Cell").Controls.Add(temporary:=True)
    .Caption = "My Macro 1"
    .OnAction = "Test1"
  End With
With Application.CommandBars("Cell").Controls.Add(temporary:=True)
    .Caption = "My Macro 2"
```

```
    .OnAction = "Test2"
  End With
With Application.CommandBars("Cell").Controls.Add(temporary:=True)
  .Caption = "My Macro 3"
  .OnAction = "Test3"
  End With
Application.CommandBars("Cell").ShowPopup
End Sub

Sub Test1()
MsgBox "This is the Test1 macro from the ActiveX object's custom " & _
    "right-click event menu.", , "''My Macro 1'' menu item."
End Sub

Sub Test2()
MsgBox "This is the Test2 macro from the ActiveX object's custom " & _
    "right-click event menu.", , "''My Macro 2'' menu item."
End Sub

Sub Test3()
MsgBox "This is the Test3 macro from the ActiveX object's custom " & _
    "right-click event menu.", , "''My Macro 3'' menu item."
End Sub
```

Cool Applications

These last samples are interesting applications that you might be able to incorporate into your own projects.

Historical Stock/Fund Quotes

Submitted by Nathan P. Oliver.

The following code retrieves the average of a valid stock ticker or the close of a fund for the specified date (see Figure 14.18).

Figure 14.18
Retrieve stock information.

	A	B	C
1	Symbol	Date	Average/Close
2	DELL	1/12/1994	25.3125
3	MSFT	1/30/2003	48.24
4	VFINX	1/20/2000	133.21
5	WMT	1/6/2009	56.02
6			

```
Private Sub GetQuote()
Dim ie As Object, lCharPos As Long, sHTML As String
Dim HistDate As Date, HighVal As String, LowVal As String
Dim cl As Range

Set cl = ActiveCell
HistDate = cl(, 0)

If Intersect(cl, Range("C2:C" & Cells.Rows.Count)) Is Nothing Then
    MsgBox "You must select a cell in column C."
```

```
        Exit Sub
    End If

    If Not CBool(Len(cl(, -1))) Or Not CBool(Len(cl(, 0))) Then
        MsgBox "You must enter a symbol and date."
        Exit Sub
    End If

    Set ie = CreateObject("InternetExplorer.Application")

    With ie
        .Navigate _
            http://bigcharts.marketwatch.com/historical & _
            "/default.asp?detect=1&symbol=" _
            & cl(, -1) & "&close_date=" & Month(HistDate) & "%2F" & _
            Day(HistDate) & "%2F" & Year(HistDate) & "&x=31&y=26"
        Do While .Busy And .ReadyState <> 4
            DoEvents
        Loop
        sHTML = .Document.body.innertext
        .Quit
    End With

    Set ie = Nothing

    lCharPos = InStr(1, sHTML, "High:", vbTextCompare)
    If lCharPos Then HighVal = Mid$(sHTML, lCharPos + 5, 15)

    If Not Left$(HighVal, 3) = "n/a" Then
        lCharPos = InStr(1, sHTML, "Low:", vbTextCompare)
        If lCharPos Then LowVal = Mid$(sHTML, lCharPos + 4, 15)
        cl.Value = (Val(LowVal) + Val(HighVal)) / 2
    Else: lCharPos = InStr(1, sHTML, "Closing Price:", vbTextCompare)
        cl.Value = Val(Mid$(sHTML, lCharPos + 14, 15))
    End If

    Set cl = Nothing
    End Sub
```

Using VBA Extensibility to Add Code to New Workbooks

You have a macro that moves data to a new workbook for the regional managers. What if you need to also copy macros to the new workbook? You can use Visual Basic for Application Extensibility to import modules to a workbook or to actually write lines of code to the workbook.

To use any of these examples, you must first open VB Editor, select References from the Tools menu, and select the reference for Microsoft Visual Basic for Applications Extensibility 5.3. You must also trust access to VBA by going to the Developer tab, choosing Macro Security, and checking Trust Access to the VBA Project Object Model.

The easiest way to use VBA Extensibility is to export a complete module or userform from the current project and import it to the new workbook. Perhaps you have an application with thousands of lines of code. You want to create a new workbook with data for the

14

regional manager and give her three macros to enable custom formatting and printing. Place all of these macros in a module called modToRegion. Macros in this module also call the frmRegion userform. The following code transfers this code from the current workbook to the new workbook:

```
Sub MoveDataAndMacro()
    Dim WSD as worksheet
    Set WSD = Worksheets("Report")
    ' Copy Report to a new workbook
    WSD.Copy
    ' The active workbook is now the new workbook
    ' Delete any old copy of the module from C
    On Error Resume Next
    ' Delete any stray copies from hard drive
    Kill ("C:\ModToRegion.bas")
    Kill ("C:\frmRegion.frm")
    On Error GoTo 0
    ' Export module & form from this workbook
    ThisWorkbook.VBProject.VBComponents("ModToRegion").Export _
        ("C:\ModToRegion.bas")
    ThisWorkbook.VBProject.VBComponents("frmRegion").Export _
        ("C:\frmRegion.frm")
    ' Import to new workbook
    ActiveWorkbook.VBProject.VBComponents.Import ("C:\ModToRegion.bas")
    ActiveWorkbook.VBProject.VBComponents.Import ("C:\frmRegion.frm")
    On Error Resume Next
    Kill ("C:\ModToRegion.bas")
    Kill ("C:\frmRegion.bas")
    On Error GoTo 0
End Sub
```

The preceding method will work if you need to move modules or userforms to a new workbook. However, what if you need to write some code to the Workbook_Open macro in the ThisWorkbook module? There are two tools to use. The Lines method allows you to return a particular set of code lines from a given module. The InsertLines method allows you to insert code lines to a new module.

> **CAUTION**
>
> With each call to InsertLines, you must insert a complete macro. Excel will attempt to compile the code after each call to InsertLines. If you insert lines that do not completely compile, Excel may crash with a general protection fault (GPF).

```
Sub MoveDataAndMacro()
    Dim WSD as worksheet
    Dim WBN as Workbook
    Dim WBCodeMod1 As Object, WBCodeMod2 As Object
    Set WSD = Worksheets("Report")
    ' Copy Report to a new workbook
    WSD.Copy
    ' The active workbook is now the new workbook
    Set WBN = ActiveWorkbook
    ' Copy the Workbook level Event handlers
```

14

```
        Set WBCodeMod1 = ThisWorkbook.VBProject.VBComponents("ThisWorkbook") _
          .CodeModule
        Set WBCodeMod2 = WBN.VBProject.VBComponents("ThisWorkbook").CodeModule
        WBCodeMod2.insertlines 1, WBCodeMod1.Lines(1, WBCodeMod1.countoflines)
    End Sub
```

Next Steps

Excel 2007 and Excel 2010 offer fantastic new data-visualization tools, including data bars, color scales, icon sets, and improved conditional formatting rules. In Chapter 15, "Data Visualizations and Conditional Formatting," you will learn how to automate the new tools and use VBA to invoke choices not available in the Excel user interface.

14

Data Visualizations and Conditional Formatting

15

Introduction to Data Visualizations

The data visualization tools were introduced in Excel 2007. However, Microsoft has made further improvements to these tools in Excel 2010.Data visualizations appear on a drawing layer that can hold icon sets, data bars, color scales, and now sparklines. In Excel 2010, you have new icon sets and new options for data bars. Unlike SmartArt graphics, Microsoft exposed the entire object model for the data visualization tools, so you can use VBA to add data visualizations to your reports.

→ **See** Chapter 17,"Dashboarding with Sparklines in Excel 2010,"for more information about sparklines.

Excel 2010 provides a variety of data visualizations. A description of each appears here, with an example shown in Figure 15.1:

- **Data bars**—The data bar adds an in-cell bar chart to each cell in a range. The largest numbers have the largest bars, and the smallest numbers have the smallest bars. You can control the bar color as well as the values that should receive the smallest and largest bar. New in Excel 2010, bars can be solid or a gradient. The gradient bars can have a border. In addition, negative bars can appear for the first time.

- **Color scales**—Excel applies a color to each cell from among a two- or three-color gradient. The two-color gradients are best for reports that are presented in monochrome. The three-color gradients require a presentation in color, but can represent a report in a traditional traffic light color combination of red-yellow-

IN THIS CHAPTER

Introduction to Data Visualizations............ 367

VBA Methods and Properties for Data Visualizations 368

Adding Data Bars to a Range 369

Adding Color Scales to a Range................... 374

Adding Icon Sets to a Range 375

Using Visualization Tricks........................... 378

Using Other Conditional Formatting Methods 382

green. You can control the points along the continuum where each color begins, and you can control the two or three colors.

■ **Icon sets**—Excel assigns an icon to each number. Icon sets can contain three icons such as the red, yellow, green traffic lights; four icons; or five icons such as the cell phone power bars. Excel 2010 adds the 3-stars icon set and the 4-boxes icon set. With icon sets, you can control the numeric limits for each icon, reverse the order of the icons, or choose to show only the icons.

■ **Above/below average**—Found under the top/bottom rules fly-out menu, these rules make it easy to highlight all of the cells that are above average. You can choose the formatting to apply to the cells. Note in Column G of Figure 15.1 only 30 percent of the cells are above average. Contrast with the top 50 percent in Column I.

■ **Top/bottom rules**—Excel highlights the top or bottom *n* percent of cells or highlights the top or bottom *n* cells in a range.

■ **Duplicate values**—Excel highlights any values that are repeated within a dataset. Because the Delete Duplicates command on the Data tab of the Ribbon is so destructive, you might prefer to highlight the duplicates and then intelligently decide which records to delete.

■ **Highlight cells**—The legacy conditional formatting rules such as greater than, less than, between, and text that contains are still available in Excel 2010. The powerful Formula conditions are also available, although you might have to use these less frequently with the addition of the average and top/bottom rules.

Figure 15.1

Visualizations such as data bars, color scales, icon sets, and top/bottom rules are controlled in the Excel user interface from the Conditional Formatting drop-down on the Home tab of the Ribbon.

	A	B	C	D	E	F	G	H	I	J	K	L	M
	Data Bar		Color Scale		Icon Set		Above Average		Top 50 Percent		Duplicate Values		Bottom 2
1													
2	8		8		8		8		8		8		8
3	437		437		437		437		437		437		437
4	-200		-200		-200		-200		-200		8		8
5	364		364		364		364		364		364		364
6	99		99		99		99		99		99		99
7	59		59		59		59		59		59		59
8	66		66		66		66		66		66		66
9	1211		1211		1211		1211		1211		1211		1211
10	1409		1409		1409		1409		1409		1409		1409
11	4		4		4		4		4		4		4

VBA Methods and Properties for Data Visualizations

All the data visualization settings are managed in VBA with the FormatConditions collection. Conditional formatting has been in Excel since Excel 97. In Excel 2010, Microsoft expanded the FormatConditions object to handle the new visualizations. Whereas legacy versions of Excel would use the FormatConditions.Add method, Excel 2010 offers additional methods such as AddDataBar, AddIconSetCondition, AddColorScale, AddTop10, AddAboveAverage, and AddUniqueValues.

It is possible to apply several different conditional formatting conditions to the same range. For example, you can apply a two-color color scale, an icon set, and a data bar to the same range. Excel includes a Priority property to specify which conditions should be calculated first. Methods such as SetFirstPriority and SetLastPriority ensure that a new format condition is executed before or after all others.

The StopIfTrue property works in conjunction with the Priority property. In the "Using Visualization Tricks" section, later in this chapter, you see how to use the StopIfTrue property on a dummy condition to make other formatting apply only to certain subsets of a range.

Beginning with Excel 2007, the Type property was expanded dramatically. This property was formerly a toggle between CellValue and Expression, but 13 new types were added in Excel 2007. Table 15.1 shows the valid values for the Type property. Items 3 through 17 were included in Excel 2007.

Table 15.1   Valid Types for a Format Condition

Value	Description	VBA Constant
1	Cell value	xlCellValue
2	Expression	xlExpression
3	Color scale	xlColorScale
4	Data bar	xlDatabar
5	Top 10 values	xlTop10
6	Icon set	XlIconSet
8	Unique values	xlUniqueValues
9	Text string	xlTextString
10	Blanks condition	xlBlanksCondition
11	Time period	xlTimePeriod
12	Above average condition	xlAboveAverageCondition
13	No blanks condition	xlNoBlanksCondition
16	Errors condition	xlErrorsCondition
17	No errors condition	xlNoErrorsCondition

Adding Data Bars to a Range

The Data Bar command adds an in-cell bar chart to each cell in a range. Many charting experts complained to Microsoft about problems in the Excel 2007 data bars. For this reason, Microsoft changed the data bars in Excel 2010 to address these problems.

15

In Figure 15.2, Cell C37 is new in Excel 2010. Notice that this cell, which has a value of 0, has no data bar at all. In Excel 2007, the smallest value receives a 4-pixel data bar, even if that smallest value is 0. In addition, in Excel 2010 the largest bar in the dataset typically takes up the entire width of the cell.

In Excel 2007, the data bars would end in a gradient that made it difficult to tell where the bar ended. Excel 2010 offers a border around the bar. You can choose to change the color of the border or even to remove the border as shown in Column K of the figure.

Excel 2010 also offers support for negative data bars, as shown in Column G and the data bars that run right to left as shown in Cells C43:C45 of Figure 15.2. These allow comparative histograms.

TIP   Although all of these are fine improvements, they add complexity to the VBA that is required to create data bars. In addition, you run the risk that your code will use new properties that will be incompatible with Excel 2007.

Figure 15.2
Excel 2010 offers many variations on data bars.

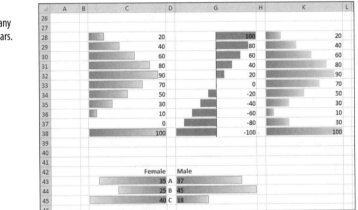

To add a data bar, you apply the `.FormatConditions.AddDataBar` method to a range containing your numbers. This method requires no arguments, and it returns an object of the `DataBar` type.

Once you add the data bar, you will most likely need to change some of its properties. One method of referring to the data bar is to assume that the recently added data bar is the last item in the collection of format conditions. This code would add a data bar, identify the data bar by counting the conditions, and then change the color:

```
Range("A2:A11").FormatConditions.AddDatabar
ThisCond = Range("A2:A11").FormatConditions.Count
With Range("A2:A11").FormatConditions(ThisCond).BarColor
```

```
      .Color = RGB(255, 0, 0) ' Red
      .TintAndShade = -0.5 ' Darker than normal
   End With
```

A safer way to go is to define an object variable of type `DataBar`. You can then assign the newly created data bar to the variable:

```
Dim DB As Databar
' Add the data bars
Set DB = Range("A2:A11").FormatConditions.AddDatabar()
' Use a red that is 25% darker
With DB.BarColor
      .Color = RGB(255, 0, 0)
      .TintAndShade = -0.25
End With
```

When specifying colors for the data bar or the border, you should use the RGB function to assign a color. You can modify the color by making it darker or lighter using the `TintAndShade` property. Valid values are from -1 to 1. A value of 0 means no modification. Positive values make the color lighter. Negative values make the color darker.

By default, Excel assigns the shortest data bar to the minimum value and the longest data bar to the maximum value. If you want to override the defaults, use the `Modify` method for either the `MinPoint` or `MaxPoint` properties. Specify a type from those shown in Table 15.2. Types 0, 3, 4, and 5 require a value. Table 15.2 shows valid types.

Table 15.2   `MinPoint` **and** `MaxPoint` **Types**

Value	Description	VBA Constant
0	Number is used.	`xlConditionNumber`
1	Lowest value from the list of values.	`xlConditionValueLowestValue`
2	Highest value from the list of values.	`xlConditionValueHighestValue`
3	Percentage is used.	`xlConditionValuePercent`
4	Formula is used.	`xlConditionValueFormula`
5	Percentile is used.	`xlConditionValuePercentile`
−1	No conditional value.	`xlConditionValueNone`

Use the following code to have the smallest bar assigned to values of 0 and below:

```
DB.MinPoint.Modify _
      Newtype:=xlConditionValueNumber, NewValue:=0
```

To have the top 20 percent of the bars have the largest bar, use this code:

```
DB.MaxPoint.Modify _
      Newtype:=xlConditionValuePercent, NewValue:=80
```

An interesting alternative is to show only the data bars and not the value. To do this, use this code:

```
DB.ShowValue = False
```

To show negative data bars in Excel 2010, use this line:

```
DB.AxisPosition = xlDataBarAxisAutomatic
```

Once you allow negative data bars, then you have the ability to specify an axis color, negative bar color, and a negative bar border color. Samples of how to change the various colors are shown in the following code that creates the data bars shown in Column C of Figure 15.3.

```
Sub DataBar2()
' Add a Data bar
' Include negative data bars
' Control the min and max point
'
    Dim DB As Databar
    With Range("C2:C11")
        .FormatConditions.Delete
        ' Add the data bars
        Set DB = .FormatConditions.AddDatabar()
    End With

    ' Set the lower limit
    DB.MinPoint.Modify newtype:=xlConditionFormula, NewValue:="-600"
    DB.MaxPoint.Modify newtype:=xlConditionValueFormula, NewValue:="600"

    ' Change the data bar to Green
    With DB.BarColor
        .Color = RGB(0, 255, 0)
        .TintAndShade = -0.15
    End With

    ' All of this is new in Excel 2010
    With DB
        ' Use a gradiant
        .BarFillType = xlDataBarFillGradient
        ' Left to Right for direction of bars
        .Direction = xlLTR
        ' Assign a different color to negative bars
        .NegativeBarFormat.ColorType = xlDataBarColor
        ' Use a border around the bars
        .BarBorder.Type = xlDataBarBorderSolid
        ' Assign a different border color to negative
        .NegativeBarFormat.BorderColorType = xlDataBarSameAsPositive
        ' All borders are solid black
        With .BarBorder.Color
            .Color = RGB(0, 0, 0)
        End With
        ' Axis where it naturally would fall, in black
        .AxisPosition = xlDataBarAxisAutomatic
        With .AxisColor
            .Color = 0
            .TintAndShade = 0
```

```
            End With
            ' Negative bars in red
            With .NegativeBarFormat.Color
                .Color = 255
                .TintAndShade = 0
            End With
            ' Negative borders in red
        End With

End Sub
```

In Excel 2010, you have a choice of showing a gradient or a solid bar. To show a solid bar, use the following:

```
DB.BarFillType = xlDataBarFillSolid
```

The following code sample produces the solid bars shown in Column E of Figure 15.3:

```
Sub DataBar3()
' Add a Data bar
' Show solid bars
' Allow negative bars
' hide the numbers, show only the data bars
'
    Dim DB As Databar
    With Range("E2:E11")
        .FormatConditions.Delete
        ' Add the data bars
        Set DB = .FormatConditions.AddDatabar()
    End With

    With DB.BarColor
        .Color = RGB(0, 0, 255)
        .TintAndShade = 0.1
    End With
    ' Hide the numbers
    DB.ShowValue = False

    ' New in Excel 2010
    DB.BarFillType = xlDataBarFillSolid
    DB.NegativeBarFormat.ColorType = xlDataBarColor
    With DB.NegativeBarFormat.Color
        .Color = 255
        .TintAndShade = 0
    End With
    ' Allow negatives
    DB.AxisPosition = xlDataBarAxisAutomatic
    ' Negative border color is different
    DB.NegativeBarFormat.BorderColorType = xlDataBarColor
    With DB.NegativeBarFormat.BorderColor
        .Color = RGB(127, 127, 0)
        .TintAndShade = 0
    End With

End Sub
```

To allow the bars to go right to left, use this code:

```
DB.Direction = xlRTL ' Right to Left
```

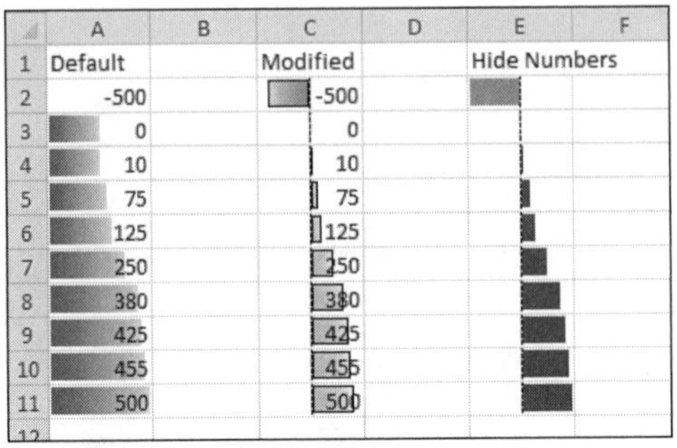

Figure 15.3
Data bars created by the macros in this section.

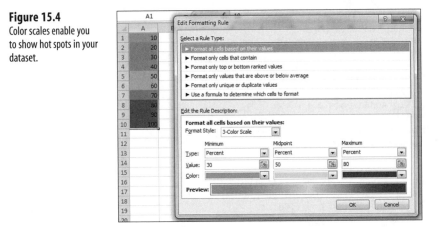

Adding Color Scales to a Range

Color scales can be added in either two-color or three-color scale varieties. Figure 15.4 shows the available settings in the Excel user interface for a color scale using three colors.

Figure 15.4
Color scales enable you to show hot spots in your dataset.

Like the data bar, a color scale is applied to a range object using the AddColorScale method. You should specify a ColorScaleType of either 2 or 3 as the only argument of the AddColorScale method.

Next, you can indicate a color and tint for both or all three of the color scale criteria. You can also specify if the shade is applied to the lowest value, highest value, a particular value, a percentage, or at a percentile using the values shown previously in Table 15.2.

The following code generates a three-color color scale in Range A1:A10:

```
Sub Add3ColorScale()
    Dim CS As ColorScale

    With Range("A1:A10")
        .FormatConditions.Delete
        ' Add the Color Scale as a 3-color scale
        Set CS = .FormatConditions.AddColorScale(ColorScaleType:=3)
    End With

    ' Format the first color as light red
    CS.ColorScaleCriteria(1).Type = xlConditionValuePercent
    CS.ColorScaleCriteria(1).Value = 30
    CS.ColorScaleCriteria(1).FormatColor.Color = RGB(255, 0, 0)
    CS.ColorScaleCriteria(1).FormatColor.TintAndShade = 0.25

    ' Format the second color as green at 50%
    CS.ColorScaleCriteria(2).Type = xlConditionValuePercent
    CS.ColorScaleCriteria(2).Value = 50
    CS.ColorScaleCriteria(2).FormatColor.Color = RGB(0, 255, 0)
    CS.ColorScaleCriteria(2).FormatColor.TintAndShade = 0

    ' Format the third color as dark blue
    CS.ColorScaleCriteria(3).Type = xlConditionValuePercent
    CS.ColorScaleCriteria(3).Value = 80
    CS.ColorScaleCriteria(3).FormatColor.Color = RGB(0, 0, 255)
    CS.ColorScaleCriteria(3).FormatColor.TintAndShade = -0.25
End Sub
```

Adding Icon Sets to a Range

Icon sets in Excel come with three, four, or five different icons in the set. Figure 15.5 shows the settings for an icon set with five different icons.

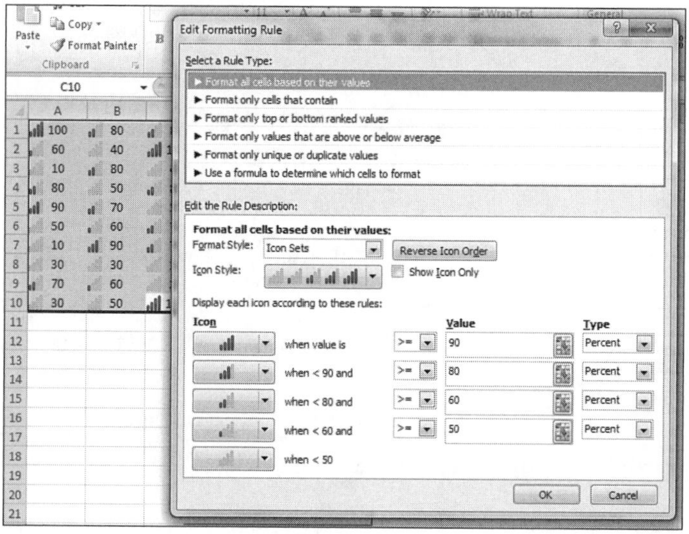

Figure 15.5
With additional icons, the complexity of the code increases.

To add an icon set to a range, use the AddIconSet method. No arguments are required. You can then adjust three properties that apply to the icon set. You then use several additional lines of code to specify the icon set in use and the limits for each icon.

Specifying an Icon Set

After adding the icon set, you can control whether the icon order is reversed, whether Excel shows only the icons, and then specify one of the 20 built-in icon sets:

```
Dim ICS As IconSetCondition
With Range("A1:C10")
    .FormatConditions.Delete
    Set ICS = .FormatConditions.AddIconSetCondition()
End With

' Global settings for the icon set
With ICS
    .ReverseOrder = False
    .ShowIconOnly = False
    .IconSet = ActiveWorkbook.IconSets(xl5CRV)
End With
```

> **NOTE** It is somewhat curious that the IconSets collection is a property of the active workbook. This seems to indicate that in future versions of Excel, new icon sets might be available.

Table 15.3 shows the complete list of icon sets.

Table 15.3   Available Icon Sets and Their VBA Constants

Icon	Value	Description	Constant
	1	3 arrows	xl3Arrows
	2	3 arrows gray	xl3ArrowsGray
	3	3 flags	xl3Flags
	4	3 traffic lights 1	xl3TrafficLights1
	5	3 traffic lights 2	xl3TrafficLights2
	6	3 signs	xl3Signs

Icon	Value	Description	Constant
	7	3 symbols	x13Symbols
	8	3 symbols 2	x13Symbols2
	9	4 arrows	x14Arrows
	10	4 arrows gray	x14ArrowsGray
	11	4 red to black	x14RedToBlack
	12	4 power bars	x14CRV
	13	4 traffic lights	x14TrafficLights
	14	5 arrows	x15Arrows
	15	5 arrows gray	x15ArrowsGray
	16	5 power bars	x15CRV
	17	5 quarters	x15Quarters
	18	3 stars	x13Stars
	19	3 Triangles	x13Triangles
	20	5 Boxes	x15Boxes

Specifying Ranges for Each Icon

After specifying the type of icon set, you can then specify ranges for each icon within the set. By default, the first icon starts at the lowest value. You can adjust the settings for each of the additional icons in the set:

```
' The first icon always starts at 0

' Settings for the second icon - start at 50%
With ICS.IconCriteria(2)
    .Type = xlConditionValuePercent
    .Value = 50
```

```
        .Operator = xlGreaterEqual
    End With
    With ICS.IconCriteria(3)
        .Type = xlConditionValuePercent
        .Value = 60
        .Operator = xlGreaterEqual
    End With
    With ICS.IconCriteria(4)
        .Type = xlConditionValuePercent
        .Value = 80
        .Operator = xlGreaterEqual
    End With
    With ICS.IconCriteria(5)
        .Type = xlConditionValuePercent
        .Value = 90
        .Operator = xlGreaterEqual
    End With
```

Valid values for the `Operator` property are `XlGreater` or `xlGreaterEqual`.

CAUTION

With VBA, it is easy to create overlapping ranges such as icon 1 from 0 to 50 and icon 2 from 30 to 90. Even though the Edit Formatting Rule dialog box will prevent overlapping ranges, VBA allows them. However, keep in mind that your icon set will display unpredictably if you create invalid ranges.

Using Visualization Tricks

If you use an icon set or a color scale, Excel applies a color to all cells in the dataset. Two tricks in this section enable you to apply an icon set to only a subset of the cells or to apply two different color data bars to the same range. The first trick is available in the user interface, but the second trick is only available in VBA.

Creating an Icon Set for a Subset of a Range

Sometimes, you might want to apply only a red X to the bad cells in a range. This is tricky to do in the user interface.

In the user interface, follow these steps to apply a red X to values greater than 80:

1. Add a three-symbols icon set to the range.
2. Specify that the symbols should be reversed.
3. Indicate that the third icon appears for values greater than 80. You now have a mix of all three icons, as shown in Figure 15.6.
4. Add a new conditional format to highlight cells less than or equal to 80. Because you don't want any icons for these values, do not specify any special formatting for the cells that match this rule.

Figure 15.6
First, add a three-icon set, paying particular attention to the value for the red X.

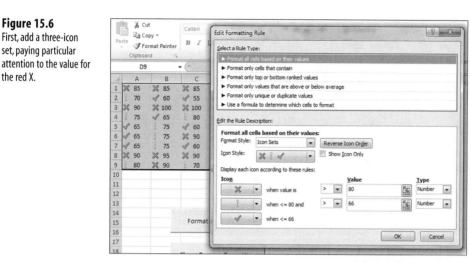

5. In the Conditional Formatting Rule Manager, indicate that Excel should stop evaluating conditions if the new condition is true. This prevents Excel from getting to the icon set rule for any cell with a value of 80 or less. The result is that only cells greater than 80 appear with a red X, as shown in Figure 15.7.

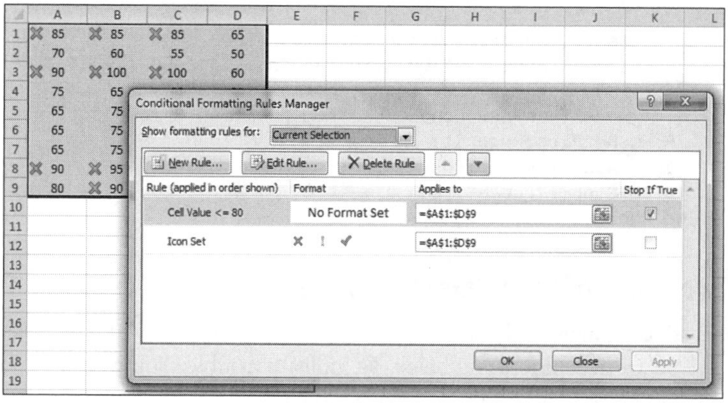

Figure 15.7
When you tell Excel to stop evaluating rules after the <=80 rule is true, Excel never has a chance to add the check mark or exclamation point to the other cells.

The code to create this effect in VBA is straightforward. A great deal of the code is spent making sure that the icon set has the red X symbols on the cells greater than 80.

You will use the FormatConditions.Add method to add the second condition. However, you need to make sure this condition is executed first. For this reason, you need to use the SetFirstPriority method to move the new condition to the top of the list. The final step is to turn on the StopIfTrue property.

The code to highlight values greater than 80 with a red X is shown here:

```
Sub TrickyFormatting()
    ' mark the bad cells
    Dim ICS As IconSetCondition
    Dim FC As FormatCondition
    With Range("A1:D9")
        .FormatConditions.Delete
        Set ICS = .FormatConditions.AddIconSetCondition()
    End With
    With ICS
        .ReverseOrder = True
        .ShowIconOnly = False
        .IconSet = ActiveWorkbook.IconSets(xl3Symbols2)
    End With
    ' The threshhold for this icon doesn't really matter,
    ' but you have to make sure that it does not overlap the 3rd icon
    With ICS.IconCriteria(2)
        .Type = xlConditionValue
        .Value = 66
        .Operator = xlGreater
    End With
    ' Make sure the red X appears for cells above 80
    With ICS.IconCriteria(3)
        .Type = xlConditionValue
        .Value = 80
        .Operator = xlGreater
    End With

    ' Next, add a condition to catch items <=80
    Set FC = Range("A1:D9").FormatConditions.Add(Type:=xlCellValue, _
        Operator:=xlLessEqual, Formula1:="=80")
    ' Move this new condition from position 2 to position 1
    FC.SetFirstPriority
    '   Add Stop if True.
    FC.StopIfTrue = True
End Sub
```

Using Two Colors of Data Bars in a Range

This trick is particularly cool because it can only be achieved with VBA. Say that values above 90 are acceptable and below 90 indicate trouble. You would like acceptable values to have a green bar and others to have a red bar.

Using VBA, you first add the green data bars. Then, without deleting the format condition, you add red data bars.

In VBA, every format condition has a Formula property that defines whether the condition is displayed for a given cell. Therefore, the trick is to write a formula that defines when the green bars are displayed. When the formula is not True, the red bars are allowed to show through.

In Figure 15.8, the effect is being applied to Range A1:D10. You need to write the formula in A1 style, as if it applies to the top-left corner of the selection. The formula needs to evaluate to True or False. Excel automatically copies the formula to all the cells in the range. The formula for this condition is =IF(A1>90,True,False).

> **TIP** The formula is evaluated relative to the current cell pointer location. Even though it is not usually necessary to select cells before adding a FormatCondition, in this case, selecting the range ensures that the formula will work.

Figure 15.8
The dark bars are red, and the lighter bars are green. VBA was used to create two overlapping data bars, and then the Formula property hid the top bars for cells below 90.

	A	B	C	D
1	92	96	81	88
2	88	84	82	99
3	99	85	92	88
4	84	84	82	84
5	90	90	82	99
6	90	80	98	88
7	81	97	81	85
8	89	89	91	93
9	81	94	88	83
10	87	82	86	85

The following code creates the two-color data bars:

```
Sub AddTwoDataBars()
    ' passing values in green, failing in red
    Dim DB As Databar
    Dim DB2 As Databar
    With Range("A1:D10")
        .FormatConditions.Delete
        ' Add a Light Green Data Bar
        Set DB = .FormatConditions.AddDatabar()

        DB.BarColor.Color = RGB(0, 255, 0)
        DB.BarColor.TintAndShade = 0.25
        ' Add a Red Data Bar
        Set DB2 = .FormatConditions.AddDatabar()
        DB2.BarColor.Color = RGB(255, 0, 0)
        ' Make the green bars only
        .Select ' Required to make the next line work
        .FormatConditions(1).Formula = "=IF(A1>90,True,False)"
        DB.Formula = "=IF(A1>90,True,False)"
        DB.MinPoint.Modify newtype:=xlConditionFormula, NewValue:="60"
        DB.MaxPoint.Modify newtype:=xlConditionValueFormula, NewValue:="100"
        DB2.MinPoint.Modify newtype:=xlConditionFormula, NewValue:="60"
        DB2.MaxPoint.Modify newtype:=xlConditionValueFormula, NewValue:="100"
    End With
End Sub
```

The Formula property works for all the conditional formats, which means you could potentially create some obnoxious combinations of data visualizations. In Figure 15.9, five different icon sets are combined in a single range. No one will be able to figure out whether a red flag is worse than a gray down arrow. Even so, this ability opens interesting combinations for those with a little creativity.

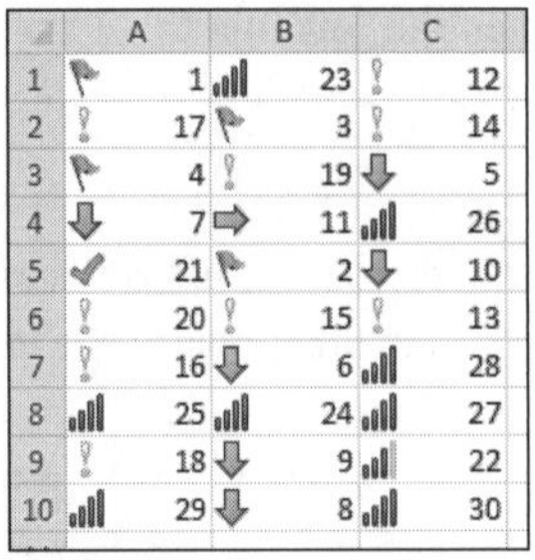

	A	B	C
1	1	23	12
2	17	3	14
3	4	19	5
4	7	11	26
5	21	2	10
6	20	15	13
7	16	6	28
8	25	24	27
9	18	9	22
10	29	8	30

Figure 15.9
VBA created this mixture of five different icon sets in a single range. The `Formula` property in VBA is the key to combining icon sets.

```
Sub AddCrazyIcons()
    With Range("A1:C10")
        .Select ' The .Formula lines below require .Select here
        .FormatConditions.Delete

        ' First icon set
        .FormatConditions.AddIconSetCondition
        .FormatConditions(1).IconSet = ActiveWorkbook.IconSets(xl3Flags)
        .FormatConditions(1).Formula = "=IF(A1<5,TRUE,FALSE)"

        ' Next icon set
        .FormatConditions.AddIconSetCondition
        .FormatConditions(2).IconSet = ActiveWorkbook.IconSets(xl3ArrowsGray)
        .FormatConditions(2).Formula = "=IF(A1<12,TRUE,FALSE)"

        ' Next icon set
        .FormatConditions.AddIconSetCondition
        .FormatConditions(3).IconSet = ActiveWorkbook.IconSets(xl3Symbols2)
        .FormatConditions(3).Formula = "=IF(A1<22,TRUE,FALSE)"

        ' Next icon set
        .FormatConditions.AddIconSetCondition
        .FormatConditions(4).IconSet = ActiveWorkbook.IconSets(xl4CRV)
        .FormatConditions(4).Formula = "=IF(A1<27,TRUE,FALSE)"

        ' Next icon set
        .FormatConditions.AddIconSetCondition
        .FormatConditions(5).IconSet = ActiveWorkbook.IconSets(xl5CRV)
    End With
End Sub
```

Using Other Conditional Formatting Methods

Although the icon sets, data bars, and color scales get most of the attention, there are still plenty of other uses for conditional formatting.

The remaining examples in this chapter show some of the prior conditional formatting rules and some of the new methods available.

Formatting Cells That Are Above or Below Average

Use the `AddAboveAverage` method to format cells that are above or below average. After adding the conditional format, specify whether the `AboveBelow` property is `xlAboveAverage` or `xlBelowAverage`.

The following two macros highlight cells above and below average:

```
Sub FormatAboveAverage()
    With Selection
        .FormatConditions.Delete
        .FormatConditions.AddAboveAverage
        .FormatConditions(1).AboveBelow = xlAboveAverage
        .FormatConditions(1).Interior.Color = RGB(255, 0, 0)
    End With
End Sub

Sub FormatBelowAverage()
    With Selection
        .FormatConditions.Delete
        .FormatConditions.AddAboveAverage
        .FormatConditions(1).AboveBelow = xlBelowAverage
        .FormatConditions(1).Interior.Color = RGB(255, 0, 0)
    End With
End Sub
```

Formatting Cells in the Top 10 or Bottom 5

Four of the choices on the Top/Bottom Rules fly-out menu are controlled with the `AddTop10` method. After you add the format condition, you need to set three properties that control how the condition is calculated:

- `TopBottom`—Set this to either `xlTop10Top` or `xlTop10Bottom`.

- `Value`—Set this to 5 for the top 5, 6 for the top 6, and so on.

- `Percent`—Set this to `False` if you want the top 10 item. Set this to `True` if you want the top 10 percent of the items.

The following code highlights top or bottom cells:

```
Sub FormatTop10Items()
    With Selection
        .FormatConditions.Delete
        .FormatConditions.AddTop10
        .FormatConditions(1).TopBottom = xlTop10Top
        .FormatConditions(1).Value = 10
        .FormatConditions(1).Percent = False
        .FormatConditions(1).Interior.Color = RGB(255, 0, 0)
    End With
End Sub

Sub FormatBottom5Items()
    With Selection
        .FormatConditions.Delete
        .FormatConditions.AddTop10
```

```
            .FormatConditions(1).TopBottom = xlTop10Bottom
            .FormatConditions(1).Value = 5
            .FormatConditions(1).Percent = False
            .FormatConditions(1).Interior.Color = RGB(255, 0, 0)
        End With
    End Sub

    Sub FormatTop12Percent()
        With Selection
            .FormatConditions.Delete
            .FormatConditions.AddTop10
            .FormatConditions(1).TopBottom = xlTop10Top
            .FormatConditions(1).Value = 12
            .FormatConditions(1).Percent = True
            .FormatConditions(1).Interior.Color = RGB(255, 0, 0)
        End With
    End Sub
```

Formatting Unique or Duplicate Cells

The Remove Duplicates command on the Data tab of the Ribbon is a destructive command. You might want to mark the duplicates without removing them. If so, the AddUniqueValues method marks the duplicate or unique cells.

After calling the method, set the DupeUnique property to either xlUnique or xlDuplicate.

As I have ranted about in *Excel 2010 In Depth* (Que, ISBN 9780789743084), I do not really like either of these options. Choosing duplicate values marks both cells that contain the duplicate, as shown in Column A of Figure 15.10. For example, both A2 and A8 are marked, when A8 is really the only duplicate value.

Choosing unique values marks only the cells that do not have a duplicate, as shown in Column B of Figure 15.10. This leaves several cells unmarked. For example, none of the cells containing 17 is marked.

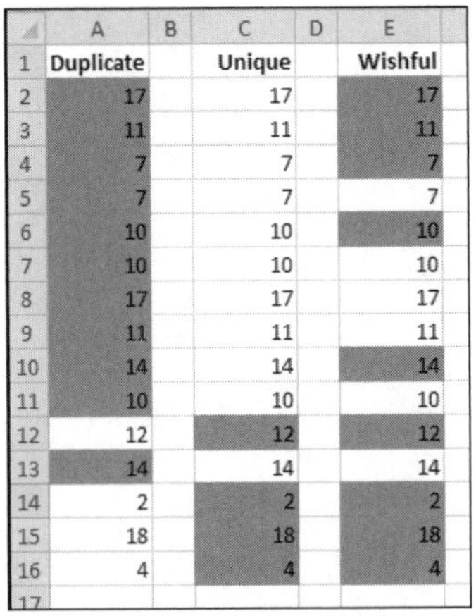

Figure 15.10
The AddUniqueValues method can mark cells such as those in Columns A and C. Unfortunately, it cannot mark the truly useful pattern in Column E.

	A	B	C	D	E
1	Duplicate		Unique		Wishful
2	17		17		17
3	11		11		11
4	7		7		7
5	7		7		7
6	10		10		10
7	10		10		10
8	17		17		17
9	11		11		11
10	14		14		14
11	10		10		10
12	12		12		12
13	14		14		14
14	2		2		2
15	18		18		18
16	4		4		4
17					

As any data analyst knows, the truly useful option would have been to mark the first unique value. In this wishful state, Excel would mark one instance of each unique value. In this case, the 17 in E2 would be marked, but any subsequent cells that contain 17 such as E8, would remain unmarked.

The code to mark duplicates or unique values is shown here:

```
Sub FormatDuplicate()
    With Selection
        .FormatConditions.Delete
        .FormatConditions.AddUniqueValues
        .FormatConditions(1).DupeUnique = xlDuplicate
        .FormatConditions(1).Interior.Color = RGB(255, 0, 0)
    End With
End Sub

Sub FormatUnique()
    With Selection
        .FormatConditions.Delete
        .FormatConditions.AddUniqueValues
        .FormatConditions(1).DupeUnique = xlUnique
        .FormatConditions(1).Interior.Color = RGB(255, 0, 0)
    End With
End Sub

Sub HighlightFirstUnique()
    With Range("E2:E16")
        .Select
        .FormatConditions.Delete
        .FormatConditions.Add Type:=xlExpression, _
            Formula1:="=COUNTIF(E$2:E2,E2)=1"
        .FormatConditions(1).Interior.Color = RGB(255, 0, 0)
    End With
End Sub
```

To see a demo of marking duplicates, search for *Excel VBA 15* at YouTube.

Formatting Cells Based on Their Value

The value conditional formats have been around for several versions of Excel. Use the Add method with the following arguments:

- Type—In this section, the type will be xlCellValue.
- Operator—Can be xlBetween, xlEqual, xlGreater, xlGreaterEqual, xlLess, xlLessEqual, xlNotBetween, xlNotEqual.
- Formula1—Formula1 is used with each of the operators specified to provide a numeric value.
- Formula2—This is used for xlBetween and xlNotBetween.

The following code sample highlights cells based on their values:

```
Sub FormatBetween10And20()
    With Selection
        .FormatConditions.Delete
        .FormatConditions.Add Type:=xlCellValue, Operator:=xlBetween, _
            Formula1:="=10", Formula2:="=20"
        .FormatConditions(1).Interior.Color = RGB(255, 0, 0)
    End With
End Sub

Sub FormatLessThan15()
    With Selection
        .FormatConditions.Delete
        .FormatConditions.Add Type:=xlCellValue, Operator:=xlLess, _
            Formula1:="=15"
        .FormatConditions(1).Interior.Color = RGB(255, 0, 0)
    End With
End Sub
```

Formatting Cells That Contain Text

When you are trying to highlight cells that contain a certain bit of text, you will use the Add method, the xlTextString type, and an operator of xlBeginsWith, xlContains, xlDoesNot-Contain, or xlEndsWith.

The following code highlights all cells that contain a capital letter *A*:

```
Sub FormatContainsA()
    With Selection
        .FormatConditions.Delete
        .FormatConditions.Add Type:=xlTextString, String:="A", _
            TextOperator:=xlContains
        ' other choices: xlBeginsWith, xlDoesNotContain, xlEndsWith
        .FormatConditions(1).Interior.Color = RGB(255, 0, 0)
    End With
End Sub
```

Formatting Cells That Contain Dates

The date conditional formats were new in Excel 2007. The list of available date operators is a subset of the date operators available in the new pivot table filters. Use the Add method, the xlTimePeriod type, and one of these DateOperator values: xlYesterday, xlToday, xlTomorrow, xlLastWeek, xlLast7Days, xlThisWeek, xlNextWeek, xlLastMonth, xlThisMonth, xlNextMonth.

The following code highlights all dates in the past week:

```
Sub FormatDatesLastWeek()
    With Selection
        .FormatConditions.Delete
        ' DateOperator choices include xlYesterday, xlToday, xlTomorrow,
        ' xlLastWeek, xlThisWeek, xlNextWeek, xlLast7Days
        ' xlLastMonth, xlThisMonth, xlNextMonth,
        .FormatConditions.Add Type:=xlTimePeriod, DateOperator:=xlLastWeek
        .FormatConditions(1).Interior.Color = RGB(255, 0, 0)
    End With
End Sub
```

Formatting Cells That Contain Blanks or Errors

Buried deep within the Excel interface are options to format cells that contain blanks, contain errors, do not contain blanks, or do not contain errors. If you use the macro recorder, Excel uses the complicated xlExpression version of conditional formatting. For example, to look for a blank, Excel will test to see whether the =LEN(TRIM(A1))=0. Instead, you can use any of these four self-explanatory types. You are not required to use any other arguments with these new types:

```
.FormatConditions.Add Type:=xlBlanksCondition
.FormatConditions.Add Type:=xlErrorsCondition
.FormatConditions.Add Type:=xlNoBlanksCondition
.FormatConditions.Add Type:=xlNoErrorsCondition
```

Using a Formula to Determine Which Cells to Format

The most powerful conditional format is still the xlExpression type. In this type, you provide a formula for the active cell that evaluates to True or False. Make sure to write the formula with relative or absolute references so that the formula will be correct when Excel copies the formula to the remaining cells in the selection.

An infinite number of conditions can be identified with a formula. Two popular conditions are shown here.

Highlight the First Unique Occurrence of Each Value in a Range

In Column A of Figure 15.11, you would like to highlight the first occurrence of each value in the column. The highlighted cells will then contain a complete list of the unique numbers found in the column.

The macro should select Cells A1:A15. The formula should be written to return a True or False value for Cell A1. Because Excel logically copies this formula to the entire range, a careful combination of relative and absolute references should be used.

The formula can use the COUNTIF function. Check to see how many times the range from A$1 to A1 contains the value A1. If the result is equal to 1, the condition is True, and the cell is highlighted. The first formula is =COUNTIF(A$1:A1,A1)=1. As the formula is copied down to, say A12, the formula changes to =COUNTIF(A$1:A12,A12)=1.

The following macro creates the formatting shown in Column A of Figure 15.11:

```
Sub HighlightFirstUnique()
    With Range("A1:A15")
        .Select
        .FormatConditions.Delete
        .FormatConditions.Add Type:=xlExpression, _
            Formula1:="=COUNTIF(A$1:A1,A1)=1"
        .FormatConditions(1).Interior.Color = RGB(255, 0, 0)
    End With
End Sub
```

Figure 15.11
A formula-based condition can mark the first unique occurrence of each value, as shown in Column A, or the entire row with the largest sales, as shown in D:F.

	D	E	F
	Region	Invoice	Sales
	West	1001	112
	East	1002	321
	Central	1003	332
	West	1004	596
	East	1005	642
	West	1006	700
	West	1007	253
	Central	1008	529
	East	1009	122
	West	1010	601
	Central	1011	460
	East	1012	878
	West	1013	763
	Central	1014	193

Highlight the Entire Row for the Largest Sales Value

Another example of a formula-based condition is when you want to highlight the entire row of a dataset in response to a value in one column. Consider the dataset in Cells D2:F15 of Figure 15.11. If you want to highlight the entire row that contains the largest sale, you select Cells D2:F15 and write a formula that works for Cell D2: =$F2=MAX($F$2:$F$15). The code required to format the row with the largest sales value is as follows:

```
Sub HighlightWholeRow()
    With Range("D2:F15")
        .Select
        .FormatConditions.Delete
        .FormatConditions.Add Type:=xlExpression, _
            Formula1:="=$F2=MAX($F$2:$F$15)"
        .FormatConditions(1).Interior.Color = RGB(255, 0, 0)
    End With
End Sub
```

Using the New NumberFormat Property

In legacy versions of Excel, a cell that matched a conditional format could have a particular font, font color, border, or fill pattern. Starting in Excel 2007, you can also specify a number format. This can prove useful for selectively changing the number format used to display the values.

For example, you might want to display numbers above 999 in thousands, numbers above 999,999 in hundred thousands, and numbers above 9 million in millions.

If you turn on the macro recorder and attempt to record setting the conditional format to a custom number format, the Excel 2007 VBA macro recorder actually records the action of executing an XL4 macro! Skip the recorded code and use the NumberFormat property as shown here:

```
Sub NumberFormat()
    With Range("E1:G26")
        .FormatConditions.Delete
```

```
    .FormatConditions.Add Type:=xlCellValue, Operator:=xlGreater, _
        Formula1:="=9999999"
    .FormatConditions(1).NumberFormat = "$#,##0,""M"""
    .FormatConditions.Add Type:=xlCellValue, Operator:=xlGreater,
        Formula1:="=999999"
    .FormatConditions(2).NumberFormat = "$#,##0.0,""M"""
    .FormatConditions.Add Type:=xlCellValue, Operator:=xlGreater,
        Formula1:="=999"
    .FormatConditions(3).NumberFormat = "$#,##0,K"
    End With
End Sub
```

Figure 15.12 shows the original numbers in Columns A:C. The results of running the macro are shown in Columns E:G. The dialog box shows the resulting conditional format rules.

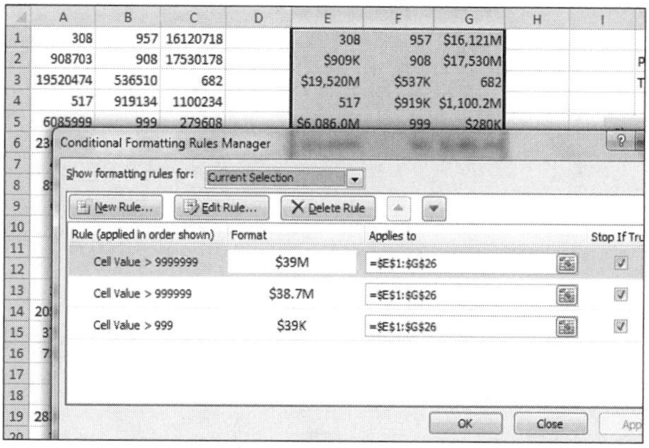

Figure 15.12
Since Excel 2007, conditional formats can specify a specific number format.

Next Steps

In Chapter 16, "Reading from and Writing to the Web," you learn how to use web queries to import data from the Internet to your Excel applications automatically.

Reading from and Writing to the Web

16

The Internet has become pervasive and has changed our lives. From your desktop, millions of answers are available at your fingertips. In addition, publishing a report on the Web allows millions of others to instantly access your information.

This chapter discusses automated ways to pull data from the Web into spreadsheets, using web queries. You will learn how to use VBA to call a website repeatedly to gather information for many data points. It also shows how to save data from your spreadsheet directly to the Web.

IN THIS CHAPTER

Getting Data from the Web.........................391

Using `Application.OnTime` to Periodically Analyze Data...399

Publishing Data to a Web Page..................404

Getting Data from the Web

There is an endless variety of data on the Internet. You can gather stock quotes from Quotes.com. You can download historical temperatures from weather underground. You can get fantasy football stats from NFL.com. Whatever your interest, there is probably a website somewhere with that information online.

Sometimes the websites make it difficult by putting the information on many different pages. You can use VBA to automate the process of visiting all those pages and collecting the data.

Instead of manually downloading data from a website every day and then importing it into Excel, you can use the Web Query feature in Excel to allow it to automatically retrieve the data from a web page.

Web queries can be set up to refresh the data from the Web every day or even every minute. While they were originally fairly hard to define, the Excel user interface now includes a web browser that you can use to build the web query.

As Web 2.0 evolves, there are some sites that are not suitable for web queries. You want to look for web pages where the URL tells you about the selections that you made while getting to that page.

For example, I searched for NFL stats. In the process of getting to an interesting page, I had asked for 2008 regular season data. I had asked for passing stats and then the complete list. I ended up at a page with a very long URL, as follows:

```
http://www.nfl.com/stats/categorystats?tabSeq=0&statisticCategory=PASSING&co
nference=null&season=2008&seasonType=REG&d-447263-s=PASSING_YARDS&d-447263-
o=2&d-447263-n=1
```

This looks like an excellent candidate for web queries because all of my choices are embedded in that URL. I can see 2008, REG, PASSING YARDS in the URL.

Go to the address bar, change 2008 to 2007, and press Enter. If the correct page comes up with 2007 passing yards, you know that you have a winner.

Another example: Suppose you wanted currency exchange rates from XE.com. On the XE.com page, you specify 100, CAD for Canadian dollars and USD for U.S. dollars. Click Go. The URL of the returned page is http://www.xe.com/ucc/convert.cgi?Amount=100&From=CAD&To=USD. You can see how you can alter this URL by changing USD to GBP to get British pounds.

In contrast, take a look at http://www.Easy-XL.com. There are several videos that you can watch there. As you navigate to each video, the URL stays exactly the same:

```
http://www.easy-xl.com/iaplayer.cgi?v=Query&x=play&p=ez%2Fvideos&i=ezVideos.
csv
```

There is nothing in that URL which tells you which video you chose. The site is using some Web 2.0 magic via java to serve up the correct video. A site built like this is not ideal for web queries.

Manually Creating a Web Query and Refreshing with VBA

The easiest way to get started with web queries is to create your first one manually while the macro recorder is running.

Excel 2010 includes the PowerPivot add-in that allows you to mash-up disparate datasets. One of the favorite demo applications is to mash up daily sales data from a store with daily weather for that city. You probably already have daily sales data for your stores. The hard part is finding daily weather data.

The Weather Underground website has a historical weather query. After browsing to find the data for the Akron Canton airport (code = CAK) for June 16, 2006, you will have this URL:

```
http://www.wunderground.com/history/airport/KCAK/2006/6/16/DailyHistory.html
```

You can see all the variables in the URL; the airport code of CAK and the date from which you need the weather, albeit in a bizarre format of YYYY/M/D.

Open Excel. Go to a blank worksheet. Rather than leave the cellpointer in A1, move down to about Cell A10 to leave room for some work variables later.

Turn on the macro recorder. Record a new macro called WeatherQuery. From the Data tab of the Ribbon, select Get External Data, from Web. Excel shows the New Web Query dialog with your Internet Explorer home page displayed.

Using the browser, go to your desired website. Make the selections necessary to get the data. In the case of Weather Underground, select history, the city, the date, and click Go. In a moment, the desired web page will display in the dialog box.

Note that in addition to the web page there are a number of yellow squares with a black arrow. These squares are in the upper-left corner of various tables on the web page. Click the square that contains the data that you want to import to Excel. In this case, you want the weather information. As shown in Figure 16.1, click the square by the weather. While you are clicking, a blue border confirms the table that will be imported. After you click, the yellow arrow changes to a green check mark.

Click the Import button on the New Web Query dialog. Click OK on the Import Data dialog. In a few seconds, you will see the live data imported into a range on your spreadsheet. Because you import the entire section of the web page, there will be the data that you want as well as extraneous data. In Figure 16.2, you will see that I've manually highlighted the statistics that I think would be relevant in northeastern Ohio. If you live in Maui or Trinidad, you might not care about snowfall. Figure 16.2 shows the returned web query.

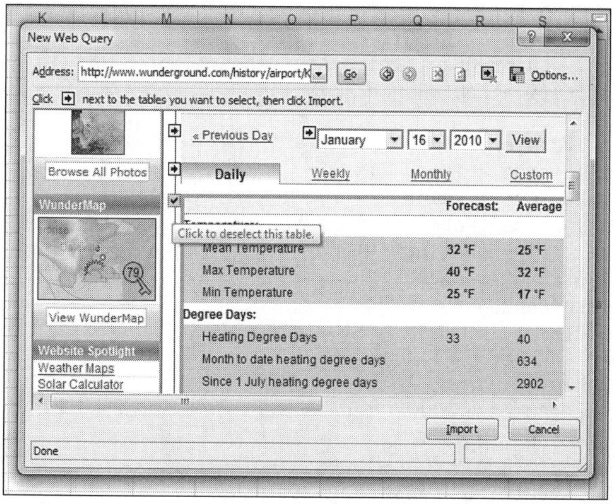

Figure 16.1
Use the New Web Query dialog to browse to a web page. Highlight the table that you want to import to Excel by clicking on a yellow arrow adjacent to the table.

Figure 16.2
Data from the web page is automatically copied to your worksheet. You can now use VBA to automatically refresh this data at your command or periodically.

	A	B	C	D
10		Actual:	Average :	Record :
11	Temperature:			
12	Mean Temperature	33 °F	25 °F	
13	Max Temperature	43 °F	32 °F	55 °F (1953)
14	Min Temperature	23 °F	17 °F	-16 °F (1982)
15	Degree Days:			
16	Heating Degree Days	32	40	
17	Month to date heating degree days	429	634	
18	Since 1 July heating degree days	2701	2902	
19	Cooling Degree Days	0	0	
20	Month to date cooling degree days	0	0	
21	Year to date cooling degree days	0	0	
22	Moisture:			
23	Dew Point	17 °F		
24	Average Humidity	57		
25	Maximum Humidity	81		
26	Minimum Humidity	33		
27	Precipitation:			
28	Precipitation	0.00 in	0.08 in	- ()
29	Month to date precipitation	1.66	1.28	
30	Year to date precipitation	1.66	1.28	
31	Snow:			
32	Snow	0.00 in	0.50 in	- ()
33	Month to date snowfall	1.6	6.9	
34	Since 1 July snowfall	18	20.7	

The recorded macro:

```
Sub WeatherQuery()
'
' WeatherQuery Macro
'
    CS = " URL;http://www.wunderground.com/history/airport/KCAK/"
    CS = CS & "2006/6/16/DailyHistory.html"
    With ActiveSheet.QueryTables.Add(Connection:= _
        CS, Destination:=Range("A10"))
        .Name = _
        "DailyHistory.html"
        .FieldNames = True
        .RowNumbers = False
        .FillAdjacentFormulas = False
        .PreserveFormatting = True
        .RefreshOnFileOpen = False
        .BackgroundQuery = True
        .RefreshStyle = xlInsertDeleteCells
        .SavePassword = False
        .SaveData = True
        .AdjustColumnWidth = True
        .RefreshPeriod = 0
        .WebSelectionType = xlSpecifiedTables
        .WebFormatting = xlWebFormattingNone
        .WebTables = "11"
        .WebPreFormattedTextToColumns = True
        .WebConsecutiveDelimitersAsOne = True
        .WebSingleBlockTextImport = False
        .WebDisableDateRecognition = False
        .WebDisableRedirections = False
        .Refresh BackgroundQuery:=False
    End With
End Sub
```

The important parts of this macro are the connect string, the location of the data returned from the web query, the web table, and the `Refresh BackgroundQuery:=False`.

The connect string is the URL that you found in the address bar of Internet Explorer (preceded by URL:).

The output location for the web query is specified in the destination property.

Setting Background Query to False means that the macro will not proceed until the data comes back from the web page. This is the appropriate setting. You macro might go on to pull certain pieces of data from the results. If you allowed the query to run in the background, the macro would be pulling from a blank web page.

In the recorded code, you will see WebTables as 11. This means that when you select the check box for the weather table, it happened to be the 11th table on the web page. The best way to figure out this table number is to record a macro and have the macro recorder tell you the table number that corresponds to the check box that you selected.

> **CAUTION**
>
> If web query macros are going to break over time, it will be because of a website redesign. If the web owner decides to ad a new advertising box at the top of the website, it might move the good data from table #11 to table #12. If you are designing a web query that will be run once a day for the next five years, you should add some code to make sure that you are actually getting the correct data.

In this example, if the word *Actual* does not appear in Cell B10, stop the macro and alert someone:

```
If Not Range("B10") = "Actual" then
    MsgBox "It looks like the underlying website changed. Call Bill at " _
        & "ext 1234. It should only take a few minutes to fix up the " _
        & "macro and have you on your way."
    Exit Sub
End Sub
```

Using VBA to Update an Existing Web Query

To update all web queries on the current sheet, use this code:

```
Sub RefreshAllWebQueries()
    Dim QT As QueryTable
    For Each QT In ActiveSheet.QueryTables
        Application.StatusBar = "Refreshing " & QT.Connection
        QT.Refresh
    Next QT
    Application.StatusBar = False
End Sub
```

You can assign this macro to a hot key or to a macro button and refresh all queries on demand.

Building Many Web Queries with VBA

To gather weather data for 24 months, you have to repeat the web query process more than 700 times. This would be tedious to do manually.

Instead, you can use VBA to build and execute the web queries. It is fairly simple to build a web query on-the-fly. The connect string to get weather for any airport for any day can be broken down into four parts.

The first part can be hard-coded because it never changes:

```
"URL;http://www.wunderground.com/history/airport/K"
```

The next part is the 3-letter airport code. If you are retrieving data for many cities, this part will change:

```
CAK
```

The third part is a slash, the date in YYYY/M/D format and a slash:

```
/2006/6/16/
```

The final part can be hard-coded:

```
DailyHistory.html"
```

Insert a new worksheet and build an output table. In Cell A2, enter the first date for which you have sales history. Use the fill handle to drag the dates down to the current date.

The formula in B2 is `="/"&Text(A2,"YYYY/M/D")&"/"`.

Add friendly headings across Row 1 for the statistics that you will collect.

The data worksheet is shown in Figure 16.3.

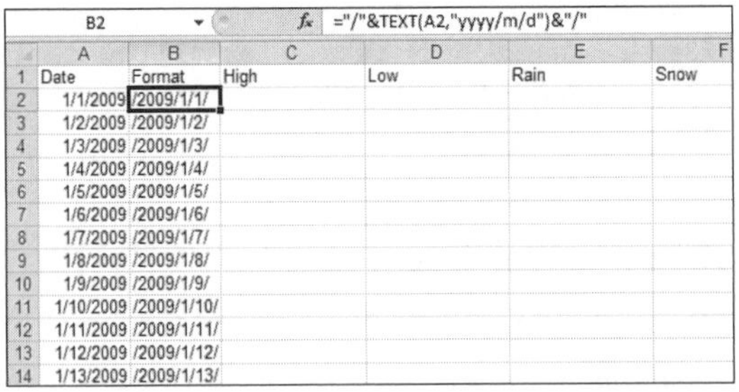

B2 fx ="/"&TEXT(A2,"yyyy/m/d")&"/"

	A	B	C	D	E	F
1	Date	Format	High	Low	Rain	Snow
2	1/1/2009	/2009/1/1/				
3	1/2/2009	/2009/1/2/				
4	1/3/2009	/2009/1/3/				
5	1/4/2009	/2009/1/4/				
6	1/5/2009	/2009/1/5/				
7	1/6/2009	/2009/1/6/				
8	1/7/2009	/2009/1/7/				
9	1/8/2009	/2009/1/8/				
10	1/9/2009	/2009/1/9/				
11	1/10/2009	/2009/1/10/				
12	1/11/2009	/2009/1/11/				
13	1/12/2009	/2009/1/12/				
14	1/13/2009	/2009/1/13/				

Figure 16.3
Build a data worksheet to hold the results of the web query.

Finding Results from Retrieved Data

Next, you have a decision to make. It looks like the weather underground website is fairly static. The snow statistic even shows up if I ask for JHM airport in Maui. If you are positive that rainfall is always going to appear in Cell B28 of your results sheet, you could write the macro to get data from there.

However, to be safe, you can build some VLOOKUP formulas at the top of the worksheet to look for certain row labels and to pull that data. In Figure 16.4, 7 VLOOKUP formulas in A2:G2 grab the necessary statistics from the web query.

> **NOTE**
>
> The variable web location of the web data happens more often than you might think. If you are pulling name and address information, some addresses have three lines and some have four lines. Anything that appears after that address might be off by a row. Some stock quote sites show a different version of the data depending on whether the market is open or closed. If you kick off a series of web queries at 3:45 p.m., the macro might work until 4 p.m. and then stop working. For these reasons, it is often safer to take the extra steps of retrieving the correct data from the web query using VLOOKUP statements.

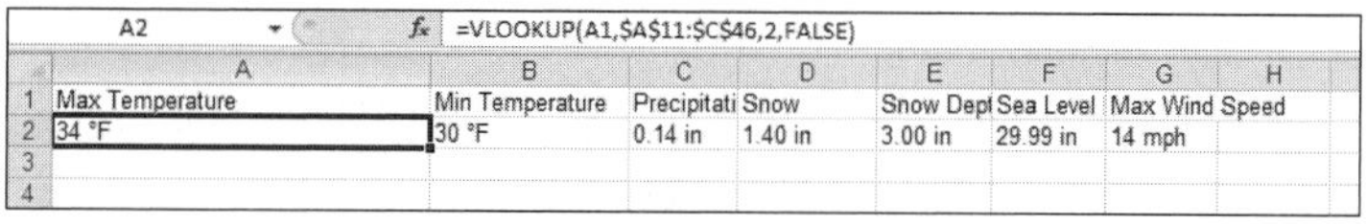

Figure 16.4

VLOOKUPs at the top of the web worksheet find and pull the relevant data from a web page.

To build the macro, you will add some code before the recorded code:

```
Dim WSD as worksheet
Dim WSW as worksheet
Set WSD = Worksheets("Data")
Set WSW = Worksheets("Web")
FinalRow = WSD.Cells(Rows.Count, 1).End(xlUp).Row
```

Then add a loop to go through all of the dates in the data worksheet.

```
For I = 2 to FinalRow
    ThisDate = WSD.Cells(I, 2).value
    ' Build the ConnectString
    CS = "URL: URL;http://www.wunderground.com/history/airport/KCAK
    CS = CS & ThisDate & "DailyHistory.html"
```

If a web query is about to overwrite existing data on the worksheet, it will move that data to the right. You want to clear the previous web query and all of the contents:

```
For Each qt In WSD.QueryTables
    qt.Delete
Next qt
WSD.Range("A10:A100").EntireRow.Clear
```

You can now go into the recorded code. Change the QueryTables.Add line to the following:

```
With WSD.QueryTables.Add(Connection:= CS, Destination:=WSW.Range("A10"))
```

After the recorded code, add some lines to calculate the VLOOKUPs, copy the results, and finish the loop:

```
WSW.Calculate
WSD.Cells(I, 3).Resize(1, 7).Value = WSW.Range("A2:G2").Value
Next i
```

Step through the code as it goes through the first loop to make sure that everything is working. You should notice that the actual `.Refresh` line takes about 5 to 10 seconds. To gather 2 or 3 years' worth of web pages, it will require more than an hour of processing time. Run the macro, head to lunch, and then come back to a good dataset.

Putting It All Together

In the final macro here, I turned off screen updating and showed the row number that the macro is processing in the status bar. I also deleted some unnecessary properties from the recorded code:

```
Sub GetData()
'
' GetData Macro
'


'
Dim WSD As Worksheet
Dim WSW As Worksheet
Dim qt As QueryTable
    Set WSD = Worksheets("Data")
    Set WSW = Worksheets("Web")
    FinalRow = WSD.Cells(Rows.Count, 1).End(xlUp).Row

For i = 2 To FinalRow
    Application.StatusBar = i
    Application.ScreenUpdating = False
    For Each qt In WSW.QueryTables
        qt.Delete
    Next qt
    WSW.Range("A10:A100").EntireRow.Clear
    CS = "URL;http://www.wunderground.com/history/airport/KCAK" _
        & WSD.Cells(i, 2).Value & "DailyHistory.html"

    With WSW.QueryTables.Add(Connection:=CS, Destination:=WSW.[A10])
        .Name = "DailyHistory"
        .FieldNames = True
        .BackgroundQuery = True
        .WebSelectionType = xlSpecifiedTables
        .WebFormatting = xlWebFormattingNone
        .WebTables = "10"
        .Refresh BackgroundQuery:=False
    End With

    WSW.Calculate

    ' Save the results from this query
    WSD.Cells(i, 3).Resize(1, 7).Value = WSW.Range("A2:G2").Value

Next i
End Sub
```

After an hour, you will have data retrieved from hundreds of web pages (see Figure 16.5).

Figure 16.5
The results of running
the web query hundreds
of times.

	A	B	C	D	E	F	G	H	I
1	Date	Format	High	Low	Rain	Snow	Snow Depth	Pressure	Max Wind
23	1/22/2009	/2009/1/22/	34 °F	15 °F	0.00 in	0.00 in	6.00 in	30.00 in	18 mph
24	1/23/2009	/2009/1/23/	43 °F	23 °F	0.00 in	0.00 in	6.00 in	29.88 in	26 mph
25	1/24/2009	/2009/1/24/	28 °F	5 °F	0.04 in	0.80 in	4.00 in	30.23 in	20 mph
26	1/25/2009	/2009/1/25/	15 °F	3 °F	0.07 in	1.10 in	4.00 in	30.35 in	13 mph
27	1/26/2009	/2009/1/26/	21 °F	3 °F	0.00 in	0.00 in	4.00 in	30.43 in	8 mph
28	1/27/2009	/2009/1/27/	23 °F	17 °F	0.15 in	1.50 in	4.00 in	30.26 in	13 mph
29	1/28/2009	/2009/1/28/	30 °F	10 °F	0.85 in	7.10 in	6.00 in	29.81 in	22 mph
30	1/29/2009	/2009/1/29/	24 °F	8 °F	T in	0.20 in	9.00 in	29.99 in	21 mph
31	1/30/2009	/2009/1/30/	25 °F	8 °F	0.02 in	0.40 in	9.00 in	29.94 in	26 mph
32	1/31/2009	/2009/1/31/	27 °F	1 °F	T in	T in	8.00 in	30.03 in	23 mph

Examples of Scraping Websites Using Web Queries

Over the years, I have used the web query trick many times. Examples include the
following:

- Names and company address for all Fortune 1000 CFOs so that I could pitch my
  Power Excel seminars to them.

- The complete membership roster for a publishing association of which I am a member.
  (I already had the printed roster, but with an electronic database, I could filter to find
  publishers in certain cities).

- The complete list of Chipotle restaurants (which later ended up in my GPS, but that is
  a story for the (yet unwritten) Microsoft MapPoint book).

Using Application.OnTime to Periodically Analyze Data

VBA offers the OnTime method for running any VBA procedure at a specific time of day or
after a specific amount of time has passed.

You can write a macro that would capture data every hour throughout the day. This macro
would have times hard-coded. The following code will, theoretically, capture data from a
website every hour throughout the day:

```
Sub ScheduleTheDay()
    Application.OnTime EarliestTime:=TimeValue("8:00 AM"), _
        Procedure:=CaptureData
    Application.OnTime EarliestTime:=TimeValue("9:00 AM"), _
        Procedure:=CaptureData
    Application.OnTime EarliestTime:=TimeValue("10:00 AM"), _
        Procedure:=CaptureData
    Application.OnTime EarliestTime:=TimeValue("11:00 AM"), _
        Procedure:=CaptureData
    Application.OnTime EarliestTime:=TimeValue("12:00 AM"), _
        Procedure:=CaptureData
    Application.OnTime EarliestTime:=TimeValue("1:00 PM"), _
        Procedure:=CaptureData
    Application.OnTime EarliestTime:=TimeValue("2:00 PM"), _
        Procedure:=CaptureData
    Application.OnTime EarliestTime:=TimeValue("3:00 PM"), _
        Procedure:=CaptureData
```

16

```
        Application.OnTime EarliestTime:=TimeValue("4:00 PM"), _
            Procedure:=CaptureData
        Application.OnTime EarliestTime:=TimeValue("5:00 PM"), _
            Procedure:=CaptureData
    End Sub

    Sub CaptureData()
        Dim WSQ As Worksheet
        Dim NextRow As Long
        Set WSQ = Worksheets("MyQuery")
        ' Refresh the web query
        WSQ.Range("A2").QueryTable.Refresh BackgroundQuery:=False
        ' Make sure the data is updated
        Application.Wait (Now + TimeValue("0:00:10"))
        ' Copy the web query results to a new row
        NextRow = WSQ.Cells(Rows.Count, 1).End(xlUp).Row + 1
        WSQ.Range("A2:B2").Copy WSQ.Cells(NextRow, 1)
    End Sub
```

Scheduled Procedures Require Ready Mode

The OnTime method will run provided only that Excel is in Ready, Copy, Cut, or Find mode at the prescribed time. If you start to edit a cell at 7:59:55 a.m. and keep that cell in Edit mode, Excel cannot run the CaptureData macro at 8:00 a.m. as directed.

In the preceding code example, I specified only the start time for the procedure to run. Excel waits anxiously until the spreadsheet is returned to Ready mode and then runs the scheduled program as soon as it can.

The classic example is that you start to edit a cell at 7:59 a.m., and then your manager walks in and asks you to attend a surprise staff meeting down the hall. If you leave your spreadsheet in Edit mode and attend the staff meeting until 10:30 a.m., the program cannot run the first three scheduled hours of updates. As soon as you return to your desk and press Enter to exit Edit mode, the program runs all previously scheduled tasks. In the preceding code, you will find that the first three scheduled updates of the program all happen between 10:30 and 10:31 a.m.

Specifying a Window of Time for an Update

One alternative is to provide Excel with a window of time within which to make the update. The following code tells Excel to run the update at anytime between 8:00 a.m. and 8:05 a.m. If the Excel session remains in Edit mode for the entire five minutes, the scheduled task is skipped:

```
    Application.OnTime EarliestTime:=TimeValue("8:00 AM"), Procedure:=CaptureData,
        LatestTime:=TimeValue("8:05 AM")
```

Canceling a Previously Scheduled Macro

It is fairly difficult to cancel a previously scheduled macro. You must know the exact time that the macro is scheduled to run. To cancel a pending operation, call the OnTime method again, using the `Schedule:=False` parameter to unschedule the event. The following code cancels the 11:00 a.m. run of CaptureData:

```
Sub CancelEleven()
Application.OnTime EarliestTime:=TimeValue("11:00 AM"), _
    Procedure:=CaptureData, Schedule:=False
End Sub
```

It is interesting to note that the OnTime schedules are remembered by a running instance of Excel. If you keep Excel open but close the workbook with the scheduled procedure, it still runs. Consider this hypothetical series of events:

1. Open Excel at 7:30 a.m.
2. Open Schedule.XLS and run a macro to schedule a procedure at 8:00 a.m.
3. Close Schedule.xls but keep Excel open.
4. Open a new workbook and begin entering data.

At 8:00 a.m., Excel reopens Schedule.xls and runs the scheduled macro. Excel doesn't close Schedule.xls. As you can imagine, this is fairly annoying and alarming if you are not expecting it. If you are going to make extensive use of `Application.Ontime`, you might want to have it running in one instance of Excel while you work in a second instance of Excel.

> **NOTE** If you are using a macro to schedule a macro a certain amount of time in the future from the current time, you could remember the time in an out-of-the way cell to be able to cancel the update. See an example in the "Scheduling a Macro to Run x Minutes in the Future" section of this chapter.

Closing Excel Cancels All Pending Scheduled Macros

If you close Excel with File, Exit, all future scheduled macros are automatically canceled. When you have a macro that has scheduled a bunch of macros at indeterminate times, closing Excel is the only way to prevent the macros from running.

Scheduling a Macro to Run x Minutes in the Future

You can schedule a macro to run at a time at a certain point in the future. The macro uses the TIME function to return the current time and adds 2 minutes and 30 seconds to the time. The following macro runs something 2 minutes and 30 seconds from now:

```
Sub ScheduleAnything()
    ' This macro can be used to schedule anything
    WaitHours = 0
    WaitMin = 2
    WaitSec = 30
    NameOfScheduledProc = "CaptureData"
    ' --- End of Input Section -------
```

```
' Determine the next time this should run
NextTime = Time + TimeSerial(WaitHours, WaitMin, WaitSec)

' Schedule ThisProcedure to run then
Application.OnTime EarliestTime:=NextTime, Procedure:=NameOfScheduledProc

End Sub
```

Later, if you need to cancel this scheduled event, it would be nearly impossible. You won't know the exact time that the macro grabbed the TIME function. You might try to save this value in an out-of-the-way cell:

```
Sub ScheduleWithCancelOption
    NameOfScheduledProc = "CaptureData"

    ' Determine the next time this should run
    NextTime = Time + TimeSerial(0,2,30)
    Range("ZZ1").Value = NextTime

    ' Schedule ThisProcedure to run then
    Application.OnTime EarliestTime:=NextTime, Procedure:=NameOfScheduledProc

End Sub

Sub CancelLater()
        NextTime = Range("ZZ1").value
        Application.OnTime EarliestTime:=NextTime, _
    Procedure:=CaptureData, Schedule:=False
End Sub
```

Scheduling a Verbal Reminder

The text to speech tools in Excel can be fun. The following macro sets up a schedule that will remind you when it is time to go to the staff meeting:

```
Sub ScheduleSpeak()
    Application.OnTime EarliestTime:=TimeValue("9:14 AM"), _
        Procedure:="RemindMe"
End Sub

Sub RemindMe()
    Application.Speech.Speak Text:="Bill. It is time for the staff meeting."
End Sub
```

If you want to pull a prank on your manager, you can schedule Excel to automatically turn on the Speak on Enter feature. Follow this scenario:

1. Tell your manager that you are taking him out to lunch to celebrate April 1.

2. At some point in the morning, while your manager is getting coffee, run the ScheduleSpeech macro. Design the macro to run 15 minutes after your lunch starts.

3. Take your manager to lunch.

4. While the manager is away, the scheduled macro will run.

5. When the manager returns and starts typing data in Excel, the computer will repeat the cells as they are entered. This is slightly reminiscent of the computer on *Star Trek* that repeated everything that Lieutenant Uhura would say.

After this starts happening, you can pretend to be innocent; after all, you have a firm alibi for when the prank began to happen:

```
Sub ScheduleSpeech()
    Application.OnTime EarliestTime:=TimeValue("12:15 PM"), _
        Procedure:="SetUpSpeech"
End Sub

Sub SetupSpeech())
    Application.Speech.SpeakCellOnEnter = True
End Sub
```

> NOTE To turn off Speak on Enter, you can either dig out the button from the QAT Customization panel (look in the category called Commands Not on the Ribbon) or, if you can run some VBA, change the SetupSpeech macro to change the True to False.

Scheduling a Macro to Run Every 2 Minutes

My favorite method is to ask Excel to run a certain macro every 2 minutes. However, I realize that if a macro gets delayed because I accidentally left the workbook in Edit mode while going to the staff meeting, I don't want dozens of updates to happen in a matter of seconds.

The easy solution is to have the `ScheduleAnything` procedure recursively schedule itself to run again in 2 minutes. The following code schedules a run in 2 minutes and then performs CaptureData:

```
Sub ScheduleAnything()
    ' This macro can be used to schedule anything
    ' Enter how often you want to run the macro in hours and minutes
    WaitHours = 0
    WaitMin = 2
    WaitSec = 0
    NameOfThisProcedure = "ScheduleAnything"
    NameOfScheduledProc = "CaptureData"
    ' --- End of Input Section -------

    ' Determine the next time this should run
    NextTime = Time + TimeSerial(WaitHours, WaitMin, WaitSec)

    ' Schedule ThisProcedure to run then
    Application.OnTime EarliestTime:=NextTime, Procedure:=NameOfThisProcedure

    ' Get the Data
    Application.Run NameOfScheduledProc

End Sub
```

This method has some advantages. I have not scheduled a million updates in the future. I have only one future update scheduled at any given time. Therefore, if I decide that I am tired of seeing the national debt every 15 seconds, I only need to comment out the `Application.OnTime` line of code and wait 15 seconds for the last update to happen.

Publishing Data to a Web Page

This chapter has highlighted many ways to capture data from the Web. It is also useful for publishing Excel data back to the Web.

In Chapter 14, "Excel Power," the RunReportForEachCustomer macro was able to produce reports for each customer in a company. Instead of printing and faxing the report, it would be cool to save the Excel file as HTML and post the results on a company intranet so that the customer service reps could instantly access the latest version of the report.

Consider a report like the one shown in Figure 16.6. With the Excel user interface, it is easy to use save the report as a web page to create an HTML view of the data.

Figure 16.6

A macro from Chapter 14 was used to automatically generate this Excel workbook. Rather than e-mail the report, we could save it as a web page and post it on the company intranet.

	A	B	C	D	E
1	**Report of Sales to DEF, LLC**				
2					
3	Date	Quantity	Product	Revenue	
4	8/29/2011	1000	XYZ	25350	
5	9/29/2011	1000	XYZ	25080	
6	11/19/2011	1000	XYZ	24070	
7	9/25/2011	1000	XYZ	23990	
8	7/17/2011	1000	XYZ	22530	

In Excel 2010, use File, Save As. Select Web Page (*.htm, *html) in the Save as Type dropdown (see Figure 16.7).

> **NOTE**
> The Excel 2003 option to add interactivity to a web page has been deprecated and is no longer available.

After Microsoft removed the interactivity option, you only have control over the title that appears in the window title bar. Annoyingly, in Excel 2010, this title also gets written to the top center of your web page.

Click the Change Title button to change the <Title> tag for the web page. Type a name that ends in either .html or .html and click Publish.

Figure 16.7
When saving as a web page, you can control the file name and a title.

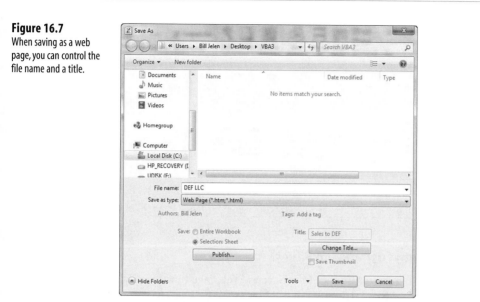

The result is a file that can be viewed in any web browser. The web page accurately shows our number formats and font sizes (see Figure 16.8).

Where the macro from Chapter 14 did `WBN.SaveAs`, the new macro uses this code to write out each web page:

```
HTMLFN = "C:\Intranet\" & ThisCust & ".html"
On Error Resume Next
Kill HTMLFN
On Error GoTo 0
With WBN.PublishObjects.Add( _
    SourceType:=xlSourceSheet, _
    Filename:=HTMLFN, _
    Sheet:="Sheet1", _
    Source:="", _
    HtmlType:=xlHtmlStatic, _
    DivID:="A", _
    Title:="Sales to " & ThisCust)
    .Publish True
    .AutoRepublish = False
End With
```

Although the data is accurately presented in Figure 16.8, it is not extremely fancy. We don't have a company logo or navigation bar to examine other reports.

Figure 16.8
The formatting is close to the original worksheet.

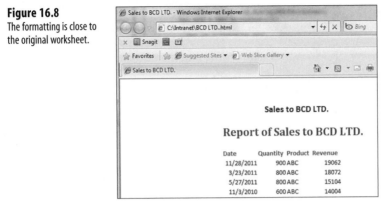

Using VBA to Create Custom Web Pages

Long before Microsoft introduced the Save as Web Page functionality, people had been using VBA to take Excel data and publish it as HTML. The advantage of this method is that you can write out specific HTML statements to display company logos and navigation bars.

Consider a typical web page template:

- There is code to display a logo and navigation bar at the top/side.
- There is content for the page.
- There is some HTML code to finish the page.

This macro will read the code behind a web page and write it to Excel:

```
Sub ImportHTML()
    ThisFile = "C:\Intranet\schedule.html"
    Open ThisFile For Input As #1
    Ctr = 2
    Do
        Line Input #1, Data
        Worksheets("HTML").Cells(Ctr, 2).Value = Data
        Ctr = Ctr + 1
    Loop While EOF(1) = False
    Close #1
End Sub
```

If you import the text of a web page into Excel, even if you don't understand the HTML involved, you can probably find the first lines that contain your page content.

Examine the HTML code in Excel. Copy the lines needed to draw the top part of the web page to a worksheet called Top. Copy the lines of code needed to close the web page to a worksheet called Bottom.

You can use VBA to write out the top, then generate content from your worksheet, and then write out the bottom.

Using Excel as a Content Management System

Five hundred million people are proficient in Excel. Companies everywhere have data in Excel, and many staffers who are comfortable in maintaining that data. Rather than force these people to learn how to create HTML pages, why not build a content management system to take their Excel data and write out custom web pages?

You probably already have data for the web page in Excel. Using the HTML to read the HTML into Excel from above, you know the top and bottom portions of the HTML needed to render the web page.

Building a content management system with these tools is simple. To the existing Excel data, I added two worksheets. In the worksheet called Top, I copied the HTML needed to generate the navigation bar of the website. To the worksheet called Bottom, I copied the HTML needed to generate the end of the HTML page. Figure 16.9 shows the simple Bottom worksheet.

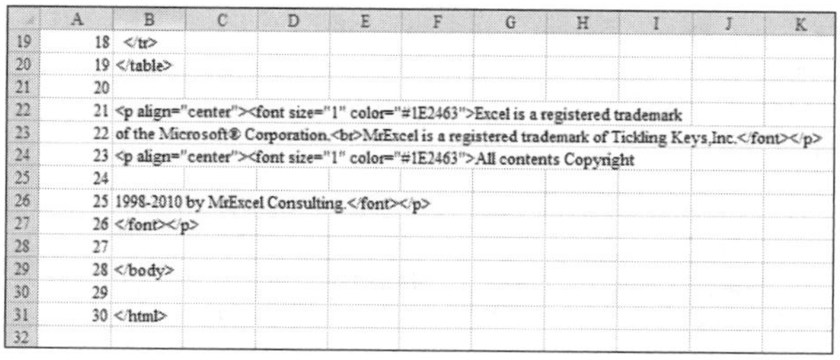

Figure 16.9

Companies everywhere are maintaining all sorts of data in Excel and are comfortable updating the data in Excel. Why not marry Excel with a simple bit of VBA so that custom HTML can be produced from Excel?

The macro code opens a text file called directory.html for output. First, all the HTML code from the Top worksheet is written to the file.

Then the macro loops through each row in the membership directory, writing data to the file.

After completing this loop, the macro writes out the HTML code from the Bottom worksheet to finish the file:

```
Sub WriteMembershipHTML()
    ' Write web Pages
    Dim WST As Worksheet
    Dim WSB As Worksheet
    Dim WSM As Worksheet
    Set WSB = Worksheets("Bottom")
    Set WST = Worksheets("Top")
    Set WSM = Worksheets("Membership")

    ' Figure out the path
    MyPath = ThisWorkbook.Path

    LineCtr = 0
```

```
FinalT = WST.Cells(Rows.Count, 1).End(xlUp).Row
FinalB = WSB.Cells(Rows.Count, 1).End(xlUp).Row
FinalM = WSM.Cells(Rows.Count, 1).End(xlUp).Row

MyFile = "sampleschedule.html"

ThisFile = MyPath & Application.PathSeparator & MyFile
ThisHostFile = MyFile

' Delete the old HTML page
On Error Resume Next
Kill (ThisFile)
On Error GoTo 0

' Build the title
ThisTitle = "<Title>LTCC Membership Directory</Title>"
WST.Cells(3, 2).Value = ThisTitle

' Open the file for output
Open ThisFile For Output As #1

' Write out the top part of the HTML
For j = 2 To FinalT
    Print #1, WST.Cells(j, 2).Value
Next j

' For each row in Membership, write out lines of data to HTML file
For j = 2 To FinalM
    ' Surround Member name with bold tags
    Print #1, "<li>" & WSM.Cells(j, 1).Value
Next j

' Close old file
Print #1, "This page current as of " & Format(Date, "mmmm dd, yyyy") & _
    " " & Format(Time, "h:mm AM/PM")

' Write out HTML code from Bottom worksheet
For j = 2 To FinalB
    Print #1, WSB.Cells(j, 2).Value
Next j
Close #1

Application.StatusBar = False
Application.CutCopyMode = False
MsgBox "web pages updated"

End Sub
```

Figure 16.10 shows the finished web page. This web page looks a lot better than the
generic page created by Excel's Save as Web Page option. It can maintain the look and feel
of the rest of the site.

This system has many advantages. The person who maintains the schedule data is comfortable working in Excel. She has already been maintaining the data in Excel on a regular
basis. Now, after updating some records, she presses a button to produce a new version of
the web page.

Figure 16.10
A simple content-management system in Excel was used to generate this web page. The look and feel matches the rest of the website. Excel achieved it without any expensive web database coding.

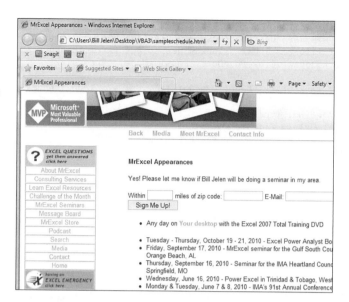

Of course, the web designer is clueless about Excel. However, if he ever wants to change the web design, it is a simple matter to open his new sample.html file in Notepad and copy the new code to the Top and Bottom worksheet.

The resulting web page has a small file size—about one-sixth the size of the equivalent page created by Excel's Save as Web Page.

> **NOTE**
> In real life, the content-management system in this example was extended to allow easy maintenance of the organization's calendar, board members, and so on. The resulting workbook made it possible to maintain 41 web pages at the click of a button.

Bonus: FTP from Excel

After you are able to update web pages from Excel, you still have the hassle of using an FTP program to upload the pages from your hard drive to the Internet. Again, we have lots of people proficient in Excel, but not so many comfortable with using an FTP client.

Ken Anderson has written a cool command-line FTP freeware utility. Download WCL_FTP from http://www.softlookup.com/display.asp?id=20483. Save WCL_FTP.exe to the root directory of your hard drive, and then use this code to automatically upload your recently created HTML files to your web server:

```
Sub DoFTP(fname, pathfname)
' To have this work, copy wcl_ftp.exe to the C:\ root directory
' Download from http://www.softlookup.com/display.asp?id=20483
```

```
' Build a string to FTP. The syntax is
' WCL_FTP.exe "Caption" hostname username password host-directory _
' host-filename local-filename get-or-put 0Ascii1Binanry 0NoLog _
' 0Background 1CloseWhenDone 1PassiveMode  1ErrorsText

If Not Worksheets("Menu").Range("I1").Value = True Then Exit Sub

s = """c:\wcl_ftp.exe "" " _
    & """Upload File to website"" " _
    & "ftp.MySite.com FTPUser FTPPassword www " _
    & fname & " " _
    & """" & pathfname & """ " _
    & "put " _
    & "0 0 0 1 1 1"

Shell s, vbMinimizedNoFocus
End Sub
```

Next Steps

Chapter 17 shows how to create tiny, word-sized charts in Excel 2010 VBA.

Dashboarding with Sparklines in Excel 2010

One of the new features in Excel 2010 is the ability to create tiny, word-size charts. If you are creating dashboards, you will want to leverage these charts.

The concept of sparklines was first introduced by Professor Edward Tufte. Tufte promoted sparklines as way to show a maximum amount of information with a minimal amount of ink.

Microsoft supports three types of sparklines:

IN THIS CHAPTER

Creating Sparklines 412

Scaling Sparklines 414

Formatting Sparklines 418

Creating a Dashboard 427

- **Line**—A sparkline shows a single series on a line chart within a single cell. On a sparkline, you can add markers for the highest point, the lowest point, the first point, or the last point. Each of those points can have a different color. You can also choose to mark all of the negative points or even all points.

- **Column**—A sparkcolumn shows a single series on a column chart. You can choose to show a different color for the first bar, the last bar, the lowest bar, the highest bar, and/or all negative points.

- **Win/Loss**—This is a special type of column chart where every positive point is plotted at a 100% height and every negative point is plotted as –100% height. The theory is that positive columns represent wins and negative columns represent losses. With these charts you will always want to change the color of the negative columns. It is possible to highlight the highest/lowest point based on the underlying data.

Creating Sparklines

Microsoft figures that you will usually be creating a group of sparklines. The main VBA object for sparklines is the `SparklineGroup`. To create sparklines, you apply the `SparklineGroups.Add` method to the range where you want the sparklines to appear.

In the `Add` method, you will specify a type for the sparkline and the location of the source data.

Say that you apply the add method to a three-cell range of B2:D2. Then the source must be a range that is either three columns wide or three rows tall.

The type parameter can be `xlSparkLine` for a line, `xlSparkColumn` for a column, or `xlSpark-Column100` for Win/Loss.

If the `SourceData` parameter is referring to ranges on the current worksheet, it can be as simple as `"D3:F100"`. If it is pointing to another worksheet, use `"Data!D3:F100"` or `"'My Data'!D3:F100"`. If you've defined a named range, you can specify the name of the range as the source data.

Figure 17.1 shows a table of NASDAQ closing prices for three years. Notice that the actual data for the sparklines is in three contiguous Columns, D, E, and F.

Figure 17.1
Arrange the data for the sparklines in a contiguous range.

D	E	F
2596.03	1589.89	2180.05
2601.01	1579.31	2211.69
2640.86	1552.37	2237.66
2691.99	1564.32	2252.67
2713.5	1532.35	2269.64
2724.41	1521.54	2285.69

Because each column might have one or two extra points, the code to find the final row is slightly different than usual.

```
FinalRow = WSD.[A1].CurrentRegion.Rows.Count
```

The `.CurrentRegion` property will start from Cell A1 and extend in all directions until it hits the edge of the worksheet or the edge of the data.

In this case, the `CurrentRegion` will report that row 253 is the final row, even though A253 and D253 are blank (see Figure 17.2).

For this example, the sparklines will be created in a row of three cells. Because each cell is showing 250 points, I am going with fairly large sparklines. The sparkline will grow to the size of the cell, so this code will make each cell fairly wide and tall:

```
With WSL.Range("B1:D1")
    .Value = array(2007,2008,2009)
    .HorizontalAlignment = xlCenter
    .Style = "Title"
    .ColumnWidth = 39
    .Offset(1, 0).RowHeight = 100
End With
```

Figure 17.2
The sparkline source
should extend to row 253.

	A	B	C	D	E	F
244	12/18/2007	12/16/2008	12/17/2009	2596.03	1589.89	2180.05
245	12/19/2007	12/17/2008	12/18/2009	2601.01	1579.31	2211.69
246	12/20/2007	12/18/2008	12/21/2009	2640.86	1552.37	2237.66
247	12/21/2007	12/19/2008	12/22/2009	2691.99	1564.32	2252.67
248	12/24/2007	12/22/2008	12/23/2009	2713.5	1532.35	2269.64
249	12/26/2007	12/23/2008	12/24/2009	2724.41	1521.54	2285.69
250	12/27/2007	12/24/2008	12/28/2009	2676.79	1524.9	2291.08
251	12/28/2007	12/26/2008	12/29/2009	2674.46	1530.24	2288.4
252	12/31/2007	12/29/2008	12/30/2009	2652.28	1510.32	2291.28
253		12/30/2008	12/31/2009		1550.7	2269.15

The following code will create three default sparklines. These won't be perfect, but the next section shows you how to format them.

```
Dim SG as SparklineGroup
Set SG = WSL.Range("B2:D2").SparklineGroups.Add( _
    Type:=xlSparkLine, _
    SourceData:="Data!D2:F" & FinalRow
```

The three sparklines are shown in Figure 17.3. There are a number of problems with the default sparklines. Think about the vertical axis of a chart. Sparklines always default to have the scale automatically selected. Because you never really get to see what the scale is, you cannot tell the range of the change.

Figure 17.3
Three default sparklines.

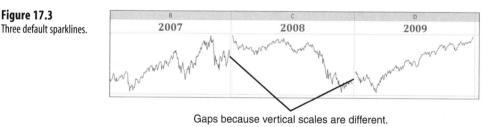

Gaps because vertical scales are different.

Figure 17.4 shows the min and max for each year. From this data, you can guess that the sparkline for 2007 probably goes from about 2300 to 2900. The sparkline for 2008 probably goes from 1300 to 2650. The sparkline for 2009 probably goes from 1250 to 2300.

Figure 17.4
Each sparkline will
assign the minimum and
maximum scale to be just
outside of these limits.

fx	=MIN(D2:D253)			
C	D	E	F	G
Date 09	Close 07	Close 08	Close 09	
Min	2,341	1,316	1,269	1,269
Max	2,859	2,610	2,291	2,859

Scaling the Sparklines

The default choice for the sparkline vertical axis is that each sparkline will have a different minimum and maximum.

There are two other choices available.

One choice is to group all the sparklines together, but to continue to allow Excel to choose the minimum and maximum scale. You still won't know exactly what values are chosen for the minimum and maximum. Looking at Figure 17.5 it seems to be roughly 1200 to 2900, but there is absolutely no way to tell for sure.

Figure 17.5
What is scale? It is hard to tell.

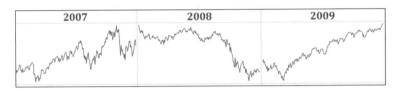

To force the sparklines to have the same automatic scale, use this code:

```
' Allow automatic axis scale, but all three of them the same
With SG.Axes.Vertical
    .MinScaleType = xlSparkScaleGroup
    .MaxScaleType = xlSparkScaleGroup
End With
```

Note that the .Axes belongs to the sparkline group, not to the individual sparklines themselves. In fact, almost all of the good properties are applied at the SparklineGroup level. This has some interesting ramifications. If you wanted one sparkline to have automatic scale and another sparkline to have a fixed scale, you would have to create each of those sparklines separately, or at least ungroup them.

Figure 17.6 shows the sparklines when both the minimum and maximum scales are set to act as a group. All three lines nearly meet now, which is a good sign. You can guess that the scale runs from about 1250 up to perhaps 1300. Again, there is no way to tell.

Figure 17.6
All three sparklines have the same minimum and maximum scale, but we don't know what it is.

Another choice is to take absolute control and assign a minimum and maximum for the vertical axis scale. The following code forces the sparklines to run from a minimum of 0 up to a maximum that rounds up to the next 100 above the largest value:

```
Set AF = Application.WorksheetFunction
AllMax = AF.Max(WSD.Range("D2:F" & FinalRow))
AllMax = Int(AllMax / 100) * 100 + 100

' Allow automatic axis scale, but all three of them the same
With SG.Axes.Vertical
     .MinScaleType = xlSparkScaleCustom
     .MaxScaleType = xlSparkScaleCustom
     .CustomMinScaleValue = 0
     .CustomMaxScaleValue = AllMax
End With
```

Figure 17.7 shows the resulting sparklines. Now, *you* know the minimum and the maximum, but you need a way to communicate this to the reader.

Figure 17.7
You've manually assigned a min and max scale, but it does not appear on the chart.

One choice is to put the minimum scale on the lower left and the upper scale on the upper right, as shown in Figure 17.8.

Figure 17.8
Labels in A2 and E2 show the upper and lower limits.

Text in A2 and E2

The code for Figure 17.8 is as follows:

```
' Add two labels to show minimum and maximum
With WSL.Range("A2")
     .Value = AllMin
     .HorizontalAlignment = xlRight
     .VerticalAlignment = xlBottom
     .Font.Size = 8
     .Font.Bold = True
     .WrapText = True
End With

With WSL.Range("E2")
     .Value = AllMax
```

```
        .HorizontalAlignment = xlLeft
        .VerticalAlignment = xlTop
        .Font.Size = 8
        .Font.Bold = True
    End With
```

Alternatively, you could put the minimum and maximum value in A2. With 8-point bold Calibri, a row height of 113 will allow 10 rows of wrapped text in the cell. So you could put the max value, then VbLf 8 times, then the min value. (vbLf is the equivalent of pressing Alt+Enter when you are entering values in a cell).

On the right side, you can put the final point's value and attempt to position it within the cell so that it falls roughly at the same height as the final point.

Figure 17.9 shows this option.

Figure 17.9
Labels on the left show the min and max. Labels on the right show the final value.

Min   Max   Final

The code to produce Figure 17.9 is shown here:

```
Sub NASDAQMacro()
' NASDAQMacro Macro
'

Dim SG As SparklineGroup
Dim SL As Sparkline
Dim WSD As Worksheet ' Data worksheet
Dim WSL As Worksheet ' Dashboard

    On Error Resume Next
    Application.DisplayAlerts = False
    Worksheets("Dashboard").Delete
    On Error GoTo 0

    Set WSD = Worksheets("Data")
    Set WSL = ActiveWorkbook.Worksheets.Add
    WSL.Name = "Dashboard"

    FinalRow = WSD.Cells(1, 1).CurrentRegion.Rows.Count
    WSD.Cells(2, 4).Resize(FinalRow - 1, 3).Name = "MyData"

    WSL.Select
    ' Set up Headings
    With WSL.Range("B1:D1")
        .Value = Array(2007, 2008, 2009)
        .HorizontalAlignment = xlCenter
```

```
            .Style = "Title"
            .ColumnWidth = 39
            .Offset(1, 0).RowHeight = 100
        End With

        Set SG = WSL.Range("B2:D2").SparklineGroups.Add( _
            Type:=xlSparkLine, _
            SourceData:="Data!D2:F250")

        Set SL = SG.Item(1)

        Set AF = Application.WorksheetFunction
        AllMin = AF.Min(WSD.Range("D2:F" & FinalRow))
        AllMax = AF.Max(WSD.Range("D2:F" & FinalRow))
        AllMin = Int(AllMin)
        AllMax = Int(AllMax + 0.9)

'       ' Allow automatic axis scale, but all three of them the same
'       With SG.Axes.Vertical
'           .MinScaleType = xlSparkScaleGroup
'           .MaxScaleType = xlSparkScaleGroup
'       End With

        ' Allow automatic axis scale, but all three of them the same
        With SG.Axes.Vertical
            .MinScaleType = xlSparkScaleCustom
            .MaxScaleType = xlSparkScaleCustom
            .CustomMinScaleValue = AllMin
            .CustomMaxScaleValue = AllMax
        End With

        ' Add two labels to show minimum and maximum
        With WSL.Range("A2")
            .Value = AllMax & vbLf & vbLf & vbLf & vbLf _
                & vbLf & vbLf & vbLf & vbLf & AllMin
            .HorizontalAlignment = xlRight
            .VerticalAlignment = xlTop
            .Font.Size = 8
            .Font.Bold = True
            .WrapText = True
        End With

        ' Put the final value on the right
        FinalVal = Round(WSD.Cells(Rows.Count, 6).End(xlUp).Value, 0)
        Rg = AllMax - AllMin
        RgTenth = Rg / 10
        FromTop = AllMax - FinalVal
        FromTop = Round(FromTop / RgTenth, 0) - 1
        If FromTop < 0 Then FromTop = 0

        Select Case FromTop
            Case 0
                RtLabel = FinalVal
            Case 1
                RtLabel = vbLf & FinalVal
            Case 2
                RtLabel = vbLf & vbLf & FinalVal
            Case 3
```

```
                    RtLabel = vbLf & vbLf & vbLf & FinalVal
            Case 4
                    RtLabel = vbLf & vbLf & _
                        vbLf & vbLf & FinalVal
            Case 5
                    RtLabel = vbLf & vbLf & _
                        vbLf & vbLf & vbLf & FinalVal
            Case 6
                    RtLabel = vbLf & vbLf & _
                        vbLf & vbLf & vbLf & vbLf & FinalVal
            Case 7
                    RtLabel = vbLf & vbLf & vbLf & vbLf _
                        & vbLf & vbLf & vbLf & FinalVal
            Case 8
                    RtLabel = vbLf & vbLf & vbLf & vbLf _
                        & vbLf & vbLf & vbLf & vbLf & FinalVal
            Case 9
                    RtLabel = vbLf & vbLf & vbLf & _
                        vbLf & vbLf & vbLf & vbLf & _
                        vbLf & vbLf & FinalVal
        End Select

        With WSL.Range("E2")
            .Value = RtLabel
            .HorizontalAlignment = xlLeft
            .VerticalAlignment = xlTop
            .Font.Size = 8
            .Font.Bold = True
        End With
    End Sub
```

Formatting Sparklines

Most of the formatting available with sparklines involves setting the color of various elements of the sparkline.

There are a few methods for assigning colors in Excel 2010. Before diving into the sparkline properties, you can read about the two methods of assigning colors in Excel VBA.

Using Theme Colors

Excel 2007 introduced the concept of a theme for a workbook. A theme is comprised of a body font, a headline font, a series of effects, and then a series of colors.

The first four colors are used for text and backgrounds. The next six colors are the accent colors. The 20 built-in themes include colors that work well together. There are also two colors used for hyperlinks and followed hyperlinks. For now, focus on the accent colors.

Go to Page Layout, Themes, and choose a theme. Next to the theme drop-down is a Colors drop-down. Open that drop-down and select Create New Theme Colors from the bottom of the drop-down. Excel will show the Create New Theme Colors dialog as shown in Figure 17.10. This gives you a good picture of the 12 colors associated with the theme.

Four Font Colors

Figure 17.10
The current theme
includes 12 colors.

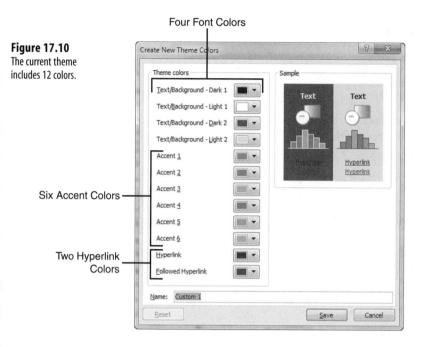

Six Accent Colors ———

Two Hyperlink
Colors

Throughout Excel, there are many color chooser drop-downs (see Figure 17.11). There is a section of the drop-down called Theme Colors. The top row under Theme colors shows the four font and six accent colors.

xlThemeColorAccent1

Figure 17.11
All but the hyperlink
colors from the theme
appear across the top row.

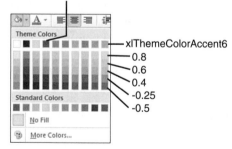

If you want to choose the last color in the first row, the VBA is as follows:

```
ActiveCell.Font.ThemeColor = xlThemeColorAccent6
```

Going across that top row of Figure 17.11, the 10 colors are as follows:

```
xlThemeColorDark1
xlThemeColorLight1
xlThemeColorDark2
```

```
xlThemeColorLight2
xlThemeColorAccent1
xlThemeColorAccent2
xlThemeColorAccent3
xlThemeColorAccent4
xlThemeColorAccent5
xlThemeColorAccent6
```

On your computer, open the fill drop-down on the Home tab and look at it in color. If you are using the Office theme, the last column is various shades of orange. The top row is the orange from the theme.

There are then five rows that go from a light orange to a very dark orange.

Excel lets you modify the theme color by lightening or darkening it. The values range from -1 which is very dark to +1 which is very light. If you look at the very light orange in Row 2, that has a tint and shade value of 0.8, which is almost completely light. The next row has a tint and shade level of 0.6. The next row has a tint and shade level of 0.4. That gives you three choices that are lighter than the theme color.

The next two rows are darker than the theme color. Because there are only two darker rows, they have values of -.25, and -.5.

If you turn on the macro recorder and choose one of these colors, it looks like a confusing bunch of code.

```
.Pattern = xlSolid
.PatternColorIndex = xlAutomatic
.ThemeColor = xlThemeColorAccent6
.TintAndShade = 0.799981688894314
.PatternTintAndShade = 0
```

If you are using a solid fill, you can leave out the first, second, and fifth lines of code. The `.TintAndShade` looks confusing because computers cannot round decimal tenths very well. Remember that computers store numbers in binary. In binary, a simple number like 0.1 is a repeating decimal. As the macro recorder tries to convert 0.8 from binary to decimal, it "misses" by a bit and comes up with a very close number: 0.7998168894314. This is really saying that it should be 80 percent lighter than the base number.

If you are writing code by hand, you only have to assign two values to use a theme color. Assign the `.ThemeColor` property to one of the six xlThemeColorAccent1 through xlThemeColorAccent6 values. If you want to use a theme color from the top row of the drop-down, the `.TintAndShade` should be 0 and can be omitted. If you want to lighten the color, use a positive decimal for `.TintAndShade`. If you want to darken the color, use a negative decimal.

> **TIP**
>
> Note that the five shades in the color palette drop-downs are not the complete set of variations. In VBA, you can assign any decimal value from -1 to 1. Figure 17.12 shows 200 variations of one theme color created using the `.TintAndShade` property in VBA.

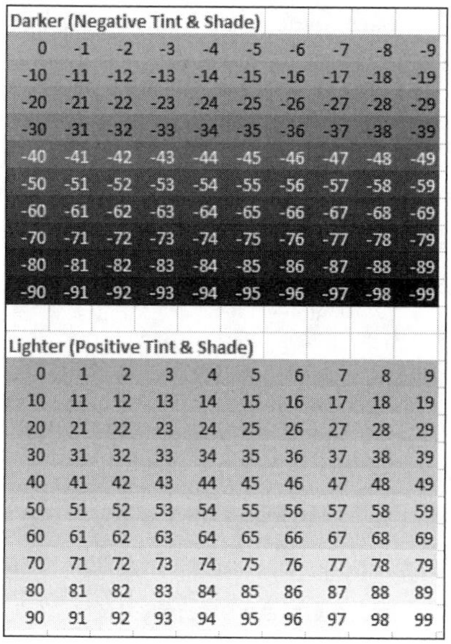

Figure 17.12
Two hundred shades of orange.

Darker (Negative Tint & Shade)									
0	-1	-2	-3	-4	-5	-6	-7	-8	-9
-10	-11	-12	-13	-14	-15	-16	-17	-18	-19
-20	-21	-22	-23	-24	-25	-26	-27	-28	-29
-30	-31	-32	-33	-34	-35	-36	-37	-38	-39
-40	-41	-42	-43	-44	-45	-46	-47	-48	-49
-50	-51	-52	-53	-54	-55	-56	-57	-58	-59
-60	-61	-62	-63	-64	-65	-66	-67	-68	-69
-70	-71	-72	-73	-74	-75	-76	-77	-78	-79
-80	-81	-82	-83	-84	-85	-86	-87	-88	-89
-90	-91	-92	-93	-94	-95	-96	-97	-98	-99

Lighter (Positive Tint & Shade)									
0	1	2	3	4	5	6	7	8	9
10	11	12	13	14	15	16	17	18	19
20	21	22	23	24	25	26	27	28	29
30	31	32	33	34	35	36	37	38	39
40	41	42	43	44	45	46	47	48	49
50	51	52	53	54	55	56	57	58	59
60	61	62	63	64	65	66	67	68	69
70	71	72	73	74	75	76	77	78	79
80	81	82	83	84	85	86	87	88	89
90	91	92	93	94	95	96	97	98	99

17

To recap, if you want to work with theme colors, you will generally change two properties, the theme color in order to choose one of the six accent colors, then tint and shade to lighten or darken the base color.

```
.ThemeColor = xlThemeColorAccent6
.TintAndShade = 0.4
```

> **NOTE**
> Note that one advantage of using theme colors is that your sparklines will change color based on the theme. If you later decide to switch from the Office theme to the Metro theme, the colors will change to match the theme.

To see a demo of using theme colors, search for Excel VBA 17 at YouTube.

Using RGB Colors

For the last decade, computers have offered a palette of 16 million colors. These colors derive from adjusting the amount of red, green, and blue light in a cell.

Do you remember back in art class in elementary school? You probably learned that the three primary colors were red, yellow, and blue. You could make green by mixing some yellow and blue paint. You could make purple by mixing some red and blue paint. You could make orange by mixing some yellow and red paint. As all of my male classmates and I soon discovered, you could make black by mixing all of the paint colors. Those rules all work with pigments in paint, but they don't work with light.

Those pixels on your computer screen are made of up light. In the light spectrum, the three primary colors are red, green, and blue. You can make the 16 million colors of the RGB color palette by mixing various amounts of red, green, and blue light. Each of the three colors is assigned an intensity from 0 (no light) to 255 (full light).

You will often see a color described using the RGB function. In the function, the first value is the amount of red, then green, then blue.

- To make red, you use =RGB(255,0,0).
- To make green, use =RGB(0,255,0).
- To make blue, use =RGB(0,0,255).
- What happens if you mix 100% of all three colors of light? You get white!
- To make white, use =RGB(255,255,255).
- If you shine no light in a pixel? You get black =RGB(0,0,0).
- To make purple, it is some red, a little green, some blue: RGB(139,65,123).
- To make yellow, use full red and green and no blue: =RGB(255,255,0).
- To make orange, use less green than the yellow: =RGB(255,153,0).

In VBA, you can use the RGB function just as it is shown here. The macro recorder is not a big fan of using the RGB function. It instead shows the result of the RGB function.

You can assign a number to each of the 16,777,216 colors by doing this math with the three RGB values:

- Take the red value times 1.
- Add the green value times 256.
- Add the blue value times 65,536.

> **NOTE**
> In case you were wondering, 65,536 is 256 raised to the second power.

If you choose a red for your sparkline, you will frequently see the macro recorder assign a .Color = 255. This is because =RGB(255,0,0) is 255.

When the macro recorder assigns a value of 5287936, it is pretty tough to figure that color out. Here are the steps I use:

In Excel, enter =Dec2Hex(5287936). You will get an answer of 50B000. This is the color that web designers refer to as #50B000.

Go to your favorite search engine and search for color chooser. You will find many utilities where you can type in the hex color code and see the color.

In Figure 17.13, ColorSchemer.com shows that #50B000 is RGB(80,176,0). This is a somewhat dark green color.

Figure 17.13
Convert hex to RGB.

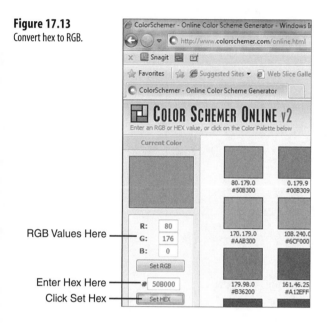

RGB Values Here ——

Enter Hex Here ——
Click Set Hex ——

While you are at the web page, you can click around to find other shades of colors and see the RGB values for those.

To recap, to skip theme colors and use RGB colors, you will set the .Color property to the result of an RGB function.

Formatting Sparkline Elements

Figure 17.14 shows a plain sparkline. The data is created from 12 points that show performance versus a budget. You really have no idea about the scale from this sparkline.

If your sparkline includes both positive and negative numbers, it will help to show the horizontal axis. This will allow you to figure out which points are above budget and which points are below budget.

To show the axis, use the following:

```
SG.Axes.Horizontal.Axis.Visible = True
```

Figure 17.15 shows the horizontal axis. This helps to show which months were above or below budget.

	A	B	C	D	E
1					
2					
3					
4					
5	Jan	17			
6	Feb	12			
7	Mar	1			
8	Apr	-45			
9	May	-32			
10	Jun	-5			
11	Jul	7			
12	Aug	-7			
13	Sep	12			
14	Oct	22			
15	Nov	18			
16	Dec	15			
17					

Figure 17.14
A default sparkline.

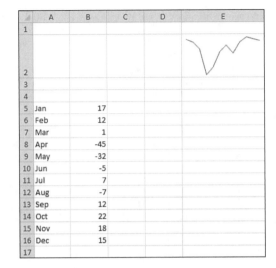

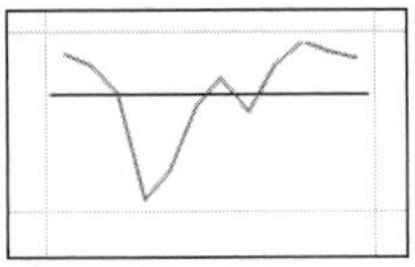

Figure 17.15
Add the horizontal axis to show which months were above or below budget.

Using code from "Scaling the Sparklines," you can add high and low labels to the cell to the left of the sparkline:

```
Set AF = Application.WorksheetFunction
MyMax = AF.Max(Range("B5:B16"))
MyMin = AF.Min(Range("B5:B16"))
LabelStr = MyMax & vbLf & vbLf & vbLf & vbLf & MyMin

With SG.Axes.Vertical
    .MinScaleType = xlSparkScaleCustom
    .MaxScaleType = xlSparkScaleCustom
    .CustomMinScaleValue = MyMin
    .CustomMaxScaleValue = MyMax
End With

With Range("D2")
    .WrapText = True
    .Font.Size = 8
    .HorizontalAlignment = xlRight
    .VerticalAlignment = xlTop
    .Value = LabelStr
    .RowHeight = 56.25
End With
```

The result of this macro is shown in Figure 17.16.

Figure 17.16
Use a nonsparkline feature to label the vertical axis.

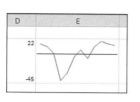

To change the color of the sparkline, use this:

```
SG.SeriesColor.Color = RGB(255, 191, 0)
```

The Show group of Sparkline Tools Design tab offers six options. You can further modify those elements by using the Marker Color drop-down.

You can choose to turn on a marker for every point in the data set, as shown in Figure 17.17.

Figure 17.17
Show All Markers.

The code to show a black marker at every point is as follows:

```
With SG.Points
    .Markers.Color.Color = RGB(0, 0, 0) ' black
    .Markers.Visible = True
End With
```

The code to show a black marker at every point is this:

```
With SG.Points
    .Markers.Color = RGB(0, 0, 0) ' black
    .Markers.Visible = True
End With
```

Instead, you can use the markers to show only the minimum, maximum, first, and last points. This code will show the minimum in red, maximum in green, first and last in black:

```
With SG.Points
    .Lowpoint.Color.Color = RGB(255, 0, 0) ' red
    .Highpoint.Color.Color = RGB(51, 204, 77) ' Green
    .Firstpoint.Color.Color = RGB(0, 0, 255) ' Blue
    .Lastpoint.Color.Color = RGB(0, 0, 255) ' blue
    .Negative.Color.Color = RGB(127, 0, 0) ' pink
    .Markers.Color.Color = RGB(0, 0, 0) ' black
    ' Choose Which points to Show
    .Highpoint.Visible = True
```

```
            .Lowpoint.Visible = True
            .Firstpoint.Visible = True
            .Lowpoint.Visible = True
            .Negative.Visible = False
            .Markers.Visible = False
        End With
```

Figure 17.18 shows the sparkline with the only the high, low, first, and last chosen.

Figure 17.18
Show only key markers.

One other element is the negative markers. These come in particularly handy when you are formatting Win/Loss charts.

Formatting Win/Loss Charts

Win/Loss charts are a special type of sparkline for tracking binary events. The Win/Loss chart shows an upward-facing marker for a positive value and a downward-facing marker for any negative value. For a zero, no marker is shown.

You can use these charts to track proposal wins versus losses. In Figure 17.19, a Win/Loss chart is showing the last 25 regular-season baseball games of the famed 1951 pennant race between the Brooklyn Dodgers and the New York Giants. This chart shows how the Giants went on a 7-game winning streak to finish the regular season. The Dodgers went 3-4 during this period and ended in a tie with the Giants, forcing a three-game playoff. The Giants won the first game, lost the second, and then advanced to the World Series by winning the third playoff game. The Giants leapt out to a 2-1 lead over the Yankees but then lost three straight.

Figure 17.19
This Win-Loss chart documents the most famous pennant race in history.

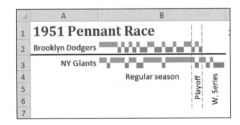

> **NOTE**
> The words *Regular season*, *Playoff*, and *W. Series*, as well as the two dotted lines, are not part of the sparkline. The lines are drawing objects manually added with Insert, Shapes.

To create the chart, you use .Add a SparkLineGroup with a type of xlSparkColumn-Stacked100:

```
Set SG = Range("B2:B3").SparklineGroups.Add( _
    Type:=xlSparkColumnStacked100, _
    SourceData:="C2:AD3")
```

You will generally show the wins and losses as different colors. One obvious color scheme is red for losses and green for wins.

There is no specific way to change only the "up" markers, so change the color of all markers to be green:

```
' Show all points as green
SG.SeriesColor.Color = 5287936
```

Then change the color of the negative markers to red:

```
'Show losses as red
With SG.Points.Negative
    .Visible = True
    .Color.Color = 255
End With
```

It is easier to create the Up/Down charts. You don't have to worry about setting the line color. The vertical axis is always fixed.

Creating a Dashboard

Sparklines have the benefit of communicating a lot of information in a very tiny space. In this section, you see how to fit 130 charts on one page.

Figure 17.20 shows a data set that summarizes a 1.8 million row dataset. I used the new PowerPivot add-in for Excel to import the records and then calculated three new measures:

- YTD Sales by month by store
- YTD Sales by month for the previous year
- % increase of YTD Sales versus previous year

This is a key statistic in retail stores; how are you doing versus the same time last year. Also this analysis has the benefit of being cumulative. The final number for December represents if the store was up or down versus the previous year.

Figure 17.20
This summary of 1.8 million records is a sea of numbers.

Store	Jan	Feb	Mar	Apr	May	Jun	Jul	Aug
YTD Sales - % Change from Previous Year								
Sherman (	1.9%	-1.3%	-0.8%	-0.2%	-0.1%	-0.1%	0.2%	-0.1%
Brea Mall	6.3%	-0.5%	-0.2%	0.1%	0.1%	-0.8%	-0.1%	-0.7%
Park Place	4.4%	-0.8%	-0.4%	-0.5%	-0.4%	-0.4%	-0.3%	-0.8%
Galleria at	-0.3%	-3.5%	-3.2%	-1.8%	-1.0%	-0.8%	-0.5%	-0.4%
Mission V	7.3%	-0.1%	-1.2%	-0.8%	-0.2%	-0.3%	0.0%	0.0%
Corona De	5.2%	-0.2%	-1.0%	-0.1%	0.4%	0.6%	0.4%	0.1%
San Franci	0.6%	-1.8%	-2.0%	-0.9%	-0.6%	-0.9%	-0.5%	-1.1%

Observations About Sparklines

After working with sparklines for a while, some observations come to mind:

- Sparklines are transparent. You can see through to the underlying cell. This means that the fill color of the underlying cell will show through and the text in the underlying cell will show through.

- If you make the font really small and align the text with the edge of the cell, you can make the text look like a title or a legend.

- If you turn on wrap text and make the cell tall enough for 5 or 10 lines of text in the cell, you can control the position of the text in the cell by using vbLf characters in VBA.

- Sparklines work better when they are bigger than a typical cell. All the examples in this chapter either made the column wider, the height taller, or both.

- Sparklines created together are grouped. Changes made to one sparkline are made to all sparklines.

- Sparklines can be created on a separate worksheet than the data.

- Sparklines look better when there is some white space around the cells. This would be tough to do manually because you would have to create each sparkline one at a time. It is easy to do here because you can leverage VBA.

Creating 100's of Individual Sparklines in a Dashboard

All those issues can be taken into account when creating this dashboard. The plan will be to create each store's sparkline individually. This will allow a blank row and column to appear between every sparkline.

After inserting a new worksheet for the dashboard, you can format the cells with this code:

```
' Set up the dashboard as alternating cells for sparkline then blank
For c = 1 To 11 Step 2
    WSL.Cells(1, c).ColumnWidth = 15
    WSL.Cells(1, c + 1).ColumnWidth = 0.6
Next c
For r = 1 To 45 Step 2
    WSL.Cells(r, 1).RowHeight = 38
    WSL.Cells(r + 1, 1).RowHeight = 3
Next r
```

Keep track of which cell will contain the next sparkline with two variables:

```
NextRow = 1
NextCol = 1
```

Figure out how many rows of data there are on the Data worksheet. Loop from row 4 to the final row. For each row, you will make a sparkline.

Build a text string that points back to the correct row on the data sheet using this code. Use that source when defining the sparkline:

```
ThisSource = "Data!B" & i & ":M" & i
Set SG = WSL.Cells(NextRow, NextCol).SparklineGroups.Add( _
    Type:=xlSparkColumn, _
    SourceData:=ThisSource)
```

You want to show a horizontal axis at the zero location. The range of values for all stores was -5 percent to +10 percent. The maximum scale value here is being set to 0.15 to allow extra room for the "title" in the cell:

```
SG.Axes.Horizontal.Axis.Visible = True
With SG.Axes.Vertical
    .MinScaleType = xlSparkScaleCustom
    .MaxScaleType = xlSparkScaleCustom
    .CustomMinScaleValue = -0.05
    .CustomMaxScaleValue = 0.15
End With
```

Like in the previous example with the Win/Loss chart, you will want the positive columns to be green and the negative columns to be red:

```
' All columns green
SG.SeriesColor.Color = RGB(0, 176, 80)
' Negative columns red
SG.Points.Negative.Visible = True
SG.Points.Negative.Color.Color = RGB(255, 0, 0)
```

Remember that the sparkline has a transparent background. Thus, you can write really small text to the cell, and it behaves almost like chart labels.

The following code joins together the store name and the final percentage change for the year into a title for the chart. The program writes this title to the cell but makes it small, centered, and vertically aligned.

```
ThisStore = WSD.Cells(i, 1).Value & " " & _
    Format(WSD.Cells(i, 13), "+0.0%;-0.0%;0%")
' Add a label
With WSL.Cells(NextRow, NextCol)
    .Value = ThisStore
    .HorizontalAlignment = xlCenter
    .VerticalAlignment = xlTop
    .Font.Size = 8
    .WrapText = True
End With
```

The final element is to change the background color of the cell based on the final percentage. If it is up, then the background is light green. If it is down, then the background is light red:

```
FinalVal = WSD.Cells(i, 13)
' Color the cell light red for negative, light green for positive
With WSL.Cells(NextRow, NextCol).Interior
    If FinalVal <= 0 Then
        .Color = 255
        .TintAndShade = 0.9
```

17

```
        Else
            .Color = 14743493
            .TintAndShade = 0.7
        End If
    End With
```

Once that sparkline is done, the column and/or row positions are incremented to prepare for the next chart:

```
NextCol = NextCol + 2
If NextCol > 11 Then
    NextCol = 1
    NextRow = NextRow + 2
End If
```

After this, the loop continues with the next store.

The complete code is shown here:

```
Sub StoreDashboard()
Dim SG As SparklineGroup
Dim SL As Sparkline
Dim WSD As Worksheet ' Data worksheet
Dim WSL As Worksheet ' Dashboard

    On Error Resume Next
    Application.DisplayAlerts = False
    Worksheets("Dashboard").Delete
    On Error GoTo 0

    Set WSD = Worksheets("Data")
    Set WSL = ActiveWorkbook.Worksheets.Add
    WSL.Name = "Dashboard"

    ' Set up the dashboard as alternating cells for sparkline then blank
    For c = 1 To 11 Step 2
        WSL.Cells(1, c).ColumnWidth = 15
        WSL.Cells(1, c + 1).ColumnWidth = 0.6
    Next c
    For r = 1 To 45 Step 2
        WSL.Cells(r, 1).RowHeight = 38
        WSL.Cells(r + 1, 1).RowHeight = 3
    Next r

    NextRow = 1
    NextCol = 1

    FinalRow = WSD.Cells(Rows.Count, 1).End(xlUp).Row

    For i = 4 To FinalRow
        ThisStore = WSD.Cells(i, 1).Value & " " & _
            Format(WSD.Cells(i, 13), "+0.0%;-0.0%;0%")
        ThisSource = "Data!B" & i & ":M" & i
        FinalVal = WSD.Cells(i, 13)
```

```
        Set SG = WSL.Cells(NextRow, NextCol).SparklineGroups.Add( _
            Type:=xlSparkColumn, _
            SourceData:=ThisSource)

        SG.Axes.Horizontal.Axis.Visible = True
        With SG.Axes.Vertical
            .MinScaleType = xlSparkScaleCustom
            .MaxScaleType = xlSparkScaleCustom
            .CustomMinScaleValue = -0.05
            .CustomMaxScaleValue = 0.15
        End With

        ' All columns green
        SG.SeriesColor.Color = RGB(0, 176, 80)
        ' Negative columns red
        SG.Points.Negative.Visible = True
        SG.Points.Negative.Color.Color = RGB(255, 0, 0)

        ' Add a label
        With WSL.Cells(NextRow, NextCol)
            .Value = ThisStore
            .HorizontalAlignment = xlCenter
            .VerticalAlignment = xlTop
            .Font.Size = 8
            .WrapText = True
        End With

        ' Color the cell light red for negative, light green for positive
        With WSL.Cells(NextRow, NextCol).Interior
            If FinalVal <= 0 Then
                .Color = 255
                .TintAndShade = 0.9
            Else
                .Color = 14743493
                .TintAndShade = 0.7
            End If
        End With

        NextCol = NextCol + 2
        If NextCol > 11 Then
            NextCol = 1
            NextRow = NextRow + 2
        End If
    Next i
End Sub
```

Figure 17.21 shows the final dashboard. This prints on a single page and summarizes 1.8 million rows of data.

If you zoom in, you can see that every cell tells a story. In Figure 17.22, Park Meadows had a great January, managed to stay ahead of last year through the entire year, and finished up 0.8 percent. Lakeside also had a positive January, but then a bad February and a worse March. They struggled back toward 0 percent for the rest of the year but ended up off seven-tenths of a percent.

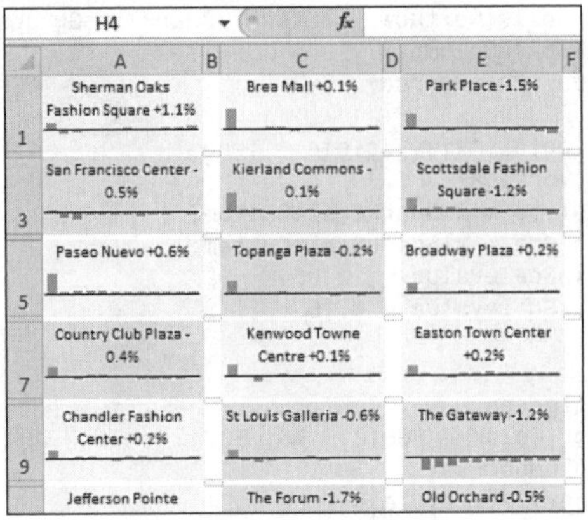

Figure 17.21
One page summarizes the sales from 140 stores.

The report is addictive. I find myself studying all sorts of trends, but then I have to remind myself that I created the 1.8 million row dataset using RandBetween just a few weeks ago! The report is so compelling I am getting drawn into studying fictional data.

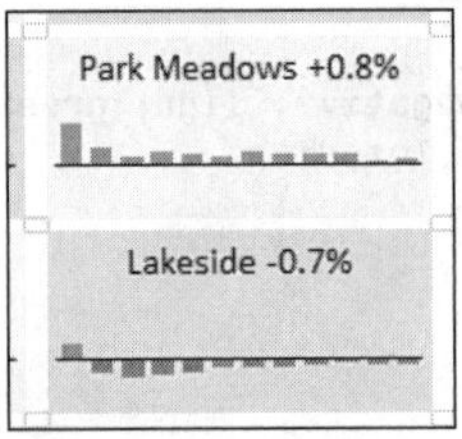

Figure 17.22
Detail of two sparkline charts.

Next Steps

The next chapter steps outside the world of Excel to talk about how to transfer Excel data into Microsoft Word documents. Chapter 18, "Automating Word," looks at using Excel VBA to automate and control Microsoft Word.

Automating Word

Word, Excel, PowerPoint, Outlook, and Access all use the same VBA language. The only difference is their object models. For example, Excel has a `Workbooks` object and Word has `Documents`. Any one of these applications can access another application's object model as long as the second application is installed.

To access Word's object library, Excel must establish a link to it by using either early binding or late binding. With *early binding*, the reference to the application object is created when the program is compiled. With *late binding*, the reference is created when the program is run.

This chapter is an introduction to accessing Word from Excel.

18

IN THIS CHAPTER

Early Binding 433

Late Binding 436

Creating and Referencing Objects 437

Using Constant Values 439

Understanding Word's Objects 441

Controlling Form Fields in Word 450

> **NOTE**
> Because this chapter does not review Word's entire object model or the object models of other applications, refer to the VBA Object Browser in the appropriate application to learn about other object models.

Early Binding

Code written with early binding executes faster than code with late binding. A reference is made to Word's object library before the code is written so that Word's objects, properties, and methods are available in the Object Browser. Tips such as a list of members of an object also appear, as shown in Figure 18.1.

The disadvantage of early binding is that the referenced object library must exist on the system. For example, if you write a macro referencing Word 2010's object library and someone with Word 2003 attempts to run the code, the program fails because the program cannot find the Word 2010 object library.

Figure 18.1
Early binding allows access to the Word object's syntax.

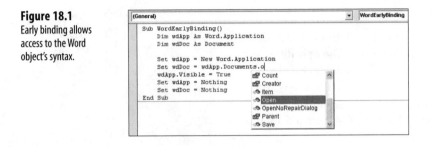

The object library is added through the VB Editor, as follows:

1. Select Tools, References.
2. Check Microsoft Word 14.0 Object Library in the Available References list (see Figure 18.2).
3. Click OK.

Figure 18.2
Select the object library from the References list

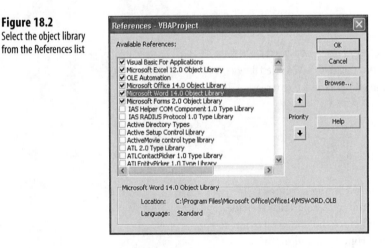

> **NOTE** If the object library is not found, Word is not installed. If another version is found in the list such as 10.0, another version of Word is installed.

After the reference is set, Word variables can be declared with the correct Word variable type. However, if the object variable is declared As Object, this forces the program to use late binding:

```
Sub WordEarlyBinding()
Dim wdApp As Word.Application
Dim wdDoc As Document
Set wdApp = New Word.Application
Set wdDoc = wdApp.Documents.Open(ThisWorkbook.Path & _
    "\Chapter 18 - Automating Word.docx")
wdApp.Visible = True
Set wdApp = Nothing
Set wdDoc = Nothing
End Sub
```

> **TIP** Excel searches through the selected libraries to find the reference for the object type. If the type is found in more than one library, the first reference is selected. You can influence which library is chosen by changing the priority of the reference in the listing.

This example creates a new instance of Word and opens an existing Word document from Excel. The declared variables, wdApp and wdDoc, are of Word object types. wdApp is used to create a reference to the Word application in the same way the Application object is used in Excel. New Word.Application is used to create a new instance of Word.

> **TIP** If you are opening a document in a new instance of Word, Word is not visible. If the application needs to be shown, it must be unhidden (wdApp.Visible = True).

When finished, it's a good idea to set the object variables to Nothing and release the memory being used by the application, as follows:

```
Set wdApp = Nothing
Set wdDoc = Nothing
```

Compile Error: Can't Find Object or Library

If the referenced version of Word does not exist on the system, an error message appears, as shown in Figure 18.3. View the References list; the missing object is highlighted with the word *MISSING* (see Figure 18.4).

Figure 18.3
Attempting to compile a
program with a missing
reference library will generate an error message.

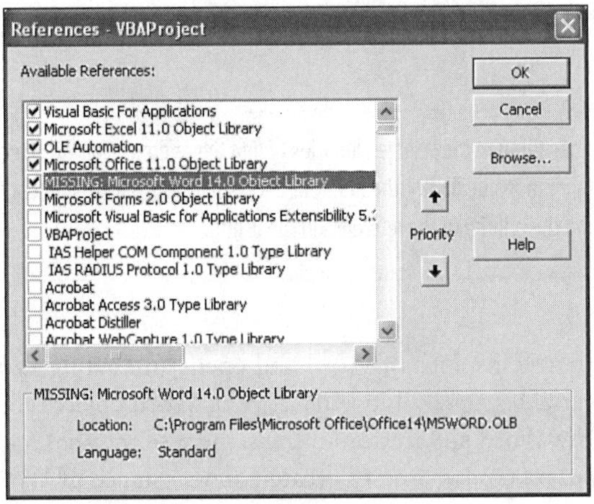

Figure 18.4
Excel will list the missing
library for you.

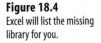

If a previous version of Word is available, you can try running the program with that version referenced. Many objects are the same between versions.

Late Binding

When using late binding, you are creating an object that refers to the Word application
before linking to the Word library. Because you do not set up a reference beforehand, the
only constraint on the Word version is that the objects, properties, and methods must exist.
In the case where there are differences, the version can be verified and the correct object
used accordingly.

The disadvantage of late binding is that because Excel does not know what is going on, it
does not understand that you are referring to Word. This prevents the tips from appearing when referencing Word objects. In addition, built-in constants are not available. This
means that when Excel is compiling, it cannot verify that the references to Word are correct. After the program is executed, the links to Word begin to build, and any coding errors
are detected at that point.

The following example creates a new instance of Word, and then opens and makes visible an existing Word document:

```
Sub WordLateBinding()
Dim wdApp As Object, wdDoc As Object
Set wdApp = CreateObject("Word.Application")
Set wdDoc = wdApp.Documents.Open(ThisWorkbook.Path & _
"\Chapter 18 - Automating Word.docx")
wdApp.Visible = True
Set wdApp = Nothing
Set wdDoc = Nothing
End Sub
```

An object variable (wdApp) is declared and set to reference the application (CreateObject("Word.Application")). Other required variables are then declared (wdDoc), and the application object is used to refer these variables to Word's object model.

> **CAUTION**
>
> Declaring wdApp and wdDoc as objects forces the use of late binding. The program cannot create the required links to the Word object model until it executes the CreateObject function.

Creating and Referencing Objects

The following sections describe how to create new objects and how to reference currently open objects.

The New Keyword

In the early binding example, the keyword New was used to reference the Word application. The New keyword can be used only with early binding; it does not work with late binding. CreateObject or GetObject would also work, but New is best for this example. If an instance of the application is running and you want to use it, use the GetObject function instead.

> **CAUTION**
>
> If your code to open Word runs smoothly, but you don't see an instance of Word (and should because you code it to be Visible), open your Task Manager and look for the process WinWord.exe. If it exists, from the Immediate window in Excel's VB Editor, type the following (which uses early binding):
>
> ```
> Word.Application.Visible = True
> ```
>
> If multiple instances of WinWord.exe are found, you need to make each instance visible and close the extra instance(s) of WinWord.exe.

18

CreateObject **Function**

The CreateObject function was used in the late binding example. However, this function can also be used in early binding. CreateObject has a class parameter consisting of the name and type of the object to be created (Name.Type). For example, the examples in this chapter have shown you (Word.Application), in which Word is the Name and Application is the Type.

The CreateObject function creates a new instance of the object. In this case, the Word application is created.

GetObject **Function**

The GetObject function can be used to reference an instance of Word that is already running. It creates an error if no instance can be found.

GetObject's two parameters are optional. The first parameter specifies the full path and file-name to open, while the second parameter specifies the application program. The following example leaves off the application, allowing the default program, which is Word, to open the document:

```
Sub UseGetObject()
Dim wdDoc As Object
Set wdDoc = GetObject(ThisWorkbook.Path & "\Chapter 18 - Automating _
   Word.docx")
wdDoc.Application.Visible = True
Set wdDoc = Nothing
End Sub
```

This example opens a document in an existing instance of Word and ensures the Word application's Visible property is set to True. Note that to make the document visible, you have to refer to the application object (wdDoc.Application.Visible) because wdDoc is refer-encing a document rather than the application.

> **NOTE** Although the Word application's Visible property is set to True, this code does not make the Word application the active application. In most cases, the Word application icon stays in the taskbar, and Excel remains the active application on the user's screen.

The following example uses errors to learn whether Word is already open before pasting a chart at the end of a document. If Word is not open, it opens Word and creates a new document:

```
Sub IsWordOpen()
Dim wdApp As Word.Application

ActiveChart.ChartArea.Copy

On Error Resume Next
Set wdApp = GetObject(, "Word.Application")
```

```
If wdApp Is Nothing Then
    Set wdApp = GetObject("", "Word.Application")
    With wdApp
        .Documents.Add
        .Visible = True
    End With
End If
On Error GoTo 0

With wdApp.Selection
    .EndKey Unit:=wdStory
    .TypeParagraph
    .PasteSpecial Link:=False, DataType:=wdPasteOLEObject, _
        Placement:=wdInLine, DisplayAsIcon:=False
End With

Set wdApp = Nothing
End Sub
```

Using On Error Resume Next forces the program to continue even if it runs into an error. In this case, an error occurs when we attempt to link wdApp to an object that does not exist. wdApp will have no value. The next line, If wdApp Is Nothing then, takes advantage of this and opens an instance of Word, adding an empty document and making the application visible.

> **TIP**
>
> Note the use of empty quotes for the first parameter in GetObject("", "Word. Application"). This is how to use the GetObject function to open a new instance of Word. Use On Error Goto 0 to return to normal VBA handling behavior.

18

Using Constant Values

The previous example used constants that are specific to Word such as wdPasteOLEObject and wdInLine. When you are programming using early binding, Excel helps by showing these constants in the tip window.

With late binding, these tips will not appear. So what can you do? You might write your program using early binding, and then change it to late binding after you compile and test the program. The problem with this method is that the program will not compile because Excel does not recognize the Word constants.

The words wdPasteOLEObject and wdInLine are for your convenience as a programmer. Behind each of these text constants is the real value that VBA understands. The solution to this is to retrieve and use these real values with your late binding program.

Using the Watch Window to Retrieve the Real Value of a Constant

One way to retrieve the value is to add a watch for the constants. Then, step through your code and check the value of the constant as it appears in the Watch window, as shown in Figure 18.5.

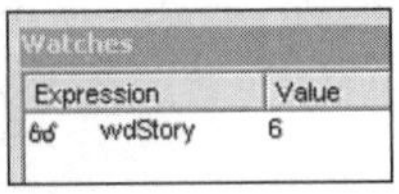

Figure 18.5
Use the Watch window to get the real value behind a Word constant.

Using the Object Browser to Retrieve the Real Value of a Constant

Another way to retrieve the value is to look up the constant in the Object Browser. However, you need the Word library set up as a reference to use this method. To set up the Word library, right-click in the constant and select Definition. The Object Browser opens to the constant that shows the value in the bottom window, as shown in Figure 18.6.

> **NOTE**
> You can set up the Word reference library to be accessed from the Object Browser. However, you do not have to set up your code with early binding. In this way, the reference is at your fingertips, but your code is still late binding. Turning off the reference library is just a few clicks away.

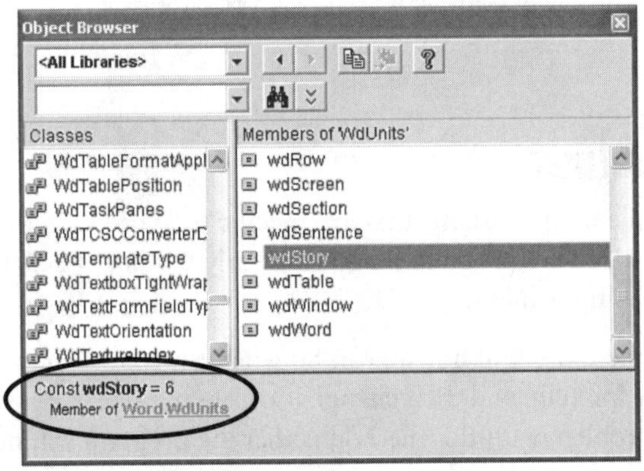

Figure 18.6
User the Object Browser to get the real value behind a Word constant.

Replacing the constants in the earlier code example with their real values would look like this:

```
With wdApp.Selection
    .EndKey Unit:=6
    .TypeParagraph
    .PasteSpecial Link:=False, DataType:=0, _
        Placement:=0, DisplayAsIcon:=False
End With
```

However, what happens a month from now when you return to the code and you try to remember what those numbers mean? The solution is up to you. Some programmers add comments to the code referencing the Word constant. Other programmers create their own variables to hold the real value and use those variables in place of the constants, like this:

```
Const xwdStory As Long = 6
Const xwdPasteOLEObject As Long = 0
Const xwdInLine As Long = 0

With wdApp.Selection
    .EndKey Unit:=xwdStory
    .TypeParagraph
    .PasteSpecial Link:=False, DataType:=xwdPasteOLEObject, _
        Placement:=xwdInLine, DisplayAsIcon:=False
End With
```

Understanding Word's Objects

Word's macro recorder can be used to get a preliminary understanding of the Word object model. However, much like Excel's macro recorder, the results will be long-winded. Keep this in mind and use the recorder to lead you toward the objects, properties, and methods in Word.

> **CAUTION**
>
> The macro recorder is limited in what it allows you to record. The mouse cannot be used to move the cursor or select objects, but there are no limits in doing so with the keyboard.

The following example is what the Word macro recorder produces when adding a new, blank document.

```
Documents.Add Template:="Normal", NewTemplate:=False, DocumentType:=0
```

Making this more efficient in Word produces this:

```
Documents.Add
```

`Template`, `NewTemplate`, and `DocumentType` are all optional properties that the recorder includes but are not required unless you need to change a default property or ensure that a property is what you require.

To use the same line of code in Excel, a link to the Word object library is required, as you learned earlier. After that link is established, an understanding of Word's objects is all you need. The next section is a review of *some* of Word's objects—enough to get you off the ground. For a more detailed listing, refer to the object model in Word's VB Editor.

18

Document **Object**

Word's Document object is equivalent to Excel's Workbook object. It consists of characters, words, sentences, paragraphs, sections, and headers/footers. It is through the Document object that methods and properties affecting the entire document such as printing, closing, searching, and reviewing, are accomplished.

Create a New Blank Document

To create a blank document in an existing instance of Word, use the Add method. We already learned how to create a new document when Word is closed—refer to GetObject and CreateObject:

```
Sub NewDocument()
Dim wdApp As Word.Application

Set wdApp = GetObject(, "Word.Application")

wdApp.Documents.Add

Set wdApp = Nothing
End Sub
```

This example opens a new, blank document that uses the default template. To create a new document that uses a specific template, use this:

```
wdApp.Documents.Add Template:="Contemporary Memo.dotx"
```

This creates a new document that uses the Contemporary Memo template. Template can either be the name of a template from the default template location or the file path and name.

Open an Existing Document

To open an existing document, use the Open method. Several parameters are available including Read Only and AddtoRecentFiles. The following example opens an existing document as Read Only, but prevents the file from being added to the Recent File List under the File menu:

```
wdApp.Documents.Open _
    Filename:="C:\Excel VBA 2007 by Jelen & Syrstad\Chapter 19 - _
    Arrays.docx", ReadOnly:=True, AddtoRecentFiles:=False
```

Save Changes to a Document

After changes have been made to a document, most likely you will want to save it. To save a document with its existing name, use this:

```
wdApp.Documents.Save
```

If the Save command is used with a new document without a name, the Save As dialog box appears. To save a document with a new name, you can use the SaveAs method instead:

```
wdApp.ActiveDocument.SaveAs "C:\Excel VBA 2007 by Jelen & _
    Syrstad\MemoTest.docx"
```

SaveAs requires the use of members of the Document object, such as ActiveDocument.

Close an Open Document

Use the Close method to close a specified document or all open documents. By default, a Save dialog appears for any documents with unsaved changes. The SaveChanges argument can be used to change this. To close all open documents without saving changes, use this code:

```
wdApp.Documents.Close SaveChanges:=wdDoNotSaveChanges
```

To close a specific document, you can close the active document or you can specify a document name:

```
wdApp.ActiveDocument.Close
```

or

```
wdApp.Documents("Chapter 19 - Arrays.docx").Close
```

Print a Document

Use the PrintOut method to print part or all of a document. To print a document with all the default print settings, use this:

```
wdApp.ActiveDocument.PrintOut
```

By default, the print range is the entire document, but this can be changed by setting the Range and Pages arguments of the PrintOut method:

```
wdApp.ActiveDocument.PrintOut Range:=wdPrintRangeOfPages, Pages:="2"
```

Selection Object

The Selection object represents what is selected in the document, such as a word, sentence, or the insertion point. It also has a Type property that returns the type that is selected such as wdSelectionIP, wdSelectionColumn, and wdSelectionShape.

HomeKey/EndKey

The HomeKey and EndKey methods are used to change the selection; they correspond to using the Home and End keys, respectively, on the keyboard. They have two parameters: Unit and Extend. Unit is the range of movement to make, to either the beginning (Home) or end (End) of a line (wdLine), document (wdStory), column (wdColumn), or row (wdRow). Extend is the type of movement: wdMove moves the selection, wdExtend extends the selection from the original insertion point to the new insertion point.

To move the cursor to the beginning of the document, use this code:

```
wdApp.Selection.HomeKey Unit:=wdStory, Extend:=wdMove
```

To select the document from the insertion point to the end of the document, use this code:

```
wdApp.Selection.EndKey Unit:=wdStory, Extend:=wdExtend
```

18

TypeText

The TypeText method is used to insert text into a Word document. User settings, such as the Overtype setting, can affect what will happen when text is inserted into the document:

```
Sub InsertText()
Dim wdApp As Word.Application
Dim wdDoc As Document
Dim wdSln As Selection

Set wdApp = GetObject(, "Word.Application")
Set wdDoc = wdApp.ActiveDocument
Set wdSln = wdApp.Selection

wdDoc.Application.Options.Overtype = False
With wdSln
    If .Type = wdSelectionIP Then
        .TypeText ("Inserting at insertion point. ")
    ElseIf .Type = wdSelectionNormal Then
            If wdApp.Options.ReplaceSelection Then
                .Collapse Direction:=wdCollapseStart
            End If
            .TypeText ("Inserting before a text block. ")
    End If
End With
Set wdApp = Nothing
Set wdDoc = Nothing
End Sub
```

Range **Object**

The Range object uses the following syntax:

```
Range(StartPosition, EndPosition)
```

The Range object represents a contiguous area or areas in the document. It has a starting character position and an ending character position. The object can be the insertion point, a range of text, or the entire document including nonprinting characters such as spaces or paragraph marks.

The Range object is similar to the Selection object, but in some ways it is better. For example, the Range object requires less code to accomplish the same tasks, and it has more capabilities. In addition, it saves time and memory because the Range object does not require Word to move the cursor or highlight objects in the document to manipulate them.

Define a Range

To define a range, enter a starting and ending position, as shown in this code segment:

```
Sub RangeText()
Dim wdApp As Word.Application
Dim wdDoc As Document
Dim wdRng As Word.Range

Set wdApp = GetObject(, "Word.Application")
Set wdDoc = wdApp.ActiveDocument
```

```
Set wdRng = wdDoc.Range(0, 22)
wdRng.Select

Set wdApp = Nothing
Set wdDoc = Nothing
Set wdRng = Nothing
End Sub
```

Figure 18.7 shows the results of running this code. The first 22 characters are selected including nonprinting characters such as paragraph returns.

The range was selected (wdRng.Select) for easier viewing. It is not required that the range be selected to be manipulated. For example, to delete the range, do this:

```
wdRng.Delete
```

Figure 18.7
The Range object selects everything in its path.

```
12
```
Data Mining with Advanced Filter

(c) Advanced Filter Is Easier in VBA Than in Excel

The arcane Advanced Filter command is so hard in the Excel
user interface that it is pretty rare to find someone who
enjoys using it regularly. In prior editions of Excel, the
AutoFilter command was probably used by most people instead
of the Advanced Filter. In Excel 2007, Microsoft renamed the
AutoFilter as a Filter and made advances in the types of
filters possible, making the Advanced Filter a less likely
choice in the user interface.

The first character position in a document is always zero, and the last is equivalent to the number of characters in the document.

The Range object also selects paragraphs. The following example copies the third paragraph in the active document and pastes it in Excel. Depending on how the paste is done, the text can be pasted into a text box (see Figure 18.8) or into a cell (see Figure 18.9):

```
Sub SelectSentence()
Dim wdApp As Word.Application
Dim wdRng As Word.Range

Set wdApp = GetObject(, "Word.Application")

With wdApp.ActiveDocument
    If .Paragraphs.Count >= 3 Then
        Set wdRng = .Paragraphs(3).Range
        wdRng.Copy
    End If
End With

'This line pastes the copied text into a text box
```

```
'because that isthe default PasteSpecial method for Word text
Worksheets("Sheet2").PasteSpecial

'This line pastes the copied text in cell A1
Worksheets("Sheet2").Paste Destination:=Worksheets("Sheet2").Range("A1")

Set wdApp = Nothing
Set wdRng = Nothing
End Sub
```

Figure 18.8

Paste Word text into an
Excel text box.

Figure 18.9

Paste Word text into an
Excel cell.

Format a Range

After a range is selected, formatting can be applied to it (see Figure 18.10). The following
program loops through all the paragraphs of the active document and bolds the first word
of each paragraph:

```
Sub ChangeFormat()
Dim wdApp As Word.Application
Dim wdRng As Word.Range
Dim count As Integer

Set wdApp = GetObject(, "Word.Application")

With wdApp.ActiveDocument
    For count = 1 To .Paragraphs.count
        Set wdRng = .Paragraphs(count).Range
        With wdRng
            .Words(1).Font.Bold = True
        .Collapse
        End With
    Next count
End With

Set wdApp = Nothing
Set wdRng = Nothing
End Sub
```

Figure 18.10

Format the first word of each paragraph in a document.

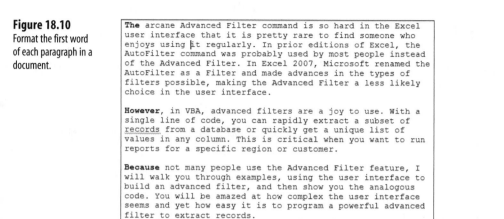

> **The** arcane Advanced Filter command is so hard in the Excel user interface that it is pretty rare to find someone who enjoys using it regularly. In prior editions of Excel, the AutoFilter command was probably used by most people instead of the Advanced Filter. In Excel 2007, Microsoft renamed the AutoFilter as a Filter and made advances in the types of filters possible, making the Advanced Filter a less likely choice in the user interface.
>
> **However**, in VBA, advanced filters are a joy to use. With a single line of code, you can rapidly extract a subset of records from a database or quickly get a unique list of values in any column. This is critical when you want to run reports for a specific region or customer.
>
> **Because** not many people use the Advanced Filter feature, I will walk you through examples, using the user interface to build an advanced filter, and then show you the analogous code. You will be amazed at how complex the user interface seems and yet how easy it is to program a powerful advanced filter to extract records.

A quick way of changing the formatting of entire paragraphs is to change the style (see Figures 18.11 and 18.12). The following program finds the paragraph with the NO style and changes it to HA:

```
Sub ChangeStyle()
Dim wdApp As Word.Application
Dim wdRng As Word.Range
Dim count As Integer

Set wdApp = GetObject(, "Word.Application")

With wdApp.ActiveDocument
    For count = 1 To .Paragraphs.count
        Set wdRng = .Paragraphs(count).Range
        With wdRng
            If .Style = "NO" Then
                .Style = "HA"
            End If
        End With
    Next count
End With

Set wdApp = Nothing
Set wdRng = Nothing
End Sub
```

18

Figure 18.11

Before: A paragraph with the NO style needs to be changed to the HA style.

Using advanced filters to get a unique set of values is usually the only case where you will perform an advanced filter without using criteria cells.	NL	¶
	NO	¶
	Normal	¶
	NX	¶

Figure 18.12

After: Apply styles with code to change paragraph formatting quickly.

Using advanced filters to get a unique set of values is usually the only case where you will perform an advanced filter without using criteria cells.	FTN	¶
	HA	¶
	HB	¶
	HC	¶

Bookmarks

Bookmarks are members of the Document, Selection, and Range objects. They can help make it easier to navigate around Word. Instead of having to choose words, sentences, or paragraphs, use bookmarks to manipulate sections of a document swiftly.

> **NOTE**
> You are not limited to using only existing bookmarks. Instead, bookmarks can be created using code.

Bookmarks appear as gray I-bars in Word documents. In Word, click the Microsoft Office Button, and then select Options, Advanced, Show Document Contents to turn on bookmarks (see Figure 18.13).

After you have set up bookmarks in a document, you can use the bookmarks to move quickly to a range. The following code automatically inserts text after four bookmarks that were previously set up in the document. Figure 18.14 shows the results.

```
Sub UseBookmarks()
Dim myArray()
Dim wdBkmk As String

Dim wdApp As Word.Application
Dim wdRng As Word.Range

myArray = Array("To", "CC", "From", "Subject")
Set wdApp = GetObject(, "Word.Application")

Set wdRng = wdApp.ActiveDocument.Bookmarks(myArray(0)).Range
wdRng.InsertBefore ("Bill Jelen")
Set wdRng = wdApp.ActiveDocument.Bookmarks(myArray(1)).Range
wdRng.InsertBefore ("Tracy Syrstad")
Set wdRng = wdApp.ActiveDocument.Bookmarks(myArray(2)).Range
wdRng.InsertBefore ("MrExcel")
Set wdRng = wdApp.ActiveDocument.Bookmarks(myArray(3)).Range
wdRng.InsertBefore ("Fruit & Vegetable Sales")
Set wdApp = Nothing
Set wdRng = Nothing
End Sub
```

Bookmarks can also be used as markers for bringing in charts created in Excel. The following code pastes an Excel chart (see Figure 18.15) into the memo:

```
Sub CreateMemo()
Dim myArray()
Dim wdBkmk As String

Dim wdApp As Word.Application
Dim wdRng As Word.Range

myArray = Array("To", "CC", "From", "Subject", "Chart")
Set wdApp = GetObject(, "Word.Application")
```

```
Set wdRng = wdApp.ActiveDocument.Bookmarks(myArray(0)).Range
wdRng.InsertBefore ("Bill Jelen")
Set wdRng = wdApp.ActiveDocument.Bookmarks(myArray(1)).Range
wdRng.InsertBefore ("Tracy Syrstad")
Set wdRng = wdApp.ActiveDocument.Bookmarks(myArray(2)).Range
wdRng.InsertBefore ("MrExcel")
Set wdRng = wdApp.ActiveDocument.Bookmarks(myArray(3)).Range
wdRng.InsertBefore ("Fruit & Vegetable Sales")

Set wdRng = wdApp.ActiveDocument.Bookmarks(myArray(4)).Range
ActiveSheet.ChartObjects("Chart 1").Copy
wdRng.PasteAndFormat Type:=wdPasteOLEObject

wdApp.Activate

Set wdApp = Nothing
Set wdRng = Nothing
End Sub
```

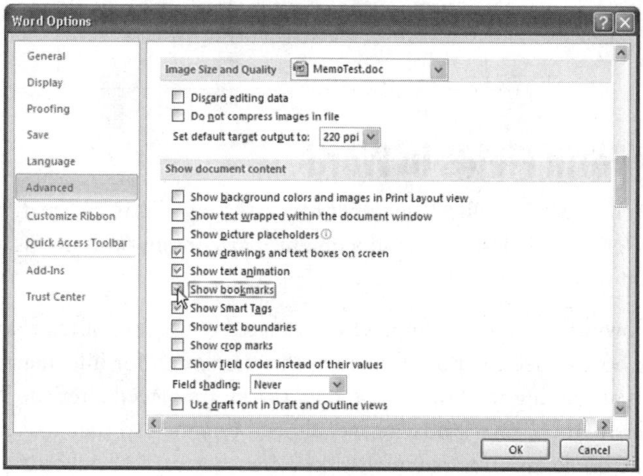

Figure 18.13
Turn on bookmarks to find them in a document.

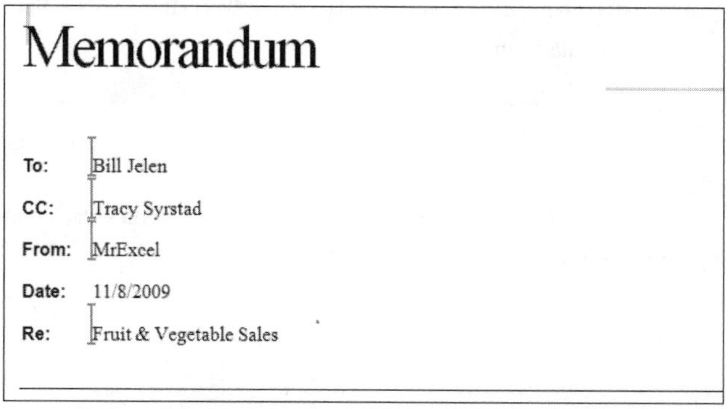

Figure 18.14
Use bookmarks to enter text quickly into a Word document.

Figure 18.15
Use bookmarks to bring charts into Word documents.

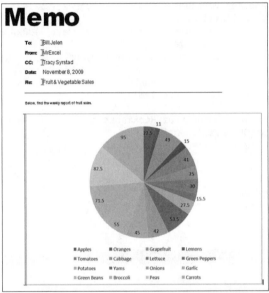

Controlling Form Fields in Word

You have seen how to modify a document by inserting charts and text, modifying formatting, and deleting text. However, a document may contain other items such as controls that you can modify.

For the following example, a template was created consisting of text, bookmarks, and Form Field check boxes. (See the note following this paragraph for information on where the Form Fields are hiding in Word.) The bookmarks are placed after the Name and Date fields. Notice that the check boxes have all been renamed so they make more sense. For example, one bookmark was renamed chk401k rather than Checkbox5. Save the template.

> **NOTE**
> The Word Form Fields are found on the Controls section of the Developer tab under Legacy Forms, as shown in Figure 18.16.

> **TIP**
> To rename a bookmark, right-click the check box, select Properties, and type a new name in the Bookmark field.

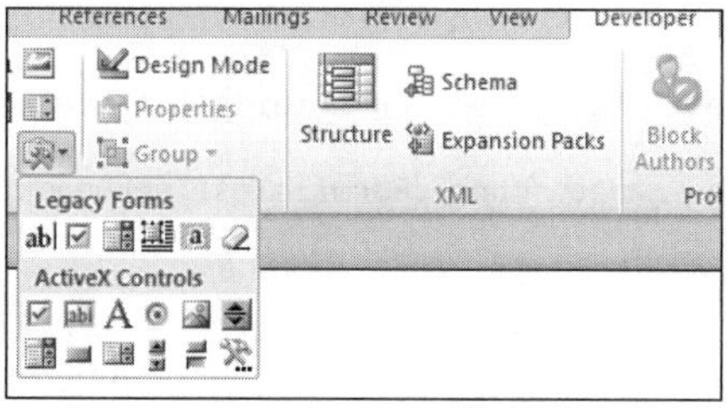

Figure 18.16
You can use the Form Fields found under the Legacy Tools to add check boxes to a document.

The questionnaire was set up in Excel, allowing the user to enter free text in B1 and B2, but setting up data validation in B3 and B5:B8, as shown in Figure 18.17.

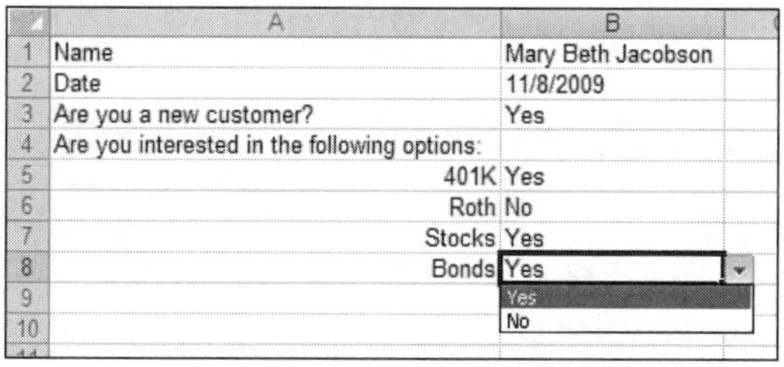

	A	B
1	Name	Mary Beth Jacobson
2	Date	11/8/2009
3	Are you a new customer?	Yes
4	Are you interested in the following options:	
5	401K	Yes
6	Roth	No
7	Stocks	Yes
8	Bonds	Yes
9		Yes
10		No

Figure 18.17
Create an Excel sheet to collect your data.

The code goes into a standard module. The name and date go straight into the document. The check boxes use logic to verify whether the user selected Yes or No to confirm whether the corresponding check box should be checked. Figure 18.18 shows a sample document that has been completed.

```
Sub FillOutWordForm()
Dim TemplatePath As String
Dim wdApp As Object
Dim wdDoc As Object

'Open the template in a new instance of Word
TemplatePath = ThisWorkbook.Path & "\New Client.dotx"
Set wdApp = CreateObject("Word.Application")
Set wdDoc = wdApp.documents.Add(Template:=TemplatePath)

'Place our text values in document
With wdApp.ActiveDocument
    .Bookmarks("Name").Range.InsertBefore Range("B1").Text
    .Bookmarks("Date").Range.InsertBefore Range("B2").Text
End With

'Using basic logic, select the correct form object
If Range("B3").Value = "Yes" Then
    wdDoc.formfields("chkCustYes").CheckBox.Value = True
Else
    wdDoc.formfields("chkCustNo").CheckBox.Value = True
End If

With wdDoc
    If Range("B5").Value = "Yes" Then .Formfields("chk401k").CheckBox.Value = _
      True
```

```
        If Range("B6").Value = "Yes" Then .Formfields("chkRoth").CheckBox.Value _
           = True
        If Range("B7").Value = "Yes" Then .Formfields("chkStocks"). _
    CheckBox.Value = True
        If Range("B7").Value = "Yes" Then .Formfields("chkBonds"). _
    CheckBox.Value = True
        End With

    wdApp.Visible = True

    ExitSub:

        Set wdDoc = Nothing
        Set wdApp = Nothing

    End Sub
```

Figure 18.18
Excel can control Word's form fields.

Name: ⌐Mary Beth Jacobson

Date: ⌐11/8/2009

New Customer: ☒Yes ☐No

Interested in the following:

| ☒ 401k | ☐ Roth | ☒ Stocks | ☒ Bonds |

CAUTION

Due to new security precautions, if the location is not trusted in the file's parent application, the code might run into an error when opening a template containing macros or controls. For example, the previous code will run into an error when opening the template on a network. Therefore users need to either configure Word to trust the network location or save the files to a local drive before running the program. Another option is to use a document instead of a template and set the `ReadOnly:=True` when opening the file.

Next Steps

In Chapter 19, "Arrays," you learn how to use multidimensional arrays. Reading data into a multidimensional array, performing calculations on the array, and then writing the array back to a range can speed up your macros dramatically.

Arrays

An *array* is a type of variable that can be used to hold more than one piece of data. For example, if you have to work with the name and address of a client, your first thought might be to assign one variable for the name and another for the address of the client. Instead, consider using an array, which can hold both pieces of information—and not for just one client, but for hundreds.

Declare an Array

Declare an array by adding parentheses after the array name. The parentheses contain the number of elements in the array:

```
Dim myArray (2)
```

This creates an array, `myArray`, which contains three elements. Three elements are included because, by default, the index count starts at 0:

```
myArray(0) = 10
myArray(1) = 20
myArray(2) = 30
```

If the index count needs to start on 1, use `Option Base 1`. This forces the count to start at 1. To do this, place the `Option Base` statement in the declarations section of the module:

```
Option Base 1
Dim myArray(2)
```

This now forces the array to have only two elements.

You can also create an array independent of the Option Base statement by declaring its lower bound:

```
Dim myArray (1 to 10)
Dim BigArray (100 to 200)
```

Every array has a lower bound (`Lbound`) and an upper bound (`Ubound`). When you declare `Dim myArray (2)`, you are declaring the upper bound and

19

IN THIS CHAPTER

Declare an Array 453

Fill an Array 455

Empty an Array 456

Arrays Make It Easier to Manipulate Data, but Is That All? 457

Dynamic Arrays 459

Passing an Array 460

allowing the option base to declare the lower bound. By declaring `Dim myArray (1 to 10)`, you declare the lower bound, 1, and the upper bound, 10

Multidimensional Arrays

The arrays just discussed are considered *one-dimensional arrays* because only one number designates the location of an element of the array. The array is like a single row of data, but because there can be only one row, you do not have to worry about the row number—only the column number. For example, to retrieve the second element (Option Base 0), use `myArray (1)`.

In some cases, a single dimension is not enough. This is where multidimensional arrays come in. Where a one-dimensional array is a single row of data, a multidimensional array contains rows *and* columns.

> **NOTE** Another word for array is *matrix*, which is what a spreadsheet is. The `Cells` object refers to elements of a spreadsheet—and a cell consists of a row and a column. You have been using arrays all along!

To declare another dimension to an array, add another argument. The following creates an array of 10 rows and 20 columns:

```
Dim myArray (1 to 10, 1 to 20)
```

This places values in the first two columns of the first row, as shown in Figure 19.1:

```
myArray (1,1) = 10
myArray (1,2) = 20
```

Figure 19.1

The VB Editor Watches window shows the first "row" of the array being filled from the previous lines of code.

This places values in first two columns of the second row:

```
myArray (2,1) = 20
myArray (2,2) = 40
```

And so on. Of course, this is time-consuming and can require many lines of code. Other ways to fill an array are discussed in the next section.

Fill an Array

Now that you can declare an array, you need to fill it. One method discussed earlier is to enter a value for each element of the array individually. However, there is a quicker way, as shown in the following sample code and Figure 19.2:

```
Option Base 1

Sub ColumnHeaders()
Dim myArray As Variant 'Variants can hold any type of data
Dim myCount As Integer

' Fill the variant with array data
myArray = Array("Name", "Address", "Phone", "Email")

' Empty the array
With Worksheets("Sheet2")
    For myCount = 1 To UBound(myArray)
        .Cells(1, myCount).Value = myArray(myCount)
    Next myCount
End With
End Sub
```

Figure 19.2

Use an array to create column headers quickly.

	A	B	C	D
1	Name	Address	Phone	Email
2				

Variant variables can hold any type of information. Create a `Variant`-type variable that can be treated like an array. Use the Array function to shove the data into the variant, forcing the variant to take on the properties of an array.

If the information needed in the array is on the sheet already, use the following to fill an array quickly:

```
Dim myArray As Variant

myArray = Worksheets("Sheet1").Range("B2:C17")
```

19

Although these two methods are quick and straightforward, they might not always suit the situation. For example, if you need every other row in the array, use the following code (see Figure 19.3):

```
Sub EveryOtherRow()
'there are 16 rows of data, but we are only filling every other row
'half the table size, so our array needs only 8 rows
Dim myArray(1 To 8, 1 To 2)
Dim i As Integer, j As Integer, myCount As Integer

'Fill the array with every other row
For i = 1 To 8
    For j = 1 To 2
'i*2 directs the program to retrieve every other row
        myArray(i, j) = Worksheets("Sheet1").Cells(i * 2, j + 1).Value
```

```
      Next j
    Next i

    'Empty the array
    For myCount = LBound(myArray) To UBound(myArray)
        Worksheets("Sheet1").Cells(myCount * 2, 4) = _
        WorksheetFunction.Sum(myArray(myCount, 1), myArray(myCount, 2))
    Next myCount
    End Sub
```

Figure 19.3

Fill the array with only the data needed.

	A	B	C	D
1		Dec '08	Jan '09	Sum
2	Apples	45	0	45
3	Oranges	12	10	
4	Grapefruit	86	12	98
5	Lemons	15	15	
6	Tomatoes	58	24	82

LBound finds the start location, the lower bound, of the array (myArray). UBound finds the end location, the upper bound, of the array. The program can then loop through the array and sum the information as it writes it to the sheet. How to empty an array is explained in the following section.

Empty an Array

After an array is filled, the data needs to be retrieved. However, before you do that, you can manipulate the data or return information about it such as the maximum integer, as shown in the following code (see Figure 19.4):

```
    Sub QuickFillMax()
    Dim myArray As Variant

    myArray = Worksheets("Sheet1").Range("B2:C17")
    MsgBox "Maximum Integer is: " & WorksheetFunction.Max(myArray)

    End Sub
```

Figure 19.4

Return the Max variable in an array.

	A	B	C	D	E
1		Dec '08	Jan '09		
2	Apples	45	0		
3	Oranges	12	10		
4	Grapefruit	86	12		
5	Lemons	15	15		
6	Tomatoes	58	24		
7	Cabbage	24	26		
8	Lettuce	31	29		
9	Peppers	0	31		
10	Potatoes	10	45		
11	Yams	61	46		
12	Onions	26	58		
13	Garlic	29	61		
14	Green Beans	46	64		
15	Broccoli	64	79		
16	Peas	79	86		
17	Carrots	95	95		
18					

Microsoft Excel

Maximum Integer is: 95

OK

Data can also be manipulated as it is returned to the sheet. In the following example, Lbound and Ubound are used with a For loop to loop through the elements of the array and average each set. The result is placed on the sheet in a new column (see Figure 19.5).

> **NOTE** MyCount + 1 is used to place the results back on the sheet because the Lbound is 1 and the data starts in Row 2.

```
Sub QuickFillAverage()
Dim myArray As Variant
Dim myCount As Integer
'fill the array
myArray = Worksheets("Sheet1").Range("B2:C17")

'Average the data in the array just as it is placed on the sheet
For myCount = LBound(myArray) To UBound(myArray)
'calculate the average and place the result in column E
    Worksheets("Sheet1").Cells(myCount + 1, 5).Value = _
    WorksheetFunction.Average(myArray(myCount, 1), myArray(myCount, 2))
Next myCount

End Sub
```

Figure 19.5
Calculations can be done on the data as it is returned to the sheet.

	A	B	C	D	E
1		Dec '08	Jan '09	Sum	Average
2	Apples	45	0	45	22.5
3	Oranges	12	10		11
4	Grapefruit	86	12	98	49
5	Lemons	15	15		15
6	Tomatoes	58	24	82	41
7	Cabbage	24	26		25
8	Lettuce	31	29	60	30
9	Peppers	0	31		15.5
10	Potatoes	10	45	55	27.5
11	Yams	61	46		53.5
12	Onions	26	58	84	42
13	Garlic	29	61		45
14	Green Beans	46	64	110	55
15	Broccoli	64	79		71.5
16	Peas	79	86	165	82.5
17	Carrots	95	95		95

Arrays Make It Easier to Manipulate Data, but Is That All?

So far you have learned that arrays can make it easier to manipulate data and get information from it—but is that all they are good for? No, arrays are so powerful because they can actually make the code run faster!

Typically, when there are columns of data to average such as in the preceding example, your first thought might be the following:

```
Sub SlowAverage()
Dim myCount As Integer, LastRow As Integer
```

```
LastRow = Worksheets("Sheet1").Cells(Worksheets("Sheet1").Rows.Count, 1). _
    End(xlUp).Row

For myCount = 2 To LastRow
    With Worksheets("Sheet1")
        .Cells(myCount, 6).Value = _
        WorksheetFunction.Average(Cells(myCount, 2), Cells(myCount, 3))
    End With
Next myCount

End Sub
```

Although this works fine, the program has to look at each row of the sheet individually, get the data, do the calculation, and then place it in the correct column. Wouldn't it be easier to grab all the data at one time, and then do the calculations and place it back on the sheet? Also, with the slower version of the code, you need to know which columns on the sheet to manipulate, which in this example are Columns 2 and 3. With an array, you need to know only what element of the array you want to manipulate.

To make arrays even more useful, rather than use an address range to fill the array, you can use a named range. With a named range in an array, it does not matter where on the sheet the range is.

For example, instead of

```
myArray = Range("B2:C17")
```

Use this:

```
myArray = Range("myData")
```

With the slow method, you need to know where myData is so you can return the correct columns. However, with an array all you need to know is that you want the first and second columns.

> **TIP**
>
> You can make your array even faster! Technically, if you place a column of data into an array, it is a two-dimensional array. If you want to process it, you must process the row and column.
>
> However, you can process the column more quickly if it is just a single row, as long as it does not exceed 16,384 columns. To do this, use the Transpose function to turn the one column into one row (see Figure 19.6)
>
> ```
> Sub TransposeArray()
>     Dim myArray As Variant
>
>     myArray = WorksheetFunction.Transpose(Range("myTran"))
>
>     'return the 5th element of the array
>     MsgBox "The 5th element of the Array is: " & myArray(5)
>     End Sub
> ```

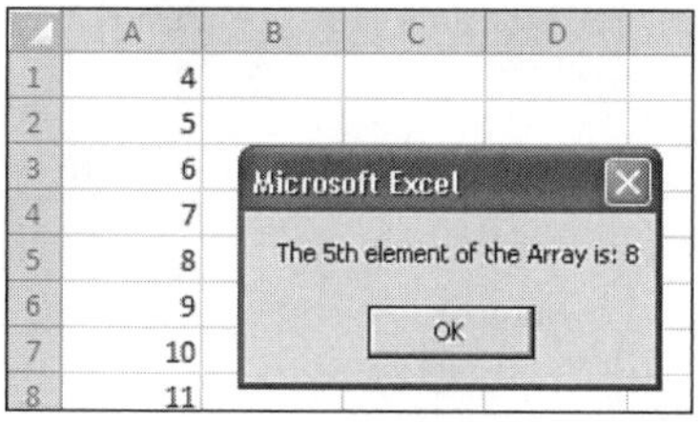

Figure 19.6

Use the `Transpose` function to turn a two-dimensional array into a one-dimensional array.

Dynamic Arrays

You cannot always know how big of an array you will need. You could create an array based on how big it could ever need to be, but that's not only a waste of memory; what if it turns out it needs to be even bigger? To avoid this problem, you can use a *dynamic array*.

A dynamic array is an array that does not have a set size. In other words, you declare the array; but leave the parentheses empty:

```
Dim myArray ()
```

Later, as the program needs to use the array, `Redim` is used to set the size of the array. The following program, which returns the names of all the sheets in the workbook, first creates a boundless array, and then it sets the upper bound after it knows how many sheets are in the workbook:

```
Option Base 1
Sub MySheets()
Dim myArray() As String
Dim myCount As Integer, NumShts As Integer

NumShts = ActiveWorkbook.Worksheets.Count

' Size the array
ReDim myArray(1 To NumShts)

For myCount = 1 To NumShts
    myArray(myCount) = ActiveWorkbook.Sheets(myCount).Name
Next myCount

End Sub
```

Using `Redim` reinitializes the array. Therefore, if you were to use it many times such as in a loop, you would lose all the data it holds. To prevent this from happening, you need to use `Preserve`. The `Preserve` keyword allows you to resize the last array dimension, but you cannot use it to change the number of dimensions.

The following example looks for all the Excel files in a directory and puts the results in an array. Because you do not know how many files there will be until you actually look at them, you can't size the array before the program is run:

```
Sub XLFiles()
Dim FName As String
```

```
Dim arNames() As String
Dim myCount As Integer

FName = Dir("C:\Contracting Files\Excel VBA 2007 by Jelen & Syrstad\*.xls*")
Do Until FName = ""
    myCount = myCount + 1
    ReDim Preserve arNames(1 To myCount)
    arNames(myCount) = FName
    FName = Dir
Loop

End Sub
```

> **CAUTION**
>
> Using `Preserve` with large amounts of data in a loop can slow down the program. If possible, use code to figure out the maximum size of the array.

Passing an Array

Just like strings, integers, and other variables, arrays can be passed into other procedures. This makes for more efficient and easier-to-read code. The following sub, `PassAnArray`, passes the array, `myArray`, into the function `RegionSales`. The data in the array is summed for the specified region and the result returned to the sub:

```
Sub PassAnArray()
Dim myArray() As Variant
Dim myRegion As String

myArray = Range("mySalesData") 'named range containing all the data
myRegion = InputBox("Enter Region - Central, East, West")
MsgBox myRegion & " Sales are: " & Format(RegionSales(myArray, _
    myRegion), "$#,#00.00")

End Sub

Function RegionSales(ByRef BigArray As Variant, sRegion As String) As Long
Dim myCount As Integer

RegionSales = 0
For myCount = LBound(BigArray) To UBound(BigArray)
'The regions are listed in column 1 of the data, hence the 1st column of the
array
    If BigArray(myCount, 1) = sRegion Then
'The data to sum is the 6th column in the data
        RegionSales = BigArray(myCount, 6) + RegionSales
    End If
Next myCount

End Function
```

Next Steps

Arrays are a type of variable used for holding more than one piece of data. Chapter 20, "Text File Processing," covers importing from a text file and writing to a text file. Being able to write to a text file is useful when you need to write out data for another system to read or even when you need to produce HTML files.

19

Text File Processing

VBA simplifies both reading and writing from text files. This chapter covers importing from a text file and writing to a text file. Being able to write to a text file proves useful when you need to write out data for another system to read, or even when you need to produce HTML files.

Importing from Text Files

There are two basic scenarios when reading from text files. If the file contains fewer than 1,048,576 records, it is not difficult to import the file using the Workbooks.OpenText method. If the file contains more than 1,048,576 records, you have to read the file one record at a time.

Importing Text Files with Fewer Than 1,048,576 Rows

Text files typically come in one of two formats. In one format, the fields in each record are separated by some delimiter such as a comma, pipe, or tab. In the second format, each field takes a particular number of character positions. This is called a *fixed-width file* and was very popular in the days of COBOL.

Excel can import either type of file. You can also open both types using the OpenText method. In both cases, it is best to record the process of opening the file and use the recorded snippet of code.

Opening a Fixed-Width File

Figure 20.1 shows a text file where each field takes up a certain amount of space in the record. Writing the code to open this type of file is slightly arduous because you need to specify the length of each field. In my collection of antiques, I still have the metal ruler used by COBOL programmers to measure the

IN THIS CHAPTER

Importing from Text Files 463

Writing Text Files 473

number of characters in a field printed on a greenbar printer. In theory, you could change the font of your file to a monospace font and use this same method. However, using the macro recorder is a slightly more up-to-date method.

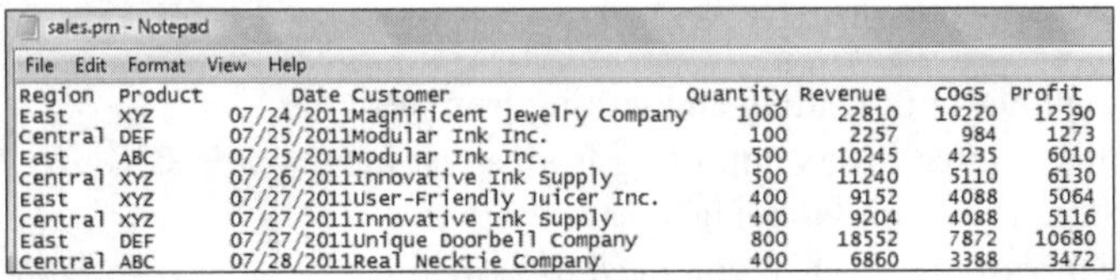

Figure 20.1
This file is fixed width. Because you must specify the exact length of each field in the file, opening this file is quite involved.

Turn on the macro recorder by selecting Record Macro from the Developer tab. From the File menu, select Open. Change the Files of Type to All Files and find your text file.

In the Text Import Wizard's step 1, specify that the data is Fixed Width and click Next.

Excel then looks at your data and attempts to figure out where each field begins and ends. Figure 20.2 shows Excel's guess on this particular file. Because the Date field is too close to the Customer field, Excel missed drawing that line.

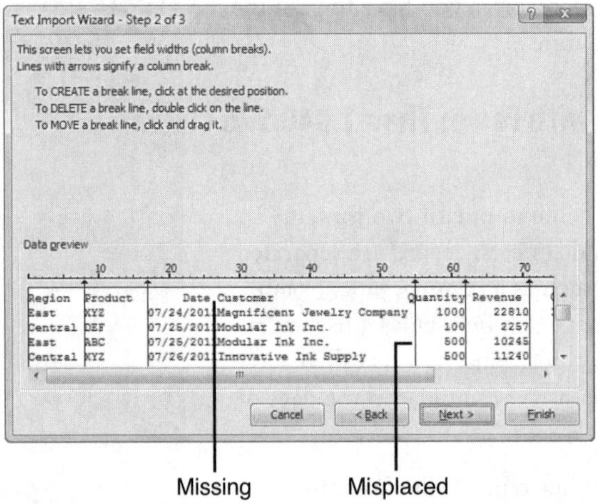

Figure 20.2
Excel guesses at where each field starts. In this case, it missed two fields and probably did not leave enough room for a longer product name.

To add a new field indicator in step 2 of the wizard, click in the appropriate place in the Data Preview window. If you click in the wrong column, click the line and drag it to the right place. If Excel inadvertently put in an extra field line, double-click the line to remove it. Figure 20.3 shows the data preview after the appropriate changes have been made. Note the little ruler above the data. When you click to add a field marker, Excel is actually handling the tedious work of figuring out that the Customer field starts in position 27 for a length of 27.

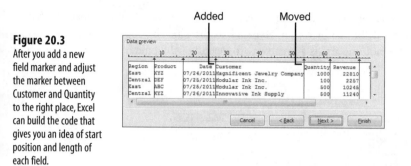

Figure 20.3
After you add a new field marker and adjust the marker between Customer and Quantity to the right place, Excel can build the code that gives you an idea of start position and length of each field.

In step 3 of the wizard, Excel always assumes that every field is in General format.

Change the format of any fields that require special handling. Click the third column and choose the appropriate format from the Column Data Format section of the dialog box. Figure 20.4 shows the selections for this file.

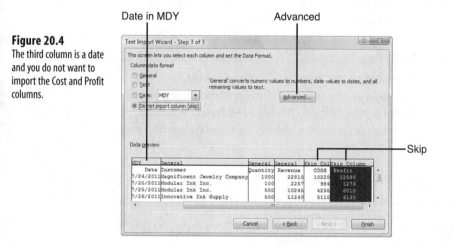

Figure 20.4
The third column is a date and you do not want to import the Cost and Profit columns.

If you have date fields, click the heading above that column, and change the column data format choice to a date. If you have a file with dates in year-month-day format or day-month-year format, select the drop-down next to date and choose the appropriate date sequence.

If you prefer to skip some fields, click that column and select Do Not Import Column (Skip) from the Column Data Format selection. There are a couple of instances when this is useful. If the file includes sensitive data that you do not want to show to the client, you can leave it out of the import. For example, perhaps this report is for a customer to whom you do not want to show the cost of goods sold or profit. In this case, you can choose to skip these fields in the import. In addition, occasionally you will encounter a text file that is both fixed width and delimited by a character such as the pipe character. Setting the 1-wide pipe columns as "do not import" is a great way to get rid of the pipe characters, as shown in Figure 20.5

Figure 20.5
This file is both fixed width and pipe delimited. Liberal use of the Do Not Import Column setting for each pipe column eliminates the pipe characters from the file.

If you have text fields that contain alphabetic characters, you can choose the General format. The only time you should choose the Text format is if you have a numeric field that you explicitly need imported as text. One example of this is an account number with leading zeros or a column of zip codes. In this case, change the field to Text format to ensure that zip code 01234 does not lose the leading zero.

CAUTION ──

After you import a text file and specify that one field is text, that field will exhibit seemingly bizarre behavior. Try inserting a new row and entering a formula in the middle of a column imported as text. Instead of getting the results of the formula, Excel enters the formula as text. The solution is to delete the formula, format the entire column as General, and then enter the formula again.

After opening the file, turn off the macro recorder and examine the recorded code:

```
Workbooks.OpenText Filename:="C:\sales.prn", Origin:=437, StartRow:=1, _
    DataType:=xlFixedWidth, FieldInfo:=Array(Array(0, 1), Array(8, 1), _
    Array(17, 3), Array(27, 1), Array(54, 1), Array(62, 1), Array(71, 9), _
    Array(79, 9)), TrailingMinusNumbers:=True
```

The most confusing part of this code is the `FieldInfo` parameter. You are supposed to code an array of two-element arrays. Each field in the file gets a two-element array to identify both where the field starts and the field type.

The field start position is zero based. Because the Region field is in the first character position, its start position is listed as zero.

The field type is a numeric code. If you were coding this by hand, you would use the `xlColumnDataType` constant names; but for some reason, the macro recorder uses the harder-to-understand numeric equivalents.

With Table 20.1, you can decode the meaning of the individual arrays in the `FieldInfo` array. `Array(0, 1)` means that this field starts zero characters from the left edge of the file and is a general format. `Array(8, 1)` indicates that the next field starts eight characters from the left edge of the file and is General format. `Array(17, 3)` indicates that the next field starts 17 characters from the left edge of the file and is a date format in month-day-year sequence.

Table 20.1   `xlColumnDataType` **Values**

Value	Constant	Used For
1	xlGeneralFormat	General
2	xlTextFormat	Text
3	xlMDYFormat	MDY date
4	xlDMYFormat	DMY date
5	xlYMDFormat	YMD date
6	xlMYDFormat	MYD date
7	xlDYMFormat	DYM date
8	xlYDMFormat	YDM date
9	xlSkipColumn	Skip Column
10	xlEMDFormat	EMD date

As you can see, the `FieldInfo` parameter for fixed-width files is arduous to code and confusing to look at. This is one situation where it is easier to record the macro and copy the code snippet.

> **CAUTION**
>
> The `xlTrailingMinusNumbers` parameter was new in Excel 2002. If you have any clients who might be using Excel 97 or Excel 2000, take the recorded parameter out. The code runs fine without the parameter in newer versions. However, if left in, it leads to a compile error on older versions. In my experience, this is the number one cause for code to crash on earlier versions of Excel.

Opening a Delimited File

Figure 20.6 shows a text file where each field is comma separated. The main task in opening such a file is to tell Excel that the delimiter in the file is a comma and then identify any special processing for each field. In this case, we definitely want to identify the third column as being a date in mm/dd/yyyy format.

20

┌─ C A U T I O N ──

If you try to record the process of opening a comma-delimited file where the filename ends in .csv, Excel records the `Workbooks.Open` method rather than `Workbooks.OpenText`. If you need to control the formatting of certain columns, rename the file to have a .txt extension before recording the macro.

└───

Figure 20.6
This file is comma delimited. Opening this file involves telling Excel to look for a comma as the delimiter and then identifying any special handling, such as treating the third column as a date. This is much easier than handling fixed-width files.

```
Region,Product,Date,Customer,Quantity,Revenue,COGS,Profit
East,XYZ,07/24/2011,Magnificent Jewelry Company,1000,22810,102
Central,DEF,07/25/2011,Modular Ink Inc.,100,2257,984,1273
East,ABC,07/25/2011,Modular Ink Inc.,500,10245,4235,6010
Central,XYZ,07/26/2011,Innovative Ink Supply,500,11240,5110,61
East,XYZ,07/27/2011,User-Friendly Juicer Inc.,400,9152,4088,50
Central,XYZ,07/27/2011,Innovative Ink Supply,400,9204,4088,511
East,DEF,07/27/2011,Unique Doorbell Company,800,18552,7872,106
```

Turn on the macro recorder and record the process of opening the text file. In step 1 of the wizard, specify that the file is delimited.

In the Text Import Wizard—step 2 of 3, the data preview may initially look horrible. This is because Excel defaults to assuming that each field is separated by a tab character (see Figure 20.7).

After clearing the Tab check box and selecting the proper delimiter choice, which in this case is a comma, the data preview in step 2 looks perfect, as shown in Figure 20.8

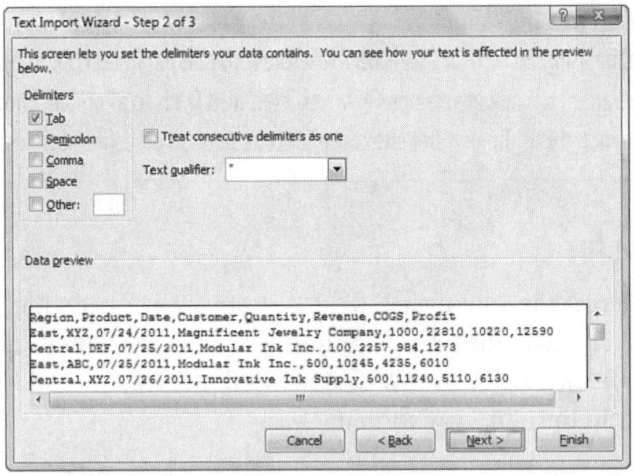

Figure 20.7
Before you import a delimited text file, the initial data preview looks like a confusing mess of data because Excel is looking for tab characters between each field when a comma is actually the delimiter in this file.

Figure 20.8
After changing the delimiter field from a tab to a comma, the data preview looks perfect. This is certainly easier than the cumbersome process in step 2 for a fixed-width file.

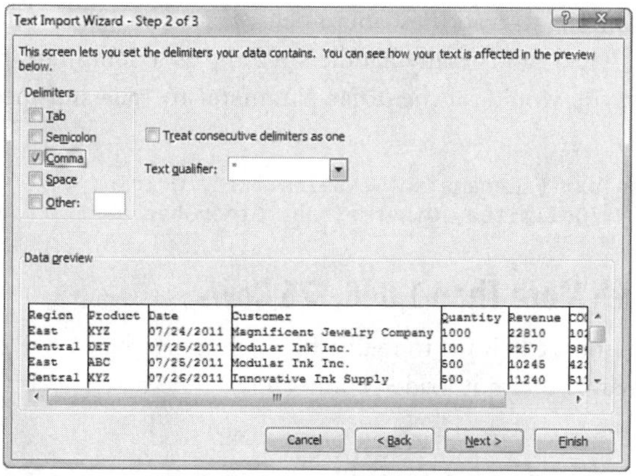

Step 3 of the wizard is identical to step 3 for a fixed-width file. In this case, specify that the third column has a date format. Click Finish, and you will have this code in the macro recorder:

```
Workbooks.OpenText Filename:="C:\sales.txt", Origin:=437, _
    StartRow:=1, DataType:=xlDelimited, TextQualifier:=xlDoubleQuote, _
    ConsecutiveDelimiter:=False, Tab:=False, Semicolon:=False, Comma:=True _
    , Space:=False, Other:=False, FieldInfo:=Array(Array(1, 1), Array(2, 1), _
    Array(3, 3), Array(4, 1), Array(5, 1), Array(6, 1), Array(7, 1), _
    Array(8, 1)), TrailingMinusNumbers:=True
```

Although this code appears longer, it is actually simpler. In the `FieldInfo` parameter, the two element arrays consist of a sequence number, starting at 1 for the first field, and then an `xlColumnDataType` from Table 20.1. In this example, `Array(2, 1)` is saying "the second field is of general type." `Array(3, 3)` is saying, "the third field is a date in M-D-Y format." The code is longer because it explicitly specifies that each possible delimiter is set to `False`. Because `False` is the default for all delimiters, you really need only the one that you will use. The following code is equivalent:

```
Workbooks.OpenText Filename:= "C:\sales.txt", DataType:=xlDelimited,
Comma:=True, _
    FieldInfo:=Array(Array(1, 1), Array(2, 1), Array(3, 3), Array(4, 1), _
    Array(5, 1), Array(6, 1), Array(7, 1), Array(8, 1))
```

Finally, to make the code more readable, you can use the constant names rather than the code numbers:

```
Workbooks.OpenText Filename:="C:\sales.txt", DataType:=xlDelimited, _
Comma:=True, _
FieldInfo:=Array(Array(1, xlGeneralFormat), Array(2, xlGeneralFormat), _
Array(3, xlMDYFormat), Array(4, xlGeneralFormat), Array(5, xlGeneralFormat), _
Array(6, xlGeneralFormat), Array(7, xlGeneralFormat), Array(8, _
xlGeneralFormat))
```

20

Excel has built-in options to read files where fields are delimited by tabs, semicolons, commas, or spaces. Excel can actually handle anything as a delimiter. If someone sends pipe-delimited text, you would set the Other parameter to True and specify an OtherChar parameter:

```
Workbooks.OpenText Filename:= "C:\sales.txt", Origin:=437, _
    DataType:=xlDelimited, Other:=True, OtherChar:= "¦", FieldInfo:=...
```

Reading Text Files with More Than 1,048,576 Rows

If you use the Text Import Wizard to read a file with more than 1,048,576 rows of data, you will get an error saying "File not loaded completely." The first 1,048,576 rows of the file will load correctly.

If you use Workbooks.OpenText to open a file with more than 1,048,576 rows of data, you are given no indication that the file did not load completely. Excel 2010 loads the first 1,048,576 rows and allows macro execution to continue. Your only indication there is a problem is if someone notices that the reports are not reporting all the sales. If you think that your files will ever get this large, it would be good to check to see whether cell A1048576 is nonblank after an import. If it is, the odds are that the entire file was not loaded.

Reading Text Files One Row at a Time

You might run into a text file with more than 1,048,576 rows. When this happens, the alternative is to read the text file one row at a time. The code for doing this is the same code you might remember in your first high school BASIC class.

You need to open the file for INPUT as #1. You can then use the Line Input #1 statement to read a line of the file into a variable. The following code opens sales.txt, reads 10 lines of the file into the first 10 cells of the worksheet, and closes the file:

```
Sub Import10()
    ThisFile = "C\sales.txt"
    Open ThisFile For Input As #1
    For i = 1 To 10
        Line Input #1, Data
        Cells(i, 1).Value = Data
    Next i
    Close #1
End Sub
```

Rather than read only 10 records, you will want to read until you get to the end of the file. A variable called EOF is updated by Excel automatically. If you open a file for input as #1, checking EOF(1) will tell you whether you have read the last record.

Use a Do...While loop to keep reading records until you have reached the end of the file:

```
Sub ImportAll()
    ThisFile = "C:\sales.txt"
    Open ThisFile For Input As #1
```

```
        Ctr = 0
        Do
            Line Input #1, Data
            Ctr = Ctr + 1
            Cells(Ctr, 1).Value = Data
        Loop While EOF(1) = False
        Close #1
    End Sub
```

After reading records with code such as this, you will note in Figure 20.9 that the data is not parsed into columns. All the fields are in Column A of the file.

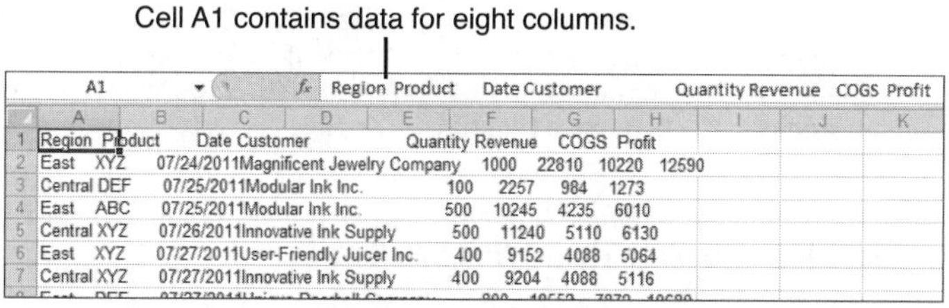

Cell A1 contains data for eight columns.

Figure 20.9

When you are reading a text file one row at a time, all the data fields end up in one long entry in Column A.

Use the TextToColumns method to parse the records into columns. The parameters for TextToColumns are nearly identical to the OpenText method:

```
Cells(1, 1).Resize(Ctr, 1).TextToColumns Destination:=Range("A1"), _
DataType:=xlDelimited, Comma:=True, FieldInfo:=Array(Array(1, _
xlGeneralFormat), Array(2, xlMDYFormat), Array(3, xlGeneralFormat), _
Array(4, xlGeneralFormat), Array(5, xlGeneralFormat), Array(6, _
xlGeneralFormat), Array(7,xlGeneralFormat), Array(8, xlGeneralFormat), _
Array(9, xlGeneralFormat), Array(10,xlGeneralFormat), Array(11, _
xlGeneralFormat))
```

CAUTION

For the remainder of your Excel session, Excel will remember the delimiter settings. There is an annoying bug (feature?) in Excel. After Excel remembers that you are using a comma or a tab as a delimiter, any time that you attempt to paste data from the Clipboard to Excel, the data is parsed automatically by the delimiters specified in the OpenText method. Therefore, if you attempted to paste some text that includes the customer ABC, Inc., the text will be parsed automatically into two columns, with text up to ABC in one column and Inc. in the next column.

20

Rather than hard-code that you are using the #1 designator to open the text file, it is safer to use the FreeFile function. This returns an integer representing the next file number available for use by the Open statement. The complete code to read a text file smaller than 1,048,576 rows is as follows:

```
Sub ImportAll()
    ThisFile = "C:\sales.txt"
    FileNumber = FreeFile
```

```
Open ThisFile For Input As #FileNumber
Ctr = 0
Do
    Line Input #FileNumber, Data
    Ctr = Ctr + 1
    Cells(Ctr, 1).Value = Data
Loop While EOF(FileNumber) = False
Close #FileNumber
Cells(1, 1).Resize(Ctr, 1).TextToColumns Destination:=Range("A1"), _
    DataType:=xlDelimited, Comma:=True, _
    FieldInfo:=Array(Array(1, xlGeneralFormat), _
    Array(2, xlMDYFormat), Array(3, xlGeneralFormat), _
    Array(4, xlGeneralFormat), Array(5, xlGeneralFormat), _
    Array(5, xlGeneralFormat), Array(6, xlGeneralFormat), _
    Array(7, xlGeneralFormat), Array(8, xlGeneralFormat), _
    Array(9, xlGeneralFormat), Array(10, xlGeneralFormat), _
    Array(10, xlGeneralFormat), Array(11, xlGeneralFormat))
End Sub
```

Reading Text Files with More Than 1,048,576 Rows

You can use the Line Input method for reading a large text file. A good strategy is to read rows into cells A1:A1048575, and then begin reading additional rows into cell AA2. You can start in Row 2 on the second set so that the headings can be copied from Row 1 of the first data set. If the file is large enough that it fills up Column AA, move to BA2, CA2, and so on.

Also, you should stop writing columns when you get to Row 1048574, leaving two blank rows at the bottom. This ensures that the code Cells(Rows.Count, 1)""".End(xlup).Row finds the final row. The following code reads a large text file into several sets of columns:

```
Sub ReadLargeFile()
    ThisFile = "C:\sales.txt"
    FileNumber = FreeFile
    Open ThisFile For Input As #FileNumber

    NextRow = 1
    NextCol = 1
    Do While Not EOF(1)
        Line Input #FileNumber, Data
        Cells(NextRow, NextCol).Value = Data
        NextRow = NextRow + 1
        If NextRow = (Rows.Count -2)  Then
            ' Parse these records
            Range(Cells(1, NextCol), Cells(Rows.Count, NextCol)).TextToColumns _
                Destination:=Cells(1, NextCol), DataType:=xlDelimited, _
                Comma:=True, FieldInfo:=Array(Array(1, xlGeneralFormat), _
                Array(2, xlMDYFormat), Array(3, xlGeneralFormat), _
                Array(4, xlGeneralFormat), Array(5, xlGeneralFormat), _
                Array(6, xlGeneralFormat), Array(7, xlGeneralFormat), _
                Array(8, xlGeneralFormat), Array(9, xlGeneralFormat), _
                Array(10, xlGeneralFormat), Array(11, xlGeneralFormat))
            ' Copy the headings from section 1
            If NextCol > 1 Then
                Range("A1:K1").Copy Destination:=Cells(1, NextCol)
```

```
                End If
                ' Set up the next section
                NextCol = NextCol + 26
                NextRow = 2
            End If
        Loop
        Close #FileNumber
        ' Parse the final Section of records
        FinalRow = NextRow - 1
        If FinalRow = 1 Then
            ' Handle if the file coincidentally had 1084574 rows exactly
            NextCol = NextCol - 26
        Else
            Range(Cells(2, NextCol), Cells(FinalRow, NextCol)).TextToColumns _
                    Destination:=Cells(1, NextCol), DataType:=xlDelimited, _
                    Comma:=True, FieldInfo:=Array(Array(1, xlGeneralFormat), _
                    Array(2, xlMDYFormat), Array(3, xlGeneralFormat), _
                    Array(4, xlGeneralFormat), Array(5, xlGeneralFormat), _
                    Array(6, xlGeneralFormat), Array(7, xlGeneralFormat), _
                    Array(8, xlGeneralFormat), Array(9, xlGeneralFormat), _
                    Array(10, xlGeneralFormat), Array(11, xlGeneralFormat))
            If NextCol > 1 Then
                Range("A1:K1").Copy Destination:=Cells(1, NextCol)
            End If
        End If

        DataSets = (NextCol - 1) / 26 + 1

    End Sub
```

Usually you should write the DataSets variable to a named cell somewhere in the workbook so that you know how many datasets you have in the worksheet later.

As you can imagine, using this method it is possible to read 660,601,620 rows of data into a single worksheet. The code that you formerly used to filter and report the data now becomes more complex. You might find yourself creating pivot tables from each set of columns to create a data set summary, and then finally summarizing all the summary tables with a final pivot table. At some point, you need to consider whether the application really belongs in Access. You can also consider whether the data should be stored in Access with an Excel front end, which is discussed in Chapter 21, "Using Access as a Back End to Enhance Multi-User Access to Data."

Writing Text Files

The code for writing text files is similar to reading text files. You need to open a specific file for output as #1. Then, as you loop through various records, you write them to the file using the Print #1 statement.

Before you open a file for output, make sure that any prior examples of the file have been deleted. You can use the Kill statement to delete a file. Kill returns an error if the file was not there in the first place. In this case, you will want to use On Error Resume Next to prevent an error.

The following code writes out a text file for use by another application:

```
Sub WriteFile()
    ThisFile = "C:\Results.txt"

    ' Delete yesterday's copy of the file
    On Error Resume Next
    Kill ThisFile
    On Error GoTo 0

    ' Open the file
    Open ThisFile For Output As #1
    FinalRow = Cells(Rows.Count, 1).End(xlUp).Row
    ' Write out the file
    For j = 1 To FinalRow
        Print #1, Cells(j, 1).Value
    Next j
End Sub
```

This is a somewhat trivial example. You can use this method to write out any type of text-based file. The code at the end of Chapter 16, "Reading from and Writing to the Web," uses the same concept to write out HTML files.

Next Steps

There will be times when you write to text files out of necessity—either to import data from another system or to produce data compatible with another system. Using text files is a slow method for reading and writing data. In Chapter 21 you learn about writing to Access Multidimensional Database (MDB) files. These files are faster, indexable, and allow multi-user access to data.

20

Using Access as a Back End to Enhance Multiuser Access to Data

21

The example near the end of Chapter 20, "Text File Processing," proposed a method for storing 683 million records in an Excel worksheet. At some point, you need to admit that even though Excel is the greatest product in the world, there is a time to move to Access and take advantage of the Access Multidimensional Database (MDB) files.

Even before you have more than one million rows, another compelling reason to use MDB data files is to allow multiuser access to data without the headaches associated with shared workbooks.

Microsoft Excel offers an option to share a workbook, but you automatically lose a number of important Excel features when you share one. After you share a workbook, you cannot use automatic subtotals, pivot tables, Group and Outline mode, scenarios, protection, Autoformat, Styles, Pictures, Add Charts, or Insert Worksheets.

By using an Excel VBA front end and storing data in an MDB database, you have the best of both worlds. You have the power and flexibility of Excel and the multiuser access capability available in Access.

IN THIS CHAPTER

ADO Versus DAO 476

The Tools of ADO 478

Adding a Record to the Database 480

Retrieving Records from the Database 481

Updating an Existing Record 483

Deleting Records via ADO 485

Summarizing Records via ADO 485

Other Utilities via ADO 487

SQL Server Examples 490

> **NOTE**
> MDB is the official file format of both Microsoft Access and Microsoft Visual Basic. This means that you can deploy an Excel solution that reads and writes from an MDB to customers who do not have Microsoft Access. Of course, it helps if you as the developer have a copy of Access because you can use the Access front end to set up tables and queries.

> **CAUTION**
>
> The examples in this chapter make use of the jet engine for reading from and writing to the Access database. The jet engine works with access data stored in Access 97 through 2010. If you are sure that all of the people running the macro will have Office 2007 or newer, you could instead use the ACE engine.
>
> The troubling issue is that when this book goes to press, Microsoft is not committed to releasing 64-bit versions of either the jet or ACE ADO interface. This is perplexing because it would leave hundreds of thousands of Access applications without a path to work in 64-bit Office. This will either prevent people from upgrading to 64-bit Office or force people into SQL Server.
>
> To use code in this chapter with 64-bit versions of Office, type `Microsoft.Jet.OLEDB` and 64-bit into a search engine to see whether Microsoft has relented and provided a 64-bit version.
>
> If you are running 64-bit Excel, you might have to switch over to SQL Server Express for storing this data. See examples at the end of the chapter for adapting this code for SQL Server.

ADO Versus DAO

For several years, Microsoft recommended data access objects (DAO) for accessing data in external database. DAO became very popular, and a great deal of code was written for it. When Microsoft released Excel 2000, they started pushing ActiveX data objects (ADO). The concepts are similar, and the syntax differs only slightly. I use ADO in this chapter. Realize that if you start going through code written a decade ago, you might run into DAO code. Other than a few syntax changes, the code for both ADO and DAO looks similar.

If you discover that you have to debug some old code using DAO, check out the Microsoft Knowledge Base articles that you can find at the following address, which discuss the differences: http://support.microsoft.com/kb/225048.

The following two articles provide the Rosetta Stone between DAO and ADO. The ADO code is shown at http://support.microsoft.com/kb/q146607.

The equivalent DAO code is shown at http://support.microsoft.com/kb/q142938.

To use any code in this chapter, open the VB Editor. Select Tools, References from the main menu, and then select Microsoft ActiveX Data Objects Library from the Available References list, as shown in Figure 21.1.

> **TIP**
>
> If you have Vista or newer, you will have access to version 6.0 of this library. If you will be distributing the application to anyone who is still on Windows XP, you should choose version 2.8 instead.

Figure 21.1
To read or write from an
Access MDB file, add the
reference for Microsoft
ActiveX Data Objects
Library or higher.

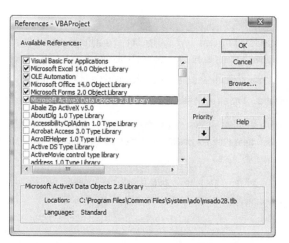

CASE STUDY: CREATING A SHARED ACCESS DATABASE

Linda and Janine are two buyers for a retail chain of stores. Each morning, they import data from the cash registers to get current information on sales and inventory for 2,000 styles. Throughout the day, either buyer may enter transfers of inventory from one store to another. It would be ideal if Linda could see the pending transfers entered by Janine and vice versa.

Each buyer has an Excel application with VBA running on her desktop. They each import the cash register data and have VBA routines that facilitate the creation of pivot table reports to help them make buying decisions.

Attempting to store the transfer data in a common Excel file causes problems. When either buyer attempts to write to the Excel file, the entire file becomes read-only for the other buyer. With a shared workbook, Excel turns off the capability to create pivot tables, and this is required in their application.

Neither Linda nor Janine have the professional version of Office, so they do not have Access running on their desktop PCs.

The solution is to produce an Access database on a network drive that both Linda and Janine can see:

1. Using Access on another PC, produce a new database called `transfers.mdb` and add a table called `tblTransfer`, as shown in Figure 21.2.

Figure 21.2
Multiple people using
their own Excel work-
books will read and write
to this table inside an
MDB file on a network
drive.

Field Name	Data Type
ID	AutoNumber
Style	Text
FromStore	Number
ToStore	Number
Qty	Number
TDate	Date/Time
Sent	Yes/No
Receive	Yes/No

21

2. Move the Transfers.mdb file to a network drive. You might find that this common folder uses different drive letter mappings on each machine. It might be H:\Common\ on Linda's machine and I:\Common\ on Janine's machine.

3. On both machines, go to the VB Editor and under Tools, References, add a reference to ActiveX Data Objects Library.

4. In both of their applications, find an out-of-the-way cell to store the path to transfers.mdb. Name this cell TPath.

The application provides nearly seamless multiuser access to both buyers. Both Linda and Janine can read or write to the table at the same time. The only time a conflict would occur is if they both happened to try to update the same record at the same time.

Other than the out-of-the-way cell reference to the path to transfers.mdb, neither buyer is aware that her data is being stored in a shared Access table, and neither computer needs to have Access installed.

The remainder of this chapter gives you the code necessary to allow the application included in the previous case study to read or write data from the tblTransfer table.

The Tools of ADO

You encounter several terms when using ADO to connect to an external data source.

- **Recordset**—When connecting to an Access database, the recordset will either be a table in the database or a query in the database. Most of the ADO methods will reference the recordset. You might also want to create your own query on-the-fly. In this case, you would write a SQL statement to extract only a subset of records from a table.

- **Connection**—Defines the path to the database and the type of database. In the case of Access databases, you specify that the connection is using the Microsoft Jet Engine.

- **Cursor**—Think of the cursor as a pointer that keeps track of which record you are using in the database. There are several types of cursors and two places for the cursor to be located (described in the following bullets).

- **Cursor type**—A dynamic cursor is the most flexible cursor. If you define a recordset and someone else updates a row in the table while a dynamic cursor is active, the dynamic cursor will know about the updated record. Although this is the most flexible, it requires the most overhead. If your database doesn't have a lot of transactions, you might specify a static cursor—this type of cursor returns a snapshot of the data at the time the cursor is established.

- **Cursor location**—The cursor can be located either on the client or on the server. For an Access database residing on your hard drive, a server location for the cursor means that the Access Jet Engine on your computer is controlling the cursor. When you specify a client location for the cursor, your Excel session is controlling the cursor. On a very large external dataset, it would be better to allow the server to control the cursor. For small datasets, a client cursor is faster.

- **Lock type**—The point of this entire chapter is to allow multiple people to access a dataset at the same time. The lock type defines how ADO will prevent crashes when two people try to update the record at the same time. With an optimistic lock type, an individual record is locked only when you attempt to update the record. If your application will be doing 90 percent reads and only occasionally updating, then an optimistic lock is perfect. However, if you know that every time you read a record you will soon update the record, then you would use a pessimistic lock type. With pessimistic locks, the record is locked as soon as you read it. If you know that you will never write back to the database, you can use a read-only lock. This allows you to read the records without preventing others from writing to the records.

The primary objects needed to access data in an MDB file are an ADO connection and an ADO recordset.

The ADO connection defines the path to the database and specifies that the connection is based on the Microsoft Jet Engine.

After you have established the connection to the database, you usually will use that connection to define a recordset. A recordset can be a table or a subset of records in the table or a predefined query in the Access database. To open a recordset, you have to specify the connection and the values for the CursorType, CursorLocation, LockType, and Options parameters.

Assuming that you have only two users trying to access the table at a time, I generally use a dynamic cursor and an optimistic lock type. For large datasets, the adUseServer value of the CursorLocation property allows the database server to process records without using up RAM on the client machine. If you have a small dataset, it might be faster to use adUseClient for the CursorLocation. When the recordset is opened, all the records are transferred to memory of the client machine. This allows faster navigation from record to record.

Reading data from the Access database is easy. You can use the CopyFromRecordset method to copy all selected records from the recordset to a blank area of the worksheet.

To add a record to the Access table, use the AddNew method for the recordset. You then specify the value for each field in the table and use the Update method to commit the changes to the database.

To delete a record from the table, you can use a pass-through query to delete records that match a certain criteria.

> **NOTE**
> If you ever find yourself frustrated with ADO and think, "If I could just open Access, I could knock out a quick SQL statement that will do exactly what I need," then the pass-through query is for you. Rather than use ADO to read through the records, the pass-through query sends a request to the database to run the SQL statement that your program builds. This effectively enables you to handle any tasks that your database might support but that are not handled by ADO. The types of SQL statements handled by the pass-through query are dependent on which database type you are connecting to.

Other tools are available that let you make sure a table exists or that a particular field exists in a table. You can also use VBA to add new fields to a table definition on-the-fly.

Adding a Record to the Database

Going back to our case study earlier in the chapter, the application we are creating has a userform where buyers can enter transfers. To make the calls to the Access database as simple as possible, a series of utility modules handle the ADO connection to the database. This way, the userform code can simply call AddTransfer(Style, FromStore, ToStore, Qty).

The technique for adding records after the connection is defined is as follows:

1. Open a recordset that points to the table. In the code that follows, see the sections commented Open the Connection, Define the Recordset, and Open the Table.

2. Use AddNew to add a new record.

3. Update each field in the new record.

4. Use Update to update the recordset.

5. Close the recordset, and then close the connection.

The following code adds a new record to the tblTransfer table:

```
Sub AddTransfer(Style As Variant, FromStore As Variant, _
    ToStore As Variant, Qty As Integer)
    Dim cnn As ADODB.Connection
    Dim rst As ADODB.Recordset

    MyConn = "J:\transfers.mdb"

    ' open the connection
    Set cnn = New ADODB.Connection
    With cnn
        .Provider = "Microsoft.Jet.OLEDB.4.0"
        .Open MyConn
    End With

    ' Define the Recordset
    Set rst = New ADODB.Recordset
    rst.CursorLocation = adUseServer

    ' open the table
    rst.Open Source:="tblTransfer", _
        ActiveConnection:=cnn, _
        CursorType:=adOpenDynamic, _
        LockType:=adLockOptimistic, _
        Options:=adCmdTable

    ' Add a record
    rst.AddNew

    ' Set up the values for the fields. The first four fields
    ' are passed from the calling userform. The date field
    ' is filled with the current date.
```

21

```
        rst("Style") = Style
        rst("FromStore") = FromStore
        rst("ToStore") = ToStore
        rst("Qty") = Qty
        rst("tDate") = Date
        rst("Sent") = False
        rst("Receive") = False

        ' Write the values to this record
        rst.Update

        ' Close
        rst.Close
        cnn.Close

    End Sub
```

Retrieving Records from the Database

Reading records from the Access database is easy. As you define the recordset, you pass a SQL string to return the records in which you are interested.

> **TIP**
>
> A great way to generate the SQL is to design a query in Access that retrieves the records. While viewing the query in Access, select SQL View from the View drop-down on the Query Tools Design tab of the Ribbon. Access shows you the proper SQL statement required to execute that query. You can use this SQL statement as a model for building the SQL string in your VBA code.

After the recordset is defined, use the CopyFromRecordSet method to copy all the matching records from Access to a specific area of the worksheet.

The following routine queries the Transfer table to find all records where the Sent flag is not yet set to True. The results are placed on a blank worksheet. The final few lines display the results in a userform to illustrate how to update a record in the next section:

```
Sub GetUnsentTransfers()
    Dim cnn As ADODB.Connection
    Dim rst As ADODB.Recordset
    Dim WSOrig As Worksheet
    Dim WSTemp As Worksheet
    Dim sSQL as String
    Dim FinalRow as Long

    Set WSOrig = ActiveSheet

    'Build a SQL String to get all fields for unsent transfers
    sSQL = "SELECT ID, Style, FromStore, ToStore, Qty, tDate FROM tblTransfer"
    sSQL = sSQL & " WHERE Sent=FALSE"

    ' Path to Transfers.mdb
    MyConn = "J:\transfers.mdb"

    Set cnn = New ADODB.Connection
```

21

```
    With cnn
        .Provider = "Microsoft.Jet.OLEDB.4.0"
        .Open MyConn
    End With

    Set rst = New ADODB.Recordset
    rst.CursorLocation = adUseServer
    rst.Open Source:=sSQL, ActiveConnection:=cnn, _
        CursorType:=AdForwardOnly, LockType:=adLockOptimistic, _
            Options:=adCmdText

    ' Create the report in a new worksheet
    Set WSTemp = Worksheets.Add

    ' Add Headings
    Range("A1:F1").Value = Array("ID", "Style", "From", "To", "Qty", "Date")

    ' Copy from the recordset to row 2
    Range("A2").CopyFromRecordset rst

    ' Close the connection
    rst.Close
    cnn.Close

    ' Format the report
    FinalRow = Range("A65536").End(xlUp).Row

    ' If there were no records, then stop
    If FinalRow = 1 Then
        Application.DisplayAlerts = False
        WSTemp.Delete
        Application.DisplayAlerts = True
        WSOrig.Activate
        MsgBox "There are no transfers to confirm"
        Exit Sub
    End If

    ' Format column F as a date
    Range("F2:F" & FinalRow).NumberFormat = "m/d/y"

    ' Show the userform - used in next section
    frmTransConf.Show

    ' Delete the temporary sheet
    Application.DisplayAlerts = False
    WSTemp.Delete
    Application.DisplayAlerts = True

End Sub
```

The CopyFromRecordSet method copies records that match the SQL query to a range on the worksheet. Note that you receive only the data rows. The headings do not come along automatically. You must use code to write the headings to Row 1. Figure 21.3 shows the results.

Figure 21.3

Range("A2").
CopyFromRecordSet
brought matching records
from the Access database
to the worksheet.

	A	B	C	D	E
1	ID	Style	From	To	Qty
2	1935	B11275	340000	340000	8
3	1936	B10133	340000	340000	4
4	1937	B15422	340000	340000	5
5	1938	B10894	340000	340000	9
6	1939	B10049	340000	340000	3
7	1941	B18722	340000	340000	10
8	1944	B12886	340000	340000	10
9	1947	B17947	340000	340000	7
10	1950	B16431	340000	340000	9
11	1953	B19857	340000	340000	7
12	1954	B11562	340000	340000	1

Updating an Existing Record

To update an existing record, you need to build a recordset with exactly one record. This requires that the user select some sort of unique key when identifying the records. After you have opened the recordset, use the Fields property to change the field in question and then the Update method to commit the changes to the database.

The earlier example returned a recordset to a blank worksheet and then called a userform frmTransConf. This form uses a simple Userform_Initialize to display the range in a large list box. The list box's properties have the MultiSelect property set to True:

```
Private Sub UserForm_Initialize()

    ' Determine how Records we have
    FinalRow = Cells(Rows.Count, 1).End(xlUp).Row
    If FinalRow > 1 Then
        Me.lbXlt.RowSource = "A2:F" & FinalRow
    End If

End Sub
```

After the initialize procedure is run, the unconfirmed records are displayed in a list box. The logistics planner can mark all the records that have actually been sent, as shown in Figure 21.4.

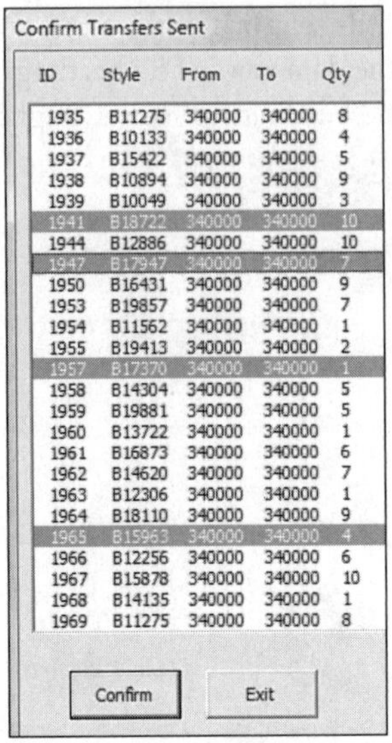

Figure 21.4
This userform displays particular records from the Access recordset. When the buyer selects certain records and then chooses the Confirm button, you'll have to use ADO's Update method to update the Sent field on the selected records.

The code attached to the Confirm button follows. Including the ID field in the fields returned in the prior example is important if you want to narrow the information down to a single record:

```
Private Sub cbConfirm_Click()
    Dim cnn As ADODB.Connection
    Dim rst As ADODB.Recordset

    ' If nothing is selected, warn them
    CountSelect = 0
    For x = 0 To Me.lbXlt.ListCount - 1
        If Me.lbXlt.Selected(x) Then
            CountSelect = CountSelect + 1
        End If
    Next x

    If CountSelect = 0 Then
        MsgBox "There were no transfers selected. " & _
            "To exit without confirming any tranfers, use Cancel."
        Exit Sub
    End If

    ' Establish a connection transfers.mdb
    ' Path to Transfers.mdb is on Menu
    MyConn = "J:\transfers.mdb"

    Set cnn = New ADODB.Connection

    With cnn
        .Provider = "Microsoft.Jet.OLEDB.4.0"
        .Open MyConn
    End With
```

```
        ' Mark as complete
        For x = 0 To Me.lbXlt.ListCount - 1
            If Me.lbXlt.Selected(x) Then
                ThisID = Cells(2 + x, 1).Value
                ' Mark ThisID as complete
                'Build SQL String
                sSQL = "SELECT * FROM tblTransfer Where ID=" & ThisID
                Set rst = New ADODB.Recordset
                With rst
                    .Open Source:=sSQL, ActiveConnection:=cnn, _
                        CursorType:=adOpenKeyset, LockType:=adLockOptimistic
                    ' Update the field
                    .Fields("Sent").Value = True
                    .Update
                    .Close
                End With
            End If
        Next x

        ' Close the connection
        cnn.Close
        Set rst = Nothing
        Set cnn = Nothing

        ' Close the userform
        Unload Me

End Sub
```

Deleting Records via ADO

Like updating a record, the key to deleting records is being able to write a bit of SQL to uniquely identify the records to be deleted. The following code uses the Execute method to pass the Delete command through to Access:

```
Public Sub ADOWipeOutAttribute(RecID)
    ' Establish a connection transfers.mdb
    MyConn = "J:\transfers.mdb"

    With New ADODB.Connection
        .Provider = "Microsoft.Jet.OLEDB.4.0"
        .Open MyConn
        .Execute "Delete From tblTransfer Where ID = " & RecID
        .Close
    End With
End Sub
```

Summarizing Records via ADO

One of Access's strengths is running summary queries that group by a particular field. If you build a summary query in Access and examine the SQL view, you will see that complex queries can be written. Similar SQL can be built in Excel VBA and passed to Access via ADO.

The following code uses a fairly complex query to get a net total by store:

```
Sub NetTransfers(Style As Variant)
    ' This builds a table of net open transfers
    ' on Styles AI1
    Dim cnn As ADODB.Connection
    Dim rst As ADODB.Recordset

    ' Build the large SQL query
    ' Basic Logic:  Get all open Incoming Transfers by store,
    ' union with -1* outgoing transfers by store
    ' Sum that union by store, and give us min date as well
    ' A single call to this macro will replace 60 _
    ' calls to GetTransferIn, GetTransferOut, TransferAge
    sSQL = "Select Store, Sum(Quantity), Min(mDate) From " & _
        "(SELECT ToStore AS Store, Sum(Qty) AS Quantity, " & _
        "Min(TDate) AS mDate FROM tblTransfer where Style='" & Style " & _
        "& "' AND Receive=FALSE GROUP BY ToStore "
    sSQL = sSQL & " Union All SELECT FromStore AS Store, " & _
        "Sum(-1*Qty) AS Quantity, Min(TDate) AS mDate " & _
        "FROM tblTransfer where Style='" & Style & "' AND " & _
        "Sent=FALSE GROUP BY FromStore)"
    sSQL = sSQL & " Group by Store"

    MyConn = "J:\transfers.mdb"

    ' open the connection.
    Set cnn = New ADODB.Connection
    With cnn
        .Provider = "Microsoft.Jet.OLEDB.4.0"
        .Open MyConn
    End With

    Set rst = New ADODB.Recordset

    rst.CursorLocation = adUseServer

    ' open the first query
    rst.Open Source:=sSQL, _
        ActiveConnection:=cnn, _
        CursorType:=AdForwardOnly, _
        LockType:=adLockOptimistic, _
        Options:=adCmdText

    Range("A1:C1").Value = Array("Store", "Qty", "Date")
    ' Return Query Results
    Range("A2").CopyFromRecordset rst
    rst.Close
    cnn.Close

End Sub
```

Other Utilities via ADO

Consider the application we created for our case study; the buyers now have an Access database located on their network but possibly no copy of Access. It would be ideal if you could deliver changes to the Access database on-the-fly as their application opens.

> **TIP**
>
> If you are wondering how you would ever coax the person using the application to run these queries, consider using an Update macro hidden in the Workbook_Open routine of the client application. Such a routine might first check to see whether a field does not exist and then add the field.

→ For details on the mechanics of hiding the update query in the Workbook_Open routine, **see** the "Using a Hidden Code Workbook to Hold All Macros and Forms" case study, **p. 594**.

Checking for the Existence of Tables

If the application needs a new table in the database, you can use the code in the next section. However, because we have a multiuser application, only the first person who opens the application has to add the table on-the-fly. When the next buyer shows up, the table may have already been added by the first buyer's application.

This code uses the OpenSchema method to actually query the database schema:

```
Function TableExists(WhichTable)
    Dim cnn As ADODB.Connection
    Dim rst As ADODB.Recordset
    Dim fld As ADODB.Field
    TableExists = False


    ' Path to Transfers.mdb is on Menu
    MyConn = "J:\transfers.mdb"

    Set cnn = New ADODB.Connection

    With cnn
        .Provider = "Microsoft.Jet.OLEDB.4.0"
        .Open MyConn
    End With

    Set rst = cnn.OpenSchema(adSchemaTables)

    Do Until rst.EOF
        If LCase(rst!Table_Name) = LCase(WhichTable) Then
            TableExists = True
            GoTo ExitMe
        End If
        rst.MoveNext
    Loop
```

21

```
ExitMe:
    rst.Close
    Set rst = Nothing
    ' Close the connection
    cnn.Close

End Function
```

Checking for the Existence of a Field

Sometimes you will want to add a new field to an existing table. Again, this code uses the
OpenSchema method but this time looks at the columns in the tables:

```
Function ColumnExists(WhichColumn, WhichTable)
    Dim cnn As ADODB.Connection
    Dim rst As ADODB.Recordset
    Dim WSOrig As Worksheet
    Dim WSTemp As Worksheet
    Dim fld As ADODB.Field
    ColumnExists = False

    ' Path to Transfers.mdb is on menu
    MyConn = ActiveWorkbook.Worksheets("Menu").Range("TPath").Value
    If Right(MyConn, 1) = "\" Then
        MyConn = MyConn & "transfers.mdb"
    Else
        MyConn = MyConn & "\transfers.mdb"
    End If

    Set cnn = New ADODB.Connection

    With cnn
        .Provider = "Microsoft.Jet.OLEDB.4.0"
        .Open MyConn
    End With

    Set rst = cnn.OpenSchema(adSchemaColumns)

    Do Until rst.EOF
        If LCase(rst!Column_Name) = LCase(WhichColumn) And _
            LCase(rst!Table_Name) = LCase(WhichTable) Then
            ColumnExists = True
            GoTo ExitMe
        End If
        rst.MoveNext
    Loop

ExitMe:
    rst.Close
    Set rst = Nothing
    ' Close the connection
    cnn.Close

End Function
```

Adding a Table On the Fly

This code uses a pass-through query to tell Access to run a `Create Table` command:

```
Sub ADOCreateReplenish()
    ' This creates tblReplenish
    ' There are five fields:
    ' Style
    ' A = Auto replenishment for A
    ' B = Auto replenishment level for B stores
    ' C = Auto replenishment level for C stores
    ' RecActive = Yes/No field
    Dim cnn As ADODB.Connection
    Dim cmd As ADODB.Command

    ' Define the connection
    MyConn = "J:\transfers.mdb"

    ' open the connection
    Set cnn = New ADODB.Connection
    With cnn
        .Provider = "Microsoft.Jet.OLEDB.4.0"
        .Open MyConn
    End With

    Set cmd = New ADODB.Command
    Set cmd.ActiveConnection = cnn
    'create table
    cmd.CommandText = "CREATE TABLE tblReplenish " & _
        "(Style Char(10) Primary Key, " & _
        "A int, B  int, C Int, RecActive YesNo)"
    cmd.Execute , , adCmdText
    Set cmd = Nothing
    Set cnn = Nothing
    Exit Sub
End Sub
```

Adding a Field On the Fly

If you determine that a field does not exist, you can use a pass-through query to add a field to the table:

```
Sub ADOAddField()
    ' This adds a grp field to tblReplenish
    Dim cnn As ADODB.Connection
    Dim cmd As ADODB.Command

    ' Define the connection
    MyConn = "J:\transfers.mdb"

    ' open the connection
    Set cnn = New ADODB.Connection
    With cnn
        .Provider = "Microsoft.Jet.OLEDB.4.0"
```

```
        .Open MyConn
    End With


    Set cmd = New ADODB.Command
    Set cmd.ActiveConnection = cnn
    'create table
    cmd.CommandText = "ALTER TABLE tblReplenish Add Column Grp Char(25)"
    cmd.Execute , , adCmdText
    Set cmd = Nothing
    Set cnn = Nothing

End Sub
```

SQL Server Examples

If you have 64-bit versions of Office and if Microsoft does not provide the 64-bit Microsoft. Jet.OLEDB.4.0 drivers, you will have to switch over to using SQL Server or another database technology:

```
Sub DataExtract()

Application.DisplayAlerts = False

'clear out all previous data
Sheet1.Cells.Clear

' Create a connection object.
Dim cnPubs As ADODB.Connection
Set cnPubs = New ADODB.Connection

' Provide the connection string.
Dim strConn As String

'Use the SQL Server OLE DB Provider.
strConn = "PROVIDER=SQLOLEDB;"

'Connect to the Pubs database on the local server.
strConn = strConn & "DATA SOURCE=a_sql_server;INITIAL CATALOG=a_database;"

'Use an integrated login.
strConn = strConn & " INTEGRATED SECURITY=sspi;"

'Now open the connection.
cnPubs.Open strConn

' Create a recordset object.
Dim rsPubs As ADODB.Recordset
Set rsPubs = New ADODB.Recordset

With rsPubs
    ' Assign the Connection object.
    .ActiveConnection = cnPubs
```

21

```
         ' Extract the required records.
         .Open "exec a_database..a_stored_procedure"
         ' Copy the records into cell A1 on Sheet1.
         Sheet1.Range("A2").CopyFromRecordset rsPubs


Dim myColumn As Range
'Dim title_string As String
Dim K As Integer
For K = 0 To rsPubs.Fields.Count - 1
   'Sheet1.Columns(K).Value = rsPubs.Fields(K).Name
   'title_string = title_string & rsPubs.Fields(K).Name & Chr(9)
   'Sheet1.Columns(K).Cells(1).Name = rsPubs.Fields(K).Name
   'Sheet1.Columns.Column(K) = rsPubs.Fields(K).Name
   'Set myColumn = Sheet1.Columns(K)
   'myColumn.Cells(1, K).Value = rsPubs.Fields(K).Name
   'Sheet1.Cells(1, K) = rsPubs.Fields(K).Name
   Sheet1.Cells(1, K + 1) = rsPubs.Fields(K).Name
   Sheet1.Cells(1, K + 1).Font.Bold = "TRUE"
Next K
'Sheet1.Range("A1").Value = title_string


      ' Tidy up
      .Close
End With

cnPubs.Close
Set rsPubs = Nothing
Set cnPubs = Nothing

'clear out errors
Dim cellval As Range
Dim myRng As Range
Set myRng = ActiveSheet.UsedRange
For Each cellval In myRng
   cellval.Value = cellval.Value
   'cellval.NumberFormat = "@" 'this works as well as setting
   'HorizontalAlignment
   cellval.HorizontalAlignment = xlRight
Next

End Sub
```

Next Steps

In Chapter 22, "Creating Classes, Records, and Collections," you learn about the powerful technique of setting up your own Class module. With this technique, you can set up your own object with its own methods and properties.

21

Creating Classes, Records, and Collections

Excel already has many objects available, but there are times when a custom object would be better suited for the job at hand. You can create custom objects that you use in the same way as Excel's built-in objects. These special objects are created in *class modules*.

Class modules are used to create custom objects with custom properties and methods. They can trap application events, embedded chart events, ActiveX control events, and more.

Inserting a Class Module

From the VB Editor, select Insert, Class Module. A new module, Class1, is added to the VBAProject workbook and can be seen in the Project Explorer window (see Figure 22.1). Two things to keep in mind concerning class modules:

- Each custom object must have its own module. (Event trapping can share a module.)
- The class module should be renamed to reflect the custom object.

IN THIS CHAPTER

Inserting a Class Module 493

Trapping Application and Embedded Chart Events 494

Creating a Custom Object 497

Using a Custom Object 498

Using Property Let and Property Get to Control How Users Utilize Custom Objects 499

Collections 501

User-Defined Types 506

Figure 22.1
Custom objects are created in class modules.

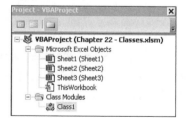

Trapping Application and Embedded Chart Events

Chapter 9, "Event Programming," showed you how certain actions in workbooks, worksheets, and nonembedded charts could be trapped and used to activate code. Briefly, it reviewed how to set up a class module to trap application and chart events. The following goes into more detail about what was shown in that chapter.

Application Events

The Workbook_BeforePrint event is triggered when the workbook in which it resides is printed. If you want to run the same code in every workbook available, you have to copy the code to each workbook. Alternatively, you can use an application event, Workbook_BeforePrint, which is triggered when any workbook is printed.

The application events already exist, but a class module must be set up first so that they can be seen. To create a class module, follow these steps:

1. Insert a class module into the project. Rename it to something that will make sense to you such as clsAppEvents. Select View, Properties Window to rename a module.

2. Enter the following into the class module:

   ```
   Public WithEvents xlApp As Application
   ```

   The name of the variable, xlApp, can be any variable name. The WithEvents keyword exposes the events associated with the Application object.

3. xlApp is now available from that class module's Object drop-down list. Select it from the drop-down, and then click the Procedure drop-down menu to its right to view the list of events that is available for the xlApp's object type (Application), as shown in Figure 22.2.

→ For a review of the various application events, **see** the "Application-Level Events" section, **p. 176**.

Any of the events listed can by captured, just as workbook and worksheet events were captured in an earlier chapter. The following example uses the NewWorkbook event to set up footer information automatically. This code is placed in the class module, below the xlApp declaration line you just added:

Figure 22.2
Events are made available after the object is created.

xlApp	▼	NewWorkbook	▼
		NewWorkbook	
Option Explicit		ProtectedViewWindowActivate	
		ProtectedViewWindowBeforeClose	
Public WithEvents xlApp As Application		ProtectedViewWindowBeforeEdit	
		ProtectedViewWindowDeactivate	
Private Sub xlApp_NewWorkbook(ByVal Wb		ProtectedViewWindowOpen	
		ProtectedViewWindowResize	
End Sub		SheetActivate	
		SheetBeforeDoubleClick	
		SheetBeforeRightClick	
		SheetCalculate	
		SheetChange	

```
Private Sub xlApp_NewWorkbook(ByVal Wb As Workbook)
Dim wks As Worksheet

With Wb
    For Each wks In .Worksheets
        wks.PageSetup.LeftFooter = "Created by: " & .Application.UserName
        wks.PageSetup.RightFooter = Now
    Next wks
End With

End Sub
```

The procedure placed in a class module does not run automatically as events in workbook or worksheet modules would. An instance of the class module must be created and the Application object assigned to the xlApp property. After that is complete, the TrapAppEvent procedure needs to run. As long as the procedure is running, the footer will be created on each sheet every time a new workbook is added. Place the following in a standard module:

```
Public myAppEvent As New clsAppEvents

Sub TrapAppEvent()

Set myAppEvent.xlApp = Application

End Sub
```

> **CAUTION**
>
> The application event trapping can be terminated by any action that resets the module level or public variables including editing code in the VB Editor. To restart, run the procedure that creates the object (TrapAppEvent).

In this example, the public myAppEvent declaration was placed in a standard module with the TrapAppEvent procedure. To automate the running of the entire event trapping, all the modules could be transferred to the Personal.xlsb and the procedure transferred to a Workbook_Open event. In any case, the Public declaration of myAppEvent *must* remain in a standard module so it can be shared between modules.

Embedded Chart Events

Preparing to trap embedded chart events is the same as preparing for trapping application events. Create a class module, insert the public declaration for a chart type, create a procedure for the desired event, and then add a standard module procedure to initiate the trapping. The same class module used for the application event can be used for the embedded chart event.

Place the following line in the declaration section of the class module. The available chart events are now viewable (see Figure 22.3):

```
Public WithEvents xlChart As Chart
```

→   For a review of the various charts events, **see** "Chart Sheet Events" on **p. 172**.

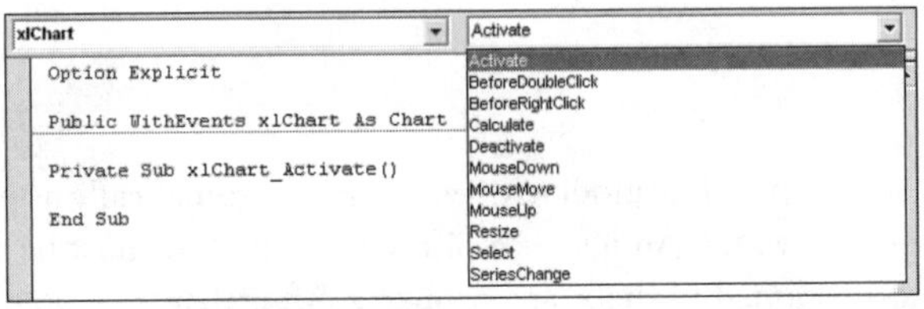

Figure 22.3
The chart events are available after the chart type variable has been declared.

Let's create a program to change the chart scale. Three events are set up. The primary event, MouseDown, changes the chart scale with a right-click or double-click. Because these actions also have actions associated with them, you need two more events: BeforeRightClick and BeforeDoubleClick, which prevent the usual action from taking place.

The following BeforeDoubleClick event prevents the normal result of a double-click from taking place:

```
Private Sub xlChart_BeforeDoubleClick(ByVal ElementID As Long, _
    ByVal Arg1 As Long, ByVal Arg2 As Long, Cancel As Boolean)
Cancel = True
End Sub
```

The following BeforeRightClick event prevents the normal result of a right-click from taking place:

```
Private Sub xlChart_BeforeRightClick(Cancel As Boolean)
Cancel = True
End Sub
```

Now that the normal actions of the double-click and right-click have been controlled, ChartMouseDown rewrites the actions initiated by a right-click and double-click:

```
Private Sub xlChart_MouseDown(ByVal Button As Long, ByVal Shift As Long, _
    ByVal x As Long, ByVal y As Long)
    If Button = 1 Then 'left mouse button
       xlChart.Axes(xlValue).MaximumScale = _
    xlChart.Axes(xlValue).MaximumScale - 50
    End If

    If Button = 2 Then 'right mouse button
       xlChart.Axes(xlValue).MaximumScale = _
    xlChart.Axes(xlValue).MaximumScale + 50
    End If

End Sub
```

After the events are set in the class module, all that is left to do is declare the variable in a standard module, as follows:

```
Public myChartEvent As New clsEvents
```

Then create a procedure that will capture the events on the embedded chart:

```
Sub TrapChartEvent()

Set myChartEvent.xlChart = Worksheets("EmbedChart"). _
    ChartObjects("Chart 2").Chart

End Sub
```

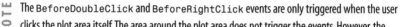

> **NOTE** The BeforeDoubleClick and BeforeRightClick events are only triggered when the user clicks the plot area itself. The area around the plot area does not trigger the events. However, the MouseDown event is triggered from anywhere on the chart.

Creating a Custom Object

Class modules are useful for trapping events, but they are also valuable because they can be used to create custom objects. When you are creating a custom object, the class module becomes a template of the object's properties and methods. To understand this better, in the following example you create an employee object to track employee name, ID, hourly wage rate, and hours worked.

Insert a class module and rename it to clsEmployee. The clsEmployee object has four properties:

- EmpName—Employee name
- EmpID—Employee ID
- EmpRate—Hourly wage rate
- EmpWeeklyHrs—Hours worked

Properties are variables that can be declared Private or Public. If declared Private, the properties are only accessible within the module they are declared in. These properties need to be accessible to the standard module, so they will be declared Public. Place the following lines at the top of the class module:

```
Public EmpName As String
Public EmpID As String
Public EmpRate As Double
Public EmpWeeklyHrs As Double
```

Methods are actions that the object can take. In the class module, these actions take shape as procedures and functions. The following code creates a method, EmpWeeklyPay(), for the object that calculates weekly pay:

```
Public Function EmpWeeklyPay() As Double
EmpWeeklyPay = EmpRate * EmpWeeklyHrs
End Function
```

The object is now complete. It has four properties and one method. The next step is using the object in an actual program.

Using a Custom Object

After a custom object is properly configured in a class module, it can be referenced from another module. Declare a variable as the custom object type in the declarations section:

```
Dim Employee As clsEmployee
```

In the procedure, set the variable to be a New object:

```
Set Employee = New clsEmployee
```

Continue entering the rest of the procedure. As you refer to the properties and method of the custom object, a screen tip appears, just as with Excel's standard objects (see Figure 22.4).

Figure 22.4

The properties and method of the custom object are just as easily accessible as they are for standard objects.

```
(General)                                              ▼  EmpPay

  Option Explicit

  Dim Employee As clsEmployee
  Sub EmpPay()
  Set Employee = New clsEmployee

  With Employee
       .EmpName = "Tracy Syrstad"
       .EmpID = "1651"
       .EmpRate = 25
       .|
       🔲 EmpID        & " earns $" & .EmpWeeklyPay & " per week."
  Enc 🔲 EmpName
       🔲 EmpRate
  Enc 🔲 EmpWeeklyHrs
       🔲 EmpWeeklyPay
```

```
Option Explicit

Dim Employee As clsEmployee

Sub EmpPay()

Set Employee = New clsEmployee

With Employee
    .EmpName = "Tracy Syrstad"
    .EmpID = "1651"
    .EmpRate = 25
    .EmpWeeklyHrs = 40
```

```
        MsgBox .EmpName & " earns $" & .EmpWeeklyPay & " per week."
    End With

    End Sub
```

The procedure declares an object `Employee` as a new instance of `clsEmployee`. It then assigns values to the four properties of the object and generates a message box displaying the employee name and weekly pay (see Figure 22.5). The object's method, `EmpWeeklyPay`, is used to generate the displayed pay.

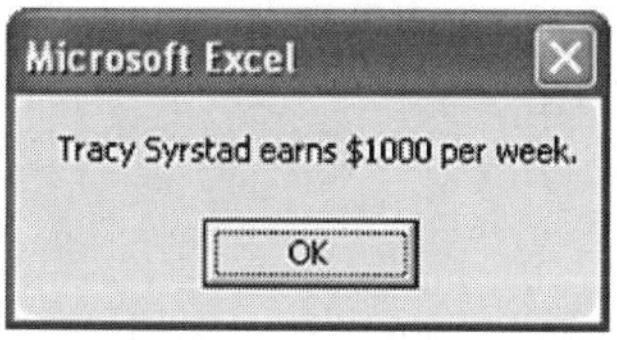

Figure 22.5
Create custom objects to make code more efficient.

Microsoft Excel

Tracy Syrstad earns $1000 per week.

OK

Using Property Let and Property Get to Control How Users Utilize Custom Objects

As declared in the earlier example, public variables have read/write properties. When they are used in a program, the values of the variables can be retrieved or changed. To assign read/write limitations, use `Property Let` and `Property Get` procedures.

`Property Let` procedures give you control of how properties can be assigned values. `Property Get` procedures give you control of how the properties are accessed. In the custom object example, there is a public variable for weekly hours. This variable is used in a method for calculating pay for the week but doesn't consider overtime pay. Variables for normal hours and overtime hours are needed, but the variables must be read-only.

To accomplish this, the class module must be reconstructed. It needs two new properties, `EmpNormalHrs` and `EmpOverTimeHrs`. However, because these two properties are to be confined to read-only, they are not declared as variables. `Property Get` procedures are used to create them.

If `EmpNormalHrs` and `EmpOverTimeHrs` are going to be read-only, they must have values assigned somehow. Their values are a calculation of the `EmpWeeklyHrs`. Because `EmpWeeklyHrs` will be used to set the property values of these two object properties, it can no longer be a public variable. There are two private variables, `NormalHrs` and `OverHrs`, which are used within the confines of the class module:

```
    Public EmpName As String
    Public EmpID As String
    Public EmpRate As Double

    Private NormalHrs As Double
    Private OverHrs As Double
```

22

A `Property Let` procedure is created for `EmpWeeklyHrs` to break the hours down into normal and overtime hours:

```
Property Let EmpWeeklyHrs(Hrs As Double)

NormalHrs = WorksheetFunction.Min(40, Hrs)
OverHrs = WorksheetFunction.Max(0, Hrs - 40)

End Property
```

The `Property Get EmpWeeklyHrs` totals these hours and returns a value to this property. Without it, a value cannot be retrieved from `EmpWeeklyHrs`:

```
Property Get EmpWeeklyHrs() As Double

EmpWeeklyHrs = NormalHrs + OverHrs

End Property
```

`Property Get` procedures are created for `EmpNormalHrs` and `EmpOverTimeHrs` to set their values. If you use `Property Get` procedures only, the values of these two properties are read-only. They can be assigned values only through the `EmpWeeklyHrs` property:

```
Property Get EmpNormalHrs() As Double

EmpNormalHrs = NormalHrs

End Property


Property Get EmpOverTimeHrs() As Double

EmpOverTimeHrs = OverHrs

End Property
```

Finally, the method `EmpWeeklyPay` is updated to reflect the changes in the properties and goal:

```
Public Function EmpWeeklyPay() As Double

EmpWeeklyPay = (EmpNormalHrs * EmpRate) + (EmpOverTimeHrs * EmpRate * 1.5)

End Function
```

Update the procedure in the standard module to take advantage of the changes in the class module. Figure 22.6 shows the new message box resulting from this updated procedure:

```
Sub EmpPayOverTime()
Dim Employee As New clsEmployee

With Employee
    .EmpName = "Tracy Syrstad"
    .EmpID = "1651"
    .EmpRate = 25
    .EmpWeeklyHrs = 45
```

```
        MsgBox .EmpName & Chr(10) & Chr(9) & _
        "Normal Hours: " & .EmpNormalHrs & Chr(10) & Chr(9) & _
        "OverTime Hours: " & .EmpOverTimeHrs & Chr(10) & Chr(9) & _
        "Weekly Pay : $" & .EmpWeeklyPay
    End With

    End Sub
```

Figure 22.6
Use Property Let and Property Get procedures for more control over custom object properties.

Microsoft Excel

Tracy Syrstad
    Normal Hours: 40
    OverTime Hours: 5
    Weekly Pay : $1187.5

OK

Collections

Up to now, you have been able to have only one record at a time of the custom object. To create more, a *collection* that allows more than a single record to exist at a time is needed. For example, Worksheet is a member of the Worksheets collection. You can add, remove, count, and refer to each worksheet in a workbook by item. This functionality is also available to your custom object.

Creating a Collection in a Standard Module

The quickest way to create a collection is to use the built-in Collection method. By setting up a collection in a standard module, you can access the four default collection methods: Add, Remove, Count, and Item.

The following example reads a list of employees off a sheet and into an array. It then processes the array, supplying each property of the object with a value, and places each record in the collection:

```
Sub EmpPayCollection()
Dim colEmployees As New Collection
Dim recEmployee As New clsEmployee
Dim LastRow As Integer, myCount As Integer
Dim EmpArray As Variant

LastRow = ActiveSheet.Cells(ActiveSheet.Rows.Count, 1).End(xlUp).Row
EmpArray = ActiveSheet.Range(Cells(1, 1), Cells(LastRow, 4))

For myCount = 1 To UBound(EmpArray)
    Set recEmployee = New clsEmployee
    With recEmployee
        .EmpName = EmpArray(myCount, 1)
        .EmpID = EmpArray(myCount, 2)
        .EmpRate = EmpArray(myCount, 3)
```

```
                .EmpWeeklyHrs = EmpArray(myCount, 4)
                colEmployees.Add recEmployee, .EmpID
        End With
    Next myCount

    MsgBox "Number of Employees: " & colEmployees.Count & Chr(10) & _
        "Employee(2) Name: " & colEmployees(2).EmpName
    MsgBox "Tracy's Weekly Pay: $" & colEmployees("1651").EmpWeeklyPay

    Set recEmployee = Nothing

End Sub
```

The collection, colEmployees, is declared as a new collection and the record, recEmployee, as a new variable of the custom object type.

After the object's properties are given values, the record, recEmployee, is added to the collection. The second parameter of the Add method applies a unique key to the record, which, in this case, is the employee ID number. This allows a specific record to be accessed quickly, as shown by the second message box (colEmployees("1651").EmpWeeklyPay) (see Figure 22.7).

Figure 22.7
Individual records in a collection can be easily accessed.

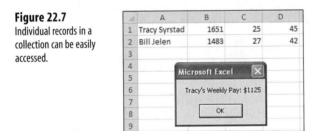

> **NOTE**
> The unique key is an optional parameter. An error message appears if a duplicate key is entered.

Creating a Collection in a Class Module

Collections can be created in a class module. In this case, the innate methods of the collection (Add, Remove, Count, Item) are not available; they need to be created in the class module. The advantages of creating a collection in a class module are

- The entire code is in one module.
- You have more control over what is done with the collection.
- You can prevent access to the collection.

Insert a new class module for the collection and rename it `clsEmployees`. Declare a private collection to be used within the class module:

```
Option Explicit
Private AllEmployees As New Collection
```

Add the new properties and methods required to make the collection work. The innate methods of the collection are available within the class module and can be used to create the custom methods and properties:

Insert an `Add` method for adding new items to the collection:

```
Public Sub Add(recEmployee As clsEmployee)

AllEmployees.Add recEmployee, recEmployee.EmpID

End Sub
```

Insert a `Count` property to return the number of items in the collection:

```
Public Property Get Count() As Long

Count = AllEmployees.Count

End Property
```

Insert an `Items` property to return the entire collection:

```
Public Property Get Items() As Collection

Set Items = AllEmployees

End Property
```

Insert an `Item` property to return a specific item from the collection:

```
Public Property Get Item(myItem As Variant) As clsEmployee

Set Item = AllEmployees(myItem)

End Property
```

Insert a `Remove` property to remove a specific item from the collection:

```
Public Sub Remove(myItem As Variant)

AllEmployees.Remove (myItem)

End Sub
```

`Property Get` is used with `Count`, `Item`, and `Items` because these are read-only properties. `Item` returns a reference to a single member of the collection, whereas `Items` returns the entire collection so it can be used in `For Each Next` loops.

After the collection is configured in the class module, a procedure can be written in a standard module to use it:

```
Sub EmpAddCollection()
Dim colEmployees As New clsEmployees
Dim recEmployee As New clsEmployee
Dim LastRow As Integer, myCount As Integer
Dim EmpArray As Variant

LastRow = ActiveSheet.Cells(ActiveSheet.Rows.Count, 1).End(xlUp).Row
EmpArray = ActiveSheet.Range(Cells(1, 1), Cells(LastRow, 4))

For myCount = 1 To UBound(EmpArray)
    Set recEmployee = New clsEmployee
    With recEmployee
        .EmpName = EmpArray(myCount, 1)
        .EmpID = EmpArray(myCount, 2)
        .EmpRate = EmpArray(myCount, 3)
        .EmpWeeklyHrs = EmpArray(myCount, 4)
        colEmployees.Add recEmployee
    End With
Next myCount

MsgBox "Number of Employees: " & colEmployees.Count & Chr(10) & _
    "Employee(2) Name: " & colEmployees.Item(2).EmpName
MsgBox "Tracy's Weekly Pay: $" & colEmployees.Item("1651").EmpWeeklyPay

For Each recEmployee In colEmployees.Items
    recEmployee.EmpRate = recEmployee.EmpRate * 1.5
Next recEmployee

MsgBox "Tracy's Weekly Pay (after Bonus): $" & colEmployees.Item("1651"). _
    EmpWeeklyPay

Set recEmployee = Nothing

End Sub
```

This program is not that different from the one used with the standard collection, but there are a few key differences.

■ Instead of declaring colEmployees as Collection, declare it as type clsEmployees, the new class module collection.

■ The array and collection are filled the same way, but the way the records in the collection are referenced has changed. When referencing a member of the collection, such as employee record 2, the Item property must be used.

Compare the syntax of the message boxes in this program to the previous program. The For Each Next loop goes through each record in the collection and multiplies the EmpRate by 1.5, changing its value. The result of this "bonus" is shown in a message box similar to the one shown previously in Figure 22.7.

CASE STUDY: HELP BUTTONS

You have a complex sheet that requires a way for the user to get help. You can place the information in comment boxes, but they are not very obvious, especially to the novice Excel user. Another option is to create help buttons.

To do this, create small labels with a question mark in each one on the worksheet. To get the button-like appearance shown in Figure 22.8, set the `SpecialEffect` property of the labels to `Raised` and darken the `BackColor`. Place one label per row. Two columns over from the button, enter the help text you want to appear when the label is clicked. Hide this help text column.

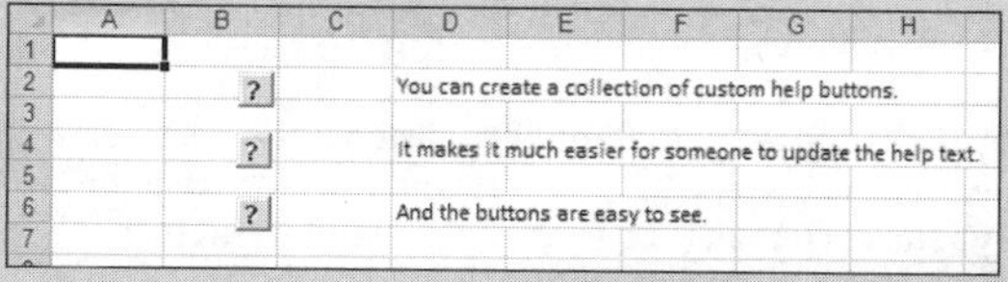

Figure 22.8
Attach help buttons to the sheet and enter help text.

Create a simple userform with a label and a Close button. Rename the form `HelpForm`, the button `CloseHelp`, and the label `HelpText`. Size the label large enough to hold the help text. Add a macro behind the form to hide it when the button is clicked. At this point, you could program each button separately. If you have many buttons, this would be tedious. If you ever need to add more buttons, you also will have to update the code. Or you could create a class module and a collection that will automatically include all the help buttons on the sheet, now and in the future.

```
Private Sub CloseHelp_Click()
Unload Me
End Sub
```

Insert a class module named `clsLabel`. You will need a variable, Lbl, to capture the control events:

```
Public WithEvents Lbl As MSForms.Label
```

In addition, you need a method of finding and displaying the corresponding help text:

```
Private Sub Lbl_Click()
Dim Rng As Range

Set Rng = Lbl.TopLeftCell

If Lbl.Caption = "?" Then
    HelpForm.Caption = "Label in cell " & Rng.Address(0, 0)
    HelpForm.HelpText.Caption = Rng.Offset(, 2).Value
    HelpForm.Show
End If

End Sub
```

In the ThisWorkbook module, create a `Workbook_Open` procedure to create a collection of the labels in the workbook:

```
Option Explicit
Option Base 1
Dim col As Collection
Sub Workbook_Open()
Dim WS As Worksheet
Dim cLbl As clsLabel
Dim OleObj As OLEObject

Set col = New Collection

For Each WS In ThisWorkbook.Worksheets
    For Each OleObj In WS.OLEObjects
        If OleObj.OLEType = xlOLEControl Then
'in case you have other controls on the sheet, include only the labels
            If TypeName(OleObj.Object) = "Label" Then
                Set cLbl = New clsLabel
                Set cLbl.Lbl = OleObj.Object
                col.Add cLbl
            End If
        End If
    Next OleObj
Next WS

End Sub
```

Run `Workbook_Open` to create the collection. Click a label on the worksheet. The corresponding help text appears in the help form, as shown in Figure 22.9.

Figure 22.9
Help text is only a click away.

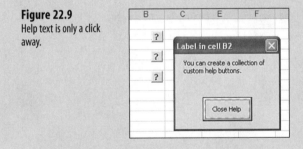

User-Defined Types

User-defined types (UDTs) provide some of the power of a custom object, but without the need of a class module. A class module allows the creation of custom properties and methods, while a UDT allows only custom properties. However, sometimes that is all you need.

A UDT is declared with a `Type..End Type` statement. It can be `Public` or `Private`. A name that is treated like an object is given to the UDT. Within the `Type`, individual variables are declared that become the properties of the UDT.

Within an actual procedure, a variable is defined of the custom type. When that variable is used, the properties are available, just as they are in a custom object (see Figure 22.10).

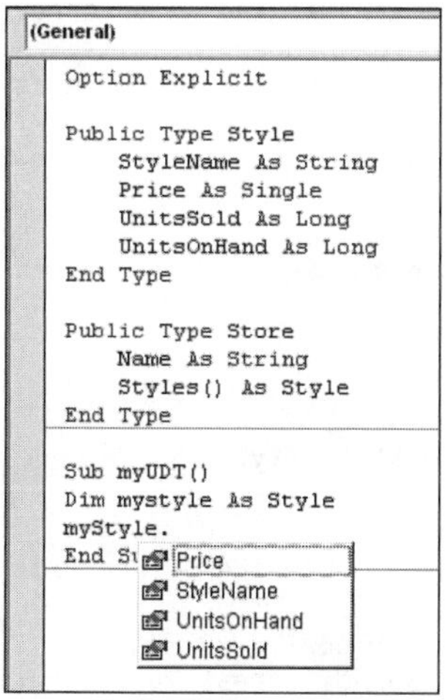

Figure 22.10
The properties of a UDT are available as they are in a custom object.

```
(General)

Option Explicit

Public Type Style
        StyleName As String
        Price As Single
        UnitsSold As Long
        UnitsOnHand As Long
End Type

Public Type Store
        Name As String
        Styles() As Style
End Type

Sub myUDT()
Dim mystyle As Style
myStyle.
End S⌐  Price
         StyleName
         UnitsOnHand
         UnitsSold
```

The following example uses two UDTs to summarize a report of product styles in various stores. The first UDT consists of properties for each product style:

```
Option Explicit
Public Type Style
        StyleName As String
        Price As Single
        UnitsSold As Long
        UnitsOnHand As Long
End Type
```

The second UDT consists of the store name and an array whose type is the first UDT:

```
Public Type Store
        Name As String
        Styles() As Style
End Type
```

After the UDTs are established, the main program is written. Only a variable of the second UDT type, Store, is needed because that type contains the first type, Style (see Figure 22.11). However, all the properties of the UDTs are easily available. In addition, with the use of the UDT, the various variables are easy to remember—they are only a dot (.) away:

```
Sub Main()
Dim FinalRow As Integer, ThisRow As Integer, ThisStore As Integer
Dim CurrRow As Integer, TotalDollarsSold As Integer, TotalUnitsSold As Integer
Dim TotalDollarsOnHand As Integer, TotalUnitsOnHand As Integer
Dim ThisStyle As Integer
Dim StoreName As String
```

```
ReDim Stores(0 To 0) As Store ' The UDT is declared

FinalRow = Cells(Rows.Count, 1).End(xlUp).Row

' The following For loop fills both arrays. The outer array is filled with the
' store name and an array consisting of product details.
' To accomplish this, the store name is tracked and when it changes,
'the outer array is expanded.
'The inner array for each outer array expands with each new product
For ThisRow = 2 To FinalRow
    StoreName = Range("A" & ThisRow).Value
' Checks whether this is the first entry in the outer array
    If LBound(Stores) = 0 Then
        ThisStore = 1
        ReDim Stores(1 To 1) As Store
        Stores(1).Name = StoreName
        ReDim Stores(1).Styles(0 To 0) As Style
    Else
        For ThisStore = LBound(Stores) To UBound(Stores)
            If Stores(ThisStore).Name = StoreName Then Exit For
        Next ThisStore
        If ThisStore > UBound(Stores) Then
            ReDim Preserve Stores(LBound(Stores) To UBound(Stores) + 1) As _
                Store
            Stores(ThisStore).Name = StoreName
            ReDim Stores(ThisStore).Styles(0 To 0) As Style
        End If
    End If
    With Stores(ThisStore)
        If LBound(.Styles) = 0 Then
            ReDim .Styles(1 To 1) As Style
        Else
            ReDim Preserve .Styles(LBound(.Styles) To _
        UBound(.Styles) + 1) As Style
        End If
        With .Styles(UBound(.Styles))
            .StyleName = Range("B" & ThisRow).Value
            .Price = Range("C" & ThisRow).Value
            .UnitsSold = Range("D" & ThisRow).Value
            .UnitsOnHand = Range("E" & ThisRow).Value
        End With
    End With
Next ThisRow

' Create a report on a new sheet
Sheets.Add
Range("A1:E1").Value = Array("Store Name", "Units Sold", _
    "Dollars Sold", "Units On Hand", "Dollars On Hand")
CurrRow = 2

For ThisStore = LBound(Stores) To UBound(Stores)
    With Stores(ThisStore)
        TotalDollarsSold = 0
        TotalUnitsSold = 0
        TotalDollarsOnHand = 0
        TotalUnitsOnHand = 0
' Go through the array of product styles within the array
' of stores to summarize information
```

```
        For ThisStyle = LBound(.Styles) To UBound(.Styles)
            With .Styles(ThisStyle)
                TotalDollarsSold = TotalDollarsSold + .UnitsSold * .Price
                TotalUnitsSold = TotalUnitsSold + .UnitsSold
                TotalDollarsOnHand = TotalDollarsOnHand + .UnitsOnHand *
    .Price
                TotalUnitsOnHand = TotalUnitsOnHand + .UnitsOnHand
            End With
        Next ThisStyle
        Range("A" & CurrRow & ":E" & CurrRow).Value = _
        Array(.Name, TotalUnitsSold, TotalDollarsSold, _
        TotalUnitsOnHand, TotalDollarsOnHand)
      End With
      CurrRow = CurrRow + 1
    Next ThisStore

    End Sub
```

Figure 22.11
UDTs can make a poten-
tially confusing multivari-
able program easier to
write.

	A	B	C	D	E
1	Store	Style	Price	Units Sold	Units On Hand
2	Store A	Style C	96.87	16	45
3	Store A	Style A	38.43	7	94
4	Store A	Style B	91.24	5	18
5	Store A	Style E	19.89	0	96
6	Store A	Style D	2.45	20	66
7	Store B	Style B	92.59	4	83
8	Store B	Style A	15.75	9	66
9	Store B	Style F	13.12	2	35
10	Store B	Style G	30.86	22	37
11	Store B	Style H	37.38	21	77
12					
13					
14					
15					
16					
17	Store Name	Units Sold	Dollars Sold	Units On Hand	Dollars On Hand
18	Store A	48	$ 2,324	319	$ 11,684
19	Store B	58	$ 2,002	298	$ 13,203

> **NOTE**
> The results of this program have been combined with the raw data for convenience.

Next Steps

In Chapter 23, "Advanced Userform Techniques," you learn about more controls and techniques you can use in building userforms.

Advanced Userform Techniques

23

Chapter 10, "Userforms: An Introduction," covered the basics of adding controls to userforms. This chapter continues this topic by looking at more advanced controls and methods for making the most out of userforms.

IN THIS CHAPTER

Using the UserForm Toolbar in the Design of
Controls on Userforms 511

More Userform Controls 511

Controls and Collections 519

Modeless Userforms 521

Using Hyperlinks in Userforms 522

Adding Controls at Runtime 523

Adding Help to the Userform 529

Transparent Forms 533

Using the UserForm Toolbar in the Design of Controls on Userforms

In the VB Editor, hidden under the View menu in the Toolbars command are a few toolbars that do not appear unless the user intervenes. One of these is the UserForm toolbar, shown in Figure 23.1. It has functionality useful for organizing the controls you add to a userform; for example, it will make all the controls you select the same size.

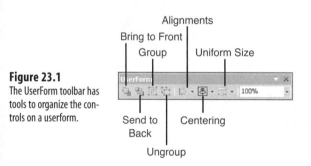

Figure 23.1
The UserForm toolbar has tools to organize the controls on a userform.

More Userform Controls

Chapter 10 began a review of some of the controls available on userforms. The review is continued here. At the end of each control review is a table listing that control's events.

Check Boxes

Check boxes allow the user to select one or more options on a userform. Unlike the option buttons discussed in Chapter 10, a user can select one or more check boxes at a time.

The value of a checked box is `True`; the value of an un checked box is `False`. If you clear the value of a check box (`Checkbox1.value = ""`), when the userform runs, the check box will have a faded check in it, as shown in Figure 23.2. This can be useful to verify that users have viewed all options and made a selection.

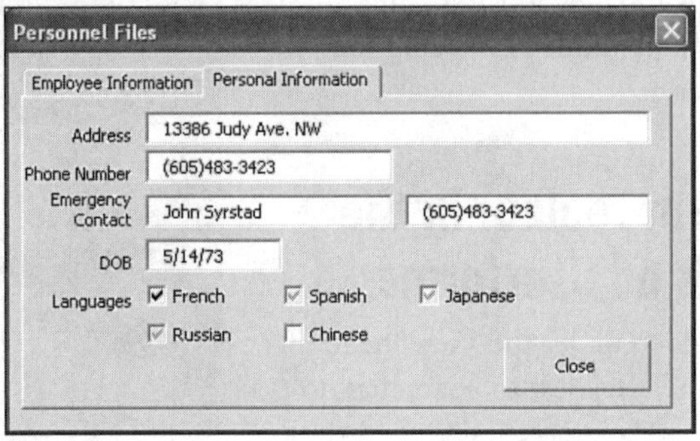

Figure 23.2
Use the null value of the check box to verify that users have viewed and answered all options.

The following code reviews all the check boxes in the language group. If a value is null, the user is prompted to review the selections:

```
Private Sub btnClose_Click()

Dim Msg As String
Dim Chk As Control

Set Chk = Nothing

'narrow down the search to just the 2nd page's controls
For Each Chk In frm_Multipage.MultiPage1.Pages(1).Controls
    'only need to verify checkbox controls
    If TypeName(Chk) = "CheckBox" Then
        'and just in case we add more check box controls,
    'just check the ones in the group
        If Chk.GroupName = "Languages" Then
            'if the value is null (the property value is empty)
            If IsNull(Chk.Object.Value) Then
                'add the caption to a string
                Msg = Msg & vbNewLine & Chk.Caption
            End If
        End If
    End If
Next Chk

If Msg <> "" Then
    Msg = "The following check boxes were not verified:" & vbNewLine & Msg
    MsgBox Msg, vbInformation, "Additional Information Required"
```

```
    End If
    Unload Me
    End Sub
```

Table 23.1 lists the events for CheckBox controls.

Table 23.1   Events for CheckBox Controls

Event	Description
AfterUpdate	Occurs after a check box has been selected/cleared.
BeforeDragOver	Occurs while the user drags and drops data onto the check box.
BeforeDropOrPaste	Occurs right before the user is about to drop or paste data onto the check box.
BeforeUpdate	Occurs before the check box is selected/cleared.
Change	Occurs when the value of the check box is changed.
Click	Occurs when the user clicks the control with the mouse.
DblClick	Occurs when the user double-clicks the check box with the mouse.
Enter	Occurs right before the check box receives the focus from another control on the same userform.
Error	Occurs when the check box runs into an error and cannot return the error information.
Exit	Occurs right after the check box loses focus to another control on the same userform.
KeyDown	Occurs when the user presses a key on the keyboard.
KeyPress	Occurs when the user presses an ANSI key. An ANSI key is a typeable character such as the letter *A*.
KeyUp	Occurs when the user releases a key on the keyboard.
MouseDown	Occurs when the user presses the mouse button within the borders of the check box.
MouseMove	Occurs when the user moves the mouse within the borders of the check box.
MouseUp	Occurs when the user releases the mouse button within the borders of the check box.

Tab Strips

The MultiPage control allows a userform to have several pages. Each page of the form can have its own set of controls, unrelated to any other control on the form. A TabStrip control also allows a userform to have many pages, but the controls on a tab strip are identical; they are drawn only once. Yet when the form is run, the information changes according to the tab strip that is active (see Figure 23.3).

Figure 23.3
A tab strip allows a user-form with multiple pages to share controls but not information.

➔ To learn more about MultiPage controls, **see** "Using the MultiPage Control to Combine Forms" on **p. 198**.

By default, a tab strip is thin with two tabs at the top. Right-clicking a tab enables you to add, remove, rename, or move that tab. The tab strip should also be sized to hold all the controls. A button for closing the form should be drawn outside the tab strip area.

The tabs can also be moved around the strip. This is done by changing the TabOrientation property. The tabs can be at the top, bottom, left, or right side of the userform.

The following lines of code were used to create the tab strip form shown in Figure 23.3. The Initialize sub calls the sub SetValuestoTabStrip, which sets the value for the first tab:

```
Private Sub UserForm_Initialize()
SetValuesToTabStrip 1 'As default
End Sub
```

These lines of code handle what happens when a new tab is selected.

```
Private Sub TabStrip1_Change()
Dim lngRow As Long

lngRow = TabStrip1.Value + 1
SetValuesToTabStrip lngRow

End Sub
```

This sub provides the data shown on each tab. A sheet was set up, with each row corresponding to a tab.

```
Private Sub SetValuesToTabStrip(ByVal lngRow As Long)
With frm_Staff
    .lbl_Name.Caption = Cells(lngRow, 2).Value
    .lbl_Phone.Caption = Cells(lngRow, 3).Value
    .lbl_Fax.Caption = Cells(lngRow, 4).Value
    .lbl_Email.Caption = Cells(lngRow, 5).Value
    .lbl_Website.Caption = Cells(lngRow, 6).Value
    .Show
End With
End Sub
```

The tab strip's values are automatically filled in. They correspond to the tab's position in the strip; moving a tab changes its value. The value of the first tab of a tab strip is 0, which is why in the preceding code, we add 1 to the tab strip value when the form is initialized.

> **TIP**
>
> If you want a single tab to have an extra control, the control could be added at runtime when the tab is activated and removed when the tab is deactivated.

Table 23.2 lists the events for the TabStrip control.

Table 23.2   Events for TabStrip **Controls**

Event	Description
BeforeDragOver	Occurs while the user drags and drops data onto the control.
BeforeDropOrPaste	Occurs right before the user drops or pastes data into the control.
Change	Occurs when the value of the control is changed.
Click	Occurs when the user clicks the control with the mouse.
DblClick	Occurs when the user double-clicks the control with the mouse.
Enter	Occurs right before the control receives the focus from another control on the same userform.
Error	Occurs when the control runs into an error and cannot return the error information.
Exit	Occurs right after the control loses focus to another control on the same userform.
KeyDown	Occurs when the user presses a key on the keyboard.
KeyPress	Occurs when the user presses an ANSI key. An ANSI key is a typeable character, such as the letter *A*.
KeyUp	Occurs when the user releases a key on the keyboard.
MouseDown	Occurs when the user presses the mouse button within the borders of the control.
MouseMove	Occurs when the user moves the mouse within the borders of the control.
MouseUp	Occurs when the user releases the mouse button within the borders of the control.

RefEdit

The RefEdit control allows the user to select a range on a sheet; the range is returned as the value of the control. It can be added to any form. The userform disappears after it is activated by a click of the button on the right side of the field. The userform is replaced with the range selection form that is used when selecting ranges with Excel's many wizard tools. Click the button on the right to show the userform once again.

The form in Figure 23.4 and the following code allow the user to select a range, which is then made bold.

Figure 23.4

Use RefEdit to enable the user to select a range on a sheet.

```
Private Sub cb1_Click()
Range(RefEdit1.Value).Font.Bold = True
End Sub
```

Table 23.3 lists the events for RefEdit controls.

Table 23.3   Events for RefEdit Controls

Event	Description
BeforeDragOver	Occurs while the user drags and drops data onto the control.
BeforeDropOrPaste	Occurs right before the user drops or pastes data into the control.
Change	Occurs when the value of the control is changed.
Click	Occurs when the user clicks the control with the mouse.
DblClick	Occurs when the user double-clicks the control with the mouse.
Enter	Occurs right before the control receives the focus from another control on the same userform.
Error	Occurs when the control runs into an error and cannot return the error information.
Exit	Occurs right after the control loses focus to another control on the same userform.
KeyDown	Occurs when the user presses a key on the keyboard.
KeyPress	Occurs when the user presses an ANSI key. An ANSI key is a typeable character, such as the letter A.
KeyUp	Occurs when the user releases a key on the keyboard.
MouseDown	Occurs when the user presses the mouse button within the borders of the control.
MouseMove	Occurs when the user moves the mouse within the borders of the control.
MouseUp	Occurs when the user releases the mouse button within the borders of the control.

Toggle Buttons

A toggle button looks like a normal command button, but when the user presses it, it stays pressed until it is selected again. This allows a `True` or `False` value to be returned based on the status of the button. Table 23.4 lists the events for the `ToggleButton` controls.

Table 23.4 Events for `ToggleButton` Controls

Event	Description
AfterUpdate	Occurs after the control's data has been changed by the user.
BeforeDragOver	Occurs while the user drags and drops data onto the control.
BeforeDropOrPaste	Occurs right before the user drops or pastes data into the control.
BeforeUpdate	Occurs before the data in the control is changed.
Change	Occurs when the value of the control is changed.
Click	Occurs when the user clicks the control with the mouse.
DblClick	Occurs when the user double-clicks the control with the mouse.
Enter	Occurs right before the control receives the focus from another control on the same userform.
Error	Occurs when the control runs into an error and cannot return the error information.
Exit	Occurs right after the control loses focus to another control on the same userform.
KeyDown	Occurs when the user presses a key on the keyboard.
KeyPress	Occurs when the user presses an ANSI key. An ANSI key is a typeable character, such as the letter *A*.
KeyUp	Occurs when the user releases a key on the keyboard.
MouseDown	Occurs when the user presses the mouse button within the borders of the control.
MouseMove	Occurs when the user moves the mouse within the borders of the control.
MouseUp	Occurs when the user releases the mouse button within the borders of the control.

Using a Scrollbar As a Slider to Select Values

Chapter 10 discussed using a `SpinButton` control to allow someone to choose a date. The spin button is useful, but it allows clients to adjust up or down by only one unit at a time. An alternative method is to draw a horizontal or vertical scrollbar in the middle of the userform and use it as a slider. Clients can use arrows on the ends of the scrollbar like the spin button arrows, but they can also grab the scrollbar and instantly drag it to a certain value.

The userform shown in Figure 23.5 includes a label named Label1 and a scrollbar called ScrollBar1.

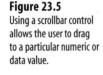

Figure 23.5
Using a scrollbar control allows the user to drag to a particular numeric or data value.

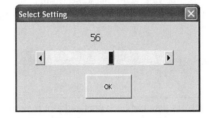

The userform's Initialize code sets up the Min and Max values for the scrollbar. It initializes the scrollbar to a value from Cell A1 and updates the Label1.Caption:

```
Private Sub UserForm_Initialize()
    Me.ScrollBar1.Min = 0
    Me.ScrollBar1.Max = 100
    Me.ScrollBar1.Value = Range("A1").Value
    Me.Label1.Caption = Me.ScrollBar1.Value
End Sub
```

Two event handlers are needed for the scrollbar. The Change event handles if users click the arrows at the ends of the scrollbar. The Scroll event handles if they drag the slider to a new value:

```
Private Sub ScrollBar1_Change()
    ' This event handles if they touch
    ' the arrows on the end of the scrollbar
    Me.Label1.Caption = Me.ScrollBar1.Value
End Sub

Private Sub ScrollBar1_Scroll()
    ' This event handles if they drag the slider
    Me.Label1.Caption = Me.ScrollBar1.Value
End Sub
```

Finally, the event attached to the button writes the scrollbar value out to the worksheet:

```
Private Sub btnClose_Click()
    Range("A1").Value = Me.ScrollBar1.Value
    Unload Me
End Sub
```

Table 23.5 lists the events for Scrollbar controls.

Table 23.5   Events for `Scrollbar` **Controls**

Event	Description
AfterUpdate	Occurs after the control's data has been changed by the user.
BeforeDragOver	Occurs while the user drags and drops data onto the control.
BeforeDropOrPaste	Occurs right before the user drops or pastes data into the control.
BeforeUpdate	Occurs before the data in the control is changed.
Change	Occurs when the value of the control is changed.
Enter	Occurs right before the control receives the focus from another control on the same userform.
Error	Occurs when the control runs into an error and cannot return the error information.
Exit	Occurs right after the control loses focus to another control on the same userform.
KeyDown	Occurs when the user presses a key on the keyboard.
KeyPress	Occurs when the user presses an ANSI key. An ANSI key is a typeable character, such as the letter *A*.
KeyUp	Occurs when the user releases a key on the keyboard.
Scroll	Occurs when the slider is moved.

Controls and Collections

In Chapter 22, "Creating Classes, Records, and Collections," several labels on a sheet were grouped together into a collection. With a little more code, these labels were turned into help screens for the users. Userform controls can also be grouped into collections to take advantage of class modules. The following example selects or clears all the check boxes on the userform, depending on which label the user chooses.

Place the following code in the class module, `clsFormEvents`. It consists of one property, `chb`, and two methods, `SelectAll` and `UnselectAll`.

The `SelectAll` method selects a check box by setting its value to `True`:

```
Option Explicit
Public WithEvents chb As MSForms.CheckBox

Public Sub SelectAll()
chb.Value = True
End Sub
```

The UnselectAll method clears the check box:

```
Public Sub UnselectAll()
chb.Value = False
End Sub
```

That sets up the class module. Next, the controls need to be placed in a collection. The following code, placed behind the form, frm_Movies, places the check boxes into a collection. The check boxes are part of a frame, f_Selection, which makes it easier to create the collection because it narrows the number of controls that need to be checked from the entire userform to just those controls within the frame:

```
Option Explicit
Dim col_Selection As New Collection

Private Sub UserForm_Initialize()
Dim ctl As MSForms.CheckBox
Dim chb_ctl As clsFormEvents

' Go thru the members of the frame and add them to the collection
For Each ctl In f_Selection.Controls
    Set chb_ctl = New clsFormEvents
    Set chb_ctl.chb = ctl
    col_Selection.Add chb_ctl
Next ctl

End Sub
```

When the form is opened, the controls are placed into the collection. All that's left now is to add the code for labels to select and clear the check boxes:

```
Private Sub lbl_SelectAll_Click()
Dim ctl As clsFormEvents

For Each ctl In col_Selection
    ctl.SelectAll
Next ctl

End Sub
```

The following code clears the check boxes in the collection:

```
Private Sub lbl_unSelectAll_Click()
Dim ctl As clsFormEvents

For Each ctl In col_Selection
    ctl.Unselectall
Next ctl

End Sub
```

All the check boxes can be selected and cleared with a single click of the mouse, as shown in Figure 23.6.

If your controls cannot be placed in a frame, you can use a `tag` to create an improvised grouping. A `tag` is a property that holds more information about a control. Its value is of type `string`, so it can hold any type of information. For example, it can be used to create an informal group of controls from different groupings.

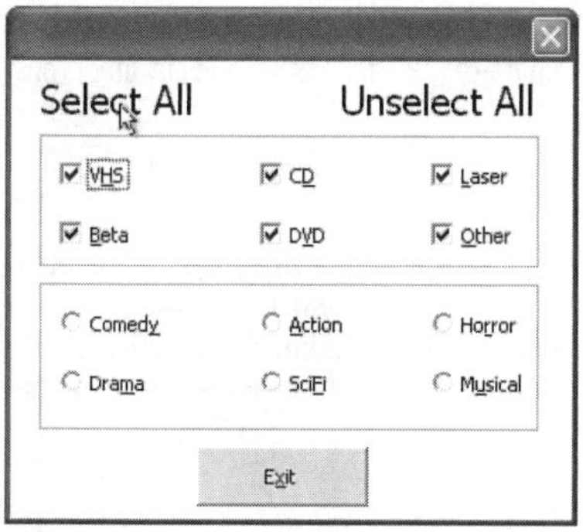

Figure 23.6
Use frames, collections, and class modules together to create quick and efficient userforms.

Modeless Userforms

Have you ever had a userform active but needed to look at something on a sheet? There was a time when the form had to be shut down before anything else in Excel could be done. No longer! Forms can now be *modeless*, which means they don't have to interfere with the functionality of Excel. The user can type in a cell, switch to another sheet, copy/paste data, and use the ribbon—it is as if the userform were not there.

By default, a userform is modal, which means that there is no interaction with Excel other than the form. To make the form modeless, change the `ShowModal` property to `False`. After it is modeless, the user can select a cell on the sheet while the form is active, as shown in Figure 23.7.

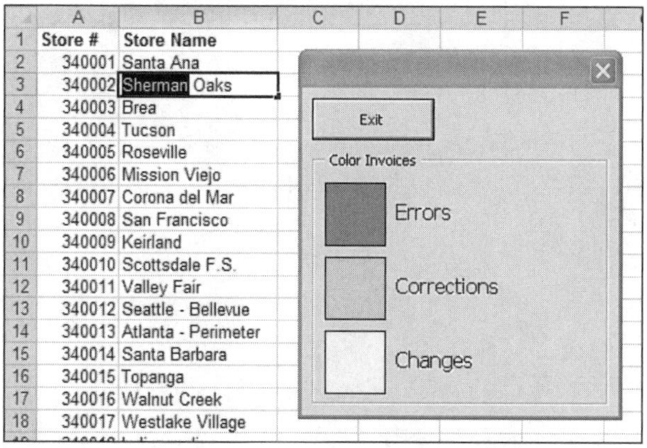

Figure 23.7
A modeless form enables the user to enter a cell while the form is still active.

Using Hyperlinks in Userforms

In the userform example shown in Figure 23.3, there is a field for e-mail and a website address. It would be nice to click these and have a blank e-mail message or web page appear automatically. You can do this by using the following program, which creates a new message or opens a web browser when the corresponding label is clicked.

> **TIP**
>
> The application programming interface (API) declaration, and any other constants, go at the very top of the code.

```
Private Declare Function ShellExecute Lib "shell32.dll" Alias _
    "ShellExecuteA"(ByVal hWnd As Long, ByVal lpOperation As String, _
    ByVal lpFile As String, ByVal lpParameters As String, _
    ByVal lpDirectory As String, ByVal nShowCmd As Long) As Long

Const SWNormal = 1
```

This sub controls what happens when the e-mail label is clicked, as shown in Figure 23.8:

```
Private Sub lbl_Email_Click()
Dim lngRow As Long

lngRow = TabStrip1.Value + 1
ShellExecute 0&, "open", "mailto:" & Cells(lngRow, 5).Value, _
    vbNullString, vbNullString, SWNormal

End Sub
```

This sub controls what happens when the website label is clicked:

```
Private Sub lbl_Website_Click()
Dim lngRow As Long

lngRow = TabStrip1.Value + 1
ShellExecute 0&, "open", Cells(lngRow, 6).Value, vbNullString, _
    vbNullString, SWNormal

End Sub
```

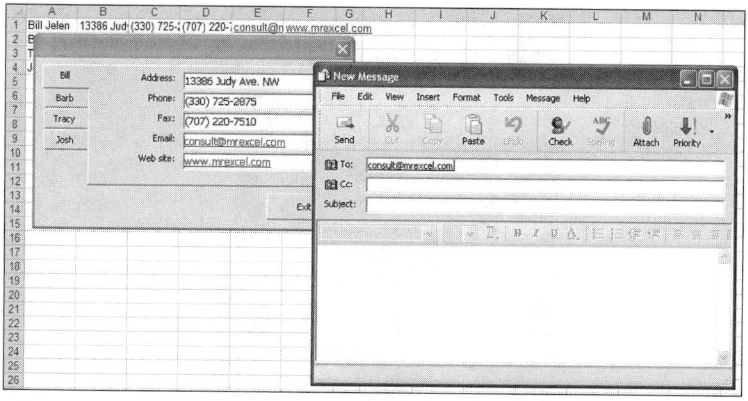

Figure 23.8
Turn e-mail addresses and websites into clickable links.

Adding Controls at Runtime

It is possible to add controls to a userform at runtime. This is convenient if you are not sure how many items you will be adding to the form.

Figure 23.9 shows a plain form with only one button. This plain form is used to display any number of pictures from a product catalog. The pictures and accompanying labels appear at runtime, as the form is being displayed.

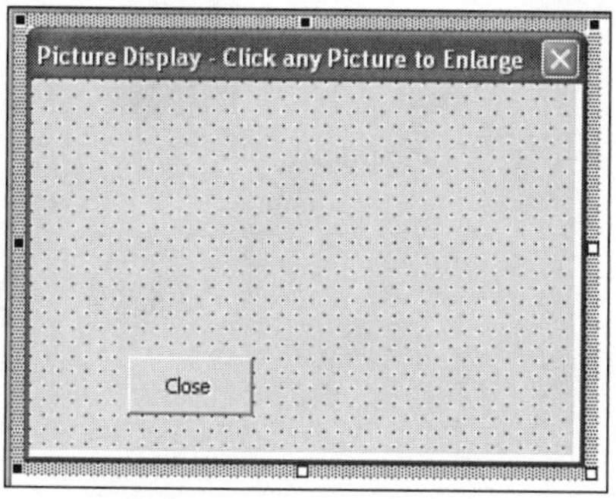

Figure 23.9
Flexible forms can be created if you add most controls at runtime.

A sales rep making a sales presentation uses this form to display a product catalog. He can select any number of SKUs from an Excel worksheet and press a hot key to display the form. If he selects 18 items on the worksheet, the form displays with a small version of each picture, as shown in Figure 23.10.

If the sales rep selects fewer items, the images are displayed larger, as shown in Figure 23.11.

A number of techniques are used to create this userform on-the-fly. The initial form contains only one button, called cbClose. Everything else is added on-the-fly.

Figure 23.10
The sales rep asked to see photos of 18 SKUs. The `UserForm_Initialize` procedure adds each picture and label on-the-fly.

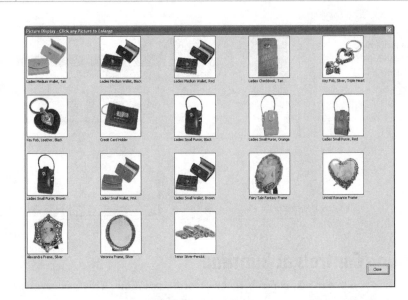

Figure 23.11
The logic in `Userform_Initialize` decides how many pictures are being displayed and adds the appropriate size controls.

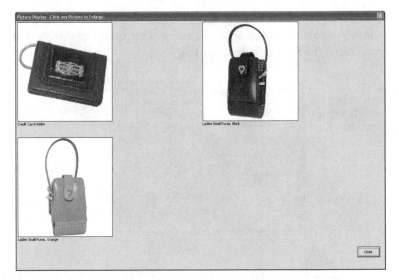

Resizing the Userform On-the-fly

One goal is to give the best view of the images in the product catalog. This means having the form appear as large as possible. The following code uses the form's Height and Width properties to make sure the form fills almost the entire screen:

```
' resize the form
Me.Height = Int(0.98 * ActiveWindow.Height)
Me.Width = Int(0.98 * ActiveWindow.Width)
```

Adding a Control On-the-fly

For a normal control added at design time, it is easy to refer to the control by using its name:

```
Me.cbSave.Left = 100
```

However, for a control that is added at runtime, you have to use the Controls collection to set any properties for the control. For this reason, it is important to set up a variable to hold the name of the control. Controls are added with the .Add method. The important parameter is the bstrProgId. This code name dictates whether the added control is a label, text box, command button, or something else.

The following code adds a new label to the form. PicCount is a counter variable used to ensure that each label has a new name. After the form is added, specify a position for the control by setting the Top and Left properties. You should also set a Height and Width for the control:

```
LC = "LabelA" & PicCount
Me.Controls.Add bstrProgId:="forms.label.1", Name:=LC, Visible:=True
Me.Controls(LC).Top = 25
Me.Controls(LC).Left = 50
Me.Controls(LC).Height = 18
Me.Controls(LC).Width = 60
Me.Controls(LC).Caption = cell.value
```

> **CAUTION**
>
> You lose some of the AutoComplete options with this method. Normally, if you would start to type Me.cbClose., the AutoComplete options would present the valid choices for a command button. However, when you use the Me.Controls(LC) collection to add controls on-the-fly, VBA does not know what type of control is referenced. In this case, it is helpful to know you need to set the Caption property rather than the Value property for a label.

Sizing On-the-fly

In reality, you need to be able to calculate values for Top, Left, Height, and Width on-the-fly. You would do this based on the actual height and width of the form and on how many controls are needed.

Adding Other Controls

To add other types of controls, change the ProgId used with the Add method. Table 23.6 shows the ProgIds for various types of controls.

Table 23.6   Userform Controls and Corresponding ProgIds

Control	ProgId
CheckBox	Forms.CheckBox.1
ComboBox	Forms.ComboBox.1
CommandButton	Forms.CommandButton.1
Frame	Forms.Frame.1
Image	Forms.Image.1
Label	Forms.Label.1
ListBox	Forms.ListBox.1
MultiPage	Forms.MultiPage.1
OptionButton	Forms.OptionButton.1
ScrollBar	Forms.ScrollBar.1
SpinButton	Forms.SpinButton.1
TabStrip	Forms.TabStrip.1
TextBox	Forms.TextBox.1
ToggleButton	Forms.ToggleButton.1

Adding an Image On-the-fly

There is some unpredictability in adding images. Any given image might be shaped either landscape or portrait. The image might be small or huge. The strategy you might want to use is to let the image load full size by setting the .AutoSize parameter to True before loading it:

```
TC = "Image" & PicCount
Me.Controls.Add bstrProgId:="forms.image.1", Name:=TC, Visible:=True
Me.Controls(TC).Top = LastTop
Me.Controls(TC).Left = LastLeft
Me.Controls(TC).AutoSize = True
On Error Resume Next
Me.Controls(TC).Picture = LoadPicture(fname)
On Error GoTo 0
```

After the image has loaded, you can read the control's Height and Width properties to determine whether the image is landscape or portrait and whether the image is constrained by available width or available height:

```
' The picture resized the control to full size
' determine the size of the picture
Wid = Me.Controls(TC).Width
Ht = Me.Controls(TC).Height
WidRedux = CellWid / Wid
HtRedux = CellHt / Ht
If WidRedux < HtRedux Then
```

```
        Redux = WidRedux
    Else
        Redux = HtRedux
    End If
    NewHt = Int(Ht * Redux)
    NewWid = Int(Wid * Redux)
```

After you find the proper size for the image so that it draws without distortion, set the `AutoSize` property to `False`. Use the correct height and width to have the image not appear distorted:

```
    ' Now resize the control
    Me.Controls(TC).AutoSize = False
    Me.Controls(TC).Height = NewHt
    Me.Controls(TC).Width = NewWid
    Me.Controls(TC).PictureSizeMode = fmPictureSizeModeStretch
```

23

Putting It All Together

This is the complete code for the Picture Catalog userform:

```
Private Sub UserForm_Initialize()
    ' Display pictures of each SKU selected on the worksheet
    ' This may be anywhere from 1 to 36 pictures
    PicPath = "C:\qimage\qi"
    Dim Pics ()

    ' resize the form
    Me.Height = Int(0.98 * ActiveWindow.Height)
    Me.Width = Int(0.98 * ActiveWindow.Width)

    ' determine how many cells are selected
    ' We need one picture and label for each cell
    CellCount = Selection.Cells.Count
    ReDim Preserve Pics(1 To CellCount)

    ' Figure out the size of the resized form
    TempHt = Me.Height
    TempWid = Me.Width

    ' The number of columns is a roundup of SQRT(CellCount)
    ' This will ensure 4 rows of 5 pictures for 20, etc.
    NumCol = Int(0.99 + Sqr(CellCount))
    NumRow = Int(0.99 + CellCount / NumCol)

    ' Figure out the ht and wid of each square
    ' Each column will have 2 pts to left & right of pics
    CellWid = Application.WorksheetFunction.Max(Int(TempWid / NumCol) - 4, 1)
    ' each row needs to have 33 points below it for the label
    CellHt = Application.WorksheetFunction.Max(Int(TempHt / NumRow) - 33, 1)

    PicCount = 0 ' Counter variable
    LastTop = 2
    MaxBottom = 1
    ' Build each row on the form
    For x = 1 To NumRow
        LastLeft = 3
```

23

```
' Build each column in this row
For Y = 1 To NumCol
    PicCount = PicCount + 1
    If PicCount > CellCount Then
        ' There are not an even number of pictures to fill
        ' out the last row
        Me.Height = MaxBottom + 100
        Me.cbClose.Top = MaxBottom + 25
        Me.cbClose.Left = Me.Width - 70
        Repaint 'redraws the form
        Exit Sub
    End If
    ThisStyle = Selection.Cells(PicCount).Value
    ThisDesc = Selection.Cells(PicCount).Offset(0, 1).Value
    fname = PicPath & ThisStyle & ".jpg"
    TC = "Image" & PicCount
    Me.Controls.Add bstrProgId:="forms.image.1", Name:=TC, _
        Visible:=True
    Me.Controls(TC).Top = LastTop
    Me.Controls(TC).Left = LastLeft
    Me.Controls(TC).AutoSize = True
    On Error Resume Next
    Me.Controls(TC).Picture = LoadPicture(fname)
    On Error GoTo 0

    ' The picture resized the control to full size
    ' determine the size of the picture
    Wid = Me.Controls(TC).Width
    Ht = Me.Controls(TC).Height
    WidRedux = CellWid / Wid
    HtRedux = CellHt / Ht
    If WidRedux < HtRedux Then
        Redux = WidRedux
    Else
        Redux = HtRedux
    End If
    NewHt = Int(Ht * Redux)
    NewWid = Int(Wid * Redux)

    ' Now resize the control
    Me.Controls(TC).AutoSize = False
    Me.Controls(TC).Height = NewHt
    Me.Controls(TC).Width = NewWid
    Me.Controls(TC).PictureSizeMode = fmPictureSizeModeStretch
    Me.Controls(TC).ControlTipText = "Style " & _
            ThisStyle & " " & ThisDesc

    ' Keep track of the bottom-most & right-most picture
    ThisRight = Me.Controls(TC).Left + Me.Controls(TC).Width
    ThisBottom = Me.Controls(TC).Top + Me.Controls(TC).Height
    If ThisBottom > MaxBottom Then MaxBottom = ThisBottom

    ' Add a label below the picture
    LC = "LabelA" & PicCount
```

```
              Me.Controls.Add bstrProgId:="forms.label.1", Name:=LC, _
                 Visible:=True
              Me.Controls(LC).Top = ThisBottom + 1
              Me.Controls(LC).Left = LastLeft
              Me.Controls(LC).Height = 18
              Me.Controls(LC).Width = CellWid
              Me.Controls(LC).Caption = "Style " & ThisStyle & " " & ThisDesc

              ' Keep track of where the next picture should display
              LastLeft = LastLeft + CellWid + 4
          Next Y ' end of this row
          LastTop = MaxBottom + 21 + 16
      Next x

      Me.Height = MaxBottom + 100
      Me.cbClose.Top = MaxBottom + 25
      Me.cbClose.Left = Me.Width - 70
      Repaint
  End Sub
```

Adding Help to the Userform

Even though you designed a great userform, there is one thing missing: guidance for the
users. The following sections show four ways you can help users fill out the form properly.

Showing Accelerator Keys

Built-in forms often have keyboard shortcuts that allow actions to be triggered or fields
selected with a few keystrokes. These shortcuts are identified by an underlined letter on a
button or label.

You can add this same capability to custom userforms by entering a value in the
Accelerator property of the control. Alt + the accelerator key selects the control. For example, in Figure 23.12, Alt+H selects the VHS check box. Repeating the combination clears
the box.

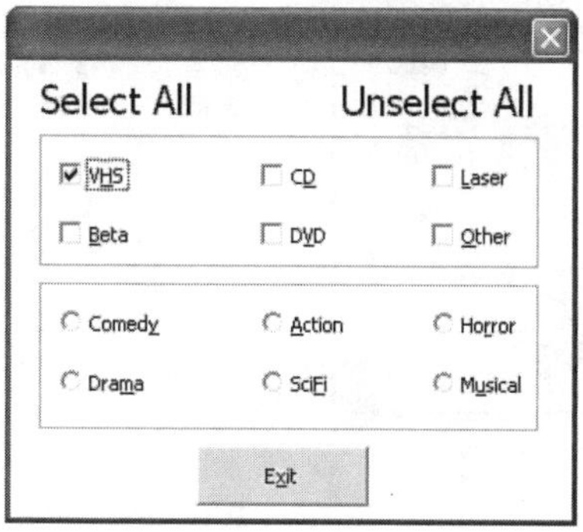

Figure 23.12
Use accelerator key
combinations to give
userforms the power of
keyboard shortcuts.

Adding Control Tip Text

When a cursor is waved over a toolbar, tip text appears, hinting at what the control does. You can also add tip text to userforms by entering a value in the `ControlTipText` property of a control. In Figure 23.13, tip text has been added to the frame surrounding the various categories.

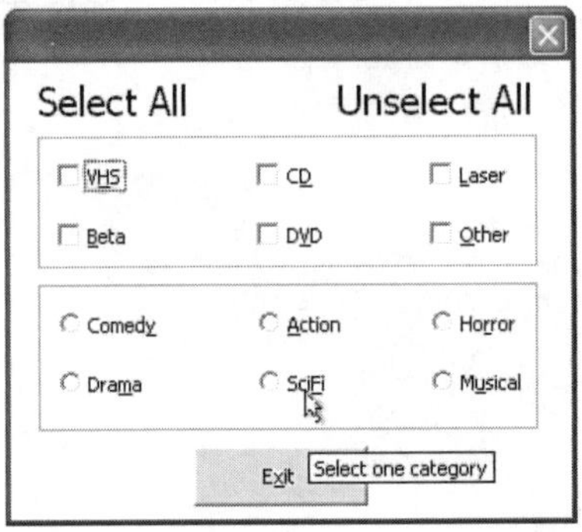

Figure 23.13
Add tips to controls to provide help to users.

Creating the Tab Order

Users can also tab from one field to another. This is an automatic feature in a form. To control which field the next tab brings a user to, you can set the `TapStop` property value for each control.

The first tab stop is zero, and the last tab stop is equal to the number of controls in a group. Remember, a group can be created with a frame. Excel does not allow multiple controls to have the same tab stop. After tab stops are set, the user can use the Tab key and Spacebar to select/deselect various options, as shown in Figure 23.14.

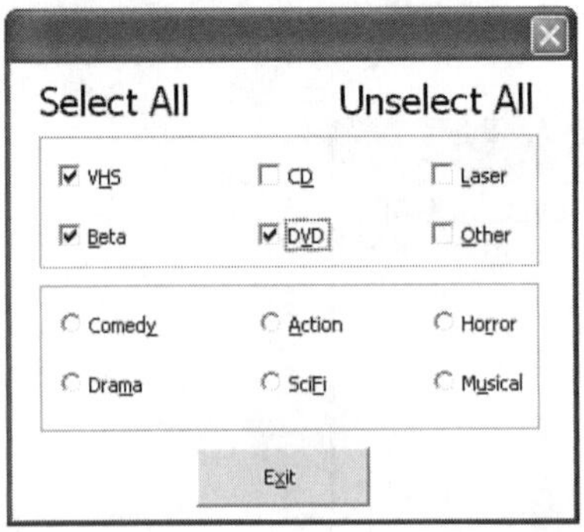

Figure 23.14
The options in this form were selected with the Tab key and Spacebar.

Coloring the Active Control

Another method for helping a user fill out a form is to color the active field. The following example changes the color of a text box or combo box when it is active.

Place the following in a class module called `clsCtlColor`:

```
Public Event GetFocus()
Public Event LostFocus(ByVal strCtrl As String)
Private strPreCtr As String

Public Sub CheckActiveCtrl(objForm As MSForms.UserForm)

With objForm
    If TypeName(.ActiveControl) = "ComboBox" Or _
        TypeName(.ActiveControl) = "TextBox" Then
        strPreCtr = .ActiveControl.Name
        On Error GoTo Terminate
        Do
            DoEvents
            If .ActiveControl.Name <> strPreCtr Then
                If TypeName(.ActiveControl) = "ComboBox" Or _
                    TypeName(.ActiveControl) = "TextBox" Then
                    RaiseEvent LostFocus(strPreCtr)
                    strPreCtr = .ActiveControl.Name
                    RaiseEvent GetFocus
                End If
            End If
        Loop
    End If
End With

Terminate:
    Exit Sub

End Sub
```

Place the following behind the userform:

```
Private WithEvents objForm As clsCtlColor

Private Sub UserForm_Initialize()
Set objForm = New clsCtlColor
End Sub
```

This sub changes the `BackColor` of the active control when the form is activated:

```
Private Sub UserForm_Activate()
If TypeName(ActiveControl) = "ComboBox" Or _
    TypeName(ActiveControl) = "TextBox" Then
    ActiveControl.BackColor = &HC0E0FF
End If
objForm.CheckActiveCtrl Me
End Sub
```

This sub changes the `BackColor` of the active control when it gets the focus:

```
Private Sub objForm_GetFocus()
ActiveControl.BackColor = &HC0E0FF
End Sub
```

23

This sub changes the `BackColor` back to white when the control loses the focus:

```
Private Sub objForm_LostFocus(ByVal strCtrl As String)
Me.Controls(strCtrl).BackColor = &HFFFFFF
End Sub
```

This sub clears the `objForm` when the form is closed:

```
Private Sub UserForm_QueryClose(Cancel As Integer, CloseMode As Integer)
Set objForm = Nothing
End Sub
```

CASE STUDY: MULTICOLUMN LIST BOXES

You have created several spreadsheets containing store data. The primary key of each set is the store number. The workbook is used by several people, but not everyone memorizes stores by his or her store numbers. You need some way of letting a user select a store by its name. At the same time, you need to return the store number to be used in the code. You could use VLOOKUP or MATCH, but there is another way.

A list box can have more than one column, but not all the columns need to be visible to the user. In addition, the user can select an item from the visible list, but the list box returns the corresponding value from another column.

Draw a list box and set the `ColumnCount` property to 2. Set the `RowSource` to a two-column range called `Stores`. The first column of the range is the store number; the second column is the store name. At this point, the list box is displaying both columns of data. To change this, set the column width to `0`, `20`—the text automatically updates to 0 pt;20 pt. The first column is now hidden. Figure 23.15 shows the list box properties as they need to be.

The appearance of the list box has now been set. When the user activates the list box, she will see only the store names. To return the value of the first column, set the `BoundColumn` property to 1. This can be done through the Properties window or through code. This example uses code to maintain the flexibility of returning the store number (see Figure 23.16):

```
Private Sub UserForm_Initialize()
    lb_StoreName.BoundColumn = 1
End Sub
Private Sub lb_StoreName_Click()
lbl_StoreNum.Caption = lb_StoreName.Value
End Sub
```

Figure 23.15
Setting the list box properties creates a two-column list box that appears to be a single column of data.

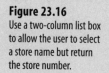

Figure 23.16
Use a two-column list box to allow the user to select a store name but return the store number.

Store Number Search

Store Names
| Santa Ana |
| Sherman Oaks |
| Brea |
| Tucson |

Active Store Number   340002

Exit

23

Transparent Forms

Have you ever had a form that you had to keep moving out of the way so you could see the data behind it? The following code sets the userform at a 50 percent transparency (see Figure 23.17) so that you can see the data behind it without moving the form somewhere else on the screen (and blocking more data).

Figure 23.17
Create a 50 percent transparent form to view the data on the sheet behind it.

MrExcel Staff

Bill	Address:	13386 Judy Ave. NW
Barb	Phone:	(330) 715-2875
	Fax:	(707) 220-4510
Tracy	Email:	consult@mrexcel.com
Juan	Website:	www.mrexcel.com

You can see text on the other side of the form

CLOSE

Place the following in the declarations section of the userform:

```
Private Declare Function GetActiveWindow Lib "USER32" () As Long
Private Declare Function SetWindowLong Lib "USER32" Alias _
    "SetWindowLongA" (ByVal hWnd As Long, ByVal nIndex As Long, _
    ByVal dwNewLong As Long) As Long
Private Declare Function GetWindowLong Lib "USER32" Alias _
    "GetWindowLongA" (ByVal hWnd As Long, ByVal nIndex As Long) As Long
Private Declare Function SetLayeredWindowAttributes Lib "USER32" _
    (ByVal hWnd As Long, ByVal crKey As Integer, _
    ByVal bAlpha As Integer, ByVal dwFlags As Long) As Long
Private Const WS_EX_LAYERED = &H80000
Private Const LWA_COLORKEY = &H1
Private Const LWA_ALPHA = &H2
Private Const GWL_EXSTYLE = &HFFEC
Dim hWnd As Long
```

Place the following behind a userform. When the form is activated, the transparency will be set:

```
Private Sub UserForm_Activate()
Dim nIndex As Long

hWnd = GetActiveWindow
nIndex = GetWindowLong(hWnd, GWL_EXSTYLE)
SetWindowLong hWnd, GWL_EXSTYLE, nIndex Or WS_EX_LAYERED
'50% semitransparent
SetLayeredWindowAttributes hWnd, 0, (255 * 50) / 100, LWA_ALPHA

End Sub
```

Next Steps

In Chapter 24, "Windows Application Programming Interface (API)," you learn how to access functions and procedures hidden in files on your computer.

Windows API

What Is the Windows API?

With all the wonderful things you can do in Excel VBA, there are some things that are out of VBA's reach or are just too difficult to do, such as finding out what the user's screen resolution setting is. This is where the Windows application programming interface (API) can help.

If you look in the folder \Winnt\System32 (Windows NT systems), you will see many files with the extension .dll. These files, which are dynamic link libraries (dll), contain various functions and procedures that other programs can access, including VBA. They give the user access to functionality used by the Windows operating system and many other programs.

24

IN THIS CHAPTER

What Is the Windows API? 535

Understanding an API Declaration 536

Using an API Declaration 537

API Examples 537

Finding More API Declarations 547

> **NOTE**
>
> Keep in mind that Windows API declarations are accessible only on computers running the Microsoft Windows operating system.

This chapter does not teach you how to write API declarations, but it does teach you the basics of interpreting and using them. Several useful examples have also been included, and you are shown how to find more.

Understanding an API Declaration

The following line is an example of an API function:

```
Private Declare Function GetUserName _
   Lib "advapi32.dll" Alias "GetUserNameA"  _
   (ByVal lpBuffer As String, nSize As Long) _
   As Long
```

There are two types of API declarations:

- **Functions**—Return information
- **Procedures**—Do something to the system

The declarations are structured similarly.

Basically, what this declaration is saying is

- It is Private; therefore, it can be used only in the module in which it is declared. Declare it Public in a standard module if you want to share it among several modules.

> **CAUTION**
>
> API declarations in standard modules can be public or private. API declarations in class modules must be private.

- It will be referred to as GetUserName in your program. This is the variable name assigned by you.
- The function being used is found in advapi32.dll.
- The alias, GetUserNameA, is what the function is referred to in the DLL. This name is case-sensitive and cannot be changed; it is specific to the DLL. There are often two versions of each API function. One version uses the ANSI character set and has aliases that end with the letter *A*. The other version uses the Unicode character set and has aliases that end with the letter *W*. When specifying the alias, you are telling VBA which version of the function to use.
- There are two parameters: lpBuffer and nSize. These are two arguments that the DLL function accepts.

> **CAUTION**
>
> The downside of using APIs is that there may be no errors when your code compiles or runs. This means that an incorrectly configured API call can cause your computer to crash or lock up. For this reason, it is a good idea to save often.

Using an API Declaration

Using an API is no different from calling a function or procedure you created in VBA. The following example uses the GetUserName declaration in a function to return the UserName in Excel:

```
Public Function UserName() As String
Dim sName As String * 256
Dim cChars As Long

cChars = 256
If GetUserName(sName, cChars) Then
    UserName = Left$(sName, cChars - 1)
End If
End Function
Sub ProgramRights()
Dim NameofUser As String

NameofUser = UserName

Select Case NameofUser
    Case Is = "Administrator"
        MsgBox "You have full rights to this computer"
    Case Else
        MsgBox "You have limited rights to this computer"
End Select

End Sub
```

Run the ProgramRights macro, and you will learn whether you are currently signed on as the administrator. The result shown in Figure 24.1 indicates an administrator sign-on.

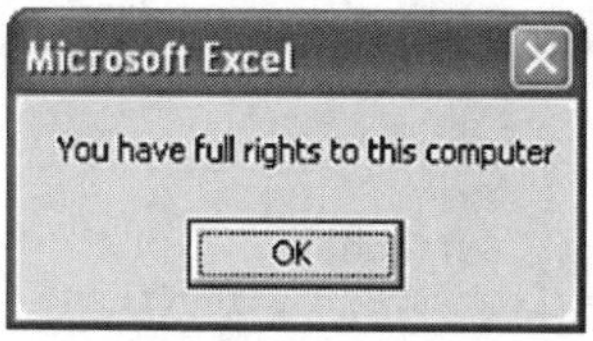

Figure 24.1
The GetUserName API function can be used to get a user's Windows login name—which is more difficult to edit than the Excel username.

API Examples

The following sections provide more examples of useful API declarations you can use in your Excel programs. Each example starts with a short description of what the example can do, followed by the actual declarations, and an example of its use.

┌─ CAUTION ───┐

The examples in this book are 32-bit API declarations and may not work in 64-bit Excel. For example, if in a 32-bit version we have this declaration:

```
Private Declare Function GetWindowLongptr Lib "USER32" Alias _
        "GetWindowLongA" (ByVal hWnd As Long, ByVal nIndex As _
        Long) As Long
```

It will need to be changed to the following to work in the 64-bit version:

```
        Private Declare PtrSafe Function GetWindowLongptr Lib _
    "USER32" Alias _
        "GetWindowLongA" (ByVal hWnd As LongPtr, ByVal nIndex As _
        Long) As LongPtr
```

But how can you know whether a Long needs to be changed to a LongPtr or to Long, Long? It might not even need to be changed at all! Because of the confusion that has ensued, Jan Karel Pieterse of JKP Application Development Services (www.jkp-ads.com) is working on an ever-growing web page listing the proper syntax for the 64-bit declarations. It can be found at www.jkp-ads.com/articles/apideclarations.asp.

└──┘

Retrieve the Computer Name

This API function returns the computer name. This is the name of the computer found under MyComputer, Network Identification:

```
Private Declare Function GetComputerName Lib "kernel32" Alias _
    "GetComputerNameA" (ByVal lpBuffer As String, ByRef nSize As Long) As Long
Private Function ComputerName() As String

Dim stBuff As String * 255, lAPIResult As Long
Dim lBuffLen As Long

lBuffLen = 255
lAPIResult = GetComputerName(stBuff, lBuffLen)
If lBuffLen > 0 Then ComputerName = Left(stBuff, lBuffLen)

End Function

Sub ComputerCheck()
Dim CompName As String

CompName = ComputerName

If CompName <> "BillJelenPC" Then
    MsgBox _
    "This application does not have the right to run on this computer."
        ActiveWorkbook.Close SaveChanges:=False
End If

End Sub
```

The ComputerCheck macro uses an API call to get the name of the computer. In Figure 24.2, the program refuses to run for any computer except the hard-coded computer name of the owner.

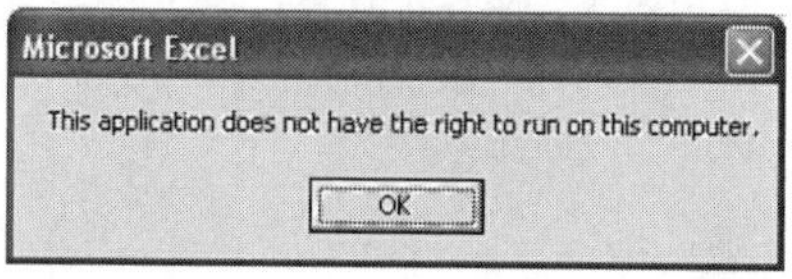

Figure 24.2
Use the computer name to verify that an application has the rights to run on the installed computer.

Check Whether an Excel File Is Open on a Network

You can check whether you have a file open in Excel by trying to set the workbook to an object. If the object is Nothing (empty), you know the file is not opened. However, what if you want to see whether someone else on a network has the file open? The following API function returns that information:

```
Private Declare Function lOpen Lib "kernel32" Alias "_lopen" _
    (ByVal lpPathName As String, ByVal iReadWrite As Long) As Long

Private Declare Function lClose Lib "kernel32" _
    Alias "_lclose" (ByVal hFile As Long) As Long

Private Const OF_SHARE_EXCLUSIVE = &H10
Private Function FileIsOpen(strFullPath_FileName As String) As Boolean
Dim hdlFile As Long
Dim lastErr As Long

hdlFile = -1

hdlFile = lOpen(strFullPath_FileName, OF_SHARE_EXCLUSIVE)

If hdlFile = -1 Then
    lastErr = Err.LastDllError
Else
    lClose (hdlFile)
End If

FileIsOpen = (hdlFile = -1) And (lastErr = 32)

End Function

Sub CheckFileOpen()

If FileIsOpen("C:\XYZ Corp.xlsx") Then
    MsgBox "File is open"
Else
    MsgBox "File is not open"
End If

End Sub
```

Calling the FileIsOpen function with a particular path and filename as the parameter will tell you whether someone has the file open.

Retrieve Display-Resolution Information

The following API function retrieves the computer's display size:

```
Declare Function DisplaySize Lib "user32" Alias _
    "GetSystemMetrics" (ByVal nIndex As Long) As Long

Public Const SM_CXSCREEN = 0
Public Const SM_CYSCREEN = 1

Function VideoRes() As String
Dim vidWidth
Dim vidHeight

vidWidth = DisplaySize(SM_CXSCREEN)
vidHeight = DisplaySize(SM_CYSCREEN)

Select Case (vidWidth * vidHeight)
    Case 307200
        VideoRes = "640 x 480"
    Case 480000
        VideoRes = "800 x 600"
    Case 786432
        VideoRes = "1024 x 768"
    Case Else
        VideoRes = "Something else"
End Select

End Function

Sub CheckDisplayRes()
Dim VideoInfo As String
Dim Msg1 As String, Msg2 As String, Msg3 As String

VideoInfo = VideoRes

Msg1 = "Current resolution is set at " & VideoInfo & Chr(10)
Msg2 = "Optimal resolution for this application is 1024 x 768" & Chr(10)
Msg3 = "Please adjust resolution"

Select Case VideoInfo
    Case Is = "640 x 480"
        MsgBox Msg1 & Msg2 & Msg3
    Case Is = "800 x 600"
        MsgBox Msg1 & Msg2
    Case Is = "1024 x 768"
        MsgBox Msg1
    Case Else
        MsgBox Msg2 & Msg3
End Select

End Sub
```

The CheckDisplayRes macro warns the client that the display setting is not optimal for the application.

Custom About Dialog

If you go to Help, About Windows in Windows Explorer, you get a nice little About dialog with information about the Windows Explorer and a few system details. With the following code, you can pop up that window in your own program and customize a few items, as shown in Figure 24.3.

Figure 24.3
You can customize the About dialog used by Windows for your own program.

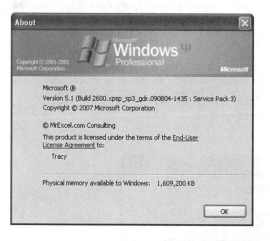

```
Declare Function ShellAbout Lib "shell32.dll" Alias "ShellAboutA" _
    (ByVal hwnd As Long, ByVal szApp As String, ByVal szOtherStuff As _
    String, ByVal hIcon As Long) As Long
Declare Function GetActiveWindow Lib "user32" () As Long

Sub AboutMrExcel()
    Dim hwnd As Integer
    On Error Resume Next
    hwnd = GetActiveWindow()
    ShellAbout hwnd, Nm, vbCrLf + Chr(169) + "" & " MrExcel.com Consulting" _
        + vbCrLf, 0
    On Error GoTo 0
End Sub
```

Disable the X for Closing a Userform

The X button located in the upper-right corner of a userform can be used to shut down the application. The following API declarations work together to disable that X, forcing the user to use the Close button. When the form is initialized, the button is disabled. After the form is closed, the X button is reset to normal:

```
Private Declare Function FindWindow Lib "user32" Alias "FindWindowA" _
    (ByVal lpClassName As String, ByVal lpWindowName As String) As Long
Private Declare Function GetSystemMenu Lib "user32" (ByVal hWnd As Long, _
    ByVal bRevert As Long) As Long
Private Declare Function DeleteMenu Lib "user32" _
```

```
     (ByVal hMenu As Long, ByVal nPosition As Long, _
        ByVal wFlags As Long) As Long
Private Const SC_CLOSE As Long = &HF060

Private Sub UserForm_Initialize()
Dim hWndForm As Long
Dim hMenu As Long

hWndForm = FindWindow("ThunderDFrame", Me.Caption)    'XL2000
hMenu = GetSystemMenu(hWndForm, 0)
DeleteMenu hMenu, SC_CLOSE, 0&

End Sub
```

The DeleteMenu macro in the UserForm_Initialize procedure causes the X in the corner of the userform to be grayed out, as shown in Figure 24.4. This forces the client to use your programmed Close button.

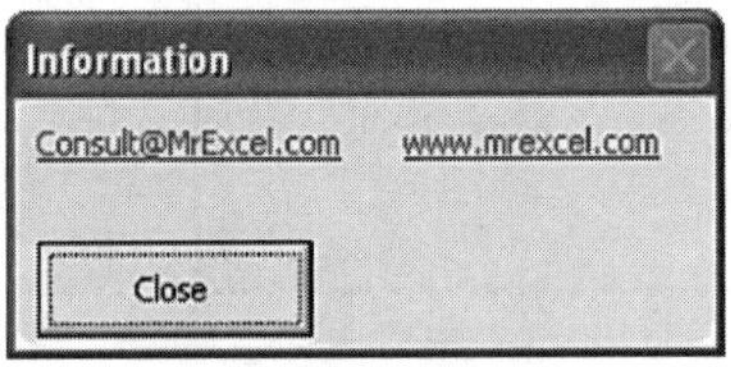

Figure 24.4
Disable the X button on a userform, forcing users to use the Close button to shut down the form properly and rendering them unable to bypass any code attached to the Close button.

Running Timer

You can use the NOW function to get the time, but what if you needed a running timer displaying the exact time as the seconds tick by? The following API declarations work together to provide this functionality. The timer is placed in Cell A1 of Sheet1.

```
Public Declare Function SetTimer Lib "user32" _
     (ByVal hWnd As Long, ByVal nIDEvent As Long, _
      ByVal uElapse As Long, ByVal lpTimerFunc As Long) As Long
Public Declare Function KillTimer Lib "user32" _
     (ByVal hWnd As Long, ByVal nIDEvent As Long) As Long
Public Declare Function FindWindow Lib "user32" _
     Alias "FindWindowA" (ByVal lpClassName As String, _
     ByVal lpWindowName As String) As Long

Private lngTimerID As Long
Public datStartingTime As Date

Public Sub StartTimer()
lngTimerID = SetTimer(0, 1, 10, AddressOf RunTimer)
End Sub

Public Sub StopTimer()
Dim lRet As Long
lRet = KillTimer(0, lngTimerID)
End Sub
```

```
Private Sub RunTimer(ByVal hWnd As Long, _
    ByVal uint1 As Long, ByVal nEventId As Long, _
    ByVal dwParam As Long)
On Error Resume Next
Sheet1.Range("A1").Value = Now - datStartingTime
End Sub
```

Run the StartTimer macro to have the current date and time constantly updated in cell A1.

Playing Sounds

Have you ever wanted to play a sound to warn users or congratulate them? You could add a sound object to a sheet and call that sound. However, it would be easier to use the following API declaration and specify the proper path to a sound file:

```
Public Declare Function PlayWavSound Lib "winmm.dll" _
    Alias "sndPlaySoundA" (ByVal LpszSoundName As String, _
    ByVal uFlags As Long) As Long

Public Sub PlaySound()
Dim SoundName As String

SoundName = "C:\WinNT\Media\Chimes.wav"
PlayWavSound SoundName, 0

End Sub
```

Retrieving a File Path

The following API enables you to create a custom file browser. The program example using the API customizes the function call to create a browser for a specific need. In this case, it will return the file path of a user-selected file:

```
Type tagOPENFILENAME
    lStructSize As Long
    hwndOwner As Long
    hInstance As Long
    strFilter As String
    strCustomFilter As String
    nMaxCustFilter As Long
    nFilterIndex As Long
    strFile As String
    nMaxFile As Long
    strFileTitle As String
    nMaxFileTitle As Long
    strInitialDir As String
    strTitle As String
    Flags As Long
    nFileOffset As Integer
    nFileExtension As Integer
    strDefExt As String
    lCustData As Long
    lpfnHook As Long
    lpTemplateName As String
End Type
```

24

```
Declare Function aht_apiGetOpenFileName Lib "comdlg32.dll" _
    Alias "GetOpenFileNameA" (OFN As tagOPENFILENAME) As Boolean
Declare Function aht_apiGetSaveFileName Lib "comdlg32.dll" _
    Alias "GetSaveFileNameA" (OFN As tagOPENFILENAME) As Boolean
Declare Function CommDlgExtendedError Lib "comdlg32.dll" () As Long

Global Const ahtOFN_READONLY = &H1
Global Const ahtOFN_OVERWRITEPROMPT = &H2
Global Const ahtOFN_HIDEREADONLY = &H4
Global Const ahtOFN_NOCHANGEDIR = &H8
Global Const ahtOFN_SHOWHELP = &H10
Global Const ahtOFN_NOVALIDATE = &H100
Global Const ahtOFN_ALLOWMULTISELECT = &H200
Global Const ahtOFN_EXTENSIONDIFFERENT = &H400
Global Const ahtOFN_PATHMUSTEXIST = &H800
Global Const ahtOFN_FILEMUSTEXIST = &H1000
Global Const ahtOFN_CREATEPROMPT = &H2000
Global Const ahtOFN_SHAREAWARE = &H4000
Global Const ahtOFN_NOREADONLYRETURN = &H8000
Global Const ahtOFN_NOTESTFILECREATE = &H10000
Global Const ahtOFN_NONETWORKBUTTON = &H20000
Global Const ahtOFN_NOLONGNAMES = &H40000
Global Const ahtOFN_EXPLORER = &H80000
Global Const ahtOFN_NODEREFERENCELINKS = &H100000
Global Const ahtOFN_LONGNAMES = &H200000

Function ahtCommonFileOpenSave( _
            Optional ByRef Flags As Variant, _
            Optional ByVal InitialDir As Variant, _
            Optional ByVal Filter As Variant, _
            Optional ByVal FilterIndex As Variant, _
            Optional ByVal DefaultExt As Variant, _
            Optional ByVal FileName As Variant, _
            Optional ByVal DialogTitle As Variant, _
            Optional ByVal hwnd As Variant, _
            Optional ByVal OpenFile As Variant) As Variant

' This is the entry point you'll use to call the common
' file Open/Save As dialog. The parameters are listed
' below, and all are optional.
'
' In:
' Flags: one or more of the ahtOFN_* constants, OR'd together.
' InitialDir: the directory in which to first look
' Filter: a set of file filters
'    (Use AddFilterItem to set up Filters)
' FilterIndex: 1-based integer indicating which filter
' set to use, by default (1 if unspecified)
' DefaultExt: Extension to use if the user doesn't enter one.
' Only useful on file saves.
' FileName: Default value for the filename text box.
' DialogTitle: Title for the dialog.
' hWnd: parent window handle
' OpenFile: Boolean(True=Open File/False=Save As)
' Out:
' Return Value: Either Null or the selected filename

Dim OFN As tagOPENFILENAME
```

```
Dim strFileName As String
Dim strFileTitle As String
Dim fResult As Boolean

' Give the dialog a caption title.
If IsMissing(InitialDir) Then InitialDir = CurDir
If IsMissing(Filter) Then Filter = ""
If IsMissing(FilterIndex) Then FilterIndex = 1
If IsMissing(Flags) Then Flags = 0&
If IsMissing(DefaultExt) Then DefaultExt = ""
If IsMissing(FileName) Then FileName = ""
If IsMissing(DialogTitle) Then DialogTitle = ""
If IsMissing(OpenFile) Then OpenFile = True

' Allocate string space for the returned strings.
strFileName = Left(FileName & String(256, 0), 256)
strFileTitle = String(256, 0)

' Set up the data structure before you call the function
With OFN
    .lStructSize = Len(OFN)
    .strFilter = Filter
    .nFilterIndex = FilterIndex
    .strFile = strFileName
    .nMaxFile = Len(strFileName)
    .strFileTitle = strFileTitle
    .nMaxFileTitle = Len(strFileTitle)
    .strTitle = DialogTitle
    .Flags = Flags
    .strDefExt = DefaultExt
    .strInitialDir = InitialDir
    .hInstance = 0
    .lpfnHook = 0
    .strCustomFilter = String(255, 0)
    .nMaxCustFilter = 255
End With

' This passes the desired data structure to the
' Windows API, which will in turn display
' the Open/Save As dialog.
If OpenFile Then
    fResult = aht_apiGetOpenFileName(OFN)
Else
    fResult = aht_apiGetSaveFileName(OFN)
End If

' The function call filled in the strFileTitle member
' of the structure. You have to write special code
' to retrieve that if you're interested.
If fResult Then
' You might care to check the Flags member of the
' structure to get information about the chosen file.
' In this example, if you bothered to pass a
' value for Flags, we'll fill it in with the outgoing
' Flags value.
    If Not IsMissing(Flags) Then Flags = OFN.Flags
        ahtCommonFileOpenSave = TrimNull(OFN.strFile)
    Else
```

```
            ahtCommonFileOpenSave = vbNullString
        End If

End Function

Function ahtAddFilterItem(strFilter As String, _
        strDescription As String, Optional varItem As Variant) As String
' Tack a new chunk onto the file filter.
' That is, take the old value, stick onto it the description,
' (like "Databases"), a null character, the skeleton
' (like "*.mdb;*.mda"), and a final null character.

If IsMissing(varItem) Then varItem = "*.*"
ahtAddFilterItem = strFilter & strDescription & _
    vbNullChar & varItem & vbNullChar

End Function

Private Function TrimNull(ByVal strItem As String) As String
Dim intPos As Integer

intPos = InStr(strItem, vbNullChar)

If intPos > 0 Then
    TrimNull = Left(strItem, intPos - 1)
Else
    TrimNull = strItem
End If

End Function
```

This is the actual program created to use this information:

```
Function GetFileName(strPath As String)
Dim strFilter As String
Dim lngFlags As Long

strFilter = ahtAddFilterItem(strFilter, "Excel Files (*.xls)")
GetFileName = ahtCommonFileOpenSave(InitialDir:=strPath, _
    Filter:=strFilter, FilterIndex:=3, Flags:=lngFlags, _
    DialogTitle:="Please select file to import")

End Function
```

Next, create the userform. The following code is attached to the Browse button, as shown in Figure 24.5. Note that the function specifies the starting directory:

```
Private Sub cmdBrowse_Click()

txtFile = GetFileName("c:\")

End Sub
```

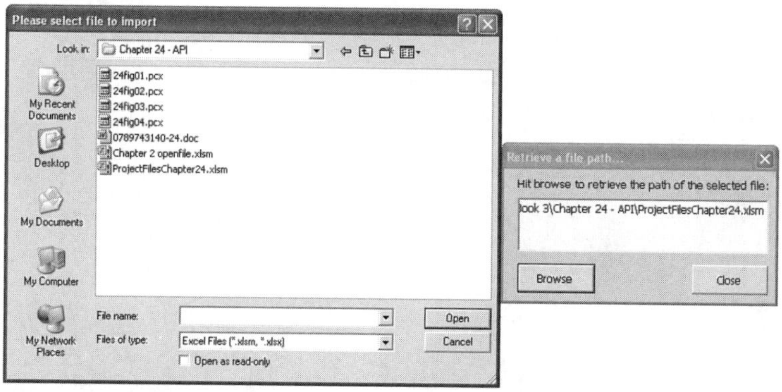

Figure 24.5
Create a custom browse window to return the file path of a user-selected file. This can be used to ensure the user does not select the wrong file for import.

Finding More API Declarations

There are many more API declarations than the ones discussed in this chapter. In fact, this chapter barely scratched the surface of the wealth of procedures and functions available. Microsoft has many tools available to help you create your own APIs (search Platform SDK). Many programmers, such as Ivan F. Moala, have also developed declarations to share (http://xcelfiles.homestead.com/APIIndex.html). Ivan has created a site full of examples that include instructions.

Next Steps

In Chapter 25, "Handling Errors," you learn about error handling. In a perfect world, you want to be able to hand your applications off to a co-worker, leave for vacation, and not have to worry about an unhandled error appearing while you are on the beach. Chapter 25 discusses how to handle obvious and not-so-obvious errors.

Handling Errors

Errors are bound to happen. Even when you test and retest your code, after a report is put into daily production and used for hundreds of days, something unexpected will eventually happen. Your goal should be to try to head off obscure errors as you code. For this reason, you should always be thinking of what unexpected things could happen someday that could make your code not work.

What Happens When an Error Occurs?

When VBA encounters an error and you have no error-checking code in place, the program stops and presents you or your client with the "Continue, End, Debug, Help" error message, as shown in Figure 25.1.

When presented with the choice to end or debug, you should click Debug. The VB Editor highlights the line that caused the error in yellow. When you hover the cursor over any variable, you will see the current value of the variable, which provides a lot of information about what could have caused the error (see Figure 25.2).

Excel is notorious for returning errors that are not very meaningful. For example, dozens of situations can cause a 1004 error. Seeing the offending line highlighted in yellow and examining the current value of any variables will help you discover the real cause of an error.

After examining the line in error, click the Reset button to stop execution of the macro. The Reset button is the square button under the Run item in the main menu, as shown in Figure 25.3.

25

IN THIS CHAPTER

What Happens When an Error Occurs?..........549

Basic Error Handling with the On Error Goto Syntax................................552

Generic Error Handlers................................554

Train Your Clients 557

Errors While Developing Versus Errors Months Later 557

The Ills of Protecting Code 559

More Problems with Passwords 560

Errors Caused by Different Versions.............561

Figure 25.1
An unhandled error in an unprotected module presents you with a choice to end or debug.

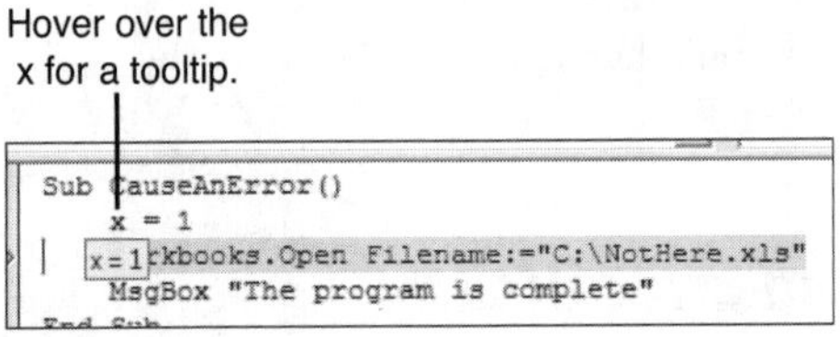

Hover over the x for a tooltip.

Figure 25.2
After clicking Debug, the macro is in break mode. Hover the cursor over a variable; after a few seconds, the current value of the variable is shown.

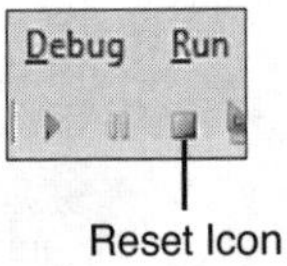

```
Sub CauseAnError()
    x = 1
    x = 1 rkbooks.Open Filename:="C:\NotHere.xls"
    MsgBox "The program is complete"
End Sub
```

Figure 25.3
The Reset button looks like the Stop button in the set of three buttons that resemble a VCR control panel.

Reset Icon

25

CAUTION

If you fail to click Reset to end the macro, and then attempt to run another macro, you are presented with the annoying error message shown in Figure 25.4. The message is annoying because you start in Excel, but when this message window is displayed, the screen automatically switches to display the VB Editor. However, immediately after you click OK, you are returned to the Excel user interface instead of being left in the VB Editor. Because this error message occurs quite often, it would be more convenient if you could be returned to the VB Editor after clicking OK.

Figure 25.4
This message appears if you forget to click Reset to end a debug session and then attempt to run another macro.

```
= WS.Cells(Rows.Count, 1).End(xlUp).Row
1, 1).S   Microsoft Visual Basic              :=xlYes
=WS.Cel
.Show
        ⚠  Can't execute code in break mode
acro co

              OK        Help

rror()
e As Va

a special error handler
```

Debug Error Inside Userform Code Is Misleading

After you click Debug, the line highlighted as the error can be misleading in one situation. For example, suppose you call a macro that displays a userform. Somewhere in the userform code, an error occurs. When you click Debug, instead of showing the problem inside the userform code, Excel highlights the line in the original macro that displayed the userform. Follow these steps to find the real error:

1. After the error message box shown in Figure 25.5 is displayed, click the Debug button.

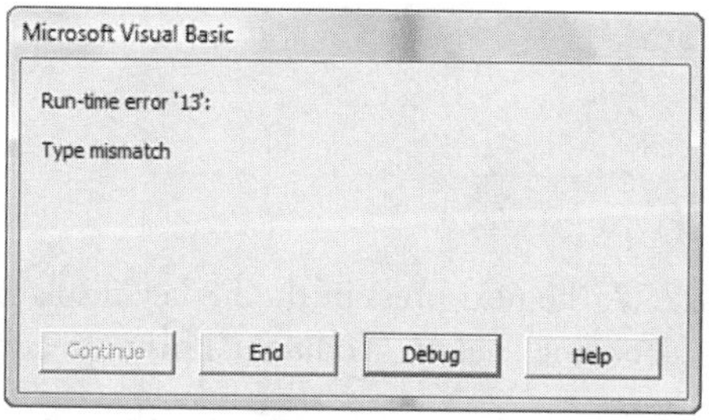

Figure 25.5
Select Debug in response to this error 13.

Microsoft Visual Basic

Run-time error '13':

Type mismatch

[Continue] [End] [Debug] [Help]

You will see that the error allegedly occurred on a line that shows a userform, as shown in Figure 25.6. Because you have read this chapter, you know that this is not the line in error.

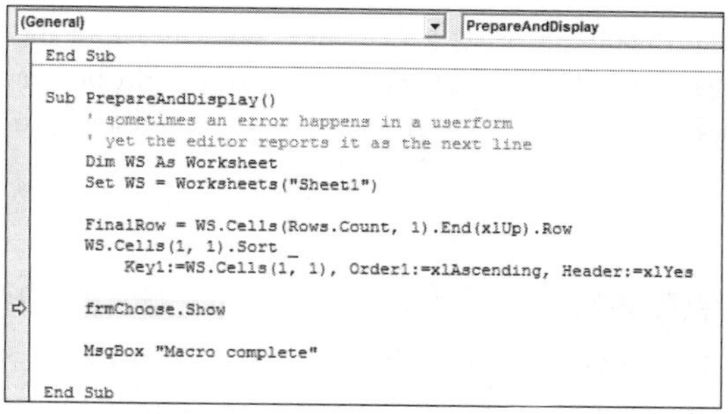

Figure 25.6
The line in error is indicated as the frm-Choose.Show line.

```
(General)                                          PrepareAndDisplay
    End Sub

    Sub PrepareAndDisplay()
        ' sometimes an error happens in a userform
        ' yet the editor reports it as the next line
        Dim WS As Worksheet
        Set WS = Worksheets("Sheet1")

        FinalRow = WS.Cells(Rows.Count, 1).End(xlUp).Row
        WS.Cells(1, 1).Sort _
            Key1:=WS.Cells(1, 1), Order1:=xlAscending, Header:=xlYes

        frmChoose.Show

        MsgBox "Macro complete"

    End Sub
```

2. Press F8 to execute the Show method. Instead of getting an error, you are taken into the Userform_Initialize procedure.

3. Keep pressing F8 until you get the error message again. Stay alert because as soon as you encounter the error, the error message box is displayed. Click Debug and you are returned to the userform.Show line. It is particularly difficult to follow the code when the error occurs on the other side of a long loop, as shown in Figure 25.7.

Imagine trying to step through the code in Figure 25.7. You carefully press F8 five times with no problems through the first pass of the loop. Because the problem could be in future iterations through the loop, you continue to press F8. If there are 25 items to add to the list box, 48 more presses of F8 are required to get through the loop safely. Each time before pressing F8, you should mentally note that you are about to run some specific line.

Loop

Figure 25.7
With 25 items to add to the list box, you must press F8 53 times to get through this 3-line loop.

```
UserForm                                    ▼  Initialize
  Private Sub CommandButton1_Click()
      Unload Me
  End Sub


  Private Sub UserForm_Initialize()
      Dim WS As Worksheet
      Set WS = Worksheets("Sheet1")

      FinalRow = WS.Cells(Rows.Count, 1).End(xlUp).Row
      For i = 2 To FinalRow
          Me.ListBox1.AddItem WS.Cells(i, 1)
      Next i

      ' The next line is actually the line that causes an error
      Me.ListBox1(0).Selected = True


  End Sub
```

At the point shown in Figure 25.7, the next press of the F8 key displays the error and returns you to the frmChoose.Show line back in Module1. This is an annoying situation.

When you click Debug and see that the line in error is a line that displays a userform, you need to start pressing the F8 key to step into the userform code until you get the error. Invariably, you will get incredibly bored pressing F8 a million times and forget to pay attention to which line caused the error. However, as soon as the error happens, you will be thrown back to the Debug message, which returns you to the frmChoose.Show line of code.

At that point, you need to start pressing F8 again. If you can recall the general area where the debug error occurred, click the mouse cursor in a line right before that section and use Ctrl+F8 to run the macro up to the cursor. Alternatively, right-click that line and choose Run to Cursor.

Basic Error Handling with the On Error GoTo Syntax

The basic error-handling option is to tell VBA that in the case of an error you want to have code branch to a specific area of the macro. In this area, you might have special code that alerts users of the problem and enables them to react.

A typical scenario is to add the error-handling routine at the end of the macro. To set up an error handler, follow these steps:

1. After the last code line of the macro, insert the code line Exit Sub. This makes sure that the execution of the macro does not continue into the error handler.

2. After the Exit Sub line, add a label. A label is a name followed by a colon. For example, you might create a label called MyErrorHandler:.

3. Write the code to handle the error. If you want to return control of the macro to the line after the one that caused the error, use the statement Resume Next.

In your macro, just before the line that may likely cause the error, add a line reading On Error GoTo MyErrorHandler. Note that in this line, you do not include the colon after the label name.

Immediately after the line of code that you suspect will cause the error, add code to turn off the special error handler. Because this is not intuitive, it tends to confuse people. The code to cancel any special error handling is On Error GoTo 0. There is no label named 0. Instead, this line is a fictitious line that instructs Excel to go back to the normal state of displaying the End/Debug error message when an error is encountered. This is why it is important to cancel the error handling.

> **NOTE** The following code includes a special error handler to handle the necessary action if the file has been moved or is missing. You definitely do not want this error handler invoked for another error later in the macro such as division by zero.

```
Sub HandleAnError()
    Dim MyFile as Variant
    ' Set up a special error handler
    On Error GoTo FileNotThere
    Workbooks.Open Filename:="C:\NotHere.xls"
    ' If we get here, cancel the special error handler
    On Error GoTo 0
    MsgBox "The program is complete"

    ' The macro is done. Use Exit sub, otherwise the macro
    ' execution WILL continue into the error handler
    Exit Sub

    ' Set up a name for the Error handler
FileNotThere:
    MyPrompt = "There was an error opening the file. It is possible the "
    MyPrompt = MyPrompt & " file has been moved. Click OK to browse for the "
    MyPrompt = MyPrompt & "file, or click Cancel to end the program"
    Ans = MsgBox(Prompt:=MyPrompt, VbMsgBoxStyle:=vbOKCancel)
    If Ans = vbCancel Then Exit Sub

    ' The client clicked OK. Let him browse for the file
    MyFile = Application.GetOpenFilename
    If MyFile = False Then Exit Sub

    ' What if the 2nd file is corrupt? We do not want to recursively throw
    ' the client back into this error handler. Just stop the program
    On Error GoTo 0
    Workbooks.Open MyFile
    ' If we get here, then return the macro execution back to the original
    ' section of the macro, to the line after the one that caused the error.
    Resume Next


End Sub
```

25

> TIP
>
> It is possible to have more than one error handler at the end of a macro. Make sure that each error handler ends with either Resume Next or Exit Sub so that macro execution does not accidentally move into the next error handler.

Generic Error Handlers

Some developers like to direct any error to a generic error handler to make use of the Err object. This object has properties for error number and description. You can offer this information to the client and prevent them from getting a Debug message:

```
On Error GoTo HandleAny
Sheets(9).Select

Exit Sub

HandleAny:
    Msg = "We encountered " & Err.Number & " - " & Err.Description
    MsgBox Msg
    Exit Sub
```

Handling Errors by Choosing to Ignore Them

Some errors can simply be ignored. For example, suppose you are going to use the HTML Creator macro from Chapter 16, "Reading from and Writing to the Web." Your code erases any existing index.html file from a folder before writing out the next file.

The Kill (FileName) statement returns an error if FileName does not exist. This probably is not something about which you need to worry. After all, you are trying to delete the file, so you probably do not care whether someone already deleted it before running the macro. In this case, tell Excel to just skip over the offending line and resume macro execution with the next line. The code to do this is On Error Resume Next:

```
Sub WriteHTML()
    MyFile = "C:\Index.html"
    On Error Resume Next
    Kill MyFile
    On Error Goto 0
    Open MyFile for Output as #1
    ' etc...
End Sub
```

> CAUTION
>
> Be careful with On Error Resume Next. It can be used selectively in situations where you know that the error can be ignored. You should immediately return error checking to normal after the line that might cause an error with On Error GoTo 0.
>
> If you attempt to have On Error Resume Next skip an error that cannot be skipped, the macro immediately steps out of the current macro. If you have a situation where MacroA calls MacroB and MacroB encounters a nonskippable error, the program jumps out of MacroB and continues with the next line in MacroA. This is rarely a good thing.

CASE STUDY: PAGE SETUP PROBLEMS CAN BE OVERLOOKED

When you record a macro and perform a page setup, even if you change just one item in the Page Setup dialog, the macro recorder records two dozen settings for you. These settings notoriously differ from printer to printer. For example, if you record the PageSetup on a system with a color printer, it might record a setting for .BlackAndWhite = True. This setting will fail on another system where the printer does not offer the choice. Your printer may offer a .PrintQuality = 600 setting. If the client's printer offers only a 300 resolution setting, this code will fail. For this reason, you should surround the entire PageSetup with On Error Resume Next to ensure that most settings happen but the trivial ones that fail will not cause a runtime error. Here is how to do this:

```
On Error Resume Next
Application.PrintCommunication = False
With ActiveSheet.PageSetup
    .PrintTitleRows = ""
    .PrintTitleColumns = ""
End With
 ActiveSheet.PageSetup.PrintArea = "$A$1:$L$27"
 With ActiveSheet.PageSetup
    .LeftHeader = ""
    .CenterHeader = ""
    .RightHeader = ""
    .LeftFooter = ""
    .CenterFooter = ""
    .RightFooter = ""
    .LeftMargin = Application.InchesToPoints(0.25)
    .RightMargin = Application.InchesToPoints(0.25)
    .TopMargin = Application.InchesToPoints(0.75)
    .BottomMargin = Application.InchesToPoints(0.5)
    .HeaderMargin = Application.InchesToPoints(0.5)
    .FooterMargin = Application.InchesToPoints(0.5)
    .PrintHeadings = False
    .PrintGridlines = False
    .PrintComments = xlPrintNoComments
    .PrintQuality = 300
    .CenterHorizontally = False
    .CenterVertically = False
    .Orientation = xlLandscape
    .Draft = False
    .PaperSize = xlPaperLetter
    .FirstPageNumber = xlAutomatic
    .Order = xlDownThenOver
    .BlackAndWhite = False
    .Zoom = False
    .FitToPagesWide = 1
    .FitToPagesTall = False
    .PrintErrors = xlPrintErrorsDisplayed
End With
Application.PrintCommunication = True
On Error GoTo 0
```

25

Suppressing Excel Warnings

Some messages appear even if you have set Excel to ignore errors. For example, try to delete a worksheet using code and you will still get the message "Data may exist in the sheet(s) selected for deletion. If you want to delete the data permanently, click Delete." This is annoying. You do not want your clients to have to answer this warning. In fact, this is not an error but an alert. To suppress all alerts and force Excel to take the default action, use `Application.DisplayAlerts = False`:

```
Sub DeleteSheet()
    Application.DisplayAlerts = False
    Worksheets("Sheet2").Delete
    Application.DisplayAlerts = True
End Sub
```

To see a demo of using DisplayAlerts, search for Excel VBA 25 at YouTube.

Encountering Errors on Purpose

Because programmers hate errors, this concept might seem counterintuitive, but errors are not always bad. Sometimes it is faster to simply encounter an error.

Suppose, for example, that you want to find out whether the active workbook contains a worksheet named Data. To find this out without causing an error, you could code this:

```
DataFound = False
For each ws in ActiveWorkbook.Worksheets
    If ws.Name = "Data" then
        DataFound = True
        Exit For
    End if
Next ws
If not DataFound then Sheets.Add.Name = "Data"
```

This takes eight lines of code. If your workbook has 128 worksheets, the program would loop through 128 times before deciding that the data worksheet is missing.

The alternative is to try to reference the data worksheet. If you have error checking set to resume next, the code runs, and the `Err` object is assigned a number other than zero:

```
On Error Resume Next
X = Worksheets("Data").Name
If Err.Number <> 0 then Sheets.Add.Name = "Data"
On Error GoTo 0
```

This code runs much faster. Errors usually make programmers cringe. However, in this case and in many other cases, the errors are perfectly acceptable.

Train Your Clients

Suppose you are developing code for a client across the globe or for the administrative assistant so that he can run the code while you are on vacation. In both cases, you might find yourself trying to debug code remotely while you are on the telephone with the client.

For this reason, it is important to train clients about the difference between an error and a simple MsgBox. Even though a MsgBox is a planned message, it still appears out of the blue with a beep. Teach your users that even though error messages are bad, not everything that pops up is an error message. For example, I had a client who kept reporting to her boss that she was getting an error from my program. In reality, she was getting an informational MsgBox. Both Debug errors and Msgbox messages beep at the user.

When clients get Debug errors, train them to call you while the Debug message is still on the screen. This allows you to get the error number and description. You also can ask the client to click Debug and tell you the module name, procedure name, and the line in yellow. Armed with this information, you can usually figure out what is going on. Without this information, it is unlikely that you will be able to resolve the problem. Getting a call from a client saying that there was a 1004 error is of little help—1004 is a catchall error that can mean any number of things.

Errors While Developing Versus Errors Months Later

When you have just written code that you are running for the first time, you expect errors. In fact, you may decide to step through code line by line to watch the progress of the code the first time through.

It is another thing to have a program that has been running daily in production suddenly stop working because of an error. This can be perplexing. The code has been working for months. Why did it suddenly stop working today?

It is easy to blame the client. However, when you get right down to it, it is really the fault of developers for not considering the possibilities.

The following sections describe a couple of common problems that can strike an application months later.

Runtime Error 9: Subscript Out of Range

You set up an application for a client and you provided a Menu worksheet where some settings are stored. Then one day this client reports the error message shown in Figure 25.8.

Your code expected there to be a worksheet named Menu. For some reason, the client either accidentally deleted the worksheet or renamed it. As soon as you tried to select the sheet, you received an error:

```
Sub GetSettings()
    ThisWorkbook.Worksheets("Menu").Select
    x = Range("A1").Value
End Sub
```

Figure 25.8
The Runtime Error 9 is often caused when you expect a worksheet to be there and it has been deleted or renamed by the client.

This is a classic situation where you cannot believe the client would do something so crazy. After you have been burned by this one a few times, you might go to these lengths to prevent an unhandled Debug error:

```
Sub GetSettings()
    On Error Resume Next
    x = ThisWorkbook.Worksheets("Menu").Name
    If Not Err.Number = 0 Then
        MsgBox "Expected to find a Menu worksheet, but it is missing"
        Exit Sub
    End If
    On Error GoTo 0

    ThisWorkbook.Worksheets("Menu").Select
    x = Range("A1").Value
End Sub
```

RunTime Error 1004: Method Range of Object Global Failed

You have code that imports a text file each day. You expect the text file to end with a Total row. After importing the text, you want to convert all the detail rows to italics.

The following code works fine for months:

```
Sub SetReportInItalics()
    TotalRow = Cells(Rows.Count,1).End(xlUp).Row
    FinalRow = TotalRow - 1
    Range("A1:A" & FinalRow).Font.Italic = True
End Sub
```

Then one day, the client calls with the error message shown in Figure 25.9.

Upon examination of the code, you discover that something bizarre went wrong when the text file was transferred via FTP to the client that day. The text file ended up as an empty file. Because the worksheet was empty, `TotalRow` was determined to be Row 1. If you assume the last detail row was `TotalRow - 1`, the code is set up to attempt to format Row 0, which clearly does not exist.

Figure 12.9
The Runtime Error 1004 can be caused by a number of things.

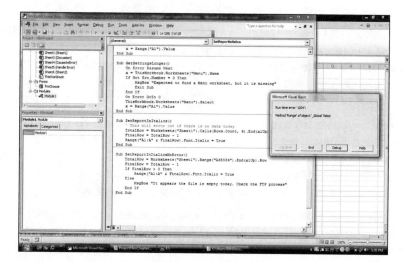

After an episode like this, you will find yourself writing code that preemptively looks for this situation:

```
Sub SetReportInItalics()
    TotalRow = Cells(Rows.Count,1).End(xlUp).Row
    FinalRow = TotalRow - 1
    If FinalRow > 0 Then
        Range("A1:A" & FinalRow).Font.Italic = True
    Else
        MsgBox "It appears the file is empty today. Check the FTP process"
    End If
End Sub
```

The Ills of Protecting Code

It is possible to lock a VBA project so that it cannot be viewed. However, this is not recommend. When code is protected and an error is encountered, your user is presented with an error message but no opportunity to debug. The Debug button is there, but it is grayed out. This is useless in helping you discover the problem.

Further, the Excel VBA protection scheme is horribly easy to break. Programmers in Estonia offer $40 software that lets you unlock any project. For this reason, you need to understand that office VBA code is not secure and get over it.

CASE STUDY: PASSWORD CRACKING

The password-hacking schemes were very easy in Excel 97 and Excel 2000. The password-cracking software could immediately locate the actual password in the VBA project and report it to the software user.

Then, in Excel 2002, Microsoft offered a brilliant protection scheme that temporarily appeared to foil the password-cracking utilities. The password was tightly encrypted. For several months after the release of Excel 2002, password-cracking programs had to try brute-force combinations. The software could crack a password like blue in 10 minutes. However, given a 24-character password such as *A6%kJJ542(9$GgU44#2drt8, the program would take 20 hours to find the password. This was a fun annoyance to foist upon other VBA programmers who would potentially break into your code.

However, the next version of the password-cracking software was able to break a 24-character password in Excel 2002 in about 2 seconds. When I tested my 24-character password-protected project, the password utility quickly told me that my password was XVII. I thought this was certainly wrong, but after testing, I found the project had a new password of XVII. Yes, this latest version of the software resorted to another approach. Instead of using brute force to crack the password, it simply wrote a new random four-character password to the project and saved the file.

Now, this causes an embarrassing problem for whoever cracked the password. The developer has a sign on his wall reminding him the password is *A6%kJJ542(9$GgU44#2drt8. However, in the cracked version of the file, the password is now XVII. If there is a problem with the cracked file and it is sent back to the developer, the developer can no longer open the file. The only person getting anything from this is the programmer in Estonia who wrote the cracking software.

There are not enough Excel VBA developers in the world, and there are more projects than there are programmers. In my circle of developer friends, we acknowledge that business prospects slip through the cracks because we are too busy with other customers.

Therefore, the situation of a newbie developer is common. This new developer does an adequate job of writing code for a customer and then locks the VBA project.

The customer needs some changes. The original developer does the work. A few weeks later, the developer delivers some requested changes. A month later, the customer needs more work. Either the developer is busy with other projects or he has underpriced these maintenance jobs and has more lucrative work. The client tries to contact the programmer a few times before realizing he needs to get the project fixed, so he calls another developer—you!

You get the code. It is protected. You break the password and see who wrote the code. This is a tough call. You have no interest in stealing the new developer's customer. In fact, you prefer to do this one job and then have the customer return to the original developer. However, because of the password hacking, you have created a situation where the two developers have different passwords. Your only choice is to remove the password entirely. This will tip off the other developer that someone else has been in his or her code. Maybe you could try to placate the other developer with a few lines of comment that the password was removed after the customer could not contact the original developer.

More Problems with Passwords

The password scheme for any version of Excel from 2002 forward is incompatible with Excel 97. If you protected code in Excel 2002, you cannot unlock the project in Excel 97. Many people are still using Excel 97. As your application is given to more employees in a company, you will invariably find an employee using Excel 97. Of course, that user will come up with a runtime error. However, if you locked the project in Excel 2002 or newer, you will not be able to unlock the project in Excel 97, which means that you cannot debug the program in Excel 97.

Bottom line: Locking code causes more trouble than it is worth.

> **NOTE** If you are using a combination of Excel 2003, Excel 2007, and Excel 2010, the passwords transfer easily back and forth. This holds true even if the file is saved as an XLSM file and opened in Excel 2003 using the file converter. You can change code in Excel 2003, save the file, and successfully round-trip back to Excel 2010.

Errors Caused by Different Versions

Microsoft improves VBA in every version of Excel. Pivot table creation was improved dramatically between Excel 97 and Excel 2000. Sparklines and slicers are new in Excel 2010. Certain chart features were improved between Excel 97 and Excel 2000, and charting was completely rewritten in Excel 2007. Excel started supporting XML in Excel 2003 and stopped supporting interactivity in saved web pages in Excel 2007.

The `TrailingMinusNumbers` parameter was new in Excel 2002. This means that if you write code in Excel 2010 and then send the code to a client with Excel 2000, that user will get a compile error as soon as she tries to run any code in the same module as the offending code. For this reason, you need to consider this application in two modules.

Module1 has macros ProcA, ProcB, and ProcC. Module2 has macros ProcD and ProcE. It happens that ProcE has an `ImportText` method with the `TrailingMinusNumbers` parameter.

The client can run ProcA and ProcB on the Excel 2000 machine without problem. As soon as she tries to run ProcD, she will get a compile error reported in ProcD because Excel tries to compile all of Module2 when she tries to run code in that module. This can be incredibly misleading: An error being reported when the client runs ProcD is actually caused by an error in ProcE.

One solution is to have access to every supported version of Excel, plus Excel 97, and test the code in all versions. Note that Excel 97 SR-2 was far more stable than the initial releases of Excel 97. Even though many clients are hanging on to Excel 97, it is frustrating when you find someone who does not have the stable service release.

Macintosh users will believe that their version of Excel is the same as the Excel for Windows. Microsoft promised compatibility of files, but that promise ends in the Excel user interface. VBA code is not compatible between Windows and the Mac. Excel VBA on the Mac in Excel 2004 is close to Excel 97 VBA but annoyingly different. Excel 2008 for the Mac uses AppleScript instead of supporting VBA. However, VBA will be back in the next version of Excel for the Mac. For this reason, anything you do with the Windows API is not going to work on a Mac.

25

Next Steps

This chapter discussed how to make your code more bullet-proof for your clients. In Chapter 26, "Customizing the Ribbon to Run Macros," you learn how to customize the ribbon to allow your clients to enjoy a professional user interface.

25

Customizing the Ribbon to Run Macros

Out with the Old, In with the New

If you have been working with a legacy version of Excel, one of the first changes you notice when you open Excel 2010 is the Ribbon toolbar that was introduced in Excel 2007. Gone are the menus and toolbars of old. And this change isn't just visual—the method of modifying custom menu controls was changed just as radically. One of the biggest bonuses of the Ribbon is that you no longer have to worry about your custom toolbar sticking around after the workbook is closed because the custom toolbar is now part of the inner workings of the workbook.

The original `CommandBars` object still works, but the customized menus and toolbars are all placed on the Add-ins tab. If you had custom menu commands, they will appear on the Menu Commands group, as shown in Figure 26.1. In Figure 26.2, the custom toolbars from two different workbooks appear together on the Custom Toolbars group.

If you want to modify the Ribbon and add your own tab, you need to modify the Excel file itself, which isn't as impossible as it sounds. The new Excel file is actually a zipped file, containing various files and folders. All you need to do is unzip it, make your changes, and you're done. Okay, it's not *that* simple—a few more steps are involved—but it's not impossible.

Before we begin, go to the File tab and select Options, Advanced, General, and select Show Add-In User Interface Errors. This will allow error messages to appear so that you can troubleshoot errors in your custom toolbar.

→ **See** the "Troubleshooting Error Messages" section, **p. 577**, for more details.

IN THIS CHAPTER

Out with the Old, In with the New 563

Creating the Tab and Group 565

Adding a Control to Your Ribbon 566

Accessing the File Structure......................571

Understanding the RELS File......................571

Renaming the Excel File and Opening the Workbook 572

Using Images on Buttons...........................572

Troubleshooting Error Messages 577

Other Ways to Run a Macro.......................580

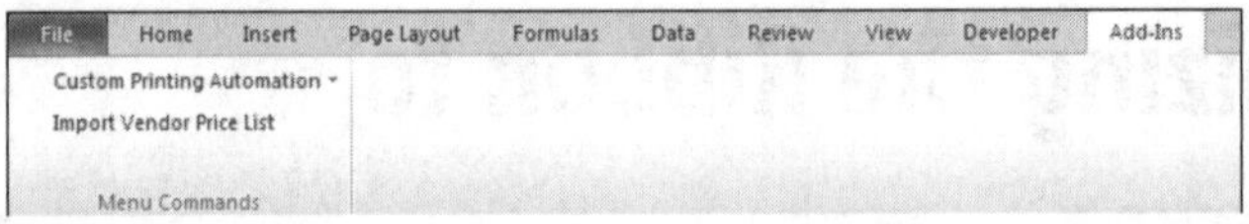

Figure 26.1
Legacy version custom menus will be grouped together under the Menu Commands group.

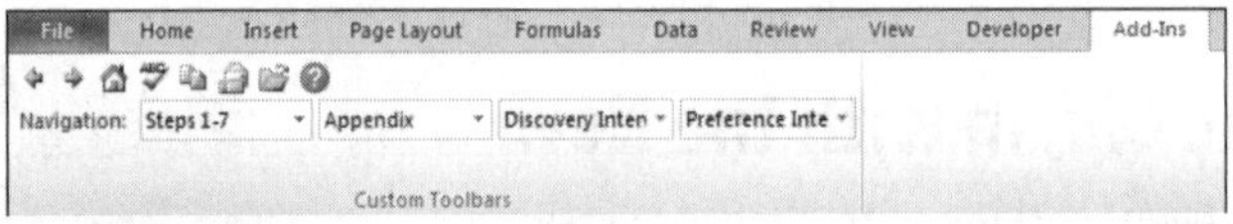

Figure 26.2
Custom toolbars from legacy versions of Excel appear in the Custom Toolbars group.

CAUTION

Unlike programming in the VB Editor, you won't have any assistance with automatic correction of letter case, and the XML code, which is what the ribbon code is, is very particular. Note the case of the XML-specific words, such as id—using ID will generate an error.

Where to Add Your Code: customui Folder and File

Create a folder called customui. This folder will contain the elements of your custom Ribbon tab. Within the folder, create a text file and call it `customUI14.xml`, as shown in Figure 26.3. Open the XML file in a text editor; either Notepad or WordPad will work.

Figure 26.3
Create a `customuUI14.xml` file within a customui folder.

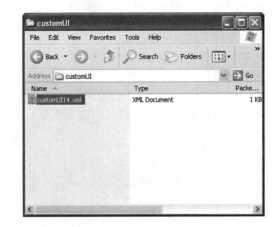

Insert the basic structure for the XML code, shown here, into your XML file. For every opening tag grouping, such as `<ribbon>`, there must be a closing tag, `</ribbon>`:

```
<customUI xmlns="http://schemas.microsoft.com/office/2009/07/customui">
  <ribbon startFromScratch="false">
    <tabs>

      <!-- your ribbon controls here -->
```

```
      </tabs>
    </ribbon>
  </customUI>
```

startFromScratch is optional with a default value of false. It's how you tell the code the other tabs in Excel will not be shown, only yours. True means to show only your tab; false means to show your tab and all the other tabs.

> **CAUTION**
>
> Note the case of the letters in startFromScratch—the small s at the beginning followed by the capital F in From and capital S in Scratch. It is crucial you do not deviate from this.

The <!-- your ribbon controls here --> you see in the previous code is commented text. Just enter your comments between <!-- and -->, and the program will ignore the line when it runs.

Creating the Tab and Group

Before you can add a control to a tab, you need to identify the tab and group. A tab can hold many different controls on it, which you can group together, like the Font group on the Home tab, as shown in Figure 26.4.

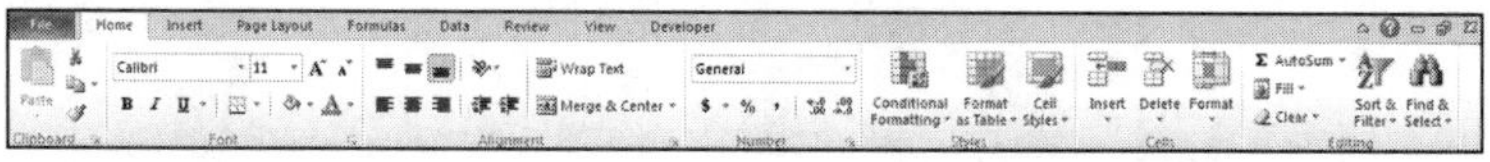

Figure 26.4
Individual controls are placed in groups on a tab. A tab may contain several such groups.

We'll name our tab MrExcel Add-ins and add a group called Reports to it, as shown in Figure 26.5:

```
<customUI xmlns="http://schemas.microsoft.com/office/2009/07/customui">
  <ribbon startFromScratch="false">
    <tabs>
      <tab id="CustomTab" label="MrExcel Add-ins">
        <group id="CustomGroup" label="Reports">

          <!-- your ribbon controls here -->

        </group>
      </tab>
    </tabs>
  </ribbon>
</customUI>
```

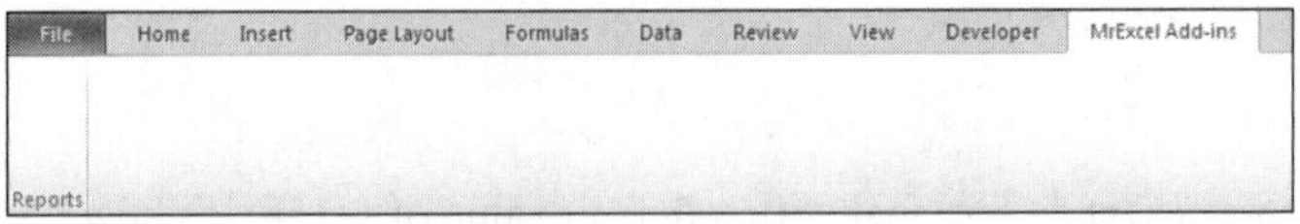

Figure 26.5
Add Tab and Group tags
to your code to create a
custom tab and group.

The id is a unique identifier for the control (in this case, the tab and group). The label is
the text you want to appear on your ribbon for the specified control.

Adding a Control to Your Ribbon

After you've set up the ribbon and group, you can add controls. Depending on the type of
control, there are different attributes you can include in your XML code. (Refer to Table
26.1 for more information on various controls and their attributes.)

The following code adds a normal-sized button to the Reports group, set to run the sub
called HelloWorld when the button is clicked (see Figure 26.6):

```
<customUI xmlns="http://schemas.microsoft.com/office/2009/07/customui">
  <ribbon startFromScratch="false">
    <tabs>
      <tab id="CustomTab" label="MrExcel Add-ins">
        <group id="CustomGroup" label="Reports">

          <button id="button1" label="Click to run"
              onAction="Module1.HelloWorld" size="normal"   />

        </group>
      </tab>
    </tabs>
  </ribbon>
</customUI>
```

The id is a unique identifier for the control button. The label is the text you want to
appear on your button. Size is the size of the button. normal is the default value, and the
other option is large. onAction is the sub, HelloWorld, to call when the button is clicked.
The sub, shown here, goes in a standard module, Module1, in the workbook:

```
Sub HelloWorld(control As IRibbonControl)
MsgBox "Hello World"
End Sub
```

Notice the argument control As IRibbonControl. This is the standard argument for a sub
called by a button control using the onAction attribute. Refer to Table 26.2 for the required
arguments for other attributes and controls.

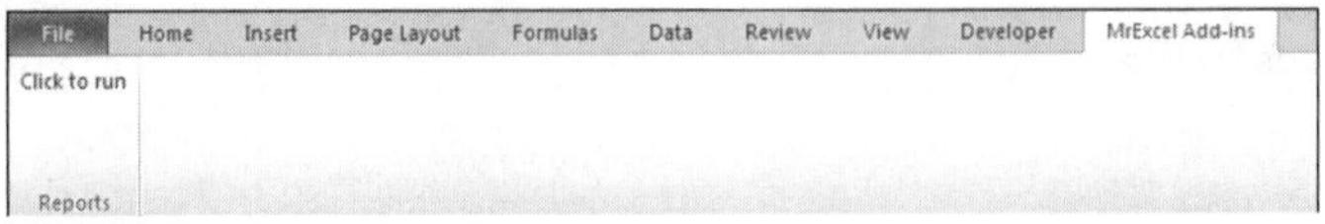

Figure 26.6
Run a program with a
click of a button on your
custom ribbon.

Table 26.1   Ribbon Control Attributes

Attribute	Type or Value	Description
description	String	Specifies description text displayed in menus when the item-Size attribute is set to Large
enabled	true, false	Specifies whether the control is enabled
getContent	Callback	Retrieves XML content that describes a dynamic menu
getDescription	Callback	Gets the description of a control
getEnabled	Callback	Gets the enabled state of a control
getImage	Callback	Gets the image for a control
getImageMso	Callback	Gets a built-in control's icon by using the control ID
getItemCount	Callback	Gets the number of items to be displayed in a combo box, drop-down list, or gallery
getItemID	Callback	Gets the ID for a specific item in a combo box, drop-down list, or gallery
getItemImage	Callback	Gets the image of a combo box, drop-down list, or gallery
getItemLabel	Callback	Gets the label of a combo box, drop-down list, or gallery
getItemScreentip	Callback	Gets the ScreenTip for a a combo box, drop-down list, or gallery
getItemSupertip	Callback	Gets the Enhanced ScreenTip for a combo box, drop-down list, or gallery
getKeytip	Callback	Gets the KeyTip for a control
getLabel	Callback	Gets the label for a control
getPressed	Callback	Gets a value that indicates whether a toggle button is pressed or not pressed Gets a value that indicates whether a check box is selected or cleared
getScreentip	Callback	Gets the ScreenTip for a control
getSelectedItemID	Callback	Gets the ID of the selected item in a drop-down list or gallery
getSelectedItemIndex	Callback	Gets the index of the selected item in a drop-down list or gallery
getShowImage	Callback	Gets a value specifying whether to display the control image
getShowLabel	Callback	Gets a value specifying whether to display the control label
getSize	Callback	Gets a value specifying the size of a control (normal or large)
getSupertip	Callback	Gets a value specifying the Enhanced ScreenTip for a control
getText	Callback	Gets the text to be displayed in the edit portion of a text box or edit box
getTitle	Callback	Gets the text to be displayed (rather than a horizontal line) for a menu separator
getVisible	Callback	Gets a value that specifies whether the control is visible

26

Table 26.1   Continued

Attribute	Type or Value	Description
id	String	A user-defined unique identifier for the control (mutually exclusive with idMso and idQ—specify only one of these values)
idMso	Control id	Built-in control ID (mutually exclusive with id and idQ—specify only one of these values)
idQ	Qualified id	Qualified control ID, prefixed with a namespace identifier (mutually exclusive with id and idMso—specify only one of these values)
image	String	Specifies an image for the control
imageMso	Control id	Specifies an identifier for a built-in image
insertAfterMso	Control id	Specifies the identifier for the built-in control after which to position this control
insertAfterQ	Qualified id	Specifies the identifier of a control whose idQ property was specified after which to position this control
insertBeforeMso	Control id	Specifies the identifier for the built-in control before which to position this control
insertBeforeQ	Qualified id	Specifies the identifier of a control whose idQ property was specified before which to position this control
itemSize	large, normal	Specifies the size for the items in a menu
keytip	String	Specifies the KeyTip for the control
label	String	Specifies the label for the control
onAction	Callback	Called when the user clicks the control
onChange	Callback	Called when the user enters or selects text in an edit box or combo box
screentip	String	Specifies the control's ScreenTip
showImage	true, false	Specifies whether the control's image is shown
showItemImage	true, false	Specifies whether to show the image in a combo box, drop-down list, or gallery
showItemLabel	true, false	Specifies whether to show the label in a combo box, drop-down list, or gallery
showLabel	true, false	Specifies whether the control's label is shown
size	large, normal	Specifies the size for the control
sizeString	String	Indicates the width for the control by specifying a string, such as "xxxxxx"
supertip	String	Specifies the Enhanced ScreenTip for the control
tag	String	Specifies user-defined text
title	String	Specifies the text to be displayed, rather than a horizontal line, for a menu separator
visible	true, false	Specifies whether the control is visible

26

Table 26.2 Control Arguments

Control	Callback Name	Signature
Various controls	getDescription	Sub GetDescription(control as IRibbonControl, ByRef description)
	getEnabled	Sub GetEnabled(control As IRibbonControl, ByRef enabled)
	getImage	Sub GetImage(control As IRibbonControl, ByRef image)
	getImageMso	Sub GetImageMso(control As IRibbonControl, ByRef imageMso)
	getLabel	Sub GetLabel(control As IRibbonControl, ByRef label)
	getKeytip	Sub GetKeytip (control As IRibbonControl, ByRef label)
	getSize	sub GetSize(control As IRibbonControl, ByRef size)
	getScreentip	Sub GetScreentip(control As IRibbonControl, ByRef screentip)
	getSupertip	Sub GetSupertip(control As IRibbonControl, ByRef screentip)
	getVisible	Sub GetVisible(control As IRibbonControl, ByRef visible)
button	getShowImage	Sub GetShowImage (control As IRibbonControl, ByRef showImage)
	getShowLabel	Sub GetShowLabel (control As IRibbonControl, ByRef showLabel)
	onAction	Sub OnAction(control As IRibbonControl)
checkBox	getPressed onAction	Sub GetPressed(control As IRibbonControl, ByRef returnValue)
		Sub OnAction(control As IRibbonControl, pressed As Boolean)
comboBox	getItemCount	Sub GetItemCount(control As IRibbonControl, ByRef count)
	getItemID	Sub GetItemID(control As IRibbonControl, index As Integer, ByRef id)
	getItemImage	Sub GetItemImage(control As IRibbonControl, index As Integer, ByRef image)
	getItemLabel	Sub GetItemLabel(control As IRibbonControl, index As Integer, ByRef label)
	getItemScreenTip	Sub GetItemScreenTip(control As IRibbonControl, index As Integer, ByRef screentip)
	getItemSuperTip	Sub GetItemSuperTip (control As IRibbonControl, index As Integer, ByRef supertip)
	getText	Sub GetText(control As IRibbonControl, ByRef text)
	onChange	Sub OnChange(control As IRibbonControl, text As String)

26

Table 26.2   Continued

Control	Callback Name	Signature
customUI	loadImage	Sub LoadImage(imageId As string, ByRef image)
	onLoad	Sub OnLoad(ribbon As IRibbonUI)
dropDown	getItemCount	Sub GetItemCount(control As IRibbonControl, ByRef count)
	getItemID	Sub GetItemID(control As IRibbonControl, index As Integer, ByRef id)
	getItemImage	Sub GetItemImage(control As IRibbonControl, index As Integer, ByRef image)
dropDown	getItemLabel	Sub GetItemLabel(control As IRibbonControl, index As Integer, ByRef label)
	getItemScreenTip	Sub GetItemScreenTip(control As IRibbonControl, index As Integer, ByRef screenTip)
	getItemSuperTip	Sub GetItemSuperTip (control As IRibbonControl, index As Integer, ByRef superTip)
	getSelectedItemID	Sub GetSelectedItemID(control As IRibbonControl, ByRef index)
	getSelectedItemIndex	Sub GetSelectedItemIndex(control As IRibbonControl, ByRef index)
	onAction	Sub OnAction(control As IRibbonControl, selectedId As String, selectedIndex As Integer)
dynamicMen	getContent	Sub GetContent(control As IRibbonControl, ByRef content)
editBox	getText	Sub GetText(control As IRibbonControl, ByRef text)
	onChange	Sub OnChange(control As IRibbonControl, text As String)
gallery	getItemCount	Sub GetItemCount(control As IRibbonControl, ByRef count)
	getItemHeight	Sub getItemHeight(control As IRibbonControl, ByRef height)
	getItemID	Sub GetItemID(control As IRibbonControl, index As Integer, ByRef id)
	getItemImage	Sub GetItemImage(control As IRibbonControl, index As Integer, ByRef image)
	getItemLabel	Sub GetItemLabel(control As IRibbonControl, index As Integer, ByRef label)
	getItemScreenTip	Sub GetItemScreenTip(control As IRibbonControl, index as Integer, ByRef screen)
	getItemSuperTip	Sub GetItemSuperTip (control As IRibbonControl, index as Integer, ByRef screen)
	getItemWidth	Sub getItemWidth(control As IRibbonControl, ByRef width)
	getSelectedItemID	Sub GetSelectedItemID(control As IRibbonControl, ByRef index)
	getSelectedItemIndex	Sub GetSelectedItemIndex(control As IRibbonControl, ByRef index)
	onAction	Sub OnAction(control As IRibbonControl, selectedId As String, selectedIndex As Integer)

26

Control	Callback Name	Signature
menuSeparator	getTitle	`Sub GetTitle (control As IRibbonControl, ByRef title)`
toggleButton	getPressed	`Sub GetPressed(control As IRibbonControl, ByRef returnValue)`
	onAction	`Sub OnAction(control As IRibbonControl, pressed As Boolean)`

Accessing the File Structure

The new Excel file types are actually zipped files containing various files and folders to create the workbook and worksheets you see when you open the workbook. To view this structure, rename the file, adding a .zip extension to the end of the filename. For example, if your filename is Chapter 26 – Simple Ribbon.xlsm, rename it to Chapter 26 – Simple Ribbon.xlsm.zip. You can then use your zip utility to access the folders and files within.

Copy into the zip file your customui folder and file, as shown in Figure 26.7. After placing them in the XLSM file, we need to let the rest of the Excel file know that they are there and what their purpose is. To do that, we modify the RELS file.

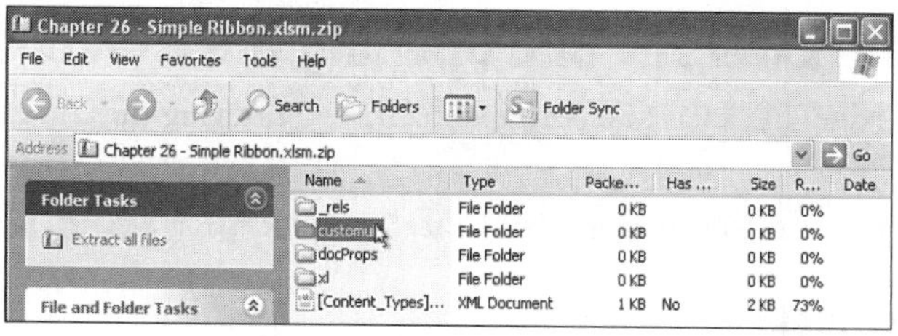

Figure 26.7
Using a zip utility, open the XLSM file and copy over the customui folder and file.

Understanding the RELS File

The RELS file, found in the _rels folder, contains the various relationships of the Excel file. Extract this file from the zip and open it using a text editor.

The file already contains existing relationships that we do not want to change. Instead, we need to add one for the customui folder. Scroll all the way to the right of the <Relationships line and place your cursor before the </Relationships> tag, as shown in Figure 26.8. Insert the following syntax:

```
<Relationship Id="rAB67989" _
Type="http://schemas.microsoft.com/office/2007/relationships/ui/_
extensibility"Target="customui/customUI14.xml"/>
```

Figure 26.8
Place your cursor in the correct spot for entering your custom ribbon relationship.

> **CAUTION**
>
> Even though the previous code appears as three lines in this book, it should appear as a single line in the RELS file. If you want to enter it as three separate lines, do not separate the lines within the quoted strings. The preceding examples are correct breaks. An incorrect break of the third line, for example, would be this:
>
> ```
> Target = "customui/
> customUI14.xml"
> ```
>
> Note that Excel will merge these three separate lines into one, when the workbook is opened.

`Id` is any unique string to identify the relationship. If Excel has a problem with the string you enter, it may change it when you open the file. `Target` is the customui folder and file. Save your changes and add the RELS file back into the zip file.

→ See the troubleshooting section, "Excel Found Unreadable Content," **p. 579**, for more information.

Renaming the Excel File and Opening the Workbook

Rename the Excel file back to its original name by removing the .zip extension. Open your workbook.

→ If any error messages appear when you rename an Excel file, **see** "Troubleshooting Error Messages," **p. 577**.

Custom UI Editor Tool

It can be a little time-consuming to perform all the steps involved in adding a custom ribbon, especially if you make little mistakes and have to keep renaming your workbook, opening the zip file, extracting your file, modifying, adding it back to the zip, renaming, and testing. To aid in this, OpenXMLDeveloper.org offers the Custom UI Editor Tool, which you can learn more about at http://openxmldeveloper.org/articles/CustomUIeditor.aspx. It also updates the RELS file, helps with using custom images, and has other useful aids to customizing the ribbon.

Using Images on Buttons

The image that appears on a button can be either an image from the Microsoft Office icon library or a custom image you create and include within the workbook's customui folder.

With a good icon image, you can hide the button label but still have a friendly ribbon with images that are self-explanatory.

Microsoft Office Icons

Remember in legacy versions of Excel if you wanted to reuse an icon from an Excel button, you had to identify the faceid? It was a nightmare to do manually, though thankfully there were many tools out there to help you retrieve the information. Well, Microsoft must have heard the screams of agony because they've made it so much easier to reuse their icons. Not only that, instead of some meaningless number, they've provided easy-to-understand text!

Select File, Options, Customize Ribbon. Place your cursor over any menu command in the list, and a ScreenTip will appear, providing more information about the command. Included at the very end in parentheses is the image name, as shown in Figure 26.9.

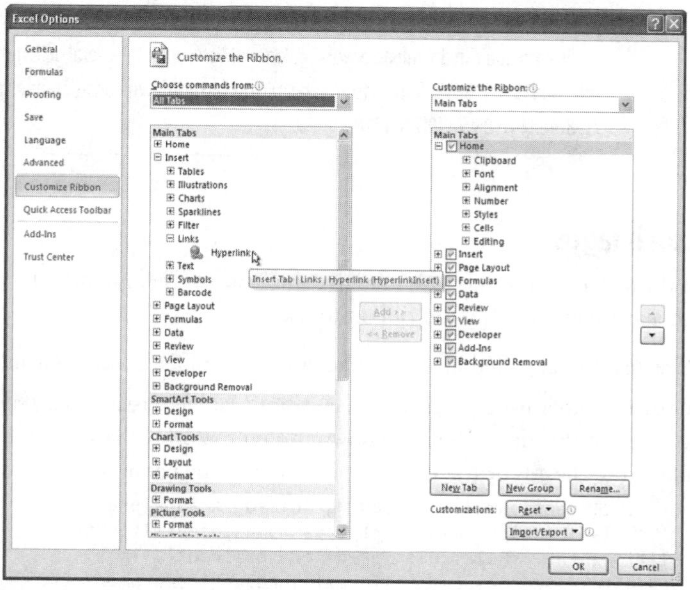

Figure 26.9

Placing your cursor over a command, such as Insert Hyperlink, brings up the icon name, HyperlinkInsert.

To place an image on our button, we need to go back into the customUI14.xml file and advise Excel of what we want. The following code uses the HyperlinkInsert icon for the HelloWorld button and also hides the label, as shown in Figure 26.10. Note that the icon name is case sensitive:

```
<customUI xmlns="http://schemas.microsoft.com/office/2009/07/customui">
  <ribbon startFromScratch="false">
    <tabs>
      <tab id="CustomTab" label="MrExcel Add-ins">
        <group id="CustomGroup" label="Reports">

          <button id="button1" label="Click to run"
            onAction="Module1.HelloWorld" imageMso="HyperlinkInsert"
```

```
                          showLabel = "false" />

                </group>
            </tab>
          </tabs>
        </ribbon>
      </customUI>
```

Figure 26.10
You can apply the image from any Microsoft Office icon to your custom button.

You aren't limited to just the icons available in Excel. You can use the icon for any installed Microsoft Office application. You can download a workbook from Microsoft with several galleries showing the icons available (and their names) from http://www.microsoft.com/downloads/details.aspx?familyid=12b99325-93e8-4ed4-8385-74d0f7661318.

Custom Icon Images

What if the icon library just doesn't have the icon you're looking for? You can create your own image file and modify the ribbon to use it:

1. Create a folder called images in the customui folder. Place your image in this folder.

2. Create a folder called _rels in the customui folder. Create a text file called customUI14. xml.rels in this new folder, as shown in Figure 26.11. Place the following code in the file. Note the Id for the image relationship is the name of the image file, mrexcellogo:

```
<?xml version="1.0" encoding="UTF-8" standalone="yes"?>
<Relationships xmlns="http://schemas.openxmlformats.org/package/2006/_
relationships"><Relationship Id="mrexcellogo"_
Type=http://schemas.openxmlformats.org/officeDocument/2006/relationships/image_
Target="images/mrexcellogo.jpg"/></Relationships>
```

Figure 26.11
Create a _rels and an images folder within the customui folder to hold files relevant to your custom image.

3. Open the customUI14.xml file and add the image attribute to the control, as shown here. Save and close the file:

```
<customUI xmlns="http://schemas.microsoft.com/office/2009/07/customui">
  <ribbon startFromScratch="false">
    <tabs>
      <tab id="CustomTab" label="MrExcel Add-ins">
        <group id="CustomGroup" label="Reports">

          <button id="button1" label="Click to run"
            onAction="Module1.HelloWorld" image="mrexcellogo"
            size="large" />

        </group>
      </tab>
    </tabs>
  </ribbon>
</customUI>
```

4. Open the [Content_Types].xml file and add the following at the very end of the file but before the </Types>:

```
<Default Extension="jpg" ContentType="application/octet-stream"/>
```

5. Save your changes, rename your folder, and open your workbook. The custom image appears on the button, as shown in Figure 26.12.

Figure 26.12
With a few more changes to your customui, you can add a custom image to a button.

CASE STUDY: CONVERTING AN EXCEL 2003 CUSTOM TOOLBAR TO EXCEL 2010

26

You have a workbook and custom toolbar designed in Excel 2003 with several buttons. You're now ready to transfer over to Excel 2010. When you open the workbook in 2010, the toolbar doesn't appear on the Add-ins tab because the toolbar wasn't designed with VBA; it is a manually created custom toolbar.

After saving the workbook as an XLSM file, create the `customUI14.xml file`, as shown here. The tab is called My Quick Macros, and it has two groups: Viewing Options and Shortcuts:

```
<customUI xmlns="http://schemas.microsoft.com/office/2009/07/customui">
  <ribbon startFromScratch="false">
    <tabs>
      <tab id="customMacros" label="My Quick Macros">
        <group id="customview" label="Viewing Options">

          <button id="btn_r1c1" label="Toggle R1c1"
            onAction="mod_2010.myButtons" />
```

```
                    <button id="btn_Headings" label="Show Headings."
                      onAction="mod_2010.myButtons" imageMso = "TableStyleClear"/>

                    <button id="btn_gridlines" label="Show Gridlines"
                      onAction="mod_2010.myButtons" imageMso = "BordersAll"/>

                    <button id="btn_tabs" label="Show Tabs"
                      onAction="mod_2010.myButtons" imageMso = "Connections"/>
                  </group>

                  <group id="customshortcuts" label="Shortcuts">

                    <button id="btn_formulas" label="Highlight Formulas"
                      onAction="mod_2010.myButtons" imageMso = "FunctionWizard"/>
                  </group>
                </tab>
              </tabs>
            </ribbon>
          </customUI>
```

After updating the RELS file, open the workbook to see the new tab, as shown in Figure 26.13.

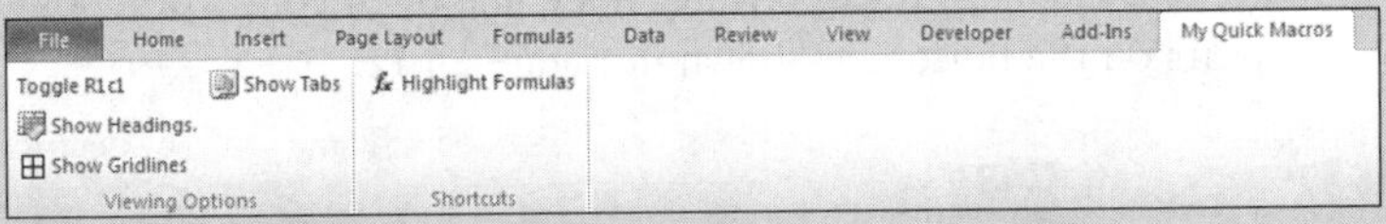

Figure 26.13
Re-create your Excel 2003 toolbar in Excel 2010 as its own ribbon.

→ **See** the "Understanding the RELS File" section, **p. 571**, to review how to update an RELS file.

Now it's time to update the code in the workbook. You'll notice the onAction in the customui folder all pointed to the same sub, mod_2010.myButtons, instead of each having a custom call. Because all the controls are of the same type, buttons and have the same argument type, iRibbonControl, we can take advantage of these facts. Create a single sub, myButtons, in a module called mod_2010 to handle all the button calls using Select Case to manage the IDs of each button:

```
Sub myButtons(control As IRibbonControl)
Select Case control.ID
    Case Is = "btn_r1c1"
        SwitchR1C1
    Case Is = "btn_Headings"
        ShowHeaders
    Case Is = "btn_gridlines"
        ShowGridlines
    Case Is = "btn_tabs"
        ShowTabs
    Case Is = "btn_formulas"
        GoToFormulas
    End Select
End Sub
```

The `control.IDs` are the `ids` assigned each button in the `customUI14.xml` file. The action within each `Case` statement is a call to the desired sub. Here is a sample of one of the subs being called, `ShowHeaders`. It is the same sub that was in the original 2003 workbook:

```
Sub ShowHeaders()
If ActiveWindow.DisplayHeadings = False Then
    ActiveWindow.DisplayHeadings = True
Else
    ActiveWindow.DisplayHeadings = False
End If
End Sub
```

Troubleshooting Error Messages

To be able to see the error messages generated by a custom ribbon, go to File, Options, Advanced, General, and select the Show Add-in User Interface Errors option, as shown in Figure 26.14.

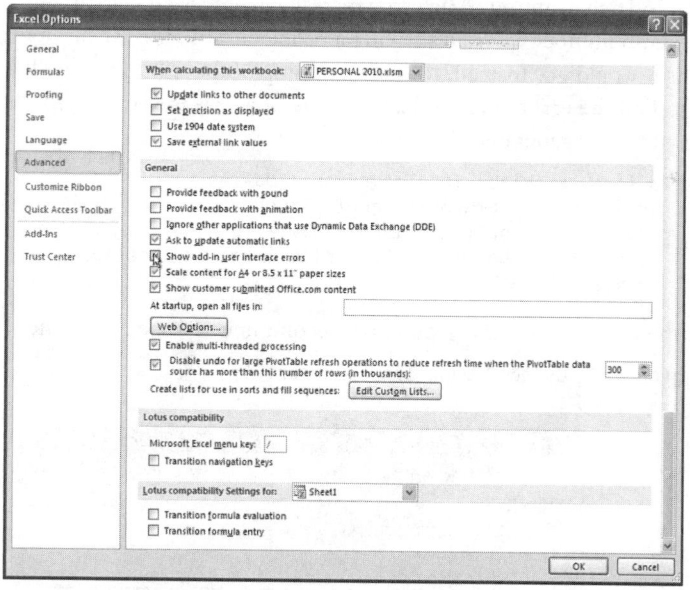

Figure 26.14
Select the Show Add-in User Interface Errors option to allow custom ribbon error messages to appear and aid you in troubleshooting.

The Attribute "Attribute Name" on the Element "customui Ribbon" Is Not Defined in the DTD/Schema

As noted in the "Where to Add Your Code: customui Folder and File" section of this chapter, the case of the attributes is very particular. If an attribute is "mis-cased," the error shown in Figure 26.15 may occur. The code in the `customUI14.xml` that generated the error had the following line:

```
<ribbon startfromscratch="false">
```

Instead of `startFromScratch`, the code contained `startfromscratch` (all lowercase letters). The error message even helps you narrow down the problem by naming the attribute with which it has a problem.

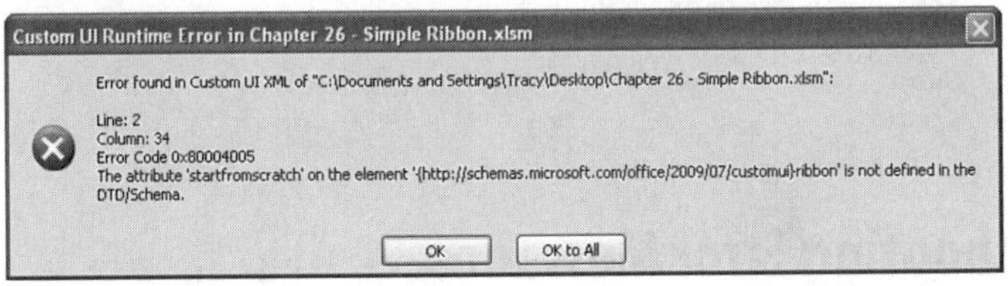

Figure 26.15
Mis-cased attributes can generate errors. Read the error message carefully; it might help you trace the problem.

Custom UI Runtime Error in Chapter 26 - Simple Ribbon.xlsm

Error found in Custom UI XML of "C:\Documents and Settings\Tracy\Desktop\Chapter 26 - Simple Ribbon.xlsm":

Line: 2
Column: 34
Error Code 0x80004005
The attribute 'startfromscratch' on the element '{http://schemas.microsoft.com/office/2009/07/customui}ribbon' is not defined in the DTD/Schema.

[OK]   [OK to All]

Illegal Qualified Name Character

For every opening <, you need a closing >. If you forget a closing >, the error shown in Figure 26.16 may appear. The error message is not specific at all, but it does provide a line and column number where it's having a problem. Still, it's not the actual spot where the missing > would go. Instead, it's the beginning of the next line. You'll have to review your code to find the error, but you have an idea of where to start. The following code in the `customUI14.xml` generated the error:

```
<tab id="CustomTab" label="MrExcel Add-ins">
  <group id="CustomGroup" label="Reports"
    <button id="button1" label="Click to run"
      onAction="Module1.HelloWorld" image="mrexcellogo"
      size="large" />
```

Note the missing > for the group line (second line of code). The line should have been this:

```
<group id="CustomGroup" label="Reports">
```

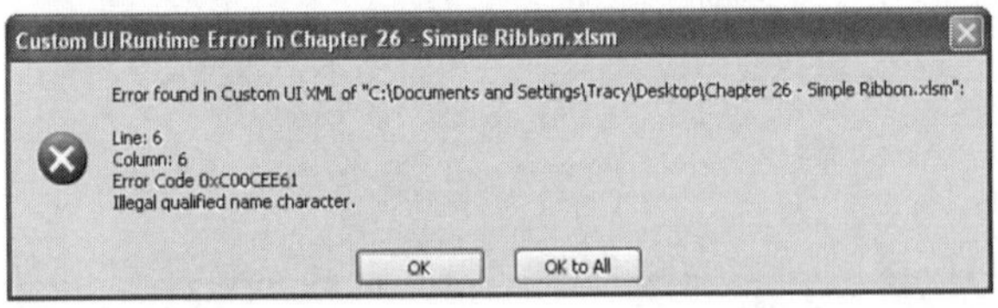

Figure 26.16
For every opening <, you need a closing >.

Custom UI Runtime Error in Chapter 26 - Simple Ribbon.xlsm

Error found in Custom UI XML of "C:\Documents and Settings\Tracy\Desktop\Chapter 26 - Simple Ribbon.xlsm":

Line: 6
Column: 6
Error Code 0xC00CEE61
Illegal qualified name character.

[OK]   [OK to All]

Element "customui Tag Name" Is Unexpected According to Content Model of Parent Element "customui Tag Name"

If your structure is in the wrong order, such as the group tag placed before the tab tag as shown here, a chain of errors will appear, beginning with the one shown in Figure 26.17:

```
<group id="CustomGroup" label="Reports">
  <tab id="CustomTab" label="MrExcel Add-ins">
```

Figure 26.17
An error in one line can lead to string of error messages because the other lines are now considered out of order.

Custom UI Runtime Error in Chapter 26 - Simple Ribbon.xlsm

Error found in Custom UI XML of "C:\Documents and Settings\Tracy\Desktop\Chapter 26 - Simple Ribbon.xlsm":

Line: 4
Column: 44
Error Code 0x80004005
Element '{http://schemas.microsoft.com/office/2009/07/customui}group' is unexpected according to content model of parent element '{http://schemas.microsoft.com/office/2009/07/customui}tabs'.
Expecting: {http://schemas.microsoft.com/office/2009/07/customui}tab.

OK   OK to All

Excel Found Unreadable Content

Figure 26.18 shows a generic catchall message for different types of problems Excel can find. If you click Yes, you then receive the message shown in Figure 26.19. If you click No, the workbook doesn't open. While creating ribbons, though, I found it appearing most often when Excel didn't like the relationship id I had assigned the customui relationship in the RELS file. What's nice is that if you click Yes, Excel will assign a new ID file, and the next time you open the file, the error should not appear.

Original relationship:

```
<Relationship Id="rId3"
Type=http://schemas.microsoft.com/office/2007/relationships/ui/extensibility
Target="customui/customUI14.xml"/>
```

Excel modified relationship:

```
<Relationship Id="rE1FA1CF0-6CA9-499E-9217-90BF2D86492F"
  Type="http://schemas.microsoft.com/office/2007/relationships/ui/extensibility"
  Target="customui/customuUI14.xml"/>
```

In the RELS file, the error also appears if you split the relationship line within a quoted string. You may recall that you were cautioned against this in the "Understanding the RELS File" section, earlier in this chapter. In this case, Excel will not fix the file, and you must make the correction yourself.

26

Figure 26.18
This rather generic message could appear for many reasons. Click Yes to try to repair the file.

Microsoft Excel

Excel found unreadable content in 'Chapter 26 - Simple Ribbon.xlsm'. Do you want to recover the contents of this workbook? If you trust the source of this workbook, click Yes.

Yes   No

Figure 26.19
Excel will let you know if it has succeeded in repairing the file.

Repairs to 'Chapter 26 - Simple Ribbon.xlsm'

Excel was able to open the file by repairing or removing the unreadable content.

Excel completed file level validation and repair. Some parts of this workbook may have been repaired or discarded.

Click to view log file listing repairs: C:\DOCUME~1\Tracy\LOCALS~1\Temp\error018480_01.xml

Close

Wrong Number of Arguments or Invalid Property Assignment

If there is a problem with the sub being called by your control, you might see the error in Figure 26.20 when you go to your ribbon. For example, the onAction of a button requires a single IRibbonControl argument such as the following:

```
Sub HelloWorld(control As IRibbonControl)
```

It would be incorrect to leave off the argument, as shown here:

```
Sub HelloWorld()
```

Figure 26.20
It's important the subs being called by your controls have the proper arguments. Refer to Table 26.2 for the various control arguments.

Microsoft Visual Basic for Applications

Wrong number of arguments or invalid property assignment

OK   Help

Nothing Happens

If you open your modified workbook, and your ribbon doesn't appear, but you don't get any error messages, double-check your RELS file. It's possible you forgot to update it with the required relationship to your custumUI14.xml.

Other Ways to Run a Macro

Custom ribbons are the best ways to run a macro; however, if you have only a couple of macros to run, it can be a bit of work to modify the file. You could have the client invoke a macro by going to the View tab, selecting Macros, View Macros, and then selecting the macro from the Macros dialog and clicking the Run button, but this is a bit unprofessional—and tedious. Other options are discussed in the following sections.

Keyboard Shortcut

The easiest way to run a macro is to assign a keyboard shortcut to a macro. From the Macro dialog box (Developer or View tab, click Macros, or press Alt+F8), select the macro and click Options. Assign a shortcut key to the macro. Figure 26.21 shows the shortcut Ctrl+Shift+C being assigned to the Clean1stCol macro. You can now conspicuously post a note on the worksheet reminding the client to press Ctrl+Shift+C to clean the first column.

┌─ CAUTION ───┐

Be careful when assigning keyboard shortcuts. Many of the keys are already mapped to important Windows shortcuts. If you would happen to assign a macro to Ctrl+C, anyone who uses this shortcut to copy the selection to the clipboard will be frustrated when your application does something else in response to this common shortcut. Letters E, J, M, and Q are usually good choices because as of Excel 2010, they have not yet been assigned to Excel's menu of "Ctrl+" shortcut combinations. Ctrl+L and Ctrl+T used to be available, but these are now used to create a table in Excel 2010.

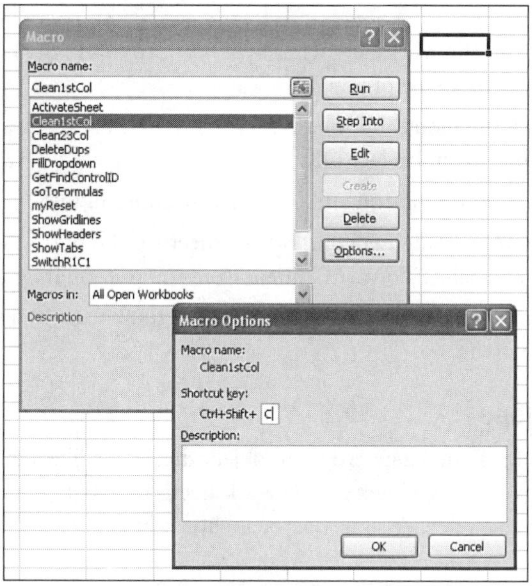

└──┘

Figure 26.21
The simplest way to enable a client to run a macro is to assign a shortcut key to the macro. Ctrl+Shift+C now runs the Clean1stCol macro.

Attach a Macro to a Command Button

Two types of buttons can be embedded in your sheet: the traditional button shape that can be found on the Forms control or an ActiveX command button. (Both can be accessed on the Developer tab under the Insert option.)

To add a Forms control button with a macro to your sheet, follow these steps:

1. On the Developer tab, click the Insert button and select the button control from the Forms section of the drop-down, as shown in Figure 26.22.

26

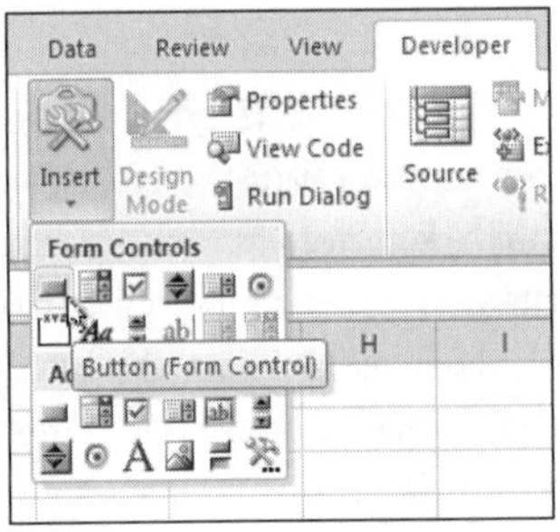

Figure 26.22
The Forms controls are found under the Insert icon on the Developers tab.

2. Place your cursor in the worksheet where you want to insert the button, and then click and drag to create the shape of your new button.

3. When you release the mouse button, the Assign Macro dialog displays. Select a macro to assign to the button and select OK.

4. Highlight the text on the button and type new meaningful text.

5. To change the font, text alignment and other aspects of the button's appearance, right-click the button and select Format Control from the pop-up menu.

6. To reassign a new macro to the button, right-click the button and select Assign Macro from the pop-up menu.

Attach a Macro to a Shape

The previous method assigned a macro to an object that looks like a button. You can also assign a macro to any drawing object on the worksheet. To assign a macro to an Autoshape, right-click the shape and select Assign Macro, as shown in Figure 26.23.

Figure 26.23
Macros can be assigned to any drawing object on the worksheet.

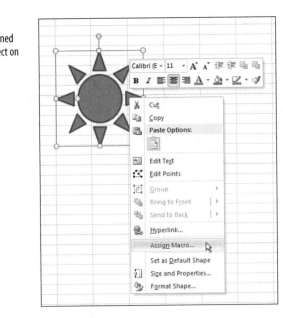

I prefer this method because I can easily add a drawing object with macro code and use the OnAction property to assign a macro to the object. There is one big drawback to this method: If you assign a macro that exists in another workbook, and the other workbook is saved and closed, Excel changes the OnAction for the object to be hard-coded to a specific folder.

Attach a Macro to an ActiveX Control

ActiveX controls are newer than Form controls and slightly more complicated to set up. Instead of simply assigning a macro to the button, you will have a button_click procedure where you can either call another macro or have the macro code actually embedded in the button_click procedure. Follow these steps:

1. On the Developer tab, click the Insert button and select the Command Button icon from the ActiveX Controls section of the drop-down Control toolbox.

2. Draw a button shape on the worksheet as described in step 2 for the Forms button.

3. To format the button, right-click the button and select Properties or select Properties from the Developer tab. You can now adjust the button's caption and color in the Properties window, as shown in Figure 26.24. If nothing happens when you right-click the button, enter Design mode by clicking the Design Mode button on the Developer tab.

> **NOTE**
> There is one annoying aspect of this Properties window: It is huge and covers a large portion of your worksheet. Eventually, if you want to use the worksheet, you are going to have to close this Properties window. When you close the Properties window, it also hides the Properties window in the VB Editor. I would prefer that I could close this Properties window without affecting my VB Editor environment.

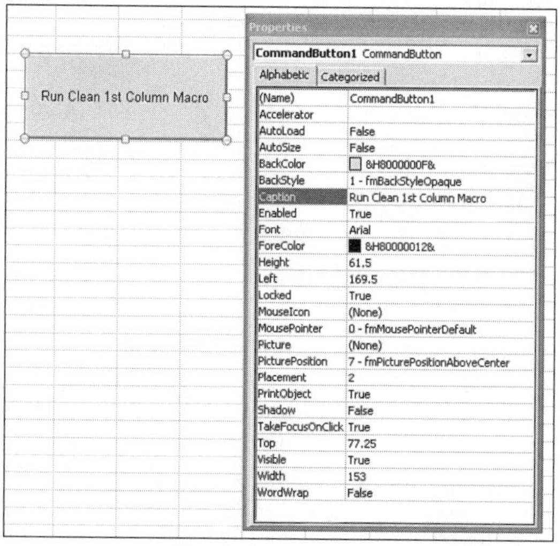

26

Figure 26.24
Clicking the Properties icon brings up the Properties window, where you can adjust many aspects of the ActiveX button.

4. To assign a macro to the button, click the View Code button on the Controls group of the Developer tab. This creates a new procedure on the code pane for the current worksheet. Type the code that you want to have run or the name of the macro you want to run in this procedure. Figure 26.25 shows the code for the button. This code appears on the code pane for the worksheet.

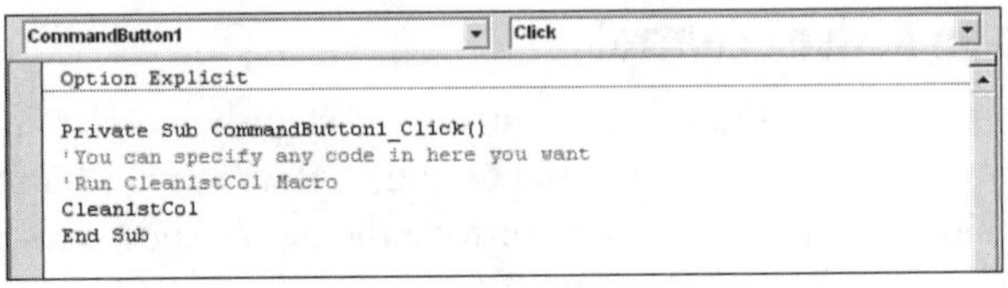

Figure 26.25
Click the View Code button in the Control Toolbox toolbar to open the macro for this button.

```
CommandButton1                          Click

Option Explicit

Private Sub CommandButton1_Click()
'You can specify any code in here you want
'Run Clean1stCol Macro
Clean1stCol
End Sub
```

Running a Macro from a Hyperlink

Using a trick, it is possible to run a macro from a hyperlink. Because many people are used to clicking a hyperlink to perform an action, this method might be more intuitive for your clients.

The trick is to set up placeholder hyperlinks that simply link back to themselves. Select a cell and from the Insert tab, select Hyperlink (or press Ctrl+K). In the Insert Hyperlink dialog, click Place in This Document. Figure 26.26 shows a worksheet with four hyperlinks. Each hyperlink points back to its own cell.

When a client clicks a hyperlink, you can intercept this action and run any macro by using the FollowHyperlink event. Enter the following code on the code module for the worksheet:

```
Private Sub Worksheet_FollowHyperlink(ByVal Target As Hyperlink)
Select Case Target.TextToDisplay
    Case "Widgets"
        RunWidgetReport
    Case "Gadgets"
        RunGadgetReport
    Case "Gizmos"
        RunGizmoReport
    Case "Doodads"
        RunDooDadReport
End Select
End Sub
```

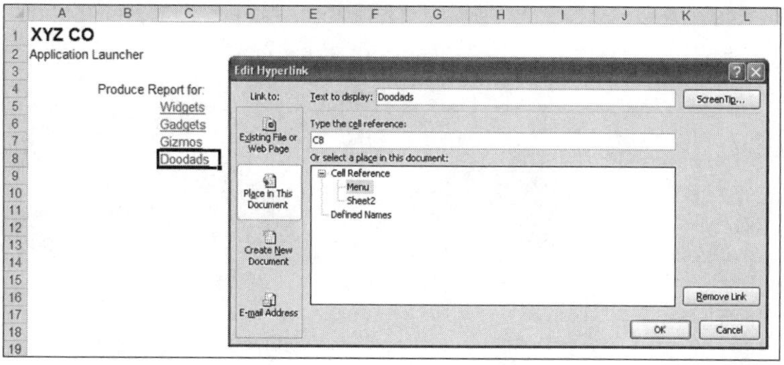

Figure 26.26
To run a macro from a hyperlink, you must create placeholder hyperlinks that link back to their cells. Then, using an event handler macro on the worksheet's code pane, you can intercept the hyperlink and run any macro.

Next Steps

From custom ribbons to simple buttons or hyperlinks, there are plenty of ways to ensure your clients never need to see the Macro dialog box. In Chapter 27, "Creating Add-Ins," you learn how to package your macros into add-ins that can be easily distributed to others.

Creating Add-Ins

Using VBA, you can create standard add-in files for your clients to use. After the client installs the add-in on his PC, the program will be available to Excel and loads automatically every time he opens Excel.

This chapter discusses standard add-ins.

Be aware that there are two other kinds of add-ins: COM add-ins and DLL add-ins. Neither of these can be created with VBA. To create these types of add-ins, you need either Visual Basic.NET or Visual C++.

Characteristics of Standard Add-Ins

If you are going to distribute your applications, you might want to package the application as an add-in. Typically saved with an .xlam extension for Excel 2007-10 or an .xla extension for Excel 97-2003, the add-in offers several advantages:

■ Usually, clients can bypass your Workbook_Open code by holding down the Shift key while opening the workbook. With an add-in, they cannot bypass the Workbook_Open code in this manner.

■ After the Add-Ins dialog is used to install an add-in (select File, Options, Add-Ins, Manage Excel Add-Ins, Go), the add-in will always be loaded and available.

■ Even if the macro security level is set to disallow macros, programs in an installed add-in can still run.

■ Generally, custom functions work only in the workbook in which they are defined. A custom function added to an add-in is available to all open workbooks.

27

IN THIS CHAPTER

Characteristics of Standard Add-Ins 587

Converting an Excel Workbook to an Add-In 588

Having Your Client Install the Add-In 591

Using a Hidden Workbook as an Alternative to an Add-In 593

■ The add-in does not show up in the list of open files in the Window menu item. The client cannot unhide the workbook by choosing Window, Unhide.

> **CAUTION**
>
> There is one strange rule for which you need to plan. The add-in is a hidden workbook. Because the add-in can never be displayed, your code cannot select or activate any cells in the add-in workbook. You are allowed to save data in your add-in file, but you cannot select the file. Also, if you do write data to your add-in file that you want to be available in the future, your add-in codes need to handle saving the file. Because your clients will not realize that the add-in is there, they will never be reminded or asked to save an unsaved add-in. You might add `ThisWorkbook.Save` to the add-in's `Workbook_BeforeClose` event.

Converting an Excel Workbook to an Add-In

Add-ins are typically managed by the Add-Ins dialog. This dialog presents an add-in name and description. You can control these by entering two specific properties for the file before you convert it to an add-in.

> **NOTE**
>
> The file must have already been saved at least once for the properties to appear.

To change the title and description shown in the Add-Ins dialog, follow these steps:

1. Select File. Excel displays the Document Properties pane on the right side of the window.

2. From the Properties drop-down, select Show All Properties

3. Enter the name for the add-in in the Title field.

4. Enter a short description of the add-in in the Comments field (see Figure 27.1).

5. Select another tab such as the Home tab, to return to your workbook.

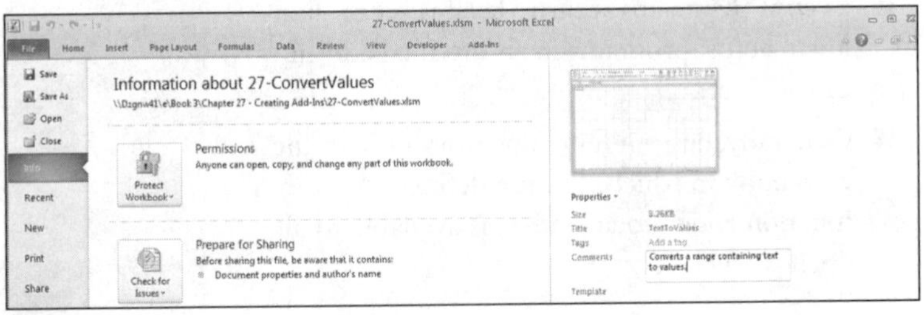

Figure 27.1
Fill in the Title and Comments fields before converting a workbook to an add-in.

There are two ways to convert the file to an add-in. The first method, using Save As, is easier, but has an annoying by-product. The second method uses the VB Editor and requires two steps, but gives you some extra control. The sections that follow describe the steps for using these methods.

Using Save As to Convert a File to an Add-In

Select File, Save As. In the Save as Type field, scroll through the list and select Excel Add-In (*.xlam).

> **NOTE**
>
> If your add-in might be used in Excel 97 through Excel 2010, choose Excel 97-2003 Add-In (*.xla).

As shown in Figure 27.2, the filename changes from Something.xlsm to Something.xlam. Also note that the save location automatically changes to an AddIns folder. This folder location varies by operating system, but it will be something along the lines of C:\Documents and Settings\Customer\Application Data\Microsoft\AddIns. It is also confusing that, after saving the XLSM file as an XLAM type, the unsaved XLSM file remains open. It is not necessary to keep an XLSM version of the file because it is easy to change an XLAM back to an XLSM for editing.

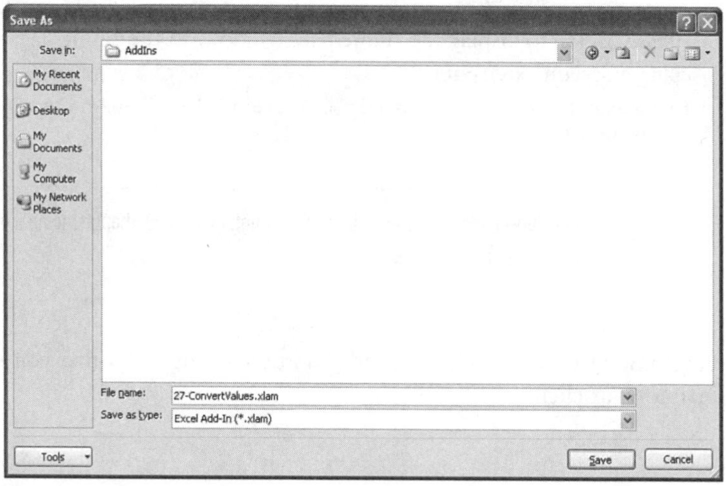

Figure 27.2
If you are creating an add-in for your own use, the Save As method changes the IsAddIn property, changes the name, and automatically saves the file in your AddIns folder.

> **CAUTION**
>
> When using the Save As method to create an add-in, a worksheet must be the active sheet. The Add-In file type is not available if a Chart sheet is the active sheet.

Using the VB Editor to Convert a File to an Add-In

The Save As method is great if you are creating an add-in for your own use. However, if you are creating an add-in for a client, you probably want to keep the add-in stored in a folder with all the client's application files. It is fairly easy to bypass the Save As method and create an add-in using the VB Editor:

1. Open the workbook that you want to convert to an add-in.

2. Switch to the VB Editor.

3. In the Project Explorer, click ThisWorkbook.

4. In the Properties window, find the property called IsAddIn and change its value to True, as shown in Figure 27.3.

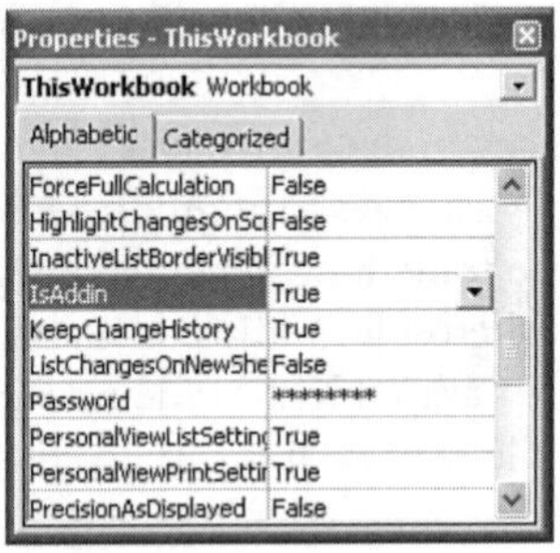

Figure 27.3
Creating an add-in is as simple as changing the IsAddIn property of ThisWorkbook.

Properties - ThisWorkbook	
ThisWorkbook Workbook	

Alphabetic	Categorized
ForceFullCalculation	False
HighlightChangesOnScr	False
InactiveListBorderVisibl	True
IsAddin	True
KeepChangeHistory	True
ListChangesOnNewShe	False
Password	********
PersonalViewListSettin	True
PersonalViewPrintSettir	True
PrecisionAsDisplayed	False

5. Press Ctrl+G to display the Immediate window. In the Immediate window, save the file, using an .xlam extension:

```
ThisWorkbook.SaveAs FileName:="C:\ClientFiles\Chap27.xlam", FileFormat:= xlO-
penXMLAddIn
```

> **NOTE**
> If your add-in might be used in Excel 97 through Excel 2003, change the final parameter from xlO-penXMLAddIn to xlAddIn.

You've now successfully created an add-in in the client folder that you can easily find and e-mail to your client.

27

Having Your Client Install the Add-In

After you e-mail the add-in to your client, have her save it on her desktop or in another easy-to-find folder. She should then follow these steps:

1. Open Excel 2010. From the File menu, select Options.
2. Along the left navigation, select Add-Ins.
3. At the bottom of the window, select Excel Add-Ins from the Manage drop-down (see Figure 27.4).

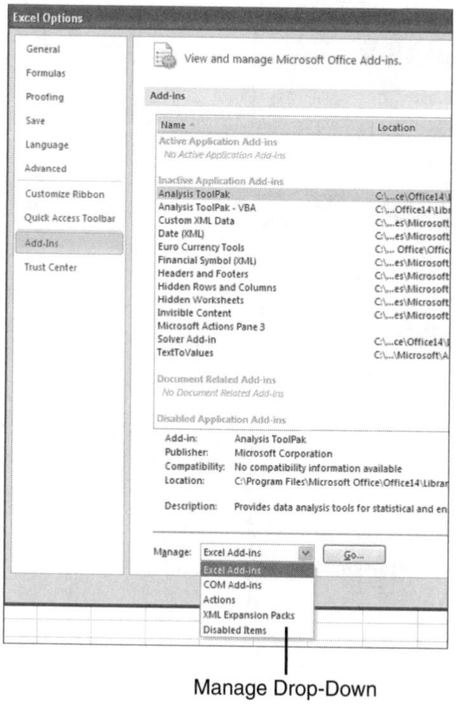

Figure 27.4

The Excel 2010 Add-Ins tab in Options is significantly more complex than in Excel 2003. Select Excel Add-Ins from the bottom and click Go.

Manage Drop-Down

4. Click Go. Excel displays the familiar Add-Ins dialog.
5. In the Add-Ins dialog, click the Browse button (see Figure 27.5).
6. Browse to where you saved the file. Highlight your add-in and select OK.

The add-in is now installed. If you allow it, Excel copies the file from where you saved it to the proper location of the AddIns folder. In the Add-Ins dialog, the title of the add-in and comments as specified in the File Properties dialog are displayed (see Figure 27.6).

Figure 27.5
Your client selects Browse
from the Add-Ins dialog.

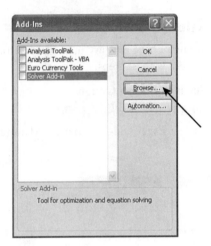

Figure 27.6
The add-in is now avail-
able for use.

Standard Add-Ins Are Not Secure

Remember that anyone can go to the VB Editor, select your add-in, and change the
IsAddin property to False to unhide the workbook. You can discourage this process by
locking the XLAM project for viewing and protecting it in the VB Editor, but be aware that
plenty of vendors sell a password-hacking utility for less than $40. To add a password to
your add-in, follow these steps:

1. Go to the VB Editor.
2. From the Tools menu, select VBAProject Properties.
3. Select the Protection tab.
4. Select the Lock Project For Viewing check box.
5. Enter the password twice for verification.

Closing Add-Ins

Add-ins can be closed in three ways:

1. Clear the add-in from the Add-Ins dialog. This closes the add-in for this session and ensures that it does not open during future sessions.

2. Use VB Editor to close the add-in. In the VB Editor's Immediate pane, type this code to close the add-in:

```
Workbooks("YourAddinName.xlam").Close
```

3. Close Excel. All add-ins are closed when Excel is closed.

Removing Add-Ins

You might want to remove an add-in from the list of available add-ins in the Add-In dialog box. There is no effective way to do this within Excel. Follow these steps:

1. Close all running instances of Excel.

2. Use Windows Explorer to locate the file. The file might be located in %AppData%\Microsoft\AddIns\.

3. In Windows Explorer, rename the file or move it to a different folder.

4. Open Excel. You get a note warning you that the add-in could not be found. Click OK to dismiss this box.

5. Go to File, Options, Add-Ins, Manage Excel Add-Ins, Go. In the Add-Ins dialog box, clear the name of the add-in you want to remove. Excel notifies you that the file cannot be found and asks whether you want to remove it from the list. Select Yes.

Using a Hidden Workbook as an Alternative to an Add-In

One cool feature of an add-in is that the workbook is hidden. This keeps most novice users from poking around and changing formulas. However, it is possible to hide a workbook without creating an add-in.

It is easy enough to hide a workbook by selecting Hide from the Window menu in Excel. The trick is to then save the workbook as Hidden. Because the file is hidden, the normal File, Save choice does not work. This can be done from the VB Editor window. In the VB Editor, make sure that the workbook is selected in the Project Explorer. Then, in the Immediate window, type the following:

```
ThisWorkbook.Save
```

27

CASE STUDY: USING A HIDDEN CODE WORKBOOK TO HOLD ALL MACROS AND FORMS

Access developers routinely use a second database to hold macros and forms. They place all forms and programs in one database and all data in a separate database. These database files are linked through the Link Tables function in Access.

For large projects in Excel, I recommend the same method. You use a little bit of VBA code in the Data workbook to open the Code workbook.

The advantage to this method is that when it is time to enhance the application, you can mail a new code file without affecting the client's data file.

I once encountered a single-file application rolled out by another developer that the client had sent out to 50 sales reps. The reps replicated the application for each of their 10 largest customers. Within a week, there were 500 copies of this file floating around the country. When they discovered a critical flaw in the program, patching 500 files was a nightmare.

We designed a replacement application that used two workbooks. The data workbook ended up with about 20 lines of code. This code was responsible for opening the code workbook and passing control to the code workbook. As the files were being closed, the data workbook would close the code workbook.

There were many advantages to this method. First, the customer data files were kept to a very small size. Each sales rep now has one workbook with program code and ten or more data files for each customer. As enhancements are completed, we distribute new program code workbooks. The sales rep opens his or her existing customer data workbook, which automatically grabs the new code workbook.

Because the previous developer had been stuck with the job of trying to patch 500 workbooks, we were extremely careful to have as few lines of code in the customer workbook as possible. There are maybe ten lines of code, and they were tested extremely thoroughly before being sent out. By contrast, the code workbook contains 3,000+ lines of code. So if something goes wrong, I have a 99 percent chance that the bad code will be in the easy-to-replace code workbook.

In the customer data workbook, the Workbook_Open procedure has this code:

```
Private Sub Workbook_Open()
    On Error Resume Next
    X = Workbooks("Code.xlsm").Name
    If Not Err = 0 then
        On Error Goto 0
        Workbooks.Open Filename:= _
            ThisWorkbook.Path & Application.PathSeparator & "Code.xlsm"
    End If
    On Error Goto 0
    Application.Run "Code.xlsm!CustFileOpen"
End Sub
```

The CustFileOpen procedure in the code workbook handles adding a custom menu for the application. It also calls a macro named DeliverUpdates. If we ever have to change the 500 customer data files, the DeliverUpdates macro will handle this via code.

This dual-workbook solution works well and allows updates to be seamlessly delivered to the client without touching any of the 500 customer files.

Next Steps

If as authors we've done our job correctly, you now have the tools you need to design your own VBA applications in Excel. You understand the shortcomings of the macro recorder yet know how to use it as an aid in learning how to do something. You know how to use Excel's power tools in VBA to produce workhorse routines that can save you hours of time per week. You've also learned how to have your application interact with others so that you can create applications to be used by others in your organization or other organizations.

If you have found any sections of the book that you thought were confusing or could have been spelled out better, we welcome your comments, and they will be given consideration as we prepare the next edition of this book. Write to us:

Bill@MrExcel.com and

Tracy@MrExcel.com.

Whether your goal was to automate some of your own tasks or to become a paid Excel consultant, we hope that we've helped you on your way. Both are rewarding goals. With 500 million potential customers, we find that being Excel consultants is a friendly business. If you are interested in joining our ranks, this book is your training manual. Master the topics, and you will be qualified to join the team of Excel consultants.

27

Index

Symbols

3-D format, changing, 230-234

3-D rotation settings, 224-229

32-bit API declarations, changing to 64-bit, 538

64-bit API declarations, changing 32-bit declarations to, 538

A

A1-style references, 127-128

About dialog, customizing, 541

AboutMrExcel() procedure, 541

above/below average cells, formatting, 383

absolute mode, 25

absolute references, 133

accelerator keys, displaying, 529

Access databases. *See* databases

Activate event, 187

active control, coloring, 530-532

ActiveFilters property, 289

ActiveX controls

attaching macros to, 583-584

right-click menu for, 360-362

ActiveX data objects. *See* ADO

Add method, 148-149, 442

Add3ColorScale() procedure, 375

AddAboveAverage method, 383

AddChart method, 203

AddControl event, 187, 195, 199

AddCrazyIcons() procedure, 382

AddGlowToTitle() procedure, 223

add-ins

Add-Ins dialog, 588

characteristics of, 587-588

closing, 593

converting workbooks to, 588-590

hidden workbooks as alternative to add-ins, 593-594

installing, 591

removing, 593

security, 592

Add-Ins dialog, 588

Addition procedure, 81

AddTransfer() procedure, 480-481

AddTwoDataBars() procedure, 381

ADO (ActiveX data objects)

compared to DOA (data access objects), 477

connections, 478

cursors, 478

fields

adding on-the-fly, 489-490

checking existence of, 488

lock type, 479

overview, 478-480

records

adding, 480-481

deleting, 485

retrieving, 481-483

summarizing, 485-486

updating, 483-485

recordsets, 478

tables

adding on-the-fly, 489

checking existence of, 487-488

ADOAddField() procedure, 489-490

ADOCreateReplenish() procedure, 489

ADOWipeOutAttribute() procedure, 485

Advanced Filter

building with Excel interface, 258

case study: creating reports for each customer, 280-283

criteria ranges

case study, 268

explained, 265-266

formula-based conditions, 268-275

logical AND criteria, 267

logical OR criteria, 267

extracting unique list of values, 258-264

getting unique combinations of two or more fields, 263-264

with user interface, 259

with VBA code, 260-263

Filter in Place, 275-276, 283-285

overview, 257

xlFilterCopy with all records, 276-280

copying all columns, 277

copying a subset of columns and reordering, 278-280

AdvancedFilter method, 260

AfterUpdate event, 190, 193-197

ahtAddFilterItem API function, 546

aht_apiGetOpenFileName API function, 544-546

aht_apiGetSaveFileName API function, 544-546

AllColumnsOneCustomer() procedure, 277

AllowMultipleFilters property, 289

API declarations

32-bit versus 64-bit, 538

ahtAddFilterItem, 546

aht_apiGetOpenFileName, 544-546

aht_apiGetSaveFileName, 544-546

calling, 537

DisplaySize, 540

explained, 535-536

finding, 547

FindWindow, 541-543

GetComputerName, 538-539

GetSystemMenu, 541-542

KillTimer, 542-543

lOpen, 539

PlayWavSound, 543

SetTimer, 542-543

ShellAbout, 541

AppEvent_AfterCalculate() event, 176

AppEvent_NewWorkbook() event, 177

AppEvent_ProtectedViewWindowActivate() event, 177

AppEvent_ProtectedViewWindowBeforeClose() event, 177

AppEvent_ProtectedViewWindowDeactivate() event, 177

AppEvent_ProtectedViewWindowOpen() event, 177

AppEvent_ProtectedViewWindowResize() event, 177

AppEvent_SheetActivate() event, 177

AppEvent_SheetBeforeDoubleClick() event, 178

AppEvent_SheetBeforeRightClick() event, 178

AppEvent_SheetCalculate() event, 178

AppEvent_SheetChange() event, 178

AppEvent_SheetDeactivate() event, 178

AppEvent_SheetFollowHyperlink() event, 178

AppEvent_SheetPivotTableUpdate() event, 178

AppEvent_SheetSelectionChange() event, 178

AppEvent_WindowActivate() event, 179

AppEvent_WindowDeactivate() event, 179

AppEvent_WindowResize() event, 179

AppEvent_WorkbookActivate() event, 179

AppEvent_WorkbookAddinInstall() event, 179

AppEvent_WorkbookAddinUninstall() event, 179

AppEvent_WorkbookAfterXmlExport() event, 181

AppEvent_WorkbookAfterXmlImport() event, 181

AppEvent_WorkbookBeforeClose() event, 179

AppEvent_WorkbookBeforePrint() event, 180

AppEvent_WorkbookBeforeSave() event, 180

AppEvent_WorkbookBeforeXmlExport() event, 181

AppEvent_WorkbookBeforeXmlImport() event, 181

AppEvent_WorkbookNewSheet() event, 180

AppEvent_WorkbookOpen() event, 180

AppEvent_WorkbookPivotTableCloseConnection() event, 180

AppEvent_WorkbookPivotTableOpenConnection() event, 180

AppEvent_WorkbookRowsetComplete() event, 181

AppEvent_WorkbookSync() event, 181

application-level events, 176-181

trapping, 494-495

Application.OnTime, 399-400

scheduling

macros to run every two minutes, 403-404

macros to run x minutes in the future, 401-402

scheduled procedures with ready mode, 400

verbal reminders, 402

specifying a window of time for updates, 400

applications

checking version of, 144-145

compatibility issues

Compatibility mode, 145

explained, 144

historical stock/fund quotes, 362-363

ApplyLayout method, 203

ApplyTexture() procedure, 220

ApplyThemeColor() procedure, 220

Areas collection, 77

arrays

advantages of, 457-458

array formulas, 137-138

declaring, 453-454

defined, 453

dynamic arrays, 459-460

emptying, 456-457

filling, 455-456

multidimensional arrays, 454

names, 153-154

one-dimensional arrays, 454

passing, 460

art, SmartArt, 142-144

Assign3DPreset() procedure, 224

AssignBevel() procedure, 230

asterisks (*), 356-358

asymmetric pivot tables, named sets for, 322-323

attaching macros

to ActiveX controls, 583-584

to command buttons, 581-582

to shapes, 582-583

The Attribute "Attribute Name" on the Element "customui Ribbon" Is Not Defined in the DTD/Schema (error message), 577

AutoFilter

filtering by color, 253

filtering by icon, 254

replacing loops with, 249-251

selecting dynamic data range with, 254-255

selecting multiple items, 252

selecting visible cells only, 255-256

selecting with Search box, 252-255

turning off drop-downs in, 285

AutoFilterCustom() procedure, 285

automation (Word)

bookmarks, 448-449

constant values, 439-441

controlling form fields, 450-452

creating and referencing objects, 437-439

Document object, 442-443

early binding, 433-436

explained, 433

late binding, 436-437

macro recorder, 441

Range object, 444-447

Selection object, 443-444

AutoSort, 308

AutoSum button, 30-31

B

BASIC, 8

BeforeDragOver event, 187, 190, 193-199

BeforeDropOrPaste event, 187, 190, 193-199

BeforeUpdate event, 190, 193-197

below/above average cells, formatting, 383

bevel format, changing, 230-234

binding
early binding, 433-436
late binding, 436-437

bins, creating for frequency charts, 236-239

blank cells
eliminating from pivot tables, 308
formatting cells that contain blanks or errors, 387

bookmarks, 448-449

BookOpen() function, 83

Bottom 5 cells, formatting, 383-384

breakpoints, 49, 55

btnClose_Click() procedure, 512

BubbleSort() procedure, 98

built-in chart types, 208-210

buttons. *See also specific buttons*
attaching macros to, 581-582
custom icon images, 574-575
help buttons, 505-506
Microsoft Office icons, 573-574

C

.Calculation options, 306-307

calculations
calculated data fields, 324-325
calculated items, 325

changing to show percentages, 305-308

elapsed time, 353-354

calling
API declarations, 537
userforms, 186

Can't find object or library (error message), 435-436

case of text, changing, 359-360

Case statements, 124

case studies
cleaning up recorded code, 62-64
converting Excel 2003 custom toolbar to Excel 2010, 575-577
criteria ranges, 268
custom functions, 80
data visualization, 327
entering A1 versus R1C1 references, 131
entering military time into cell, 171
filtering to top five or top 10, 319
formula-based conditions, 270
Go To Special instead of looping, 256-257
help buttons, 505-506
hidden workbook to hold macros and forms, 594
looping through directory files, 119-120
multicolumn list boxes, 532
named ranges for VLOOKUP, 156-157
page setup errors, 555
password cracking, 560
recording macros, 22-23
relative references, 26-28

cells

A1-style references, 127-128

blank cells, eliminating from pivot tables, 308

checking for empty cells, 73-74

comments

charts in, 341-342

listing, 337-339

resizing, 339-341

conditional formatting. *See* conditional formatting

entering military time into, 171

noncontiguous cells, selecting/deselecting, 347-349

progress indicators, creating, 355-356

R1C1-style references

absolute references, 133

array formulas, 137-138

case study: entering A1 versus R1C1 references, 131

explained, 127-128

formulas, 129-132

mixed references, 133

multiplication table example, 134-135

referring to entire columns/rows, 134

relative references, 132-133

remembering column numbers associated with column letters, 136

switching to, 128

returning column letter of cell address, 103

reversing contents of, 101

selected cells, highlighting, 342-344, 344-345

selecting with SpecialCells, 360

setting workbook name in, 82

summing based on interior color, 89-90

Cells(), 59

Cells property

as parameters in Range property, 69

selecting ranges with, 68-69

centering cell comments, 340-341

Change event, 190, 193-199

ChangeFormat() procedure, 446

ChangeStyle() procedure, 447

ChangeTheChartLater() procedure, 207

changing

range size, 71-72

text case, 359-360

Chart_Activate() event, 173

Chart_BeforeDoubleClick() event, 173

Chart_BeforeRightClick() event, 173

Chart_Calculate() event, 173

Chart_Deactivate() event, 173

Chart_DragOver() event, 175

Chart_DragPlot() event, 175

chart events, 166-167, 172-175, 495-497

ChartFormat method, 203

ChartFormat object, 218

Chart Layout gallery, 211-213

Chart_MouseDown() event, 174

Chart_MouseMove() event, 174

Chart_MouseUp() event, 174

Chart_Resize() event, 174

charts

built-in chart types, 208-210

in cell comments, 341-342

chart events, 166-167, 172-175, 495-497

trapping, 495-497

creating, 204-207

dynamic charts, creating in userforms, 244-245

embedded charts, 172

exporting as graphics, 244-245

formatting

3-D rotation settings, 224-229

bevel and 3D format, 230-234

chart elements to which formatting applies, 218-234

Format method, 218-234

glow settings, 222-223

line settings, 222

object fill, 219-222

reflection settings, 223

shadow settings, 223

soft edges, 223-224

frequency charts, 236-239

Layout tab, 213-218

layouts, 211-213

new features (Excel 2010), 139-140

Open-High-Low-Close (OHLC) charts, 235-236

overview, 203

pivot charts, 246-247

referencing, 203-207

SetElement method, 213-218

sparklines. *See* sparklines

specifying size and location of, 204-205

stacked area charts, 239-243

styles, 211-213

template chart types, 210-211

Win/Loss charts, 426-427

Chart_Select() event, 174-175

Chart_SeriesChange() event, 175

ChartStyle property, 213

ChartType property, 208

CheckBox control, 512-513

check boxes, 512-513

CheckDisplayRes() procedure, 540

CheckForSheet() procedure, 84

checking

existence of names, 155-156

for open files, 539

whether workbook is open, 83

CheckUserRights() procedure, 86

class modules

creating collections in, 502-504

inserting, 493

cleaning up recorded code

case study, 62-64

tips for, 58-61

ClearAllFilters method, 289

ClearTable method, 289

Click event, 187, 190, 193-196, 200

clients, training about error handling, 557

Close method, 443

closing

add-ins, 593

documents, 443

Excel, 401

userform windows, 200-201

code protection, 559

collections

Areas, 77

creating

in class modules, 502-504

in standard module, 501-502

defined, 501

explained, 35

grouping controls into, 519-521

ColName() function, 103

color

color scales

adding to ranges, 374-375

explained, 367

coloring active control, 530-532

filtering by, 253

RGB colors in sparklines, 421-423

summing cells based on interior color, 89-90

theme colors for sparklines, 418-421

using two colors of data bars in range, 380-382

ColorFord() procedure, 251

ColorFruitRedBold() procedure, 121-122

ColumnExists() procedure, 488

ColumnHeaders() procedure, 455

columns

copying all columns, 277

remembering column numbers associated with column letters, 136

subset of columns, copying, 278-280

Columns property, 72

combining worksheets into workbooks, 334-335

combo boxes, 191-193

command buttons

attaching macros to, 581-582

events for, 189

CommandButton event, 191

comments

adding to names, 150

in cells

charts in, 341-342

listing, 337-339

resizing, 339-341

compact layout, 293-294

CompactLayoutColumnHeader property, 289

CompactLayoutRowHeader property, 289

CompactRowIndent property, 290

compatibility issues

checking application version with Version property, 144-145

Compatibility mode, 145

explained, 144

Compatibility mode, 145

complex expressions, 124

ComplexIf() procedure, 124-126

computer names, retrieving, 538-539

concatenation, 97-98

conceptual filters (pivot tables), 313-316

conditional formatting

color scales

adding to ranges, 374-375

explained, 367

data bars

adding to ranges, 369-374

explained, 367

determining which cells to format, 387-388

formatting cells based on value, 385

formatting cells in top 10 or bottom 5, 383-384

formatting cells that are above/below average, 383

formatting cells that contain blanks or errors, 387

formatting cells that contain dates, 386

formatting cells that contain text, 386

formatting unique or duplicate cells, 384-385

highlighting selected cell, 342-344

icon sets

adding to ranges, 375-378

explained, 368

new features (Excel 2010), 140-141

NumberFormat property, 388-389

VBA methods and properties, 368-369

conditions (If statement), 121

configuring pivot tables, 295-296

connections (ADO), 478

constant values

defined constants, 41-45

explained, 439

retrieving with Object Browser, 440-441

retrieving with Watch window, 440

ContainsText() function, 100-101

content management system, 407-409

controls. *See also* **userforms**

active control, coloring, 530-532

ActiveX controls

attaching macros to, 583-584

right-click menu for, 360-362

adding at runtime, 523-529

adding on-the-fly, 525

CheckBox, 512-513

grouping into collections, 519-521

programming, 188

RefEdit, 515

renaming, 188

Ribbon control arguments, 569-571

Ribbon control attributes, 566

running macros from, 16-17

ScrollBar, 517-519

TabStrip, 513-515

tip text, adding to userforms, 530

ToggleButton, 517

troubleshooting, 189

converting

Excel 2003 custom toolbar to Excel 2010, 575-577

pivot tables to values, 299-301

week numbers into dates, 96

workbooks to add-ins, 588-590

ConvertToFormulas method, 289

CopyFromRecordSet method, 481

copying

data into worksheets, 335-336

formulas, 129-130

macros into workbooks, 363-365

ranges, 61

subset of columns, 278-280

CopyToNewFolder() procedure, 120

counting

records, 303

unique values, 90-91

workbooks in directory, 84-85

CountMyWkbks() procedure, 85

cracking passwords, 560

CreatedStackedChart() procedure, 242-243

CreateFrequencyChart() procedure, 238-239

CreateMemo() procedure, 448-449

CreateObject() function, 438

CreateOHCLChart() procedure, 236

CreatePivot() procedure, 298-299

CreatePivotTable method, 295

CreateSummaryReportUsingPivot() procedure, 246-247, 300-301

criteria ranges

case study, 268

explained, 265-266

formula-based conditions, 268-275

logical AND criteria, 267

logical OR criteria, 267

Criteria reserved name, 155

CSV files, importing, 331-332

CurrentRegion property, 74-76

cursors, 478

custom About dialog, 541

custom functions. *See* UDFs (user-defined functions)

Custom UI Editor, 572

CustomerByProductReport() procedure, 309-312

customizing

data transposition, 345-347

icon images, 574-575

objects

creating custom objects, 497-498

Property Let/Property Get procedures, 499-501

referencing, 498-499

Ribbon to run macros

control arguments, 569-571

control attributes, 566

custom icon images, 574-575

Custom UI Editor tool, 572

customui folder, 564-565

error messages, 577-580

explained, 563-565

file structure, accessing, 571

Microsoft Office icons, 573-574

RELS file, 571-572

tab and group, 565-566

sort orders, 354-355

web pages, 406

customui folder, 564-565

D

dashboards

creating, 427-432

sparklines

creating, 412-413

creating 100's of individual sparklines in a dashboard, 428-432

formatting, 418-421

observations about, 428

scaling, 414-418

types of sparklines, 411

data

getting from the Web, 391-392

publishing to web pages, 404-406

data access objects (DAO), 477

data bars

adding to ranges, 369-374

explained, 367

using two colors of data bars in range, 380-382

data transposition, customizing, 345-347

data visualizations

applying, 327

color scales, adding to ranges, 374-375

conditional formatting

determining which cells to format, 387-388

formatting cells based on value, 385

formatting cells in top 10 or bottom 5, 383-384

formatting cells that are above/below average, 383

formatting cells that contain blanks or errors, 387

formatting cells that contain dates, 386

formatting cells that contain text, 386

formatting unique or duplicate cells, 384-385

NumberFormat property, 388-389

data bars

adding to ranges, 369-374

using two colors of data bars in range, 380-382

explained, 368

icon sets

adding to ranges, 375-378

creating for subset of range, 378-380

VBA methods and properties for, 368-369

DataBar2() procedure, 372-373

DataBar3() procedure, 373

Database reserved name, 155

databases

ADO

connections, 478

cursors, 478

lock type, 479

overview, 478-480

recordsets, 478

fields

adding on-the-fly, 489-490

checking existence of, 488

Multidimensional Database (MDB) format, 475

records

adding, 480-481

deleting, 485

retrieving, 481-483

summarizing, 485-486

updating, 483-485

shared access databases, creating, 477-478

SQL Server, 490-491

tables

adding on-the-fly, 489

checking existence of, 487-488

DataExtract() procedure, 490-491

DataSets variable, 473

dates

converting week numbers into, 96

formatting cells that contain dates, 386

grouping to months, quarters, or years, 303-305

retrieving permanent date/time, 87

retrieving saved date/time, 86-87

DateTime() function, 87

DblClick event, 187, 190, 193-197, 200

Deactivate event, 187

Debug button, 551

Debug errors, 551-552

debugging tools

breakpoints, 49

jumping forward/backward in code, 49-50

querying variable values, 50-54

Run to Cursor, 50

stepping through code, 46-48

watches, 55

declaring

arrays, 453-454

variables, 20

defined constants, 41-45

defining

pivot cache, 295

ranges, 444-446

Delete method, 149-150

DeleteFord() procedure, 251

deleting
names, 149-150
records, 485
selections from recorded code, 58

delimited files, opening, 467-470

delimited strings, separating, 96-97

deselecting noncontiguous cells, 347-349

Design tab, changing layout from, 325-326

Developer tab, viewing, 9-10

directories
counting workbooks in, 84-85
listing files in, 329-331
looping through directory files, 119-120

Disable All Macros Except Digitally Signed Macros setting, 12

Disable All Macros with Notification setting, 11-12

Disable All Macros Without Notification setting, 11

disabling X button for closing userforms, 541-542

DisplayAllMember method, 289

DisplayContextTooltips property, 290

DisplayFieldCaptions property, 290

displaying R1C1-style references, 128

DisplayMemberPropertyTooltips property, 290

display-resolution information, retrieving, 540

DisplaySize API function, 540

dll (dynamic link libraries), 535

Do loops
explained, 113-115
Until clause, 115-117
While clause, 115-117

DOA (data access objects), 477

Document object
closing documents, 443
explained, 442
opening documents, 442
printing documents, 443
saving documents, 442-443

documents
closing, 443
creating, 442
exporting to, 336-337
opening, 442
printing, 443
saving, 442-443

drilling down pivot tables, 349-350

DropButtonClick event, 190, 193

duplicate cells, formatting, 384-385

duplicates, removing from ranges, 91-92

dynamic arrays, 459-460

dynamic charts, creating in userforms, 244-245

dynamic data ranges, selecting with AutoFilter, 254-255

dynamic link libraries (dll), 535

DynamicAutoFilter() procedure, 255

E

early binding, 433-436

elapsed time, calculating, 353-354

Element "customui Tag Name" Is Unexpected (error message), 578

e-mail addresses, validating, 88-89

embedded chart events, trapping, 495-497

embedded charts, 172

EmpAddCollection() procedure, 504

EmpPayCollection() procedure, 501-502

empty cells, checking for, 73-74

emptying arrays, 456-457

Enable All Macros (Not Recommended: Potentially Dangerous Code Can Run) setting, 12

enable/disable macro settings, 11-12

enabling

events, 161

macros, 12

encountering errors on purpose, 556

EndKey method, 443

Enter event, 190, 193-197, 200

Err object, 554

Error event, 187, 190, 193-197, 200

error handling

debug errors inside userform code, 551-552

encountering errors on purpose, 556

Err object, 554

error messages

The Attribute "Attribute Name" on the Element "customui Ribbon" Is Not Defined in the DTD/Schema, 577

Can't find object or library, 435-436

Element "customui Tag Name" Is Unexpected, 578

Excel Found Unreadable Content, 579

Illegal Qualified Name Character, 578

runtime error 9: Subscript Out of Range, 557

runtime error 1004: Method Range of Object Global Failed, 558-559

Wrong Number of Arguments or Invalid Property Assignment, 580

errors caused by different versions, 561

errors while developing versus errors months later, 557

explained, 549-552

formatting cells that contain blanks or errors, 387

generic error handlers, 554

ignoring errors, 554

On Error GoTo syntax, 552-554

On Error Resume Next statement, 554-555

page setup errors, 555

problems with passwords, 560-561

protecting code, 559

suppressing Excel warnings, 556

training clients, 557

error messages

The Attribute "Attribute Name" on the Element "customui Ribbon" Is Not Defined in the DTD/Schema, 577

Can't find object or library, 435-436

Element "customui Tag Name" Is Unexpected, 578

Excel Found Unreadable Content, 579

Illegal Qualified Name Character, 578

runtime error 9: Subscript Out of Range, 557

runtime error 1004: Method Range of Object Global Failed, 558-559

Wrong Number of Arguments or Invalid Property Assignment, 580

Evaluate method, 153

events. *See also* **specific events**

application-level events, 176-181, 494-495

chart events, 172-175

CheckBox control events, 513

for combo boxes, 191-193

for command buttons, 189

embedded chart events, trapping, 495-497

enabling, 161

explained, 160

for graphics, 195-202

for labels, 189

levels of events, 159-160

for list boxes, 191-193

for MultiPage control, 198-200

for option buttons, 194-195

parameters, 160

RefEdit control events, 516

Scrollbar control events, 519

for spin buttons, 196-202

TabStrip control events, 515

for text boxes, 189

ToggleButton control events, 517

userform events, 186-187

workbook events, 161-167

worksheet events, 168-172

EveryOtherRow() procedure, 455

Excel 97-2003 Workbook file type, 18

Excel 2003 custom toolbar, converting to Excel 2010, 575-577

Excel 2007 pivot table features, 288-290

Excel 2010

file types, 18-19

pivot table features, 288

Excel Binary Workbook file type, 18

Excel Found Unreadable Content (error message), 579

Excel Macro-Enabled Workbook file type, 18

Excel Workbook file type, 18

Excel8CompatibilityMode property, 145

Execute method, 485

Exit event, 191-197, 200

exiting For...Next loop after condition is met, 111-112

ExportChart() procedure, 244

exporting

charts as graphics, 244-245

to Word document, 336-337

expressions in Case statements, 124

Extract reserved name, 155

F

FieldListSortAscending property, 290

fields

adding on-the-fly, 489-490

adding to pivot tables, 296-299

calculated data fields, 324-325

checking existence of, 488

field entry in userforms, verifying, 200

form fields, controlling in Word, 450-452

multiple value fields (pivot tables), 302-303

File menu, Save As command, 589

files

checking for open files, 539

CSV files, importing, 331-332

file structure, accessing, 571

file types in Excel 2010, 18-19

filenames, retrieving, 201-202

listing, 329-331

looping through directory files, 119-120

paths, retrieving, 543-546

RELS file, 571-572

text files

    fixed-width files, 463-467

    importing files with fewer than 1,048,576 rows, 463-470

    importing files with more than 1,048,576 rows, 470-473

    reading and parsing, 332-333

    writing, 473-474

filling arrays, 455-456

FillOutWordForm() procedure, 451-452

Filter in Place, 275-276, 283-285

FilterByFontColor() procedure, 253

FilterByIcon() procedure, 254

filtering

    data into worksheets, 335-336

    pivot tables

        conceptual filters, 313-316

        filtering to top five or top 10, 319

        manual filters, 312-313

        with named sets, 321-323

        Search filter, 316-317

        slicers, 319-321

FilterNoFontColor() procedure, 253

filters

    Advanced Filter

        building with Excel interface, 258

        case study: creating reports for each customer, 280-283

        extracting unique list of values, 258-264

        Filter in Place, 275-276

        overview, 257

        xlFilterCopy with all records, 276-280

    AutoFilter

        filtering by color, 253

        filtering by icon, 254

        replacing loops with, 249-251

        selecting dynamic data range with, 254-255

        selecting multiple items, 252

        selecting visible cells only, 255-256

        selecting with Search box, 252-255

        turning off drop-downs in, 285

finding

    API declarations, 547

    first nonzero-length cell, 93

FindJPGFilesInAFolder() procedure, 119-120

FindWindow API function, 541-543

first nonzero-length cell, finding in range, 93

FirstNonZeroLength() function, 93

fixed-width files, opening, 463-467

flow control

    complex expressions in Case statements, 124

    If statement

        conditions, 115, 121-124

        If...Then...Else, 121

        If...Then...Else...End If, 122-123

        If...Then...End If, 121-122

    nested If statements, 124-126

    Select Case...End Select statement, 123

folders, customui, 564-565

For...Next loops

    exiting early after condition is met, 111-112

    explained, 107-109

    nesting, 112

    Step clause, 110-111

    variables, 110

Format method, 218-234

Format Shape dialog, 230

Format tab. *See* formatting

FormatAboveAverage() procedure, 383

FormatBelowAverage() procedure, 383

FormatBetween10And20() procedure, 386

FormatBorder() method, 222

FormatBottom5Items() procedure, 383-384

FormatConditions object, 368

FormatContainsA() procedure, 386

FormatDatesLastWeek() procedure, 386

FormatDuplicate() procedure, 385

FormatLessThan15() procedure, 386

FormatLineOrBorders() procedure, 222

FormatShadow() procedure, 223

FormatSoftEdgesWithLoop() procedure, 224

formatting
    charts
        3-D rotation settings, 224-229
        bevel and 3D format, 230-234
        chart elements to which formatting applies, 218-234
        Format method, 218-234
        glow settings, 222-223
        line settings, 222
        object fill, 219-222
        reflection settings, 223
        shadow settings, 223
        soft edges, 223-224
    conditional. See conditional formatting
    ranges, 446-447
    sparklines
        RGB colors, 421-423
        sparkline elements, 423-426
        theme colors, 418-421
        Win/Loss charts, 426-427

FormatTop10Items() procedure, 383

FormatTop12Percent() procedure, 384

FormatUnique() procedure, 385

FormatWithPicture() procedure, 221

forms. See userforms

formulas
    array formulas, 137-138
    determining which cells to format, 387-388
    entering once and copying down the column, 129-130
    formula-based conditions, 268-275
    names, 151
    R1C1 formulas, 61

frequency charts, 236-239

FruitRedVegGreen() procedure, 122

FTP, 409-410

functions. See specific functions

G

generic error handlers, 554

GetAddress() function, 102-103

GetComputerName API function, 538-539

GetFileName() function, 546

GetObject() function, 438-439

GetSettings() procedure, 558

GetSystemMenu API function, 541-542

GetUniqueCustomers() procedure, 260

GetUnsentTransfers() procedure, 481-482

global names, 147-148

glow settings, 222-223

Go To Special dialog, 256-257

graphics. See also icons
    adding on-the-fly, 526-527
    events for, 195-202
    exporting charts as, 244-245
    SmartArt, 142-144

groups, creating for Ribbon, 565-566

H

HandleAnError() procedure, 553

handling errors. *See* error handling

hard-coding, 60-61

help

    adding to userforms, 529-532

        accelerator keys, 529

        coloring active control, 530-532

        control tip text, 530

    help buttons, 505-506

    help files, 143

        installing, 37-38

        selecting libraries in, 45

    help topics, 39

hidden workbooks

    as alternative to add-ins, 593-594

    case study: hidden workbook to hold macros and forms, 594

Hide method, 186

hiding

    hidden workbooks

        as alternative to add-ins, 593-594

        case study: hidden workbook to hold macros and forms, 594

    names, 155

    userforms, 186

HighlightFirstUnique() procedure, 385-388

highlighting selected cells, 342-345

HighlightWholeRow() procedure, 388

historical stock/fund quotes application, 362-363

HomeKey method, 443

hovering, 53

hyperlink addresses, returning, 102-103

hyperlinks

    in userforms, 522

    running macros from, 584

I

icons

    custom icon images, 574-575

    filtering by, 254

    icon sets

        adding to ranges, 375-378

        creating for subset of range, 378-380

        explained, 368

    Microsoft Office icons, 573-574

If statements

    conditions, 121

    If...Then...Else, 121

    If...Then...Else...End If, 122-123

    If...Then...End If, 121-122

    nesting, 124-126

ignoring errors, 554

Illegal Qualified Name Character (error message), 578

images. *See* graphics; icons

Immediate window, 50-53

Import10() procedure, 470

ImportAll() procedure, 470-471

ImportData function, 156-157

importing

    CSV files, 331-332

    text files

        files with fewer than 1,048,576 rows, 463-470

        files with more than 1,048,576 rows, 470-473

IncrementRotationHorizontal property, 229

IncrementRotationVertical property, 229

IncrementRotationX property, 229

IncrementRotationY property, 229

IncrementRotationZ property, 229

InGridDropZones property, 290

Initialize event, 187

input boxes, 183-184

InputBox function, 183-184

inserting class modules, 493

InsertText() procedure, 444

installing
add-ins, 591
help files, 37-38

Intersect method, 73

IsEmailValid() function, 88-89

ISEMPTY function, 73-74

IsWordOpen() procedure, 438

J

jet engine, 476

joining multiple ranges, 72-73

jumping forward/backward in code, 49-50

K

keyboard shortcuts, running macros with, 580-581

KeyDown event, 187, 191-197, 200

KeyPress event, 187, 191-197, 200

KeyUp event, 187, 191-200

keywords, New, 437

KillTimer API function, 542-543

L

Label event, 191, 194-195

labels, 189

last row, determining, 59-60

LastSaved() function, 86-87

late binding, 436-437

Layout event, 187, 195

Layout tab, 213-218

LayoutRowDefault property, 290

layouts
charts, 211-213
compact layout, 293-294
pivot table layout, 325-327

lbl_Email_Click() procedure, 522

lbl_SelectAll_Click() procedure, 520

lbl_unSelectAll_Click() procedure, 520

lbl_Website_Click() procedure, 522

learning curve for VBA, 8

levels of events, 159-160

libraries
dynamic link libraries (dll), 535
selecting in help files, 45

lighting, VBA constants for, 233-234

Line Input method, 472

line settings, 222

LineFormat object, 222

list boxes
combo boxes versus, 191-193
multicolumn list boxes, 532

listing
cell comments, 337-339
files in directories, 329-331

lists, sorting, 354-355

Load method, 186

local names, 147-148

location of charts, specifying, 204-205

lock type (ADO), 479

logical AND criteria, 267

logical OR criteria, 267

loops
Do
explained, 113-115
Until clause, 115-117
While clause, 115-117
For Each, 117-119

For...Next
exiting early after condition is met, 111-112
explained, 107-109
nesting, 112
Step clause, 110-111
variables, 110
Go To Special instead of looping, 256-257
looping through directory files, 119-120
replacing with AutoFilter, 249-251
While...Wend, 117
lOpen API function, 539
Lotus 1-2-3 macros, 29

M

macro recorder, 441
cleaning up recorded code
case study, 62-64
tips for, 58-61
examining code from, 39-46
flaws in, 7-8, 21-31
absolute mode, 25
AutoSum button, 30-31
examining code in Programming window, 23-25
recording macros case study, 22-23
relative references, 26-29
relative references case study, 26-28
tips for, 31
Macro Security icon (Developer tab), 9
macros. *See also* **specific procedures**
attaching
to ActiveX controls, 583-584
to command buttons, 581-582
to shapes, 582-583
canceling previously scheduled, 400-401
closing, 401
copying into workbooks, 363-365
holding in hidden workbooks, 594
recording, 12-14, 22-23
running, 14-17
from form controls, 16-17
from hyperlinks, 584
with keyboard shortcuts, 580-581
from Quick Access toolbar, 15-16
from Ribbon. *See* Ribbon
scheduling
to run every two minutes, 403-404
to run x minutes in the future, 401-402
security, 10-12
Disable All Macros with Notification setting, 12
enable/disable settings, 11-12
trusted locations, 10-11
testing, 25
Macros icon (Developer tab), 9
manual filters (pivot tables), 312-313
manually creating web queries, 392-395
material types, 232
maximum values in range, returning addresses of, 101-102
MaxPoint property, 371
MDB (Multidimensional Database) format, 475
Me keyword, 186
message boxes, 184
methods. *See specific methods*
Microsoft Office icons, adding to buttons, 573-574
military time, entering into cells, 171

MinPoint property, 371

mixed references, 133

mixed text

retrieving numbers from, 95

sorting numeric and alpha characters, 99-100

modeless userforms, 521

Modify method, 371

modules, 21

MouseDown event, 187, 191-196, 200

MouseMove event, 187, 191, 194-196, 200

MouseUp event, 187, 191, 194-196, 200

MoveAfterTheFact() procedure, 205

MoveAndFormatSlicer() procedure, 321

MsgBox function, 184

MSubstitute() function, 94-95

multicolumn list boxes, 532

multidimensional arrays, 454

Multidimensional Database (MDB) format, 475

MultiPage control, 198-200

multiple actions in With...End With blocks, 61

multiple characters, substituting, 94-95

multiple items, selecting, 252

multiple row fields, suppressing subtotals for, 326-327

multiple value fields (pivot tables), 302-303

MultipleIf() procedure, 122

multiplication table, building with R1C1-style references, 134-135

MultiSelect property, 192-193

MyFullName() function, 82-83

MyName() function, 82

N

Name property, 149

named ranges, 66

named sets, 321-323

NameExists function, 155-157

names

adding comments about, 150

array names, 153-154

checking existence of, 155-156

computer names, retrieving, 538-539

creating, 148-149

deleting, 149-150

explained, 147

formula names, 151

global versus local names, 147-148

hiding, 155

named ranges for VLOOKUP, 156-157

number names, 152-153

reserved names, 154-155

storing values in, 152

string names, 151-152

table names, 153

workbook names, setting in cell, 82

NASDAQMacro() procedure, 416-418

navigation keys, 31

nesting

If statements, 124-126

loops, 112

NetTransfers() procedure, 486

new features (Excel 2010)

charts, 139-140

conditional formatting, 140-141

objects/methods, 143

pivot tables, 140

Ribbon, 139

slicers, 140

SmartArt, 142

sorting, 141-142

tables, 141

New keyword, 437

NewDocument() procedure, 442

noncontiguous cells, selecting/ deselecting, 347-349

noncontiguous ranges, returning, 77

NumberFormat() procedure, 388-389

NumberFormat property, 388-389

numbers

names, 152-153

retrieving from mixed text, 95

static random numbers, generating, 103

week numbers, converting into dates, 96

NumFilesInCurDir() function, 84-85

NumUniqueValues() function, 90-91

O

Object Browser, 56-57, 440-441

object-oriented languages, 33-34

object variables, 117-119

objects. *See also* ***specific objects***

ActiveX data objects. See ADO

bookmarks, 448-449

in collections, 35

creating and referencing

CreateObject() function, 438

GetObject() function, 438-439

New keyword, 437

custom objects

creating, 497-498

Property Let/Property Get procedures, 499-501

referencing, 498-499

explained, 34

fill, 219-222

new features (Excel 2010), 143

properties, 36, 37

returned by properties, 46

watches on, 55

ObjectThemeColor property, 219

objForm_LostFocus() procedure, 532

Offset property, 69-70, 251

OHLC (Open-High-Low-Close) charts, 235-236

OldLoop() procedure, 250

OldLoopToDelete() procedure, 250

OneColorGradient method, 221, 222

one-dimensional arrays, 454

On Error GoTo syntax, 552-554

On Error Resume Next statement, 554-555

open files, checking for, 539

Open-High-Low-Close (OHLC) charts, 235-236

Open method, 442

opening

delimited files, 467-470

documents, 442

fixed-width files, 463-467

OpenSchema method, 487

OpenText method, 40, 42, 463

optimizing

calculating elapsed time, 353-354

Page Setup, 350-353

option buttons, 194-195

optional parameters, 41

Origin parameter, 41

overlapping ranges, creating new ranges from, 73

P

Page Setup, 350-353, 555

parameters

event parameters, 160

explained, 35-36

optional parameters, 41

parsing text files, 332-333

PassAnArray() procedure, 460

passing arrays, 460

passwords

cracking, 560

password box protection, 356-358

problems with, 560-561

pasting ranges, 61

.Patterned method, 221

Peltier, Jon, 243

percentages, showing, 305-308

permanent date/time, retrieving, 87

Personal Macro Workbook, 13

pivot cache, 295

pivot charts, 246-247

pivot tables

building in Excel interface, 290-294

building in VBA, 294-301

adding fields to data area, 296-299

creating and configuring pivot table, 295-296

defining pivot cache, 295

calculated data fields, 324-325

calculated items, 325

changing calulations to show percentages, 305-308

changing layout of, 325-327

compact layout, 293-294

controlling sort order with AutoSort, 308

counting number of records, 303

data visualization, applying, 327

determining size of and converting pivot table to values, 299-301

drilling down, 349-350

eliminating blank cells in values area, 308

Excel 2007 new features, 288-290

Excel 2010 new features, 288

explained, 287

filtering data sets

conceptual filters, 313-316

filtering to top five or top 10, 319

manual filters, 312-313

Search filter, 316-317

slicers, 319-321

with named sets, 321-323

with ShowDetail, 325

grouping daily dates to months, quarters, or years, 303-305

limitations, 299

multiple value fields, 302-303

new features (Excel 2010), 140

replicating reports for every product, 309-312

supressing subtotals for multiple row fields, 326-327

PivotColumnAxis property, 290

PivotRowAxis property, 290

playing sounds, 543

PlayWavSound API function, 543

Pope, Andy, 243

PresetGradient method, 222

PresetTextured method, 220

Print_Area reserved name, 155

Print_Titles reserved name, 155

PrintDrillIndicators property, 290

printing documents, 443

PrintOut method, 443

Priority property, 369

private properties, 497

procedural languages, 33-34

procedures. *See specific procedures*

Programming window, examining macro recorder code in, 23-25

progress indicators, 355-356

Project Explorer, 20-21

properties. *See also specific properties*

 explained, 36-37

 return values, 46

Properties window, 21

Property Get procedure, 499-501

Property Let procedure, 499-501

protecting

 code, 559

 password boxes, 356-358

public properties, 497

publishing data to web pages, 404-406

Q

queries, 391-395

QueryClose event, 187, 201

querying variable values, 50-54

Quick Access toolbar, 15-16

QuickFillMax() procedure, 456

QuickSort() procedure, 99-100

R

R1C1-style references, 61

 absolute references, 133

 array formulas, 137-138

 case study: entering A1 versus R1C1 references, 131

 explained, 127-128

 formulas, 129-132

 mixed references, 133

 multiplication table example, 134-135

 referring to entire columns/rows, 134

 relative references, 132-133

 remembering column numbers associated with column letters, 136

 switching to, 128

random numbers, generating, 103

Range object, 65-66, 444-447

 defining ranges, 444-446

 formatting ranges, 446-447

Range property, 69

ranges

 color scales, adding, 374-375

 copying/pasting in one statement, 61

 creating from overlapping ranges, 73

 criteria ranges

  case study, 268

  explained, 265-266

  formula-based conditions, 268-275

  logical AND criteria, 267

 data bars, adding, 369-374

 defining, 444-446

 first nonzero-length cell, finding, 93

 formatting, 446-447

 icon sets, adding, 375-378

  specifying icon set, 376

  specifying ranges for each icon, 377-378

 joining multiple ranges, 72-73

 named ranges, 66, 156-157

 names

  adding comments about, 150

  creating, 148-149

  deleting, 149-150

 Range object, 65-66, 444-447

referencing, 59

with Offset property, 69-70

in other sheets, 67

relative to another range, 68

shortcuts, 66-67

removing duplicates from, 91-92

resizing, 71-72

returning addresses of maximum values in range, 101-102

returning noncontiguous ranges, 77

selecting

with AutoFilter, 254-255

with Cells property, 68-69

with CurrentRegion property, 74-76

specifying

syntax, 66

with Columns/Rows properties, 72

Ranges(), 59

RangeText() procedure, 444

reading text files, 332-333

files with fewer than 1,048,576 rows, 463-470

importing files with more than 1,048,576 rows, 470-473

ReadLargeFile() procedure, 472-473

Record Macro dialog box, 13

Record Macro icon (Developer tab), 9

recorded code, cleaning up, 58-64

recording macros, 12-14, 22-23. See also **macro recorder**

records

adding to databases, 480-481

counting number of, 303

deleting, 485

retrieving from databases, 481-483

showing after Filter in Place, 276

summarizing, 485-486

updating, 483-485

recordsets, 325, 478

RefEdit control, 515

references

A1-style references, 127-128

case study: entering A1 versus R1C1 references, 131

R1C1-style references

absolute references, 133

array formulas, 137-138

explained, 127-128

formulas, 129-132

mixed references, 133

multiplication table example, 134-135

referring to entire columns/rows, 134

relative references, 132-133

remembering column numbers associated with column letters, 136

switching to, 128

referencing

charts, 203-207

custom objects, 498-499

objects

CreateObject() function, 438

GetObject() function, 438-439

New keyword, 437

ranges, 59

with Offset property, 69-70

in other sheets, 67

relative to another range, 68

shortcuts, 66-67

tables, 77-78

reflection settings, 223

refreshing web queries, 392-395

relative references, 26-31

  case study, 26-28

  R1C1-style references, 132-133

RELS file, 571-572

RememberTheName() procedure, 206

Remove Duplicates command, 384-385

RemoveControl event, 187, 195, 200

removing

  add-ins, 593

  duplicates from ranges, 91-92

renaming controls, 188

replacing loops with AutoFilter, 249-251

replicating reports for every product, 309-312

reports

  creating with Advanced Filter, 280-283

  replicating for every product, 309-312

reserved names, 154-155

Reset button, 549-550

ResetRotation method, 229

Resize event, 187

Resize property, 71-72

resizing

  cell comments, 339-341

  ranges, 71-72

  userforms, 524

resolution, 540

RetrieveNumbers() function, 95

retrieving

  file paths, 543-546

  filenames, 201-202

  records, 481-483

return values of properties, 46

ReturnsMaxs() function, 101-102

RevenueByCustomers() procedure, 261

ReverseContents() function, 101

reversing cell contents, 101

RGB colors, 421-423

Ribbon

  changes in Excel 2010, 139

  customizing to run macros

    control arguments, 569-571

    control attributes, 566

    custom icon images, 574-575

    Custom UI Editor tool, 572

    customui folder, 564-565

    error messages, 577-580

    explained, 563-565

    file structure, accessing, 571

    Microsoft Office icons, 573-574

    RELS file, 571-572

    tab and group, 565-566

  macro buttons, creating, 14-15

rotation, 224-229

RotationX property, 228

RotationY property, 229

RotationZ property, 229

RowAxisLayout method, 289

rows, determining last row, 59-60

Rows property, 72

Run to Cursor debugging tool, 50

RunCustReport() procedure, 278-279

running

  macros, 14-17

    from form controls, 16-17

    from Quick Access toolbar, 15-16

    from Ribbon, 14-15

  timers, 542-543

RunReportForEachCustomer() procedure, 281-283

runtime

adding controls at, 523-529

errors

runtime error 9: Subscript Out of Range, 557

runtime error 1004: Method Range of Object Global Failed, 558-559

S

Save As command (File menu), 589

Save method, 442

saved date/time, retrieving, 86-87

saving documents, 442-443

sbX_Change() procedure, 245

sbY_Change() procedure, 245

scaling sparklines, 414-418

scheduling

macros

to run every two minutes, 403-404

to run x minutes in the future, 401-402

verbal reminders, 402

Scroll event, 187, 195, 200

ScrollBar control, 517-519

Search box, 252-255

Search filter (pivot tables), 316-317

searching for strings within text, 100-101

security

add-ins, 592

macro security

Disable All Macros with Notification setting, 12

enable/disable settings, 11-12

trusted locations, 10-11

password box protection, 356-358

Select Case...End Select statement, 123

Select...Case statement, 104

Select statements, 123

SelectCase() procedure, 123

selected cells, highlighting, 342-345

selecting

cells, 360

libraries, 45

multiple items, 252

noncontiguous cells, 347-349

ranges

with Cells property, 68-69

with CurrentRegion property, 74-76

Selection object, 443-444

SelectSentence() procedure, 445

separating

delimited strings, 96-97

worksheets into workbooks, 333-334

SetElement method, 203, 213-218

SetPresetCamera values, 225-229

SetReportInItalics() procedure, 559

SetTimer API function, 542-543

SetValuesToTabStrip() procedure, 514

shadow settings, 223

shapes, attaching macros to, 582-583

shared access databases, creating, 477-478

sharing UDFs (user-defined functions), 81-82

sheet events (workbook level), 166-167

SheetExists() function, 83-84

sheets, verifying existence of, 83-84

ShellAbout API function, 541

Show method, 186

ShowAllData method, 276

ShowCustForm() procedure, 263

ShowDetail, 325

ShowDrillIndicators property, 290

ShowTableStyleColumnHeaders property, 290

ShowTableStyleColumnStripes property, 290

ShowTableStyleLastColumn property, 290

ShowTableStyleRowHeaders property, 290

ShowTableStyleRowStripes property, 290

SimpleFilter() procedure, 285

size
    of charts, 204-205
    of pivot tables, 299-301

slicers, 319-321

SmartArt, 142

soft edges, formatting, 223-224

SortConcat() function, 97-98

sorter() function, 99-100

sorting
    AutoSort, 308
    with custom sort orders, 354-355
    new features (Excel 2010), 141-142
    numeric and alpha characters, 99-100
    with SortConcat() function, 97-98

SortUsingCustomLists property, 290

sounds, playing, 543

sparklines
    creating, 412-413, 428-432
    formatting
        RGB colors, 421-423
        sparkline elements, 423-426
        theme colors, 418-421
        Win/Loss charts, 426-427
    observations about, 428
    scaling, 414-418
    types of sparklines, 411

SpecialCells method, 276, 360

SpecifyExactLocation() procedure, 205

SpecifyLocation() procedure, 205

speed testing, 350-353

spin button events, 196-202

SpinDown event, 198

SpinUp event, 198

SQL Server, 490-491

stacked area charts, 239-243

standard modules, creating collections in, 501-502

StartRow parameter, 41

statements. *See also* loops
    Case, 124
    If
        conditions, 115, 121-124
        If...Then...Else, 121
        If...Then...Else...End If, 122-123
        If...Then...End If, 121-122
        nesting, 124-126
    On Error GoTo, 552-554
    On Error Resume Next, 554-555
    Select...Case, 104
    Select Case...End Select, 123
    Type..End Type, 506

state_period() function, 103

static random numbers, generating, 103

StaticRAND() function, 103

Step clause (For statement), 110-111

stepping through code, 46-48

stock quotes, historical stock/fund quotes application, 362-363

StopIfTrue property, 369

StoreDashboard() procedure, 430-431

StoreTheName() procedure, 207

storing values in names, 152

StringElement() function, 96-97

strings

delimited strings, separating, 96-97

finding within text, 100-101

names, 151-152

Styles gallery, 212-213

Sub cbConfirm_Click() procedure, 484-485

subsets of ranges, creating icon sets for, 378-380

substituting multiple characters, 94-95

SubtotalLocation method, 289

subtotals, suppressing for multiple row fields, 326-327

SumColor() function, 89-90

summarizing records, 485-486

summing cells based on interior color, 89-90

suppressing

Excel warnings, 556

subtotals for multiple row fields, 326-327

SwapElements() procedure, 100

switching to R1C1-style references, 128

T

tab strips, 513-515

TableExists() procedure, 487-488

tables

adding on-the-fly, 489

checking existence of, 487-488

exporting to, 336-337

names, 153

new features (Excel 2010), 141

pivot tables. *See* pivot tables

referencing, 77-78

TableStyle2 property, 290

tabs

creating for Ribbon, 565-566

tab order for userforms, 530

TabStrip control, 513-515

template chart types, 210-211

Terminate event, 187

testing

macros, 25

speed testing, 350-353

text

case, changing, 359-360

control tip text, 530

formatting cells that contain text, 386

mixed text, sorting numeric and alpha characters, 99-100

retrieving numbers from mixed text, 95

searching for strings within, 100-101

text boxes, 189

text files

delimited files, opening, 467-470

fixed-width files, opening, 463-467

importing, 463-473

reading and parsing, 332-333

writing, 473-474

text files

delimited files, opening, 467-470

fixed-width files, opening, 463-467

importing

files with fewer than 1,048,576 rows, 463-470

files with more than 1,048,576 rows, 470-473

reading and parsing, 332-333

writing, 473-474

Text Import Wizard, 42, 464-467

Text to Columns Wizard, 43

TextBox event, 191, 195

TextToColumns method, 471

theme colors for sparklines, 418-421

time

   elapsed time, calculating, 353-354

   military time, entering into cells, 171

   permanent date/time, retrieving, 87

   saved date/time, retrieving, 86-87

timers, 542-543

ToggleButton control, 517

toolbars

   converting Excel 2003 custom toolbar to Excel 2010, 575-577

   UserForm toolbar, 511

ToolTips, 53

Top 10 cells

   filtering to, 319

   formatting, 383-384

Top5Customers() procedure, 317-319

Top10Filter() procedure, 252

Top/Bottom Rules, 383-384

TrailingMinusNumbers parameter, 42, 561

training clients about error handling, 557

transparent forms, 533-534

TransposeArray() procedure, 458

transposing data, 345-347

TrapChartEvent() procedure, 497

trapping

   application events, 494-495

   embedded chart events, 495-497

TrickyFormatting() procedure, 380

troubleshooting. *See* error handling; error messages

trusted locations, 10-11

TwoColorGradient() procedure, 221

Type..End Type statement, 506

types, user-defined types (UDTs), 506-509

TypeText method, 444

U

UDFs (user-defined functions)

   BookOpen(), 83

   case study, 80

   ColName(), 103

   ContainsText(), 100-101

   creating, 79-81

   DateTime(), 87

   FirstNonZeroLength(), 93

   GetAddress(), 102-103

   IsEmailValid(), 88-89

   LastSaved(), 86-87

   MSubstitute(), 94-95

   MyFullName(), 82-83

   MyName(), 82

   NumFilesInCurDir(), 84-85

   NumUniqueValues(), 90-91

   RetrieveNumbers(), 95

   ReturnsMaxs(), 101-102

   ReverseContents(), 101

   sharing, 81-82

   SheetExists(), 83-84

   SortConcat(), 97-98

   sorter(), 99-100

   state_period(), 103

   StaticRAND(), 103

   StringElement(), 96-97

   SumColor(), 89-90

   UniqueValues(), 91-92

   Weekday(), 96

   WinUserName(), 85-86

UDTs (user-defined types), 506-509

Union method, 72-73

unique cells, formatting, 384-385

Unique Records Only, 283-285

unique values

counting, 90-91

extracting with Advanced Filter, 258-264

getting unique combinations of two or more fields, 263-264

with user interface, 259

with VBA code, 260-263

UniqueCustomerProduct() procedure, 263-264

UniqueCustomerRedux() procedure, 261

UniqueProductsOneCustomer() procedure, 266

UniqueValues() function, 91-92

Unload method, 186

Until clause (Do loops), 115-117

updating

records, 483-485

web queries, 395

Use Relative Reference icon (Developer tab), 9

UseBookmarks() procedure, 448

UseGetObject() procedure, 438

user-defined functions. *See* UDFs

user-defined types (UDTs), 506-509

UserForm toolbar, 511

UserForm_Initialize() procedure, 527-528

UserForm_QueryClose() procedure, 532

userforms, 183-202

calling, 186

command buttons, 189

controls

adding at runtime, 523-529

adding on-the-fly, 525

CheckBox, 512-513

grouping into collections, 519-521

programming, 188

RefEdit, 515

ScrollBar, 517-519

TabStrip, 513-515

ToggleButton, 517

troubleshooting, 189

creating, 184-185

Debug errors inside userform code, 551-552

disabling X button for closing userforms, 541-542

dynamic charts, creating, 244-245

field entry, verifying, 200

filenames, retrieving, 201-202

help, adding, 529-532

accelerator keys, 529

coloring active control, 530-532

control tip text, 530

hiding, 186

hyperlinks in, 522

images

adding on-the-fly, 526-527

graphics events, 195-202

input boxes, 183-184

labels, 189

list boxes, 191-193

message boxes, 184

modeless userforms, 521

MultiPage control, 198-200

option buttons, 194-195

resizing on-the-fly, 524

spin buttons, 196-202

tab order, 530

text boxes, 189

transparent forms, 533-534

UserForm toolbar, 511

viewing code, 186

windows, closing, 200-201

USERID function, 85-86

UserIDs, retrieving, 85-86

V

validating e-mail addresses, 88-89

values

constant values

explained, 439

retrieving with Object Browser, 440-441

retrieving with Watch window, 440

converting pivot tables to, 299-301

duplicates, removing from ranges, 91-92

formatting cells based on, 385

maximum values in range, returning addresses of, 101-102

storing in names, 152

unique values

counting, 90-91

extracting with Advanced Filter, 258-264

variables

DataSets, 473

hard-coding versus, 60-61

in For statements, 110

object variables, 117-119

querying values of, 50-54

requiring declaration, 20

wdApp, 435

wdDoc, 435

VB Editor, 19-21

converting files to add-ins, 590-591

debugging tools

breakpoints, 49

jumping forward/backward in code, 49-50

querying variable values, 50-54

Run to Cursor, 50

stepping through code, 46-48

watches, 55

Object Browser, 56-57

Programming window, 23-25

Project Explorer, 20-21

Properties window, 21

settings, 19-20

VBA (Visual Basic for Applications)

advantages of, 8-9

learning curve, 8

syntax, 34-37

VBA Extensibility, 363-365

verbal reminders, scheduling, 402

verifying field entry, 200

Version property, 144-145

versions, errors caused by different versions, 561

viewing

Developer tab, 9-10

Project Explorer, 20

Properties window, 21

userform code, 186

visible cells, selecting with AutoFilter, 255-256

Visual Basic for Applications. *See* **VBA (Visual Basic for Applications)**

Visual Basic icon (Developer tab), 9

visualizations. *See* **data visualizations**

VLOOKUP function, 156-157

W

warnings, suppressing, 556
Watch window, 440
watches
  querying variable values with, 53-54
  setting breakpoints, 55
wdApp variable, 435
wdDoc variable, 435
web pages
  creating custom, 406
  publishing data to, 404-406
web queries, 391-392
  building, 396-399
  creating manually and refreshing with
    VBA, 392-395
  scraping, 399
  updating, 395
week numbers, converting into dates, 96
Weekday() function, 96
While clause (Do loops), 115-117
While...Wend loops, 117
Window API declarations
Windows API declarations
  32-bit versus 64-bit, 538
  ahtAddFilterItem, 546
  aht_apiGetOpenFileName, 544-546
  aht_apiGetSaveFileName, 544-546
  calling, 537
  DisplaySize, 540
  explained, 535-536
  finding, 547
  FindWindow, 541-543
  GetComputerName, 538-539
  GetSystemMenu, 541-542
  KillTimer, 542-543
  lOpen, 539

  PlayWavSound, 543
  SetTimer, 542-543
  ShellAbout, 541
windows for userforms, closing, 200-201
Win/Loss charts, 426-427
WinUserName() function, 85-86
With...End With blocks, 61
wizards, Text Import Wizard, 464-467
Word automation
  bookmarks, 448-449
  constant values
    explained, 439
    retrieving with Watch window,
      440
  controlling form fields, 450-452
  creating and referencing objects
    CreateObject() function, 438
    GetObject() function, 438-439
    New keyword, 437
  Document object
    closing documents, 443
    creating documents, 442
    explained, 442
    opening documents, 442
    printing documents, 443
    saving documents, 442-443
  early binding, 433-436
  explained, 433
  late binding, 436-437
  macro recorder, 441
  Range object, 444-447
    defining ranges, 444-446
    formatting ranges, 446-447
  Selection object, 443-444
Word documents, exporting to, 336-337
WordEarlyBinding() procedure, 435
WordLateBinding() procedure, 437

Workbook_Activate() event, 161

Workbook_AddInInstall() event, 165

Workbook_AddInUninstall event, 165

Workbook_AfterXmlExport() event, 166

Workbook_AfterXmlImport() event, 166

Workbook_BeforeClose() event, 163-164

Workbook_BeforePrint() event, 163, 494

Workbook_BeforeSave() event, 162

Workbook_BeforeXmlExport() event, 166

Workbook_BeforeXmlImport() event, 166

Workbook_Deactivate() event, 161

Workbook_NewSheet() event, 164

Workbook_Open() event, 161

Workbook_Open() procedure, 594

Workbook_PivotTableCloseConnection() event, 165

Workbook_PivotTableOpenConnection() event, 165

Workbook_RowsetComplete() event, 165

Workbook_SheetActivate() event, 166

Workbook_SheetBeforeDoubleClick() event, 167

Workbook_SheetBeforeRightClick() event, 167

Workbook_SheetCalculate() event, 167

Workbook_SheetChange () event, 167

Workbook_SheetDeactivate() event, 167

Workbook_SheetFollowHyperlink() event, 167

Workbook_SheetPivotTableUpdate() event, 167

Workbook_SheetSelectionChange() event, 167

Workbook_Sync() event, 165

Workbook_WindowActivate() event, 165

Workbook_WindowDeactivate() event, 165

Workbook_WindowResize() event, 164

workbooks

checking whether open, 83

combining worksheets into, 334-335

converting to add-ins, 588-590

copying macros into, 363-365

counting number of workbooks in directory, 84-85

events

Workbook_Activate(), 161

Workbook_AddInInstall(), 165

Workbook_AddInUninstall, 165

Workbook_AfterXmlExport(), 166

Workbook_AfterXmlImport(), 166

Workbook_BeforeClose(), 163-164

Workbook_BeforePrint(), 163

Workbook_BeforeSave(), 162

Workbook_BeforeXmlExport(), 166

Workbook_BeforeXmlImport(), 166

Workbook_Deactivate(), 161

Workbook_NewSheet(), 164

Workbook_Open(), 161

Workbook_PivotTableCloseConnection(), 165

Workbook_PivotTableOpenConnection(), 165

Workbook_RowsetComplete(), 165

Workbook_Sync(), 165

Workbook_WindowActivate(), 165

Workbook_WindowDeactivate(), 165

Workbook_WindowResize(), 164

hidden workbooks

as alternative to add-ins, 593-594

case study: hidden workbook to hold macros and forms, 594

permanent date/time, retrieving, 87

saved date/time, retrieving, 86-87

separating worksheets into, 333-334

Workbooks object, 40

Worksheet_Activate() event, 168

Worksheet_BeforeDoubleClick() event, 168

Worksheet_BeforeRightClick() event, 169

Worksheet_BeforeRightClick() procedure, 160

Worksheet_Calculate() event, 169

Worksheet_Change() event, 170

Worksheet_Change() procedure, 161

Worksheet_Deactivate() event, 168

Worksheet_FollowHyperlink() event, 171

Worksheet_PivotTableUpdate() event, 172

Worksheet_SelectionChange() event, 170

worksheets

combining into workbooks, 334-335

events, 168-172

filtering/copying data into, 335-336

referencing ranges in other sheets, 67

Select...Case statements on, 104

separating into workbooks, 333-334

WriteFile() procedure, 474

WriteHTML() procedure, 554

writing text files, 473-474

Wrong Number of Arguments or Invalid Property Assignment (error message), 580

X-Y-Z

X button, disabling, 541-542

xlApp_NewWorkbook() procedure, 495

XLFilterInPlace constant, 275

.xls file type, 18

.xlsb file type, 18

.xlsm file type, 18

.xlsx file type, 18

Zoom event, 187, 195, 200

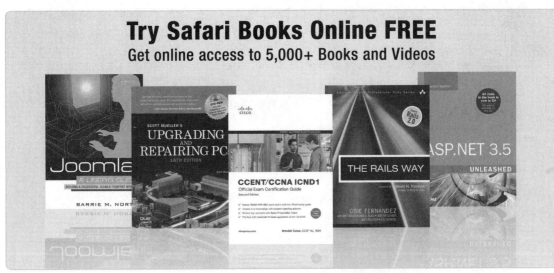

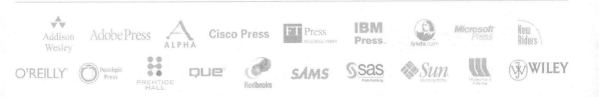

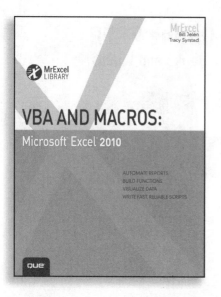